Cases on Technological Adaptability and Transnational Learning:
Issues and Challenges

Siran Mukerji
IGNOU, India

Purnendu Tripathi
IGNOU, India

Information Science REFERENCE

INFORMATION SCIENCE REFERENCE
Hershey · New York

Director of Editorial Content:	Kristin Klinger
Director of Book Publications:	Julia Mosemann
Acquisitions Editor:	Lindsay Johnston
Development Editor:	Beth Ardner
Publishing Assistant:	Keith Glazewski
Typesetter:	Michael Brehm
Production Editor:	Jamie Snavely
Cover Design:	Lisa Tosheff
Printed at:	Yurchak Printing Inc.

Published in the United States of America by
Information Science Reference (an imprint of IGI Global)
701 E. Chocolate Avenue
Hershey PA 17033
Tel: 717-533-8845
Fax: 717-533-8661
E-mail: cust@igi-global.com
Web site: http://www.igi-global.com/reference

Library of Congress Cataloging-in-Publication Data

Cases on technological adaptability and transnational learning : issues and challenges / Siran Mukerji and Purnendu Tripathi, editors. p. cm.

Includes bibliographical references and index.

Summary: "The case studies in this volume enforce technology is a principle catalysts for transnational collaborative interventions in providing learning and professional development opportunities to the people of both developed and developing countries"--Provided by publisher. ISBN 978-1-61520-779-4 (hardcover) -- ISBN 978-1-61520-780-0 (ebook) 1. Educational technology--Cross-cultural studies. I. Mukerji, Siran. II. Tripathi, Purnendu, 1975-

LB1028.3.C327 2010

371.33--dc22

2009036915

British Cataloguing in Publication Data

A Cataloguing in Publication record for this book is available from the British Library.

Editorial Advisory Board

List of Reviewers

Table of Contents

Foreword xiii

Preface xv

Chapter 1
Learning across Social Spaces 1
Gilbert Ahamer, Austrian Academy of Sciences, Austria
Josef Strobl, Austrian Academy of Sciences, Austria

Chapter 2
Online Teaching Partnerships in Diverse Socio-Cultural Institutions 27
Julian Scheinbuks, Chicago State University, USA
Anthony A Pina, The Sullivan University System, USA

Chapter 3
Balanced Assessment of Flexible E-Learning versus Face-to-Face Campus Delivery
Courses at an Australian University 42
Kenneth David Strang, University of Technology, Australia

Chapter 4
Planning a Quality University System: Using Technology to Increase Access
to University Education 69
C. W. S. Sukati, University of Swaziland, Swaziland

Chapter 5
Using Portable DVD Players to Deliver Interactive Simulations for Training
Health Care Workers in Kenya 87
Hannum Wallace, The University of North Carolina at Chapel Hill, USA

Chapter 6
Transnational Postgraduate Study for Development Workers: Using Technology to Bridge the Gap 103
Elizabeth A. Beckmann, The Australian National University, Australia
Patrick Kilby, The Australian National University, Australia

Chapter 7
Learning Patterns of Learner's Interaction in the Learning Management Systems: A Comparative Study of China and Malaysia 123
Wu Bing, The University of Shanghai for Science and Technology, China
Teoh Ai Ping, Wawasan Open University, Malaysia
Ye Chun Ming, The University of Shanghai for Science and Technology, China

Chapter 8
EPICT: Transnational Teacher Development through Blended Learning 147
Katalin Csoma, Embassy of Canada in Budapest, Hungary

Chapter 9
Japanese Students' Digitally Enabled Futures Images: A Synergistic Approach to Developing Academic Competencies 162
Michael Vallance, Future University Hakodate, Japan
David L. Wright, Future University Hakodate, Japan

Chapter 10
Development of a Transnational Framework for E-Learning Technologies 187
Deryn Graham, University of Greenwich, UK

Chapter 11
Second Life Brought to Life: A Case of Usability In-World 203
Kevin Yee, University of Central Florida, USA
Jace Hargis, University of the Pacific, USA

Chapter 12
Perspectives on the Influences of Social Capital upon Internet Usage of Rural Guatemalan Teachers 218
Douglas Tedford, Fundación Rigoberta Menchú Tum, Guatemala

Chapter 13
Interactive Hypermedia-Based Learning Environment: Models of Making Sense of Dynamic Visualization 244
Billie Eilam, University of Haifa, Israel
Ofir Gortler, University of Haifa, Israel

Chapter 14
Using Email as a Cultural Bridge in the Learning Process for Transnational Students 264
Sandra Wilson Smith, Rowan University and Union College, USA

Chapter 15
Integrated Cross-Cultural Virtual Classroom Exchange Program:
How Adaptable Public Schools are in Korea and the USA? 284
Eunhee Jung O'Neil, Center for International Virtual Schooling, USA

Chapter 16
Live Interactive Virtual Explorations via the High Performance Wireless Research
and Education Network.. 311
Kimberly Mann Bruch, University of California at San Diego, USA
Hans-Werner Braun, University of California at San Diego, USA
Susan Teel, Southern California Research Learning Center, USA

Chapter 17
Effectiveness of Problem Based Learning for Engineering Curriculum 333
J.I. Rojas, Universitat Politècnica de Catalunya (UPC), Spain
X. Prats, Universitat Politècnica de Catalunya (UPC), Spain
A. Montlaur, Universitat Politècnica de Catalunya (UPC), Spain
M. Valero, Universitat Politècnica de Catalunya (UPC), Spain
E. García-Berro, Universitat Politècnica de Catalunya (UPC), Spain

Chapter 18
Using the How People Learn Framework for Online Course Design in Teacher Education.............. 360
Sharon Dole, Western Carolina University, USA
Lisa Bloom, Western Carolina University, USA

Compilation of References 377

About the Contributors 409

Index 417

Detailed Table of Contents

Foreword xiii

Preface xv

Chapter 1
Learning across Social Spaces 1
Gilbert Ahamer, Austrian Academy of Sciences, Austria
Josef Strobl, Austrian Academy of Sciences, Austria

The case explores the mutual link between education, structural evolution, social spaces and institutional change from theoretical perspectives as well as by practical applications. A series of cases in this chapter are for learning settings, especially dialogic intercultural learning and identified as a key path to a harmonious development of nations.

Chapter 2
Online Teaching Partnerships in Diverse Socio-Cultural Institutions 27
Julian Scheinbuks, Chicago State University, USA
Anthony A Pina, The Sullivan University System, USA

It is a case of an inter-institutional online teaching partnership through synchronous and asynchronous distance learning technologies so as to provide a way to teaching and learning that is socially accessible, technologically adaptable, economically viable, and politically agreeable.

Chapter 3
Balanced Assessment of Flexible E-Learning versus Face-to-Face Campus Delivery
Courses at an Australian University 42
Kenneth David Strang, University of Technology, Australia

This case highlights the values in using formal methodologies to gain an objective balanced perspective of actual practice and objectively measure whether flexible e-learning was at least as effective as campus delivery mode. It not only provides some ideas and benchmarks for competitive higher education but also explores the viability of Australian higher education model from international perspective.

Chapter 4
Planning a Quality University System: Using Technology to Increase Access to University Education 69
C. W. S. Sukati, University of Swaziland, Swaziland

This case analyses problems and challenges that now confront the Institute of Distance Education, University of Swaziland which work against the realization of its goals and it evaluates these challenges towards use of ICTs in the delivery of content. It also argues for the use of online learning, and the need for a new strategic plan for the university.

Chapter 5
Using Portable DVD Players to Deliver Interactive Simulations for Training Health Care Workers in Kenya 87
Hannum Wallace, The University of North Carolina at Chapel Hill, USA

This case focuses on a project in Kenya utilizing portable DVD players as a technology-based learning solution for providing continuing education to nurses by taking the instruction directly to the workplace of the nurses rather than by removing them from their villages and clinics. It explores how interactive simulations delivered by Technology-based learning using simulations holds great promise as an alternative or supplement to traditional classroom-based training in low-resource settings.

Chapter 6
Transnational Postgraduate Study for Development Workers: Using Technology to Bridge the Gap 103
Elizabeth A. Beckmann, The Australian National University, Australia
Patrick Kilby, The Australian National University, Australia

This case describes the STEP factors impacting on transnational learning in Master level program at the Australian National University. The case shows how flexible delivery of education allows development workers to continue their career progression while remaining fully active in the field, and enables them to engage in stimulating high-level discourse with their development practitioner peers as they apply theory to practice and thus enhances their day-to-day work activities.

Chapter 7
Learning Patterns of Learner's Interaction in the Learning Management Systems: A Comparative Study of China and Malaysia 123
Wu Bing, The University of Shanghai for Science and Technology, China
Teoh Ai Ping, Wawasan Open University, Malaysia
Ye Chun Ming, The University of Shanghai for Science and Technology, China

This case study looks at the understanding, expectation and experience of learners from China and Malaysia based on vital aspects of learning in the web-based environment which are reflected in the learning patterns and behavior of online learners. It also highlights the influence of national culture towards learners' interaction as displayed in their online learning activities.

Chapter 8
EPICT: Transnational Teacher Development through Blended Learning 147
Katalin Csoma, Embassy of Canada in Budapest, Hungary

This case aims to focus at the transnational teacher development program, the European Pedagogical ICT License (EPICT), which empowers teachers to use information technologies with greater efficiency in their everyday practice in overall perspective of the Hungarian experience, the present state of teacher training in line with the Bologna process and the joint European harmonization of education systems. It also examines how alternative forms of learning and networking bring about changes to the teaching profession in Europe and other affiliated countries.

Chapter 9
Japanese Students' Digitally Enabled Futures Images: A Synergistic Approach to Developing Academic Competencies 162
Michael Vallance, Future University Hakodate, Japan
David L. Wright, Future University Hakodate, Japan

This case illustrates how a Futures Studies approach encourages Japanese students to strategically analyze their futures by anticipating problems and stimulating collaborative solutions supported by creative digital media integration in the fore sighting contexts of local community and personal employment futures and thus analyzes the effectiveness of digitally enabled Futures Studies in promoting academic competencies of students in Japanese Higher Education.

Chapter 10
Development of a Transnational Framework for E-Learning Technologies.. 187
Deryn Graham, University of Greenwich, UK

This case by Deryn Graham attempts to look at the creation of a Transnational Framework for e-Learning Technologies in a United Kingdom institution from considering e-Tutoring/e-Moderating from a Human-Computer Interaction (HCI) point of view, to the adoption of Blended Learning as a solution to problems revealed by the Framework. It attempts to evaluate e-Learning in terms of STEP factors, which led to the realization of major external issues for e-Learning. Most recently, the study evolved to revisit e-Learning from an HCI and Computer-Supported Cooperative Work (CSCW) perspective, by applying a Cooperative Work Framework.

Chapter 11
Second Life Brought to Life: A Case of Usability In-World 203
Kevin Yee, University of Central Florida, USA
Jace Hargis, University of the Pacific, USA

This case on Second Life by Jace and Kevin presents the challenges and successes encountered when a university attempts to offer a course in a new online virtual learning environment (VLE) which needs to be unique and innovative. It discusses the rationality of significant STEP parameters involved in this process in order to provide an innovative, individualized teaching and learning model.

Chapter 12
Perspectives on the Influences of Social Capital upon Internet Usage
of Rural Guatemalan Teachers 218
Douglas Tedford, Fundación Rigoberta Menchú Tum, Guatemala

This case of Internet Usage of Rural Guatemalan Teachers by Douglas identifies the influences of bonding, bridging and linking social capital upon teacher Internet usage in the rural Guatemalan town of San Lucas Toliman. It highlights that the bonding and bridging social capital influences of family, friends, technology experts and school administrators have significant positive and negative effects upon teacher decisions to use the Internet.

Chapter 13
Interactive Hypermedia-Based Learning Environment: Models of Making
Sense of Dynamic Visualization 244
Billie Eilam, University of Haifa, Israel
Ofir Gortler, University of Haifa, Israel

This case by Billie and Ofir on Interactive Hypermedia-Based Learning Environment illustrates the processes involved in the interpretation of a dynamic performance art in a hypermedia-based learning environment, followed by learning a hypermedia–based curriculum unit concerning this complex skill, and concluding by transferring this acquired knowledge for interpreting a new and different artwork. It also discusses how this learning environment enabled most students to overcome some of the difficulties involved in this dynamic visualization, but presented them with other difficulties. A careful consideration of these issues as related to the design, by curriculum developers and teachers may yield a successful students' performance.

Chapter 14
Using Email as a Cultural Bridge in the Learning Process for Transnational Students 264
Sandra Wilson Smith, Rowan University and Union College, USA

This case emphasizes on theme-based American composition and rhetoric courses with an embedded focus on social, political, and/or popular cultural issues can be especially challenging for transnational students who are less conversant with this cultural information than many of their native-born peers. Sandra Wilson Smith in this case makes an effort to focus how email discussion can be incorporated organically into a learning/writing task, and how this discussion can be student-framed as the students are empowered to act autonomously and construct their own learning activity.

Chapter 15
Integrated Cross-Cultural Virtual Classroom Exchange Program:
How Adaptable Public Schools are in Korea and the USA? 284
Eunhee Jung O'Neil, Center for International Virtual Schooling, USA

Eunhee Jung O'Neil views that the educational institutions need to provide students with cultural learning opportunities and ICT skills. In this case, she discusses a cross-cultural virtual classroom exchange program using an online course management system in public schools in Korea and the USA. The case analyzes the adaptability of public schools in Korea and the USA with respect to integrating cross-cultural virtual exchange activities within their respective curricula and recommends solutions for increasing adaptability, and invites international collaboration among education stakeholders to disseminate the cross-cultural virtual learning worldwide.

Chapter 16
Live Interactive Virtual Explorations via the High Performance Wireless Research and Education Network 311
Kimberly Mann Bruch, University of California at San Diego, USA
Hans-Werner Braun, University of California at San Diego, USA
Susan Teel, Southern California Research Learning Center, USA

Kimberly, Hans and Susan, the researchers affiliated with the National Science Foundation funded High Performance Wireless Research and Education Network (HPWREN), are conducting case studies and facilitating technology transfer activities that enable Live Interactive Virtual Explorations (LIVE) between hard-to-reach science sites and an array of education communities. This chapter discusses lessons learned – both technological and pedagogical – during a longitudinal study of HPWREN LIVE case studies and technology transfer activities.

Chapter 17
Effectiveness of Problem Based Learning for Engineering Curriculum 333
J.I. Rojas, Universitat Politècnica de Catalunya (UPC), Spain
X. Prats, Universitat Politècnica de Catalunya (UPC), Spain
A. Montlaur, Universitat Politècnica de Catalunya (UPC), Spain
M. Valero, Universitat Politècnica de Catalunya (UPC), Spain
E. García-Berro, Universitat Politècnica de Catalunya (UPC), Spain

This case of Problem Based Learning (PBL) experience covers a wide spectrum of educational aspects, ranging from theoretical disciplines, such as fluid dynamics and rocket dynamics, to topics more related to experimental work and hardware utilization like the certification of the rockets, as well as the rocket altitude measurements. The case study shows some problems and improvements, academic results and lessons learned from the PBL approach. Finally, a series of new ideas related to Model Rocket Workshop (MRW) and the subject it belongs to are presented. The objective is to expand the MRW so that it embraces the totality of the activities that constitute this mother-subject. As a consequence, the former would then become a new subject entirely based on PBL.

Chapter 18
Using the How People Learn Framework for Online Course Design in Teacher Education 360
Sharon Dole, Western Carolina University, USA
Lisa Bloom, Western Carolina University, USA

This case study by Sharon and Lisa uses the How People Learn (HPL) framework as the conceptual model to examine online courses in a teacher education program for evidence of high level learning outcomes. The outcome of the study demonstrates that the HPL framework provides a powerful structure for creating and assessing environments conducive to the work of prospective professionals.

Compilation of References 377

About the Contributors 409

Index 417

Foreword

Since at least the Industrial Revolution, the imperative for people, communities and nations to adapt to technological change has been unceasing. Initially, some people could hide from the consequences of technological change, others—notably the Luddites— criticised and resisted its consequences, and some were outside of its reach. Indeed, even today there are some people who live their lives in relatively isolated communities 'free' from the demands and resources of contemporary life. It is difficult, however, to say that anyone or any place is 'free' of the consequences of post-industrial society. The entire world is 'governed' in some form or another, even if in some places it is through weak or contested governance. Also, we have known for decades that the consequences for the environment of industrialisation and some of its disasters know no boundaries. A damaged ozone layer affected the planet over previous decades, and rising carbon dioxide levels are doing likewise now. It is difficult for anyone to 'hide' from these global consequences. For the majority of the world's citizens the developments led by scientific and intellectual innovation have been just that: developments. Notwithstanding the costs and consequences, social and economic change has broadly benefited the world's citizens. In particular, the technical and technological advances in computing and communications have been so significant and widespread that they have required a new term to be coined to conceptualise and understand their consequences: globalisation.

The enormous development of electronic communications and, later, computer technology over the past century has encased the globe in an invisible and untouchable atmosphere. An atmosphere that it is crowded with signals and signs of human activity yet is unobservable and unknowable without the technical means (radio, mobile phone, computers) to receive the signals. Most importantly in the context of this book—*Cases on Technological Adaptability and Transnational Learning: Issues and Challenges*—it is unknowable without the knowledge and skills to read and understand the signs. This requires sufficient good education being provided to the world's citizens so that they can read and understand the signals and signs, and create and transmit their own in a purposeful and knowledgeable way. Many of these same citizens are required for the creation and use of the next new technologies. So, although we tend think that we are the generation facing technological change here and now, we are merely the current generation of a succession that extends back to late 18th Century England. Hence, technological change isn't new and it isn't going away!

Education and its systems are themselves processes and products of technological change. As noted above, without the knowledge and skills it is impossible for citizens to participate in contemporary society, and without advanced specialist skills and knowledge it is impossible to create the ideas, conduct the research and develop the products and systems that enable future social and economic developments. For education to remain pertinent to the emerging world, it is necessary for it to continuously adapt and reform. It is this context that this book—*Cases on Technological Adaptability and Transnational Learning: Issues and Challenges*— addresses. It provides cases of education adapting to, and adapting, new technologies to provide learning conditions and opportunities for students from a variety of backgrounds and circumstances. In particular, it provides examples where the aforementioned educational practices and technological adaptations are addressed to transnational audiences and circumstances. Undertaking such developments requires, not just technical adaptability and technological understanding, but also social and cultural understanding and sensitivity.

The capacity of new computer and communications technologies to 'deliver' courses internationally and globally is well-recognised and underpins this book. In many respects, distances are irrelevant to the 'delivery' of course-materials in electronic form over the internet. Students 'on-campus' may receive their material or participate in online discussions simultaneously with students half a world away. However, transnational educational activities need to be built on mutual national understandings and respect otherwise they risk being forms of cultural invasion and colonization. These are part of the 'issues and challenges' reflected and/or addressed explicitly by *Cases on Technological Adaptability and Transnational Learning: Issues and Challenges.* There is an implicit invitation here for readers to reflect critically on the substance of the chapters and on the implications for their own practice. Which new computer and communications technologies are appropriate and efficacious for their own educational practices? What are the personal, social and cultural implications of their (intended) transnational educational practices? What can they identify and learn from the contributions to this book in these respects? There are many 'gems' to be 'mined' from the contributions to *Cases on Technological Adaptability and Transnational Learning: Issues and Challenges*. It is important, however, that readers bring their own perspectives and contexts to 'cutting and polishing' these gems to 'set' them into their own educational contexts. Good transnational education demands no less.

Professor Terry Evans
Deakin University, Australia

***Terry Evans** is a Professor of Education at Deakin University, Geelong, Australia. He is Chief Investigator on two Australian Research Council Projects: Research capacity-building: the development of the Australian PhD programs in national and emerging global contexts (with M Pearson & P Macauley); Australian doctoral graduates' publication, professional and community outcomes (with P Macauley), and an AusAID Australian Development Research Grant entitled, Identifying strategies to sustain professional learning communities for teachers in remote primary schools in Papua New Guinea (with E Honan, S Muspratt, A Kukari & P Paraide). Terry Evans has published widely on distance education and doctoral education, in particular he has co-edited (with M Haughey & D Murphy) The International Handbook of Distance Education, (2008, Bingley, UK, Emerald Publishing), and (with C Denholm) Doctorates Downunder: Keys to successful doctoral study in Australia and New Zealand (Melbourne, ACER, 2006), Supervising doctorates downunder: Keys to effective supervision in Australia and New Zealand (Melbourne, ACER, 2007) and Beyond Doctorates Downunder: maximising the impact of your Australian or New Zealand doctorate (Melbourne, ACER, 2009).*

Preface

Technology is the very essence of development and it holds the key for bridging the gap between access to quality education and the need for enhanced learning experiences. Can we have a platform wherein we can share our experiences for technological adaptability and collaborative strategies for sustained development of education across the globe? How are the organizations and institutions of learning in the developing and developed world adapting to advancements in technology for providing educational opportunities with a transnational perspective? Can there be an international platform for policy makers, educators and trainers, educational administrators and researchers contributing and sharing their experiences, ideas, attitudes and perspectives on how institutions in their respective countries are addressing Social, Technological, Economical and Political (STEP) dimensions? In a single volume, is it possible to have case studies on one hand from developed world for innovation and application of technology in education and transnational learning and on the other from the developing world for cost effective technology towards improved access and equity to education and transnational learning experience through international collaboration? These were the core questions in our mind when we thought of developing this book.

These thoughts have now given a shape to a book with case studies on divergent themes of personalized learning environments, e-learning and virtual learning, inclusive learning for social change, innovative learning and assessment techniques, technology in training and development, cost effective technology for access and equity in learning and growth, collaborated and networked learning environments, virtual learning in transnational perspectives, emerging technologies and accessibility, technology enhanced learning, technology and international partnership and transnational collaboration for enhanced access under the core domain of technological adaptability and transnational learning.

In all, 18 chapters in this book provide excellent case studies from the USA, New Zealand, Japan, Swaziland, Austria, Australia, China, Malaysia, Hungary, Guatemala, Israel and Spain. In a single book, it is interesting to read thought provoking cases on future studies, social spaces, virtual explorations via the high performance wireless research and education network, interactive simulation for training, online course for teacher education, Second Life, performance art in hypermedia and transnational collaborative cases on e-learning technologies, e-mail bridging the cultural gap, virtual classroom exchange programs, teacher development, online teaching partnerships and development workers. Besides, this volume has case studies on problem based learning, influences of social capital upon internet usage in Guatemala, comparative perspective of learning patterns and assessment of flexible e-learning vis-a-vis face-to-face campus and technology for enhanced access in Swaziland.

The first chapter by Gilbert Ahamer and Josef Strobl in this compilation of cases explores the mutual link between education, structural evolution, social spaces and institutional change. It builds a theoretical perspective on "Space" which according to the authors is understood as being created by social, specially communicative action and can hence be generated anew by pervasive learning processes.

Learning across social spaces means both intercultural and interdisciplinary learning and places learners into diverse systems of meaning. This approach is then substantiated with the help of a series of cases exemplifying international and cross-cultural exchanges for learning which is thought to be the key to a harmonious development of nations.

The chapter *Online Teaching Partnerships in Diverse Socio-Cultural Institutions* by Julian Scheinbuks and Anthony A. Pina, is a case of Online Teaching Partnership (OTP) involving three public universities in the United States which possess diverse student population. This online cross-disciplinary collaborative initiative facilitated interactions amongst students and faculty through synchronous and asynchronous distance learning technologies. Scheinbuks and Pina believe that this partnership resulted into many positive outcomes and met the basic goals of providing enhanced technological exposure to the students, making the faculty better competent in using technology for creation and modification of courses that use technology in different settings, developing online courses for degree completion, and encouraging and providing an enriched learning experience. This inter-institutional effort positively affected the students and faculty resulting into better educational experience, broadened outlook and made the course more interesting.

This chapter objectively measures whether flexible e-learning is as effective as campus delivery mode. This case study *Balanced Assessment of Flexible e-learning versus Face-to-face Campus Delivery Courses at an Australian University* by Kenneth Strang assesses this important aspect not only by performance and student satisfaction but by six factors linked to Australian university accreditation, namely, industry focus, resources/content materials, critical thinking activities, teaching quality, student satisfaction, and student performance (including completion). During the research, Strang observed that due to 2008 global economic crises, the international student market is changing which is forcing the universities to change what and how they offer higher education in the future. While the case provides some ideas and benchmarks for competitive higher education, simultaneously it also explores the viability of Australian higher education model from international perspective.

With the increasing number of students at the post-secondary level, a need has been felt for developing viable alternative mode of providing education in developing world. This will help to provide adequate quality higher education facilities to the students. So more and more universities are turning towards distance education (DE) and/or a blend of conventional face to face (CF2F) and online learning methods for imparting education. Responding to similar needs, the University of Swaziland established the Institute of Distance Education (IDE) in 1994 to increase access to university education by offering its programmes through distance education. This successful attempt has however led to a number of challenges facing IDE that hinder in the realization of its goals. This chapter by Walter Sukati argues for the use of online learning, and the need for a new strategic plan for the University. The author believes there is a need for harnessing the new technologies in DE and in CF2F learning methods and thereby blur the boundaries between the two modes.

The author of *Using Portable DVD Players to Deliver Interactive Simulations for Training Health Care Workers in Kenya*, Hannum Wallace believes technology-based learning using simulations such as portable DVD players holds great promise as an alternative or supplement to traditional classroom-based training in low-resource settings. This case study looks into technological interventions for providing training to heath care workers in Kenya. It reports on a project in Kenya for using interactive simulations by portable DVD players for providing continuing education to nurses at their workplace without compromising with their professional commitments. This study demonstrates that technology can bring learner-centered interactive video simulations for consistent content and uniform learning experiences towards significant learning gains.

Elizabeth A. Beckmann and Patrick Kilby in the present case study describe the STEP factors impacting on transnational learning in Master of Applied Anthropology and Participatory Development program at the Australian National University. The case shows how flexible delivery of education allows development workers to continue their career progression while remaining fully active in the field, and enables them to engage in stimulating high-level discourse with their development practitioner peers as they apply theory to practice and thus enhances their day-to-day work activities.

The seventh chapter of the book by Wu Bing, Teoh Ai Ping and Ye Chun Ming provides a comparative study on vital aspects of learning and learner's interaction in the Learning Management System of universities in China and Malaysia. It looks into the varied and important dimensions of online learning such as teaching and learning, the role of the teacher, communication patterns in the virtual scenario, learner-tutor relationships and attitudes towards learning achievement. This case also explores the influence of national culture on learners' interaction in virtual learning environment.

This case focuses on a transnational teacher development program, the European Pedagogical ICT License (EPICT), which equips the teachers with the requisite skills to use information technologies with greater efficiency in their everyday practice. Beyond introducing the program through the Hungarian experience, the present state of teacher training is discussed by Katalin Csoma, under transformation in line with the Bologna process and the joint European harmonization of education systems. It examines how alternative forms of learning and international collaboration and networking bring about changes to the teaching profession in Europe and other affiliated countries.

Can the systematic and analytical study of the future help the students to shape their future with desired set of outcomes? The ninth chapter of this book by Michael Vallance and David L. Wright attempts to address this strategic question. It illustrates how a Futures Studies approach encourages Japanese students to strategically analyze their futures by anticipating problems and stimulating collaborative solutions. The studies in the chapter *Japanese Students' Digitally Enabled Futures Images: A Synergistic Approach to Developing Academic Competencies* support that the students become active participants of a learning process by creative digital media integration which results into measurable outcomes of academic competencies. The case explores two foresighting contexts i.e. local community and personal employment futures and the data from both the contexts are analyzed to assess the effectiveness of digitally enabled Futures Studies so that academic competencies of students in Japanese Higher Education can be promoted. The article concludes with personal critiques from digitally enabled learning and Futures Studies perspectives.

The tenth chapter of the book is a case study by Deryn Graham that looks at the creation of a Transnational Framework for e-Learning Technologies. The author attempts to describe how the original study which aimed to "Develop a Framework for e-Learning" has gone through several iterations from e-Tutoring/e-Moderating to the adoption of Blended Learning as a solution to problems revealed by the Framework. The author also highlights challenges of e-learning such as other forms of interaction and their requirements in developing the framework. The author has explored e-Learning in terms of PESTE (Political, Economic, Social, Technical and Environmental) factors, and led to the realization of major external issues for e-Learning. Most recently, the study evolved to revisit e-Learning from an HCI and Computer-Supported Cooperative Work (CSCW) perspective, by applying a Cooperative Work Framework.

This case study presents the challenges and successes experienced by a university while attempting to offer a course in Second Life, a new online virtual learning environment (VLE), which is community driven and connects individuals through a new, avatar-driven interface offering spontaneous experience and companionship. The authors in this chapter Jace Hargis and Kevin Yee are of the view that overcoming the resistance towards change requires many aspects—innovation, expertise, funds, culture, persistence, attitude, collaboration, willingness to take risk and possibly open to experiencing a failed event and above all, a necessity for addressing the individual needs of student learning. The authors also believe that the success of this new VLE in higher education largely depends on the ability of the institutions to develop networks and reach outside of those networks for expertise, input, and commitments.

The subsequent chapter by Douglas Tedford is a case study for identifying the influences of bonding, bridging and linking social capital upon teacher Internet usage in the rural Guatemalan town of San Lucas Toliman by a collaborative effort of the author as a facilitator here with the Fundación Rigoberta Menchú Tum in Guatelmala. Employing Participatory Rural Appraisal, community perspectives were invited for identifying the study problem, designing interview questions, and evaluating data. The research findings revealed that bonding and bridging social capital influences of family, friends, technology experts and school administrators were found to have significant positive and negative implications on teacher decisions to use the Internet in a region with inadequate buying power and limited telecommunications infrastructure.

The present case is an example of learning the performance art i.e. a dynamic, ill-structured knowledge domain in a hypermedia environment. The authors Billie Eilam and Ofir Gortler opine that interpretation of performance art is highly complex, but is important in visual culture. Generally, this learning environment enabled most students to overcome some of the difficulties involved in this dynamic visualization, but presented them with other difficulties. A careful consideration of these issues as related to the design, by curriculum developers and teachers may yield a successful students' performance. This case examines the students' performance art interpretation when they are learning and interacting with information in a hypermedia-based environment. The case illustrates how students learning art experienced for the first time the processes involved in the interpretation of a dynamic performance art in a hypermedia-based learning environment. The case explores learning a hypermedia–based curriculum unit concerning this complex skill, and concludes how to transfer this acquired knowledge for interpreting a new, different artwork. Cognitive aspects of students' profiles of understanding and models of enactment i.e. the multi-stage interactive model, the model of intermediate stages, and the deficient stages model are described in this chapter.

Sandra Wilson Smith in this study focuses on the ways by which discussion through email can be incorporated organically into a learning/writing task, and how this discussion can be student-framed. She states that the fact that the students initiate the email communication of their own volition taps into the positive qualities that computer-mediated communication (CMC) has and it can assist in bridging the cultural gap experienced in the learning process by transnational students who are less familiar with social, political, and cultural issues in theme based composition and rhetoric courses.

In the next chapter *Integrated Cross-cultural Virtual Classroom Exchange Program: How Adaptable Public Schools are in Korea and the USA* authored by Eunhee Jung O'Neil, the author discusses the adaptability of public schools in Korea and USA in a cross-cultural virtual classroom exchange program i.e. International Virtual Elementary Classroom Activities (IVECA) which is designed to provide cross-cultural learning opportunities by using ICT to effectively develop intercultural competence through public school curricula. The overall objective of this paper is to suggest strategies for international collaboration with education stakeholders to disseminate the cross-cultural virtual learning in public schools worldwide. This paper attempts to investigate technological, pedagogical, and organizational factors responsible for the adaptability of public schools in Korea and the USA with respect to integrating cross-cultural virtual exchange activities within their respective curricula.

Kimberly Mann Bruch and Hans-Werner Braun of San Diego Supercomputer Center and Susan Teel of National Park Service, California Mediterranean Research Learning Center have authored this chapter wherein they have discussed case studies of distance learning experiments conducted at National

Science Foundation funded High Performance Wireless Research and Education Network (HPWREN) connected science sites such as California Wolf Center, Cabrillo National Monument, the Palomar Observatory, and the Santa Margarita Ecological Reserve. The paper also explores the technology transfer activities that enable Live Interactive Virtual Explorations (LIVE) hard-to-reach science sites and an array of education communities.

This case study illustrates the practical experience in a Model Rocket Workshop (MRW), where students design, simulate, build, test and launch a small model rocket. The workshop itself provides a learning experience which is a Problem Based Learning (PBL) involving group puzzle technique and covering a wide spectrum of educational aspects, ranging from theoretical disciplines, such as fluid dynamics and rocket dynamics, to topics more related to experimental work and hardware utilization like the certification of the rockets, as well as the rocket altitude measurements. The case in this chapter attempts to explore some problems and improvements, academic results and lessons learned from the PBL approach in MRW. Finally, a series of new ideas related to MRW and the subject it belongs to are presented.

Finally, the chapter on using How People Learn (HPL) framework as the conceptual model to examine online courses in a teacher education program for evidence of high level learning outcomes by Sharon Dole and Lisa Bloom, demonstrates that this framework provides a powerful structure for creating and assessing environments conducive to the work of prospective professionals. This study assumes significance in the wake of growing demand for online teacher education programs not only in the United States but also in other countries.

The case studies in this volume evidently point towards an important fact that the technology is one of the principle catalysts for transnational collaborative interventions in providing learning and professional development opportunities to the people both in developed as well as in developing world. More so, collaborations with the help of technological innovations are instrumental in bringing the educational prospects to the people in the lesser developed part of the world thus providing them the much needed support required for their socio-economic development.

Finally, we as editors of this volume would like to extend our sincere thanks and gratitude to the authors of the case studies who shared their valuable experiences and insightful thoughts making this an excellent platform for presenting innovations in technological adaptability with a transnational perspective. It is hoped that the readers will find this book useful and it will prove to be an interesting reading for all those in the field of education and technology. We also take this opportunity to thank the IGI-Global team for being so supportive and helpful in every phase of the development of this book.

Siran Mukerji
Purnendu Tripathi
Editors

Chapter 1
Learning across Social Spaces

Gilbert Ahamer
Austrian Academy of Sciences, Austria

Josef Strobl
Austrian Academy of Sciences, Austria

ABSTRACT

This case explores the mutual link between education, structural evolution, social spaces and institutional change. It develops theoretical perspectives and illustrates them by practical cases. Three approaches of learning (psychological, evolutionist and ontological) lead to specific targets for successful learning settings, both for individual and societal learning. A series of structural transitions seems to best characterize the genesis of economies, civilizations and targets. "Space" is here understood as being created by social, esp. communicative action and can hence be generated anew by pervasive learning processes. Learning across social spaces means both intercultural and interdisciplinary learning and places learners into diverse systems of meaning. In a series of cases for learning settings, especially dialogic intercultural learning is identified as a key path to a harmonious development of nations.

QUESTIONS AND ANSWERS

1. What theoretical standpoint should we adopt towards learning?
2. Can our lessons learned from individual learning also be applied to societal learning?
3. What does civilisational evolution tell us about suitable targets and methods of learning?
4. Does "institution building" have a natural place in civilisational evolution?
5. Is it helpful to think of social space as a substrate and tool for our learning procedures?
6. Will the emerging "network society" support the creation of meaning, i.e. societal learning?

The following chapters will provide answers and the case studies will show implementations.

DOI: 10.4018/978-1-61520-779-4.ch001

WHAT IS LEARNING?

Several basic approaches can be taken towards learning. The direction in which one understands learning predetermines the learning setting considered as optimal. Consequently, it is a prerequisite to reach clarity about how one might understand "learning". This chapter proposes:

1. learning as mental structural change (psychological approach)
2. learning as leapfrogging biological and evolutionary cycles (evolutionist approach)
3. learning as creating new (mental, existential) spaces by reflection (ontological approach).

In any case, it will be useful to keep in mind both *learning of individuals* and *learning of society*.

Learning is Mental Structural Change

According to a psychological approach, learning is understood as *mental structural change* that leads to change in real-world behaviour. In this view, learning would be only successful if it results in changes of the person's real actions. Let us undertake a "tour d'horizon", in which contexts we may find a similar viewpoint and how fixed or loose border conditions for such learning should be:

Here we examine any type of learning, especially life-long learning for adults (Strobl & Car, 2009, Lenz, 2005) and we draw conclusions from decades of our own teaching, learning and training experience in both roles, active and passive. Often, learning is most productive when taking the role of a trainer. We adopt a constructivist stance, under the philosophical auspices of John Dewey's *Pragmatism* (Berding, 2000, Haack, 2004, Grippe, 2002). In the resulting picture, in order to reach the mentioned structural mental change, the *core action is dialogue* and *exchange of views in a discourse*, constituting Dewey's "education for responsible democracy".

As does democracy, education deeply involves ethics: it is based on the "principle of responsibility" (Jonas, 1984, Stähli, 1998, 2005, Werner, 2003). Here, preference is given to *teleologic* (target oriented) ethics as opposed to *deontologic* (duty oriented) ethics – stressing the result of any human action as preferred to theoretical and subjective conviction.

For facilitating such dialogue, a very helpful approach is: "learning through gaming" (Prensky, 2001, Ahamer, 2004). Symbolically, a gaming setting means to leave a "play" in the rigid mechanisms of traditional reproduction of content by allowing for trial and error in a modelled ("game") scenario. Coherent with the affiliation of the authors, such endeavour of responsibility-oriented teaching encompasses both the area of e-learning and (human) geography (Popke, 2003: 298, Cloke, 2002: 589). An "*ethics of encounter*" (Popke, 2003: 300, Cutchin, 2002: 660) is both facilitated by *e-learning tools* and *geo-referenced* in a multicultural sense. Supported by web-based tools and e-learning didactics (and especially by virtual globes: Strobl, 2007a, 2001, Strobl & Linder-Fally, 2007), we are led to say: "out of sight, but *in* mind".

Let us consider another perspective on learning: according to design literature, iterative oscillation occurs between the *problem* space and the *solution* space (Maher, 2003; Dorst & Cross, 2001: 434). Such loose type of oscillating interaction between the two "spaces", namely to act and to reflect, is also well characterized by the pedagogic concept of "*reflection-in-action*", a pedagogical and managerial principle combining sequences of contemplative and actionist aspects (Schön, 1983, 1986: 62, Lawless & Roth, 2001) that has been applied to learning individuals but also to learning organisations.

In an influential article that has prompted a series of responses and comments, Roth et al. (2001) instead propose the notion of "*Spielraum*"

– a word that the Canadian authors import into English language from German. It has the meaning "room to play" both in the sense of game-based learning (Pivec et al., 2004) and in the sense of machinery as the desired clearance a joint has in order to allow for motion. So, there should be a playful element or "game" in learning in both senses. The symbolic usage of the word "play" suggests allowing students to enjoy a near-to-real-life situation without fearing the merciless real-world sanctions of suboptimal behaviour (Fresner et al., 2007: 21).

Concluding from the above, "leeway for wits and senses" (Tröhler, 2007) should be allowed in any learning setting. *Spielraum* is "elbow room" (an effective existence radius of the self) according to Jaros (2007) who stems from spatial planning and argues that "the self depends for its ability to recognise itself primarily on collisions that suspend the flow of spatialised complexity".

After decades of classroom experience narrated in vivid examples, Roth et al. (2001: 183) "propose 'Spielraum' as room to manoeuvre, as a concept that describes the reality of teaching much better than reflection-in-action, especially when there is no time out for reflection." They "therefore see [themselves as teachers] always at some point in time and space which means for them to take into account the specific individual situation of students in the given classroom. Readiness for appropriate action, whatever the unfolding events, means that the agent has Spielraum, the room to manoeuvre appropriately in the current situation. According to Heidegger (1977), *Dasein* (being here) "combines self and world into a single irreducible entity, being-in-the-world, in the face of all the contingencies real-time interactions pose to the participants involved" (Roth et al. 2001: 186) and "constitutes the location from which a person negotiates the world" (Popke, 2003, 302). Not the teacher's but "the students' own questions guide or scaffold students because they always test the outer edge of their students' current reality. The questions therefore can neither be completely in the teacher's reality nor completely internal to students' reality, but always along the interface of the two. Students are the builders of their own reality" (Roth et al., 2001: 186-201).

Summing up this subchapter 1.1, readers may believe that the following views are helpful:

- learners construct their own reality
- learners benefit from less pressure of real-life consequences
- in the optimal case, trainers and teachers have a set of reactions at their disposal ready to implement them even without lengthy reflections
- learning individuals proceed on a largely unpredictable path; and trying to understand learners' unforeseen explanatory constructions dissolves and replaces immature concepts in teachers' mindsets. No theory whatsoever sufficiently describes real learning paths of individuals.

To continue, we propose one step of reasoning: what applied to individual learning (i.e. of students), may apply also to societal learning, namely to the long-term evolution of countries.

The findings for individual learning deduced from this section in the above four bullets will be adapted to societal learning in the four bullets of the following subchapter 1.2.

Learning is Leapfrogging Biological and Evolutionary Cycles

Recently several universities have launched initiatives in "intercultural learning" (e.g. Global Studies, 2009) which means that students are trained to better understand divergent cultural and ethical concepts. Thinking of states, countries, economies and cultures (instead of students), we may conclude:

- countries construct their own realities and their own national rationalities and sense

– which might harmonise or not with concepts of sense in other countries or other populations (Castells & Arsenault, 2006: 285)

- the understanding of other cultures and their civilisational trajectories is likely to benefit from loosening the tightness of pre-fabricated explanatory patterns – for example macro-economic theories of one kind or another that state "how economies develop and grow" (Mankiw, 1990: 1646, Coats, 1985: 1718) and believe to be correct even in a historical sense (Heilbronner, 1990: 1097)
- the ones considering themselves as leaders are not likely to act based on thorough, reflected or even scientific understanding of ongoing complex procedures but rather based on "preconceptive understandings", visions, or "preanalytic cognitive acts" (Schumpeter, 1949, Heilbronner, 1990: 1109), similar to an elbow room in the strict sense
- economies proceed on a largely unpredictable path when developing; trying to understand such real techno-socio-economic development quickly unveils the tremendous limitations of economic theories, be they (neo-)classical or Keynesian. No theory whatsoever sufficiently describes real learning paths of societies.

As a consequence, it is proposed to follow the real-world paths of evolutionary development instead of following the results of theoretical concepts boiled down to a set of formulas. Purely formula-centred understanding of economics tumbles down the abyss of non-perceived complexity, it remains painfully simple. *Priority to phenomena!* Freedom from formulas! To promote "reflective science", the sociologist Bourdieu has created a method of letting the phenomena speak for themselves (Robbins, 2007: 87).

Complexity is the major challenge in multi-actor networks where one actor forms the framework condition and context for the other. Complexity might be seen as a major challenge of slowly maturing rational science (Ahamer et al., 2009: 7). Robust knowledge is always situated and situating (Roth et al., 2001: 203). Foresight has to be trained especially for entrepreneurs as an art involving intuition and creativity (Fontela et al., 2006: 11).

Current Theorising on Global Structural Evolution

Learning on the societal level means also the creation, development and strengthening of new emerging societal institutions (Papenhausen, 2009: 5). These might be likely to appear cyclically (Freeman & Louca, 2001), according to Kondratieff's famous analysis of economic long waves that he performed in the 1920s. Which other shape could a developing trend show? Linear, curvilinear, a sequence of saturation states (Menzel, 1996: 35ff, Mensch, 1975, Wagner-Döbler, 1998: 67) or just a complex pattern of syndromes? No single "theory" (reducing itself to a simple cause-and-effect style) is capable of explaining consistently the complexity of global historical dynamics – even if several explanatory patterns were applied, such as the unsatisfying "climatic explanation" for differences in economic and cultural development (Landes, 2000, Mokyr, 1990).

Hence we take the pragmatic standpoint to just take into account what we see in civilisational evolution, even without being able to explain it. A series of saturation states is proposed (Figure 1) as a long-term meta-pattern of civilisational evolution (and hence of "societal learning") that hypothesizes that institution building and generation of societal structures takes place after each saturation phase has matured (compare Raskin et al., 2002, Mensch, 1995 cited after Menzel, 1995: 35). The evolutionary magnitudes in Figure 1 might be for example population, nutrition

Figure 1. A series of saturation states is hypothesized as the long-term dynamic pattern of civilisational evolution along centuries

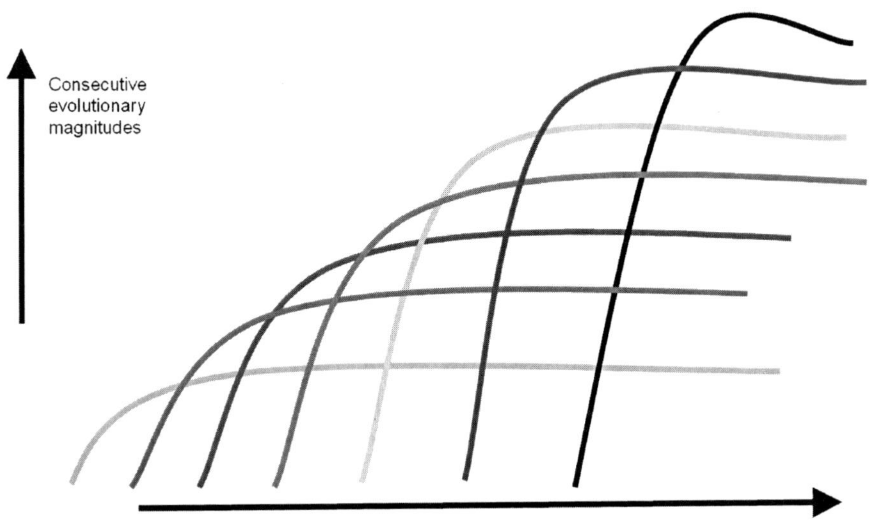

per person, meat share in nutrition, agricultural efficiency or similar systemic variables.

Sometimes it is believed that data series not covering complete centuries are the main obstacle to describing a wide range of evolutionary stages (Menzel, 1996: 15) because they cover only some decades. Instead, the method of the "Global Change Data Base" GCDB (Ahamer, 2001) suggests ordering countries along GDP/cap instead of historic time. This allows to reconstruct patterns along "evolutionary time" (approximated by GDP/cap) in the same way as reconstructing an antique vase from several fragments with supposedly repetitive design. Additionally, such waves of development do not run in parallel for all countries within historic time (Menzel, 1996: 16) but rather within recalibrated "evolutionary time". As shown by data analysis, to the approach of evolutionary economics (Saviotti, 2007: 2), *economic development creates new structures, new institutions and organisations* – also educational institutions – which is at the heart of the theme of this entire volume (Mukerji & Tripathi, 2009).

Therefore this paper tries to derive pedagogical targets from long-term dynamics of social development, namely that learners should become apt to master the specific challenges of their countries' evolutionary phase.

Other attempts have been made relying on a cyclical historical world view (Papenhausen, 2009: 12) identifying pedagogical trends characteristic for each Kondratieff cycle; but we prefer an evolutionary world view suggesting a series of maturing civilisational themes leading towards a "society of sense" (Horx, 2007). In any case, the innovation of institutions, especially the genesis, development and maturisation of educational institutions (Tripathi & Mukerji, 2008) might still be co-determined by long economic waves (Papenhausen, 2009: 7).

The following three sub-chapters provide quantitative examples for the hypothesis of global structural evolution behaving in the pattern hypothesised in Figure 1: both the agricultural and energy system are described by a simple array of quotients that allows attributing change rates to each one of the logical subsystems quantified by the respective quotient.

Figure 2. The agronomical chain of cause and effect leading from the variable area (supply side) to the variable population (demand side)

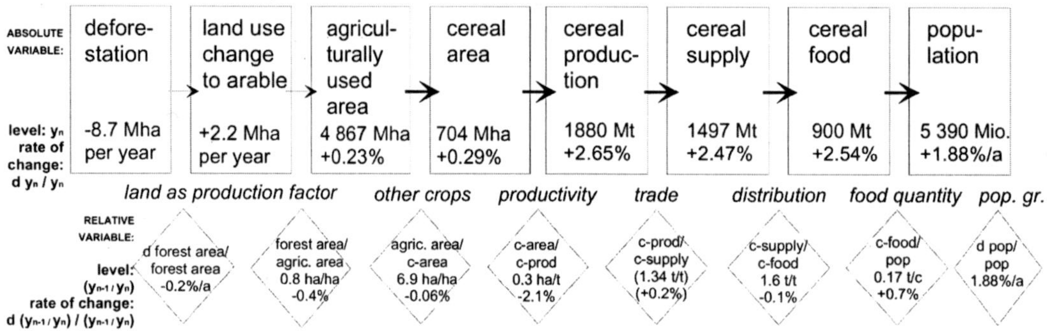

The Example of Global Agricultural Evolution

The example of the evolving global agroeconomic system is graphically shown in Figure 2. The main logical chain of cause and effect is demonstrated by a sequence of parameters (y_n, global levels and their change rates, see in the rectangles). However, the structural properties of the system are better described by the quotients of subsequent rectangles (y_{n-1} / y_{n-1}, global levels and change rates, see in the rhombuses).

The sequence of themes along this logical chain of rhombuses reads: land as production factor in the economic sense (first three boxes), percentage of crops other than cereals, cereal area productivity, cereal trade, cereal distribution, cereal amount for food, and population (growth); or as formula:

Arable land use =

(arable land / cereal area) × (cereal area / cereals produced) × (cereals produced / cereals supplied) × (cereals supplied / cereals as food) × (cereals as food / capita) × population

This logical structure of Figure 2 is very simple, but allows already to describe the development over the course of historic time for each of the mentioned themes (e.g. quotients as a function of time). However, much clearer patterns of graphs are obtained when these quotients are depicted as functions of GDP/capita – which may be cautiously interpreted as economic level or "evolutionary time".

Figure 3 shows each of the quotients of the above formula as a function of GDP/cap for each country for the past decades as one averaged line. It can be seen that (1) even if there is considerable dispersion of the levels due to individual characteristics of the country, (2) the change rates for each country seem to unfold along almost the same direction which is suggested by the structure of parallel lines. In other words: may the global agronomical system show considerable divergences, yet its movement into the future is much less divergent. The "underlying law of motion" for the global agricultural system seems to exhibit rather constant change rates, even if starting from different levels.

Especially the parameters "area efficiency of cereal production", "the share of crops other than cereals", "cereal distribution" and "cereal intake per person" show parallel geometric structures.

This allows imagining that underlying societal structures develop in a largely analogous way in all countries of the world, a hypothesis that could even be extended to educational structures and institutions. Synchronicity is defined not so much by historical time t (such images would be tremen-

Figure 3. Land use as arable land is understood here as the product of six quotients which allows to discern dynamics arising from different aspects of life, as described in the text above. Each country shows an averaged path of development along the past decades along the horizontal direction describing the economic level (GDP/cap). For many of the six quotients, a visible increase of decrease of these six structural variables occurs on the path to higher GDP/cap

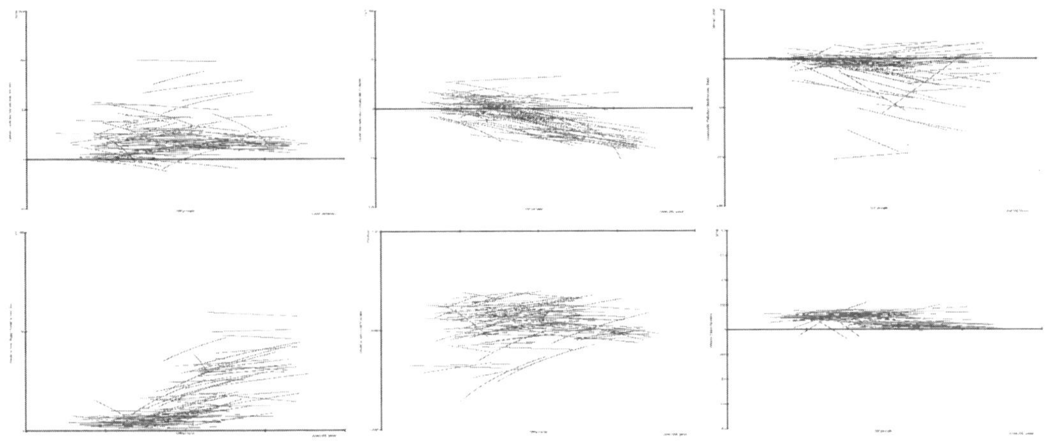

dously scattered) but by GDP/cap. Consequently, institutions might be both the (1) result and (2) precondition of suitable humanitarian and social development; the first mechanism being suggested by the above findings (sometimes correlated with "social capital", Mohan & Mohan, 2002: 196, Burt, 2000, Adler & Kwon, 2002) and the second mechanism lying at the core of any institutional educational promotion, often soberly labelled as "human resources" or "human capital" (Mukerji & Tripathi, 2004: 14, 2005) and representing one of the key findings of classical "growth theory". For "growth theories", GDP grows by investment in "human capital", in other words education: authors such as Barro (1991, 2001), Mankiw et al. (1992), Nonneman & VanHoudt (1996), Stokey (1991), Rosenzweig (1990), Becker et al. (1990) stress the importance of schooling, higher education and technological know-how as key factors to economic progress.

In this evolutionary picture of Figure 3, "successful societal learning" would mean that a country jumps forward on the path of developing its systemic parameters towards values that would normally correlate to a higher GDP/cap. In brief, learning means "leapfrogging material evolution by enhanced mental and social restructuring".

The Example of the Global Economic Structure

If a similar quantitative analysis of the long-term structural shift in the sectoral structure of the global economic system is undertaken (analogous figures in Ahamer, 2005a: 10-14), again a fundamental underlying trend of historic dimension can be detected: the percentages of sectoral GDP are significantly changing along the move towards a higher GDP/cap. When examining the subject in more depth (versus seeing only the widely known transition from agricultural to industrial and further on to service oriented economic structures), one perceives the following trends:

- Needs of the individual → needs of society
- Single (building) projects → implementation of a collective (built) structure

Figure 4.

$$CO_2 = (CO_2/E_{prim}) \cdot (E_{prim}/E_{end}) \cdot (E_{end}/GNP) \cdot (GNP/QL) \cdot (QL/P) \cdot P$$

Legend: CO_2 = CO_2 emissions, E = (primary or final) energy, GNP = Gross National Product, QL = quality of life, P = population.

- Material targets (quantitative growth) → well-being (qualitative growth).

Also here, long-term developments are not proceeding on a linear path but are characterised by saturation effects similar to Figure 1. According to evolutionary economics, co-evolutive autopoietic structural change is reorganising institutions (Saviotti, 2007). The economic sector "education" is situated at the very end of the detected evolutionary chain and can therefore be expected to increase in GDP share in all economies worldwide in the long run. Such a general diagnosis tends to positively impact on any tedious effort of improving educational structures in any world region.

The Example of the Global Energy System

... Each wreath of smoke

Appeared to him but as the magic vapour

Of some alchymic furnace, from whence broke

The wealth of worlds

Lord Byron (1818–24), 'Don Juan', Canto the tenth; cited after Bickerstaff & Walker, 2003: 45)

In analogy to the global agricultural system in above sections, this section quantitatively analyses the long-term structural changes of the global energy system. Also here, the logical chain of cause and effects for the global CO_2 emissions (formula below) stretches across several scientific disciplines described by the quotients in the following formula: carbon content of fuels, technological efficiency of energy conversion, economic effectivity of energy use, economic input per quality of life, quality of life of the population (See Figure 4).

When looking at quantitative figures (Ahamer, 2005a: 15-24), it becomes apparent that each of the consecutive quotients starts to optimise in a given evolutionary period and then reaches saturation. Starting from "smoking stacks" (CO_2/E) in Charles Dickens' and Lord Byron's times (see poem above), to the eras of ever more efficient machinery in the 19th and 20th centuries (E_{prim}/E_{final}), to "demand oriented energy management" (E_{final}/GDP) at the end of the 20th century, to our present period when no longer the target of optimising GDP/cap but rather of QL/cap decently comes into sight – a *global long-term shift occurs from maximising material targets towards optimizing qualitative targets*. Such shifts are called "transitions". This perception is not inferred from an a priori perspective but deduced from the data in the interdisciplinary "Global Change Data Base" (GCDB).

Figure 5 shows these "transitions of targets" again in a graphical manner, which we read from left to right: to the extent that one quotient was optimised (i.e. nolens volens having represented a target), it becomes fulfilled, levels out and falls out of the focus of societal perception because "the story is finished up". Even the sign of optimisation changes: smokestacks no longer denote areas of progress but of environmental pollution.

What was a desired value in an earlier phase (e.g. GDP), is likely to turn into an undesired effort after a transition has occurred. Mathematically, the

Figure 5. The hypothesis is made that societal targets shift from left to right to the extent they are fulfilled along civilisational evolution

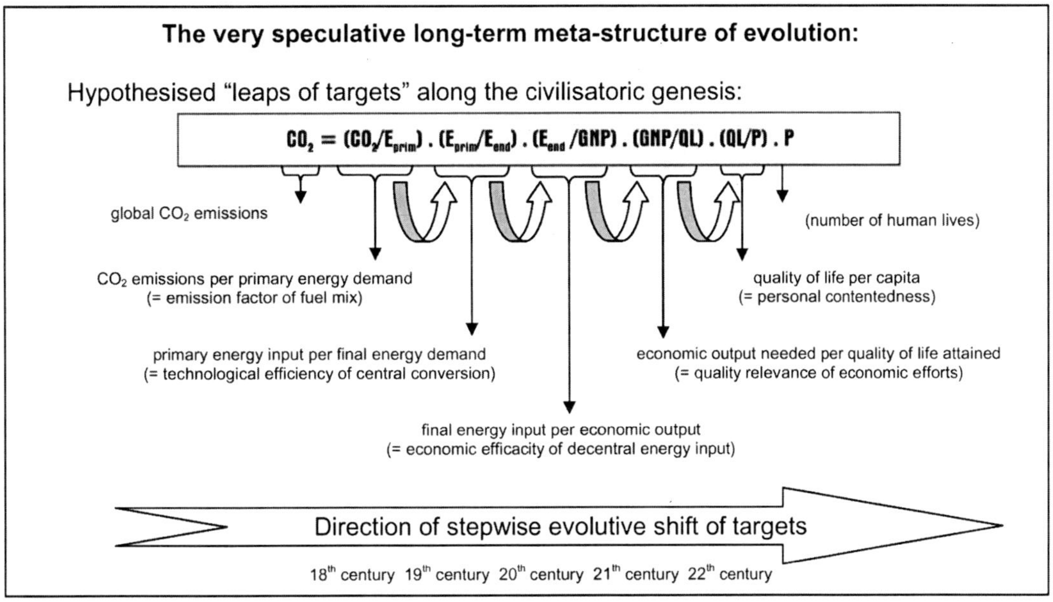

parameter changes its position and goes under the fraction line. In other words, societal values in a growth phase stand in contrast to societal values in the saturation phase. By evolutionary necessity(!), societal values change along evolution.

Thinking further radically, a consequence would be that "improving the world" could mean: speeding up (structural) evolution. Societal "learning" in this picture would mean to accelerate evolutionary time (as opposed to physical time) – which *means to accelerate structure building.* Precisely this is the target of the present volume for educational structure building.

In the next section we will see that (social) structures are enhanced by enhanced density of (communicative) interaction among the system's elements and sub-systems.

Learning Means to Create New Spaces by Reflection

In this section, we will understand learning as the creation of new spaces (ontological approach), be they "only" mental or existential spaces.

The opening of "spaces of understanding" is evident especially in *intercultural learning*, where more than one different type of learner is to understand more than one "object" of learning", namely the individual perspectives in complex interdisciplinary and international matters (logically m:n learning, such as peace research or diplomacy). Much more simple structures are scientific learning (1:1 learning: viewing one object from the perspective of one discipline, e.g. mechanics) or interdisciplinary learning (1:n learning: viewing one object from the perspective of several disciplines, e.g. environmental protection).

Learning means to *create perspectives*. Perspectives – in an audacious definition – are the elements of reality (Ahamer et al., 2009: 1), not atoms. Analysing space is a core activity of geography, more interestingly the intrinsic connection of space and time (Car, 2009). What composes space? This question can be answered with more than just "North, South, East, West".

Fundamentally, space is a social product, a way to view reality. Space is the result of the interaction of the viewer and the viewed object – and therefore an object even of quantum mechanics. Space is the genuine outcome of an interaction (i.e. the perceiving and acting human) – not only the prerequisite for an interaction taking place some*where*.

Adopting a system analytic standpoint (Sterman, 2000, Umpleby, 2009, ASC, 2009, Ossimitz, 2009) leads to the assumption that the crucial parameter is the density of interactions in a system (the number of interactions between elements divided by the number of the system's elements) which increases the likelihood of (positive and negative) feedback circles which are ultimately responsible for the endogenous and intrinsic autopoietic dynamic of the system. Consequently, increasing interactions within a system makes a system (i) more dynamic in the systems analytic sense, (ii) more mature in the evolutionary sense and (iii) more stable in the ecological sense. At this point, it is easy to apply such logical deduction to systems of learners and learning – optimally to m:n (i.e. intercultural) learning settings: the higher the density of interaction, i.e. dialogue, i.e. reflection (cf. from the section titled "Learning is mental structural change") is during the learning endeavour, the more mature and vital will be the outcome – namely the *dialogically learned mutual understanding of individual world views*. Along this train of thought, we have again reached the conviction of the section titled "Learning is mental structural change", namely that an optimal learning strategy is to optimize dialogue and discourse.

Exactly this is an opportunity to make use of asynchronous and synchronous web based technology: discussion forums and chats as described in Ahamer (2005b).

Regarding the "ever new construction of space", the journal "Progress in Human Geography" contains several articles redefining space; e.g. for Smith (2003: 562) it seems likely that spaces and times are multiple. "Space is an ontology of movement, networks, flows, fluids and folds". "If spaces and times are created, there is no particular reason why they should be consistent with one another" – how true, especially in intercultural settings or political conflicts.

One of the most widely read writers redefining space is Manuel Castells (2001) who speaks of the *space of flows* and fluids (apart from the usual *space of places*) as a distinctive entity in the upcoming network society and renders the conviction of "the one and objective space" obsolete.

Smith (2003: 546) sees other fathers of abundance in space models: "In short, with Dandieu we learn that geographical scales (or spaces) are no more than degrees of abstraction. With Foucault, we move beyond the duality of space proposed by Dandieu between concrete and abstract scales to begin to argue for a skein of networks that is characterized by non-linear experiences". Smith (2003: 574) quotes Latour: "time and space are the consequences of the way in which bodies relate to one another".

In the same journal – and with a view to deriving quality criteria for learning – Cutchin (2002: 661) supports an 'ethic of encounter': "A geographical pragmatist ethic is not relativistic [but] it suggests moral rules as principles that need to be creatively, flexibly and intelligently applied in ever-changing circumstances."

Summing up, valid learning means to *understand formerly foreign spaces* (of understanding) and to be able to move and live in them, unconsciously, without effort, just as an experienced car driver is capable of conversation while driving. In short, learning means to harmonize perspectives with reality and to create common spaces of understanding.

What is Social Space?

In this section, we will pose the question: "What are (social) spaces?"

To start from scratch, we must ask: what is "space" at all? Most basically, "being not on the same spot" hinders communication for a paleolithic human. All the rest is more difficult to think and construct: the superimposed metric equals *hypothesized travel time* from spot to spot, on foot and on even ground. Already, very high grass, high snow and not so high mountains overthrow any simple metric even for paleolithians. The paleolithic deconstruction of space consisted already in fire signals, bow and arrow and did not have to wait for theoretical geographers in the 21st century (Demeritt, 2002). Even long before that monkeys swinging from branch to branch might have become jealous seeing birds flying over which made them consider revenge by creating other means of communication birds might not have...

Let us merely recapitulate: "space" enables communication (when being on the same spot) but hinders communication when being "spatially" separated. At the moment, we do not know much more than that. Following Piaget (1955), the construction of space is one of the earliest achievements in childhood. "Space" is created by the wish to eliminate it through travel. We are not really sure if we will ever define "space" much better than this, but for the sake of continuing this article we will adhere to said assumption for now.

Inspired by pre-paleolithic monkeys, e-learning strategies (Strobl, 2007b, Ahamer, 2004: 39) play a vital role in enlarging social and communicative spaces.

Hence *space is a projection of one's own communicational possibilities*.

Similarly, theoretical physics and quantum mechanics speak of the "space of options" ("*Möglichkeitsraum*" after Sander & Vollbrecht, 2000, as a realm of possibility for development) which spans up all possibilities of a particle to move and accelerate. *Space* means reified options, decisions, bifurcations, implementable paths through time.

If time reduces itself to the substrate in which procedures happen (Ahamer et al., 2009: 2), then in the same vein space would reduce itself to the substrate in which interaction and communication happens. In any system, *space is what embeds interaction*.

Space is the substrate for decisions, whereas ***time is the substrate for processes.*** This is why space has several dimensions, whereas time has only one.

Such a definition is not new: reviewing Lefebvre (1991), Canete (2004) identifies *space as a social construct* founded on interactions, especially the communication procedures taking place in this space (Strobl, 2004, 2007a: 7). Lefebvre does not believe in abstract space. He develops what he calls "a conceptual triad" in explaining how space is produced: (1) Spatial practice, (2) Representations of space, (3) Representational spaces. Similarly, from a spatial planning perspective Taylor (2007: 198) claims that *spaces are constructed.*

To implement such theoretical convictions, contemporary technology extends a helping hand: According to Castells (2001, p. 4), "the *Network Society* deals with the 'new techno-economic system' and is defined "as a social structure which is characterised by networked communications technologies". "This includes such social phenomena as economic interdependence among nations as well as globalisation and social movements related to individual identity. Based on this definition, Castells hypothesises that "the network society is organized around two new forms of time and space: timeless time and the space of flows. Space of flows infers that physical distances are closer among organizations in the society, and information can be easily transmitted from one point to another by new communication technologies. This means abandoning the logical concept of space. For example, the hyperlink on a webpage eliminates the succession of things in time and space, because it takes one from one location to another in an instant. Space and time, the material foundations of human experience, have been transformed, as the space of flows dominates the space of places, and timeless time supersedes clock time of the industrial era." Castells is defining *space* as the physical support of the way we live in time. The space and time we are used to, 'real world time', is referred to by him as a space of places." (Wikibook, 2009).

Manuel Castells (2001: 4) calls "a *complex system of institutional relations* 'the network state', because, in fact, it's a network of interactions of shared sovereignty". "In a world of global flows of wealth, power, and images, the search for identity becomes the fundamental source of social meaning." Such a view is excellently compatible with what Figure 5 proposes, namely the epochal shift towards non-material targets, towards human well-being, towards meaning, towards a "society of sense" – as Horx (2007) puts it. For the extremely long run single authors see space and time even as an illusion in the sense of the dissolution of time and space as we know it now (Renard, 2003).

In this view, **the basic civilisatoric aim is to create meaning.**

The linkage to e-learning becomes still more visible. For Castells (2004, 5), "the human consciousness is the source and the networks are programmed by human minds". "Network patterns are characteristic for the most advanced economic sectors (this links directly to results of the above section titled "The example of the global economic structure"), highly competitive corporations as well as for communities and social movements. Identity-building itself is a dynamic motor in forming society. Identity is defined as 'the process of construction of meaning'. The way social groups define their identity *shapes the institutions of society*" (Stalder, 2000). This brings us back to the subject of this entire volume (Mukerji & Tripathi, 2009), just formulated in the words of Manuel Castells.

Summing up, geography can be seen as the branch of science offering *perspectives on reality* by "mapping reality". In this sense, geography might extend its scope to creating spaces (of common understanding), that may be converging in the best case, namely in successful intercultural learning. The main tool for converging such spaces of understanding is the *dialogue*. Again the circle of argumentation is closed.

After having reached these general definitions and after having taken into account additional, partly novel views, it is just an easy activity of breaking down the above theoretical statement in order to clearly attribute a position to the following case studies inside the theoretical concept: *(e-)learning strategies are able to bridge such spaces.*

HOW TO LEARN?

Based on the theoretical deliberations in the first section, in this part of the paper, their practical implications are analysed in a structured manner, following the four basic characteristics of learning put forth by the editors of this volume (Mukerji & Tripathi, 2009) – these are equivalent to the STEP factors described in the following four sub-sections.

Social Factor S: The Procedural Factors for Learning

The social factors (S) largely correspond to the procedural factors for learning and answer the question: how to design learning?

They coincide with Castell's *space of flows* and they regulate the *interaction* between students and trainers and among students. We propose to:

- facilitate an interactive *dialogue* between trainers & learners and among learners
- make use of the chances of ODL to render the exchange of "flows" more massive
- allow for *self-guidedness* of learners (key word of self-adaptive e-learning material)
- suitably *rhythmise* procedures in order to facilitate optimal learning as suggested by

"Surfing Global Change" SGC (Ahamer & Schrei, 2006)

- establish clear and well-defined procedural rules and criteria for success for students in order to safeguard quality control
- use the concept of "*spatial citizens*" to denote the approach of personal responsibility of learners (Strobl, 2008)
- to make use of evolutionary long-term trends for the target of learning
- to promote *leap-frogging* matter-centred *evolution* by faster evolving mental and social reorganization of a country (inner re-crystallisation of a country's society).

Technological Factor T: The Tools for Learning

- Web platforms (such WebCT or others) have been the object of suitability studies already a decade ago and have entered their annual routine at most universities. From being a critical bottleneck for communication-centred e-learning (because of alleged self-restriction to a mere behaviourist learning model) most platforms have made a consistent step forward to enabling communication-centred learning
- For the UniGIS curriculum (Strobl & Car, 2009, Car, 2008) the decision was made to use two technologies (Blackboard & MS live) in order to enhance e-literacy of learners.
- Promote formation of teachers and trainers to incorporate peer communication among learners
- To enhance autopoiesis, i.e. self-creation of (knowledge) structures such as wikis
- Include digital globes for learning.

Economic Factor E: The Material Basis for Learning

- Which resources are necessary for learning? In Europe, many universities provide each resource in the necessary amount.
- In the view of the GCDB analysis (section titled "The example of the global economic structure"): Education is part of the sector "social services" encompassing personal care-taking, (mental) health and communication services and can be expected to grow further as a long-term global tendency. Analysis of the evolution of forerunning economic sectors calls for suitable maturity of both learning infrastructures and learning motivation, namely to "create meaning by education".
- In the view of the section on social space life meant the generation of meaning and sense. "Sense" equals forward-linking of values into the future (in Latin: re-ligio). Investments in e-learning therefore are based on a minimum accountability and foreseeability of individual careers. Vice versa, e-learning should foster skills that are independent of short-term business cycles.
- Evolutionarily, we slide into an "era of a society of sense": acting in order to produce meaning becomes gradually more important than acting for a material target – to the extent that material targets are already fulfilled. A "natural succession" of life's targets for any learner may be hypothesized.

Political Factor T: The Structural Basis for Learning

- Connectedness to other organisational entities on the labour market, among firms, within administration is the materialization

of the "network society" (section "Learning means to create new spaces by reflection)
- Human, social, institutional structures and tissues complement traditional "hard skills"
- The reliability and openness of political structures must guarantee that learners can implement their democratic social skills in real-life careers in real-life institutions.

THE CASES

List of Cases

The following cases are explained in the coming sections. More insight is available from the literature and the links provided as well as in (Ahamer & Jekel, 2010):

- UniGIS ("Learn, but learn together") – a collaborative web-based study framework
- Twinning Projects ("Learn while living together") are the main programming tools for EU accession and applied also to European Neighbourhood Nations: examples with the authors' collaboration range from Slovakia and Slovenia to Armenia, Georgia and Azerbaijan.
- "Global Studies" are curriculum initiatives in Graz, Vienna and Salzburg ("Learn, how to live together") training professionally for intercultural understanding and in-depth cooperation.
- UniNET ("Live together, but while learning") is the largest bilateral university network between a European country and Asia; the authors have organized several conferences in Kyrgyzstan and Nepal
- ESD (= European Forum for the Promotion of Sustainable Development) creates radically new visions prompted by the economic-environmental crisis by dialogic authoring of a book
- Environmental Systems Analysis (USW) is a unique curriculum in Graz focusing on interdisciplinary dialogue.

Details on characteristics and on results of these cases can be found in Table 1.

UniGIS

What started as several local initiatives for open and distance learning (ODL) of Geographic Information Science and Systems (GIS) has become the largest global network of highly professional GIS curricula (Unigis, 2009) that are internationally not only recognised but defining standards.

The characteristic is a very clear definition of rules, criteria and procedures which allows to reach standardisation across a wide range of countries, universities and related working styles and cultures.

This networked and networking social system keeps proliferating: last year, the Central Asian node was formally founded as the "Austria-Central Asia Centre for GIScience" ACA*GIS (2009) in Bishkek, Kyrgyzstan after a series of preparatory workshops, conferences, projects and common projects that have constituted an evolution of networking flows.

Twinning Projects

We move from the world of education to the world of administration and national strategies. The European Union has developed a successful "tool" called "Twinning" for enhancing institution building in neighbouring countries that has been initially applied to preparing candidate countries for their accession to the Union. The core issue is "institution building" (EU, 2009) – again very similar to the intention of the present volume.

Twinning principles are: "Twinning must aim at developing structural reforms. At the end of a project, any new or adapted system must be self-

Table 1. How the STEP factors apply to the cases of this article; these are explained in the earlier section

Cases	S = Social factors	T =Technological factors	E = Economical factors	P = Political factors
UniGIS	Easy access for individuals, international network embeds	normalised catalogue of criteria for achievements	Costs paid by learners and supporting institutions	UniGIS is embedded in intl. and EU networks
UniNet	Lecturers and students are networking agents	Thematic orientation is secondary, real persons travel	One-way financial transfer from Austria to Asian universities	Developmental aid on academic level in mutual partnership
- Kyrgyzstan	Promote GIS and solar energy	Strengthen local institutions	~ODA + own effort to organise	Young democratic republic
- Nepal	Apply GIS for mountain areas	Divert natural hazards' menaces	Cooperation with Himalaya states	Strengthen local self-governance
Global Studies	Response to increasing students' awareness and NGO work	Partly e-learning, but focus on face2face, students travelling	Efforts made by students who also participate in practicals	The guiding idea of global collaboration is implemented
ESD	A NGO creates itself and provides orientation to others	Only "social software" directs interplay of self-responsible actors	No economic weight. "Just" development of societal strategies	Includes senior political figures with high profile & individualism
USW (= Environmental Systems Analysis)	Institutionalising a pioneering university curriculum	Strong e-learning component but only as blended learning	Synergism with classical curricula boosts attractivity for students	Slow diffusion through the traditional university system
Twinning tool	Main tool of EU enlargement & reduce barriers	Self-motivated implementation of EU legislation	Better mutual exchange increases development	Smooth transition from EU to neighb. countries
- Slovakia	Candidate country wants to join	Improve air quality legislation	Reduced pollution improves life	Ex-communist country's rebirth
- Slovenia	New EU member state joined	Implement water quality legislation	Water price covers external costs	New market economy stabilises
- Armenia	Discontinue Soviet safety syst.	Aviation security must be compatible	Switch from old to EU system	European neighbourhood policy
- Georgia	Leave behind Soviet security	Aviation will be compatible to EU	Integration in larger aviation area	Equilibration of strategic contacts
- Azerbaijan	Re-build agr. vocational training	Agriculture employs 40% of pop.	Agricult. value added is minimal	Wish to modennise non-oil sect.

sufficient and function under the auspices of the beneficiary country" (EU, 2009).

A very clearly defined set of procedural rules has been moulded into a "Twinning handbook" a decade ago. Annually, over 100 Twinning projects with a typical budget of 1M€ take place on almost any aspect of administrative life. In the meantime, this instrument for strengthening institutions by sourcing from the own strength and conviction of the beneficiary country is also applied to interested non-candidate countries in the so-called European Neighbourhood Policy (ENP, 2009)

The main strategy is to create understanding by (i) daily collaboration for complex issues by peer-oriented collaboration with equal rights and mutual respect, (ii) keeping the driving force the main interest of the beneficiary administration, (iii) generous funding by the European Commission, (iv) personal contacts emerging after week-long repeated on-site collaboration of experts and (v) clear focus on voluntary adoption of parts of the European legal system for easier bilateral exchange.

One author has worked during the last decades in such Twinnings on the subjects of air quality (Slovakia, 2000-01), water quality (Slovenia, 2007-08); and prepared Twinnings on the subjects of aviation security (Armenia, Georgia, 2008) and vocational formation (Azerbaijan, 2009) and is convinced of high suitability and appropriateness of such programmes of international co-operation.

Global Studies

Several independent initiatives of Austrian universities have led to the establishment of curricula on "Global Studies" (Graz and Salzburg) or "International Development" (Vienna). The national umbrella organisation "Mattersburg Circle of Developmental Studies" acts as forum for exchange while maintaining a critical stance towards globalisation. The speed of a genesis of structures here is much slower that in both above cases because the underlying tissue of convictions is still in the making, in a co-evolutionary sense. Three high-quality series of books and an internationally reviewed journal are the result of a decade of work in the Vienna initiative. No direct profit was generated from "developmental studies" in the home country, therefore the economic basis is modest and success is based on idealistic activity of individuals over decades.

Eurasia-Pacific UniNet

A facilitator of a very wide range of university co-operations is the Eurasia-Pacific UniNet that developed out of the China Centre of Salzburg University. UniNet (2009) supports initiatives aimed at establishing lasting structures and has already resulted in at least five bilateral institutions on environment, medicine and technology.

UniNet's procedural strategy dwells on a series of annual meetings, workshops and conferences that produces the communicational substrate for further institution building. Reiterated personal contact together with selecting areas of collaboration that promise mutual benefit lies at the heart of this very personalised strategic concept of building intercultural institutions on a peer level.

Personal contacts on the individual level constitute protective shells of social space in

Figure 6. A three-dimensional portfolio for all mentioned cases with axes named: one or more universities, single or multi-disciplines, one's own or others' motivation

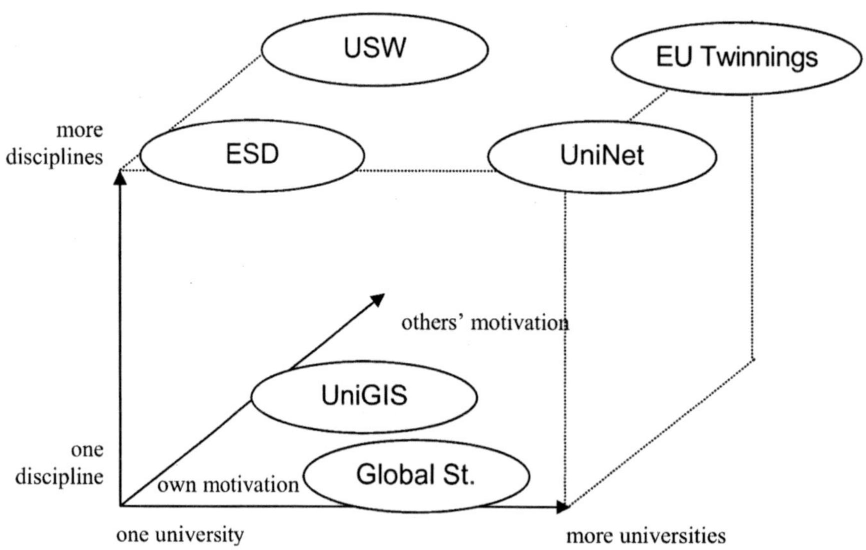

*Table 2. Experiences with the cases of this article ordered approximately along the STEP factors, while taking the perspective as seen from the "**learners**"*

Cases	S ~ collaboration	T ~ dialogue tech.	E ~interculturality	P ~ results
UniGIS	Occasional questions among individual learners	An internal discussion forum + annual meetings	Only among German speaking students	Technical & background GIS knowledge
UniNet	Among occasional Austro-Asian working groups	Co-author future project proposals with Asia	On the university level only; scientific exchange	Transfer of knowledge and skills
- Kyrgyzstan	Bridge heads in civil engineering university	Along annual conferenc-es and staff exchanges	Review of papers in a scientific journal	Common publiccation and mutual insight
- Nepal	Bridge to an Asian mul-tilateral research centre	Only personal exchange on the conference	Very broad range of cultures along the Himalayas	Scientific assessment harmonised on a confer-ence
Global Studies	Students with strong multicultural inclination	Integrative core lectures + isolated specialised lectures	Interculturality extends to differrent scient. culture	Integration of explicitly opposing views
ESD	Panel of self-motivated idealists & authors	Discussing chapters of the own visionary book	Representatives from academia & industry discuss	Consensus view on very radical societal changes
USW (= Environmental Systems Analysis)	Five disciplines: economics, business administrat., chemistry, physics, geography	30% integrative core lectures done jointly plus 70% specialised lectures done in isolation	Offering a systemic approach to overcome barriers between social & natural sci.	Environmental scientists mastering divergent scientific approaches
Twinning tool	Administrative repre-sentatives from EU & candidate countries	Clear definition of delib-erable results worked out in 2 years project	Experts from diverse political cultures col-laborate personally	Harmonisation of legal systems and their factual implementation
- Slovakia (SK)	8 SK + 8 AT authors:12 reports	Monthly 1-day visits during 1 year	Ex-communist working habits	Air quality laws are on EU level
- Slovenia (SI)	10 SI + 10 DE + 6 AT authors: 3 r.	Permanent 3-days visits during 1 yr.	Similar approach, demo-cratic state	Water quality & pricing law is ok
- Armenia	Define workplan for EU aviation	Daily interviews with AM experts	Clear technical targets are easy	Defined results for future Twinn.
- Georgia	Define workplan for EU aviation	Daily interviews with GE experts	Clear technical targets are easy	Defined results for future Twinn.
- Azerbaijan	Define workplan for vocational education in agriculture	Trying to identify part-ners for daily interviews with AZ experts	Difficulties due to unclarity of own targets, low familiarity w. EU	Defined results for future Twinning including pilot voc. school

which professional and personal contacts on the group level and later on the corporate level may mature.

ESD

Another organically grown mycelium continuously working on novel views on globalisation and reworking them in a structured process (including publication of books) is the Vienna-based European Association for the Promotion of Sustainable Development ESD (2009). ESD strives to develop radically new concepts in the face of the global economic and environmental crisis and shows its rare strength in combining both challenges. Several dozen individuals have contributed to the normative book "Turn of the Titanic" (Rauch & Strigl, 2005) that has reached the highest ranking for national environmental and future books and serves as a starting point for ongoing peer-oriented pluri-disciplinary discussions in Austrian NGO networks.

Environmental Systems Analysis: SGC & GCDB

At Graz University, the unique curriculum of "Environmental Systems Sciences" incorporates the faculties of natural, social and educational sciences and includes the five curricula of economics, business administration, geography, chemistry and physics.

The target is to provide students with the capacity to understand interdisciplinary matters from several scientific points of views. Therefore, a core feature is to actively participate in the "Interdisciplinary Practicals" (IP, 2009) that serve as a forum for debate, peer review, and consensus building. The most often used dramaturgic pattern for IPs is the web-based negotiation game "Surfing Global Change" SGC (Ahamer, 2004) that trains interdisciplinary consensus building in a five-level procedure among the 20 students. Material of the "Global Change Data Base" GCDB (Ahamer, 2005a) provides quantitative backing for building consensus on themes such as passive houses, locally disputed highway projects, future research, climate change and technology assessment.

Relevance of the STEP Structure for these Cases

This section views the described institutional case studies along the four criteria proposed by the editors of this book: S, T, E, P (= Social, Technological, Economical and Political): *Table 1*.

It is possible to arrange these case studies in a portfolio (Figure 6) in order to make visible their relative position within the descriptors "one vs. more universities", "one vs. more disciplines", "own vs. others' motivation". This portfolio shows that societal learning strategies may be implemented adjusted to the most variable framework conditions of our social reality.

Practical experiences from these case studies are described from the perspective of "learners" (Table 2) and the perspective of "trainers" (Table 3) while approximately using the STEP factors.

*Table 3. Experiences with the cases of this article ordered approximately along the STEP factors, while taking the perspective as seen from the "***trainers***"*

Cases	S ~ How the (social, economic, technological) space is bridged	T ~what kind of difficulties are encountered in practice	E ~ how/whether technology helped in overcoming barriers	P ~ how to learn from such international interventions
UniGIS	By a tight compulsory schedule & clear exercises	Lack of previous experience with GIS can be fatal	Online chats, webspace, tutors, annual meetings	Create strong personal initial committment
UniNet	By own developmental interest	Shortage of time during pers. visits	Joint proceedings define achievemt.	A clear, narrow discipline helps
Global Studies	By being in the same curriculum	Initially romantic attitudes prevail	Only personal experience ripens	Own long-year studies equilibrate
ESD	Weekly structured discussion rounds	Divergent value systems preferred	Book publication focused all ideas	Intensive personal dedication
USW (= Environmental Systems Analysis)	By drawing own identity from the first pioneering student generation	Lack of enthusiasm and working motivation of some students	Web platforms allow detailed communication between courses	To create a strong identity as pioneering entity within university
Twinning tool	By jointly defining the targets of the Twinning future project	Fundamentally different political views in different countries	Dialogic review during joint authoring of legislation and reports	Online cooperation helps only if intact personal ties exist

CONCLUSION

This text has provided an extensive overview of diverse concepts, philosophies and views.

Based on multiple experiences of "learning" of individuals and societies, a general view of the sense and the procedure of learning is proposed in this contribution: The target of learning is to maximise the change of real-world behaviour. Consequently, an optimal learning methodology is to put learners in a situation of dialogue with stakeholders having another view of the complex interdisciplinary issue at stake.

Such conclusion of seeing "facilitated dialogue" in the centre of any learning endeavour results from all three understandings proposed here (psychological, evolutionist and ontological approaches). Dialogue is the unit activity of approximating world views between persons.

The role of technology receives a clear place, namely to facilitate dialogue and discourse. Such has been corroborated by a series of cases of individual, societal and international learning.

Attempts to implement technology-centred learning environments without foregoing generation of the strong wish and persistent will of learners to reflect, exchange, discuss and reformulate own convictions would not yield optimal learning results.

This sequence seems promising: first create human attitudes for a dialogue and second support such dialogue by technological means.

Dialogue is the key element and the will to arrive at a consensus is the key motor for learning.

When designed in this order, technological support may become valuable for learning which is a deeply human act of questioning oneself and redirecting one's behaviour.

A symbolic description of such learning effect is "to create new spaces of understanding".

REFERENCES

ACA*GIS. (2009). *Austria-Central Asia Centre for GIScience*. Retrieved from http://www.aca-giscience.org/

Adler, P. S., & Kwon, S.-W. (2002). Social Capital: Prospects for a New Concept. *Academy of Management Review*, *27*(1), 17–40. doi:10.2307/4134367

Ahamer, G. (2001). A Structured Basket of Models for Global Change. In C. Rautenstrauch & S. Patig (Eds.), Environmental Information Systems in Industry and Public Administration, (pp.101-136). Hershey, PA: Idea Group Publishing.

Ahamer, G. (2004). Negotiate your Future: Web Based Role Play. *Campus-Wide Information Systems*, *21*(1), 35–58. doi:10.1108/10650740410512329

Ahamer, G. (2005a). *Structural change in global energy economics*. University course materials. Retrieved from http://www.uni-graz.at/globalstudies/deposit/USW_VisionWirtschaftsEnergiekapitel.pdf

Ahamer, G. (2005b). 'Surfing Global Change': How didactic visions can be implemented. *Campus-Wide Information Systems, 22*(5), 298-319. Retrieved from http://www.emeraldinsight.com/1065-0741.htm

Ahamer, G., Car, A., Marschallinger, R., Wallentin, G., & Zobl, F. (2009). *How to map perspectives: Moving GISc to IISc. 4th International Conference on Information Technology ICIT'09*, Al-Zaytoonah University of Jordan, Amman, June 3rd – 5th, 2009. Retrieved from http://www.alzaytoonah.edu.jo/ICIT/pages/index.aspx

Ahamer, G., & Jekel, T. (2010). Make a Change by Exchanging Views. In S. Mukerji & P. Tripathi, (Eds.) Cases on Transnational Learning and Technologically Enabled Environments, pp x-x.

Ahamer, G., & Schrei, C. (2006). Exercise 'Technology Assessment' through a gaming procedure. *Journal of Desert Research*, *5*(2), 224–252. doi:10.1504/JDR.2006.011364

ASC. (2009). American Society for Cybernetics. Retrieved from http://www.asc-cybernetics.org/

Barro, R. J. (1991). Economic growth in a cross section of countries. *The Quarterly Journal of Economics*, *106*(2), 407–443. doi:10.2307/2937943

Barro, R. J. (2001). Human Capital and Growth. *The American Economic Review*, *91*(2), 12–17.

Becker, G. S., Murphy, K. M., & Tamura, R. (1990). Human capital, fertility, and economic growth. *The Journal of Political Economy*, *98*(S5), 12–38. doi:10.1086/261723

Berding, J. W. A. (2000). John Dewey's participatory philosophy of education – Education, experience and curriculum. The history of education and childhood, Nijmegen University, http://www.socsci.kun.nl/ped/whp/histeduc/misc/dewey01.html.

Bickerstaff, K., & Walker, G. (2003). The place(s) of matter: matter out of place – public understandings of air pollution. *Progress in Human Geography*, *27*(1), 45–67. doi:10.1191/0309132503ph412oa

Burt, R. S. (2000). The network structure of social capital. *Research in Organizational Behavior*, *22*, 345–423. doi:10.1016/S0191-3085(00)22009-1

Canete, A. (2004). Book Report on: The Production of Space by H. Lefebvre. *Thinking Culture*. Retrieved from http://thinkingculture.blogspot.com/2004/12/production-of-space-by-h-lefebvre-aloy.html

Car, A. (2008). Towards a Quality Assurance Concept for Postgraduate Distance Learning Programmes for Professionals. In T. Jekel, A. Koller, J. Strobl (Eds.), Lernen mit Geoinformation II, (pp. 172-178). Heidelberg, Germany: Wichmann.

Car, A. (2009). *Time and Space*. GIScience, Austrian Academy of Sciences. Retrieved from http://www.oeaw-giscience.org/index.php?option=com_content&task=blogcategory&id=27&Itemid=38

Castells, M. (2001). *Identity and Change in the Network Society*. Institute of International Studies, UC Berkeley. Retrieved from http://globetrotter.berkeley.edu/people/Castells/castells-con0.html

Castells, M., & Arsenault, A. (2006). Conquering the Minds, Conquering Iraq. *Information, Communication & Society*, *9*(3), 284–307. Retrieved from http://annenberg.usc.edu/Home/Faculty/Communication/~/media/Faculty/Facpdfs/Castells%20Iraq%20misinformation%20pdf.ashx

Cloke, P. (2002). Deliver us from evil? Prospects for living ethically and acting politically in human geography. *Progress in Human Geography*, *26*(5), 587–604. doi:10.1191/0309132502ph391oa

Coats, A. W. (1985). The American Economic Association and the Economics Profession. *Journal of Economic Literature*, *23*(4), 1697–1727.

Cutchin, M. P. (2002). Ethics and geography: continuity and emerging syntheses. *Progress in Human Geography*, *26*(5), 656–664. doi:10.1191/0309132502ph393pr

Demeritt, D. (2002). What is the 'social construction of nature'? A typology and sympathetic critique. *Progress in Human Geography*, *26*(6), 767–790. doi:10.1191/0309132502ph402oa

Dennis, L. (1970). Dewey's Brief for the Fine Arts. *Studies in Art Education, 11*(3), 3-8. Retrieved from http://www.jstor.org/stable/1319771

Dorst, K., & Cross, N. (2001). Creativity in the design process: co-evolution of problem-solution. *Design Studies*, *22*(5), 425–437. doi:10.1016/S0142-694X(01)00009-6

ENP. (2009). *European Neighbourhood Policy*. Retrieved from http://ec.europa.eu/world/enp/

ESD. (2009). European Association for the Promotion of Sustainable Development, Vienna. Retrieved from http://www.esd-eu.org/

EU. (2009). *Boosting Co-operation through Twinning*. European Commission, EuropeAid. Retrieved from http://ec.europa.eu/europeaid/where/neighbourhood/overview/twinning_en.htm

Fontela, E. Guzmán, J., Pérez, M., Santos, F.J. (2006). The art of entrepreneurial foresight. *Foresight, 8*(6), 3-13. Retrieved from http://www.emeraldinsight.com/

Fresner, J., Angerbauer, C., Möller, M., Wolf, P., Dielacher, T., Schnitzer, H., et al. (2007). *ZERMEG III – Decision guidance for the visualisation of the achievements of sustainable corporate strategies*. Final report by STENUM, Austrian Federal Ministry of Traffic, Infrastructure and Technology, Vienna. Retrieved from http://www.fabrikderzukunft.at/results.html/id4132

Global Studies. (2009). *Bundle of Electives and New Master Curriculum on "Global Studies" at Graz University*. Retrieved from http://www.uni-graz.at/globalstudies/

Grippe, E. J. (2002). Pragmatism, Perspectivism and Education: A Critique of Habitual Social Constructivism. *Insights, 34*(3), 2–14.

Haack, S. (2004). Pragmatism, Old and New. *Contemporary Pragmatism, 1*(1), 3–41.

Heidegger, M. (1977). Sein und Zeit. Tübingen, Germany.

Horx, M. (2007). *How We Will Live*. Vienna: Signum. Retrieved from http://www.zukunftsinstitut.de/verlag/medien_detail.php?nr=9

Jonas, H. (1984). The Imperative of Responsibility. *Search of Ethics for the Technological Age*, [transl. of "Das Prinzip Verantwortung"], University of Chicago Press; see also http://www.hans-jonas-zentrum.de/

Landes, D. S. (2000). The Wealth and Poverty of Nations: Why Some Are So Rich and Some So Poor. New York: W.W. Norton.

Lawless, D. V., & Roth, W.-M. (2001). The Spiel on "Spielraum and Teaching". *Curriculum Inquiry, 31*(2), 229–235. doi:10.1111/0362-6784.00194

Lefebvre, H. (1991). The Production of Space. Oxford, UK: Blackwell.

Lenz, W. (2005). Bildung im Wandel. Wien, Germany: LIT Verlag.

Maher, M. L., & Tang, H.-H. (2003). Co-evolution as a computational and cognitive model of design. *Research in Engineering Design, 14*(1), 47–63.

Mankiw, N. G., Romer, D., & Weil, D. N. (1992). A contribution to the empirics of economic growth. *The Quarterly Journal of Economics, 107*(2), 407–438. doi:10.2307/2118477

Mensch, G. (1975). Das technologische Patt: Innovationen überwinden die Depression. Frankfurt/Main: Umschau.

Menzel, U. (1996). *Lange Wellen und Hegemonie*. Inst. for Social Science. TU Brunswick, http://www-public.tu-bs.de:8080/~umenzel/inhalt/forschungsberichte/BlaueReihe13.PDF

Mohan, G., & Mohan, J. (2002). Placing social capital. *Progress in Human Geography, 26*(2), 191–210. doi:10.1191/0309132502ph364ra

Mokyr, J. (1990). The lever of riches. Technological creativity and economic progress. New York: Oxford University Press.

Mukerji, S., & Tripathi, P. (2004). Academic Program Life Cycle: A Redefined Approach to Understanding Market Demands. *Journal of Distance Education, 19*(2), 14-27. Retrieved from http://www.jofde.ca/index.php/jde/article/view/97/76

Mukerji, S., & Tripathi, P. (2005). Quality of life of labour: a collaborative ODL approach towards humanising the society. In *ICDE International Conference*, November 19-23, New Delhi.

Mukerji, S., & Tripathi, P. (2009). *Editorial: Cases on Technological Adaptability and Transnational Learning: Issues & Challenges*, Riyadh. Retrieved from http://www.igi-global.com/requests/details.asp?ID=588

Nonneman, W., & Vanhoudt, P. (1996). A further augmentation of the Solow model and the empirics of economic growth for OECD countries. *The Quarterly Journal of Economics*, *111*(3), 943–953. doi:10.2307/2946677

Ossimitz, G. (2009). *System Dynamics*. Retrieved from http://wwwu.uni-klu.ac.at/gossimit/pap.php?uk=6

Papenhausen, C. (2009). A cyclical model of institutional change. *Foresight*, *11*(3), 4–13. doi:10.1108/14636680910963909

Piaget, J. (1955). The Child's Construction of Reality. London: Routledge and Kegan Paul.

Pivec, M., Koubek, A., & Dondi, C. (2004). Guidelines for Game-Based Learning. Lengerich, Germany: Pabst Science Publishers.

Popke, E. J. (2003). Poststructuralist ethics: subjectivity, responsibility and the space of community. *Progress in Human Geography*, *27*(3), 298–316. doi:10.1191/0309132503ph429oa

Prensky, M. (2001). Digital Game-Based Learning. New York: McGraw-Hill.

Raskin, P., Banuri, T., Gallopín, G., Gutman, P., Hammond, A., Kates, R., & Swart, R. (2002). *The Great Transition. The Promise and Lure of the Times Ahead*. Stockholm Environmental Institute, Global Scenario Group. See http://www.tellus.org/seib/publications/Great_Transitions.pdf or http://www.sei.se

Rauch, H., & Strigl, A. (2005). *Die Wende der Titanic. Wiener Deklaration für eine zukunftsfähige Weltordnung*. [The Turn of the Titanic. Vienna Declaration of a Sustainable World Order.], Munich, Germany: oekom verlag. Retrieved from http://www.oekom.de/buecher/buchprogramm/

Renard, G. (2003). The Disappearance of the Universe. Fearless Books.

Robbins, D. (2007). Sociology as reflective science - On Bourdieu's Project. *Theory, Culture & Society*, *24*(5), 77–98. doi:10.1177/0263276407081284

Rosenzweig, M. R. (1990). Population growth and human capital investments: Theory and evidence. *The Journal of Political Economy*, *98*(S5), 38–71. doi:10.1086/261724

Roth, W.-M., Lawless, D. V., & Masciotra, D. (2001). Spielraum and Teaching. *Curriculum Inquiry*, *31*(2), 183–207. doi:10.1111/0362-6784.00191

Sander, U., & Vollbrecht, R. (2000). Jugend im 20. Jahrhundert. München, Germany: Reinhardt.

Saviotti, P. P. (2007). *Diversity, efficiency and economic development & Variety, structural change and economic development*. Two lectures at the Graz Schumpeter School. Retrieved from http://www.uni-graz.at/schumpeter.centre/summerschool.php

Schön, D. (1983). The reflective practitioner. New York: Basic Books.

Schön, D. A. (1986). Leadership as Reflection-in-Action. In T.J. Sergiovanni, J.E. Corbally. Leadership and Organizational Culture: New Perspectives on Administrative Theory and Practice, (pp. 59). Chicago: University of Illinois Press.

Schumpeter, J. A. (1949). The theory of economic development. Cambridge, MA: Harvard Univ. Press.

Smith, R. G. (2003). World city topologies. *Progress in Human Geography*, *27*(5), 561–582. doi:10.1191/0309132503ph447oa

Stähli, F. (1998). Ingenieurethik an Fachhochschulen [Ethics for Engineers at Universities of Applied Science]. Fortis FH, Verlag Sauerländer AG, Aarau.

Stähli, F. (2005). *Warum muss Technik ein Gegenstand der Ethik sein?* [Why must technology be an object of ethics?]. Aarau. Retrieved from http://web.fhnw.ch/personenseiten/fridolin.staehli/_html/publ.html

Stalder, F. (2000). The Network Paradigm: Social Formations in the Age of Information. *The Information Society, 14*(1). Retrieved from http://www.indiana.edu:80/~tisj/readers/full-text/14-4%20 Stalder.html

Sterman, J. D. (2000). Business Dynamics. System Thinking and Modeling for a Complex World. Boston: McGraw-Hill.

Stokey, N. L. (1991). Human capital, product quality, and growth. *The Quarterly Journal of Economics*, *106*(2), 587–616. doi:10.2307/2937948

Strobl, J. (2001). *Information Spaces – Individualized Information in Context.* GIS and Remote Sensing Conference in Sopron, Hungary, 6-8 September 2001, http://www.geo.info.hu/sat/presentations/InfoSpaces_Sopron_elemei/frame.htm

Strobl, J. (2004). GIScience Education for Professionals – the UNIGIS Distance Learning Model. *Geospatial Today, 6*/2004.

Strobl, J. (2006). Regional Energy Potentials: Spatial Optimization of Renewable Resources. In *26th Annual ESRI User Conference, Track Ecology and Conservation.* Retrieved from http://proceedings.esri.com/library/userconf/proc06/papers/abstracts/a1818.html

Strobl, J. (2007a). Geographic Learning. *Geoconnexion, 6*(5-6), 42–43.

Strobl, J. (2007b). Geographic Learning in Social Web Environments. In S. Catling & L. Taylor (eds.), Changing Geographies: Innovative Curricula, (pp. 327-332). Oxford, UK: IGU Commission for Geographical Education and Oxford Brookes University.

Strobl, J. (2008). Digital Earth Brainware. A Framework for Education and Qualification Requirements. In J. Schiewe, U. Michel, (Eds.), Geoinformatics paves the Highway to Digital Earth, (pp. 134-138). Osnabrück, Germany: Universität Osnabrück.

Strobl, J., & Car, A. (2009). Continuing Professional Education via Distance Learning: Success Factors and Challenges. In *FIG International Workshop on Professional Education 2009*, Vienna, 26-28 February 2009. Retrieved from http://www.fig.net/commission2/vienna_2009_proc/ppt/02_car_et_al_ppt.pdf

Strobl, J., & Lindner-Fally, M. (2007). *Global Learning - Pedagogical Concepts involving Virtual Globes.* Presentation at the conference "Geography for Society: Putting Bologna into Action", http://www.herodot.net/conferences/stockholm/esri/Lindner-Fally_Strobl(paper).pdf

Taylor, P. (2007). Space and sustainability: an exploratory essay on the production of social spaces through city-work. *The Geographical Journal*, *173*(3), 197–206. doi:10.1111/j.1475-4959.2007.00241.x

Tripathi, P., & Mukerji, S. (2008). *Access and Equity to Education in India through Synergy of Conventional and ODL Systems: A Step towards Democratization of Education.* IGNOU. Retrieved from http://www.distanceetdroitaleducation.org/contents/OP2008-IGNOU.pdf

Tröhler, M. (2007). Leeway for wits and sense [Spielraum für Sinne und Sinn]. *Du: Zeitschrift Der Kultur, 778*, 45-61. Retrieved from http://www.du-magazin.com/

Umpleby, S. (2007). Management Cybernetics: Tutorial on 5 DVDs. *The 11th World Multi-Conference on Systemics, Cybernetics and Informatics, July 8-11, Orlando, Florida*, organized by the International Institute of Informatics and Systemics (IIIS).

UniGIS. (2009). UNIGIS International Association. *Curricula*, Retrieved from http://www.unigis.net/

UniNet. (2009). *Eurasia-Pacific UNINET*. Retrieved from http://www.eurasiapacific.net/

Wagner-Döbler, R. (1998). Innovationsebben und Innovationsfluten: xxx. In S. Greif, H. Laitko, H. Parthey (eds.), Wissenschaftsforschung: Yearbook 96/97. Marburg, Germany: BdWi-Verlag.

Werner, M. H. (2003). Hans Jonas' Prinzip Verantwortung [H. Jonas' principle of responsibility]. In M. Düwell, K. Steigleder (Eds.), *Bioethik: Eine Einführung* (pp. 41-56). Frankfurt, Germany: Suhrkamp. Retrieved from http://www.micha-h-werner.de/jonas.pdf

Wikibook. (2009). *Communication Theory / Network Society*. Retrieved from http://en.wikibooks.org/wiki/Communication_Theory/Network_Society

ADDITIONAL READING

Academy for New Media. (2006). 3x7=21: *A discursive structure for quality enhancement in interdisciplinary university courses*. Academy for New Media and Technology Transfer http://www.uni-graz.at/anmwww/anmwww_fachbereiche/anmwww_fachdidaktik.htm, Graz University.

Ahamer, G. (2001a). *Twinning: a tool for enhancing the accession process in the environmental sector. Meteorologický Časopis*, 4(3), 3-17, see title in http://metmag.shmu.sk.

Ahamer, G. (2005c). *How the use of web based tools may evolve along three generations of WBT*, ICL05 conference in Villach/Austria, see http://www.icl-conference.org/accepted.htm.

Badke-Schaub, P. (2004). Strategies of experts in engineering design: between innovation and routine behaviour. *Journal of Desert Research, 4*(2).

Csikszentmihalyi, M. (1990). Flow - psychology of optimal experience. New York: Harper and Row.

Dorst, K., & Cross, N. (2001). Creativity in the Design Process: co-evolution of problem-solution. *Design Studies, 22*(5), 425–437. doi:10.1016/S0142-694X(01)00009-6

Grunwald, A. (1999). Technology Assessment or Ethics of Technology? Reflections on Technology Development between Social Sciences and Philosophy. *Ethical Perspectives, 6*(2), 170–182. doi:10.2143/EP.6.2.505355

Herder, P. M., Turk, A. L., Subrahmanian, E., & Westerberg, A. W. (2003). Collaborative Learning in a Cross-Atlantic Design Course. *Journal of Desert Research, 3*(2).

Hofmeyer, H., Rutten, H. S., & Fijneman, H. J. (2006). Interaction of spatial and structural design, an automated approach. *Design Studies, 27*(4), 423–438. doi:10.1016/j.destud.2005.07.002

IPCC. (2007). Fourth Assessment Report. www.ipcc.ch and http://ipcc-wg1.ucar.edu/

Jarvenpaa, S. L., & Leidner, D. E. (1998). Communication and Trust in Global Virtual Teams, *Journal of Computer-Mediated Communication*, 3(4), see http://jcmc.indiana.edu/

Klabbers, J. H. G. (2003). Gaming and simulation: Principles of a science of design. *Simulation & Gaming: An Interdisciplinary Journal*, *34*(4), 569–591. doi:10.1177/1046878103258205

Mayer, I., & Veenemann, W. (2002). Games in a World of Infrastructures. Simulation-games for Research, Learning and Intervention, Eburon, Delft.

Mayer, I. S., van Bueren, E. M., Bots, P. W. G., & van der Voort, H. (2005). Collaborative decision-making for sustainable urban renewal projects: a simulation-gaming approach. *Environment and Planning. B, Planning & Design*, *32*, 403–423. doi:10.1068/b31149

Naidu, S., Ip, A., & Linser, R. (2003). Dynamic Goal-Based Role-Play Simulation on the Web – A Case Study. University of Melbourne, Australia, see http://www.roleplaysim.org/papers/Naidu_etal.html.

Ono, M. M. (2006). Cultural diversity as a strategic source for designing pleasurable and competitive products, within the globalisation context. *Journal of Desert Research*, *5*(1), 3–15. doi:10.1504/JDR.2006.010793

Ossimitz, G. (2000). Development of Systemic Thinking. Theoretical Concepts and empirical Investigations. Klagenfurt University, http://www.uni-klu.ac.at/~gossimit.

Strobl, J. (2007). Geospatial Awareness, Skills and Knowledge - Managing Our Future. (Oct 29, 2007). Plenary keynote, Map Africa Conference, Cape Town.

Strobl, J. (2007). Regional Models for Renewable Energy Potentials. (May 15, 2007). Conference on "Eco-Energies for Future Generations" Northwest Agricultural and Forestry University, Yangling, China.

Thérivel, R. (2004). Strategic Environmental Assessment in Action, Earthscan, London.

KEY TERMS AND DEFINITIONS

Autopoiesis: Self-steered generation of structures by living organisms; e.g. bio-molecules create membranes, individuals create states, cultures create meaningful values.

Civilisational Evolution: When understanding history as evolution (towards higher complexity, towards more meaning in individual lives and towards more humanity), not only biological species undergo evolution, bur also society and societal patterns and institutions.

Dialogue: Exchange of views between individuals; explaining each other the understanding of reality in a repeated manner that includes repositioning of own views.

Leap-Frogging: Jumping a long leap across a way that usually has to be "gone on foot" with much slower speed. Symbolic for jumping across evolutionary phases as a result of societal learning that leads to much more developed societal structures than would be typical for the societies economic level (e.g. by means of information technology).

Intercultural Learning: Learning and understanding, how individuals in other cultures think, what values are developed and esteemed and what procedures can be followed in case of conflict.

OntologicalApproach: Perceived realities are considered as being created by reflection.

Social Space: The entirety of social interactions that leads to cognising reality in a certain and individual perspective.

Societal Learning: Learning not of an individual, but of an entire society, nation or culture

Spaces of Understanding: An individuals perspectives onto reality constitutes it's own "space". If individuals (or societies) share some perspectives, their "worlds" are overlapping and they have in common "spaces of understanding".

Spatial Citizens: Members of the "civil society" (i.e. individual showing strong responsibilities) that are very much aware of the spatial aspects of any social procedures (e.g. in spatial planning).

Spatial Planning: Ordering infrastructure (such as buildings, roads, railways, harbours, parks) within a city in a planned manner, depending on administrative planning procedures.

Structure Building: It is hypothesised that during evolution gradually ever more structures are generated by the living organisms: biochemical compounds, algae, cells, organisms, states of ants, economic units, philosophical convictions, systems of values etc. – Also institution building (i.e. the genesis of differentiated administration) is a case of structure building.

Twinning: The European Union creates this project type as main program line for the enlargement of the EU. In Twinnings, administrations collaborate link brother and sisters (twins) and jointly master complex interdisciplinary and intercultural tasks, such as environmental protection, democracy reform etc. while empowering the EU candidate's own administrative abilities. Twinning means "institution building".

Chapter 2
Online Teaching Partnerships in Diverse Socio-Cultural Institutions

Julian Scheinbuks
Chicago State University, USA

Anthony A. Piña
Sullivan University System, USA

ABSTRACT

In this chapter, the authors present the case of an inter-institutional online teaching partnership. The partnership has allowed faculty and students from racially and socio-economically diverse institutions to interact with each other through synchronous and asynchronous distance learning technologies. Courses were developed and team-taught by faculty from the three partner institutions. Faculty who were new to the online teaching environment collaborated with and were mentored by experienced online instructors. These instructors became more experienced in teaching a diverse student population and more comfortable and competent within technology-mediated teaching environments. Students from diverse socio-economic, racial and experiential backgrounds engaged in a more heterogeneous learning environment and learned how to be more effective online learners. Cross-discipline partnerships resulted in new courses being added to the curriculum. The inter-institutional online teaching partnership is a way to provide teaching and learning that is socially accessible, technologically adaptable, economically viable, and politically agreeable.

ORGANIZATION BACKGROUND

The Online Teaching Partnership (OTP) was sponsored by a four-year grant-funded project involving three Illinois public universities, each with distinct and unique student populations. The OTP provided the opportunity for students and faculty to join across geographic, cultural, socio-economic, institutional and racial boundaries. The overall goal of the project was to assist the three partner institutions to meet the challenges associated with educating a diverse student population, provide enhanced curricular offerings, develop instructor capability and address under-enrollment, student retention and time-to-graduation issues (Scheinbuks & Piña, 2009).

DOI: 10.4018/978-1-61520-779-4.ch002

In 2002, the Illinois Board of Higher Education (IBHE) funded a collaborative effort between the University of Illinois at Springfield and Chicago State University to promote the use of online learning to reach previously underserved student populations. The Higher Education Cooperation Act (HECA) grant (**IBHE**, 2005) was initiated by Chicago State University as a vehicle to assist in building its online learning program and allow the University of Illinois at Springfield to meet an institutional goal of reaching out to underserved populations. In 2004, the proposal was amended to include online teaching partnerships, allowing for online collaborations between individual faculty and students at the two universities. In 2005, the partnership was expanded to include Northeastern Illinois University as a third partner institution (Piña & Scheinbuks, 2008b).

The University of Illinois at Springfield (UIS) is a small, rural campus with a predominantly white student population of about 5,000. Its online program has been highly successful, with 17 fully online degree programs and an annual student enrollment growth of 30%. Retention of students in online courses at UIS is equivalent to that of students enrolled in face-to-face courses (Oakley, 2004). Training, development and technical support for online courses and faculty is provided by the UIS Office of Technology-Enhanced Learning (OTEL). In 2007, the University was awarded the 2007 Sloan-C Award for Excellence in Institution-Wide Online Teaching & Learning (Sloan Consortium, 2009).

Chicago State University (CSU) is an urban campus in the southern end of the country's third largest city, with the largest minority student population in the state. More than 80% of CSU's 7,000 students are African-American. The University had a developing distance learning program that offered several online courses, but no online degrees. CSU's instructors were less experienced in teaching within a virtual environment than those at UIS. Training, development and technical support for online courses and faculty is provided by the CSU Office of Distance Learning (ODL) (Piña & Scheinbuks, 2008b).

Northeastern Illinois University (NEIU), the newest partner institution, is an urban public campus on Chicago's north side with a student population of approximately 12,000 (about the same as UIS and CSU combined). NEIU is recognized by US News and World Report as the most racially and culturally diverse campus in the Midwestern United States, with a population that is 26% Hispanic, 13% African-American and 11% Asian (U.S. News, 2005). Unlike UIS and CSU, NEIU had no dedicated distance learning department and offered no fully online courses or online degree programs when it joined the partnership. Training, development and support services for faculty participating in the OTP were provided by NEIU's Center for Teaching and Learning (CTL) (Piña & Scheinbuks, 2008b).

SETTING THE STAGE

The nature of the OTP involved the establishment of mentor-mentee relationships in planning and implementing the instructional partnership. The faculty partners did not assume exclusive roles of mentee and mentor, but shared these roles as they exposed each other to their strengths and weaknesses (Gatliff & Wendel, 1998). In working together, the faculty partners were introduced to new instructional technologies and their own best practices. Some faculty members had developed expertise using these technologies and served as mentors for the other faculty members. Some faculty members served as content experts for collaborative projects. This was especially important for partnerships that served a cross-disciplinary theme (Piña & Scheinbuks, 2007).

A faculty partnership was established when the partners agreed to the extent of collaboration (full semester or unique units). The partners cooperated to develop a syllabus containing assignments meeting the individual course objectives and the goals of the partnership. These were supported by an agreement to team teach and facilitate student activities and research in both synchronous and asynchronous modes. Students enrolled at their own university, so that there were no problems related to tuition and participation in programs leading toward a degree or certification. The instructors assigned by that institution were responsible for evaluating their own students' efforts.

The OTP was made publically available on the UIS-sponsored OTP website (http://online.uis.edu/partners/csu) where faculty members at the member universities made contact and provided information about the disciplines in which they taught and their specific topic areas of interest. Once faculty members contacted each other, they notified the distance learning support offices: OTEL at UIS, ODL at CSU, and CTL at NEIU. The staff of these offices assisted faculty members in planning the partnerships and in authoring proposals for inter-institutional collaborations.

Faculty collaborators possessed varied backgrounds: Some of the participating faculty had considerable experience teaching online or in using technology within their face-to-face courses, while others had little or no experience. OTEL, ODL and CTL staff provided training and support in the use of the Blackboard Learning Management System's asynchronous tools. These included uploading course content, class announcements, threaded discussion forums, assignment management, quizzes and assessments, and the online grade book. Synchronous tools for delivering interactive real-time instruction, such as two-way audio, application and desktop sharing, whiteboards, live PowerPoint presentations and interactive polling and quizzing, were provided for by the Elluminate Live Classroom system. These technologies were made available to both faculty and students, to assist in developing and completing joint assignments and discussions by the support organizations at each institution.

Since administrative and management rights and authority for the Blackboard and Elluminate systems resided at OTEL, ODL and CTL, each partnership could be assigned to a joint Blackboard course, administered by one of the campuses. Students and partner faculty from both campuses were enrolled into the joint course. Both faculty members were given full instructor privileges in the course. Some instructors chose to use the group feature in Blackboard to separate students from the two institutions for grading purposes, but all of the courses used tools in Blackboard to allow all of the students to interact with each other and/or complete joint assignments.

CASE DESCRIPTION

The project and experiences were developed to address four primary goals that provided a meaningful experience to faculty and students involved in both synchronous and asynchronous educational experiences at a distance. These are listed below.

Project Goals

Goal 1: Increase Student Exposure to Technology

- **Objective 1.1:** The ODL, OTEL and CTL will promote integrating technology broadly into the overall curriculum of both universities to better prepare students to use technology as a learning resource.
- **Objective 1.2:** The ODL will investigate strategies for of making technology available and *affordable* to students at CSU as well as students at UIS and NEIU.

Goal 2: Train Faculty to use Technology to Enhance, Create or Modify Courses that make Use of Technology in Face-to-Face, Blended and Online Settings

- **Objective 2.1:** Faculty will be exposed to the Blackboard Learning Management System and Elluminate live classroom tools and instructed in best practices of online pedagogy prior to the development and the creation of web-enhanced, blended or online courses.
- **Objective 2.2:** When interdepartmental mentoring is not available for the creation of an online, blended or web-enhanced course, a partnership will be formed between instructors at two of the three partner campuses in the same or compatible discipline. A mentor/mentee relationship will be formed to create an online course that will be shared between both campuses. Such a course will be team-taught by faculty from both campuses. Students will enroll in the course from both campuses and be hosted in the mentor's single course shell.

Goal 3: Focus on the Development of Online Courses for Degree Completion

- **Objective 3:** The development of online courses will focus on courses required for degree completion. Online formats for general education courses as well as courses required for a degree will be sought.

Goal 4: Encourage and Provide a Rich and Diverse Learning Experience

- **Objective 4:** Technology will be used to bring together students and faculty from different socio-cultural backgrounds and institutions. Students and faculty of differing ethnicities, urban/rural settings, technology experience, discipline, work setting, age, gender, class standing, etc., will be involved in collaborative learning and instructional activities that will expose each to the others' points of view.

Overview of Collaborations

All faculty and students participating in the program have diverse ethnic, racial, educational, and technological backgrounds. It was expected that the mix of diverse backgrounds would enhance teaching and learning for all the collaborative groups studied. Eight teaching partnerships were implemented and completed during the first three years of the HECA program. These partnerships involved faculty from a number of disciplines:

1. Technology in the Curriculum and Cooperative Education
2. Internet and American Life
3. Creative Writing and Black Women Authors
4. Environmental Studies and Science Teaching Methods
5. Training for Pre-service and Post-Service Teachers
6. Educational Leadership and Future Teachers Academy
7. Instructional Design and Educational Leadership
8. Latin American Studies and the Studies of the Latin American Barrio

Of the eight OTPs completed, one partnership was implemented for an entire semester. Other collaborations took place for as few as a couple of weeks to as long as six weeks. Partnership #8 above was uniquely designed to focus on diversity, while others integrated diversity themes within the courses' normal instructional activities.

Each of the collaborations involved in the OTP consisted of two faculty members, each from a different university. Attempts were made to develop partnerships involving faculty at all three institutions; however, these did not come to fruition due to problems associated with the scheduling of classes and instructional assignments. These same reasons also prevented several two-campus partnerships from forming. Only one partnership did not follow the partnership proposal and ended prematurely. A ninth collaboration has been proposed between an introductory biology health course, the Illinois Department of Public Health and anthropology and medicine courses. This partnership has not yet been implemented because of the unavailability of a second faculty member to complete the partnership.

Faculty who participated in the OTP agreed that it promoted a well-rounded education that provides access to a diverse student population. It also provided opportunities for faculty to enhance and develop teaching skills. They felt that the OTP strategy has the potential for retaining students who may register for classes which could be dropped for lack of registration. The sharing of a faculty member team between two institutions could be the basis for a state-wide initiative for providing classes that students need for graduation. Students likewise help positive views of the OTP, stating in course evaluations, interviews and focus groups that they enjoyed interacting with students from other schools and that the technology enhanced their educational experience.

Information regarding the establishment of the OTP, overviews of the three partner institutions, resources provided by the three support units, and descriptions of individual collaborations, has been disseminated locally, nationally and internationally via presentations at conferences. These include the Association for Educational Communications and Technology (AECT)(Piña & Scheinbuks, 2007; 2008b), Association for the Advancement of Computing in Education (AACE)(McCurdy & Schroeder, 2005a), Syllabus (McCurdy & Schroeder, 2005b), Distance Teaching & Learning (DTL)(McCurdy & Schroeder, 2005c), Supporting Learning and Technology in Education (SLATE) (Scheinbuks, Schroeder, McCurdy & Piña, 2006) TechEd Events (Piña, McCurdy & Scheinbuks, 2007, Piña & Scheinbuks, 2008a; Scheinbuks & Piña, 2009) and EDUCAUSE (Schroeder & McCurdy, 2005).

Description of Collaborations

Described below are the individual HECA-sponsored teaching partnerships that took place between Chicago State University, the University of Illinois at Springfield and Northeastern Illinois University, with training, resources and support by the staff members of OTEL, ODL and CTL. Each of the faculty participating in these partnerships responded to a request for proposal, composed a joint proposal and team-taught a course using asynchronous and synchronous online technologies.

1. Technology in the Curriculum (UIS) and Cooperative Education (CSU) provided an opportunity for both faculty members to develop a unique assignment unit for all members of the collaborative class. The class consisted of students who had varying experiences, backgrounds, and cultural differences. Students from CSU were pre-service education majors and the students from UIS were in-service educators. They were divided into several research groups, which included students from both UIS and CSU. Group discussions were facilitated in real-time by the use of Elluminate. Due to the differences in student service background, the concerns of CSU students were different than those of the UIS students. The groups worked well together in a professional manner and successfully carried out a series of surveys of concerning technologically advanced high schools in three areas: Northern Illinois, Central Illinois, and the Greater Chicago area. The extent of the study was novel for this class and had an impact on reaching class objectives for the course. The students learned to effectively use the Elluminate tool in working well together by complementing each other's skills and interests. In conclusion, the students felt that the collaboration

between the classes was a rewarding experience that enhanced learning.

2. Internet and American Life (UIS) and Special Topics in Technology and Education (CSU) provided an opportunity for one faculty member to mentor another in online pedagogy as their students collaborate in an online course environment. CSU students and a CSU instructor were enrolled within a UIS Blackboard course shell. Activities were also shared by using the Elluminate software. The faculty agreed to a common syllabus with similar expectations for both UIS and CSU students. Readings of the *Pew Charitable Trust Project* served as the basis for student discussion of their own experiences. In describing the tone of the class, one of the instructors (UIS) noted, "The perspectives reflected in the discussions were far more rich with the addition of the CSU students. Extended exchanges were common as the students sorted through the impact of the Internet on such aspects of American life as health care, government, elections, and education" (Schroeder & McCurdy, 2005). '

The collaborating CSU faculty member provided a different but relevant perspective. As time progressed, he developed experience and confidence in the role of an online collaborative faculty member and began to recognize some significant differences in the computer literacy and online course expectations between CSU and UIS students. Other CSU online faculty confirmed these observations. The CSU faculty member plans to adapt this UIS course and offer it as a unique CSU course that will expand course offerings by the Technology and Education Department (Scheinbuks, Schroeder, McCurdy & Piña, 2006).

3. Creative Writing (CSU) and Black Women Authors (UIS) provided a unique opportunity for both faculty members who were interested in Black women authors to create a unit for discussion between their two classes. In preparation for this unit, both classes were assigned to read *Mama Day*, by Gloria Naylor and view the film, *Julie Dash's Daughter of the Dust*. Real-time collaboration and discussion occurred in two sessions using Elluminate Live Classroom. The software permitted considerable input from most members of both classes. In addition, there were several sidebar conversations (implemented by written chat that related to the ongoing speaker's discussion). Unfortunately, the timing of the collaboration was a bit rushed and not sufficient time was planned to develop additional asynchronous collaborative exercises using the Blackboard discussion boards. However, the students reported that they had enjoyed the collaborative sessions and felt that it helped them understand the issues and relative to the novel, Mama Day. Both instructors were excited about the results of the collaborations and indicated that they would be willing to collaborate again.

4. Technology for School Leaders (NEIU) and Cougar Academy for Teachers (CSU) provided an opportunity for one faculty member to mentor the other concerning the implementation of pedagogical techniques used with technology. The two faculty members had agreed to a blended learning approach where a component of the collaboration was asynchronous using Blackboard for online discussions between students in the two courses and synchronous lessons, where the instructors provided live step-by-step instruction in the creation of instructional materials using PowerPoint software in both linear and non-linear formats. In implementing the synchronous presentations and exercises, the presence of faculty members to assist students was an important issue in providing a successful student experience.

This partnership was proposed originally as a three-way collaboration between classes offered in the Colleges of Education at each of the CSU, NEIU and UIS campuses. Unfortunately, these plans could not be implemented because of programmatic issues in scheduling the classes during the summer session, so it was determined that the partnership would continue with NEIU and CSU, NEIU serving as the lead institution. The two faculty members who remained did not effectively communicate the differences that had occurred as a result of instructional assignment changes at Chicago State University. As a result, the class of pre-service teachers at CSU was replaced by a class of pre-college students who were interested in entering a career in education—unbeknownst to the NEIU instructor. The students at NEIU were graduate students who were principally professional educators in the last stages of their master's degrees. As a result of the gap in communication, some miscalculation occurred in developing collaborative assignments that would be equally useful and beneficial to both classes. In reality, both classes had a very unique experience in understanding the differences in the capabilities and maturities of the collaborative class. The collaboration was also a challenging experience for both instructors who had to do some "on the fly" adaptation of their instruction to match the backgrounds of the students in each of the classes. The pre-college students tended to be a bit overwhelmed, while the graduate level students were amused and understanding of their younger colleagues located on the other side of the city.

5. Instructional Design in Human Resource Development (NEIU) and Educational Leadership (CSU) was an instance where a teaching partnership had been planned and one of the instructors' courses did not have sufficient enrollments to be offered that semester. In its place, another course was selected after the semester had begun. The original full-semester partnership was modified to four weeks of collaborative instruction.

This partnership provided two faculty members the opportunity to collaborate in teaching two different courses, one offered by Departments of Human Resource Development at NEIU and the other by the Department of Educational Leadership at CSU. Students in the NEIU were undergraduates who were interested in training and development in business and industry settings, while the CSU students were studying the integration of technology into school curriculum and instruction. Both courses were blended courses, which implemented both asynchronous activities using Blackboard and synchronous sessions using Elluminate. This teaching partnership involved a number of collaborative events: 1) a discussion forum related to interviews with technology coordinators at local K-12 school districts by the CSU class. Both classes discussed the results of several research findings and proposed an optimal type of arrangement for a local K-12 institution. The students discovered that some of these institutions were lacking in technology (implicating a digital divide) while others were well supported. Students compared and contrasted K-12 technology training and support with that provided in industry settings.

A second asynchronous unit dealt with the advantages and disadvantages of online verses blended learning modalities. The discussions indicated that both are appropriate, but the blended class would be the most acceptable to the group. They discussed what types of learning should take place in synchronous verses asynchronous sessions. A further discussion related to recent research on the use of mobile technology, such as iPods, PDAs, MP3 players and cell phones by minority students and Caucasian students. The finding that minority students tended to use the advanced features of mobile technology at higher rates than Caucasian students led students from both courses to conclude that mobile delivery of online content should be a priority of minority-serving institutions (Rainie & Keeter, 2006; Rainie & Madden, 2005).

A synchronous presentation of the history of distance learning in the state of Illinois was presented using Elluminate followed by a discussion of the presentation using the tools made available by Elluminate. At the conclusion of the course, both of the instructors and the students concluded that, despite the rocky start of the partnership, it was a success and the instructors were looking forward to future collaborations with each other.

6. Environmental Studies (NEIU) and Science Teaching Methods (CSU). Both classes in related disciplines provided an opportunity to focus on various points of views related to the collaboration. The CSU class had a greater focus on the development of instructional techniques related to the various scientific disciplines. One of the disciplines considered appropriate for the collaboration was the area of environmental sciences. The NEIU class provided students at that institution with an opportunity to fulfill their general education requirements for an undergraduate degree by being exposed to real environmental issues and understanding how these can be studied to resolve environmental problems. The instructors agreed upon a syllabus that provided an opportunity to collaborate and team-teach their students for three different units or areas.

The first was related to the development of concept maps as an approach to relating scientific concepts. Various biological concepts were studied and concept maps were developed relative to the regulation of the biosphere through a process called homeostasis. Life forms interact with environmental factors to produce a self-regulating system. A movie clip was used to illustrate the concept. A classroom activity was designed in which an interactive free computer program CTOOLS was used for producing the concept maps. Students from both classes evaluated each other's maps in terms of the overall effectiveness of organizing new information. The CSU class in terms of how the use of these maps could enhance learning in a high school classroom setting analyzed the learning process.

The second unit involved a class visit to the Green Technology Center in Chicago. This city-operated center provides information about how to pursue and develop green technologies. This outing permitted students in both classes to meet and interact. Up to this point, the students interacted asynchronously. This outing provided the students to meet their counterparts in the teaching partnership and interact on a different level. Many of the students in the environmental studies class have considered developing a career in education. This interaction was helpful for them to meet potential role models of students who were actively pursuing these objectives.

The third unit developed from concepts that had been discussed from the second unit. The second unit related to green technologies and the absence of hazards. While the third unit dealt with an understanding of hazards and how they affect the environment. Discussions of how hazards affect the environment were done synchronously using Elluminate. The NEIU instructor demonstrated an Air Emissions Modeling Program (ALOHA) to assist responders to emergency events. An understanding was developed of the issues related to such an environmental catastrophe. Students were then given similar problems for analysis and to develop strategic approaches for resolving these problems. As a result of the immersion into this model, each class developed different take-home lessons. The CSU students used this as a model to develop an instruction plan while the NEIU students used this as a model for understanding issues related to toxic accidents.

The students were queried about each of the three units. Their responses were positive and helpful in assessing learning associated with each of the units. Students were enthusiastic about the collaboration and said that they would participate in additional courses using similar formats. The two instructors were not experienced at using online technologies for instructor prior to the course and while they found some of the technology to be challenging initially, they were able to master a wide range of synchronous and asynchronous applications.

7. Educational Leadership (UIS) and Educational Leadership (CSU) provided two faculty members an opportunity to collaborate in teaching two educational leadership classes at the graduate level located at different institutions separated at a distance. The UIS class was populated with graduate-level in-service teachers and the CSU

class contained undergraduate-level pre-service teachers. The instructors were experienced in offering both blended course and online course modalities. The instructor at UIS had stronger technology skills than the instructor at CSU. The instructors developed a syllabus for each of their respective classes that had designated both asynchronous activities (2-3 weeks) and synchronous activities (3 weeks). The asynchronous activities were implemented easily and the students appeared to enjoy the interactions between members of both classes. Two of the three synchronous sessions using Elluminate were successfully implemented. The instructors interacted well in planning the collaboration as well as interacted well in the various collaborative sessions with the students.

The instructor of each class was responsible for setting the standards and objectives for their respective classes and evaluating their own students. Although the objectives for the two respective courses differed somewhat, the instructors agreed upon the objectives for the collaborative sessions. Students were queried both at midterm and at the end of the course by survey to obtain feedback concerning the collaboration. The students indicated that they enjoyed the collaborative activities and felt that the collaboration added an extra dimension to the content of the course. The extra dimension was related to student backgrounds—UIS is an institution located in rural Illinois while CSU is located in the Chicago urban area. Both students and faculty felt that their experiences were valuable in that they were able to obtain unique information and understanding relative to their diverse backgrounds. Both faculty members have presented papers at conferences based upon this collaborative experience.

8. Latino and Latin American Studies (NEIU) and Public Administration (UIS) provided an opportunity for 2 faculty members from UIS and NEIU to develop a teaching partnership, which was proposed to be unique. A proposal for a semester long partnership focusing on diversity (the Barrio in Latin-American communities) was submitted during the spring, 2007 semester. During this semester, the faculty team planned the nature of the course collaboration, which was implemented during the fall 2007 semester. Since a course comparable to LLAS 312 did not exist at UIS, the faculty member proposed a new course that met UIS general education requirements so that it could be scheduled for the fall, 2007 session. An agreement concerning the management of the course took place where one of the faculty members was responsible for the introduction and implementation of the technologies used to link the students together (Blackboard, videoconferencing and Elluminate) while the other faculty member was responsible for providing background and content for the course. The teaching partnership proceeded for 5 weeks before it was terminated by one of the faculty members.

The partnership focused initially on the development of web resources to study the Barrio. To accomplish this goal, an introduction to the use of technology to link the classes together was provided within the first 2 weeks. During the third week, a lecture/discussion was presented to both classes on "The Meaning of Context" relative to the study of the Barrio. The demographics of Chicago and the state of Illinois were examined in lecture/discussion using Elluminate. Students were involved in Blackboard forums related to the nature of the Barrio. Following these discussion, students were assigned to propose research projects based upon the course's introductory sessions. These research projects were discussed during the fifth week of the partnership.

After the initial two week technology introduction period was complete and the team-teaching of the course content commenced, it became clear to the two faculty partners that their teaching styles were not compatible. One instructor was very meticulous in his preparation and delivery and preferred instructor-led discussions, while the other one preferred to "go with the flow" and allow the instruction and discussion to be led by the students. Ultimately, these two styles proved to be incompatible and it was agreed that the collaboration would end after 5 weeks and the two courses would be developed and offered independently for the remainder of the semester.

Feedback from the students indicated that they were unaware of the difficulties between their two professors and assumed that the course was designed for collaboration at the beginning only. Students from both courses rated them highly, which reflected positively on the professionalism of the faculty involved.

Introductory Biology Health (CSU) and Illinois Department of Public Health'sBrothers and Sisters United Against HIV/AIDS (BASUAH) provided an opportunity to enhance an introductory level biology class focused on issues related to sexually transmitted diseases. The objectives of the course are to make the issues of contracting and treating these diseases meaningful to the minority student audience at CSU. A collaboration was begun between CSU and UIS, in partnership with the Illinois Department of Public Health to enhance learning by immersing the students in the course into the virtual worlds of Second Life. Some students in the class were familiar with Second Life and had developed Avatars while others accessed it for the first time to develop their new avatars. With the assistance of OTEL, our students were introduced to the virtual instructional world ofUIS SL Island. The process of enrolling students into SL was cumbersome because of issues related to the selection of Avatar names.

Students in the class were given access to the BASUAH Ambassador training site to learn and review basic information about sexual diseases. The course also provided a unique focus promoting the attitude of education the public about problems surrounding these diseases. Many of the students were excited about the opportunity to become BASUAH ambassadors and looked forward to educating their community within the confines of community and state organizations,

The class utilized this experience to develop skits so that they could role play how they would meet the challenges of educating members of the community about sexual disease issues. The presentations and skits were recorded on Elluminate and then converted to a format so that these could become available in the BASUAH instructional area within the UIS SL Island.

Since this collaboration involved a faculty member at CSU and a non-faculty instructional designer at UIS, it is included separately from the other eight faculty partnership included above. A teaching partnership has been proposed between CSU and UIS to collaborate with a class focused on the Anthropology of Medicine as it relates to attitudes toward diseases in other countries. Although the HECA support for the OTP has concluded, this partnership is planned to proceed in 2010. Support for the collaboration will be provided through a newly established consortium, the New Century Learning Consortium that both institutions have joined (NCLC, 2009; Scheinbuks & Piña, 2009).

Summary of Collaborations

At the completion of each course, the partner faculty members composed and submitted a final report, which included: 1) a description of the courses involved in the partnerships; 2) a description of the student and faculty participants; 3) a statement of learner objectives; 4) an overview of the process of establishing the partnership; 5) a description of what occurred during the development and implementation of the courses; 6) an evaluation of the process and 7) a summary of lessons learned and recommendations. Data for student and instructor evaluations were gathered via surveys and interviews. Interviews were also conducted with personnel involved in the administrative and support of the OTP. Online course materials in Blackboard and recorded Elluminate sessions were examined to verify and evaluate the instructional activities and interactions that occurred within the classes and the grades achieved by student in the OTP courses were compared to those of students who took the courses previously.

The results of the interviews and surveys were consistent across all classes and campuses. There was no indication that participation in an OTP course increased student grades significantly. However, the OTP experienced was reported by students, faculty, staff and administration to have been a worthwhile program that had many positive outcomes and met its basic goals. Both students and faculty felt that the interaction with students from another campus and culture positively affected their educational experience, broadened their outlook and made the course more interesting. Faculty noted that their technology skills and comfort with technology increased. They also found the exchange with a peer collaborator exposed them to ideas that helped to make their courses better. Nearly all of the faculty who participated in the OTP expressed interest in future opportunities to collaborate.

It was gratifying to note that the diverse socio-cultural differences between the student populations at UIS, CSU and NEIU did not prove to be a stumbling block. In fact, the evidence points to the conclusion that both student and instructors welcomed and valued the opinions and observations of those from the partner universities., particularly when differences were found among ethnicity, grade level, discipline, work setting or institution.

Unreliable technology also did not seem to play much of a factor in the online teaching partnerships. While some found the technology—particularly Elluminate--to be challenging to learn and operate at the beginning, all agreed that using these technologies can enhance instruction and can help to bring diverse learners and faculty together.

CHALLENGES

The following were challenges related to the implement of the OTP:

1. The funding dates for each year of the grant varied, depending upon when the state legislature passed its budget. The second year of the grant did not get funded until almost Thanksgiving. The time lost was a whole semester. Because of the late funding date, the funds requested could not be spent entirely to support the program without requesting an extension. Extensions were granted, but there was an overlap between the second and third year of the grant.
2. Introducing faculty members who wished to participate in a partnership was also challenging. We attempted to allow them to meet by video conferencing so that they may introduce themselves. Additionally, a web site was created which provided background information and interests so that faculty members could choose to contact potential partners.
3. Once faculty partnerships were considered and some planning occurred, several partnerships did not take place because of schedule changes as well as teaching assignment changes.
4. Some partnerships failed because classes were cut due to low enrollments. The possibility of picking up additional students attending from another university did not affect administrative decisions to cut some of the experimental partnerships.
5. Communication between the members of the partnerships sometimes was difficult especially when classes were cancelled and other classes were substituted. The faculty members were under pressure to adapt course syllabi and approaches due to unexpected changes in the student audiences. In one instance, an upper-level undergraduate

class was replaced by a class of high school students and the fact was not communicated to the partner teacher. In another instance, a class did not "make" due to poor enrollment and another class was substituted in its place after the semester had begun.

6. Communications between some faculty members became difficult when their teaching styles and personalities differed considerably. This led to frustration and the abandonment of the partnership.

SOLUTIONS AND RECOMMENDATIONS

The following are steps that have been taken to address the challenges of the OTP:

1. CSU has joined a consortium initiated by OTEL at UIS, the New Century Learning Consortium (NCLC, 2009). The objectives of this consortium are many-fold:
   a. Provide continuing education sessions on instructional technology through the use of Elluminate
   b. Provide opportunities to form course partnerships between the various campuses.
   c. Provide opportunities to collaborate in completing online programs leading to online certifications or online degrees. These programs will assist students in completing their course work without delays due to low enrollments.
2. The OTP institutions are members of SLATE, which is a community of practice involving over 50 institutions inside and outside of Illinois. SLATE meets monthly at member institutions, shares information and hosts its own conference (Piña, Sadowski, Scheidenhelm & Heydenburg, 2008). SLATE can be a conduit to enhance current partnerships and establish new ones.
3. The CSU Office of Distance Learning, the UIS Office of Technology-Enhanced Learning and the NEIU Center for Teaching and Learning will continue to provide training and support for the use of online and in-class technologies, such as Learning Management Systems (Blackboard, Moodle) and virtual classrooms (Elluminate). These technologies will continue to be made available to faculty by their respective institutions.
4. The ODL will provide an opportunity for faculty members to submit their courses for review in a new program called, the Exemplary Course. Courses submitted will be reviewed and exemplary courses will be recognized once a year in a Distance Learning Day program. Travel funds may be offered to the winner(s) to attend a national conference to discuss aspects of their course.

REFERENCES

Gatliff, B., & Wendel, F. C. (1998). Inter-institutional collaboration and team teaching. *American Journal of Distance Education, 12*(1). doi:10.1080/08923649809526981

IBHE. (2005). State of Illinois board of education: Higher education cooperation act, fiscal year 2005 application. Springfield, IL: State of Illinois Board of Higher Education.

McCurdy, S., & Schroeder, R. (2005a). *Achieving diversity through online inter-institutional collaborations.* Paper presented at ED-Media World Conference on Educational Multimedia, Hypermedia and Telecommunications, Association for the Advancement of Computing in Education, Montreal, Quebec, Canada.

McCurdy, S., & Schroeder, R. (2005b). *Inter-institutional online class-sharing to promote diversity.* Paper presented at the Syllabus Conference, Los Angeles, CA.

McCurdy, S., & Schroeder, R. (2005c). *Inter-institutional collaboration in the delivery of online learning.* Paper presented at the annual Distance Teaching and Learning Conference, Madison, WI.

New Century Learning Consortium (NCLC). (2009). Retrieved May 4, 2009 from http://nclc-online.ning.com

Oakley, B. (2004). The value of online learning: Perspectives from the University of Illinois at Springfield. In J. C. Moore (Ed.), Elements of quality online education: Into the mainstream. Needham, MA: Sloan Consortium.

Piña, A. A., McCurdy, S., & Scheinbuks, J. (2007). *Building virtual bridges: Implementation of a collaborative online teaching partnership.* Paper presented at the Technology in Education (TechEd) Conference, Ontario, CA.

Piña, A. A., Sadowski, K. P., Scheidenhelm, C. L., & Heydenburg, P. R. (2008). SLATE: A community of practice for supporting learning and technology in education. *International Journal of Instructional Technology and Distance Learning, 5*(7).

Piña, A. A., & Scheinbuks, J. (2007). *Creating a culture of technology through inter-institutional online teaching partnerships.* Paper presented at the Association for Educational Communications & Technology, Anaheim, CA.

Piña, A. A., & Scheinbuks, J. (2008a). *An e-learning partnership between racially and culturally different institutions.* Paper presented at the Technology in Education (TechEd) Conference, Ontario, CA.

Piña, A. A., & Scheinbuks, J. (2008b). *Case studies of e-learning partnerships between racially & culturally diverse universities.* Paper presented at the Association for Educational Communications & Technology, Orlando, FL.

Rainie, L., & Keeter, S. (2006). How Americans use their cell phones, Washington, DC: The Pew Research Center.

Rainie, L., & Madden, M. (2005). Podcasting catches on. Washington, DC: Pew Research Center.

Scheinbuks, J., & Piña, A. A. (2009). *An e-learning instructional partnership between culturally diverse minority institutions.* Paper presented at the Technology in Education (TechEd) Conference, Ontario, CA.

Scheinbuks, J., Schroeder, R., McCurdy, S., & Piña, A. A. (2006). *Online teaching partnerships.* Paper presented at the Supporting Learning and Technology in Education (SLATE) Conference. Chicago, IL.

Schroeder, R., & McCurdy, S. (2005). *Inter-institutional class collaborations online.* Paper presented at the Midwest EDUCAUSE Conference, Chicago, IL.

Sloan Consortium. (2009). *2007 Sloan-C excellence in online teaching and learning awards.* Retrieved May 12, 2009 from http://www.sloan-c.org/aboutus/awards.asp

U.S. News & World Report. (2005). Choosing a school: Campus diversity. *America's Best Colleges.* New Hudson, MI: U.S. News & World Report.

ADDITIONAL READING

Ajiferuke, I. (2005). Inter-university collaboration in Canada. *Canadian Journal of Information and Library Sciences, 29*(4).

Alexander, G. R. (2000). Issues and innovations in very large scale on-line distance learning: A case study. *International Journal of Continuing Engineering Education and Lifelong Learning, 10*(4). doi:10.1504/IJCEELL.2000.000377

Austin, A. E., & Baldwin, R. G. (1992). Faculty collaboration: Enhancing the quality of scholarship and teaching. *ERIC Digest ED347958*. Accessed May 18, 2009 from http://www.ericdigests.org/1992-2/faculty.htm

Beatty, V. (2006). Real-time communication helps online instruction. *Community College Week 18*(16).

Bers, M., & Portsmore, M. (2005). Teaching partnerships: Early childhood and engineering students *teaching* math and science through robotics. *Journal of Science Education and Technology, 14*(1). doi:10.1007/s10956-005-2734-1

Dahl, J. (2004). How to launch an inter-institutional collaboration.. *Distance Education Report 8*(3).

Dahl, J. (2005). Inter-institutional alliances lower costs and risks. *Distance Education Report 9*(20).

Dow, E. (2008). Successful inter-institutional resource sharing in a niche educational market: Formal collaboration without a contract. *Innovative Higher Education, 33*(3). doi:10.1007/s10755-008-9076-x

Evenbeck, S., & Kahn, S. (2001). Enhancing learning assessment and accountability through communities of practice. *Change, 33*(3). doi:10.1080/00091380109601797

IBHE. (1999). The Illinois commitment: Partnerships, opportunities & excellence. Springfield, IL: State of Illinois Board of Higher Education.

Jervis-Tracy, P. (2005). Inter-institutional networks and alliances: New directions in leadership. *International Journal of Leadership in Education, 8*(4).

Kahn, N., Nasti, C., Evans, E., & Chapman-Novakofski, K. (2009). Peer education, exercising, and eating right (PEER): Training of peers in an undergraduate faculty teaching partnership. *Journal of Nutrition Education and Behavior, 41*(1).

Knackendoffel, E. A. (2005). Collaborative teaming in the secondary school. *Focus on Exceptional Children 27*(5).

Lang, D. (2002). A lexicon of inter-institutional cooperation. *Higher Education, 44*(1). doi:10.1023/A:1015573429956

MacGregor, J. (2000). Teaching communities within learning communities. *Washington Center News*. Retrieved April 1, 2009, from http://learningcommons.evergreen.edu/pdf/spring2000b.pdf

McCurdy, S., & Schroeder, R. (2006). Achieving diversity through online inter-institutional collaborations. *Journal of Asynchronous Learning Networks, 10*(1).

Misanchuk, M., & Anderson, T. (2001). Building community in an online learning environment: communication, cooperation and collaboration. Retrieved April 1, 2009 from http://www.mtsu.edu/~itconf/proceed01/19.html.

Moran, L. (2000). Inter-institutional collaboration: The case of the Australian inter-university women's studies major. *Journal of Distance Education, 5*(2).

Piña, A. A. (2008). Distance learning and the institution: Foundations, importance and implementation. Saabrucken, Germany: VDM Publishing.

Quinn, A., Coe-Regan, J., & Schoech, D. (2008). Online synchronous audio and video environments for education, training, and human service delivery: A review of three products. *Journal of Technology in Human Services*, *26*(1). doi:10.1300/J017v26n01_07

Roberts, C. (2005). Partners in pedagogy. *Times Educational Supplement*, 4634.

Robson, P., & Robert, J. (2006). Strengthening partnership. *Social Work Education*, *25*(4). doi:10.1080/02615470600593469

Sullivan, M. & Schmidt, K. (2004). Online team teaching enriches instruction, instructors. *Online Classroom November 2004*.

USGAO. (2003). Distance education: Challenges for minority serving institutions and implications for federal education policy. Washington DC: United States General Accounting Office.

Verbaan, E. (2003). The multicultural society in the Netherlands: Technology-supported inquiry-based learning in an inter-institutional context. *Teaching in Higher Education*, *13*(4).

Wang, J. (1997). *Statewide collaboration in adult continuing education: A case study of distance education in Maine*. Unpublished doctoral dissertation, Northern Illinois University, Dekalb, Illinois.

Wilensky, J. (2003). Teaching partnerships promote interdisciplinary education. *Human Ecology*, *31*(1).

KEY TERMS AND DEFINITIONS

Asynchronous Instruction: Instruction that uses technology to provide content, activities, communication and interaction between teachers and learners who meet online at different times and from various locations.

Blackboard: The Enterprise Version of the Learning Management System developed by Blackboard, Inc. (*see Learning Management System below*).

Elluminate: Elluminate Live! is an online synchronous virtual classroom/meeting environment that provides live two-way audio, desktop sharing, video and other resources for conducting real-time presentations, meetings or class sessions.

Illinois Board of Higher Education (IBHE): The principal governance and regulatory body for institutions of higher education in the state of Illinois. The IBHE administers the HECA grant program (*see below*).

Higher Education Cooperation Act (HECA): Legislation passed by the State of Illinois and administered by the IBHE (*see above*) to promote effective use of resources though cooperation among institutions, to achieve an equitable distribution of education services, and to develop innovative concepts and applications. HECA provides competitive grants to cooperatives comprising at least two public and private higher education institutions.

Learning Management System: An online platform that provides for the development, delivery and management of online courses. Can deliver both synchronous and asynchronous instruction and communication. Also known as a Course Management System or Virtual Learning Environment.

Online Teaching Partnership: A HECA-funded (*see above*) collaborative effort between Chicago State University, University of Illinois at Springfield and Northeastern Illinois University to improve the teaching and learning of diverse student populations via course design and teaching collaborations between professors at the three institutions.

Synchronous Instruction: Instruction that uses technology to provide content, activities, communication and interaction between teachers and learners who meet online at the same time from different locations.

Chapter 3
Balanced Assessment of Flexible e-Learning versus Face-to-Face Campus Delivery Courses at an Australian University

Kenneth David Strang
University of Technology, Australia

ABSTRACT

This case study reminded researchers of the value in using formal methodologies to gain an objective balanced perspective of actual practice. By using models and survey instruments that gathered objective input from key stakeholders in the higher education market, several of the true underlying factors were revealed. The key instrument used in the case study allowed us to objectively measure if flexible e-learning was at least as effective as campus delivery mode. More so, the assessment was not just performance and not just student satisfaction – instead the outcomes assessed included six factors that were linked to Australian university accreditation: Industry focus, resources/content materials, critical thinking activities, teaching quality, student satisfaction, and student performance (including completion). One of the most interesting aspects of the case study was that we are seeing history in the making to some degree in that as a result of the 2008 global economic crises, the international student market is changing which will force universities to change what and how they offer higher education in the future. More countries (and their populations) in the world are seeking a credible university higher education and they do not always want to travel to holiday destinations to obtain that... the world economic model is changing, continuing to increase the demand for education, yet changing how that product/service must be delivered. Successful higher education institutions around the world are already showing the followers how to do that. This case study provides some ideas and benchmarks for becoming more competitive in higher education, and while the model was developed and used in Australia, likely it can be applied elsewhere since the majority of students feeding into this model and research were international.

DOI: 10.4018/978-1-61520-779-4.ch003

INTRODUCTION

This case study discusses unique socio cultural and political challenges faced by Australian universities in higher education course design and delivery. Many researchers abroad might be surprised to read that synchronous e-learning in higher education is not typically practiced in Australian universities, except in research pilots, at least as compared to the virtual learning environments and methods that are reported in UK (Biggs, 2003; Laurillard, 2002) and USA literature (Weller, 2007; Bates & Poole, 2003; Palloff & Pratt, 2002). Nonetheless this case compares the same e-learning course with a traditional campus version delivered to both domestic and international or multi-cultural students.

Rationale and Challenges

It is difficult to position this research into the Australian theoretical or empirical contexts because the term 'e-learning' is often applied in rudimentary and ambiguous ways, without actually meaning online synchronous student interaction for learning (Eklund, 2005; Brabazon, 2002; Manathunga, 2002). In Australian higher education theory, e-learning often refers to a student having Internet access to campus systems, primarily for convenient access to materials, asynchronous group discussions and submission of assignments (Lock & Redmond, 2008; Pauli, 2007). Exceptions do occur such as in science, business and military where synchronous interactive e-learning is being used for continuing education (Zimmer, Billaud, & Geoffroy, 2006; Newton & Ellis, 2005; Zhang, Zhao, Zhou, & Nunamaker, 2004).

Additionally, from experience and the literature (Kobas & Renzie, 2005; Karemera, Reuben, & Sillah, 2003; Stevens-Long & Crowell, 2002), comparing face-to-face with e-learning delivery for effectiveness is difficult because very little of the context may be consistent between the two modes (lack of experimental control). The instructor, materials, assessment requirements and teaching methods often differ (Drent & Meelissen, 2008; Kobas & Renzie, 2005; Grant, 2004). Students often have different levels of experience and/or learning styles, some favoring e-learning mode (executives, managers or engineers) as compared with others preferring face-to-face tutoring, like English second language (ESL) or inexperienced adolescents.

There is considerable debate in the empirical literature on whether e-learning (or online education) is as effective as traditional face-to-face (campus) delivery. Many empirical studies have found e-learning is as effective as, or better, than face-to-face mode (Strang, 2007; Cybinski & Selvanathan, 2005; Gao & Lehman, 2003; St Hill, 2000). In the literature, several meta-analysis of e-learning versus classroom effectiveness studies have been inconclusive about the '(no) significant difference' finding (Coffield, Moseley, Hall, & Ecclestone, 2004; Olson & Wisher, 2002; Russell, 2002; Joy & Garcia, 2000).

Another unresolved dimension in comparing e-learning to campus-based delivery is determining what metrics should be used: Student grades, student satisfaction, organizational costs (less faculty, less time to design/deliver), environmental impact (travel, paper usage), and so on. It was the proposition of a cost-effective blended teaching model by Laurillard (2007) that inspired documenting this case study. Most importantly, few if any empirical studies of learning use a 'balanced measure' of effectiveness. A 'balanced measure' refers to benchmarks that are valued by all relevant stakeholders. The assessment paradigm used here is a balanced one, which is conceptually linked to the key stakeholders, namely: Students, faculty, administration, and the public-at-large through university accreditation agencies.

Research Approach

A case study methodology (Yin, 2003) is applied on a single organization, with two embedded

Figure 1. Hypothetical balanced assessment rubric for course effectiveness

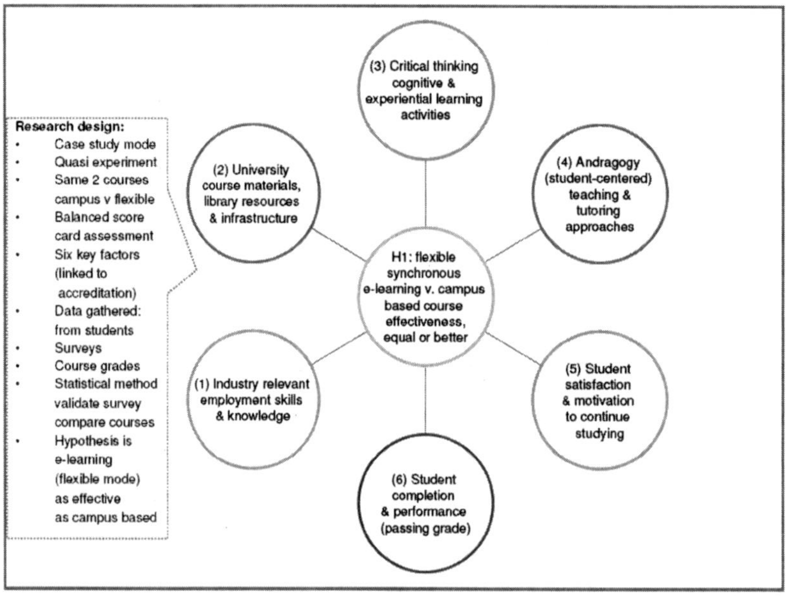

phases: action learning (Schön, 1983) and a quasi-experiment (Creswell, 2003). A logical-positivistic philosophy is engaged, meaning there is some interpretation of the context, yet the underlying motive is to prove a hypothesis using scientific methods and evidence. Unlike the popular grounded theory or interpretive philosophy of naturalistic inquiry, the logical-positivist action learning methodology starts with *a priori* educational theories and instruments, when reflecting on course design and delivery. The unit of interest is learning effectiveness while the level of analysis is course. The action learning phase applies a literature review and reflection-in-action (Schön, 1983) to reveal lesser-known challenges (and a few controversies) in Australian higher education. Drawing from applied theories in the literature and introspective reflection, a balanced model is proposed to assess the effectiveness of course delivery. The quasi experiment phase uses the balanced model to compare two identical business degree courses: the first, a traditional campus-based format; the second, an e-learning mode. Quantitative and qualitative data are gathered from students to compare the effectiveness of each course (experimental control consists of same context, same course, and same teachers).

The aim of this study is to answer the research question: How effective is e-learning for multicultural students as compared to campus mode, using a balanced assessment reflecting accreditation requirements. The unit of analysis is course effectiveness by delivery mode, at the group level of analysis (students).

Figure 1 illustrates the research design and hypothesis, with the key features summarized on the left side. At the center of the research model is a simple hypothesis (H1) that posits the flexible e-learning course offering will be at least as effective as the campus-based mode (when the same course is delivered in both modes). The six proposed factors radiating from the center represent the balanced assessment rubric. The data for each of the assessment items is gathered from students in terms of self-reported perceptions (for the first five), and as actual course performance (grade) for the sixth. The course assessment rubric consists of key course quality dimensions, namely:

(1) industry relevance, (2) resources/materials, (3) critical thinking, (4) effective teaching, (5) student satisfaction and (6) performance. These course quality dimensions are important for students and for university accreditation in Australia (Barrie & P., 2007; Ginns, Prosser, & Barrie, 2007; Fresen & Boyd, 2005). A previously validated survey is adapted.

BACKGROUND

First several critical definitions are provided. Then the key socio cultural and political challenges that face Australian higher education universities are discussed. Since the case study is in Australia, e-learning changes rapidly, and a logical-positivist ideology is applied, newer relevant empirical studies are cited.

Contemporary Definition of e-Learning

The definition of e-learning in Australian higher education is ambiguous, meaning differs across disciplines (management science versus educational psychology), and application varies from researcher to researcher. For example, e-learning has often been associated with technology-enhanced-learning (Lock & Redmond, 2008; Ginns & Ellis, 2007), with a fully digitized (online) course (Manathunga, 2002). "The term e-learning generally embraces a variety of electronic delivery media, for example web-based, multimedia on CD-Rom, interactive television, virtual classrooms and video conferencing ...Internationally, the term distance education has become synonymous with online learning, which is sometimes also referred to as technology-assisted distance learning." (Fresen & Boyd, 2005, p. 318).

Distance learning is generally described as off-site e-learning with the materials sent to the student and assessments sent to the university via post mail/courier, along with occasional one-to-one telephone and/or email communications between student and professor (Olson & Wisher, 2002). In Australia distance education is sometimes utilized at the university level by rural and/or fully employed students.

Rosenberg (2001) conducted a meta-review of e-learning definitions and suggested three underlying principles: Networked/interconnected students (allowing for timely interaction and feedback); accessible via a standard Internet browser on a standard personal computer (from anywhere anytime); and it employs educational psychology theories to facilitate learning beyond self-directed training. Rosenberg is commonly cited in Australia higher education case studies. His definition is adopted here because it differentiates e-learning from individual training, self-directed learning, and from online environments that do not permit group synchronous interaction for practicing realistic team work, development and experiential learning. Nevertheless he accepted that e-learning can be regarded as a subsection of distance education (if the above criteria were met), but not all distance education would qualify as e-learning.

Socio cultural, Economic and Technical Challenges

Australia is probably best known to the western world and highly developed countries as a pleasant safe tropical/subtropical tourist destination (since the advent of long haul jets). Oddly enough, albeit Australia was settled in the 1800's by UK convicts, since the 1990's we have been predominately influenced by USA (and their TV shows) in just about every facet of the community with exception to natural resource industries (minerals, wine growing, etc.), and a large immigrant presence has introduced us to Asian/Indonesian cuisine. A nice climate and a booming economy (until the 2008 global economic crises) brought a very significant influx of both rich and poor immigrants, mostly from countries in Asia, Indonesia, some in Africa, along with a continuing flow in Europe, as well as a few New Zealanders. Politically, Australia is similar in higher education structure and operating regulations to USA (and somewhat to UK). Geographically it is about the same size as USA but as of this writing, Australia is about 1/20th of the USA population and mostly concentrated on the coast.

Culturally, even though the Australian dialect and accent are a caricature of their UK heritage, in urban areas there is a large adoption of USA social terms and practices, especially with the under 30 year old generation (notably observed in the case study university students). Economically, Australia boomed in the 1990's (especially the urban areas of Sydney-Melbourne-Brisbane on the east coast, and later the western cities like Perth due to mineral resources). Like other well-developed countries, Australia was also hit by the 2008 global economic crises, but much less so as compared with most other G12 nations. Three severe economic handicaps during the global crises were: Heavy investment by USA companies (retail and manufacturing), the reliance of exporting minerals to China (mostly coal), as well as a stock market that (akin to social culture) tended to mirror the USA NYSE (and other USA markets).

Higher education design and delivery in the forty recognized (accredited) Australian universities follows a similar anthropological trend, borrowing heavily from the theories and materials of USA (as well as UK), yet e-learning seems prehistoric in comparison to other developed nations (especially compared to UK). In Australia the most unique application of e-learning theory and technology can be found in rural schools that interconnect remote children and their teachers through mobile GSM and satellite telecommunications. Pedagogy, problem based learning (Schunk, 2004), and ADDIE (Dick, Carey, & Carey, 2001) were respectively the key educational psychology theories and design methodologies underpinning most higher education program designs.

At the university campus level, learning related technology typically includes Blackboard or WebCT as the Learning Management System (LMS), 100mbps LAN, audio-visual-lecture system, video conferencing links to 'offshore' campuses, and common office automation software (usually the Microsoft Office Suite). There are a few instances of virtual learning environments and tools such as Moodle, SecondLife, Qik, Twitter, Wimba, ElluminateLive, FM and so on - but usually these are experimental projects or personal-faculty research.

The student populations of Australian universities are usually multicultural in terms of ethnic background (especially in the eastern states and coastal city regions surrounding Adelaide, Melbourne, Canberra, Wollongong, Sydney, Brisbane, Darwin and Perth). Internationalization of the curriculum has become one of the criteria for accreditation (AUQA, 2009). Nonetheless internationalization refers to helping foreigners be mobile, apply English grammar and appreciate culture - not embedding other cultures into materials or adjusting education delivery methods to accommodate diverse learning styles (Leask, 2004).

For example, the University of Technology Sydney - known for having one of the largest international student populations in Australia second to Central Queensland University (AUQA, 2006) - states their approach for "UTS internationalisation of the student experience" is: "To develop national and international renown for [sic] programs of teaching and learning that enable graduates to acquire knowledge and skills that assist them to live and work in a world of increased globalisation and cultural diversity." (AUQA, 2006, p. 7). This is similar to the internationalization strategies of other Australian universities (AUQA, 2009). Obviously the challenge with that goal is the broad competency focus of teaching knowledge and skills; yet there is no acknowledgement of the difficultly to achieve such an educational promise, or of appeasing the diverse learning styles of multicultural students to accomplish that. On the other hand, this also goes to explain the focus on face-to-face campus-based delivery mode in Australia. It can be very difficult to achieve effective asynchronous and synchronous e-learning with ESL students having diverse multicultural learning styles (Strang, 2008; Picciano, 2006).

Instead, the attractive subtropical climate and good economy attract immigrants for money and education as a temporary resident with a work visa (Editorial, 2005) not as an online student. Recent Australian university audits found a common theme arising from discussions with students, external stakeholders and staff was that many students – particularly international students – enrolled specifically because of the ease of entrance for Australian residency. Evidence for students' attention to residency requirements includes a shift in student enrolments away from IT to accounting courses when the DIMIA [immigration department] points structure shifted to favor accounting (AUQA, 2009). Domestic students seem satisfied with campus based learning along with a tranquil hedonistic lifestyle (and who can blame them). For example, Kennedy and colleagues examined the use of e-learning technology by undergraduate students (including Blackboard discussion, podcasts, mobile/Internet chat) and found the use of "learning technology is neither automatic nor guaranteed" (Kennedy, Judd, Churchward, Gray, & Krause, 2008, p. 119). Also there is a significant amount of high quality medical and engineering university education (and probably a few others that escape mention here), inherently and traditionally relying a campus-based delivery mode (Gilding & Martino, 2001). The typical Australian university higher education delivery infrastructure consists of lecture theatres/classes, overhead projectors, AudioVisual Lecture Systems, campus-to-campus video conferencing systems, and CMS's, the latter of which are almost entirely Blackboard or WebCT (Grushka, McLeod, & Reynolds, 2005). Most Australian universities promote ease-of-Internet connectivity at campus.

Given that the number of Australian households with broadband Internet steadily increased by almost 80% between 2005 and 2006 to 3.2 million (ACCC, 2006), it might be expected that e-learning would be a common mode of delivery for higher education, yet from experience and the literature it is not (Reding, 2003). A study by the Commonwealth Department of Education, Science and Training found that e-learning was being widely employed at 54% of Australian universities to achieve an online presence of their programs (marketing, enrollment, policies), yet with a focus on physical presence (or video conferencing to offshore sites), and knowledge competencies (such as written papers, presentation hardcopies and/or portfolios or e-portfolios) for learning (Dixon & Dixon, 2008).

These learning delivery systems are usually situated within each campus (sometimes linked to Asian or Indonesian partnered-institutions which are called international or offshore campuses). The CMS allows direct or remote access to each campus via the Internet but this is often incorrectly labeled as e-learning (e-access is a better term). The online interaction specified in the curriculum for all examined courses at universities in Australia use asynchronous discussion at best (18 campuses were visited online) - students post questions, answers, examples and/or reflections one at a time over a fixed period. This is not concurrent synchronous interaction. There are exceptions (e-learning is increasing) yet it is the status quo.

Another technical-organizational challenge is that experienced university faculty are often not familiar with e-learning tools, and vice-versa, faculty assigned to design e-learning courses are not familiar with either educational psychology theories and/or course design best practices (Stewart, Norwood, Ezell, & Waight, 2006). Feedback from early e-learning case studies indicated participants were frustrated with their inability to ask questions and get answers (Olson & Wisher, 2002). Sometimes even students are given the duty of designing online courses because they are more familiar with technology, they are interested, they have more time, and their work can be linked to their studies. Unfortunately "while graduate students are not assigned instructional responsibility for on-line courses they do provide faculty support in areas such as course enhancement, technical support, course management … [but] faculty were not willing to assume all of the issues of quality control and training that would be required…" (Stewart et al., 2006, p. 209). Many Australian universities "are hesitant about the use of e-learning due to failures, either real or perceived, within other organisations; and also because of a lack of knowledge and understanding of the possibilities." (Eklund, 2005, p. 3).

In summary, the existing higher education culture in the Australian university community of practice does not yet endorse or embrace virtual (interactive) learning environments or true synchronous e-learning context. Technology is used extensively at the campus location. Internet connectivity is promoted for research purposes. Australian universities have established their presence on the Internet for marketing and administrative/operational functions, not to promote anywhere anytime synchronous e-learning. Notwithstanding this, it is possible the market may impact this organizational culture since international and domestic higher education enrollments have plummeted after the 2008 global economic crisis.

Higher Education Compliance and Political Issues

From a compliance standpoint, Australian universities are self-accrediting but they are regulated by the Commonwealth Department of Education, Science and Training (DEST); and the Ministerial Council on Education, Employment, Training and Youth Affairs (MCEETYA), in terms of their accreditation and authority to operate. The key federal legislation governing universities mainly consists of the *National Protocols for Higher Education Approval Processes* (MCEETYA, 2009), the *Australian Qualification Framework* (DEST, 2009), the *Educational Services for Overseas Students Act* (MCEETYA, 2009), along with state level acts and regulations. Universities are independently audited by another federal government unit - Australian Universities Quality Agency (AUQA) - usually every four years, whereby AUQA convenes a panel of specialists to assist (drawn from the educational community of practice). Most universities are public. A few private higher education universities do exist in Australia (e.g. Bond), but low-fee accreditation and very active monitoring by government and agencies such as National Board of Employment, Education and Training Higher Education Council (NBEET) prevents online degree mills from operating in Australia (NBEET, 2003). However, the continuing pressure of audits (along with the evidence documentation and class attendance requirements) tends to emphasize behaviorist teaching methods and it is posited this in turn thwarts faculty creativity.

The major political impact of this context on e-learning design and delivery concerns the requirement for the university to have rigid quality compliance for course design, assessment, student enrolment, ethics, professor qualifications, and active research participation. There is no specific requirement to use a given educational theory, or e-learning. Group interaction is also not mandatory. At a higher level, there is input via periodic consultations with employers (business, government, sports, etc.), to suggest desired under and post graduate competencies. The auditing processes check for learning objectives and assessments that emphasize these student knowledge competencies. Therefore, the underlying principles of higher education design are prescriptive and behaviorist (Reding, 2003). Subsequently it is difficult to design courses that capture evidence of constructivist learning at the bachelor level especially with large classes of multicultural students (Kennedy et al., 2008). For this reason, more short-answer and multiple choice assessments are used, which ultimately reinforces memorization, behaviorist learning strategies, and prescriptive course design approaches.

Furthermore, there is a political feeling that e-learning is not accepted because the students are not observable. In Australia, "university teaching allocations are still based on lecture hours/contact hours or equivalents, and some administrators believe that if the students are not physically present for class the time is not a real part of the teaching allocation." (Eklund, 2005, p. 6). Despite the abundance of government-funded university research into online learning projects "failures of e-learning are [rampant...] at the classroom level technologies have provided little benefit, and such initiatives are commonly driven by a misplaced desire on the part of educational administrators to be a part of the movement." (Brabazon, 2002, p. 5). "This re-examination of priorities and tendency for skepticism reflects both the growing maturity of the industry and an acknowledgement of the failures of e-learning, or at least its past failures to deliver on a set of unrealistic expectations." (Eklund, 2005, p. 3).

Issues and Controversies in e-Learning Case Studies

There are several case studies in the literature of computer mediated learning pilots at Australian universities similar to this research, but most of these focus on 'old school style' asynchronous discussion forums. More so, undergraduate students were found to be using e-learning tools like Internet chatting and email, but not always as part of the prescribed curriculum (Huijser, 2006). A conference presentation shared how a Content Management System (CMS) facilitated an integrated delivery mode for material sharing, asynchronous student interaction, and assessment (online quiz, test distribution, digital assignment dropbox, grade posting), for both local and off-shore campuses (Barker, 2004). Another case study used synchronous chat rooms (and asynchronous discussion forums) to increase student interaction, with good results (Stewart et al., 2006, p. 209), yet there was no scientific evidence reported. This represents very basic use of technology in e-learning for asynchronous student tasks.

Simplistic approaches are often used to leverage e-learning tools. A case study of collaborative online learning (which included the University of Southern Queensland) leveraged a unique flexible learning model developed by the second author; the student interaction was asynchronous in an online discussion forum and the student interview feedback was supportive of the teaching methods (Lock & Redmond, 2008). Another Australian study used an online asynchronous discussion database (for courses in the Bachelor of Education degree) to promote student reflection and collaboration (Logan, 2004). A case study of flexible learning (as a blended mode) emphasized the importance of using educational theories for both design and delivery (Manathunga, 2002), but no empirical data was recorded. An interesting case study found university-level self-directed e-learning was effective for military students that were required to travel frequently (Newton & Ellis, 2005). The use of FirstClass (a CMS similar to Blackboard) was found to be helpful in allowing distance students to asynchronously discuss topics in an education master degree program (Stacey & Rice, 2002). These interesting studies were single cohorts, they focused on asynchronous student interaction and lacked empirical evidence to support their findings.

It can be difficult to achieve harmony between multicultural groups in e-learning as students with similar cultures tend to favor working with each other and could become capricious with other groups. A researcher studied e-learning at RMIT and came to similar conclusions. "It seems, that in this experiential online Organisation Behaviour course, defensive group dynamics can operate as a more potent factor on group learning, than that of the teacher as designer or facilitator." (Creese, 2003, p. 10).

Case studies of e-learning in Australia are popular and the most common methodology is action research (rather than the more controlled approaches of experiments or rigorous correlation techniques used in USA and UK), and they are usually blended with face-to-face. Many e-learning case studies focus on educating teachers about using technology, such as (Grushka et al., 2005; Manathunga, 2002; Stacey & Rice, 2002; Mak, 1995). There is some evidence of e-learning course success; Eklund and Kay (2003) examined online learning across 34 courses, reporting success as defined by "enthusiastic teacher(s)" as well as "significant institutional support in the form of relief time and/or encouragement" and "positive initial experiences".

A case study by Stacey and Rice of a Masters level program (with the e-learning component consisting of an online discussion forum in First-Class software) at an Australian university same to these insightful conclusions based on student comments. "The multiple methods of evaluation meant that we were able to triangulate student's individually expressed perspectives with content analysis and frequency statistics. A final summative discussion of results confirmed the results gathered which gave us a great deal of insight into how effectively computer conferencing had been incorporated into our course and the ways this was affecting student learning." (Stacey & Rice, 2002, p. 339).

(Robson, 2002) evaluated online learning at the Australian Catholic University citing several earlier theories (Hall, Skinner, and Piaget). She concluded with this scientific assertion: "It can be seen that the human-computer interface is playing an increasing role in open distance-learning and, as such, to ignore its impact is to lessen the validity and worth of an evaluation. (Robson, 2002, p. 170). The case study started off well but no educational theory or interesting e-learning applications were discussed.

In Australia many universities struggle with integrating technology into higher education. RMIT University is often cited in local higher education case studies and by AUQA for its $47 million ERP failure of the Peoplesoft Student Information System (Ketchell, 2003). Yet outside Australia technology problems are rarely cited; Hershey receives most attention in higher education case studies for its $112 million ERP failure of SAP R/3, Siebel CRM, and Manugistics SCM (Songini, 2000). While ERP failure is not directly related to e-learning, a Phd student (and a member of the failed RMIT ERP project) also examined their e-learning problems associated with the Distributed Learning System project (DLS). "The lack of activity within many of the subjects in the DLS points to the fact that many of the staff may be finding the time involved to develop their materials is more demanding than they realised....I didn't learn much in regards to using online programs ..." (Kenny, 2003, p. 10). "There is no doubt that a more effective planning process is needed for the development of subjects to use the DLS, particularly in this time of rapid growth." (Kenny, 2003, p. 13). This research team re-examined the RMIT DLS and found as of 2005 it was an online blackboard, catalog and enrollment system, allowing students to post comments, retrieve policies/materials and search journal databases.

A typical case study by an Australian university applying e-learning to a professional student body makes this conclusion, while citing an effective e-learning model developed by one of the authors in 2002. "The main factors that were important for respondents involved in e-learning design, development and delivery could be identified. This case study demonstrates the importance of maintaining a focus on organisational priorities and learning goals while meeting the demands of change pressures." (Newton & Ellis, 2005, p. 395).

Ironically the e-learning system and model in that case study is not used at the university.

Finally, there are a few studies of e-learning in Australia that argue the 'no significant difference' well-known finding reported in USA (Russell, 2002). This 'no difference' is a favorable condition for e-learning because it suggests the online mode is just as effective as face-to-face classes (but without the necessary commuting to/from campus for professors and students). Olson and Wisher (2002) conducted a meta-study of e-learning courses in higher education, and although these predate this case study, they found there was no statistically significant difference between e-learning versus campus-based compared effectiveness (n=47). However, only 29 of those case studies used experimental control and only one used repeated measures by having the same student take both types of delivery modes (Olson & Wisher, 2002).

Summary of Challenges and Issues

In summary, the socio cultural, economic and political factors in Australia have favored campus-based higher education delivery (not e-learning). This is the result of having a friendly culture, subtropical climate, a strong economy, high multicultural student immigration, along with a rigorously enforced behaviorist accreditation paradigm (competency and evidence driven). From the literature, some Australian scholars conclude that e-learning does not provide any benefit in the current context (Eklund, 2005; Brabazon, 2002). A review of several empirical e-learning case studies from well-known large Australian universities revealed simplistic asynchronous discussion forums were used and there was no quantitative evidence of posited benefits. This is not to say there is anything wrong with the status quo, but pointing this out illustrates the unique challenge of operating a constructivist e-learning delivery mode within a prescriptive (behaviorist) framework in higher education (Harper & Hedberg, 1997).

Nevertheless, some would say there is a cloud of suspicion on the effectiveness of e-learning in Australia which needs to be lifted. "Just as business was forced to re-examine business models for software development following the dot-com boom and bust, it is now no longer popular for futurists to make outrageous claims about the proliferation and transformation that e-learning will bring." (Eklund, 2005, p. 2). "We may be a society with far fewer learning-disabled children and far more teaching-disabled environments than currently perceived." (Negroponte, 1995, p. 198).

Balanced effectiveness of flexible e-learning

This section starts with a brief description of the underlying principles used for course design and delivery for both campus-based and flexible (e-learning) in this Australian university case study. Obviously competition and legal constraints preclude revealing all details, but the approaches are cited to the relevant theories. The balanced assessment rubric is then explained, followed by a description of the methods and techniques used to test the hypothesis. Finally the results are analyzed and discussed.

Design and Delivery of Campus and Flexible e-Learning

In the case study, the same methodology is used for both campus-based and flexible e-learning mode. Educational psychology theories are used to design the content, learning processes and assessments, based on the employer-driven and accredited graduate competencies. The case study university policy was that flexible e-learning courses could be taken only by students out of the country, otherwise they were required to report to campuses (this was also purposefully linked to immigration regulations). The only exceptions were those due to special circumstances that were approved by both the university executive and the immigration department (such as religious beliefs or medical leave). In this group there were no exceptions on file so the flexible e-learning students were all located outside of Australia. Essentially the only difference between campus and flexible mode in the case study is that the student does not have to physically go to the campus – everything else is the same: Content, learning process, assessment. Some modifications are made to allow for e-learning delivery, such as requiring the student to take two extra orientation sessions (one individually and a second with a group), to become familiar with the virtual learning environment (VLE) – which is a significant travel/time reduction when compared with having to travel to the university campus for the regular classes.

Case Study Technological Environment

Blackboard is used as the CMS. Pilots were conducted with Moodle (and other products). The reason Blackboard was chosen was because it was entrenched into the organizational and student culture –faculty, administration, technical staff and students were more familiar with Blackboard. The CMS provides all the components necessary to organize, digitize and disseminate the learning content, including gathering the assessment outcomes. The discussion forum was flexible enough to manage the asynchronous interactions. The product is so well known that one does not have to explain all the features. Microsoft WebOutlook email system was used for the university and every student is also given a student prefixed userid for use during the course and/or degree program. Obviously email is used as a communication tool between students and professors during both campus and flexible learning courses.

Most materials are digitized for both modes and the assessments require outcomes (tests, written reports, presentation power points, online presentation recordings, etc.) to be submitted in digital format inside the CMS linked to the VLE. Whenever possible, e-books are specified for courses. At least four peer reviewed journal articles no older than ten years must be provided for additional reading. Most courses require at least one group interaction event, whether it is a self-managed project (with a group outcome) or a synchronous activity such as a presentation with questions or problem based case study/role play.

The VLE enabled the synchronous e-learning environment for students and faculty. In this case study, the VLE was provided by Wimba Collaboration Suite, which provides online real-time interactive voice, chat, video, whiteboarding, application sharing, and quizzes polling. It also provides audio podcast for recording lectures and it can link to a URL where the recording is uploaded (e.g. to allow students to download into their iPod or similar product). Most importantly, Wimba interfaces with our Blackboard database allowing all student data to be shared (userid, names, course enrollments, security levels and so on). Another product (ElluminateLive) was piloted but it did not link to Blackboard data (e.g. student userids).

Case Study Course Design Framework

There is a strong emphasis on declarative knowledge content and competencies in Australian university curriculums (NBEET, 2003; Stoekel & Quirke, 1992). For this reason, most higher education design approaches at least consider the *Taxonomy of Learning* cognitive domain stages and process (Krathwohl, Bloom, & Masia, 1964; Bloom & Krathwohl, 1956), as shown in Figure 2. This theory is so well known in the university education community of practice and literature that only a brief overview is presented of its application in the case study. It should be noted that the cases study and this discussion applies to business and

Figure 2. Behaviorist-oriented course content design framework

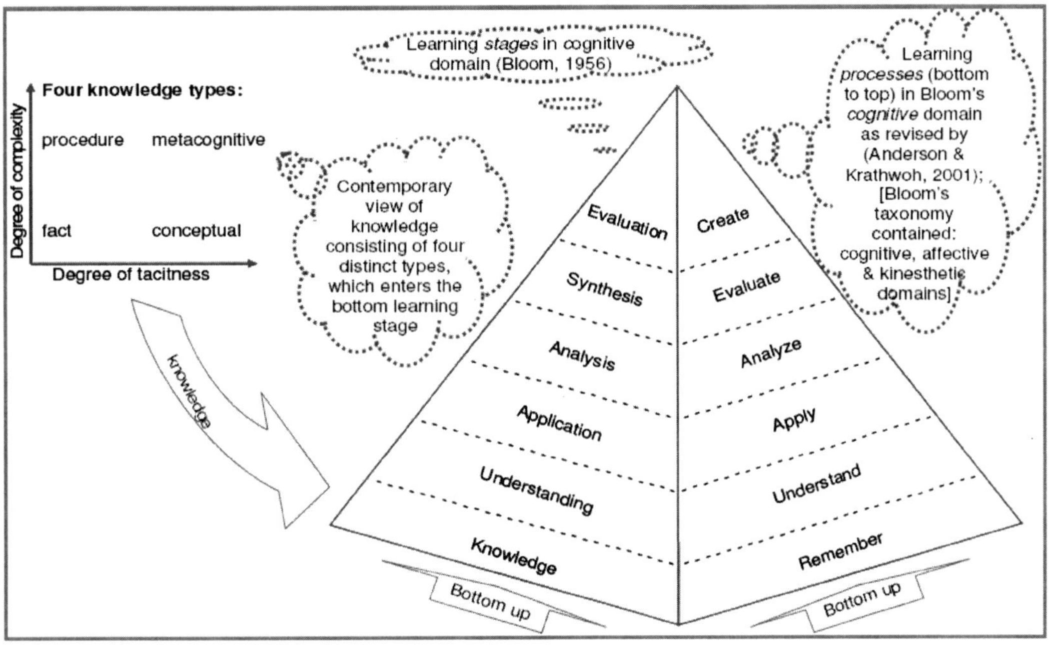

science degrees (other disciplines like sports are beyond the scope of this research).

In this model (Figure 2) the older version of the taxonomy appears on the left (emphasizing learning content), with the modern interpretation on the right (emphasizing learning process). This model illustrates that course content design takes place from the bottom up perspective. An effort is typically made to include the four types of knowledge for the given subject discipline (starting with basic facts, procedures if applicable, then conceptual perspectives and broader metacognitive variations of the subject from the literature). In this learning taxonomy, the two pyramids aim for the same thing. A course is designed such that the learning materials, activities and assessments progress from the bottom towards the top, namely: Remembering-knowledge, understanding, applying, analyzing, evaluating-synthesis, and finally creating, with the last three stages/processes involving critical thinking. It is most obvious that the model does not emphasize group problem interaction or the formative feedback on learning. Despite this, most courses are designed using individual as well as group interaction to encourage more perspectives.

The CMS is used for knowledge dissemination and organization as well as assessment response collection. In practice, a single relevant e-book is often selected that covers most of the required knowledge content for the course, then relevant supplemental readings are selected from peer-reviewed journals. The remaining five cognitive domain stages and processes constitute the learning activities and assessments. Usually there are at least three formal assessments. The sequencing and aesthetic structure of the course design in the CMS follows the generally accepted e-learning design guidelines (IEEE, 2006).

The approach and type of synchronous interactions is again identical between campus and flexible learning mode. A generally accepted model from the literature is used to guide the design of the five types of interactions, as briefly enumerated below:

- delivery of material by the teacher using digital materials where possible;
- interaction with materials by students using appropriate technology in either mode;
- interaction with the teacher by students – asynchronous and synchronous during class;
- interaction between students – asynchronous and synchronous during class with teacher present;
- intra-action by students – asynchronous and synchronous within their project teams (out of class); (MOLTA model adapted from: Caladine, 1997, pp. 3-4).

Another educational psychology model cited by many Australian researchers for course design is from Laurillard (1993, p. 50); she created a framework of five aspects for learning as outlined below:

- **Apprehending structure:** when students are exposed to discourse (usually through reading and/or listening), they need to be able to understand the structure of that discourse;
- **Integrate parts:** this aspect involves interpreting the signs of a discipline and what is signified by them. These signs may be in the form of language, diagrams, symbols etc.;
- **Acting on the world:** students engage in an activity which helps them bring together their collection of ideas to create meaning;
- Using feedback – student receive feedback on their actions, resulting in adjustment of the action/s;
- **Reflecting on goals-action-feedback:** students reflect on the relationships between the goal of their learning, the actions they took, and the feedback received.

Project management theory is leveraged to guide the course design process, ensuring on time, in scope, cost-effective, and accreditation-compliant results. Design always starts with a campus mode pilot first, then this course is migrated to the flexible e-learning platform. This allows the 'bugs' (problems) to be removed from the process by taking advantage of the immediate face-to-face feedback to make adjustments on the fly. This is especially critical given the multicultural profile of the students in the case study, so there is some customization of the materials and activities to appease the most common learning styles. A project management methodology (originating from information technology) was transformed for the education course design context by another researcher – namely: Analysis-Design-Development-Implementation-Evaluation ADDIE (Dick et al., 2001) - which was adapted and used in this case study.

ADDIE (Dick et al., 2001) was adapted by adding a sixth phase and by modifying the phases to make them systemic (through a feedback loop for both creating and maintaining a course). ADDIE was adapted by improving the phases for accreditation criteria, as briefly enumerated below (and shown in Figure 3):

1. **Learning needs analysis:** survey/interview for relevant industry employment content and skills;
2. **Employment driven goals:** resources, materials, assessments focused on above competencies;
3. **Conceptual, experiential learning development:** e-books, articles, case studies, and adult centered learning (andragogy) is enforced to ensure critical thinking and to master competencies;
4. **Asynchronous and synchronous interaction:** real-time in-class and homework activities are designed to motivate and promote the consideration of multiple perspectives leading to assessments (individual and group based projects or presentations are examples);

Figure 3. Balanced assessment model for flexible learning course design/delivery

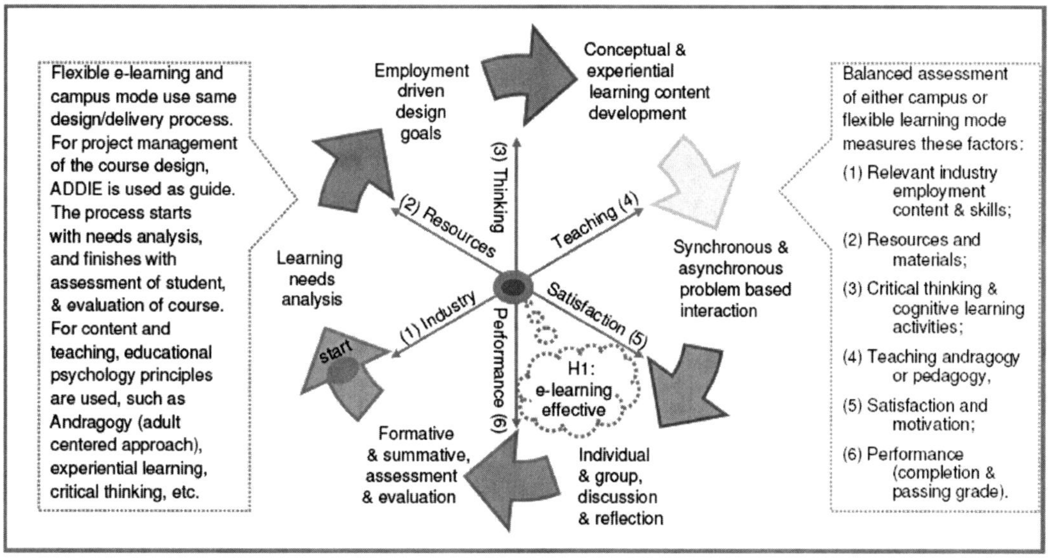

5. **Individual and group discussion:** reflection of theory and work, independently and in a group;
6. **Assessment and evaluation:** deliverables are combinations of written reports, presentations, example product/system prototypes, assessed using summative (quantitative) and formative (constructive comments) methods, evaluated in light of the whole contribution.

Balanced Assessment Framework and Methods

Logically a university wants to produce a product that will satisfy their key client – the student – yet there are other stakeholders (as mentioned earlier), namely: DEST, MCEETYA, NBEET and AUQA. This is analogous to the business environment whereby organizations design products to meet multiple goals, clients, internal strategies, and external regulatory compliance. Therefore it made sense to borrow upon the concepts from management science, such as the Intelligent Assets Monitor (from Sweden knowledge management literature) and the Balanced Scorecard (from USA business strategy literature).

The Balanced Scorecard (Kaplan & Norton, 2001) is a performance management method focused on translating strategy into action, by designing products and measuring their effectiveness on four perspectives: financial, customer, process and innovation. The Intangible Assets Monitor (Sveiby, 2001) is more scientific as it applies stock-flow and accounting theory, to measure innovation, growth/renewal, efficiency and stability across four dimensions: (1) tangible outcomes (financial), (2) internal structure (resources, processes), (3) external structure (customers, suppliers, stakeholders), and (4) competencies (skills, tacit and meta-knowledge). These ideas inform the balanced assessment model (shown in Figure 3), by linking course design/delivery to university accreditation requirements, as listed below:

1. **Industry:** relevant industry employment skills and competencies;
2. **Resources:** relevant current content and discipline specific theories, methodologies, cases;

3. **Thinking:** cognitive oriented, critical thinking, experiential learning activities;
4. **Teaching:** effective student-centered motivated teaching methods (andragogy);
5. **Satisfaction:** student confirmation of satisfaction with the product (learning experience);
6. **Performance:** student retention, course completion with passing grade.

Assessment Factors and Instrument

All of these six factors are in some way directly or indirectly mandatory for an Australian university to report to the government, which the AUQA will periodically audit by looking for evidence. The perception of the client (students) most strongly influences one critical part of the university accreditation and regulatory compliance. Student perceptions of the university are gathered through surveys and interviews by the various government agencies and departments. There is a key piece of evidence on the course level of analysis that is used for this accreditation process: Course Experience Questionnaire (CEQ), and there are variations of this instrument adapted by most universities for internal benchmarking. The CEQ is officially used by all higher education institutions in Australia as an indicator of the quality of teaching in contact learning programs (Barrie & P., 2007; Ginns et al., 2007; Prosser & Barrie, 2003).

Student performance can be measured by the completion of the course and final grade. The other five factors can be assessed using some items from CEQ. Other Australian researchers have used the CEQ to evaluate e-learning course effectiveness (Barrie & P., 2007; Ginns & Ellis, 2007; Ginns et al., 2007; Fresen & Boyd, 2005; Prosser & Barrie, 2003; Ramsden, 2003, 1991). For example, Fresen (2005) performed a similar case study of online learning using a modified CEQ.

The CEQ was originally designed to gather self-reported perceptions from students on their higher education experience (Ramsden, 2003, 1991), and has been adapted and validated for use by AUQA and Australian universities (Barrie & P., 2007; Ginns et al., 2007; Prosser & Barrie, 2003; Ramsden, 2003). The full instrument has 50 items which ask students to indicate the extent to which they agree, or disagree, with each statement, using a five-point scale where '1' represents strong disagreement and '5' indicates strong agreement. Some items are reverse worded (and the response is inverted prior to scoring); for example: "The workload was too heavy". Most universities use only 50% of the available items.

The Good Teaching Scale assesses the degree to which students perceive that their teacher(s) provided a high level of teaching quality. Higher scores are better since they mean adequate feedback was received, the course was presented in an interesting motivating manner, and teacher(s) make an effort to understand student problems as well as attempted to explain things clearly. The Generic Skills Scale assesses the extent to which the student perceives the course adds to the generic skills that might be expected for industry employment. Discipline-specific skills and knowledge are not assessed (learning of these becomes evidence in the course grade). Generic skills include decision-making skills, problem-solving skills, analytic skills, written communication skills, planning skills, and general ability to address unique problems, the ability to apply knowledge to the workplace, and the capacity to work with minimum supervision (Ramsden, 2003, 1991). There is a single Overall Satisfaction Scale item. The above constitute the three mandatory CEQ scales and items which are mandatory for AUQA accreditation. The seven optional CEQ scales are discussed below.

The Clear Goals and Standards Scale assesses additional good teaching approaches, such as setting clear goals for the course and clear expectations of the standard of work for assessment. The Appropriate Assessment Scale focuses on the extent to which assessments (tests) emphasize recall of factual information rather than higher order critical thinking. The Appropriate Workload Scale solicits student perceptions on whether the workload was too heavy. This is rationale behind this is that heavy workloads require students to adopt a skimming approach (surface learning) instead of deep learning (critical thinking). The Student Support Scale asks students to indicate their perception with support services such as library, access to information technology resources, course and careers advice, learning resources and health, welfare and counseling services. The Learning Resources Scale assesses student perceptions on support services, but focuses more on the available of library content and information technology reliability. The Learning Community Scale asks students their perception of a sense of community in the course cohort at the university, based on knowledge creation theories for community of practice. The Graduate Qualities Scale is similar to the Generic Skills Scale but it requests the student's perception of how the course contributed towards enthusiasm for further learning, and appreciation for hearing diverse perspectives and ideas. The Intellectual Motivation Scale evaluates the student perception of how well a course motivated them and the perceived degree it was intellectually stimulating.

AUQA, universities and other agencies have simplified the 5 Likert response scales for public reporting purposes, by combining levels 4 and 5 (agree and strongly agree) as 'Agreement', and joining levels 1 and 2 (strongly disagree and disagree) as 'Disagree', with the midpoint level 3 is reported as 'Neutral'. The reason that has been done is that the raw scores from interval scales are not meaningful. For example, an interval score "mean" might be 3.1 but that is not as useful as knowing that approximately 50% of the students in a course do not feel they clearly understand the goals of this course.

Measures and Techniques

CEQ has been used by this research team and found to have ambiguous items that do not pass ordinal confirmatory factor analysis, and there is considerable cross loading on several factors. Another statistical weak point with the CEQ there is only one item testing the satisfaction factor, and over five factors testing others. Nevertheless it is important to synchronize empirical case studies such as this with the literature – and as pointed out the CEQ is used by the all accredited Australian universities. Therefore, a modified version is used (changing only wording and the factor grouping) – as shown in Table 1 (sorted by factor).

The balanced learning survey (modified CEQ), was created through iterations of rewording and testing (using principal component and factor analysis) with a pilot group, separate from the students in this case study. The final version was given to students at the end of their course, using an online format, which contained ethical disclosure, and after acceptance, the student number was requested to avoid duplicate submissions. Also, this enabled the course performance score (grade) to be added to the resulting dataset using the student number as the key. An ordinal factor analysis was performed on all the responses combined since there was no need to analyze the factor compliance, but just a requirement to ensure the theoretical dimensions of the original CEQ model were basically supported (the interest here was to compare flexible versus campus mode responses). The results of the ordinal factor analysis are shown in *Table 1*, with the rows sorted by factors (e.g. industry is first followed by resources, and so on). The factor loadings are shown in the matrix (most significantly loaded on the proper factor). The factor correlations and score reliabilities are shown at the bottom of *Table 1* (these were acceptable). Since a confirmatory factor analysis was not conducted, and the responses were ordinals on a small scale, the Kaiser-Meyer-Olkin Measure of Sampling

Table 1. Balanced learning survey ordinal factor analysis loadings and reliabilities

Item	Survey question (loadings from ordinal factor analysis, sorted by balanced assessment factor)	Industry relevance	Resources for learning	Critical thinking	Effective teaching	Satisfaction motivation
09	The course helped me develop my ability to work in a team.	**0.868****	0.067	-0.322	-0.215	-0.088
22	The course helped me develop the ability to plan my work.	**0.798****	-0.202	-0.314	0.120	0.209
26	The course provided me with an overview of my career field.	**0.825****	-0.226	0.238	-0.237	0.093
45	The course provided knowledge related to my planned job.	**0.819****	0.281	-0.132	-0.124	0.102
37	I felt part of a group of professionals committed to learning.	**0.781****	0.282	0.317	-0.302	0.234
39	I learned to explore ideas confidently with other people.	**0.673***	0.371	0.132	-0.108	0.311
50	Where it was used, the information technology in teaching and learning was effective.	**0.607***	0.322	0.115	-0.321	0.268
49	Course materials were relevant and up to date.	0.214	**0.854****	-0.323	0.229	-0.392
46	The library resources were appropriate for my needs.	0.338	**0.798****	-0.017	0.203	-0.226
47	The study materials were clear and concise.	-0.332	**0.699****	0.329	0.102	0.362
32	I was able to access information technology resources when I needed them.	0.217	**0.701****	-0.302	-0.214	0.282
35	The library services were readily accessible.	0.332	**0.693***	-0.208	0.211	0.372
08 r	To do well in this course all you needed was a good memory.	0.022	-0.015	**0.822****	0.371	-0.224
12 r	The teachers seemed more interested in testing what I had memorized than what I had understood.	0.024	-0.223	**0.798****	0.342	-0.332
16 v	The assessment methods employed in this course required an in-depth understanding of the course content.	0.331	-0.017	**0.886****	-0.226	-0.308
19 r	Most assessments asked me questions just about facts.	0.218	0.329	**0.680****	0.364	0.331
02	The course developed my problem-solving skills.	-0.092	-0.092	**0.923****	0.283	0.079
05	The course sharpened my analytic skills.	-0.307	-0.308	**0.878****	0.375	0.203
11	The course improved my skills in written communication.	-0.017	-0.222	**0.907****	0.223	-0.023
10	As a result of my course, I feel confident about tackling unfamiliar problems.	-0.232	-0.215	**0864****	0.217	-0.232
29	I can apply principles from this course to new situations.	0.211	0.338	**0.798****	0.329	0.017
03	The teachers of this course motivated me to do my best work.	-0.303	0.330	-0.302	**0.799****	0.232
07	The teachers put a lot of time into commenting on my work.	-0.097	0.210	-0.209	**0.781****	-0.015
15	The teachers made a real effort to understand difficulties I might be having with my work.	0.109	0.233	0.202	**0.692***	0.223
17	The teachers normally gave me helpful feedback.	0.218	-0.023	0.317	**0.737****	0.217
18	My teachers were extremely good at explaining things.	-0.323	0.230	0.332	**0.854****	0.103

continued on following page

Table 1. continued

Item	Survey question (loadings from ordinal factor analysis, sorted by balanced assessment factor)	Industry relevance	Resources for learning	Critical thinking	Effective teaching	Satisfaction motivation
20	The teachers worked hard to make their subjects interesting.	0.108	-0.133	0.202	**0.593***	0.392
13 r	It was hard to discover what was expected of me.	0.136	-0.123	0.102	**0.692***	0.381
24	The teachers made it clear right from the start what they expected from students.	0.105	-0.024	0.092	**0.699***	0.293
25	Overall, I was satisfied with the quality of this course.	-0.117	0.212	0.015	-0.017	**0.908****
30	I consider what I learned valuable for my planned career.	-0.217	0.217	0.215	-0.015	**0.808****
42	I found the course intellectually stimulating, interesting.	-0.139	-0.137	0.323	0.393	**0.799****
43	I found the course motivating.	-0.312	-0.215	-0.017	0.317	**0.751****
44	Overall, my university course experience was worthwhile.	-0.228	0.237	0.320	0.326	**0.853****
Summary	**Polychoric factor correlation matrix**: Industry	1.000				
	Resources	**-0.111****	1.000			
	Thinking	**0.045*****	**-0.121****	1.000		
	Teaching	**-0.119****	**-0.113****	**0.098*****	1.000	
	Satisfaction	**0.039****	**-0.102****	**0.021*****	**0.169****	1.000
	Alpha reliabilities by balanced assessment factor:	0.881*	0.923**	0.939**	0.837**	0.896**
	Kaiser-Meyer-Olkin Measure of Sampling Adequacy = 0.669; Bartlett's Test of Sphericity: x^2=52.974** df=55, p=0.003					

significant p < 0.05; ** significant p < 0.01; *** significant p < 0.001; items sorted by balanced assessment factors.

Adequacy and Bartlett's Test of Sphericity were used to ensure validity (Strang, 2009; Creswell, 2003) – the estimates are also shown at the bottom of *Table 1* and can be seen from the significance level (p=0.003) they were acceptable.

Next the six balanced factors (from the student survey responses and completion grades) were compared for the same course delivered across the two modes. Two different statistical techniques were used since the data types were different. The first five balanced learning assessment factors: industry, resources, thinking, teaching and satisfaction were taken from the balanced survey by averaging the items for each factor. Factor scores were not used as a composite variable because they tend to emphasize scale covariance, while we were more interested in comparing between group average (summated) differences. Each factor mean was converted to a percent score out of 100 (similar to the AUQA procedures). Discriminate analysis (Wilks Lambda of x^2) was used to test the first five ordinal factors. Analysis of variance (ANOVA one-way f-test) was used to compare the performance (since it was a ratio data type).

Results and Discussion

The summary demographic statistics from the sample are shown in Table 2 - there were 34 students in the campus mode and 39 students in the flexible learning mode. The first obvious statistic from the demographics is only a small portion of the students were Australian-born, even

Table 2. Sample demographic statistics

Key demographic estimates	Culture %	Culture %
Sample size Campus N=34 (n=34), Flexible N= 39 (n=38) Mean Age 21.8 Standard deviation 0.17 Kurtosis** -0.01 Skewness** +0.03 Gender M=61%, F=39% Employment: Full time=17%, Part time=53%, Study=30% Languages: English+ 54% English only 46%	Philippines 0.20 India 0.18 Singapore 0.14 China 0.08 Pakistan 0.08 Thailand 0.05 Japan 0.04 Slovenia 0.04 Taiwan 0.03 NewZealand 0.03 KoreaSouth 0.03	Australia 0.02 Italy 0.01 Austria 0.01 Israel 0.01 Germany 0.01 Turkey 0.01 Nigeria 0.01 France 0.01 Greece 0.01 (Homeland culture sorted %). Countries 20

those enrolled in the campus-mode classes (the estimates include both courses). This suggests a large portion of students are international, regardless of whether the delivery mode was campus or flexible e-learning. From experience, this was a typical cohort for both modes, with 70% of them working either full or part time. As an incentive for completing the balanced learning assessment survey (in addition to proper ethical confidentiality), students were promised to be given a link to their final marks a week in advance of the official printed copy (which would assist them greatly in choosing follow up courses during enrollment in the subsequent semester). This resulted in a very good response rate with only one missing survey (campus n1=34, flexible n2=38).

The course was an introductory marketing subject in the bachelor of information management degree. The same professor and tutorial team conducted both course deliveries, and as noted earlier, the exact same materials were used (syllabus, e-book, journal articles, assessments, and so on). The only difference was that the interaction activities for the flexible learning course mode took place in Blackboard-Wimba product, which consisted of ten lectures, individual introductions, questions-answers after lectures, individual presentation, and group presentation (from their group project). All assessment rubrics were identical as well (there were four individual and group graded items: individual answers to periodic 'marketing CEO questions' posted in discussion forum, individual marketing analysis paper, group marketing strategy paper and group marketing recommendation presentation).

The results of the six factor balanced assessment is summarized in Table 3 below. One record was dropped from this analysis for the single student that did not respond (n1=34, n2=38). As explained previously, the values for the first five factors were converted from a mean of the items per factor to a score out of 100%. The performance factor was the final course grade. There were no drop outs and no failures in these groups (albeit that is not always the case for all instances of this and other courses). Nevertheless these groups were similar to other cohorts when comparing their performance (grade invariance $p>0.05$). Table 3 confirms that the flexible e-learning mode was at least as effective as the campus-based delivery, and significantly more effective for the satisfaction factor. These results also uphold the so called 'no significant difference' empirical studies in the literature in as far as there was no statistically significant difference in performance (grade) found between these two modes of delivery.

The balanced assessment statistical estimates from Table 3 were used to diagram a radar chart to visually depict the results, as shown in Figure 4. This radar chart graphically illustrates the jus-

Table 3. Balanced learning assessment results

Balanced learning factor	Campus	Flexible	Differ	Significance measure	Hypothesis
1. Industry employment focus	0.84	0.83	-0.01	Wilks λ: x^2=115.68 df=74, p=0.354	H1 accepted
2. Resource/content relevant	0.91	0.90	-0.01	Wilks λ: x^2=124.81 df=74, p=0.391	H1 accepted
3. Thinking, critical skills used	0.83	0.85	+0.02	Wilks λ: x^2=125.16 df=74, p=0.422	H1 accepted
4. Teaching approach good	0.81	0.83	+0.02	Wilks λ: x^2=120.55 df=74, p=0.361	H1 accepted
5. Satisfaction level	0.82	0.89	+0.07	Wilks λ: x^2=265.22 df=74, p=0.034	H1 accepted+
6. Performance score	0.79	0.80	+0.01	ANOVA f=1.162 df=33,37 p=0.326	H1 accepted
Sample size	n1 = 34	n2 = 38			+flexible best

Figure 4. Balanced learning assessment radar chart

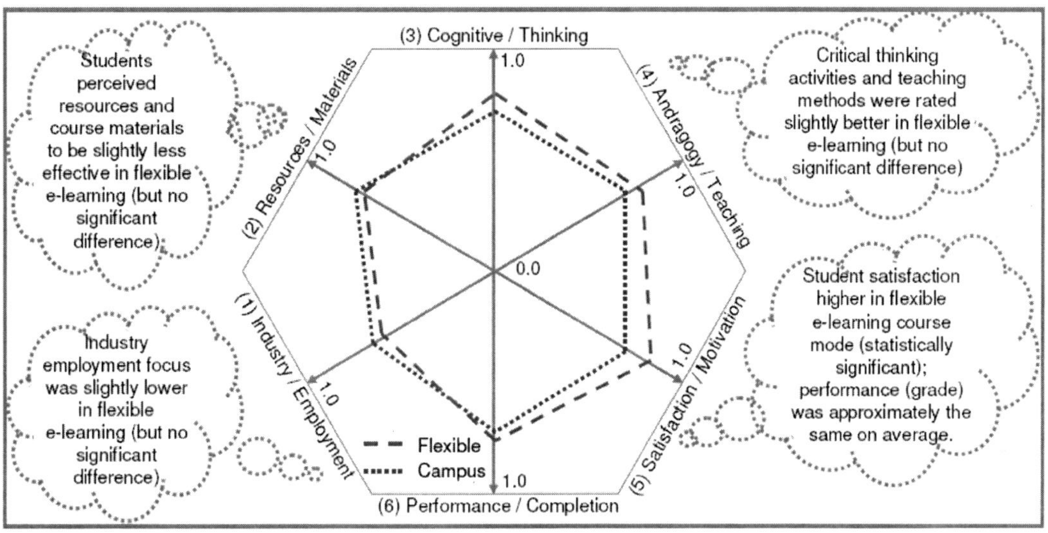

tification to accept the hypothesis that the flexible e-learning course delivery mode was as effective, or better, than the campus based method. In fact, three of the five student-rated factors were higher, with satisfaction being significantly higher (as noted by '+flexible best' in Table 3 under the hypothesis testing result column). Another critical observation was that actual student performance (grade) was very slightly higher for the flexible e-learning mode (but no statistically significant difference). Essentially both courses were approximately equal in effectiveness yet the flexible e-learning mode gained significantly higher student satisfaction ratings as compared to the campus mode.

CONCLUSIONS AND FUTURE RESEARCH DIRECTIONS

This case study made a genuine effort to expose the critical challenges facing Australian universities. In particular some of the rarely-discussed socio cultural and political issues in higher education were revealed. It was asserted that the rigorous accreditation processes, while good at reducing degree mills, actually place a behaviorist constraint on creativity by forcing university faculty to design courses that generate competency evidence and not necessarily learning. Also it was empathized in this case study that e-learning is rarely practiced in Australian higher education outside of experimental projects. Further problems included lack of faculty training/competency for e-learning design/delivery, and perhaps an unwilling client – multicultural immigrants and young students that may prefer campus mode delivery. Further to the last point, recent university audits claimed some international students commented that they enroll to physically attend an Australian campus to gain entrance and facilitate residency (AUQA, 2009), which is substantiated with the higher failure rates of international students. This was not the case in this study, but nevertheless it is a country-wide problem for Australian higher education universities.

Notwithstanding the above, it was shown that some universities are practicing e-learning, which features synchronous student interaction to promote critical thinking and experiential learning. The case study described a methodology used for course design and delivery (which is basically the same for campus and e-learning courses). The methodology cited and described well-known educational psychology theories.

The purpose of the case study was to show that flexible e-learning was at least as effective as campus delivery mode. To accomplish that, a balanced assessment model was created, informed by Swedish knowledge management and American business science theories (e.g. balanced assets/score card). The assessment model included six factors that were linked to Australian university accreditation: Industry focus, resources/content materials, critical thinking activities, teaching quality, student satisfaction, and student performance (including completion). Two identical courses were compared, one given at campus and the other in flexible e-learning mode. A survey was used to gather student perceptions of the first five factors, and along with their actual performance. Evidence was produced to show flexible e-learning was as effective, or better, than campus delivery (satisfaction was higher at a statistically significant level). There are a few limitations with this research. This was a single university context, and a business course (with relatively small sample sizes of 34 and 38). Thus it is not yet possible to generalize these findings to other universities or degrees in Australia (and no inferences can be extended abroad), without replication.

Since the balanced assessment model and survey are available to the educational community of practice, other researchers can use this improved instrument to benchmark their own courses. Also since the course design methodology was articulated, new professors have a basic model to use until they become more experienced. Finally since it was shown the same campus course could be delivered in flexible and campus modes, with as good or better results (measured with criteria used by Australian accreditation bodies), e-learning could be blended into more courses. Nonetheless, the challenges associated with social culture and politics still go answered so hopefully other researchers will join in the effort to resolve them.

REFERENCES

ACCC. (2006). *Snapshop of Broadband Deployment as at 31 March 2006* [Report]. Australian Competition and Consumer Commission; Canberra, ACT. Retrieved December 12, 2008, from the World Wide Web: http://www.accc.gov.au/content/index.phtml/itemId/693170

AUQA. (2006, August). *Report of an Audit of the University of Technology, Sydney* [Report]. Australian Universities Quality Agency. Retrieved, from the World Wide Web www.auqa.edu.au/quality audit/reports/auditreport_uts_2006.pdf

AUQA. (2009). *Report of an Audit of the Royal Melbourne Institute of Technology University* [Report]. Australian Universities Quality Agency. Retrieved, from the World Wide Web www.auqa.edu.au/quality audit/reports/auditreport_rmit_2009.pdf

Barker, S. (2004). *Using Online Facilities to Support Face-to-Face Teaching.* Paper presented at the Online Learning and Teaching Conference: exploring integrated learning environments: a national forum for sharing information on engaging, designing, assessing and collaborating in online learning and teaching, Brisbane, Australia.

Barrie, S. C., & P., G. (2007). The Linking of Institutional Performance Indicators to Improvements in Teaching in Classrooms. *Quality in Higher Education, 13*(3), 275–286. doi:10.1080/13538320701800175

Bates, A. W., & Poole, G. (2003). Effective Teaching with Technology in Higher Education: Foundations for Success. San Francisco, CA: Jossey-Bass.

Biggs, J. (2003). Teaching for Quality at University: What the Student Does (2nd ed.). Buckingham, UK: Society for Research into Higher Education and Open University Press.

Bloom, B. S., & Krathwohl, D. R. (Eds.). (1956). Taxonomy of Educational Objectives: The Classification of Educational Goals. New York: Longman, Green.

Brabazon, T. (2002). Digital Hemlock: Internet Education and the Poisioning of Teaching. Sydney, Australia: Report on e-learning for Department of Education and Training, University of New South Wales.

Caladine, R. (1997). Molta: A Model of Learning and Teaching Activities. *ultiBASE, 10*(1), 1-10.

Coffield, F. J., Moseley, D. V., Hall, E., & Ecclestone, K. (2004). Learning Styles and Pedagogy in Post-16 Learning: A Systematic and Critical Review. London: Learning and Skills Research Centre (University of Newcastle upon Tyne).

Creese, E. L. (2003). Group Dynamics and Learning in an Organisation Behaviour Virtual Learning Community: The Case of Six Virtual Peer-Learning Teams. *ultiBASE, 3*(11), 1-11.

Creswell, J. W. (2003). Research Design: Qualitative, Quantitative, and Mixed Methods Approaches (2nd ed.). New York: Sage.

Cybinski, P., & Selvanathan, S. (2005). Learning Experience and Learning Effectiveness in Undergraduate Statistics: Modeling Performance in Traditional and Flexible Learning Environments. *Decision Sciences Journal of Innovative Education, 3*(2), 251–271. doi:10.1111/j.1540-4609.2005.00069.x

DEST. (2009). *Australian Qualification Framework.* Commonwealth Department of Education, Science and Training (Sydney, NSW). Retrieved, from the World Wide Web http://www.dest.gov.au

Dick, W., Carey, L., & Carey, J. O. (2001). The Systematic Design of Instruction (5th ed.). New York: Addison-Wesley Longman.

Dixon, K., & Dixon, R. (2008). Capacity of an Electronic Portfolio to Promote Professionalism, Collaboration and Accountability in Educational Leadership. In J. Salmons & L. Wilson (Eds.), Handbook of Research on Electronic Collaboration and Organizational Synergy (pp. 472-493). Hershey, PA: IGI Global.

Drent, M., & Meelissen, M. (2008). Which Factors Obstruct or Stimulate Teacher Educators to Use Ict Innovatively? *Computers & Education, 11*(1), 53–68.

Editorial. (2005, May 8). Faking It Qualifications. *Sydney Morning Herald,* (p. 3).

Eklund, J. (2005). Driving the Future of E-Learning. Taskforce Report, University of Sydney. Canberra, ACT: Industry Taskforce on Higher Education - Ministry for Employment, Education and Training, Australian Federal Government.

Eklund, J., & May, M. (2003). Evaluation of the Usage of National Flexible Learning Tookboxes (Series 3). Canberra, ACT: Australian National Training Authority.

Fresen, J. W., & Boyd, L. G. (2005). Caught in the Web of Quality. *International Journal of Educational Development*, *25*(3), 317–331. doi:10.1016/j.ijedudev.2004.12.002

Gao, T., & Lehman, J. D. (2003). The Effects of Different Levels of Interaction on the Achievement and Motivational Perceptions of College Students in a Web-Based Learning Environment. *Journal of Interactive Learning Research*, *14*(4), 367–386.

Gilding, A., & Martino, J. (2001). *Learning About Online Learning in a Dual Sector University: Reflections, Issues and Challenges.* Paper presented at the Meeting at the crossroads: proceedings of the 18th Annual Conference of the Australasian Society for Computers in Learning in Tertiary Education (ASCILITE), Melbourne, Australia.

Ginns, P., & Ellis, R. (2007). Quality in Blended Learning: Exploring the Relations between on-Line and Face-to-Face Teaching and Learning. *The Internet and Higher Education*, *10*, 53–64. doi:10.1016/j.iheduc.2006.10.003

Ginns, P., Prosser, M., & Barrie, S. C. (2007). Students' Perceptions of Teaching Quality in Higher Education: The Perspective of Currently Enrolled Students. *Studies in Higher Education*, *32*(5). doi:10.1080/03075070701573773

Grant, M. M. (2004). Learning to Teach with the Web: Factors Influencing Teacher Education Faculty. *The Internet and Higher Education Journal*, *7*(4), 329–341. doi:10.1016/j.iheduc.2004.09.005

Grushka, K., McLeod, J. H., & Reynolds, R. (2005). Reflecting Upon Reflection: Theory and Practice in One Australian University Teacher Education Program. *Reflective Practice*, *6*(2), 239–246. doi:10.1080/14623940500106187

Harper, B., & Hedberg, J. (1997). Creating Motivating Interactive Learning Environments: A Constructivist View. In R. Kevill & R. Oliver & R. Phillips (Eds.), *What Works and Why: Proceedings of the 14th Annual Conference of Ascilite*. Perth, Australia: Curtin University of Technology.

Huijser, H. (2006). Refocusing Multiliteracies for the Net Generation. *International Journal of Pedagogies and Learning*, *2*(1), 21–33.

IEEE. (2006). *Instructional Management System (Ims) Content Packaging Best Practice and Implementation Guide*. IEEE Learning Technology Standards Committee (LTSC). Retrieved 30 June 2006, from the World Wide Web http://ltsc.ieee.org/

Joy, E. H., & Garcia, F. E. (2000). Measuring Learning Effectiveness: A New Look at No-Significant-Difference Findings. *Journal of Asynchronous Learning Networks*, *4*(1), 33–39.

Kaplan, R. S., & Norton, D. P. (2001). The Strategy-Focused Organization: How Balanced Scorecard Companies Thrive in the New Business Environment. Boston: Harvard Business School Press.

Karemera, D., Reuben, L. J., & Sillah, M. R. (2003). The Effects of Academic Environment and Background Characteristics on Student Satisfaction and Performance: The Case of South Carolina State University's School of Business. *College Student Journal*, *37*(2), 298.

Kennedy, G. E., Judd, T. S., Churchward, A., Gray, K., & Krause, K. (2008). First Year Students' Experiences with Technology: Are They Really Digital Natives? *Australasian Journal of Educational Technology*, *24*(1), 108–122.

Kenny, J. (2003). *Student Perceptions of the Use of Online Learning Technology in Their Courses.* Retrieved May, 2004, from the World Wide Web http://ultibase.rmit.edu.au/Articles/march03/kenny2.pdf

Ketchell, M. (2003, February 28). Rmit to Scrap $47m Software System. [Fairfax Digital]. *Age*, 2–3.

Kobas, J. E., & Renzie, S. (Eds.). (2005). Innovation in Web-Enhanced Learning at University. Hershey, PA: IGI Global.

Krathwohl, D. R., Bloom, B. S., & Masia, B. B. (1964). Taxonomy of Educational Objectives: The Classification of Educational Goals. Handbook Ii: Affective Domain. New York: David McKay Co., Inc.

Laurillard, D. (1993). Rethinking University Teaching: A Framework for the Effective Use of Educational Technolgy. London: Routledge.

Laurillard, D. (2002). Rethinking University Teaching: A Framework for the Effective Use of Educational Technolgy (2nd ed.). London: Routledge.

Laurillard, D. (2007). Modelling Benefits-Oriented Costs for Technology Enhanced Learnign. *Higher Education*, *54*(1), 21–39. doi:10.1007/s10734-006-9044-2

Leask, B. (2004). Internationalisation Outcomes for All Students Using Information and Communication Technologies (Icts). *Journal of Studies in International Education*, *8*(4), 336–351. doi:10.1177/1028315303261778

Lock, J. V., & Redmond, P. (2008). Working Collaboratively on the Digital Global Frontier. In J. Salmons & L. Wilson (Eds.), Handbook of Research on Electronic Collaboration and Organizational Synergy (pp. 262-277). Hershey, PA: IGI Global.

Logan, J. (2004). *Using an Online Database Searching Tutorial to Encourage Reflection on the Research Process by Undergraduate Students.* Paper presented at the Online Learning and Teaching Conference: exploring integrated learning environments: a national forum for sharing information on engaging, designing, assessing and collaborating in online learning and teaching, Brisbane, Australia.

Mak, S. (1995). *Developing a Self-Access and Self-Paced Learning Aid for Teaching Statistics.* Paper presented at the Australian World Wide Web Conference 1995, Great Coral Reef Resort, Gold Coast, Australia.

Manathunga, C. (2002). Designing Online Learning Modules: An Australian Example in Teacher Education. *International Journal of Instructional Media*, *29*(2), 185.

MCEETYA. (2009). *National Protocols for Higher Education Approval Processes*. Ministerial Council on Education, Employment, Training and Youth Affairs (Canberra, ACT). Retrieved, from the World Wide Web: http://www.mceetya.edu.au/

NBEET. (2003). Australian Graduate Studies and Higher Degrees. (Report). Canberra: National Board of Employment, Education and Training - Higher Education Council.

Negroponte, N. (1995). Being Digital. Rydalmere, Australia: Hodder & Stoughton.

Newton, D., & Ellis, A. (2005). Effective Implementation of E-Learning: A Case Study of the Australian Army. *Journal of Workplace Learning*, *17*(5/6), 385–397. doi:10.1108/13665620510606797

Olson, T. M., & Wisher, R. A. (2002). The Effectiveness of Web-Based Instruction: An Initial Inquiry. *International Review of Research in Open and Distance Learning, 3*(3).

Palloff, R. M., & Pratt, K. (2002). Beyond the Looking Glass: What Faculty and Students Need to Be Successful Online. In K. E. Rudestam & J. Schoenholtz-Read (Eds.), Handbook of Online Learning: Innovations in Higher Education and Corporate Training (pp. 171-184). Thousand Oaks, CA: Sage.

Pauli, D. (2007). Upskill on the Go [Macquarie University]. *Computerworld, 29*, 32–34.

Picciano, A. G. (2006). Blended Learning: Implications for Growth and Access. *Journal of Asynchronous Learning Networks, 10*(3), 1–14.

Prosser, M., & Barrie, S. C. (Eds.). (2003). Using a Student-Focused Learning Perspective to Strategically Align Academic Development with Institutional Quality Assurance. Buckingham, UK: Open University Press.

Ramsden, P. (1991). A Performance Indicator of Teaching Quality in Higher Education: The Course Experience Questionnaire. *Studies in Higher Education, 16*, 129–150. doi:10.1080/03075079112331382944

Ramsden, P. (2003). Learning to Teach in Higher Education. London: Routledge.

Reding, V. (2003). *Student Approaches to Learning and Studying in Australia.* Paper presented at the Proceedings of the Learning Forum, Karlsruha.

Robson, J. (2002). Evaluating on-Line Teaching. *Open Learning, 15*(2).

Rosenberg, M. J. (2001). E-Learning - Strategies for Delivering Knowledge in the Digital Age. New York: McGraw-Hill.

Russell, T. L. (2002). The No Significant Difference Phenomenon as Reported in 355 Research Reports, Summaries and Papers: A Comparative Research Annotated Bibliography on Technology for Distance Education [Updated from 1999]. NC, USA: North Carolina State University: Office of Instructional Telecommunications.

Schön, D. A. (1983). The Reflective Practitioner - How Professionals Think in Action. Aldershot, UK: BasiAshgate ARENA.

Schunk, D. H. (2004). Learning Theories: An Educational Perspective. Upper Saddle River, NJ: Pearson Prentice Hall.

Songini, M. L. (2000, November 1). Halloween Less Haunting for Hershey This Year. *Computer World.*

St Hill, R. (2000). *Modal Preference in a Teaching Strategy.* Paper presented at the Paper presented at the Effective Teaching and Learning at University Conference, Brisbane, QLD.

Stacey, E., & Rice, M. (2002). Evaluating an Online Learning Environment. *Australian Journal of Educational Technology, 18*, 323–340.

Stevens-Long, J., & Crowell, C. (2002). The Design and Delivery of Interactive Online Graduate Education. In K. E. Rudestam & J. Schoenholtz-Read (Eds.), Handbook of Online Learning: Innovations in Higher Education and Corporate Training (pp. 151-169). Thousand Oaks, CA: Sage.

Stewart, B. L., Norwood, M., Ezell, S., & Waight, C. (2006). Case Study: Collaborative Creation of an on-Line Degree Program. *Innovations in Education and Teaching International, 43*(3), 197–211. doi:10.1080/14703290600618399

Stoekel, A., & Quirke, D. (1992). Services: Setting the Agenda for Reform. Canberra, Australia: Department of Industry, Technology and Commerce, Australian Government Publishing Service.

Strang, K. D. (2007, 14-16 February). *Building Quality and Interaction into Elearning: Applying Andragogy Theory to Synchronous and Asynchronous Online Course Design.* Paper presented at the Innovation, Education, Technology, and You: Online Conference for Teaching & Learning, Chicago.

Strang, K. D. (2008). Quantitative Online Student Profiling to Forecast Academic Outcome from Learning Styles Using Dendrogram Decision. *Multicultural Education & Technology Journal*, *2*(4), 215–244. doi:10.1108/17504970810911043

Strang, K. D. (2009). Using Recursive Regression to Explore Nonlinear Relationships and Interactions: A Tutorial Applied to a Multicultural Education Study. *Practical Assessment. Research Evaluation*, *14*(3), 1–13.

Sveiby, K. E. (2001). A Knowledge-Based Theory of the Firm to Guide in Strategy Formulation. *Journal of Intellectual Capital*, *2*(4), 344–358. doi:10.1108/14691930110409651

Weller, M. (2007). Virtual Learning Environments. New York: Routledge.

Yin, R. K. (2003). Case Study Research: Design and Methods (3rd ed.). London: Sage.

Zhang, D., Zhao, J. L., Zhou, L., & Nunamaker, J. F. (2004). Can E-Learning Replace Classroom Learning? *Communications of the ACM*, *47*(5), 75–79. doi:10.1145/986213.986216

Zimmer, T., Billaud, M., & Geoffroy, D. (2006). A Remote Laboratory for Electrical Engineering Education. *International Journal of Online Engineering*, *2*(3), 1–4.

ADDITIONAL READING

Barrie, S. C., & P., G. (2007). The Linking of Institutional Performance Indicators to Improvements in Teaching in Classrooms. *Quality in Higher Education*, *13*(3), 275–286. doi:10.1080/13538320701800175

Dixon, K., & Dixon, R. (2008). Capacity of an Electronic Portfolio to Promote Professionalism, Collaboration and Accountability in Educational Leadership. In J. Salmons & L. Wilson (Eds.), Handbook of Research on Electronic Collaboration and Organizational Synergy (pp. 472-493). Hershey, PA: IGI Global.

Drent, M., & Meelissen, M. (2008). Which Factors Obstruct or Stimulate Teacher Educators to Use Ict Innovatively? *Computers & Education*, *11*(1), 53–68.

Eklund, J., & May, M. (2003). Evaluation of the Usage of National Flexible Learning Tookboxes (Series 3). Canberra, ACT: Australian National Training Authority.

Fresen, J. W., & Boyd, L. G. (2005). Caught in the Web of Quality. *International Journal of Educational Development*, *25*(3), 317–331. doi:10.1016/j.ijedudev.2004.12.002

Schunk, D. H. (2004). Learning Theories: An Educational Perspective. Upper Saddle River, NJ: Pearson Prentice Hall.

KEY TERMS AND DEFINITIONS

ADDIE: A project management methodology (originating from information technology) that was transformed for the education course design context by another researcher – it is an acronym for: Analysis-Design-Development-Implementation-Evaluation ADDIE (Dick et al., 2001).

Andragogy: A teaching method (originally founded in Europe but popularized in USA in the 1960's), emphasizing a student-centered approach for mentoring, using self-regulation, motivation, and constructivist learning strategies and materials.

AUQA: Australia University Quality Agency, a government agency responsible for auditing all Australian universities on behalf of a number of higher education departments.

Balanced Learning Assessment: Similar to and informed by the balanced scorecard idea, it includes six factors to evaluate learning effectiveness based on student perceptions and performance – these factors are also used by Australian accreditation agencies and by universities to benchmark performance; these factors are: assessment model (shown in Figure 3), by linking course to accreditation requirements, as listed below: industry employment relevance, resources/materials, critical thinking activities, teaching quality, student satisfaction and performance (passing grade).

E-Learning: Although ambiguous in the literature, Rosenberg (2001) was chosen as the source for a contemporary e-learning definition, which suggested three underlying principles are needed: Networked/interconnected students (allowing for timely interaction and feedback); accessible via a standard Internet browser on a standard personal computer (from anywhere anytime); and it employs educational psychology theories to facilitate learning beyond self-directed training.

Flexible Learning: As its namesake suggests, it provide options to students that want to take a course, such as being able to take lectures at campus or online, interact with peers at campus or online, and so on. Here it is used in conjunction with e-learning but it actually includes e-learning as an alternative mode.

Taxonomy of Learning: Framework for education design that included three domains: cognitive, affective and physical (Krathwohl et al., 1964; Bloom & Krathwohl, 1956). Here the cognitive domain stages and process were applied to course design. Course design takes place from the bottom up perspective, starting with knowledge (basic facts, procedures if applicable, then conceptual perspectives and broader meta-cognitive variations of the subject from the literature). A course is designed such that the learning materials, activities and assessments progress from the bottom towards the top, namely: Remembering-knowledge, understanding, applying, analyzing, evaluating-synthesis, and finally creating, with the last three stages/processes involving critical thinking.

Chapter 4
Planning a Quality Education System:
Using Technology to Increase Access to University Education

C. W. S. Sukati
University of Swaziland, Swaziland

ABSTRACT

Responding to the social, technological, economic and political (STEP) environmental factors, UNISWA established the Institute of Distance Education (IDE) in 1994 to increase access to university education by offering its programmes using the distance education delivery mode. The success achieved by this intervention has led to a number of problems and challenges that now confront the Institute which work against the realization of its goals. An evaluation of these challenges points to the urgent need to use new ICTs in the delivery of content. Doing this, would enable the institution to increase its enrolments at a lower cost per enrolled student. It would further lead to the blurring of the boundaries between the conventional university and the IDE. This chapter argues for the use of online learning, and the need for a new strategic plan for the university.

ORGANIZATIONAL BACKGROUND

The University of Swaziland (UNISWA) developed from the University of Botswana, Lesotho and Swaziland (UBLS), which had its headquarters in Roma, Lesotho between 1964 and 1975. UBLS was equally funded by the three Governments of Botswana, Lesotho and Swaziland, and had until 1970, little presence in Botswana and Swaziland. Following student unrest at Roma, and strained relations between the UBLS administration and the Lesotho Government over the implementation of development plans or devolution plans, the Roma Campus was withdrawn from UBLS in 1975 and named the National University of Lesotho. This led Botswana and Swaziland to form their own University in 1976, which was named the University of Botswana and Swaziland (UBS). UBS had two constituent colleges – the University College of Botswana and the University College of Swaziland, and it was planned that these two colleges would later develop to become national universities. Indeed,

DOI: 10.4018/978-1-61520-779-4.ch004

in accordance with this plan, the University of Botswana and the University of Swaziland came into being in 1982.

The chief mandate of UNISWA has been manpower production to assist in national development. Enrolment of students at UNISWA rose steadily until it reached a point where the university facilities and resources could not handle the numbers, resulting in a large number of qualifying candidates being rejected. In addition, the demand for tertiary education from people who were in full-time employment, self-employed, housewives, etc. was increasing. All these factors led to the creation of the Institute of Distance Education (IDE), which was to offer the university programmes and courses using the distance education delivery mode. The IDE was set up as one of the Faculties of UNISWA. The Institute is headed by a Director, who reports to the Vice Chancellor of the University, and performs similar duties as those of a Dean of a Faculty. Current plans, as reflected in the Draft University of Swaziland Strategic Plan (2009) are that the IDE will become a College of Distance Education and have more autonomy to carry out its mandate. The main sources of income for the University are from the Swaziland Government (about 74%) and from Student fees (about 20%). As the country's economy has grown at lower rates than in the past, funding the University has become a major problem, and the Institution has had to find ways of being more efficient and of controlling its expenditures. This case study is important therefore in that it provides one viable way that the challenges facing the University can be addressed, and the quality of education offered improved while at the same time the costs are minimised.

SETTING THE STAGE

At the Fourth Pan-Commonwealth Forum on Open Learning held at Ocho Rios, Jamaica in October/November, 2006, a special session was organized to discuss the unique challenges that face dual-mode institutions. Key papers were presented in this session by Ms. J. N. Aguti from Makerere University in Uganda, Prof. R. Siaciwena of the University of Zambia, and Dr. O. Tau from the University of Botswana. The author, who attended the session, noted that the challenges that were highlighted were similar to those faced by the IDE at UNISWA. These presentations left the author with one major question: how can these challenges be addressed, and what organizational structures, delivery modes and mechanisms should be devised and adopted to increase access to a quality education at a competitive cost? This chapter seeks to address this question.

Many Swazi nationals were unable to enrol in the conventional face-to-face (CF2F) university for several reasons, the main one being shortage of space. This necessitated that other options of broadening access to a quality university education be explored and existing barriers removed. Distance education (DE) was the option chosen as it has become a rapidly growing alternative of access to higher education in both developed and developing countries. DE is convenient as learners do not have to leave home or work, this mode of instruction is achieving institutional maturity, and it has become an important complement to the mainstream CF2F system (Srisa-An, 2006; Salawu & Ogunsola-Bandele, 2005; Perraton, 2004a; Lentell, 2004; UNESCO, 2002; Keegan, 2000; Reddy & Manjulika, 1995). Daniel (2006) further reports that it allows education to break the "iron triangle" in that it increases access, improves quality and cut costs - all at the same time. Jegede (2000) has further claimed that it is the most appropriate mode for the disadvantaged, underprivileged and underrepresented members of society. DE has moved from the margins of educational policy and practice to being a respected and widespread mode of delivery alongside full-time and part-time study (Tait & Mills, 1999). In Southern Africa, its importance has been shown by the recent increase in institutions that offer it, increases in their enrolments, and also by the increase in the membership of the Distance Education Association of Southern Africa (DEASA).

However, it is noted that despite these increases, the overall participation rates in higher education in African countries are still small when compared to those of developed countries and those of other developing regions. The participation rate in Swaziland, for example, was 4% in 2001/02 while that of developed countries like the USA, Republic of Korea, Finland, etc. were over 80% (UNESCO, 2004). Other African countries e.g. Burundi, Djibouti, Niger, etc. had rates as low as 1%, with the average African rate being generally around 1 – 4% (UNESCO, 2004). Thus, African institutions cannot be central in the creation of knowledge based economies if the institutions are only admitting less than ten percent of the children who should be accessing tertiary education and training (Dzvimbo, 2005). The current conventional universities are a relic of past elitist (ivory tower) policies, and would be unable to substantially increase these rates, as their structures, funding arrangements and levels, and teaching arrangements were not set up for this. The major challenge that then arises is: how can African countries, like Swaziland, increase access to a quality university education, taking into account their Social, Technological, Economical and Political (STEP) environment and factors?

In trying to maximise the strengths, and minimise the weaknesses of CF2F and DE delivery, many institutions, particularly in developed countries, have come up with many forms of dual-mode delivery. The advent of new information communication technologies (ICT), and the establishment and success of the United Kingdom Open University, have encouraged many CF2F institutions to become multi modal institutions. Depending on how the dual-mode offer is planned, structured, organised and implemented, there are several challenges that the institutions have had to deal with to guarantee increased access and the quality of their programmes. As UNISWA opted to become a dual-mode institution in 1994, it is now opportune and relevant to review progress and to determine the major challenges that it now faces. Such a review should articulate an appropriate plan to address these challenges, considering the STEP factors of Swaziland, and further evolve possible long term strategies and solutions, in order to increase accessibility and quality of programmes and courses.

In this regard, this chapter addresses the following questions with regard to IDE:

- What were the STEP factors that led to its creation, instructional mode and its policies to ensure quality?
- What are the STEP problems and challenges that the IDE currently faces?
- Which new technology(ies) should be chosen and used for teaching and learning to solve these challenges?

Information for this case study was collected by an in-depth examination of the IDE by the author, who is one of the staff members in this Institute. It draws on personal knowledge, observations, experience, discussions with colleagues, and published documents on IDE to ascertain the challenges and problems that the Institute faces. Using the large available literature on DE, particularly of the success stories, the researcher compares the successful experience of many dual mode Institutions, (which are mainly in the developed world), with the challenges of IDE, and an evaluation of the available new ICTs, and comes out with a possible solution to these challenges. It is argued that a well planned university system, that uses new technologies for teaching and blurs DE and CF2F offers the most appropriate solution. It is also believed that it is by understanding the STEP environment and factors that dual-mode institutions like UNISWA face, that the planning of a quality university system can really begin. The study is therefore important in that it:

(a) encourages debate among policy makers, planners, educators, and researchers on policy issues surrounding appropriate structures and modes of teaching/learning in universities. Teaching and learning that removes barriers and increases access to a quality education, and thereby allow for the achievement of Millennium Development Goals (MDGs) in a cost effective and efficient manner in developing countries considering the STEP environment;
(b) helps inform UNISWA and the Government, in articulating the major problems faced by the nation's dual-mode institution, and what appropriate technology can help address these; and
(c) contributes to the pool of knowledge upon which policy makers and educationists draw from when designing and developing their own higher education systems that have direct relevance to national and regional development and their STEP environments.

CASE DESCRIPTION: THE STEP PERSPECTIVES

Social and Political Factors: Reasons for the Creation of the IDE

In Swaziland, the use of the social demand approach to educational planning and the implementation of universal primary education has meant that larger numbers of students attend primary school. On completion, these students proceed to secondary school, and hence this level of schooling has had to be expanded to meet the demand. Expansion at secondary has increased the number of high school graduates who desire to proceed to tertiary education. Following on this, and in conformity with trends observed in many developing countries (Bates, 2005), it was noted that a number of Swazi Nationals who qualified for entry, and wanted to enter UNISWA, were unable to do so because of limited facilities and human resources. To address these inhibitors, UNISWA had to explore other options for broadening access to a quality higher education in the country. For this reason, the IDE was created in 1994 to convert and offer programmes that were taught in the conventional University using the DE delivery mode. The mission of IDE is:

to create educational and training opportunities for individuals (employed, self-employed, unemployed, and post-high school graduates) who have been unable to, for one reason or another, undertake conventional and professional education programmes and courses. For this reason, the motto of IDE is: "Taking the University education and professional programmes to the people rather than the people coming to the University. (UNISWA, 1996, p. 2)

The student enrolments in IDE have increased rapidly since inception as shown in Table 1.

Three major reasons account for the particularly large student enrolment increases between 1997/98 and 2001/02. These are:

- that following several requests and representations from the students and university officials, the Swaziland Government began to sponsor students who were admitted into IDE;
- at the beginning as there were few students applying to IDE and yet many students who qualified were being rejected in the CF2F programme, the University admitted these qualifying students into IDE, even if they had not applied to the Institute; and
- the major growth trend in post secondary education, which according to Daniel, West, D'Antoni & Uvalic-Trumbic (2005) is happening globally, of growth in demand.

The creation of IDE has however not solved the social demand for university education in

*Table 1. Student enrolment in IDE: 1996/97 to 2008/09 (***Source:** *UNISWA Full-Time and Part-Time Enrolment Yearbooks)*

Academic year	Female	Male	Total enrolment	Percent increase
1996/97	...	...	158	-
1997/98	109	115	224	41.8
1998/99	...	...	283	26.3
1999/00	314	232	546	92.9
2000/01	470	310	780	42.9
2001/02	617	438	1,055	35.3
2002/03	743	503	1,246	18.1
2003/04	824	623	1,447	16.1
2004/05	917	678	1,595	10.2
2005/06	1,106	837	1,943	21.8
2006/07	1,155	891	2,046	5.3
2007/08	1046	814	1860	- 9.09
2008/09	969	726	1695	- 8.87

Note: ... means data is not available.

the country as the IDE is also unable to absorb all students who want to enrol. In fact, as Table 1 shows, enrolments have been falling over the last two years due to low admission figures which are due to the problems and challenges that the Institute faces. The IDE then rejects a large number of candidates who qualify for entrance and want to access the Institute's programmes and courses. Hence the need to look into other more efficient modes of course delivery which can address the current challenges that are faced by the Institute, and accommodate large numbers of learners and at the same time be cost effective.

Technological Factors: IDE Delivery System

The IDE structure and delivery mode put in place at the inception of the Institute paralleled the Off-Campus Centre of Universiti' Sains Malaysia as discussed in Dhanarajan (1992). Although at the time IDE was created, many distance learning institutions were already using third and fourth generation technology for course delivery and support, IDE chose (for several reasons) to use first generation technology, i.e. the print media, in the form of self-instructional course modules. This mode was supplemented by some limited face-to-face contact. The IDE policy, according to Sukati and Chandraiah (2004), was that two-thirds of the content should be imparted through the DE mode, i.e. the self- instructional course modules, and one-third through the face-to-face contact classes. The face-to-face contact sessions composed of lectures (delivered by the course lecturers at Kwaluseni – the main campus of the university) and tutorial sessions which are conducted by part-time tutors at the three regional centres of IDE.

In addition to this technology, students were encouraged to send their assignments and questions that they had on their work to the Institute using postal mail, and could use the phone for any assistance that they required. Computers have been used by the staff of the Institute for management only and not for content delivery and/or communication with students. The Institute has gone further recently, to prepare audio tapes for the teaching of the Certificate Programme in Portuguese. The use of the face-to-face teaching and support system at IDE means that the number of students enrolled in each course is limited by the capacity of the available physical facilities and teaching personnel. As a key rationale for establishing the IDE was to accommodate demand for university education in a situation where the existing facilities on-campus were inadequate, it followed that as the IDE enrolments increased, the university facilities were inadequate to accommodate all the learners during their limited face-to-face sessions. This confirms Moon's (2005) assertion that:

The "bricks and mortar" institutions (universities and colleges) created to meet the educational needs of the twentieth century will, as currently constituted, be unable to meet the demands of the twenty-first century (p.10).

Hence the need to look into other teaching/learning/support mechanisms that are cost effective and would allow much larger numbers of students to be taught individually and/or in small groups away from the limiting facilities of the university and/or regional learning centres.

Economic Factors: Policies to Control Quality

Higher education in Swaziland, as is the case in many other countries, is much more expensive than primary and secondary schooling. The Swaziland Government therefore provides scholarships for almost all its students to do their programmes at the University. The scholarships that are given to the university students further erode the tight budgets that are allocated to the Ministry of Education. Because of this, expanding the existing facilities, increasing the staff positions, and adding more funds for other university operations has become a nightmare for the Government and the Institution. How could it go around this and offer good quality programmes to masses of students with the limited resources? To address the issue of quality control, the university set up certain policies.

Quality control and assurance plays a critical role if open and distance learning is to be accepted as equal to, or even better than, CF2F instruction. Many countries have Quality Assurance Agencies which monitor several quality parameters in both conventional and open universities (Robinson, 2004; Lawery, 2003; Sinclair, 2003; Moore, 2001; Keegan, 2000). In meeting this need, the IDE set up the following relevant policies (UNISWA, 1996, p. 7 - 12):

i) If an on-campus programme was also offered through IDE, the curriculum would be the same and the lecturer teaching the course on-campus would also teach the DE students (including setting and marking of assignments, tests and final examinations);
ii) The normal minimum required academic standards or qualifications for lecturers in the on-campus programme would be the same as those of IDE and the instructional modules were to be prepared by the academic staff members who taught the course to the on-campus students;
iii) The IDE Instructional Designer and Developer, would be responsible for converting regular on-campus courses into distance learning course materials and would plan, organize, and conduct in house training for academic staff in the preparation of distance teaching/learning materials;
iv) The IDE Board and the Boards of the relevant CF2F Departments would be responsible for the monitoring and maintenance of academic standards and equivalences between the off-campus and on-campus programmes, and in the event the on-campus students and the off-campus ones were taking the same course(s), they would write the same examination, have the same external examiners and would be awarded the same qualifications

(certificates, diplomas, or degrees); and

v) Heads of Departments that provided DE programmes and courses would automatically become members of the IDE Board and would serve as Course Coordinators or "link pins" between their CF2F Departments and IDE.

CURRENT PROBLEMS AND CHALLENGES FACING IDE

Despite its major success in increasing access to university education, to human resource development, to national development and potential to the achievement of the MDGs, the IDE therefore, like many other dual-mode institutions as confirmed in the special session at the Pan Commonwealth Forum (op. cit.), faces a number of STEP problems and challenges. The challenges, which are also compared with those presented by other African Institutions in Jamaica, can be summarized as follows:

Social Challenges

A large number of qualifying candidates apply to the Institute each year, and the IDE is able to admit only a few. The Institute is therefore failing to fulfil its mandate with the current delivery and technology mechanisms, and hence a need to review these. The irony of it all is that although many students apply, only a few really want to study using the DE mode. It is therefore a fact that the majority of students in IDE are recent school leavers, who, because of lack of space could not be admitted in the CF2F programme. They therefore applied to IDE as a last resort to getting a university education and a qualification. This IDE situation supports the observations by Perraton (2004a) and by Simonson, Smaldino, Albright & Svacek (2000) that in developing countries, many Open University students enrol in DE because there is no room for them within the conventional system, and hence do not want to study at a distance. Many reasons exist at UNISWA for this reluctance, and chief among them are that: they get lower accommodation and meal allowances than the CF2F ones, they miss the prestige of staying on campus and be seen as "university students", the IDE programmes take longer to complete than in the on-campus system, they consider themselves as adults and want to stay at the University away from the control of their parents, and the perceived quality and prestige of the CF2F programme vis-à-vis the distance one. As a result, at the end of each academic year, many IDE students apply to the Registrar of the University to transfer from IDE to the full time programme. This poses a major unique challenge for the IDE: How do you educate and motivate learners who do not want to study in the Institute after all?

Technology Challenges

While it is possible to have high quality learning and teaching using traditional technologies (e.g. print) alone, it is noted that the introduction of new technologies enhances learning, interaction and student support, and thus the quality of education offered (Bates, 2005). As noted above, IDE, just like many other universities in the African continent (Sife et al. 2007) has not yet started using new ICTs in its delivery mode. The Institute therefore needs to progress in the use of new technology and adopt a proper multi media system where the latest technology is used for teaching. In this regard, several authors such as Bates (2005), Perraton (2004 (b), and Sife et al. (2007) offer a detailed list of technologies used in open and distance learning and an idea of their related costs. The IDE therefore faces a challenge in developing and introducing ICT's in its instructional media, so that a flexible programme is offered to ensure that the learners can access their courses and get support at any time and any place. The challenge then is how to start technology based education where there is inadequate provision of physical infrastructure, laboratories, equipment and networks, financial resources and trained personnel to implement this.

Tait and Mills (1999, p. 1) correctly point out that one of the problems in introducing new learning methodologies in institutions is that of inadequate capital investment in learning materials and staff development. Siaciwena (2006) reveals that UNZA also has this information technology challenge, and that the use of ICT's in programme delivery and management is still very limited, and that this was partly due to low level ICT knowledge and skills, as well as the high cost of, and the slow erratic telephone system. Namibia also has not fully integrated technology in the development and delivery of open and distance learning (Nekongo-Nielsen, 2006).

Economic Challenges

A clear institutional comprehensive strategic plan for developing DE at the UNISWA should have been articulated at the design stage of the IDE. Such a plan would have indicated the vision, mission, objectives, the human, financial and physical facility resource needs, the organizational structure and the institutional arrangements. Such a comprehensive plan should have involved all the key stakeholders so as to get a shared understanding and commitment to the new Institute. This would have further clarified the roles and responsibilities of all the key stakeholders, future direction and needs, relationship to national developmental needs, and provided a better basis to obtain better ownership of the Institute. In the absence of such a plan, there seems to be no ownership and commitment by the other stakeholders on the work of the IDE. This challenge is one that was also faced by the University of Zambia (UNZA) (Siaciwena, 2006). The lack of a strategic plan has led to a number of problems that border on quality assurance. Rapid increase in IDE enrolments entailed that there be corresponding increases in the IDE full-time coordinating staff and in the number of part-time lecturers. This did not happen. The IDE senior management staff only has three coordinators covering materials design and development, academic studies, and student support. Such a structure cannot adequately manage all the activities of IDE as they are too few to organize and supervise the teaching in the face-to-face classes, introduce and work on new programmes, provide support services, educate lecturers and tutors, and promote the work of IDE.

The IDE does not have its own teaching staff and it relies on those from the on-campus programmes. These full time lecturers who become part-time lecturers in IDE have complained of heavy teaching loads in their mother departments and of having to teach on Saturdays and during holidays (when they are supposed to be on leave). IDE pays these lecturers to prepare the teaching modules and also teach the face-to-face classes. After all, if they refuse, where would IDE get the part-time Lecturers, as the country is small and does not have a pool of qualified people from which it could draw Lecturers? Some of the teaching in IDE classes has therefore been poor as some required course modules have not been fully developed, and as certain lecturers had low morale and lacked enthusiasm and motivation to teach the IDE classes. This problem of staffing however seems to be common among the dual-mode institutions as UNZA staff (Siaciwena, 2006) also complained about insufficient staff and the "heavy workloads" and Makerere University also lacked appropriately qualified, skilled and experienced staff (Aguti, 2006).

Siaciwena (quoted in Rumble & Latchem (2004, p. 124) described the problems of using the same lecturers. He indicated that the system of assigning the same Lecturers to both internal and external students was disadvantageous to the DE students because overworked staff tended to use the available time for internal teaching and ignore external teaching, and that such negative attitudes undermined both the status of DE and the very concept of parity of standards. Other authors, including Rumble & Latchem (2004), Ross and Klug (1999) and Calvert (1992) have reported on the lower level of interest that the CF2F academics demonstrate towards the off-campus students, the lower status that they accord to DE, and the possibility of stifling improvements in DE, and the situation in IDE seems to support these observations. In IDE the situation is made worse by the fact that most of the Departments had a limited staff resource that could not cover all their courses when offered in IDE. Similarly, in Botswana, it has been observed that one of the limitations of the process of introducing distance education was that it was difficult to get Faculties and teaching Departments to allocate the necessary time and resources to convert their programmes to DE (Tau, 2006). This lack of resources limited the expansion of DE as staff members did not cooperate with the Institute in adding new programmes because it entailed more work for their Departments.

Open and distance education has faced an ongoing struggle to establish its credibility and legitimacy, even when its quality is good, especially in contexts where it is new or faces a history of poor-quality provision. For these reasons, attention to its governance, accreditation and quality assurance is essential in establishing good practice, standards and reputation (Robinson 2004). For quality assurance, UNISWA has the tradition of relying on External Examiners, who come to the university each year to assess the quality of the courses offered and the performance of the students. This is seen as critical to making sure that the courses, certificates, diplomas and degrees that the students do are of an acceptable standard in the region and in the World. As such, it has not been seen as necessary for the Institute to set up its own quality assurance, quality control and continuous monitoring and evaluation structures. Available information seems to support this parity of standards, as studies by Magagula and Ngwenya (2004), and Sukati et. al. (2008) indicate that IDE is doing a very good job in producing educated individuals (output) and that the quality of its output is of a very high standard as they do as well as (or even better) than their counterparts on the CF2F system. It is noted however, that other dual mode Institutions, e.g. the University of Zambia, also have no framework for quality assurance, quality control and quality enhancement (Siaciwena, 2006).

The setting up and running of a DE system differs from that of the conventional system. This causes a problem when there are certain resources that the DE system requires as most (if not all) the decision makers are from the CF2F system. They often do not understand the operations, needs and arrangements of the DE system, and as a result, many DE requests are either rejected or deferred by the University Committees. This affects the operations of the Institute and the quality of its programmes, and at the end, perhaps the morale of the DE staff. The IDE has raised funds from outside sources to support its operations and innovations. However, these have not been sufficient to cater for all of the urgent needs of the Institute. These difficulties in the arrangements between IDE and the CF2F system are perhaps not unique only to IDE, as Daniel (2006, p. XVI) has observed that it is rather rare to find arrangements between the mother institution and its DE arm that are fully satisfactory.

Political Challenges

As the Institute has to offer courses and programmes that are currently offered on-campus, this has stifled the development of IDE. It cannot offer its own courses and programmes that it sees as necessary and relevant to learners and to the labour market. It has to offer the CF2F programmes with the same regulations and requirements as in the full-time programme. The lack of diversified programmes at UNISWA is perhaps the single most important reason for the high rate of unemployment among its graduates. It is therefore necessary that needs assessment studies be conducted and relevant short and long term courses and programmes offered to make the graduates more marketable. Changing this UNISWA policy, and enabling the IDE to offer its own courses (short and long term) would therefore help the Institute in providing flexible and relevant courses and reduce the unemployment rate of its graduates. It is also found that the priorities of the conventional Departments may be different from those of the DE unit, and thus they do not cooperate in the introduction of a new programme. This is currently the case with the introduction of a B.A. Social Science degree in IDE. Tau (2006) also provides an example of her Unit failing to persuade the Department of Primary Education (in the conventional system of the University of Botswana) to provide a home for the Diploma in Primary Education. Siaciwena (op. cit.) also points to the inflexibility of their programmes which often do not sufficiently respond to the professional development needs of distance learners. He further asserts that because of the concept of parity of standards and equality of treatment, both full-time and DE students follow the same curriculum offered by the same lecturers, and thus that the range of study programmes and courses offered to their DE students was determined by the capacity/ability of the conventional Departments, than the needs of the DE learners.

SOLVING THE PROBLEMS: USING APPROPRIATE TECHNOLOGY

IDE is serving an important function for Swaziland in removing barriers and making university education accessible to a large number of nationals who desire it, especially women. One is therefore overwhelmed by the power of DE, and this leads to the question of whether poor developing countries should develop CF2F Universities, DE ones, or as Croft (1992) pondered, something in-between the two? Moon's (2005) assertion that Africa needs a paradigm shift in its approach to the provision of education is therefore supported. The author believes that there has to be this shift, and it should be towards harnessing the new technologies in DE and in CF2F and thereby blur the boundaries between the two modes. That is why the IDE is involved in the Commonwealth of Learning's project on the Virtual University of Small States of the Commonwealth (VUSSC), which brings together several experts from the small Commonwealth countries to prepare course material which is then given to all the countries to offer through various modes. Many DE experts have written on the blurring of the distinction between DE and CF2F made possible by technological advances and the emergence of flexible learning opportunities for all students in dual-mode institutions (Hope, 2006; Challis, 2006; Bates, 2005, Tait & Mills, 1999; Dhanarajan, 1992). As the education providers in both CF2F and DE modes embrace the use of new ICTs to facilitate student learning, the boundaries between distance and conventional education become blurred. The challenges faced by IDE therefore, are not insurmountable, but require a paradigm shift on UNISWA's part. A careful look at these challenges, coupled with a comparison to successful institutions, reveals that the possible solution lies in the planning of university education using ICTs and blurring DE and CF2F.

Appropriate ICT's, on top of print and face-to-face that are currently used, need to be introduced and utilized for course delivery, interaction and management. The technology/s utilized would have to be accessible, flexible, affordable, cost effective and efficient, and further allow for two way communication and dialogue (whether synchronous or asynchronous). An evaluation of the new ICTs by the author reveals that a suitable mode could be online learning which utilizes the internet and the World Wide Web, which would allow the delivery of content and the two way communication between learners and their course Lecturers and/or Tutors. The regional learning centres, Tinkhundla Centres and some secondary schools, on top of the already existing computers in the three UNISWA Campuses, would have to be equipped with the necessary computers and networks that would allow for internet connectivity. This would give the students good access to computers. Hence IDE would not have to go through all the technology generations that many Institutions, particularly in the developed world, went through. It would leap-frog to the appropriate technology, and in this way save in terms of time, costs, human resources and development, expertise, etc. Why would it be necessary to go through early generation technology, e.g. radio, audio/video cassettes, TV, etc. when that technology is already getting outdated?

Once the course content is available online, all the UNISWA students (IDE and CF2F), could have access and be allowed to study online (after all it is the same content). Bates (2005) also noted this and revealed that one of the impacts of technological innovation on campuses was the convergence of on-campus and off-campus, and that once materials were developed for one group, they could, if designed with this in mind, be easily used for the other group. As this would allow both DE and CF2F students to study using the same mode, it would thus be unnecessary to offer the many hours of face to face instruction on CF2F and on the DE students, and this would blur the boundaries between the two modes. In this case, it might not even be necessary to indicate the students as DE or CF2F, as they would all register in their respective Departments and learn using the same mode. IDE would not have students and would cease to exist in its current form.

Online learning could improve the quality of learning and teaching in that it would: facilitate content delivery and two way communication and interaction, provide for greater information access and synthesis, model and simulate a range of scientific phenomena, increase collaboration and cooperation, provide video clips, graphics, sound, develop problem solving capabilities, electronic submission of assignments, aid deeper understanding, provide creative thinking and animation, assess and evaluate students, and generally motivate, engage and provide enjoyment to the learners (Sife et al., 2007; Bates, 2005, Perraton, 2004a; Melton, 2002). According to Srisa-An (2006), Information technology has revolutionized education systems and methodologies, making learning easier, more effective, more enjoyable and highly customized or "Learner Centred".

The proposed solution of making online learning the major delivery mode would not only provide the above mentioned benefits, but would further address the current challenges and problems faced by the IDE in its STEP environment in the following manner:

a. Force IDE, the University, and the Government to first work on a detailed and comprehensive strategic plan. This plan would have to involve all the relevant stakeholders in these organizations such that in the end, it is accepted and owned by all. Once owned, there would be commitment by the stakeholders to its implementation.
b. As the students would learn online, away from the Institution, very large student numbers could be accommodated. The course lecturers would have fewer class sessions and not have to teach the huge overcrowded classes. In this way they would have no reason to complain about large classes and being overworked. Furthermore, the lecturer's role would change from that of information givers to be facilitators of learning. To ensure that the quality of the teaching and learning process is maintained, all the lecturers would be trained in DE and taught and supported to use this mode of teaching, the content in all the media used would be prepared by qualified course teams, and further, there would be a quality assurance system put in place.
c. IDE would just need to have only a core staff to assist Departments in preparing the

content and converting it to online courses and also how to teach effectively using this mode. This restructuring would however need careful research and planning in order to address pertinent questions, similar to those posed by Bates (2005, p. 15) on how the institution would need to be reorganized. As the UNISWA Lecturers would teach all the students as one group, with no distinction between IDE and CF2F, it would be easy for Departments to calculate their teaching loads and request additional staff, if needed. Hence all students would be treated alike and with the same enthusiasm, and in this way, the quality of their interaction with the staff would be improved and as a result also the quality of education offered. There would also be no case of an unwilling learner.

d. The physical infrastructure would not be a barrier as the new mode of teaching and learning would mean that the demand for face-to-face interaction would diminish, and the limited physical infrastructure at the Kwaluseni main campus and at the Regional Learning Centres could just be adequate. In this way, the University could continue to admit more students without regard to existing UNISWA physical infrastructure.

e. The problems associated with the offering the same courses in IDE as in CF2F, would not exist. The University would have to conduct a needs assessment study and then offer those programmes (short or long term) that would be found to be in demand. Hence, all UNISWA offered programmes would be demand driven. As the learners would study the same content, write the same examinations, taught by the same Lecturer using the same assessment tools, it would not be possible for one to say that other students were not as good as the other.

f. Several studies have demonstrated that DE is cost effective and cost efficient (Butcher & Roberts, 2004). Introducing and mainstreaming DE to all students at UNISWA would therefore allow the University to be economic and produce graduates at lower unit costs. Funds would be further saved by blurring as the writing of modules, delivery of the content, marking of tests and examinations, etc. would all be done by the full-time course lecturers who are already in the payroll of the University. Bates (1995, p. 12) has correctly pointed out that the use of technology can allow for more students to be accommodated for the same number of faculty, with the scope for re-allocation of resources to free up faculty for the development of the teaching materials. With the flexible course offerings, students would not need to stay on campus, so the university could reduce the accommodation places and all their associated maintenance, plant and personnel costs, to become **"a University without a hotel".** Finances could therefore be released from these centres to acquire the necessary ICT's and further provide training for the staff. Again, this would involve a paradigm shift for UNISWA, to change from its traditional university image to one with equity, effectiveness, relevance, flexibility and an efficient structure.

CONCLUSION

The creation of IDE heralded a new chapter in University education in Swaziland. It turned out to be a resounding success in removing barriers and increasing access. This success has however brought about a number of challenges that need to be urgently addressed if the progress made has to be maintained. Identification of these STEP challenges facing UNISWA has led to the need for a re-assessment of university planning in Swaziland. To successfully do this, this chapter argues for a paradigm shift in the planning and provision of university education in the country.

This shift entails the introduction of new ICTs and the offering of a multi media approach to teaching and learning. In this regard, it supports Dzvimbo's (2005) and Daniel's (2005) call for Africa to innovate and apply open and distance learning and ICT's to the challenges of African Development and for the expansion of a differentiated, flexible and creative system of higher education and training. The study calls for the planning of a quality university programme for all UNISWA students that should be achieved by the introduction of online programme delivery and management.

The writer believes this would be the ideal model for a small country like Swaziland, which cannot afford two universities (if an open university was established as a solution to the challenges). Furthermore, the small population (estimated at around one million) might not warrant two universities – which if they were created, may not achieve economies of scale. Yet it is important that access be increased so that unit costs can be lowered and the country can educate more students with less, and as Renwick (1992) points out, the benefits of DE need not be confined to the distance learners only. The proposed paradigm shift further supports the increasing literature on blurring the modes and revelation by scholars that e-learning may bring down the barriers between the different modes, and that a range of convergences are taking place with rapidity that is bewildering from all perspectives (Tait and Mills (op. cit.); Perraton (2004, (a)). From the learner's perspective, the convergence of distance and conventional education would certainly bring the potential for increased access and quality, as a range of modes of study become the norm.

REFERENCES

Aguti, J. N. (2006, October/November). *Education for national development: The Makerere University dual mode experience*. Paper presented at the Fourth Pan-Commonwealth Forum on Open Learning, Ocho Rios, Jamaica.

Bates, A. W. (1995). *The Future of Learning*. Paper first presented at the Minister's Forum on Adult Learning, Edmonton, Alberta, November 30 – December 1st, 1995. Retrieved April 12, 2007, from HTTP://bates.cstudies.ubc.ca/papers/side.html

Bates, A. W. (2005). Technology, E-Learning and Distance Education, (2nd Ed.). London: Routledge Falmer.

Butcher, N., & Roberts, N. (2004). Costs, effectiveness, efficiency: A guide for sound investment. In H. Perraton & H. Lentell (Eds.), Policy for Open and Distance Learning. World review of distance education and open learning (Vol. 4, pp. 224 – 245). London: Routledge Falmer.

Calvert, J. (1992). Deakin University. In I. Mugridge (Ed.), *Perspectives on Distance Education –Distance Education in Single and Dual Mode Universities*. Papers presented to a Symposium on Reforms in Higher Education in New Delhi, India. Vancouver: The Commonwealth of Learning.

Challis, D. (2006). Eroding distinctiveness: blurring the boundaries between on- and off-campus students by the adoption of learning management systems. In M. Tulloch, S. Relf, & P. Uys, (Eds.), *Selected papers from the 17th. Biennial Conference of the Open and Distance Learning Association of Australia: Breaking down boundaries: International experience in open, distance and flexible learning*, Adelaide, Australia: November 9-11, 2005, (pp. 87-96). Charles Sturt University: Open and Distance Learning Association of Australia.

Croft, M. (1992). Single or Dual Mode: Challenges and Choices for the Future of Education. In I. Mugridge (Ed.). *Perspectives on Distance Education – Distance Education in Single and Dual Mode Universities*. Papers presented to a Symposium on Reforms in Higher Education in New Delhi, India, (pp. 49-78). Vancouver: The Commonwealth of Learning.

Daniel, J. with Naidoo, V. (2005). Open and Distance Education for Africans and by Africans. Speech made at the African Council of Distance Education on Mobilization of African Leadership, at Tshwane, South Africa. In Commonwealth of Learning (Ed.). Speeches by Sir John Daniel and Colleagues, (pp. 5 – 9). Vancouver, Canada: Editor.

Daniel, J. (2006). Foreword. In A. Hope & P. Guiton (Eds.), Strategies for Sustainable Open and Distance Learning. World review of distance education and open learning, Volume 6, p. xiv-xviii. London: Routledge.

Daniel, J., West, P., D'Antoni, S. & Uvalic-Trumbic, S. (2005). ICT's in Education: Can

Dhanarajan, G. (1992). Dual Mode Institutions: The Off-Campus Centre of Universiti Sains Malaysia. In I. Mugridge (Ed.), *Perspectives on Distance Education – Distance Education in Single and Dual Mode Universities*. Papers presented to a Symposium on Reforms in Higher Education in New Delhi, India, (pp. 79 - 92). Vancouver: The Commonwealth of Learning.

Digital Dividend Replace Digital Divide? In Commonwealth of Learning (Ed.), *Speeches by Sir John Daniel and Colleagues,* (pp. 29 – 34). Vancouver, Canada: Editor.

Dzvimbo, K. P. (2005, September). The *African Researcher, the AVU Experiences and the Limits and Possibilities of Open, Distance and Electronic Learning in Africa.* Paper presented at the 11th Cambridge International Conference on Open and Distance Learning.

Hope, A. (2006). *Factors for Success in Dual Mode Institutions*. Retrieved April, 12, 2007 from HTTP://www.col.org/colweb/site/pid/3975

Hope, A., & Guiton, P. (Eds.). (2006). Strategies for Sustainable Open and Distance Learning. World review of distance education and open learning, (Vol. 6). London: Routledge.

Jegede, O. (2000). Evolving a National Policy on Distance Education. *Education Today*, *8*(2), 109–128.

Keegan, D. (2000). Distance Training – Taking Stock at a Time of Change. London: Routledge Falmer.

Lawery, V. (2003). Quantifying quality – an examination of the factors which define 'quality' in a professional development program. In G. Davies & E. Stacey (Eds.), Quality Education @ A Distance (pp. 189 – 197). Boston: Kluwer Academic Publishers.

Lentell, H. (2004). Framing policy for open and distance learning. In H. Perraton & H. Lentell (Eds.). Policy for Open and Distance Learning. World review of distance education and open learning (Vol. 4, 249 – 259). London: Routledge Falmer.

Magagula, C. M. & Ngwenya, A. P. (2004). A Comparative Analysis of the Academic Performance of Distance and On-Campus Learners. *Turkish Online Journal of Distance Education (TOJDE)*, *5*(4).

Melton, R. F. (2002). Planning and Developing Open and Distance Learning – A Quality Assurance Approach. London: Routledge Falmer.

Moon, B. (2005, August). *Designing school-based training programmes for teachers through distance education*. Paper presented at the DETA Conference 2005, held at the University of Pretoria, South Africa.

Moore, D. (2001). Perspectives on quality assurance and distance education. In N. Baijnath, S. Maimela & P. Singh (Eds.), Quality Assurance in Open and Distance Learning. Roodeport, South Africa. A Joint publication between UNISA and Technikon SA. (pp. 55 – 63).

Nekongo-Nielsen, H. (2006, October/November). *The contributions of open and distance learning to national development in Namibia.* Paper Presented at the Fourth Pan-Commonwealth Forum on Open Learning held at Ocho Rios, Jamaica.

Perraton, H. (2004 (a)). Aims and Purpose. In H. Perraton & H. Lentell (Eds.). Policy for Open and Distance Learning. World review of distance education and open learning (Vol. 4, pp. 9 – 41). London: Routledge Falmer.

Perraton, H. (2004 (b)). Choosing Technologies for Education. In H. Perraton & H. Lentell (Eds.), Policy for Open and Distance Learning. World review of distance education and open learning (Vol. 4, pp. 142 – 150). London: Routledge Falmer.

Peters, O. (2001). Learning and teaching in distance education: Pedagogical Analyses and Interpretations in an International Perspective. Open and Distance Learning Series. London: Kogan page.

Reddy, V., & Manjulika, S. (1995). The Practice of Distance Education in Single and Dual Mode Institutions in India: Issues of Convergence and Integration. In Asian Association of Open Universities (Ed.), *Proceedings of the Asian Association of Open Universities IXth. Annual Conference. Globalized and Cooperative Distance Learning:* The National Open University, Taiwan, R.O.C.

Renwick, W. (992). Distance Education in Dual Mode Universities. In I. Mugridge (Ed.), *Perspectives on Distance Education – Distance Education in Single and Dual Mode Universities.* Papers presented to a Symposium on Reforms in Higher Education in New Delhi, India, (pp. 141 - 152). Vancouver: The Commonwealth of Learning.

Robinson, B. (2004). Governance, accreditation and quality assurance in open and distance education. In H. Perraton & H. Lentell (Eds.), Policy for Open and Distance Learning. World review of distance education and open learning (Vol. 4, pp. 181 – 206). London: Routledge Falmer.

Ross, C. J., & Klug, M. (1999). Attitudes of business college faculty and administrators toward distance education: A national survey. *Distance Education, 20*(1), 109–128. doi:10.1080/0158791990200109

Rumble, G., & Latchem, C. (2004). Organisational models for open and distance learning. In H. Perraton & H. Lentell (Eds.), Policy for Open and Distance Learning. World review of distance education and open learning, (Vol. 4, pp. 117 – 140). London: Routledge Falmer.

Salawu, O. & Ogunsola – Bandele, M. (2005). *Reminiscences on the Practice of Open and Distance Learning in Nigeria: Lessons for the Future.* Supplementary Paper Presented at the 11th. Cambridge International Conference on Open and Distance Learning, 22 – 23 September, 2005.

Siaciwena, R. (2006, October/November). *Challenges of a dual mode institution: The case of the University of Zambia (UNZA).* Paper Presented at the Fourth Pan-Commonwealth Forum on Open Learning held at Ocho Rios, Jamaica.

Sife, A.S.; Lwoga, E.T. & Sanga, C. (2007). New technologies for teaching and learning: Challenges for higher learning institutions in developing countries. *International Journal of Education and Development using ICT, 3*(2).

Simonson, M., Smaldino, S., Albright, M., & Zvacek, S. (2000). Teaching and Learning at a Distance – Foundations of Distance Education. Upper Saddle River, NJ: Prentice Hall, Inc.

Sinclair, R. (2003). Components of quality distance education – Distance education guidelines from different countries. In G. Davies & E. Stacey (Eds.), Quality Education @ A Distance, (pp. 257 – 264). Boston: Kluwer Academic Publishers.

Srisa-An, W. (2006). Making Distance Education Borderless. In S. Garg, A. R. Khan, A. K. Aggarwal, U. Kanjilal & S. Panda (Eds.), Open and Flexible Learning – Issues and Challenges – Prof. G. Ram Reddy Memorial Lecturers, (pp. 15 – 28). New Delhi: Viva Books Private Limited.

Sukati, C. W. S., & Chandraiah, E. (2004). Effectiveness of Face-To-Face Sessions for Course Delivery at IDE, UNISWA. *Staff and Educational Development International*, *8*(2 & 3), 129–141.

Sukati, C. W. S., Chandraiah, E., Simelane, H. S., Sithole, M. M., & Magagula, C. M. (2008). Comparative Analysis of the Academic Achievement of a Cohort of B.A. (Hums) Students Studying Full-Time and Those Studying by Distance Learning Mode. Unpublished Final Report Prepared for the UNISWA Research Centre.

Tait, A., & Mills, R. (1999). The Convergence of Distance and Conventional Education. In A. Tait & R. Mills (Eds.), The Convergence of Distance and Conventional Education: Patterns of flexibility for the individual learner, (pp. 1 – 4). London: Routledge.

Tau, O. (2006, October/November). *Structure and Process in Dual-Mode Institution: Implications for Development*. Paper Presented at the Fourth Pan-Commonwealth Forum on Open Learning held at Ocho Rios, Jamaica.

UNESCO. (2002). Open and Distance Learning: Trends, Policy and Strategy Considerations. Paris: UNESCO

UNESCO. (2004). Global [*Comparing Education Statistics Across the World*. Montreal: UNESCO Institute of Statistics.]. *Education Digest*, 2004.

UNISWA. (1996). Policy Guidelines and Collaboration between IDE and Conventional Faculties/ Departments. Kwaluseni, Swaziland: University of Swaziland.

UNISWA. (1996/97 – 2008/09). Full–Time and Part–Time Student Enrolment Yearbooks. Kwaluseni, Swaziland: University of Swaziland.

UNISWA. (1996). Policy Guidelines and Collaboration between IDE and Conventional Faculties/ Departments. Kwaluseni, Swaziland: University of Swaziland.

UNISWA. (2009). Draft University of Swaziland Strategic Plan 2009 – 2014 (Unpublished). Kwaluseni, Swaziland: University of Swaziland.

ADDITIONAL READING

Bates, A. W. (2000). Managing Technological Change: Strategies for College and University Leaders. San Francisco: Jossey-Bass.

Bates, A. W. (2005). Technology, E-Learning and Distance Education, 2nd. Edition. London: Routledge.

Bates, A. W., & Poole, G. (2003). Effective Teaching with Technology in Higher Education: Foundations for Success. San Francisco: Jossey-Bass.

Bernard, R. M., Abrami, P. C., Lou, Y., Borokhovski, E., Wade, A., & Wozney, L. (2004). How Does Distance Education Compare With Classroom Instruction? A Meta-Analysis of the Empirical Literature. *Review of Educational Research*, *74*(3), 379–439. doi:10.3102/00346543074003379

Daniel, J. (1996). Mega-Universities and Knowledge Media: Technology Strategies for Higher Education. London: Kogan Page.

Daniel, J. (2007). *The Expansion of Higher Education in the Developing World: Can Distance Learning Contribute*? Paper Presented at the CHEA International Commission Conference 2007. Retrieved March 18, 2008, from: http://www.col.org/colweb/site/pid/4358.

Dhanarajan, G. (2006). Face to face with Distance Education. In S. Garg, A.R. Khan, A.K. Aggarwal, U. Kanjilal, & S. Panda (eds.). Open and Flexible Learning: Issues and Challenges – Prof. G. Ram Reddy Memorial Lectures. New Delhi: Viva Books Private Limited.

Gamliel, E., & Davidovitz, L. (2005). Online versus traditional teaching evaluation: mode can matter. *Assessment & Evaluation in Higher Education*, *30*(6), 581–592. doi:10.1080/02602930500260647

Harasim, L. (Ed.). (1990). Online Education: Perspectives on a New Environment. New York: Praeger.

Johnson, G. M. (2008). The Effectiveness of Distance Education VS. Classroom Instruction: A Summary of Bernard's Meta-Analysis With Implications for Practice. *International Journal of Instructional Media*, *35*(2), 137–144.

Makhubu, L. P. (1998). Opening Remarks by Prof. L. P. Makhubu, Vice Chancellor. In C. M. Magagula (ed.), Issues on University Education in Swaziland. A Report on the National Seminar held at the University of Swaziland. Kwaluseni, Swaziland: University of Swaziland.

McGreal, R. (Ed.). (2004). Online Education Using Learning Objects. London: Routledge.

Nipper, S. (1989). Third generation distance learning and computer conferencing. In R. Mason, & A. Kaye (eds.), Mindweave: Communication, Computers and Distance Education. Oxford: Pergamon.

Palmer, R. (2006). Beyond the Basics: Balancing Education and Training Systems in Developing Countries. *Journal of Education for International Development*, 2(1). Retrieved October 20, 2007, from: http://www.equip123.net/JEID/articles/2/BeyondBasics.pdf

Perraton, H. (2004). Choosing Technologies for Education. In H. Perraton, & H. Lentell (eds.). Policy for Open and Distance Learning. World review of distance education and open learning. Volume 4. London: Routledge Falmer.

Perraton, H., & Lentell, H. (Eds.). (2004). Policy for Open and Distance Learning. World review of distance education and open learning. Volume 4. London: Routledge Falmer.

Russell, T. (2002). *"The no Significant Phenomenon" as reported in 355 research reports, summaries and papers – a comprehensive research bibliography on technology for distance education*. Retrieved June 20, 2008, from http://www.teleeducation.nb.ca/nonsignificant-difference/

Russell, T. L. (1999). *The no significant difference phenomenon.* Chapel Hill: North Carolina State University.

Schoenfeld-Tacher, R., McConnell, S., & Graham, M. (2001). Do No Harm – A comparison of the effects of on-line vs. traditional delivery media on a science course. *Journal of Science Education and Technology*, *10*(3), 257–265. doi:10.1023/A:1016690600795

Smith, P. L., & Dillon, C. L. (1999). Comparing distance learning and classroom learning: conceptual considerations. *American Journal of Distance Education*, *13*, 107–124.

South African Institute for Distance Education. (1999). Distance Education and Educational Technology Choices in South Africa. Johannesburg: South African Institute for Distance Education.

Sukati, C. W. S. (2006). *The Teaching/Learning System at the IDE (UNISWA)*. Paper presented at a Writer's Workshop held at Orion Hotel in Piggs Peak, Swaziland on 25 June, 2006.

Sukati, C. W. S., & Chandraiah, E. (2005). Use of Information and Communication Technologies (ICTS) in Distance Education: A Comparative Study. *International Journal of Open & Distance Learning*, *2*, 25–32.

Sukati, C. W. S., Esampally, C., & Vilakati, N. (2007). Factors affecting the quality of education offered by the IDE at UNISWA. *Progressio: South African Journal of Open and Distance Learning Practice*, *29*(1 & 2), 5–20.

Tait, A., & Mills, R. (Eds.). (1999): The convergence of distance and conventional Education: Patterns of flexibility for the individual learner. London: Routledge.

Twigg, C. (2003). Expanding Access to Learning: The Role of Virtual Universities. Troy, New York: Center for Academic Transformation Rensselaer Polytechnic Institute.

UNESCO. (2002). Open and Distance Learning: Trends, Policy and Strategy Considerations. Paris: UNESCO.

University of Swaziland. (1996). *Policy Guidelines and Collaboration Between IDE and Conventional Faculties / Departments*. Kwaluseni: Institute of Distance Education.

Vakalisa, N. C. G. (2005). Unemployment in South Africa on the rise: Are schools and universities to blame? *Africa Education Review*, *2*(1), 40–58. doi:10.1080/18146620508566290

KEY TERMS AND DEFINITIONS

Access: Opening up additional places at the university to allow more candidates to enrol for university courses and programmes.

Blurring Boundaries: Means that the distinction or dividing lines between face-to-face and distance education is made fuzzier and fuzzier (or converges) such that the two modes tend to be the same.

Challenges of Dual-Mode: Problems that dual-mode institutions and universities encounter in their everyday operations.

Distance Education: A method of educating learners who are away (or separated) from the institution and from the instructor offering the instruction and hence technology is used to connect the student and the teacher.

Online Learning: Means using the computer, particularly the internet and the World Wide Web, for teaching and learning.

Planning: A detailed rational and systematic method by which university education should be organized, run and developed.

Swaziland: A country in Southern Africa on which this case study is based on.

Technology: Is the mode or media that is used to communicate the subject content and instructions to the learner and allow for interaction between the teacher and the learner.

University Education: Learning that is given in an institution at the tertiary level that offers advanced learning leading to the conferment of degrees and other academic awards.

Chapter 5
Using Portable DVD Players to Deliver Interactive Simulations for Training Health Care Workers in Kenya

Wallace Hannum
University of North Carolina at Chapel Hill, USA

ABSTRACT

This chapter reports on a project in Kenya that explored the feasibility of using interactive simulations delivered by portable DVD players as a technology-based learning solution for providing continuing education to nurses by taking the instruction directly to the workplace of the nurses rather than by removing them from their villages and clinics to transport them to the capital city for training. Technology-based learning using simulations holds great promise as an alternative or supplement to traditional classroom-based training in low-resource settings. This study demonstrates that technology has the potential to deliver learner-centered interactive video simulations that provide consistent content and uniform learning experiences that produced significant learning gains in complex content and had high acceptance from participants.

ORGANIZATION BACKGROUND

This case study is based on a public health project undertaken in Kenya by a non-governmental organization (NGO) based in the United States with an office and operations in Nairobi, Kenya. The project was developed to improve health outcomes for clients by improving the skills of Kenyan nurses. The NGO involved in planning and executing this project has served the public health needs of developing countries for almost 30 years. This NGO has worked in more than 50 countries with the support of the U.S. Agency for International Development, foundations, corporations and individuals. The NGO has provided technical support and assistance to ministries of health in several developing nations with a focus on improving the performance of health care providers, especially those focusing on reproductive health as a means to enhancing the overall health status of these countries.

Several agencies in Kenya participated in this project. The Kenyan Ministry of Health (MOH) was

DOI: 10.4018/978-1-61520-779-4.ch005

involved in this project from its inception providing critical information and guidance along the way. Representatives from this project met with members of the Nursing Council of Kenya on several occasions to inform them of the project and to solicit information about the appropriateness of the methodology, the design of the simulations and the technology used to ensure a good fit with the realities of nurses across Kenya. Meetings were also held with administrators and faculty from the Kenya Medical Teaching College. They confirmed the appropriateness of the overall design of the simulations and acknowledged the potential educational benefits of the approach used. A second NGO located in the United States with experience working on health issues in a number of developing countries collaborated on scripting and development of the interactive simulations. While one organization had responsibility for conducting this project, people from many organizations were involved along the way from the initial needs assessment to the creation of the simulations and development of the DVDs and continuing through evaluation. The author served as the project director.

SETTING THE STAGE

The health care status of people in Africa continues to lag behind the health care status of people living in other areas. Undoubtedly there are many factors that contribute to this including child nutrition problems, poverty, the low quality of many health care facilities and services, an inadequate number of health care workers, and several diseases that take a substantial toll including HIV/AIDS, acute respiratory infections, diarrhea, and malaria. In this regard, Kenya suffers as other nations in the region. While Kenya had been successful in achieving health gains during the 1980s and 1990s, this trend has reversed because of these problems and the rapid population growth Kenya experienced. Kenya has been losing skilled health care workers to other countries in recent years that offer better financial packages and to the private sector. The public sector doctor to population ratio in 2004 was 3:100,000; the nurse to population ration was 49:100,000 (Chankova, et al., 2006). These numbers fall short of what is desirable for providing adequate health care.

Like many countries, both developing and developed, Kenya has an imbalance in geographic location of health care workers. This is typical in sub-Saharan Africa where skilled health care workers are predominately located in urban areas. Within Kenya, 42 percent of the doctors and 30 percent of the nurses are located in Nairobi and the Rift Valley provinces alone while more rural areas have considerably fewer doctors and nurses (Chankova, et al., 2006). Throughout the country, over half of all health personnel are urban based with four-fifths of the doctors being in urban areas. This imbalance in health care workers serves to exacerbate the shortage in health care workers that Kenya and many other nations face.

This case began with the belief that technology when appropriately used can impact social problems that developing nations face. Health stands among the most critical problems that burden developing nations. While there are many dimensions to improving the health status of people in developing nations, having adequately trained health care providers is essential. Using technology to train and support health care providers who are scattered across a country can be beneficial, perhaps even essential, in ensuring better health status of people living in developing nations. In this case, personnel from a number of countries collaborated on the design and development of a technology-based solution to help Kenyan nurses learn how to better interact with their clients and thus improve the quality and impact of their services. The rationale for this project was to bring together expertise from people in several countries to focus on using available technology to deliver potent training to nurses located at different sites in Kenya. The problem was identified in Kenya by Kenyans and served to focus all effort in this project. The project director in the NGO who had been involved in training health care workers in several developing nation, including Kenya, and who had extensive background in technology use initially suggested the technology-based solution. A multinational team of people with experience training health care workers in developing nations undertook the development of the content.

Continuing Education

This project looked to portable DVD players as a hardware that holds promise for distributing highly portable lessons in the form of digital video with audio and text all under control of the learners. This creates a stand-alone training solution that appeared appropriate for the realities of Kenya in that it was easy to use, portable, battery powered, and capable of supporting rich interactive simulations that were video-based. As Hager, Russell & Fletcher (2008) noted, "Interactive scenarios and simulations are promising approaches to CE, particularly for skills development, whether the skill is a highly technical procedure, history taking, or a physical examination technique." (p.220). This technology allows an anytime, anyplace and any pace learning environment for continuing education of nurses. Most importantly, it would support the pedagogy that was required to accomplish important learning objectives, namely presenting learners with a typical situation they would encounter when working with a client, allowing them to select what they think is the most appropriate course of action, seeing the results unfold in terms of the client's reactions and receiving informative feedback from a highly skilled mentor who explains what happened and why, all on the DVD. This feedback from the mentor is a critical part of the simulations because the differences between an appropriate action by nurses when informing or counseling a client and an inappropriate action are subtle, not dramatic or obvious.

This solution follows from the need for continuing education that many health care workers in Africa have in order to deal effectively with the problems they face. However, opportunities for providing this continuing education are severely limited for a variety of reasons (Robinson, Dodson and Sewell, 1999; Ntiro and Mrema, 2003). Access to information for continuing education such as libraries, the Internet, and universities can be difficult in this region. Another consideration in planning for continuing education of health care workers in Africa is the costs of providing the instruction. We often fail to include the most important cost of continuing education – the opportunity cost of having a health care worker away from her clinic. In many areas, especially rural areas, the health care worker is the only person with any health care training. Thus, when she or he is away for a few days to attend a continuing education event, everyone in the community is without health care. Because health care workers in Africa face complex health problems in their clients, especially with the emergence of HIV/AIDS, they often require additional training in the form of continuing education. Yet the costs of continual health education are often prohibitive and the appropriateness of traditional teaching methods are questionable. As Ntiro and Mrema (2003) note, "It is clear that rural healthcare providers - the most important asset of the healthcare system are increasingly 'disconnected' from essential learning, knowledge, and information. As a result, the quality of the care they provide suffers." p28. Furthermore, traditional classroom-based methods consisting primarily of lectures are less appropriate for teaching problem solving skills and client-provider interactions, both of which are important for health care workers. "Traditional lecture-based CE has proven to be largely ineffective in changing health professional performance and in improving patient care. Lecture formats are employed excessively relative to their demonstrated value." (Hager, Russell & Fletcher, 2008, p. 220)

CASE DESCRIPTION

Typically nurses in Kenya, as in many countries, would have to travel to a city, often the capital city, to take a continuing education course. Usually the course was taught by lecture, possibly accompanied by demonstration. This "standard" approach to meeting the continuing education needs of nurses has several limitations that constrain its appropriateness. Nurses have to leave their clinics and villages and travel some distance to attend continuing education events. They incur not only travel and per diem expenses, but often they leave people in their villages without anyone to care for them if a medical situation arose while they were away for the continuing education. The lack of flexibility in delivery of traditional continuing education ties up the health care workers for several days including the travel time and the workshop time. It also fails to recognize that within any group of nurses participating in a continuing education event there may be large variability in their background knowledge and skill. This variability makes the "one size fits all" approach to instruction problematic as some participants already know what is being "taught" while other participants may lack the necessary prerequisites to understand the new content. Even when the content is appropriate for the average nurse, the variability found within the group attending any continuing education event is typically such that the content is too elementary in some cases because it is already known to some and too advanced in other cases because some do not arrive with the necessary background knowledge to benefit from the new instruction.

In this case study we sought to develop a different approach that would use technology to alleviate some of these common problems associated with continuing medical education. As Ntiro and Mrema (2003) noted, "ICTs can bring learning resources and information to the learners, instead of making the learners travel to the places of learning. This allows health workers to learn in their own workplace and in their own time." (p. 2). They list four reasons that ICTs add value to continuing medical education. These are: 1) ICTs make continuing medical education more efficient, 2) ICTs make continuing medical education more demand responsive, 3) ICTs can make continuing medical education more sustainable by reducing costs and helping scale up training for all health workers, and 4) ICTs make participation more enjoyable and motivating for learners (Ntiro and Mrema, 2003). Traditional training approaches fail to offer these benefits, and thus are questionable for continuing medical education in many situations.

Rationale

If we are to improve the quality of healthcare in this area of the world, then we must address the continuing education needs of front-line health care providers. Without continuing medical education, health care workers experience a decline in knowledge and skill, have higher professional dissatisfaction, have lower morale, and exhibit a lack of commitment and reduced interest in their work (Ntiro and Mrema, 2003). With shortages of health care workers, it is even more important to support and sustain existing health care professionals with continuing medical education. Without this continuing medical education, the healthcare workers can become disconnected from the essential knowledge and skills that support effective practices. Continuing medical education is also the best, and often only, way to infuse new information about health practices into the care that healthcare workers provide.

There are two key elements to consider: 1) what knowledge and skill do nurses require that would enable them to produce better health outcomes in their patients/clients, and 2) what is the best way to enable nurses to acquire this knowledge and skill? The first of these two questions involves conducting some form of *needs assessment*. The second of these two questions involves determining the most appropriate form of *training delivery*. The first of these two is as, if not more, important than the second. However, we often fail to systematically attend to either, especially needs assessment. This project began with a careful needs assessment and identification of the knowledge and skill that was often missing in health care workers.

Continuing Education Challenge

The principal challenge to providing continuing education to health care workers is to identify gaps in the knowledge and/or skill that the health care workers have which limit their acceptable performance and provision of quality health care services. This recognizes there are two prerequisites conditions before undertaking training of health care workers: 1) the training must focus on areas in which the provision of services is inadequate, and 2) this inadequate provision of services must arise as a result of the health care workers' lack of knowledge and/or skill. If there is not evidence of inadequate performance that inhibits the provision of services to clients, then investing in training is an unwise waste of time and budget. If there is evidence of inadequate performance, but this problem is caused by something other than a lack of knowledge or skill, then providing training is unlikely to be a successful solution. Thus, before initiating a training program we believe that it is important to document that there is a real discrepancy in the performance of health care workers and this discrepancy arises because they lack necessary knowledge and/or skill. If so, then carefully designed that adds this knowledge and/or skill can lead to successful results. When the instructional content is based on locally identified needs, the instruction has the potential to upgrade the knowledge and skills of health care providers in critical areas that can impact the quality of health care while attending to the economic and social realities of their communities.

Training Delivery

Traditional training delivery approaches for providing continuing education are not sufficient for a variety of reasons including access and cost. The use of information and computing technologies (ICTs) offers an approach that has the potential to provide access to continuing education in rural areas of Africa. Further, when integrated with appropriate pedagogy, ICTs can form a robust learning environment allowing health care providers an opportunity to learn when they have time available at their own workplace while progressing at a pace that is comfortable and appropriate for them. They have the opportunity to interact with the instructional materials delivered through ICTs when they have time available in their clinics. There can be a striking difference in the costs of providing continuing education in the form of traditional residential training and continuing education delivered as distance education by ICTs. In a report on using ICTs for continuing medical education in Kenya, Nduba and Kinyua (2003) state that the cost of distance education for continuing medical education is a sixth of the costs of residential training.

Technology Concerns

We formulated a set of considerations that were necessary for effective delivery of the continuing medical education to nurses in Kenya. The instruction had to be delivered to the nurses at their locations without requiring travel on their part. The intent of this was to enable the nurses to stay in their villages and clinics so that they were available to clients who had any medical needs. We also wanted to eliminate or severely reduce the costs associated with providing continuing education. These costs include travel, housing, and per diem costs and especially the opportunity costs of nurses not being available. We wanted to formulate a technological-based delivery that would adjust to the variable starting points in terms of the knowledge and skills the nurses would bring to the training. That is, we wanted to have an adaptable instructional method that could accommodate the needs of nurses who had different background knowledge with regards to the teaching objectives so that no nurse would be being "taught" that which she already knows and no nurse would be "taught" that for which she is not adequately prepared. Further, the technology would have to be able to function effectively in rural areas of Kenya being used by persons who were by not regular technology users and likely would not have used ICTs other than possibly mobile phones. We recognized that the technology had to be easily used without training. Otherwise this defeats the intent of reducing the time nurses had to spend away from their clinics and clients. It is not realistic to require that nurses spend half a day or so in order to learn an operating system so they could use a laptop computer to complete a computer-based lesson.

It is not realistic to expect nurses in rural areas of Kenya to complete an online course delivered via e-learning. Despite progress with connectivity, large areas do not have Internet access. Indeed, parts of the country do not have dependable access to electricity. Thus, many technology options that are typical in distance education programs in other more developed parts of the world may not be feasible in rural Kenya. The technology approach needed to involve the concept of mobile learning, or m-learning, using small portable devices rather than e-learning because of the lack of computers and connectivity as well as the need for flexible locations.

Finally, we recognized that to be effective the training would have to extend considerably beyond disseminating information to healthcare workers. As Kanouse and Jacoby (1988) noted, simply providing information to healthcare workers is rarely sufficient to cause any change in their practices. Indeed, in evaluating the impact of continuing medical education, Davis et al. (1999) indicated that lectures by themselves do not play a significant role in changing physician performance or improving care received by patients. They noted that role-playing and practice sessions were more effective in changing these outcomes.

Needs Assessment

For a training intervention to be successful, whether it uses technology or not, the focus of the training should be on clearly identified knowledge or skill gaps on part of the people being trained. In the present project we conducted a needs assessment working with a variety of stakeholders in Kenya including governmental officials at the ministerial level and a national nurses association. Through systematic needs assessment two areas of need were identified for health care workers: working with clients who are at risk for HIV/AIDS and clients who require counseling related to reproductive health issues. Both of these needs require health care workers to understand complex issues and interact with clients in subtle ways due to the emotional content. Developing skill in interacting with clients on these issues is not likely to be accomplished in a passive learning environment such as a lecture.

Instructional Environment

Developing client-provider interaction skills requires an instructionally rich environment in which a health care provider can see the fine differences between appropriate interactions with clients regarding HIV/AIDS and those less appropriate interactions. Such an environment would allow the health care worker to see possible provider-client interactions, to select which interaction she thinks is more appropriate, and to receive detailed feedback. In short, the optimal pedagogy should include video-based simulations that show health care workers interacting with clients in a variety of ways some of which are better than others. The health care worker should choose the best way to interact with the client at that particular moment and see the result. A mentor should provide expert feedback to the health care worker on her choices and explain why certain choices produce better outcomes. This is consistent with the comments of Leach and Fletcher (2008) who stated,

A patient is seen, inevitable ambiguities are encountered, hypotheses are formed, and refuted or accepted, an intervention is accomplished, and an outcome occurs. This process repeated a thousand times constitutes the physician's work. Learning what will improve patient care must accommodate this reality. Learning, once removed from reality and composed of lectures, goals, and objectives, is anemic by comparison and, not surprisingly, has been considered to be relatively ineffective (p. 1300).

The underlying model in this project recognized that effective instruction requires more than simple transfer of information. We relied on a constructivist model that holds that learning should be an active process in which the learner has the opportunity to build more substantial knowledge structures through interacting with realistic situations he or she has, or will, encounter and making choices about how to proceed. The learner decides where and when to learn as well as the pace at which he or she feels comfortable. The challenges presented by the instruction should be realistic to the learners forcing them into more difficult areas while providing scaffolding to support them. Mistakes should be expected and seen not as failures but rather as a natural byproduct of extending into a new area of knowledge. The role of feedback is essential in helping the learners understand the nature of their mistakes and thereby build deeper understandings of the knowledge. Someone with more experience and skill should be available to explain any mistakes to the learner. Throughout the process, the learner should be in control of what to do next in order to facilitate his or her understanding. We drew from concepts associated with the cognitive apprenticeship approach to learning (Wilson, Jonassen & Cole, 1993). This asserts that we should teach tacit, heuristic knowledge as well as "textbook" knowledge and that we should teach in ways that the knowledge is used in real life. We should model and explain what we are teaching as well as provide coaching and feedback while scaffolding the learner. This view informed our instructional environment and shaped the pedagogical approach created in this project.

The simulations developed in this project were closely based on actual situations encountered regularly by nurses in Kenya including common mistakes made by these nurses. A mentor was created and included in the simulations to coach, provide feedback and explain the circumstances faced in the simulation much as a skilled worker would help a novice worker who was apprenticed to him or her. After the nurse who was learning with the simulation would make a choice, this mentor would explain and show why that was a good choice or point out some problems with that choice if it was not the most desirable one. The mentor would take the nurse back through his or her selection to provide careful, specific feedback followed by encouragement. The learner would then have the option to go back and reexamine that part of the simulation making a different choice. By situating the instruction in real cases the nurses face, or will face, giving the nurses choices for different courses of action in the simulation, and providing elaborate feedback and coaching from a skilled mentor, the instruction in this project was planned to be as effective as possible in teaching subtle job-related skills that are necessary for success.

Technology Components

Effective training would have to be delivered by ICT to achieve such an instructionally rich environment available to health care workers at their work locations. Internet-based training delivery was not an option because of the lack of Internet availability in large areas outside major cities. Requiring Internet connectivity in order to be able to participate in the continuing education offered in this project would exclude many, if not most, of the health care workers we desired to reach. Requiring stand-alone computer-based delivery was also not a realistic option due to relatively high costs of multimedia laptop computers that could support the delivery of video-based simulations. In addition, any use of laptop computers would require a major user-training effort to enable all nurses to use the operating systems and the laptops. Thus, two ICT options that would likely be considered in some countries, especially more developed countries, were not realistic in rural Kenya.

Rather than online instruction or stand-alone computer-based training, we used small, portable DVD players that were battery operated and could be solar powered. Lack of dependable electricity as well as lack of Internet availability in certain areas of Kenya made other ICT options inappropriate. The DVD players were standard consumer electronics items typical of those found in electronics stores. They had a color screen and basic start/stop/advance controls as well as the option to go to menus to navigate. These did not require any Internet connectivity, as all the material was on the DVDs. Because the controls for a DVD player are so simple, we did not have to provide any IT training that would have been the case had we used computers. The per unit costs for DVD players were considerably less than for personal computers, and the video quality was quite high. The health care workers had only to be able to start/stop the DVD and make selections from among four or fewer choices when viewing the scenarios. The portable DVD players supported all of this while being small, infinitely portable, easily stored and battery powered. The batteries could be recharged with small solar collectors or by plugging them in if electricity was available. Using portable DVD players allowed the learning to take place at anytime, anyplace and any pace thus proving flexibility in the learning approach. While use of portable DVD players is somewhat different from the current concept of mobile learning, or m-learning, they share many common elements including the use of small, portable devices that allow learning to take place in a flexible manner from anyplace at anytime. In discussing the role of m-learning for Nigeria, Boyinbode, and Akinyede (2008) distinguish m-learning from e-learning by stating that m-learning can be used everywhere at every time while e-learning cannot. They further state that m-learning uses smaller and lighter devices that are portable and less expensive. They list cell phones, smart phones, PDAs, notebook and tablet computers as mobile learning devices. While the DVDs produced and used in this project were distributed and played on portable DVD players, they could also be played on notebook or tablet computers, and thus would be consistent with this definition of mobile learning. The key for us was to create a highly portable and flexible learning environment that could be used when and where necessary by nurses.

Development of the Simulations

In the present study two interactive video simulations were developed to show scenarios of a nurse and a client interacting in which the nurse could make several choices regarding what to do next at several points during the scenario. While all these choices were plausible, one choice depicted the recommended best approach for dealing with the situation that was unfolding. The other options depicted less desirable alternatives. Some of these less desirable alternatives showed the nurse in the scenario doing something that would be better if she had not done it or failing to do something that would have improved the situation. Both options of doing something less appropriate or failing to do something that was more appropriate were based on mistakes that nurses often made in their practices. Once the nurse made a choice in the simulation, she would see the scenario continue according to that choice. After making a choice and seeing the result play out in terms of what the clients would do, a mentor comes on to explain what happened and why as well as to give pointers to the nurse. The nurse has the option to go back through a simulation multiple times and change her choices to see the results from taking a different approach. All events shown in the simulations were based on the experiences and observations of nursing and medical personnel in Kenya who served as advisors to this project to ensure that the simulations would be realistic.

The scenarios that form the basis for these simulations followed from the needs assessment and were developed through consultation and discussion with nurses in Kenya and representatives of national nursing organizations. To ensure technical accuracy of the content, both nurses and physicians reviewed the content. Instructional design specialists created scripts that reflected common situations seen by nurses in Kenya and that demonstrated both appropriate and inappropriate interactions. Feedback was developed for each interaction that the health care provider could select to explain why that choice was appropriate or less appropriate. The roles of the health care provider, the client and the mentor were scripted. These scripts underwent a thorough review process in Kenya and in the USA where they were produced. Prior to filming the scenarios, the scripts were pilot tested in Kenya to refine any aspect of the scenarios. This pilot-testing included nurses as well as several content specialists to check for technical accuracy. Professional actors were used in the filming to ensure the scripts would be enacted in a credible manner that would be engaging.

Evaluation

This learning approach was field-tested in a feasibility study that used a combination of quantitative and qualitative methods with 17 nurses in Kenya. This was a case study in naturalistic settings. Ten of these nurses were female and seven were male. These nurses were located in medical centers or clinics in seven different geographical areas of Kenya. None of the nurses had seen or used a DVD player before. An evaluation consultant observed 10 of these nurses as they participated in the technology-based approach and completed field notes on their use of the simulations and the DVD players. The remaining 7 participants were given the DVDs with the simulations and the portable DVD player to complete the lessons on their own. All participants, both those who were observed while completing the lessons and those who completed the lessons on their own, were interviewed following their use of this technology-based learning approach. In addition all participants completed a pre-test and a post-test to measure knowledge gains.

Results

Observations and interviews confirmed that nurses saw the learning approach and technology as easy-to-use, convenient and flexible. They reported that this learning method was especially effective because they were in control of when they engaged in the learning process, and they did not have to leave their facilities to update their skills. For most providers, the DVD player was easy to operate, although a few said that at first it wasn't, mostly because they were not familiar with the technology. On the other hand, all nurses agreed that the instructions on the DVD screens were easy to follow.

Most agreed that the simulations were easy to use and that the distinctions/differences between options were clear, although several found the options in one of the simulations more similar and therefore it was harder to distinguish which were the best options. This was consistent with a design goal of the simulations to show subtle mistakes and missed opportunities when interact-

Figure 1. Scores on test of knowledge

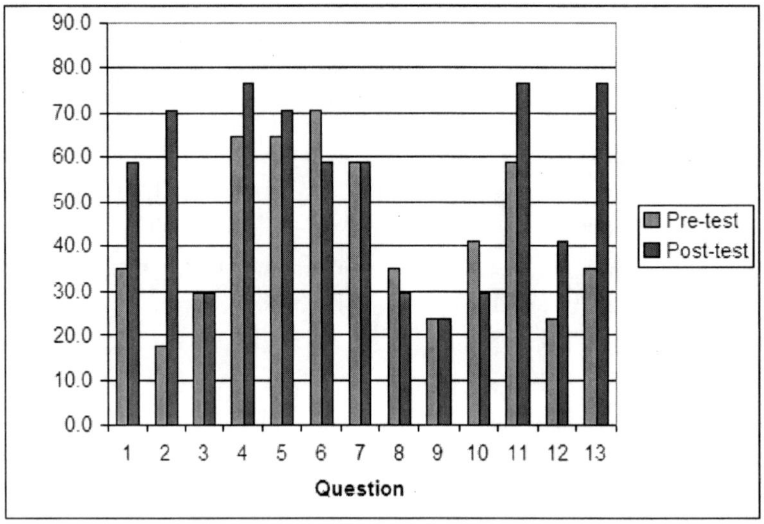

ing with clients, since this was the nature of most of the mistakes nurses made. All the nurses had previously been trained and had experience interacting with clients, so showing obvious mistakes as alternatives in the simulations would have no pedagogical value. These nurses were not making these mistakes; rather they were making more subtle mistakes when interacting with clients. The initial draft of the simulations had greater differences between the correct options in the simulations and the alternatives. During the initial review of the draft scripts and in the pilot-testing this was pointed out as being a problem because the correct choice would be obvious to any nurse with experience or training. Plus, the incorrect options did not reflect actions these nurses were taking in their practices. Based on this feedback, the scripts for the simulations were modified to show incorrect options that were less obvious and showed courses of actions that nurses were taking that could be improved upon. Thus, we were not surprised that nurses reported that it was difficult at times to distinguish the most desirable option in the simulation.

The participants indicated that the depiction of the stories shown on each DVD was believable, because they showed situations that they encounter in their daily practice. This is the result of careful planning and collaboration with others in Kenya to ensure that the simulations were high fidelity and represented typical nurses and typical clients. The circumstances of the simulated client reflected situations in Kenya as did the content and tone of the interactions. In short, the participants indicated that the simulations were believable because considerable care went into the design of the simulations so that they were realistic.

Analysis of scores on criterion-referenced pre-tests and post-tests showed an average gain of 42.6% as a result of completing the interactive simulations. The pre-test and post-test scores are shown in Figure 1. These results confirm the information collected through observation and interviews that this approach was effective for the nurses in terms of producing learning gains while allowing them the convenience of staying at their location and being available to clients at their clinics.

Specific Comments

All nurses agreed that the interactive experience held their attention and interest throughout. They indicated that they had to be very attentive so they would not miss any important points and because they were curious to know what would happen next. As one nurse said, "You are most interested to see how your colleague [in the story] solved the problem" and "you're yearning to go to the next [scene], to know what will happen."

Watching the different options unfold allowed participants to consider the possible range of options that a nurse has in any given situation. One nurse noted, "...you are able to identify the good and bad things, ...you can see where you have gone wrong." Several nurses mentioned that some of the options were very similar and had very subtle differences that made the selection difficult. This was intended as part of the design of the simulations to ensure pedagogical value.

Choosing from various options allowed nurses to control the learning experience and to learn from the feedback for each option. A nurse mentioned that, "[when counseling a client] you may have started well and then made a mistake along the way", and indicated that the options helped him see those mistakes. Another nurse said that choosing from different options allowed her to learn at her own pace because "you can pause and repeat, so you are able to choose, you can rewind and fast forward so you can get the story properly." All nurses agreed that taking notes helped them think about the options they had to choose from, writing down the strong and weak points of each option.

All nurses indicated that the mentor's feedback about the options was clear and appropriate. Many liked that the mentor explained the different nurse behaviors in the scenes by showing clips from each scene. They liked that the mentor used simple language, "she was using a simple language that one can understand. After talking [she] was able to give us a review of how the provider was behaving with the client." They felt that the mentor's feedback was appropriate for each option, and it helped them understand why some nurse behaviors were more desirable than others.

Interacting with the stories improved participants' understanding of counseling, as they gave them examples showing how important it is to ensure clients' rights such as privacy and confidentiality. The simulations showed the importance of discussing sensitive subjects with clients. One nurse said, "sometimes when you found an approach with a client, and she's not comfortable, you tend to run away from it, now I can go directly but in a different way." In addition, nurses added that they had learned how important it is to listen to the client and ask questions instead of telling them everything, "first before I used to sort of teach, but it [meaning the simulation] has helped me ask what somebody knows and I build on these most appropriate knowledge."

All nurses agreed that they would be comfortable using a DVD-based program for independent learning. One mentioned that this would enhance and reinforce the learning, "what you see you don't forget." Another added, "it's a good method of learning, to introduce [to] the community outside, a good method of providing education." All would highly recommend this interactive learning approach to their colleagues for many reasons -- because of its ease of operation, the convenience to the nurse, and the ability to watch again any scene that was not clear. As one said, she would recommend this approach to her colleagues because, "it has so much to learn about at very reasonable cost, you don't have to be absent from your facility to learn."

The overall acceptability of this learning approach was very good. All the nurses indicated that they had learned a lot from both simulations. It also, "...discourages you from the practices that are not appropriate. It helps to understand your client better in all aspects..." In addition, it is portable, easy to use, and saves the health care provider a lot time, as he or she does not need to leave their facility to attend a training workshop. Lastly, "it doesn't require a lot of technical know-how and it can be used in the office or outdoors." All participants indicated they would like to use this method of learning again on a new topic.

Participants indicated that the best aspect of this approach is that "it is easy to operate, it is portable, rechargeable, can be used with no power, and in outreach services", and whenever they have free time. One nurse added that she "… took advantage of the breaks between clients to watch, [she] was able to watch both in the time given [four days]. It's quite handy, you can use it at your own convenient time." Also, "it is time saving, it is practical, you see what happens, it is convenient, can be used without plugging it in, and easy to carry."

Most participants would not add, change, or delete elements in this learning tool. One suggested making the simulations available via the web, although not every nurse would have access to the Internet. One participant suggested that in the event this methodology was used in the future, it would be a good idea to provide participants with contact information in case anyone has questions.

This learning experience made all nurses think about how they counsel their clients. Finally, most nurses said that they had learned a lot with the simulation. In the words of one provider, "it was quite an enlightening interactive session and will help improve the services that [he] offers." Specific comments included: 1) "You feel comfortable and independent. It gives you a chance to go back/replay where one doesn't understand fully."; 2) "It is easiest to learn because you are seeing the play, and experiencing it practically, instead of someone giving a lecture. Seeing it goes straight to your head."; 3) "I can learn anywhere, for example, at my workplace or at my home."; and 4) "The feedback was constructive, including what was done well; replay of selected behaviors to justify views was very good."

In summary, some of the comments mentioned by nurses during the interviews were:

- Both simulations are very educational and highlight aspects they have overlooked.
- The simulations were very easy to use, and the instructions were very clear and easy to follow.
- They don't have to leave their facilities to update their skills, and they can watch the simulations whenever they have time.
- The experience of choosing between different options and hearing the mentor's feedback allowed them to understand which nurse behaviors are most desirable.
- The simulations are believable and show situations they've encountered in their own practice.
- All the participants liked the mentor and considered that she used very clear language when giving feedback.

Two findings are particularly noteworthy: 1) all the nurses would like very much to use this technology for other topics, and 2) as a result of participating in this project and interacting with the simulations, all the nurses indicated that it made them think about how they counsel their clients. After completing the interactive simulations, the nurses said they are considering making the following changes in their behavior:

- Spending more time with their clients: "…I should take more time with my clients, not be in a hurry", as well as making sure to write a referral letter to a VCT center instead of a brief note."
- Asking the client questions to better understand the client's situation: as one nurse responded, "…When I am … with the client, I [should] put myself at her level, ask questions that she can understand easily, not be judgmental."
- Taking more time after a procedure to counsel the client on FP, STIs, and HIV/AIDS, as one nurse said:"…especially in PAC services, I should take more time

especially after the procedure to explain in more detail especially STIs, FP, and HIV/AIDS."

- Letting clients decide on her own whether to use a contraceptive method or be tested for STIs or HIV/AIDS: "we should be giving her the reasons why we think she should visit and let her come up with that decision herself."
- Reassuring the clients about confidentiality: "during counseling, [she] know[s] confidentiality is good."
- Ensuring privacy as well as an uninterrupted counseling session: "it puts the patient and you off balance if you are interrupted. I will be locking the front door, now I will lock the door, it means a lot to you as counselor and client."

The evaluation indicated that nurses increased their knowledge a considerable amount through using these interactive simulations even though all were trained nurses with experience. They were quite favorable about the learning approach that combined portable DVD players as the delivery approach with interactive simulations as the pedagogical approach. They were enthusiastic and engaged while completing the simulations and highly recommend this mode of instruction to others. They articulated what they saw as the advantages of this approach, and interestingly their comments closely parallel what is said in the literature on technology-based learning. As a result of participating in these simulations, the nurses indicated specific behaviors on their part that they now plan to change so as to be more appropriate when interacting with clients.

SOLUTIONS AND RECOMMENDATIONS

Innovative learning approaches that use flexible delivery methods, such as technology-based learning using simulations, when applied judiciously hold great promise as an alternative or supplement to traditional classroom-based training in low-resource settings. This study demonstrates that technology has the potential to deliver learner-centered interactive video simulations that provide consistent content and uniform, but adaptable, learning experiences that produce significant learning gains in complex content. This project had the advantage of allowing nurses who were unable to leave their villages for any extended period due to economic or social reasons to participate in training in a form that was sensitive to their needs and consistent with their circumstances.

To an extent, this study affirms that persons from different countries who focus their energies and expertise on a specific problem or circumstances in one country can conduct projects successfully. Complex training problems may require complex learning solutions that employ technology. There may be significant benefits from involving personnel from several countries in creating the technology-based solution rather than drawing solely on the resources found within any single country. Kenyans played an important role in the present project, but persons from other countries were instrumental. These include the initial conceptualization for this project which was done in the United States, identification of the problem by Kenyans, content expertise from Kenyans, as well as a nurse from Senegal, script development from a person who had lived and worked in Colombia and another who had lived and worked in Botswana, technical support from developers in the United States, and a professional actor originally from Tanzania now living in the United States. The project director who had worked extensively throughout South and Central America, Africa and Asia on technology-based projects was from the United States. Persons in Kenya were essential in providing editorial guidance and approvals of the content of the DVDs. The development happened both in Kenya and the United States with the filming done on a sound stage in the United States designed from photographs of several Kenyan clinics and using artifacts from those clinics. The decision to film in the United States was based primarily on cost estimates from both countries. It was less expensive to film and produce the DVDs in the United States. That the participants viewing the DVDs indicated that the people and settings were typical of those where they work affirms that the sound stage set and actors recreated a typical Kenyan clinic.

From our experience as well as from considerable prior research, it seems clear that the emphasis should be on effective instructional design practices and appropriate pedagogy rather solely on the technology used. We have serious reservation about taking existing content whether from print or some other source and putting it onto newer technologies and expecting more effective instruction and greater learning outcomes. This is rarely the case despite however stunning the technologies may be because it is the pedagogy that drives the learning; the technology just delivers it (Clark, 1994; Hannum, 2007). For technology to be effective in instructional situations, the technology should be directed at a documented need caused by a lack of knowledge and/or skill, and the instruction delivered by technology should be based on sound empirically-based principles following an instructional design approach. Otherwise, you usually wind up with something that may look interesting, even inviting, but which will produce little or no impact. The problems are too great and resources are too scarce to follow a wishful thinking approach when using technology in learning environments in Africa by simply placing content on some technology for delivery.

In an article on m-learning in Africa, Brown (2005) indicated that mobile learning has the potential to bring learning to a wider audience making learning more available and accessible than was the case with e-learning. Drawing on their work in South Africa and Kenya, Traxler and Leach (2006) noted that often the physical infrastructure has a low density of population, poor roads and transportation systems, poor landline phone networks, unreliable electricity, little Internet bandwidth outside cities, and little PC usage. Against this backdrop, they see potential for mobile learning solutions. Others, such as Brown (2005), have proposed specific models for m-learning in Africa. Sharples, Taylor and Vavoula (2005) offer a broad definition of mobile learning that includes several elements. First, learners are on the move rather than at fixed locations, and learning happens across time and space. Second, a large amount of learning happens outside the classroom often in the learners' homes or offices. Third, to be effective mobile learning should be based on effective practices that see learning as an active process of building knowledge and skill through practice within a supportive community. Fourth, mobile learning should recognize the wide array of technology used today by the general population and especially by young adults. This definition is noteworthy because it extends beyond the technology itself.

This view was embraced in the present study as we focused more on effective pedagogy and learning than technology itself. Traxler (2007) explores the nature and possibilities of m-learning. While recognizing that mobile learning is still a new and relatively immature field, he nevertheless describes mobile learning as having enormous potential when coupled with distance learning. In a modest way, the present project serves to demonstrate that this can indeed be the case.

REFERENCES

Boyinbode, O. K., & Akinyede, R. O. (2008). Mobile Learning: An Application of Mobile and Wireless Technologies in Nigerian Learning System. *International Journal of Computer Science and Network Security*, *8*(11), 386–392.

Brown, T. H. (2005). Toward a model of m-Learning for Africa. *International Journal on E-Learning*, *4*(3), 299–315.

Chankova, S., Kombe, G., Muchiri, S., Decker, C., Kimani, G., & Pielemeier, N. (2006). *Rising to the challenges of human resources for health in Kenya: Developing empirical evidence for policy making.* Partners for Health Reformplus Project: Bethesda, MD. Retrieved May 30, 2009 from www.phrplus.org/pubs/Tech101_fin.pdf

Clark, R. E. (1994). Media will never influence learning. *Educational Technology Research and Development*, *42*(2), 21–29. doi:10.1007/BF02299088

Davis, D., O'Brien, M. A., Freemantle, N., Wolf, F. M., Mazmanian, P., & Taylor-Vaisey, A. (1999). Impact of formal continuing medical education: Do conferences, workshops, rounds, and other traditional continuing education activities change physician behavior or health care outcomes? *Journal of the American Medical Association*, *282*, 867–874. doi:10.1001/jama.282.9.867

Hager, M., Russell, S., & Fletcher, S. W. (Eds.). (2008). Continuing education in the health professions: improving healthcare through lifelong learning. Bermuda, NY: Josiah Macy, Jr. Foundation.

Hannum, W. H. (2007). When computers teach: A review of the instructional effectiveness of computers. *Educational Technology*, *47*(2), 5–13.

Kanouse, D. E., & Jacoby, I. (1988). When does information change practitioners' behavior? *International Journal of Technology Assessment in Health Care*, *4*(1), 27–33. doi:10.1017/S0266462300003214

Leach, D. C., & Fletcher, S. W. (2008). Perspectives on continuing education in the health professions: improving health care through lifelong learning. *Chest*, *134*(6), 1299–1303. doi:10.1378/chest.08-1022

Nduba, S., & Kinyu, M. (2003). *Consultative Meeting on Continuing Medical Education and the role of Information and Communication Technologies in Kenya*, AMREF International Training Centre. Retrieved May 30, 2009 from http://www.healthcomms.org/pdf/CME-ICTs-Kenya--report.pdf

Ntiro, S., & Mrema, J. (2003). *Information and Communication Technologies and Continuing Medical Education in East and Southern Africa.* Report of a Conference held in Moshi, Tanzania 8-10 April 2003.

Robinson, G., Dobson, M. & Sewell, J. (1999). Using C&IT for Continuing Medical Education in Africa - a pilot project in Zimbabwe. *Journal of Medical Internet Research*, Jul–Sep; 1(suppl1): e67.

Traxler, J. (2007). Defining, Discussing, and Evaluating Mobile Learning: The moving finger writes and having writ… *International Review of Research in Open and Distance Learning, 8*(2), Traxler, J., & Leach, J. (2006). Innovative and Sustainable Mobile Learning in Africa. Paper presented at the Fourth IEEE International Workshop on Wireless, Mobile and Ubiquitous Technology in Education (ICHIT'06).

Wilson, B. G., Jonassen, D. H., & Cole, P. (1993). Cognitive approaches to instructional design. In G. M. Piskurich (Ed.), The ASTD Handbook of Instructional Technology (pp. 21.1-21.22). New York: McGraw-Hill.

ADDITIONAL READING

Ally, M. (2009). Mobile Learning: Transforming the Delivery of Education and Training. Edmonton: Athabasca University Press.

Beldarrain, Y. (2006). Distance education trends: Integrating new technologies to foster student interaction and collaboration. *Distance Education, 27*(2), 139–153. doi:10.1080/01587910600789498

Clark, R. E., Yates, K., Early, S., & Moulton, K. (2009). An Analysis of the Failure of Electronic Media and Discovery-based learning: Evidence for the performance benefits of Guided Training Methods. In Silber, K. H. & Foshay, R. (Eds.). Handbook of Training and Improving Workplace Performance, Volume I: Instructional Design and Training Delivery. Somerset, NJ: Wiley.

Donner, J. (2008). Research Approaches to Mobile Use in the Developing World: A Review of the Literature. *The Information Society, 24*(3), 140–159. doi:10.1080/01972240802019970

Kukulska-Hulme, A., & Traxler, J. (2005). Mobile Learning: A Handbook for Educators and Trainers, London, Routledge.

Lee, M. J. W., & Chan, A. (2007). Pervasive, lifestyle-integrated mobile learning for distance learners: an analysis and unexpected results from a podcasting study. *Open Learning, 22*(3), 201–218.

Sharples, M., Taylor, J., & Vavoula, G. (2005). *Towards a Theory of Mobile Learning*. In Proceedings of mLearn 2005 Conference, Cape Town, South Africa, 2005.

Traxler, J., & Kukulska-Hulme, A. (2005). In Mobile Learning in Developing Countries (G. Chin, Ed.). Vancouver, BC: Commonwealth of Learning.

Wright, C. R., Dhanarajan, G., & Reju, S. A. (2009). Recurring Issues Encountered by Distance Educators in Developing and Emerging Nations. *International Review of Research in Open and Distance Learning, 10*(1).

KEY TERMS AND DEFINITIONS

FP (Family Planning): Refers to an approach that allows individuals and couples to anticipate and attain their desired number of children and the spacing and timing of their births.

ICTs (Information and Communications Technologies): A generic term to refer to all the technologies for the manipulation and communication of information. This includes technologies for storing information such as flash drives and CD/DVD; technologies for broadcasting information such as radio and television; technologies for communicating sound, images and video such as cameras, telephones, & cellular phones; computer hardware technologies such as PCs (Personal Compouters) – laptops, servers, & mainframes; personal devices such as MP3 players & PDAs; all categories of software; and, of course, the Internet.

NGO (Non-Governmental Organization): A private non-profit organization separate from any governmental organization or agency that provides humanitarian aid or support to impoverished or economically underdeveloped nations.

PAC (Postabortion Care): Care provided when a medical problem develops following a spontaneous or induced abortion.

STI (Sexual Transmitted Infection): Refers to infections that are spread primarily through person-to-person sexual contact. There are more than 30 different sexually transmissible bacteria, viruses and parasites.

VCT (Voluntary Counseling and Testing): Program established in which people can voluntarily decide to be tested for HIV/AIDS and receive counseling about HIV/AIDS.

Chapter 6
Transnational Postgraduate Study for Development Workers: Using Technology to Bridge the Gap

Elizabeth A. Beckmann
The Australian National University, Australia

Patrick Kilby
The Australian National University, Australia

ABSTRACT

This case describes social, technological, economic and political factors impacting on transnational learning in the Master of Applied Anthropology and Participatory Development program at the Australian National University. Using the experiences of students working in areas of conflict, poverty and injustice across the world, this case shows how flexible delivery of postgraduate education not only allows development workers to continue their career progression while remaining fully active in the field, but also enables them to engage in stimulating high-level discourse with their development practitioner peers as they apply theory to practice. Giving development workers the opportunity to engage in advanced study in a stimulating and peer-supported learning environment without leaving home both enriches their career functionality and long-term prospects, and enhances their day-to-day work activities. As a bonus, host communities benefit from a development worker with greater access to expertise, experience and support, and a reduced sense of professional and/or cultural isolation.

ORGANISATION BACKGROUND

The Australian National University (ANU) was established uniquely in Canberra by a Federal Act of Parliament in 1946. Consistently ranked highly internationally (Center for World-Class Universities, Shanghai Jiao Tong University; Times Higher Education-QS World University Rankings), the ANU is one of Australia's most research-intensive universities, with a focus on research-led teaching in both its undergraduate and postgraduate teaching. Currently the University has about 14,000 students, including some 3,000 international students from 106 countries. As with all Australian higher education, tuition fees are charged for both domestic and international students. The ANU is essentially a single-campus university with a primary focus on face-to-face teaching, and—with notable exceptions

DOI: 10.4018/978-1-61520-779-4.ch006

such as the Migration Law and Practice program; involvement in the Australia Global Development Learning Network; and the Master of Applied Anthropology and Participatory Development, which is the focus of this case—has only recently started to engage more widely with issues of flexible delivery and open learning.

SETTING THE STAGE

The Masters in Applied Anthropology and Participatory Development: Advanced Study for Development Professionals

Australia's geographic and sociopolitical context has given rise to a strong relationship with countries of the Asia-Pacific region. This includes a major focus on supporting development in many of those countries. ANU's teaching in development studies dates back to the establishment of the National Centre for Development Studies under the vision of Sir John Crawford, one of the leading development experts of the 1960s, and a strong advocate for high level teaching and research in development.

One of the foremost programs in ANU's development studies stable is the Master of Applied Anthropology and Participatory Development (MAAPD, http://rspas.anu.edu.au/maapd/). Established in 2002, this program focuses on the application of critical social inquiry and participatory processes to the design, implementation, monitoring and evaluation of development activities. It helps students explore how to combine social perspectives and participatory practices with other forms of technical expertise in development work. The MAAPD draws on the significant regional and conceptual expertise that contributes to ANU's world-class reputation in anthropological studies and development policy, with lecturers coming from specialist areas such as the School of Archaeology and Anthropology, the Research School of Pacific and Asian Studies, and the Centre for Aboriginal Economic Policy Research. All eleven lecturers are active practitioners in the development field, so the MAAPD's practical focus on current issues is paramount.

The one year full-time-equivalent program—which offers a range of fifteen different courses—offers both a general program and optional specializations in 'gender and development', 'conflict and development', 'society and environment' and 'indigenous policy'. All students undertake core courses in social mapping and social impact, at least one advanced course in their specialization, and several electives. In educational terms, the program takes a strongly constructivist approach; students are encouraged and enabled to negotiate meaning in the context of their own experiences, and assessment is focused on real-life development problems (Cunningham, 1992; Mishra, 2002). The program's success is evidenced by testimonials from its alumni (MAAPD, 2009).

Cookson (2002) noted that the fastest-growing market sector in higher education is postgraduate education delivered online to people already working in the field of study. Professionals working on aid and development projects are among those who seek the benefits of postgraduate opportunities to engage in structured, critical reflection on their work, and to learn from their peers and specialists. Yet the dilemma of pursuing such study is clear: high quality programs in development studies are generally only available on-campus in universities in developed countries, so professional development generally comes at a high economic cost. Perhaps more important for many would-be students, however, and especially those working for non-government organizations, is the social and political cost of abandoning a specific development project and its associated community in order to study, a choice many aid workers are unwilling or unable to make.

Moreover, there are political and pedagogical tensions inherent in out-of-context teaching. Oxenham (1980, p.31) noted that institutions that teach development studies in developed countries prefer students who already have working experience in relevant contexts, and focus on issues pertinent to developing countries, yet actually teach those students in 'places quite divorced from the situations of their concern'. In Oxenham's (1980) controversial view, such institutions are thus 'promoting useless learning ... deny[ing] their students the full potential benefit of what they purport to be offering.' (p.31) Two possible defences—that students can 'use their remembrances of things past as satisfactory surrogates for immediate dialectic with reality' and/or 'adapt what has been learned to particular circumstances, when they get home'—are dismissed summarily: memories, Oxenham argues, are neither comprehensive nor reliable, and the harsh reality of students returning to a position as development worker gives them little opportunity for reflection, so 'the likelihood of their being able to incorporate a substantial proportion of their learning into their practice is severely curtailed.' (Oxenham, 1980, p.31).

These concerns are 'worth revisiting by anyone teaching or studying development studies today' (Devereux and Knowles, 2009). For institutions such as ANU, any development studies program must provide authenticity of both content and context. The MAAPD program certainly capitalizes on ANU's many highly regarded development studies practitioners and researchers, and the richness of cultural and linguistic diversity on its Canberra campus, which attracts many students. However, while many current or would-be development workers are grateful to have an opportunity to immerse themselves in full-time study on-campus, or at least to attend intensive on-campus anchor courses, this is clearly not a possibility for many. In designing and reviewing the MAAPD, therefore, lecturers have been mindful of these interacting social, political, economic and pedagogical factors—prospective students' needs; Oxenham's caveats for those teaching development studies out of context; and the potential learning opportunities available by having at least some students 'on-site' in real development settings.

CASE DESCRIPTION

Transnational Online Learning

In recent years, the MAAPD has taken advantage of new teaching technologies and online learning platforms, and the increasing ubiquity of the internet, to offer its professional study opportunities in blended mode on-campus and fully online off-campus. As a result of this opportunity, about half the MAAPD's 120 currently enrolled students are development workers based in countries such as Afghanistan, Bangladesh, Cambodia, Colombia, East Timor, Indonesia, Madagascar, Nepal, Panama, Thailand, Uganda, Uzbekistan, Vanuatu and Vietnam, as well as in remote Australian indigenous communities. There are also off-campus students living in other Australian cities, and in countries such as Britain, Canada and the United States, who are planning future careers in development. The benefits of this option are clear:

[After] 18 years of professional and volunteer work in the field of development, it was a dream come true to have such an opportunity [to study] amid the very busy schedule of fulltime work and the absence of similar options in Egypt. (Off-campus student, 2008)

... flexible delivery of the MAAPD enabled me to apply the learning directly to my work. Had I taken time off to attend full-time study in Canberra, I would not have had this opportunity to apply principles and practices from the coursework. (Off-campus student in Papua New Guinea, 2008)

... the inevitable infrastructure issues that come with living in a developing country ... make things even more challenging for those studying overseas [but] I'm very glad the course is offered

by distance or I probably would never have had the chance to take it. (Off-campus student in Vanuatu, 2009)

Unequivocally FANTASTIC! I am doing three courses (and working as well) so I can really testify how great it is to be able to do some self-paced online work. (Off-campus student in Australia, 2008)

Of course, in a demanding academic program at the postgraduate level, isolation from one's lecturers, fellow students and resources can be a significant disadvantage. It is therefore essential that the intended learning outcomes of MAAPD courses are as attainable by students off-campus as by those on-campus, and that the learning experiences of both groups are as rich as possible. Central to this has been the requirement to use effective and accessible learning technology (Volery and Lord, 2000), with the aim of facilitating deep learning (Marton and Säljö, 1976; Ramsden, 1992) that encourages adaptive and conceptual change (Trigwell, Prosser and Lyons, 1999).

Using Educational Technology

The MAAPD has been very successful since its inception. As transnational enrolments increased, more thought was given to ensuring the program met the needs of off-campus students. In 2008, therefore, the program's educational design was reviewed in the context of the ANU's Flexible Learning Project. We considered the likely technological constraints and realities for students in developing countries; the need to emphasize asynchronous interactions (given the many time zones of students' locations); the technologies available on secure online platforms at ANU, including the capabilities of our learning management systems (LMS); and the way in which these technologies could be used effectively to replicate the highly participatory on-campus teaching.

We aimed for 'instruction-related elements... [that] enable interaction with and among students, and between students and the content to be learned' (Cookson, 2002), with a focus on engaging learners 'in more meaningful learning activities' rather than on the distance learning technology itself (Kimball, 2001). As few MAAPD courses are presented solely online or solely on-campus, we recognized that supporting combined on-/off-campus learning communities effectively would require lecturers to adopt new approaches to managing teaching and learning processes, and to seek out the qualitative advantages of the technologies (Kimball, 2001).

Teaching activities were redesigned to provide, as far as possible, authentic and equivalent learning experiences for both on- and off-campus students, through a more flexible and student-focused use of educational technologies available at ANU. This saw the introduction, or more effective use, of:

- course-specific password-protected websites on ANU's LMS (WebCT 4.1 from 2004 to 2008, Moodle 1.9 for 2009) providing all resources (e.g. lectures, readings) online;
- resources available in various formats (e.g. streamed and downloadable audio and narrated slide presentations for lectures; readings as pdf files or via URLs, online or on CD-ROMs) to meet students' needs under different technology and access constraints;
- small- or large-group asynchronous online discussion forums—in 2008 these were hosted on group-specific password-protected websites on ANU's online collaboration environment Alliance (Sakai), using the 'Forums' tool; in 2009 these were in group-specific formats on course sites hosted within ANU's LMS Wattle (Moodle), using the 'Discussion' tool; and
- assessment strategies that provided engaging tasks (constructively aligned with

Table 1. Student surveys 2008 and 2009: response rates and enrolment status

	Survey May 2008	Survey May 2009
Respondents	38 (32% of all enrolled MAAPD students)	59 (approx 40% of all MAAPD students and alumni who had experienced online learning)
Current students	38 (100%)	39 (66%)
Past students	n/a	20 (34%)
Full-time	16 (42%)	25 (42%)
Part-time	22 (58%)	33 (56%)
Both full/part-time*	0	1 (2%)
On-campus	26 (68%)	34 (58%)
Off-campus	11 (29%)	24 (41%)
Both off/on-campus*	1 (3%)	0

* i.e. enrolled differently in different semesters or enrolled in two or more courses in different delivery modes in the same semester

course learning outcomes); incorporated significant flexibility of content or approach; and weighted towards online rather than in-class participation.

The aim at all times was not only to provide an experience that provided richness of content and engagement as much for those off-campus as for those on-campus, but also to maximise the benefits that flowed between these two groups.

Collecting Feedback from Students

The redesigned courses were first taught in Semester 1 (February to June) 2008. We adopted an action research approach to investigate staff and student responses. Informal feedback was collected throughout the semester, with immediate action taken if an identified problem had a simple or technological solution. We ran a more formal feedback process in May 2008 (i.e. near the end of semester, when most online discussion tasks were complete) through an anonymous online survey of students enrolled in that semester's courses. Wherever possible, this feedback—reported in depth by Kilby and Beckmann (2008) and Beckmann and Kilby (2008)—was taken into account in the redesign of courses presented in second semester (July to November) 2008. More informal review occurred in early 2009, when an additional driver for restructure was the move onto ANU's new LMS (Moodle 1.9), which allowed integration of teaching resources and discussion forums onto a single platform. Some innovations occurred: for example, one course used Web 2.0 tools to put online a role-play previously only available on-campus (S. Mahanty, pers.comm., April 2009). Finally, in May 2009, we conducted a second online survey—this time aimed at both currently enrolled and recently graduated MAAPD students (i.e. students and alumni)—to collect feedback on three semesters of the specific online focus.

Both surveys comprised mostly open-ended questions, although the second also collected attitude data. In the first, 38 students responded, including students from all MAAPD courses active in that semester, while 59 students and alumni responded to the second survey, with good representation of both on- and off-campus students (Table 1).

Using feedback to inform necessary change requires careful attention to detail, and an ability to discriminate between issues pertaining to specific individuals and those likely to be representative. As the student voice is so important, respondent quotes are used extensively to illustrate the kinds of feedback obtained. Analysis of the 2008 data has already been reported in the context specifically of peer learning (Beckmann & Kilby, 2008) and open learning in conflict and justice (Kilby and Beckmann, 2008), so this case focuses on the 2009 data and the bigger picture.

Technology Concerns

Students need affordable, reliable access to high quality and appropriate hardware and software, and especially to the higher broadband speeds necessary to make full use of online technological opportunities and provisions. To provide off-campus students in developing countries with online resources available where and when the students need them depends on the availability of cost-effective and reliable technology and internet access. Despite rapid rates of change, across the Asia-Pacific region—where most of our off-shore students are located—download capacity still places significant limits on the effectiveness of online education (Marginson, 2004):

It was often hard enough getting an Internet line but keeping it open long enough to download large parcels of information, such as audio files, or to engage in meaningful chat was difficult, if not impossible. (Papua New Guinea)

It takes several hours to download the lecture. I only have internet access at work: one dial-up line for 25 people. I don't even have a phone line at home [so] I can only use the Internet for study purposes on weekends. (East Timor)

The lectures take ages to download and I often have power cuts. It often happens that I have downloaded 80% of the lecture (sometimes 4-5 hours of downloading) when I get a power cut and then I have to start again. (Indonesia)

It takes me well over an hour just to download the recordings which is very frustrating. The files from the [narrated presentation] recordings are just too big to download ... Ideally I'd love to watch a video recording of the lecture. I can download these more easily .... (Uzbekistan)

The audio recordings are great when you can actually download them! Lack of consistent internet means I need to download and save and sometimes that is not even possible. I was back in Australia for a week and was amazed at how well it worked streaming live there. (Cambodia)

My internet access here is often very good, but inconsistent. At the same time, we've had ongoing problems with our electricity ... if either the electricity or the internet got much worse I'd have a lot of trouble. (Vanuatu)

Most technological issues are addressed as far as possible when first identified, but the diversity of students' locations and needs, and especially the shift to a new university LMS in 2009, has brought to light new (largely solvable) difficulties:

... the options for listening to lectures were better on the old system. I used to stream lectures rather than download ... I could listen while [it] was still downloading and ... if my internet or electricity cut out in the middle of the download, I was still able to listen to the recording to that point. Because [the new LMS] only allows downloading, if the internet connection is terminated for any reason, I lose everything ... downloaded to that point and haven't heard anything. This can be very frustrating. (Vanuatu)

I would have liked to have been able to save the narrated slides/recordings to listen to later, rather than have to be online. (Thailand, Cambodia)

Technological limitations are not the preserve of developing countries. A London-based student complained of internet connections often timing out, and different operating systems confounded an Australian student, with disappointing outcomes:

I found downloading the lectures in 2007 easy and quick. At the time I used [computer operating system A]. I now have [operating system B] which I was using this year (2009). After many unsuccessful attempts to download the audio ..., I finally managed to do so by using someone else's [operating system A]. Previously I played the downloaded lectures in my car when I was travelling and had planned to do so again. The difficulties I encountered militated against doing this and I was a long way behind in listening to the lectures when I withdrew from the program. (remote Australia)

Unlike universities that focus extensively on distance/open learning, and therefore invest heavily in state-of-the-art technological infrastructure, the ANU uses fairly straightforward online platforms and technological interfaces. Yet any institution entering the open learning market in even a limited way knows that today's students constantly compare their online experiences across all providers—educational, government, commercial and private. Students may therefore have high technological expectations of online learning:

... when I download audio files from the Australian Broadcasting Corporation ... that are the same [duration as those from ANU] they are smaller in size, while still being good quality; files of a similar size download faster from ABC than ANU. (Indonesia)

For people sitting in a well-resourced university office or classroom in Australia, it is sometimes hard to think through the most basic of technological concerns that may affect students with constrained access to materials or quality technology:

Some people ... need to print [scanned] documents. The more black in the non-text scanned areas, the more ink is required. For some documents [in this course] up to 1/3 of the scanned area was black. This caused a lot of wastage (and expense) replacing ink cartridges.

Would be nice to be able to download and print all the readings at once, rather than having to download each one and print separately. Even better, it would be great if the readings could be accessed at the beginning of semester by way of USB stick, to save having to spend lots of time getting them off the online server.

Although it is the quality of the education being provided that is the real test, and MAAPD students are of course advised of the technology required to make best use of online learning, it still behoves all providers to think carefully about how technology will be used, and what we can do to make students' lives and learning easier:

I was and still am very impressed with the website for the MAAPD courses. I wish all my courses had such a wonderfully developed and detailed course website.

Choosing Online Discussions as a Teaching Tool

Online forums were considered an effective way to try to recreate the 'immediacy and energy' of face-to-face engagement (Meyer, 2003) experienced by on-campus students. McLeod, Dawson and Berg (2002) found that synchronous online chat incorporated into clinical field placements could 'negate the tyranny of distance and the associated feeling of isolation'. Most MAAPD courses had previously used email, recorded lectures and the LMS discussion tools to support off-campus students. However, online dialogue arising from a classroom discussion sometimes simply reinforced the feeling of isolation of off-campus students. In the review process, therefore, we chose to formalize the casual discussion formats of the classroom into more focused online forums, integrating the opportunities for peer and supportive learning more securely within the learning/assessment process.

Our redesign was guided by evidence from the literature. We addressed the major pedagogical attributes—learner centricity, asynchronous interaction, communication effectiveness and assessment facilitation (Sahu, 2008)—and noted that learning via these tools is influenced most by the extent to which the latter are effectively integrated into the teaching/learning process (Funaro and Montell, 1999). We were also aware that 'threaded' discussions increase the amount of time students spend on course objectives and on reflection (Meyer, 2003), and that meaningful discourse is improved by facilitator guidelines, evaluation rubrics and posting protocols (Gilbert and Dabbagh, 2005). Our redesign included all these features, with one of us (EB) working as educational designer one-on-one with individual MAAPD lecturers (including PK) to develop online discussion formats, assessment tasks and marking criteria/rubrics.

Notably, the formats of the online discussions for each course were often quite different, based on individual course and lecturer needs: for example, some were highly structured with groups of four to six students and specific assessment-focused objectives—often led by students—while others were guided conversation opportunities open to all 60 or so enrolled students. In all cases, however, the emphasis was on students being knowledgeable and influential in starting and steering discussion processes.

We sought to provide a differentiated learning environment, equally relevant to both on- and off-campus students, where the focus was clearly on exchanges among students rather than information flow from lecturers. Concerned that the relevant tools in ANU's LMS (then WebCT 4) were inadequate, we hosted these new forums on the more user-friendly Alliance (Sakai) platform. In early 2009, as a result of the ANU's move to a new LMS (Moodle 1.9) and the feedback received previously, the first semester MAAPD courses were slightly restructured and presented in a second iteration.

The 2008 survey found that most students—and especially transnational students—were very satisfied with the way online discussions had been incorporated into the teaching, and their impact on learning (Beckmann and Kilby, 2008; Kilby and Beckmann, 2008).

The online discussion is a really good place for topic discussion, especially for off-campus students. It also provides a space for both on- and off-campus students to exchange ideas, case studies, extra reading materials, news and personal experiences, which I consider as essential for our learning. The online forum created a virtual community for students to extend their participation and take their knowledge beyond general classroom activities and I think it is fantastic. (2008)

The 2009 survey confirmed this, with many students responding very positively:

... online discussions are great for those of us who work full-time or live in a different time zone, because they allow us to fit study more easily into our lives. (Off-campus student, East Timor, 2009)

Learning Opportunities from Online Discussions

In their teaching, MAAPD lecturers generally focus on comparing practice with theory, considering theoretical paradigms in different cultural contexts, and looking at evidence-based research. Students have many opportunities to engage in structured, critical reflection on their learning, and to share this reflection with one another. Beckmann and Kilby (2008) described specifically how the 2008 student feedback showed that online discussions significantly facilitated opportunities for peer learning (defined as 'the use of teaching and learning strategies in which students learn with and from each other without the immediate intervention of a teacher'; Boud, Cohen and Sampson, 1999, p.413).

In the 2009 survey, some 59% of respondents agreed that online discussions had provided them with additional learning opportunities, and 49% felt they benefitted more from online discussions than they expected:

... Some of the groups I participated in were ... very committed and eager and there was always a lot of interesting and challenging discussion (and also a lot of work!).

Online discussion facilitates broader understanding and learning. Many ideas are presented, makes one learn ideas that sometimes we failed to comprehend from our independent reading. It allows one to share ideas from ... other sources .... (Vietnam)

I was able to email a participant in my course and learn the troubles they were having with their work in the field. This developed into a mutually supportive acquaintanceship, as we shared personal experiences that helped each other in areas 'outside' of the course. ... Contacts are always beneficial for those in rural or remote areas who need that human contact. (Remote Australia)

Of course, the nature of the MAAPD student cohort naturally supports peer learning: most students are Australian or international mature-age professionals either already working in the development field or keen to increase their range of skills pertinent to such work. Many students—both on- and off-campus—have first-hand experience of developing country contexts, which enables them to contribute to discussions in a highly critically-informed way.

It is not surprising, therefore, that in the 2009 survey, 70% of respondents agreed that 'online discussions are especially valuable in the context of development studies, as we can communicate at first-hand with fellow students working in development roles':

It is interesting obtaining views from other students. Many of them have a wealth of experience in other countries which provides alternate insights to the discussions.

[Online discussions] facilitate sharing between students working in development overseas and those living in Canberra. (East Timor)

Overseas students related their experiences on issues which you can never get in Australia.

[Online discussions] facilitate sharing between students working in development overseas and those living in Canberra.

When the questions regarded personal field experience—that was the most intriguing.

It was definitely particularly useful to be able to interact with the off-campus students. ... they were generally older and more experienced that some of my classmates on-campus which made the discussions even richer, and made the Masters as a whole more challenging and full-encompassing. Also the fact that many of these students are at the time working on specific issues we are studying is fascinating!

... when students contribute multiple times and actually refer to others students' responses then it makes you reconsider your original posting. (Uzbekistan)

Many students described times where ideas or comments expressed by another student online enhanced their learning and encouraged deeper critical reflection. Transnational students both contributed to this enhancement—through the immediacy of their ability to apply theory to practice in their working situations—and gained from others' input, feeling less isolated in their thinking:

I drew my analysis from other comments expressed by other students. It helped me reflect on my own positions on particular readings and resources.

I learned a lot from reading other students' experiences with participatory wealth ranking. Working in a post-conflict setting in Timor-Leste, this struck me at first as something which would be very divisive. But I was interested to learn that in less fragile settings, this can be a valuable tool.

Some students commented on the opportunity to explore topics of direct relevance to their home country and/or work:

I particularly enjoy the freedom [of assessment tasks]... I've been able to do a lot of work on Madagascar, and even the Sahel. (Madagascar, 2009]

I am particularly interested to hear from students who work in reproductive health, [which] is related to my own field of experience in refugee protection, particularly for women and girls, but is an area I have had little exposure to. (Vanuatu)

There was clear strong that the flow of ideas and support was by no means one-way, neither solely from the lecturer to the student, nor always from the developed country or community to the less developed:

For me, as someone who works in a different country and culture, some of the most interesting contributions have come from people working with Indigenous communities in Australia. (Indonesia)

... when students contribute multiple times and actually refer to others students' responses then it makes you reconsider your original posting. (Uzbekistan)

One reading mentions an NGO in India who forced women to participate in committees, and in reality these women acted as proxies for their husbands or brothers (posts allocated to women were still controlled by men ...). I mentioned a program I worked on in Cambodia, where women said participating in committees gave them practice to speak in public, which in turn gave them confidence not only to speak but to engage in community affairs ... three women (out of 30) went on to be village and deputy chiefs. Someone in the forum responded that it was a good example that context does really matter: an activity in one context may have opposite results to those of the same activity somewhere else. I think exchanging experiences is an important way of learning, and those who have worked should be encouraged to use their experience more. (Madagascar)

It was interesting viewing contrasting perspectives of people in private sector in Australia, full-time university students, people working in Australia, Australians working overseas and developing country nationals working in their home country. It displayed more clearly than any journal article could the divergence of opinion in development. It also highlighted a very real difference between some academic opinions and opinions in the field. (Cambodia)

I remember someone in Indonesia talking about experiences doing focus groups discussions, which were quite different from my own experiences ... helpful both for learning and work. (Madagascar)

Personally experiencing the ways in which practice plays a crucial part in knowledge creation and learning (McFarlane, 2006) is a value-added opportunity for development workers, who need to conceive of innovative practices to engage the social process of learning at both community and institutional level (Roper and Pettit, 2002).

CURRENT CHALLENGES

Technological Factors

Almost regardless of the quality of content or teaching, the success of off-campus study is very dependent on the reliability of technology. Some of the technological problems our students encountered are not within ANU's power to solve directly (e.g. speed and reliability of internet access), while others are (e.g. downloadable files sizes and format; care in recording and scanning; educational design of assessment tasks involving online components; creating online databases of useful resources). The key responsibilities for MAAPD staff are thus to collect student feedback on technology problems early and regularly; to respond quickly to identified technological problems; and to keep a realistic view of student technological contexts and settings.

Of course, doing all this requires a significant and constant effort. In designing technology-facilitated learning, it is common to underestimate the time and effort needed by both lecturers and students to understand the practicalities, and to incorporate time for these into course design:

There is an initial steep learning curve associated with beginning the on-line program. Lecturers seemed to be aware of this but perhaps not to the extent that students actually experienced. Finding your way around the web sites took considerable time before gaining confidence that all was under control. (Off-campus student, Australia, 2009)

An assumption that I was going to be online and able to interact at least several times a week was difficult. Field trips, dodgy internet connections, busyness at work made this often impossible. Many distance students do their work in big 'bursts' when they can (e.g. when they have a couple of weeks leave or have a month of great internet connection) and the course did not sufficiently accommodate that. (Off-campus student moving between Afghanistan, East Timor and Cambodia, 2009)

Providing effective 'help' tools can reduce the time students to understand how to use the tools. Although we provided a written manual as well as a dedicated website, available to students in all courses, with clear audiovisual presentations on how to use the technology, usage records suggested few students accessed these support resources, even though they actually requested them:

I am reasonably computer-literate but would have appreciated clearer instructions on how to use all the site resources, including how to download and save the lecture recordings. Perhaps these instructions could also be given as an audio file, for those of us who are not 100% visual learners. And maybe a diagram for those who are! (Off-campus student, Australia, 2009)

Building familiarity and exploration exercises into assessment, giving students specific technology-related tasks, or asking for students to complete a checklist of competencies in the first weeks of teaching are all ways to consider addressing this issue in future.

Students' Workloads

Most (64%) 2009 respondents agreed that 'an assessable online discussion generally involves more work than most other forms of assessment'. In addition, a notable minority (32%) agreed that, for an on-campus student, it is more difficult to contribute to an online discussion than to a classroom discussion:

The use of online discussion was very useful in terms of getting my head around some of the issues and new topics encountered within the course. However the workload associated with participating ... substantially added to my semester workload i.e. having to attend on-campus tutorials and ... do [the online discussions] was too much ... working full time and doing [online discussions] equals no life! (On-campus student, 2008)

I really enjoyed the forum in general, but reading and updating opinions every second week while doing the online simulation game took a lot of time and effort. Sometimes I feel I focus so much on 'getting things done' for online forums and getting a bit nervous about the game (while trying to write essays), I feel I did not have enough time to build depth in my field as a postgraduate student. (On-campus student, 2009)

Although frequent engagement with the learning tasks in this courses probably supports conceptual change more effectively than widely-spaced efforts, reviewing the workload needed to meet the assessment requirements on a course by course basis will be useful in this context.

Access to Scholarly and Field-Based Resources

Although each course suggests many resources from the published literature, the development field is notorious for its 'grey literature' (Posnett and Baulkwill, 1982). Transnational students must often rely almost exclusively on online resources:

I don't have access to a library, so I am limited to what is available to download (i.e. generally not books). (Indonesia)

Difficulty in finding additional academic resources. Materials available online from the library are inadequate. (Afghanistan, East Timor, Cambodia)

The only constraint with being a transnational student is access to library resources. (Vietnam)

MAAPD lecturers have therefore tried to create online repositories of project reports and similar 'grey' material as well as published papers; to make full use of the ANU's capacity to provide other online library resources; and to ensure students were aware of the university's online information literacy training (for example, helping students use databases and search engines more effectively). The online discussions clearly facilitate the sharing of additional resources among students:

What I have found most valuable has been when other students have posted links to additional resources, such as articles, tool kits or websites. (on-campus student)

I've often read new materials mentioned by classmates. (on-campus student)

[A fellow student] added links to ecological demography and behavioural ecology papers which in some ways contradicted the class readings—we had a 'give and take' (we had different interpretations so it was good) and it pushed me to go to the logical ends of the arguments. (Madagascar)

However, this raises the issue of professional integrity. As with any relatively casual discussion among professionals when outcomes may be reported more widely (in this case in the form of submitted assignments or professional reports), issues of attribution and academic honesty are important considerations:

There are questions over how and to what degree other students' ideas should be cited in one's own work; the question of whether a student's idea is original to him or her is a factor.

Lecturers can obviously model appropriate ethical behaviour in this context, by ensuring that students know how to cite unpublished material and to reference a fellow student's individual ideas or experiences as 'personal communication'.

Educational Design of the Online Discussion Activities

As explained earlier, while there is uniformity in resource presentation and course structure, each lecturer developed his or her own learning activities related to the online components. With on-campus students doing up to four courses each semester (off-campus students usually do only one or two), such individuality is very valuable in ensuring that students do not become bored with any one approach, and also that the design is more closely suited to the content. However, this means that full-time on-campus students may be comparing discussion designs and developing preferences, and hence responding to superficially similar formats quite differently:

I found that it is great to have one discussion leader and then the leader facilitate the week forum. I learned a lot that way. Also, it's great that everyone updates their opinions using 'reply' ... as in the [course A] forum. However, for [course B] everyone updated their opinions separately so the discussion wasn't happening as much as everyone expected.

In my group often people posted their own thoughts, rather than responses to other's questioning. So I didn't feel it was a particularly healthy debate. But in every forum I got valuable ideas and different perspectives from others that helped increase my understanding.

Constantly thinking through the design of online learning environments is crucial in a field that is changing so rapidly. For example, MAAPD lecturers may need to consider how to establish a 'social presence' and create a greater 'sense of place', especially for on-campus students, in the online learning environment, as advocated by Northcote (2008). More evaluation at the course level, instead of at the current program level, will be useful.

Equality of On- and Off-Campus Experience: an Appreciated Goal?

A driving force in creating a more flexible and online presence for the MAAPD's teaching activities was our desire to provide an equality of experience to on- and off-campus students, especially those studying transnationally. Technological constraints excepted, student feedback suggests we are generally achieving that goal:

With the current technology I see almost no difference to being an overseas off-campus student. I think the key difference is more as being an off-campus as compared to an on-campus student. (Vietnam)

[There are] time delays with being able to download materials to participate by given dates but I knew this when I signed up. I think you've done a fantastic job with clearly outlining dates etc prior to the beginning of the course. (Uzbekistan)

Yet some on-campus students are less sure of equity of experience as a goal:

I think requiring on-campus students to participate online as well [as in class] is a classic case of mistaking novelty for progress. (on-campus student, 2008)

... too much attention is being made to make everything equally accessible and equally framed

so that in essence the on-campus and off-campus student get the same exact experience. Some may argue that this is indeed favourable, since both students pay the same fees and hence should get the same education. However I think the whole point of being on-campus is to get a closer experience, get more dialogue going with professors in class and with students. A lot of us have left jobs and careers to study, and with everything being online there seems very little benefit in having done that instead of continuing a job (perhaps part-time or 80% of the time) and undertaking the Masters from long-distance. I may be old-fashioned in my views, but I think face-to-face learning should still be the preferred method when possible and that, as such, as on-campus students we should benefit from more 'live' discussions with professors and classmates, feedback and the like. ... I don't see there is that much value (at least at this point) to be on-campus rather than off. You pretty much get the same experience and I think this should not be the case. (on-campus student, 2009)

[Online discussions] tend to be boring, hard work and not particularly beneficial for on-campus students. For off-campus students, they are an important way to interact and for lecturers to assess interaction ..., but I think the same issues still exist. (on-campus student, 2009, previously off-campus)

A particular concern voiced by these few troubled on-campus students centres on having the same online assessment tasks—and especially the online discussions—for all students:

I enrolled in Masters Coursework specifically for on-campus interaction with students and teaching staff, and feel that [the online discussions] compromises this. ... I value in-class discussions more. (on-campus student, 2009)

I can see absolutely no connection between my learning and the online discussions. I appreciate that online discussions may be useful to external students, as it presents perhaps the only opportunity to interact with other students and the lecturer. However, the situation of on-campus students is very different: we attend lectures, have active discussions in class and we can talk to the lecturer. Conversely, the lecturer can and does talk to us: so probably has a good sense of whether or not we have done the reading, and whether we are grasping the material. To me, the online discussions feel very forced (i.e: they are undertaken because they are assessable), time-consuming (it is much more time consuming to write and post a response than to ask a question in class), for little educational value. (on-campus student, 2008)

Some responses from on-campus students suggest a primary concern with the loss of face-to-face contact:

Expressions and gestures are important ... [but] not possible with online discussions.

I find face-to-face discussions more worthwhile due to immediacy of exchange and scope for debate ... often student contributions [online] amount to not much more then a summary of a reading or a non-insightful 'blog'.

However, this view is countered by others:

I think online discussions are terrific—much better ... than most of the face-to-face tutorials I attended during my undergraduate degree at ANU.... when people know they are assessed, and they can't 'waffle' so easily as they can when speaking, their input tends to be of a much higher quality. This goes for me as much as anyone else!

I personally prefer face to face interaction in the classes but I do appreciate that the online forums allow us to interact with those who are currently working abroad.

The only real loss with online discussions as compared to face-to-face tutorials is that we don't get to build friendships with other students.

Some on-campus students were dissatisfied with a perceived poorer quality of interaction online:

I often find group work in class to be a useful tool in sharing ideas and experiences and working together to complete the task. The [online] forums tend to be a general conversation more than a collaborative effort as it is in class.

I find the discussions very forced—people are trying to impress because [the discussions] are assessable, so they are rarely free-flowing and spontaneous.

Participants in online discussions either write formalised mini-essays which respond directly to the readings or [contribute] general discussions related to philosophies or principles. ... 'discussion groups' are tiresome and generally do not contribute to learning. (on-campus student, previously off-campus)

These responses may seem surprising coming from people specifically studying issues of equity and participatory involvement. However, they simply illustrate both the complexity of meeting the educational needs of professional adults who have very defined personal goals, assumptions, expectations, preferences and intentions for their own learning, and the 'hard act to follow' in blended learning when the face-to-face element is of very high quality. Ironically, having excellent lecturers (all of whom were complimented by name by different students in both surveys) can make online elements appear to offer less:

I am torn in my assessment of the value of online discussions. On the one hand they did at times give me new things to think about, [which] enhanced my learning. However, I don't think that would be different from what I would gain in a class discussion or in reading an online blog. ... If (at least for the on-campus students) we had more class time, where lecturers had more time for discussions, we could reach even better outcomes than in the online forums. Moreover we would be able to receive more pointed feedback from teachers, and incorrect assumptions could be corrected or further discussed, something that does not happen in the online forums. (on-campus student, 2009)

Despite the strength with which some of these concerns were expressed, they represent just a few on-campus students. Only 26% of the 2009 on-campus respondents (18% of all respondents) agreed with the statement that 'online discussions are really only beneficial for off-campus students'. Most of our students' feedback both in 2008 and 2009 is rather in keeping with others' findings, for example that online discussions significantly improve learners' critical thinking skills (Yang, Newby and Bill 2008) and are more likely than face-to-face encounters to elicit a critically thought-out response to a disagreement between two other parties (Chen and Chiu 2008).

Indeed, our 2008 data suggested that online discussions actually enhanced the interactions of some on-campus peers, with thoughtful interactions online often spilling over into face-to-face engagement in class tea-breaks (Beckmann and Kilby 2008):

In class [after online contact] I hear comments like 'Hey, I enjoyed reading your posting last week', 'Thanks for your comments on the discussions'. I would say the same thing to others. (on-campus student, 2008)

Moreover, less confident on-campus students sometimes found the online discussions provided a sheltered entry-point into the world of debate (Beckmann and Kilby, 2008):

[With] English as second language, I'm shy to speak up in tutorials or lectures. But with online discussions, it's more comfortable for me to express my point of view. (on-campus student, 2008)

Nevertheless, in today's free market world of higher education, understanding, and preferably meeting, the needs of students is fundamental to the economic survival of a graduate coursework program. For the MAAPD, awareness of the concerns identified above will not mean any change in our policy of seeking to provide equitable experiences for both on- and off-campus students, but it may require more careful promotion, differentiation and explanation of the two kinds of educational 'products'.

CONCLUSION

In the global education context, Australia has a vibrant focus on the education of international students (Access Economics, 2009), as well as an active engagement in the provision of aid to the Asia-Pacific region (AusAID, 2009). ANU's MAAPD is successfully taking postgraduate development studies off-campus, especially to those who are practitioners in the field, through the use of relatively simple but highly functional educational technology. The political and economic contexts of developing countries undoubtedly impose technological constraints on transnational students' access to all the educational resources on offer. Nevertheless, off-campus students are generally very satisfied with the quality of the online learning opportunities being provided:

I have been an off-campus student for my whole academic career. In comparison to my previous experience, I find the MAAPD to be quite effective at providing online learning. (Indonesia)

... thank you for your efforts in producing these [lecture audio/visual] files as I feel I can better access the learning through these rather than just being isolated and doing the readings. (Uzbekistan)

Once technological issues are addressed, educational design comes to the fore. The opportunities for democratization offered by peer interaction in online learning are well known: 'there is a multiplicity of voices or perspectives, and students are exposed to a variety of possible interpretations or solutions rather than just the 'right' or textbook' answer" (Harasim, 2000). We believe that by offering online opportunities to student professionals working in developing countries, we have introduced an exciting new dimension to the teaching of participatory development.

Our off-campus students are encouraged to engage in structured and supported reflection as they attempt to interpret and apply high-level theory in the context of their day-to-day practice. They can access ANU's research community and fellow practitioners in Canberra, ask their student peers elsewhere in the world about similar situations, and, in real time, consider and discuss the potential outcomes of different strategies to help them deal with their day-to-day work situations. Most importantly, any insights gained from this professional study and debate can be incorporated into active projects with an immediacy that directly benefits the communities with which these development worker students are working:

The online discussions give me the precious opportunity of directly discussing with my course mates [my work] activities ... in the framework of the current debates and thinking, and therefore gaining from someone else's experiences. (2008, Nepal)

MAAPD changed the whole way I did my work at the time and. .. it certainly changed the way [my co-workers] looked on the impacts of their work. [2008, Papua New Guinea]

Although we can continue to fine-tune our use of educational technology and online/blended course design, the evidence so far clearly shows that providing off-campus development studies opportunities to Australian and local aid workers in developing countries benefits both the individual students and the communities they serve (Kilby and Beckmann, 2008):

I studied by distance and was 'hooked' from the very first week—engaging lectures, thought provoking readings, and a great online space to develop, test and exchange ideas. Although juggling studies with a full-time development job, I was addicted enough to study right into the early hours. The excellent academic support is a real hallmark of the MAAPD experience, as is the opportunity to engage with other practitioners working in challenging real-life development situations. It's already been a stepping-stone for me to move into a management position. (Off-campus student testimonial; MAAPD, 2009)

It has allowed me to study a degree that is relevant to my job at a prestigious university. I would not have the financial means to stop working totally to be a fulltime on-campus student. Given the everyday relevance of the degree to my job I consider that my work enhances my MAAPD learning and that doing the MAAPD is enhancing my work performance. It allows the opportunity to network with people in other countries and causes me to put an academic critical perspective lens over some of the work I am doing (Off-campus student, Cambodia, 2009)

REFERENCES

Access Economics Pty Limited. (2009) *The Australian education sector and the economic contribution of international students.* Report for Australian Council for Private Education and Training. Retrieved from http://globalhighered.files.wordpress.com/2009/04/theaustralianeducationsectorandtheeconomiccontributionofinternationalstudents-2461.pdf

AusAID. (2009). *Where We Work.* Retrieved from http://www.ausaid.gov.au/about/ausaidmap.cfm

Beckmann, E. A., & Kilby, P. (2008). On-line, Off-campus and in the Flow: learning from peers in development studies. *Australasian Journal of Peer Learning, 1*(1), 61–69.

Boud, D., Cohen, R., & Sampson, J. (1999). Peer learning and assessment. *Assessment & Evaluation in Higher Education, 24*(4), 413–426. doi:10.1080/0260293990240405

Center for World-Class Universities, Shanghai Jiao Tong University. (2008). *Academic Ranking of World Universities 2008.* Retrieved http://www.arwu.org/rank2008/EN2008.htm

Chen, G., & Chiu, M. M. (2008). Online discussion processes: Effects of earlier messages' evaluations, knowledge content, social cues and personal information on later messages. *Computers & Education, 50*(3), 678–692. doi:10.1016/j.compedu.2006.07.007

Cookson, P. (2002). Online postgraduate education: some reflections. *International Review of Research in Open and Distance Learning, 3*(2), 1492–3831.

Cunningham, D. J. (1992). Assessing constructions and constructing assessments. In T.M. Duffy, & D.H. Jonassen, (Eds.), Constructivism and the technology of instruction: a conversation, (pp. 35-44). Mahwah, NJ: Lawrence Erlbaum Associates.

Devereux, S., & Knowles, C. (2006). Introduction: challenging orthodoxies, influencing debates. The *IDS Bulletin* at 40. *IDS Bulletin, 37*(4), 1-5.

Funaro, G. M., & Montell, F. (1999). Pedagogical roles and implementation guidelines for online communication tools. *Asynchronous Learning Network Magazine, 3*(2) 1-8. Retrieved from http://www.sloanc.org/publications/magazine/v3n2/funaro.asp

Gilbert, P. K., & Dabbagh, N. (2005). How to structure online discussions for meaningful discourse: a case study. *British Journal of Educational Technology, 36*(1), 5–18. doi:10.1111/j.1467-8535.2005.00434.x

Harasim, L. (2000). Shift happens: online education as a new paradigm in learning. *The Internet and Higher Education, 3*(1-2), 41–61. doi:10.1016/S1096-7516(00)00032-4

Kilby, P., & Beckmann, E. A. (2008). So, what happened in Kabul today? Flexible learning in conflict and social justice programs at the Australian National University. In *Proceedings from Fifth Pan-Commonwealth Forum on Open Learning: Access to Learning for Development*, 13-17 July 2008, London. Retrieved from http://www.wikieducator.org/images/b/bc/PID_359.pdf

Kimball, L. (2001). Managing distance learning: new challenges for faculty. In R. Hazemi, S. Hailes, & S. Wilbur (Eds.), The digital university: building a learning community (pp. 27-40). London: Springer.

MAAPD. (2009). *Alumni testimonials*. Retrieved from http://rspas.anu.edu.au/maapd/testimonials.php

Marginson, S. (2004). Don't leave me hanging on the Anglophone: the potential for online distance higher education in the Asia-Pacific Region. *Higher Education Quarterly, 58*(2/3), 74–113. doi:10.1111/j.1468-2273.2004.00263.x

Marton, F., & Säljö, R. (1976). On qualitative differences in learning 1: outcome and process. *The British Journal of Educational Psychology, 46*, 4–11.

McClellan, R., & Dominguez, R. (2006). The uneven march toward social justice: diversity, conflict, and complexity in educational administration programs. *Journal of Educational Administration, 44*(3), 225–238. doi:10.1108/09578230610664823

McFarlane, C. (2006). Knowledge, learning and development: a post-rationalist approach. *Progress in Development Studies, 6*, 287–305. doi:10.1191/1464993406ps144oa

McLeod, S., Dawson, S., & Berg, L. (2002). Using online chat to enhance peer learning while on fieldwork placements. *CAL-laborate, 8*. Retrieved from http://science.uniserve.edu.au/pubs/callab/vol8/mcleod.html

Meyer, K. A. (2003). Face-to-face versus threaded discussions: the role of time and higher-order thinking. *Journal of Asynchronous Learning Networks, 7* (3), 55-65. Retrieved from http://www.sloanc.org/publications/jaln/v7n3/pdf/v7n3_meyer.pdf

Mishra, S. (2002). A design framework for online learning environments. *International Journal of Educational Management, 33*(4), 493–496.

Northcote, M. (2008). Sense of place in online learning environments. In *Hello! Where are you in the landscape of educational technology? Proceedings ascilite Melbourne 2008*. Retrieved from http://www.ascilite.org.au/conferences/melbourne08/procs/northcote.pdf

Oxenham, J. (1980). Teaching development at graduate level in Britain. *IDS Bulletin, 11*(3).

Posnett, N. W., & Baulkwill, W. J. (1982). Working with Non-Conventional Literature. *Journal of Information Science*, *5*(4), 121–130. doi:10.1177/016555158200500402

Ramsden, P. (1992). Learning to Teach in Higher Education. London: Routledge.

Roper, L., & Pettit, J. (2002). Development and the learning organisation: an introduction. *Development in Practice*, *12*(3/4), 258–271. doi:10.1080/0961450220149654

Sahu, C. (2008). An evaluation of selected pedagogical attributes of online discussion boards. In *Hello! Where are you in the landscape of educational technology? Proceedings ascilite Melbourne 2008*. Retrieved from http://www.ascilite.org.au/conferences/melbourne08/procs/sahu.pdf

Volery, T., & Lord, D. (2000). Critical Success Factors in Online Education. *International Journal of Educational Management*, *14*(5), 216–223. doi:10.1108/09513540010344731

Yang, Y. C., Newby, T., & Bill, R. (2008). Facilitating interactions through structured web-based bulletin boards: A quasi-experimental study on promoting learners' critical thinking skills. *Computers & Education*, *50*(4), 1572–1585. doi:10.1016/j.compedu.2007.04.006

ADDITIONAL READING

Ally, M. (2004). Foundations of educational theory for online learning. In T. Anderson & F. Elloumi (Eds.), Theory and practice of online learning (pp. 3-31). Athabasca, Canada: Athabasca University.

Anderson, R. S., Bauer, J. F., & Speck, B. W. (Eds.). (2002). Assessment strategies for the online class: from theory to practice. San Francisco: Jossey-Bass.

Apple, M. W. (2001). Comparing neo-liberal projects and inequality in education. *Comparative Education*, *37*(4), 409–423. doi:10.1080/03050060120091229

Boud, D. (1999). Situating academic development in professional work: using peer learning. *The International Journal for Academic Development*, *4*(1), 3–10. doi:10.1080/1360144990040102

Duff, A., & Quinn, D. (2006). Retention in online courses: using a motivational framework and online peers to enlighten potential learners about learning online. *Journal of Learning Design*, *1*, 29–40.

Graham, C. R. (2002). Factors for effective learning groups in face-to-face and virtual environments. *Quarterly Review of Distance Education*, *3*, 307–319.

Gustafson, P., & Gibbs, D. (2000). Guiding or hiding? The role of the facilitator in online teaching and learning. *Teaching Education*, *11*(2), 195–210. doi:10.1080/713698967

Harris, N., & Sandor, M. (2008). Student views on participation and interaction in student centred online discussion forums. In *Hello! Where are you in the landscape of educational technology? Proceedings ascilite Melbourne 2008*. Retrieved from http://www.ascilite.org.au/conferences/melbourne08/procs/harris.pdf

Maor, D. (2007). The cognitive and social processes of university students' online learning, Proceedings Ascilite Singapore 2007: *ICT-Providing Choices for Learners and Learning* (611-623). Retrieved http://www.ascilite.org.au/conferences/singapore07/procs/maor.pdf

Maor, D., & Hendriks, V. (2001). Peer-learning and reflective thinking in an on-line community of learners. Paper presented at the Australian Association for Research in Education (AARE), Fremantle, Australia, 2-6 December, 2001. Retrieved http://www.aare.edu.au/01pap/mao01549.htm

Meyer, K. A. (2003). Face-to-face versus threaded discussions: the role of time and higher-order thinking. *Journal of Asynchronous Learning Networks*, 7 (3): 55-65. Retrieved http://www.sloan-c.org/publications/jaln/v7n3/pdf/v7n3_meyer.pdf

Nunan, T. (2005). Markets, distance education, and Australian higher education. *International Review of Research in Open and Distance Learning*, March.

Pallof, R., & Pratt, K. (2005). Collaborating online: learning together in community. San Francisco: Jossey Bass.

Tanguma, J., Liu, L. C., & Koong, K. S. (2008). Hybrid learning and effects on student assessment outcomes. *International Journal of Mobile Learning and Organisation*, *2*(1), 36–47. doi:10.1504/IJMLO.2008.018716

Trigwell, K., Prosser, M., & Lyons, F. (1999). Relations between teachers' approaches to teaching and students' approaches to learning. *Higher Education*, *37*, 57–70. doi:10.1023/A:1003548313194

Vidovich, L. (2004). Global-national-local dynamics in policy processes: a case of 'quality' policy in higher education. *British Journal of Sociology of Education*, *25*, 341–354. doi:10.1080/0142569042000216981

Wegerif, R. (1998). The social dimension of asynchronous learning networks. *Journal of asynchronous learning networks*, *2*(1). Retrieved from http://www.aln.org/alnweb/journal/vol2_issue1/wegerif.htm

KEY TERMS AND DEFINITIONS

Development Studies: A multidisciplinary branch of social science which addresses issues of concern to community development, and specifically developing countries.

Development Workers: A person who works to help a community achieve its development goals and objectives, often through formalized aid projects.

Off-Campus Study: Any form of study where the student does not have to attend campus to obtain any learning materials.

Online Discussion: A set of related postings made in an online setting that allows participants to post messages and comment on other messages

Participatory Development: Processes of community development through which stakeholders influence and share control of development initiatives and associated decision-making.

Postgraduate Study: Formal study at an institution of higher education that is designed for students who have already completed a bachelor degree, often leading to a coursework Master degree (equivalent to 'graduate study' in North America).

Transnational Study: A form of distance learning where the institution of study is in one country and the student is located in another country for all or part of the duration of study.

Chapter 7
Learning Patterns of Learner's Interaction in the Learning Management Systems:
A Comparative Study of China and Malaysia

Wu Bing
The University of Shanghai for Science and Technology, China

Teoh Ai Ping
Wawasan Open University, Malaysia

Ye Chun Ming
The University of Shanghai for Science and Technology, China,

ABSTRACT

Following the rapid development of open distance education and the enrichment of online resources and Learning Management Systems in Asia, the quality of interactions amongst learners and online content, teacher and peers has become one of the imperative factors in determining the efficacy of web-based teaching-learning. Online learning is distinctive as compared to face-to-face interaction in terms of how the course material is presented, the nature of interactions, and overall learning experience. This case study explores the understanding, expectation and experience of learners from China and Malaysia based on vital aspects of learning in the web-based environment such as the concept of teaching and learning, the role of the teacher, communication patterns in the virtual classroom, relationships with the teacher and the classmates, and attitudes towards learning achievement. These are reflected in the learning patterns and behavior of online learners as observed in their interaction with the web-based content and participation in the online forum discussions within the online Learning Management Systems. In addition, this case highlights the influence of national culture towards learners' interaction as displayed in their online learning activities.

DOI: 10.4018/978-1-61520-779-4.ch007

INTRODUCTION

The People's Republic of China, located at Eastern Asia, has a population of 1,338,612,968, with 72.1% in the age group of 15 – 64 years (male 51.4%/female 48.6%), a median age of 34.1 years, and having about 253 million Internet users (Central Intelligence Agency, 2009a). China has more than five thousand years of culture and the people in China are strong influenced by the Confucian philosophy. 'Han' is the major ethnic group in the population of China and the 'Han' language, or Mandarin language, is the official language of the country. For the past three decades, China has experienced rapid economic growth as well as a more open society. China has a nationwide system of public education, which includes primary schools, middle schools (lower and upper), and universities, with literacy rate of about 92% (Wikipedia, 2009a). Online education in China has benefited students of remote and under-developed areas in China while students who failed university entrance examinations and working people are provided with an opportunity of lifelong education. The Ministry of Education in China has approved 68 ordinary schools of higher learning and the Central Radio and TV University to pilot modern distance education. By the end of 2003, these schools had established 2,027 off-campus learning centers around China, offering 140 majors in ten disciplines, and had a total enrollment of 1.373 million (Wikipedia, 2009a). The utilization of broadband technology has also promoted online education while the China Education and Research Network started in 1994, is China's second largest Internet network, covering all major cities of China.

Malaysia, located in the Southeastern Asia, is a country with an open economy and stable socio-economic development. Malaysia has a population of 25,715,819, with 63.6% in the age group of 15-64 years (male 50.2%/female 49.8%), a median age of 24.9 years, and having about 15.868 million Internet users (Central Intelligence Agency, 2009b). The personal computer penetration level in Malaysia is about 11 per cent, i.e. below the world average of 35 percent and only 5 percent of Malaysians surf the Internet, compared with the world average of 30 percent (Netto, 2009). Malaysians comprise of three major ethnic groups, namely Malay, Chinese and Indians. The Malay language or Bahasa Malaysia is the official language of the country. Education in Malaysia broadly consists of stages which include: pre-school, primary education, secondary education, tertiary education and postgraduate, with literacy rate of about 91.5% (Wikipedia, 2009b). Enrollments in private Higher Education Institutions in Malaysia have increased by 60.1% between 1998–2000 and 20.0% between 2003–2005 (World Bank, 2006). Distance education in Malaysia started off with correspondence schools and private institutions offering correspondence courses. Distance education at tertiary level in Malaysia was first introduced and implemented by Universiti Sains Malaysia in 1971 at its then Center for Off-campus Studies, conducted mainly via printed materials and face-to-face classes. As Malaysia progresses into the information age, the Seventh Malaysian Plan put in place the necessary infrastructure and environment for the development of information and communication technology (ICT), in which a key initiative was the Multimedia Super Corridor - designed as a world test-bed for ICT development. Consequently, multimedia technologies create the infrastructure for new educational network of the entire educational system incorporating the use of modern technologies and facilities. The liberalization of education in Malaysia has been demonstrated through the policy decision by the Ministry of Higher Education on open entry to higher education accorded to three open distance education institutions, i.e. Open University Malaysia, Universiti Tun Abdul Razak and Wawasan Open University.

Education is one of the crucial transformation pillars for human capital development. In order to fulfill social agenda and broaden the tertiary education opportunities in promoting lifelong learning, open distance education (ODE) has emerged as one of the trend in both China and Malaysia. The education sector in both nations has experienced a significant shift as it enters into a new era of online learning, following the booming and rapid growth of information technology. In Asian countries, e-learning is still in its infancy stage compared to developed countries in the West. High quality and effectiveness of ODE, particularly adult teaching-learning in tertiary education has become one of the crucial determinants to realize the country's goal and agenda in today's knowledge economy. Adapted from the definition by UNESCO, the terms open learning and distance education refers to approaches that focus on 'opening access to education and training provision, freeing learners from the constraints of time and place, and offering flexible learning opportunities to individuals and groups of learners' (UNESCO, 2002, p.7). Open distance education institutions in Asia and worldwide are facing vast changes brought by the increasing availability and sophistication of information and communication technologies, as well as the way these technologies are impacting upon the delivery of ODE programs (Murphy, Walker & Webb, 2001).

There is little consensus on one specific definition of national culture (Useem & Useem, 1963; Banks & Banks, 1997; Hofstede, 1980; Hofstede, 1991) as it is a complex concept. In this case study, the national culture of a country is synthesized as the language, values, behaviors, norms, and practices shared by people in the society of the nation. National culture can be identified based on four dimensions, i.e. power distance, individualism/collectivism, masculinity/femininity, and uncertainty avoidance (Hofstede, 1980).

As defined by Hofstede (1983), power distance refers to how society deals with inequality of power and wealth as a result of unequal physical and/or mental capacity of the people, while the dimension of individualism/collectivism relates the relationship between an individual and fellow citizens. Individuals concerned only their own interest and favor autonomy in societies of high individualism but societies of collectivism prefer conformity and uniformity. The masculinity/femininity dimension refers to the fundamental issue of the social aspect, rather than biological roles of the different sexes in society. In masculine societies, the traditional social role of men permeates society and values of showing off, the need for achievement, making money are important, while in feminine societies, values of relationship, quality of life, helping others and anti-hero are dominant. The dimension of uncertainty avoidance explains how society deals with the fact that the future is and will always be unknown and uncertain. Societies with low uncertainty avoidance tolerate the idea of uncertainty and take risks easily. Hofstede (2009) reported (based on a rating of 1 – 104) that the Chinese rank lower (20) than any other Asian country in the individualism ranking which is partly due to the Communist rule being in a more collectivist community that emphasizes loyalty and close commitment and relationship to the group is fostered. On the other hand, Malaysians ranked slightly higher (26), which shows Malaysians being slightly more individualistic than the Chinese. In terms of power distance, Chinese recorded a much lower ranking (80) than Malaysians (104), this indicates there is a bigger perception of inequality of power and wealth in the society of Malaysia. For the masculinity/femininity dimension, Hofstede (2009) found the Chinese society portrays higher masculinity characteristics (66), i.e. assertiveness and competitiveness, compared to the Malaysians (50). As for uncertainty avoidance, Chinese (30) has slightly better tolerance of uncertainty compared to Malaysians (36), and both societies show much lower indicators. This depicts Asian societies are able to tolerate uncertainty and ambiguity, adapting to unstructured situations.

The importance of national culture in teaching and learning can be viewed as rooted in the political, sociological, and psychological aspects of the society (Hofstede, 1986). Nations are by nature political unit, with their own history, legal, educational, governing systems, while nationality provides identity and symbolic value, and a society's thinking is shaped by national cultures. Putting the national cultural dimensions in the context of education, Hofstede (1986) found learners from small power distance societies stresses on 'impersonal truth' in knowledge dissemination, while societies with larger power distance focuses on 'personal wisdom'. Individual students will only speak up in small group setting when called upon and education is a way of obtaining upward social mobility in a typical collectivist society, which implies that obtaining paper qualification is of more importance than acquiring competencies. Students from masculine societies behave more assertive and competitive as compared to students from feminine society who behave in a modest manner as reflected in their study behavior. For students, who are able to tolerate uncertainty in their society, they feel more comfortable and are able to adapt better to less structured learning situations. Previous studies (Pratt, 1992; Bauer, Chin & Chang, 2000; Conner, 2000; Merriam & Muhammad, 2000; Tylee, 2001; Kim & Bonk, 2002; Munro-Smith, 2002; Alfred, 2003) have found evidence on cultural influence to teaching and learning based on an analysis of national cultural characteristics. Students from different cultural background learn differently as their learning attitude and behavior are influenced by their cultural values and social factors. Learners from different national cultural backgrounds have demonstrated varied web-based interaction behavior.

ORGANIZATION BACKGROUND

Shanghai TV University (STVU) is an open university, which conducts distance education based on tele-communication, broadcasting and television, computer and other modern media as one of the progress made within the competitive environment of Shanghai. It was first established in 1960 and was temporarily closed down during the "Cultural Revolution", and was resumed in 1979. The headquarters of the university has three campuses covering an area of 60.030 square meters with a total 60,000 square meters of classrooms and office buildings. Since 1994, STVU has undertaken more than 3 million person time of the test for Shanghai resident' computer abilities and has advanced an education platform and abundant teaching resources. STVU has made great efforts in promoting the popularization of higher education and continuing education, the socialization of citizens' moralization education. It is specialized in open and distance education and is called as "A University without Bounding Walls". Until June 2009, STVU has set up 14 specialties for bachelor's degree and enrolled 25,788 students; 25 specialties for under bachelor's degree, enrolled 76,034 students. The distance education broad band connects 57 campuses in Shanghai. The principles of STVU's open education are "Orienting to people", "Progressing with society", "Enhancing openness and flexibility", and "Nurturing life-long learning". The missions of the University are to build itself into a top open university within China and an influential open university in the world at large; to serve as the teaching center, R&D center, resource center and public service platform for open and distance education in Shanghai; to provide services for the whole country with Shanghai as its base; and to contribute to the establishment of learning-type society and the life-long learning system in Shanghai. The tasks of the University include to implement the overall education policies of the Chinese Communist Party and the state; to adapt to the needs of economic and social development in Shanghai and improve the reforms in education and teaching; to develop actively both the degree and non-degree education and deliver training to nurture professionals with practical skills and the ability of innovation; and to offer timely and effective services of open and distance education for people from all walks of life who intend to update their knowledge and develop skills; to make active exploration into the managing system and operating mechanism of modern open universities, to utilize the modern information technologies and bringing the advantages of open and distance education into full play; and to contribute to the social and economic development in Shanghai by serving the needs of society, industries, institutions and organizations at basic level and communities.

STVU has formed the 6Ss quality assurance system, consisting of: (i) Concept System - for encouraging, clarifying and defining ideas about quality, principles and quality management, (ii) Criterion System - consisting of quality criterion, division of responsibilities and process, (iii) Organization System - that offers organizational assurance, (iv) Implementation Systems - brings quality management into effect, (v) Control System - examines and inspects the whole teaching process and offers feedback information for the teaching, and (vi) Evaluation System and Feedback System - evaluates the teaching results and feedbacks to the departments concerned. In taking measures for quality assurance, STVU tries to fulfill the guarantee mechanism and standardize the construction and operation of teaching resources, sets up the monitor mechanism and promotes the use of multi-media teaching equipment, improves the quality of its teaching resources, offers its teachers necessary equipments. In addition, by taking advantage of all available media (e.g. TV, Internal and the publishing resources), STVU integrates all the resources and establishes the carrier of quality-oriented education. It cultivates the campus culture and cyber culture, which are of open educational features.

Wawasan (Vision) Open University (WOU) with headquarters in Penang, is Malaysia's first private and not-for-profit open university dedicated to (working) adult learners through the open distance learning (ODL) mode. WOU opened its doors to the first batch of learners in January 2007. By January 2009, there were a total of 4,047 learners who have experienced the WOU system. WOU currently offers 11 undergraduate and 2 postgraduate programs at five WOU regional and learning centers throughout the nation. WOU aspires to be a vibrant learning community that inspires learning, supports innovation and nurtures all-round personal growth, and commits to the expansion of opportunities in higher education and to teaching excellence aimed at increasing the level of knowledge and scholarship among all Malaysians. WOU believe in upholding high institutional standards, celebrating the diversity of its students, recognizing its employees, valuing citizens and the community, as well as practice academic freedom and fairness. WOU has laid down a comprehensive governance and organizational structure to ensure that it achieves its goal of excellence in all areas, also in collaboration with experts around the world. WOU has established five strategic goals, i.e. (i) A social goal to provide access to values-based learning for all adult working Malaysians regardless of their prior academic achievements and present knowledge, age, socio-economic situation, gender and residential location, (ii) An academic goal to deliver high-quality education at the preparatory, diploma, undergraduate and postgraduate levels, (iii) A first institutional goal to build a world-class environment for learning, administration and the pursuit of scholarship, (iv) A second institutional goal to establish and strengthen institutional partnerships and community outreach, and (v) A management goal to handle the institution's human, financial and physical resources effectively and efficiently.

WOU Senate and Management Boards have developed and implemented protocols for the maintenance of quality reflecting international good practices which are subjected to constant internal and external scrutiny. Quality in WOU is monitored rigorously to ensure that the five core academic integrity and excellence are maintained, i.e. in program planning, course design, development and production, course delivery, student assessment and award, and staff development. WOU quality assurance policies are guided by the University's values and commitment to good practice, the Malaysian Quality Agency's criteria and guidelines, and the international good practices and benchmarks addressing ODL provisions. WOU have instituted into its course development, delivery and assessment protocols inputs from a wide spectrum of academic and community leaders in the form of advisory peer groups to advice on the above listed expectations; external examiner systems to ensure that appropriate exit standards are met via assessment and exam systems; external content assessors to provide expert assessment on the content of individual courses as reflected in the learning material; participation of a broad range of specialists such as academics, instructional designers, editors in the development of learning materials; external course assessor to provide expert assessment input on the content of individual course materials in order to enhance their quality; subjecting the entire system for external program appraisal once every 5 to 6 years to ensure that WOU continue to maintain its academic rigor and high standards.

Despite both institutions are operating within the context of Asian countries, STVU takes roots in the traditional framework of Chinese culture while WOU operated in a multicultural environment.

SETTING THE STAGE

The motto of STVU is "Education for all, learning with aspiration" and the aim of the University is "For All Learners and All For Learners", adopting the systems approach in expansion and use of technologies. The purpose of utilization of technologies is to serve the mission of the University, raising quality of teaching and learning. Its strategy is exploring the proper and best combination of all available, both of new and old technologies, suitable and reachable for different categories of learners in different context, rather than seeking the advancement alone of modern technologies. STVU has put forward and has been carrying out in its teaching and learning the Guided Learning, Self-directed Learning and Supported Learning Mode, shortened as 3Ls Mode, which is a three dimensionally interactive mode in the sense that it is learners' autonomous learning centered, educators' guidance premised, and multimedia sources with interactive accessibility supported to meet the needs of students in their autonomous learning. The headquarters and its branch schools function differently in their division of responsibilities in the implementation of the 3Ls teaching and learning mode. During these activities, teachers and students interact with each other via various modes such as discussions in the Bulletin Board Systems (BBS) forums, question and answer session via telephone and so on. On the basis of making use of the software of China Central Radio and TV University (a dedicated open and distance education institution, under the direct supervision of the Ministry of Education of P.R. China which offers, on a nationwide basis, multi-media courses through radio, TV, print, audio-visual materials and computer networks), STVU has designed and applied a series of information management platforms. The platforms of information management in STVU include (i) Students recruitment system on the web, (ii) Platform of teaching plan and curricula management, (iii) Application system for taking the credits of the courses without examinations in the distance education, (iv) Teaching and research platform on the web, (v) Classroom on the web, and (vi) Mobile campus on texts. STVU attaches great importance to the practical resource construction for students, including teaching texts, video order program, electronic lecture notes, self-tests, assignment tutorship, virtual experiments, distance experiments, MP3, mobile learning sub-website, case study storehouse and material storehouse.

The WOU model of delivering ODE involves the interplay of key components, i.e. course materials, assessment, open entry admission system, flexible progression pathways, multiple exit points and external peer review. In WOU's technology enhanced ODL model, the role of conventional lectures are replaced by a set of comprehensive self-contained course material (including texts books) that is provided either in print or CD form. To assist learners in their studies, WOU provides learner support consisting (i) Teachers - part-time academics with relevant subject expertise who assist students in their studies through a number of two-hour long face-to-face tutorials conducted once every 4-5 weeks at the local Learning Centre, (ii) Telephone consultation by teachers (iii) Online learning support on a 24X7 basis via *WawasanLearn* - a Learning Management System (LMS) that enables learners to access additional supplementary materials, online quizzes, and forum discussions exchanges with teachers and peers, (iv) Extensive electronic library resources, (v) The staff and facilities of the WOU Regional Offices which are equipped with computer labs, libraries and free access computer terminals. WOU seek to play a significant role in the national educational landscape and continuously strives to ensure that its curricula are relevant to the principles and ideals of life-long learning. The programs offered will be utilitarian in character, and support the nation's desire to be an active player in the Knowledge Economy through producing graduates with high levels of skills and knowledge to enhance the workforce and fulfilling human resource training needs. In utilizing technology to support the University's operation and its core function of teaching and learning, WOU has in place several technology-based systems in addition to the web-based LMS, e.g. Web-based Student Portal, Staff Portal, Digital library, Online Assignment Submission and Grading System, Video Conferencing system, Online E-enrolment and payment system etc. The main campus and regional offices IT infrastructure provides WIFI access to students and computing facility that supports web-based applications. The design of the enterprise information architecture allows for WOU IT staff to manage the infrastructure down to the desktop for each site.

The concept of ODL entails educational training and instruction that does not require a student to be physically present for classes at all time. The learning process is achieved instead through content that is transmitted electronically, over the telephone, by teleconferencing, and print and multimedia materials. Both STVU and WOU have a similar mode of delivery of courses and learners support system, i.e. printed materials and/or textbook provided to all learners, offer comprehensive learner support services e.g. face-to-face tutorials, online learning, digital library resources and regional support centers. However, face-to-face tutorial in STVU are usually held once a week for 3 hours per session, but in WOU these sessions are once a month of 2 hours each. The mastery of learning outcomes of courses are evaluated via an assessment strategy that consists of a number of assignments (10 – 40% in STVU and 50% in WOU) and a proctored final examination (60% - 90% in STVU and 50% in WOU). It is also notable that learners' participation in the LMS does not contribute towards course work marks in WOU, but may be so for some courses in STVU.

CASE DESCRIPTION

Many researchers have focused on instructional considerations in response to the need to plan, design and deliver distance and/or online courses. Nonetheless, the analysis of open distance learner's learning behavior in the web-based learning environment and the influence of national cultural diversity on this mode of learning is viewed as an area worth to be explored, particularly during the transition period for Asian learners migrating from a traditional learning approach to a new web-based learning environment. Learners' interaction with the online content, i.e. the web-based resources as well as the interaction in the forum discussions within the online learning environment is investigated based on synthesizing various literatures in the related research area, i.e. model of interaction by Moore (1989), the national cultural dimensions of Hofstede (1980) as well as the dimensions of exchanges by Oliver and McLoughlin (1997).

To ensure comparability, data from the LMS of selected courses of the Bachelor of Business Administration program offered at the two institutions was obtained. A cross sectional analysis was done at the end of the semester 2 in year 2008. This study was undertaken mainly using content analysis and quantitative analysis on indicators defined to measure the students' interaction with online content, i.e. time and frequency of assessing online learning resources, types and feedback capability of online learning resources and dimension of interaction with online learning resources. Three indicators, namely dimensions of interaction, categories of exchanges and thread level of discussion were further employed to measure the students' interaction within the online forum discussions. In addition, qualitative data was acquired and analyzed via in depth interview sessions with the learners. This case presents findings that will contribute to explore the uniqueness of the learning expectation/needs and behavior of ODL learners who are within a similar Asian context but with different national culture, as observed in their learning patterns through LMS.

Technology, Management and Organizational Concerns

The management from both the institutions has carefully considered the needs and input of all stakeholders (i.e. the key administrators, the academicians, the information technology services personnel, the instructional designers, etc.) before selecting a technological medium and its implementation. In fact, representatives of the main stakeholders participated in the planning, analyzing, evaluation, designing and implementation of the online LMSs. Several technology-related concerns were considered at both the institutions with regards to the selection, development and implementation of a web-based LMS towards supporting the learners. Among the factors in consideration include evaluating the cost versus benefits, the functions, features, usability, accessibility, technological infrastructure as well as upgrading and maintenance issues of the software. Above all, the key concern revolved the issue of how well the LMS is able to support the fulfillment of the teaching-learning objective of the institutions within its culture and existing sub-systems. Now when the LMS system has been implemented, the management/key administrators of both institutions are concerned of how effectively are the LMSs are being utilized by both the teachers and learners, and whether the substantial resources embedded in the systems actually translate into core functions of supporting the students in their learning within an ODE environment.

The Web-Based Learning Management Systems (LMS) of the Institutions

Both STVU and WOU utilize the web-based LMS to provide a facilitated web-based learning environment. Asynchronous forum boards have become one of the important features of the LMS in both institutions. The LMS of STVU ("*Olclass*") was developed in-house while the LMS of WOU ("*WawasanLearn*") used Moodle, an open-source course management system. *Olclass* was developed using .net, has been in-use since year 2000 with continuous technological up-gradations. Chinese is the main language of communication used in *Olclass*. There is a separate platform for main campus and branch schools/learning centers and accessibility to previous semester's forum discussions is possible in STVU. It was also noted that the editing capability of the LMS pages of *Olclass* can be further improved, and there is a lack of tracking mechanism and statistical report-

Figure 1. Screen capture of the main page of a sample course in the LMS of STVU

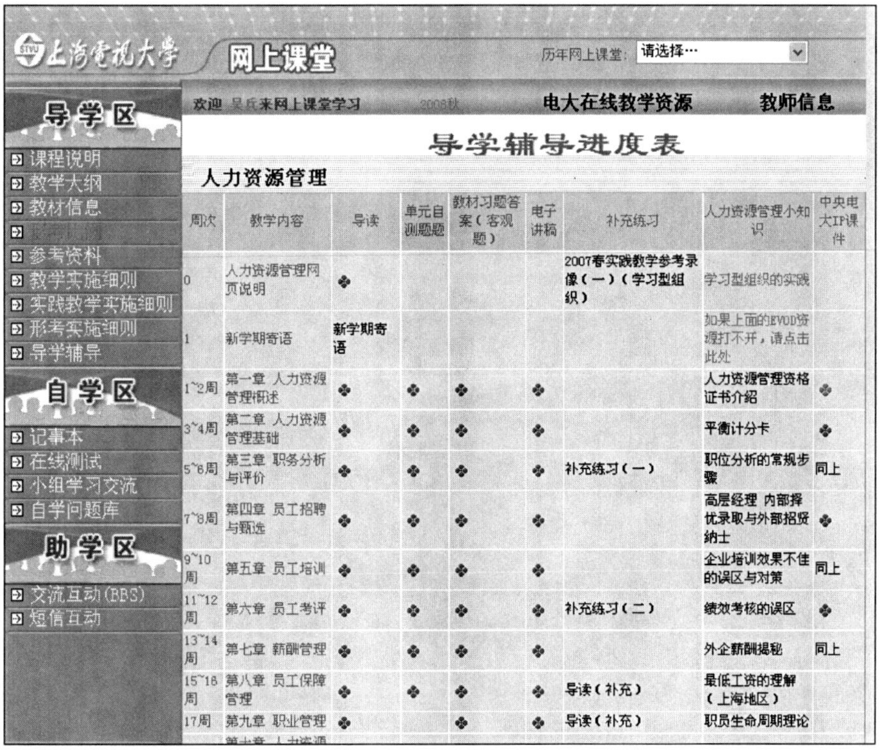

ing features (e.g. log) in the system that allows monitoring of the teaching and learning activities. *WawasanLearn* has been in-use since year 2007 and English is the medium of communication despite learners' diverse language background. The LMS of the main campus and all learning centers are integrated in the same platform, but at present, access to previous semesters' forum discussions has not been in place at WOU. *WawasanLearn* has good editing ability which is GUI-based and has strong monitoring function in place via better statistical reporting feature and log function – as per some of Moodle's capabilities. Among the common functions available in *Olclass* and *WawasanLearn* are static course materials (e.g. uploaded files, text pages, web pages, links and directories), as well as interactive and social course materials (e.g. online quizzes, asynchronous forum boards and synchronous chats).

Learners Interaction with Online Content of the LMS

Layout of the main page of the Learning Management Systems for a sample course in STVU and WOU are shown in Figure 1 and Figure 2 respectively.

The layout design in the LMS of STVU is based on its 3Ls philosophy. The left panel depicts (i) Guided learning - which provides course information, teaching outline, news, course assessment weighting, references, lesson plan - guided learning etc. (ii) Self-directed learning - that provide a notepad and online quizzes etc., and (iii) Supported learning - which provide the BBS and short message system for learners interaction with peers and teachers. The details of the resources clicked from the menu are published in the main window of the page. In the example in Figure 1, the main window of the page illustrates the Lesson Plan

Figure 2. Screen capture of the main page of a sample course in the LMS of WOU

and Schedule in guiding the learners throughout the semester. Various resources (e.g. attachments of additional notes/summaries, videos, link to the resources of CCRTVU) are planned for the learners on weekly basis.

In the LMS of WOU, the left panel of the page shows the activities (e.g. various online resources, online forums, online quizzes), the administration related functions, and a link to other courses that the learner is enrolled. On the right panel, learners are able to view the latest news of the course (which is currently set as announcements from the teacher), upcoming events (e.g. online quizzes open), calendar (which is a two-way tool that study activities are planned for the learners, and the individual learners are able to set in the calendar his/her own study plan), messaging capability (to communicate on a one-to-one basis with teacher and other learners), as well as other applications relevant to the course. The essence of the online resources designed for the course contains in the main window of the page. In this section, learners are able to access all the online forums (which serve specific purpose e.g. Announcements from the teacher, Public forum, as well as Group discussion forums based on tutorial topics of the semester). In addition, learners are able to access the supplementary course materials and other resources in place to assist their learning. These are categorized based on the five tutorial / five study units for the course. Common resources within each study unit/ tutorial include a folder that contains additional summaries/notes in presentation files and documents, hyperlinks to relevant external websites, online quizzes and other online activities.

While most of the online resources are made in place at the start of the semester, the teachers were observed to constantly post additional resources and initiating/replying to forum discussions along the semester.

Figure 3 presents a summary of the key data of the samples selected for analysis in this case study in STVU and WOU.

As shown in Figure 3, the average age of the learners enrolled in the sample courses was lower in STVU (27 years) as compared to WOU (35 years). Majority of the learners in STVU and WOU were female, accounting 53% and 55% respectively. Participation rate in the LMS (calculated as the number of students logged in and access to the online resources over the total number of students enrolled in the course) was much higher in WOU (95%) as compared to 51% in STVU. The average time spent online for 18-weeks semester was approximately 13.6 hours for STVU learners and 29.5 hours for WOU learners. The activity level /frequency of interaction with the online content was measured by the number of times the learners have accessed the online resources on the LMS during the semester, over the total number of learners who go online. In quantifying this, redundant data from the log files of the activities in LMS has been eliminated to ensure a true reflection of the learners' learning pattern with the online content. The average activity level over a semester was higher in WOU (58 times) than STVU (17 times). In terms of the pattern of activity, the frequency of learners going online was more evenly distributed (an average access rate of 15%) through out the semester in WOU. This was contrary to the pattern observed among the STVU learners in which the frequency of interaction with online content was the highest during the last couple of months of the semester, i.e. during the examination time. The examination attendance rate was slightly higher in WOU (93.7%) as compared to STVU (83.2%). Another interesting finding which was common to the learners of both the institutions that learners actively accessing and participating in the online LMS got better results as compared to that of their peers who were accessing and participating intermittently in the web-based learning environment.

Interview sessions conducted with randomly selected students (equal number of interviewees according to gender, online activity, and examination results, based on five questions to guide the interviewer) provide further insight into the learner pattern observed and are discussed along with the subsequent findings as reported in this case. Learners from STVU did not perceive the LMS as the main source of study, as they preferred to attend the face-to-face classes. They found the materials in LMS supportive to their learning, particularly when it was nearer to the examination period. Learners from WOU spent more time on the LMS due to their professional commitment and were not able to attend the face-to-face classes (tutorial attendance at an average of 79%). These students had spent most of their time (approximately 50%) on self-study while another 30% utilized their time in accessing the LMS for information and participation in the forum

Figure 3. Data summary

Indicators	STVU		WOU	
Average age of students (years)	27		35	
Gender	Male: 47% Female:53%		Male: 45% Female: 55%	
Participation rate (%) (No. Online / No. Enrolled)*100%	51%		95%	
Average time online (hours)	13.6		29.5	
Average activity level over a semester (times) (Total no. of access / Total learners online)	17		58	
Examination attendance rate (%)	83.2%		93.7%	
Patterns of Access Across Time in a Semester				
Access rate by learners (%)				
1st month	0.4		13.2	
2nd month	4.7		16.3	
3rd month	13.9		17.8	
4th month	10.5		19.1	
5th month	47.9		19.4	
6th month	22.6		14.2	
Total	*100%*		*100%*	
Learners' access to online content, examination score and passing rate	**Low access (below median)**	**High access (above median)**	**Low access (below median)**	**High access (above median)**
Examination score (%) (Mean)	63.5	65.7	58.3	71.6
Passing rate (%)	69.6	73.9	79.4	88.6

discussions. The balance of their study time was used in accessing the digital library, telephone communication with the teacher and group discussions with their peers, attending classes and working on the assignments. Majority of these learners rated the usefulness of the LMS as 80 over 100. They found the LMS enabling them to access up-to-date support materials and allowing them to stay in touch with their course mates. In fact, the learners have indicated that the forum discussions were relevant to the course content and hence they have benefitted from it.

The online resources available on the LMS of both institutions are categorized as:

M1: Text-based pages (e.g. course overview information, references, information on assessment tasks)

M2: Attachment files (e.g. additional supplementary reading materials, case studies, past year examination questions, and summaries of the study unit in the form of presentation files, word documents etc.)

M3: Video resources (e.g. For STVU – recorded lectures of teachers and guest lecturers, and videos from CCRTVU)

M4: Hyperlinks to external websites (e.g. For WOU – educational and related websites that were related to the course content)

M5: Online BBS Discussion Forums (asynchronous)

M6: Online Quizzes (not contributing to the assessment marks for the course)

The evaluation and feedback capability of the above resources were examined on the criteria of one-way non-interactive or two-way interaction between learner-content to evaluate the outcome of learning from the interaction. Online resources that are perceived to have weaker evaluation and

Figure 4. Distribution of online learning content by teachers versus access to the online content by students

Type of Online Resources	STVU			WOU		
	Distribution (%)	Access (%)	Rank	Distribution (%)	Access (%)	Rank
M1 Text	25.4	17.8	2 vs 2	4.6	0.9	5 vs 5
M2 Attachment files (E.g. .doc, .pdf, .ppt)	52.4	64.3	1 vs 1	14.4	20.1	3 vs 3
M3 Video	17.3	4	3 vs 4	-	-	-
M4 Link to External Websites	-	-	-	45.4	8.0	1 vs 4
M5 Online Forums	3.6	10.7	4 vs 3	13.9	45.4	4 vs 1
M6 Online Quizzes	1.2	3.2	5 vs 5	21.7	25.6	2 vs 2
Total	100	100		100	100	

Note:
- Rank 1 vs 1 means that the online content rank highest in distribution and also obtain the highest in access by learners
- Rank 4 vs 6 means that the online content rank 4th highest in distribution but lowest in terms of access by learners.

feedback capability include digital reading materials e.g. additional notes posted in the format of .pdf, .ppt or .doc., text and static web pages. Online resources that have stronger evaluation and feedback capability are the asynchronous discussion forums that allow interactivity compared to the previous category. The content of exchanges preserved in the online discussion forums is viewed as one of the important learning resources in the online learning environment. Thus learners' access to the online forum has been one of the indications of learners' interaction with the online content as well. Discussions in the online forums are often a reflection of learners thinking process of the course content. As learners discuss course concepts in the online forums, it creates a learning environment that reflects online collaboration effort. As a result of these exchanges, knowledge has been generated. In the forums, learners are able to view the entire process of the queries raised, the analysis of the queries and how the queries are resolved or concluded among their teacher and peers. Hence, learners are able to extend the knowledge and clear any doubts that they have about a subject, despite not posting any responses. The type of online content that provides strongest evaluation capability and real-time feedback are the online quizzes. These are means of learners' self-evaluation of learning and serve as one of the tool for teachers to assess the outcome of learners' learning process.

The extent of interaction with online materials can be viewed in terms of the various dimensions of interaction i.e. social, procedural, expository, explanatory and cognitive. Similar dimensions are adopted in analyzing the detailed forum exchanges at a later section of this case. Online content that allow social presence would be the welcoming message posted by the teacher on the main page and the learners' exchanges in the online forums. Procedural related content comprises mainly text files or web-pages that present the generic information about the course such as the learning objectives, assessment tasks and intended learning outcomes of the course. Interaction with online learning materials that involves demonstration of knowledge and facts without much further elaboration represent interaction at the expository dimension. For examples, viewing glossary of keywords for the course. Online learning resources that are contained in the explanatory dimension include materials uploaded as attachments (e.g. presentation slides and additional notes in word document) that explain the essential concepts about the course. This may also be sharing of frequently-asked questions from learners in the previous semesters which were presented in a web page. These resources help learners to clarify any doubts that they have and to reinforce their understanding on the basic principles of the course content. The final dimension of interaction with online content at cognitive level involves providing constructive feedback and detailed commentary on course content via critical thinking that leads to knowledge development. Online learning resources that permit interaction at this level include online quizzes. Exchanges in the online forums would cover the above mentioned dimensions of interaction.

Figure 4 shows the distribution and access to the various types of online resources in the LMSs of both the institutions.

As shown in Figure 4, the distribution of online resources in STVU was mostly the M2 (52.4%) category as compared to M4 (45.4%) in WOU while online content of one-way nature accounted for 95% for STVU and 64% for WOU. This explains that most of the online resources are still centered at delivery the content via one-way non-interactive communication. Online resources in attachment files (M2) category include mostly topic exercise questions, answers to the exercises in the printed materials and lecture notes. These resources mainly explain and elaborate the essential concepts of the study unit. Hence, in terms of the dimension of interaction with this type of online content, it would more be at the expository or explanatory level. High number of access to this type of resources also entails that learners at STVU are able to integrate what they have learnt from the printed learning materials and classes with the online learning resources, thus indicates an increasing adaptation of the learners to the online learning environment. In WOU, a number of hyperlinks to external websites were provided to direct the working adult learners to additional resources related to the course content. While teachers in WOU have arranged a number of hyperlinks to other websites as additional online reading related to topics discussed in the course, while serving as supplementary materials to broaden the learners' thinking, learners seem do not favor accessing these hyperlinks. While printed learning materials and online learning materials are delivered to learners, learners prefer to spend more time in reading and studying materials that are directly related to the course content. They are not willing to explore much on additional learning materials that are not directly related to the course. Generally, learners still perceived printed learning materials as most reliable and authoritative in determining their learning outcome from the course. The teachers view additional supplementary readings as assistance in learning, learners may face difficulties in grasping the main points arising from browsing and reading from the other websites due to the amount of information contained in those websites. STVU learners did not access the video much (accounted only for 4% of the total access). As discovered from the interviews, despite video being a multimedia resource that combines visual and audio elements in delivering the course content, it seems not well-received by the learners. Learners still prefer to attend face-to-face classes in physical presence, instead of spending hours in front of the computer screen to view a one-way delivered video. It is noticed that the content of these videos are mainly case studies related to the teaching of the course. Learners can either select case studies from the videos or source for other case studies to produce an assignment paper as part of the course assessment. Most learners have demonstrate the choice of sourcing their own case studies which they perceived to be more familiar with compared to what that have been prescribed. Despite containing valuable content related to the course, the ease of accessing and viewing the content of video is a concern.

Among all online content, WOU learners accessed online forums the most which account for 45.4% of their overall online activity while STVU learners preferred supplementary reading materials in the form of presentation files and document files of additional study notes. This difference can be partly explained in terms of the course delivery model of both institutions in which STVU learners attend face-to-face tutorials every week while it is once a month for WOU. STVU learners have more opportunities to interact physically with the teacher and peers. Learners from STVU prefer to resolve their doubts and queries during the face-to-face meetings when they face difficulties in their study. Learning on the web-based environment would be focusing on evaluating and reinforcing their understanding of the knowledge via accessing the supplementary materials. WOU learners meet less frequently physically and eventually utilize the online forums to discuss on matters related to the course with their teacher and peers. Based on feedback obtained from the interview sessions, learners in WOU were keen to participate in the online quizzes which was prepared by the teacher include numerous types of questions such as multiple choice questions and true/false questions. Each time the learners access the online quizzes; questions would be extracted from the questions bank in the LMS and be presented to the learners. Upon completion of the test, learners will know the score and obtained the answers to all questions attempted. Online tests have become a web-based resource that allows real-time assessment to the learners' learning. Despite scores obtained are not taken into account as part of the course marks, online tests are perceived as a valuable learning resources to test learners' basic understanding and be more well-prepared for examination particularly for distance learners. However, STVU learners were found to least access the online quizzes in this platform as further investigation revealed that they have actually accessed another platform by CCRTVU to complete the online quizzes there which were accounted for their assessment grades.

Learners Interaction with Teacher and Peers in the Online Forum Discussions

Based on Oliver and McLoughlin (1997) who explored the dimensions of interaction by classifying interaction activity into five parts, i.e. social, procedural, expository, explanatory and cognitive, social dimension can be defined as to include discussions of a social nature which are not directly associated with the course content, while procedural dimension involves explanation on course related procedures, requirements and administrative issues. Expository dimension involves demonstration of knowledge/facts without much further elaboration while explanatory dimension refers to elaborate explanation on knowledge and developed content based on learner's response. Finally, cognitive involves providing constructive feedback and detailed commentary on course content via critical thinking which leads to knowledge development.

The content of the web-based interaction - by initiator and respondents, are categorized into four groups of exchanges, i.e. from teacher to group, from teacher to individual learner, from individual learner to teacher and from individual learner to group. In a teacher to group category of exchanges, the teacher initiates a discussion and addresses it to all students in the group.

Figure 5 shows the dimension, exchanges and depth of interaction in the online forum board discussions in LMSs of STVU and WOU.

As depicted in Figure 5, the initiators of the discussions in forum were mostly female learners (61.1%) as compared to WOU in which male

Figure 5. Dimension, exchanges and depth of interactions in the online forum board discussions

Interactions	STVU (%)	WOU (%)
Initiator		
Male	38.9	62.3
Female	61.1	37.7
Total	*100.0*	*100.0*
Dimensions		
Cognitive	16.1	15.2
Explanatory	5.5	29.1
Expository	11.2	22.6
Procedural	48.7	20.7
Social	18.5	12.4
Total	*100.0*	*100.0*
Exchanges		
Teacher-Group	5.3	51.2
Teacher-Student	0.8	0
Student-Teacher	60.7	14.5
Student-Group	33.2	34.3
Total	*100.0*	*100.0*
Depth		
Thread = 1	25.3	20.3
Thread = 2	55.4	18.6
Thread = 3	9.4	20.9
Thread ≥ 4	9.9	40.2
Total	*100.0*	*100.0*

accounted for more (62.3%) in initiating online discussions. This reflects the aggressiveness of female learners in online learning and the social gender equality in the modern city of Shanghai while in the case of WOU, despite majority of the learners were female, male learners seemed to be more assertive in starting forum discussions.

The Procedural dimension of interaction was the most dominant (48.7%) in STVU, followed by Social (18.5%), Cognitive (16.1%), Expository (11.2%) and the least dominant dimension was Explanatory (5.5%). Most messages were initiated by the individual learner to the teacher (60.7%), followed by the exchanges with classmates (33.2%). The least dominant category of exchanges was teacher to individual learner (0.8%). Most forum exchanges (55.4%) remained at second thread while 25.3% topics of discussion did not receive any ensuing replies. About 10% of the discussions proceeded to the fourth thread and beyond. The Explanatory dimension of interaction (29.1%) appears to be the most dominant in WOU, followed by Expository (22.6%), Procedural (20.7%) and Cognitive (15.2%). The least dominant dimension was Social (12.4%). More than half of the messages (51.2%) were in the teacher to group category of exchanges while student to group category accounted for 34.3%. The least dominant was the category of exchanges of individual student to teacher which is 14.5%. There were no messages initiated in the teacher to student category as the students used the Message function to communicate with individual student or teacher. Most forum exchanges in WOU proceeded to the fourth thread of interactions and beyond (40.2%), with about 20.9% of the discussions with only 2 replies, while 20.3% of the discussions did not have any ensuing reply.

The demand for skilled manpower and higher education increases in tandem with China's rapid social development and economic growth. More Chinese are considering continued education program and retraining in order to gain personal prestige and improve their socio-economic standing. With many formal education setups still heavily exam-orientated, learners' questions and concerns still tend to gravitate towards examination procedures and strategies, as shown in the dominant dimension of interaction as Procedural related. The LMS, besides acting as a platform for learning materials, also enables learners to establish friendships with their counterparts. Web-based interactions not only fulfilled the learning requirement, but also fulfilled the social need for bonding and friendship. This finding also highlights the elements of collectivism in China's culture. In the depth of discussion, statistics for STVU indicate a high level of Thread 2 interaction activity. This is due to the fact that most exchanges were at the Procedural dimension level and were geared towards obtaining a single direct answer to a query. When Chinese learners encounter challenges in their studies, most of them prefer to use LMS and have direct contact with their teacher in order to gain more information. The environment of a web-based learning process offers a learning experience with a difference. Online learners are able to bridge the distance or close the gap between learners and teachers easily. Meanwhile, the high teacher to group interaction level in WOU indicates that the ODL in Asia is still very teacher-centered. The teacher plans learning tasks and follow up with directives or instructions. The findings indicate that learners in Malaysia aim to gain more knowledge in their learning activities as reflected in the exchanges at explanatory dimension. At the same time, the results also imply that the learners in Malaysia are quite independent and could easily adapt to a web-based mode of education. Based on inputs obtained from the interview sessions, Chinese learners view learning as the acquisition of knowledge or skills from others, is a fulfillment of responsibility to society, and a change in understanding of external things and oneself, while Malaysian learners indicated their preference to be collective and interdependent as they view learning as they enjoyed being in a group and related with other learners. The Malaysian learners portrayed independent thinking in articulating their views on the discussion topics and appreciated the support and sharing of knowledge by teachers and peers in the web-based learning environment and conveyed that they are intrinsically motivated in enrolling for the course to improve the economic growth and self-respect based on ability and competence. Malaysian learners seldom challenge the teachers directly, which depicts a higher degree of power distance in online learning environment of Malaysian society.

Findings from the case have shown that Asian learners in general are gradually adapting to the online learning environment, and moving away from the conventional teacher-centered learning.

CURRENT CHALLENGES FACING THE ORGANIZATIONS

The case brought forward several challenges facing both STVU and WOU with regards to better utilization of the web-based LMS in teaching and learning effectively – considering the influence of national culture of the two nations. The breadth and depth of the online resources and the capabilities, features and functions adequacy of the LMSs are areas need to be further examined. The gap between the expectation and understanding of the teacher versus the learner on the online content and support provided in the web-based learning environment needs to be addressed in order to further enhance the efficacy of the online learning environment. It has always been the concern of the management of both institutions on the access and use of the online learning platform by its learners. This in turn reflects the effectiveness of the online resources put in place and the accessibility of the LMSs. In order to better monitor and measure the effectiveness of such system in fulfilling the institution's core objective, this call for the need to enhance the monitoring log capabilities of the LMSs. Acknowledging these concerns, the management of STVU and WOU are continuously monitoring and improving the delivery of online content via the LMSs.

Particularly, among the challenges faced by STVU as found by this case study, include discovering ways to improve the learners' participation rate in the online learning platform, encourage them to spend more time in utilizing the online resources and hence improve the activity level in the LMS. While teachers may perceive the usefulness of certain online resources to the learners, the resources may not be well received (utilized) by the learners in an online setting. For example in the case of STVU, the learners were found to prefer using the online forum versus watching the videos in the LMS. This prompts the management/academicians to further investigate the concern of learners with regards to the videos (content, relevance and accessibility) in the LMS. In WOU, learners were found to favor the online forums and the online quizzes over the additional hyperlinks provided for further readings and resources. Hence, the challenge would be balancing the expectation and perception of the learners with regards to the online resources put in place, as well as to further capitalize on the preferred online study material of the learners.

Management and academicians at both institutions were also confronted by the actual utilization of the online forums as an instrument in promoting quality interaction among the teacher, learners and their peers. As found by the case, interaction in the LMS of STVU was dominantly at the procedural level, with majority of only 1 single reply to a posting initiated in the online forum. In addition, the prevailing category of exchanges that occurred was mainly learner directing questions to the teacher, rather than to the group of learners. This is common in a society that upholds strong value of Confucian which believe that neither the teacher nor students should be put in a position to suffer "loss of face" or embarrassment. Students are found to be unwilling or reluctant to comment on others' opinion or ideas posted in the forums. In the case of WOU, the more dominant interaction was in the explanatory dimension rather than the cognitive dimension which usually occurs in a face-to-face context. The online activities as observed in the forum discussion showed a teacher-centered approach as rooted in the society of very high power distance, however, the depth of most of the exchanges have progressed to thread = 4 and above.

From the perspective of information transmission, the interaction of online learning via the web lacks the range of physical expressions and the stimulus of sound. Learners do not experience the impact of live hearing and seeing, but only communication via words. This type of communication is perceived to be less intimate and animated, increasing the feeling of loneliness and alienation experienced by the learners. The learner's experience in the first few weeks of the semester is believed to deeply affect the subsequent learning behavior of the learners. This is the transition period for learners to shift from a traditional learning approach to a new web-based learning environment. Asian learners are known to have acted as readers who did not ask or field any questions. These groups of learners often wait for the teacher to define their responsibility, and may directly relay their doubts to the teacher. It is crucial to help the learner, regardless of the influence of background culture, to gain a level of confidence in learning, which will lead to greater satisfaction in acquiring and synthesizing knowledge. This factor is crucial as it boosts the learner's satisfaction and interest, and encourages participation in web-based discussions in a more meaningful way.

The above findings put forward the challenge to encourage higher order and deeper exchanges among the teacher, learner and peers in the LMS. Besides, the online learning environment need to be better designed and facilitated to allow balanced interaction among the players, and across time during the semester.

SOLUTIONS AND RECOMMENDATIONS

In addressing the issues and challenges discussed in the preceding section, several aspects should be considered in delivering online content for ODL courses. The online learning activities of learners are influenced by various factors such as the learning style, attitude of learners and capability of using computer and Internet. The selection and delivery of online content should take into consideration practical guidelines of a good web-based content such as accessibility, flexibility, interactivity, ease of navigation, motivational value and its effectiveness. In addition, the influence of regional and the role of national culture which cannot be neglected.

The online learning environment should always allow for quality interaction between the learners and content, learners and teacher, as well as learners and peers. The design and organization of online learning materials should be closely related to the intended learning outcomes, and not by merely having loads of materials to supplement the existing materials. Online learning materials need to be congruent with the learning objectives of the course. Providing as much resources as possible to the learners tends to be thought as effective teaching, however, this could actually divert the learners' attention away from focusing on the intended learning outcomes to be achieved and possibly caused information overload. The interaction with content should not just be a one-way interaction via purely text display or conversion of learning materials to digital forms. The organization of online learning materials should include other forms which have the capability of providing immediate feedback and stimulate the learning process. While hyperlinked websites serve as additional learning materials that supplement the course content, the number of hyperlinks made available on the LMS should not be too many as it may divert the learners' attention and could incurred too much time spent accessing websites that may not be directly relevant to their studies. It is more effective if teachers could summarize and arrange the main points from supplementary readings for learners. In addition, validity of the web address at the point of accessing need to be taken into account. With regards to online quizzes, teachers should incorporate more variety of question types via establishment of a questions bank to capitalize on the effectiveness of online tests. From the scores recorded and analysis of questions attempted by the learners, teachers would then be able to improve on the course content delivery.

Timely and appropriate training is crucial to equip teachers with necessary facilitation skills towards enhancing learner-centered interaction in the web-based learning environment, acknowledging the fact that teachers are managers of learners learning experience. Teachers need to capitalize on various techniques to break the ice as well as to create a friendly web-based learning environment, in order to eliminate the gap caused by distance and non-face to face communication. Once the learners are used to the web-based communication environment, they will adopt and participate in online communication as one of the crucial learning tools available to them. As ODL learners tend to feel lonely throughout their journey of acquiring knowledge, timely feedback plays a vital role to eliminate the negative feelings associated with on-line learning. Feedback can be broadly defined as the exchange of information between learner-instructor, learner-learner and learner-LMS with regard to an action, event, or process that results in enhanced student learning. Asynchronous forum board is one of the good ways to provide timely feedback.

The bearing that culture has will not be eliminated with the advancement of technologies. Information and communication technology is largely unable to provide a solution for all the problems encountered in gearing towards effective and efficient teaching and training, despite its continuous development and evolvement. Along with the progress of Asian societies and the learners' ability to adapt to new learning approaches, the behavior of Asian learners learning via the Internet is expected to change progressively. Hence, acknowledgement of this fact brings a realization of the many strategies that will need to be implemented to upgrade the effectiveness of online teaching learning environment.

REFERENCES

Alfred, M. V. (2003). Sociocultural contexts and learning: Anglophone Caribbean immigrant women in U. S. postsecondary education. *Adult Education Quarterly, 53*, 242–260. doi:10.1177/0741713603254028

Banks, J. A., & Banks, C. A. (1997). Multicultural education: Issues and perspective (3rd ed.). Boston: Allyn & Bacon.

Bauer, C., Chin, K. L., & Chang, V. (2000). *Web-based learning: Aspects of cultural differences*. Paper presented at the 8th European Conference on Information Systems, Trends in Information and Communication Systems for the 21st Century. Austria. Retrieved July 1, 2007, from http://csrc.lse.ac.uk/asp/aspecis/20000068.pdf

Central Intelligence Agency. (2009a). *The World Factbook: China*. Retrieved March 1, 2009, from https://www.cia.gov/library/publications/the-world-factbook/geos/ch.html

Central Intelligence Agency. (2009b). *The World Factbook: Malaysia*. Retrieved March 1, 2009, from https://www.cia.gov/library/publications/the-world-factbook/geos/my.html

Conner, M. (2000). *Global implications of e-learning*. Retrieved July 1, 2007 from http://www.linezine.com/2.1/features/mcgie.htm

Hofstede, G. (1980). Culture's consequences: International differences in work-related values. Beverly Hill, CA: Sage.

Hofstede, G. (1986). Cultural differences in teaching and learning. *International Journal of Intercultural Relations, 10*, 301–320. doi:10.1016/0147-1767(86)90015-5

Hofstede, G. (1991). Cultures and organizations: Software of the mind. New York: McGraw-Hill.

Hofstede, G. (2009). *Geert Hofstede Cultural Dimensions*. Retrieved March 1, 2009, from http://www.geert-hofstede.com/hofstede_dimensions.php

Kim, K. J., & Bonk, C. J. (2002). Cross-cultural comparisons of online collaboration. *Journal of Computer-Mediated Communication, 8*(1).

Meriam, S., & Muhammad, M. (2000). How cultural values shapes learning in older adulthood: The case of Malaysia. *Adult Education Quarterly, 51*, 45–63.

Moore, M. G. (1989). Three types of interaction. *American Journal of Distance Education, 3*(2), 1–7. doi:10.1080/08923648909526659

Munro-Smith, N. (2002). *A tale of two cities: Computer mediated teaching and learning in Melbourne and Singapore*. Paper presented at the 19th ASCILITE Conference, Auckland, New Zealand. Retrieved July 1, 2007 from http://www.ascilite.org.au/conferences/auckland02/proceedings/papers/105.pdf

Murphy, D., Walker, R., & Webb, G. (2001). Online learning and teaching with technology: Case studies, experience and practice. London: Kogan Page.

Netto, A. (2009). *IT Literacy High on Government Priority List in Malaysia*. Retrieved March 1, 2009. from http://www.unesco.org/education/efa/know_sharing/grassroots_stories/malaysia.shtml

Oliver, R., & McLoughlin, C. (1997). Interactions in audio-graphics and learning environments. *American Journal of Distance Education, 11*(1), 34–54. doi:10.1080/08923649709526950

Pratt, D. D. (1992). Chinese conceptions of learning and teaching: A Westerner's attempt at understanding. *International Journal of Lifelong Education, 11*, 301–319. doi:10.1080/0260137920110404

Tylee, J. (2001). *Cultural issues and the online environment*. Retrieved July 1, 2007, from http://www.csu.edu.au/division/landt/resources/documents/cultural_issues.pdf

United Nations Educational, Scientific and Cultural Organization (UNESCO). (2002). *Open and distance learning: Trends, policy and strategy considerations*. Retrieved March 1, 2009, from http://unesdoc.unesco.org/images/0012/001284/128463e.pdf

Useem, J., & Useem, R. (1963). Men in the middle of the third culture: The roles of American and non-Western people in cross-cultural administration. *Human Organization, 22*, 169–179.

Wikipedia. (2009a). *Education in the People's Republic of China*. Retrieved March 1, 2009 from http://en.wikipedia.org/wiki/Education_in_the_People's_Republic_of_China

Wikipedia. (2009b). *Education in Malaysia*. Retrieved March 1, 2009, from http://en.wikipedia.org/wiki/Education_in_Malaysia

World Bank. (2009). *Malaysia: Country Summary of Higher Education*. Retrieved March 1, 2009, from http://siteresources.worldbank.org/EDUCATION/Resources/278200-1121703274255/1439264-1193249163062/Malaysia_CountrySummary.pdf

ADDITIONAL READING

Bates, A. W. (1995). Technology, open learning and distance education. New York: Routledge.

Carter, L. M. (2009). Assessing Learners Online: A Review. *Journal of Distance Education*, 23(1), Retrieved July 1, 2009, from http://www.jofde.ca/index.php/jde/article/viewArticle/486

Cronjé, J. C. (2006). Interpreting cross-cultural blended teaching and learning along Hofstede's cultural dimensions. Retrieved March 1, 2009, from http://emerge2006.net/connect/site/UploadWSC/emerge2006/file32/Microsoft%20Word%20-%20interpretingwithhofstede.pdf

Dennen, V. P., Darabi, A. A., & Smith, L. J. (2007). Instructor–learner interaction in online courses: The relative perceived importance of particular instructor actions on performance and satisfaction. *Distance Education, 28*(1), 65–79. doi:10.1080/01587910701305319

Garrison, D. R., & Cleveland-Innes, M. (2005). Facilitating cognitive presence in online learning: Interaction is not enough. *American Journal of Distance Education, 19*(3), 133–148. doi:10.1207/s15389286ajde1903_2

Hill, J. R., Song, L., & West, R. E. (2009). Social Learning Theory and Web-Based Learning Environments: A Review of Research and Discussion of Implications. *American Journal of Distance Education, 23*(2), 88–103. doi:10.1080/08923640902857713

Hillman, D. C. A., Willis, D. J., & Gunawardena, C. N. (1994). Learner-interface interaction in distance education: An extension of contemporary models and strategies for practitioners. *American Journal of Distance Education, 8*(2), 30–42. doi:10.1080/08923649409526853

Hrastinski, S. (2009). A theory of online learning as online participation. *Computers & Education, 52*(1), 78–82. doi:10.1016/j.compedu.2008.06.009

Hutchins, H. M., & Hutchison, D. (2008). Cross-disciplinary contributions to e-learning design: a tripartite design model. *Journal of Workplace Learning, 20*(5), 364–380. doi:10.1108/13665620810882950

Hwang, A., & Arbaugh, J. B. (2009). Seeking feedback in blended learning: competitive versus cooperative student attitudes and their links to learning outcome. *Journal of Computer Assisted Learning, 25*(3), 280–293. doi:10.1111/j.1365-2729.2009.00311.x

Johnson, E. S. (2007). Promoting Learner-Learner Interactions through Ecological Assessments of the Online Environment. *MERLOT Journal of Online Learning and Teaching*, 3(2), Retrieved July 1, 2009, from http://jolt.merlot.org/vol3no2/johnson.htm.

Jones, J., Warren, S., & Robertson, M. (2009). Increasing Student Discourse to Support Rapport Building in Web and Blended Courses Using a 3D Online Learning Environment. *Journal of Interactive Learning Research, 20*(3), 269–294.

Jones, M., & Alony, I. (2007). The Cultural Impact of Information Systems – Through the Eyes of Hofstede – A Critical Journey. Issues in Informing Science and Information Technology, 4, Retrieved March 1, 2009, from http://proceedings.informingscience.org/InSITE2007/IISITv4p407-419Jone365.pdf

Moore, M. G., & Kearsley, G. (1996). Distance education: A systems view. New York: Wadsworth.

Oliver, R., & McLoughlin, C. (1997). Interactivity in telelearning environments: Using communications and dialogue meaningfully in the learning process. Retrieved July 1, 2007, from http://elrond.scam.ecu.edu.au/oliver/docs/97/ODLAA2do.pdf

Oliver, R., Omari, A., & Herrington, J. (1997). Exploring Student Interaction in Collaborative World Wide Web Learning Environments. ED-MEDIA/EDTELECOM 1997. Calgary, Canada, II, 812-817. Retrieved July 1, 2007, from http://ecu.edu.au/oliver/docs/97/EM1doc.pdf

Palaiologou, N. (2009). Needs for developing culturally oriented supportive learning with the aid of Information and Communication Technologies. *Pedagogy, Culture & Society, 17*(2), 189–200.

Picciano, A. G. (2002). Beyond student perceptions: Issues of interaction, presences and performance in an online course. *Journal of Asynchronous Learning Networks, 6*(1), 21–40.

Robson, J. (1996). The effectiveness of teleconferencing in fostering interactions in distance learning education. *Distance Education, 17*(2), 304–334. doi:10.1080/0158791960170207

Shanghai TV University http://www.shtvu.edu.cn

Tapanes, M. A., Smith, G. G., & White, J. A. (2009). Cultural diversity in online learning: A study of the perceived effects of dissonance in levels of individualism/collectivism and tolerance of ambiguity. *The Internet and Higher Education*, *12*(1), 26–34. doi:10.1016/j.iheduc.2008.12.001

Thorpe, M. (2008). Effective online interaction: Mapping course design to bridge from research to practice. *Australasian Journal of Educational Technology*, *24*(1), 57–72.

Wawasan Open University http://www.wou.edu.my

Weaver, D., Spratt, C., & Nair, C. S. (2008). Academic and student use of a learning management system: Implications for quality. *Australasian Journal of Educational Technology*, *24*(1), 30–41.

Woo, Y., & Reeves, T. C. (2007). Meaningful interaction in web-based learning: A social constructivist interpretation. *The Internet and Higher Education*, *10*(1), 15–25. doi:10.1016/j.iheduc.2006.10.005

Wu, B., & Teoh, A. P. (2008). The Influence of National Culture Toward Learner Interaction: Shanghai TV University and Wawasan Open University. *Quarterly Review of Distance Education*, *9*(3), 327–339.

Yang, Y. T. C., Newby, T., & Bill, R. (2008). Facilitating interactions through structured web-based bulletin boards: A quasi-experimental study on promoting learners' critical thinking skills. *Computers & Education*, *50*(4), 1572–1585. doi:10.1016/j.compedu.2007.04.006

Zhu, C., Valcke, M., & Schellens, T. (2009). A cross-cultural study of online collaborative learning. *Multicultural Education & Technology Journal*, *3*(1), 33–46. doi:10.1108/17504970910951138

KEY TERMS AND DEFINITIONS

Categories of Exchanges: Categories of exchanges refers to the web-based interaction - by initiator and respondents, and can be categorized into four groups of exchanges, i.e. from teacher to group, from teacher to individual learner, from individual learner to teacher and from individual learner to group.

Dimensions of Interaction: Dimension of interaction can be viewed in terms of classifying interaction activity into five levels, i.e. social, procedural, expository, explanatory and cognitive.

Interaction: Open distance learner engagement in the online learning environment involve exchanges at various dimensions, i.e. learner with online content, learner and teacher, learner and peers, as well as learner with technology interface. This encompasses the learner's adaptability and experience interacting with the online content.

Learner Interaction with Online Content: This involves the time and frequency of assessing online learning resources by the learners, types and feedback capability of online learning resources, and dimension of interaction with online learning resources.

Learner Interaction in the Online Asynchronous Discussion Forums: This relates to the learner's interaction in the online forums based on three indicators, namely dimensions of interaction, categories of exchanges and thread level of discussion.

Learning Management Systems: Learning management system refers to software that delivers, facilitates and monitor teaching and learning. A web-based learning management system provides the platform for delivery and facilitating online content in various forms, such as static course materials (e.g. uploaded files, text pages, web pages, links and directories), as well as interactive and social course materials (e.g. online quizzes, asynchronous forum boards and synchronous chats), that support the teaching and learning of courses at a distance utilizing the Internet technology.

National Culture: National culture is synthesized as the language, values, behaviors, norms, and practices shared by people in the society of a nation, and can be based on four dimensions (Hofstede, 1980), i.e. power distance, individualism/collectivism, masculinity/femininity, and uncertainty avoidance. This is among the factors that shape the online learning environment contained and faced by the open distance learners.

Online Content: Online content can be categorized into six groups, i.e. text/web pages, attachments (e.g. documents, presentation files etc.), video, hyperlink to external websites, online forums, and online quizzes.

Chapter 8
EPICT:
Transnational Teacher Development through Blended Learning

Katalin Csoma
Freelance researcher, Hungary

ABSTRACT

This case aims at introducing international professional audiences to a transnational teacher development program, the European Pedagogical ICT License (EPICT), empowering teachers to use information technologies with greater efficiency in their everyday practice. Beyond introducing the program through the Hungarian experience, the present state of teacher training will be discussed, under transformation in line with the Bologna process and the joint European harmonization of education systems. It will be examined how alternative forms of learning and networking bring about changes to the teaching profession in Europe and other affiliated countries.

INTRODUCTION

Common Technologies in the 21st Century

With the emergence of new technologies, the learning habits of today's youth have undoubtedly changed worldwide. Those born in or after the 1980s or even more so towards the end of the millennium – referred to as 'digital natives' (Prensky, 2001) – take instant access to information for granted and do not wait for authority figures, for instance educators, to enlighten them about the issues that interest them. This obvious change in attitudes towards acquiring new knowledge forces education to face the new challenges and offer a diversified pattern of delivery. Prensky (2001) extends the metaphor to those over 30, which the majority of teachers are, calling them 'digital immigrants': learning about, using and even and conforming to technology is one thing, but being born into it is another. Immigrants will almost always have accents or linguistic imperfections that natives may find amusing or at least peculiar. One digital example of this may be when the teacher prints the digital image for the students rather than projecting it in the classroom,

DOI: 10.4018/978-1-61520-779-4.ch008

or writes a URL on the board rather than posting it on his or her webpage or sending it to the students via email.

As opposed to earlier decades, it is not only the infrastructural environment that changed in schools, but students themselves arrive with a different frame of mind as well. The generation raised with computers and high-speed Internet at hand is commonly referred to as *Generation D* (D for digital), who take connectivity and immediate feedback for granted, and the way they think is completely different too.

Although the above distinction undoubtedly exists between naturally comfortable users of technology and the older generation, in his recent article, Prensky suggests that it is more important what users make of technology rather than how comfortable they feel with it.

Homo sapiens digital, then, differs from today's human in two key aspects: He or she accepts digital enhancement as an integral fact of human existence, and he or she is digitally wise, both in the considered way he or she accesses the power of digital enhancements to complement innate abilities and in the way in which he or she uses enhancements to facilitate wiser decision making. Digital wisdom transcends the generational divide defined by the immigrant/native distinction. Many digital immigrants exhibit digital wisdom. Barack Obama, who grew up in the pre-digital era, showed his digital wisdom in enlisting the power of the Internet to enhance both his fundraising ability and his connection with the American people (Prensky, 2009, www.innovateonline.info/index.php?view=article&id=705).

According to Prensky, today it is digital wisdom that makes a stronger distinction and beyond the fact that youth expects teachers to understand and be prepared for the digital era, but they should also be ready to integrate the various tools and resources into the curriculum in a manner that facilitates youngsters' multilateral thinking (Prensky, 2009). In today's classroom, the traditional setup, i.e. teacher talking, students listening and taking notes, replying to questions, is not feasible any longer. It is not only the teacher and textbooks, or even static material on the Internet that are the sources of information, but also 'unapproved' sources are relied on such as strangers' opinions in forums, wikis and blogs as well as peers.

The question arises: does school environment conform to these changes in the students' general environment? Do teachers try to synchronize their teaching practices with students' lifestyles? Or is it still the transition of an elaborated knowledge base that characterizes the learning process in schools? It has to be noted that active learning is certainly not a new phenomenon: it dates back to Socrates over 2400 years ago. In the spirit of the Socratic method, the learner is inspired to learn actively (Robinson, 1953), to question the world. Both teacher instructions and the learning environment are meant to assist the learner with constructing knowledge independently, creating a system, thus becoming part of an active, constructive participant in the learning process. Well-built study programs enable learners to discover their own learning styles and preferences, make decisions of their own time schedules, learning pace taking responsibility for their own learning at the same time. This is what teachers could expect from today's learners given the circumstances, but are educators themselves prepared for this process? Before further investigating this question, let us examine the local educational context.

Integration of New Technologies in Education in the Hungarian Context

Although once a relatively isolated country behind the Iron Curtain, Hungarian education has caught up with the methodologically more flexible and technologically more developed parts of the world by now. The days of centralized and uniformed education are over, flexible delivery methods and new modes of learning are emerging. At the same time, as one of the member states of the European Union, Hungary strives to harmonize its education system with international standards to provide more transparency, ensure the comparability and recognition of credentials, and encourage international mobility and cooperation as set forth with the aim of establishing the common European Higher Education Area by 2010.

In line with the so-called Bologna Process, the strategic harmonization of European Higher Education Systems, the country's teacher training system is presently under transformation. This re-accreditation process does not only concern the structure and pedagogical and subject content of teacher training programs, but also the integration of new technologies into teacher training programs and also the implantation of the concept of the necessity of lifelong learning in teacher trainees' and teachers' minds.

The Hungarian education system now bears very close resemblance to that of the rest of Europe and North America in terms of its tertiarity. Children leave kindergarten at the age of 6 to attend primary school for 8 years. Typically, students start secondary education at the age of 14 when they have the option to pursue an academic track by attending a grammar school preparing for higher education studies. There are also alternative high schools where students can start more advanced studies as early as at the age of 10 or 12 on a competitive basis. Those not wishing to continue their studies at university but rather wanting to learn a trade or vocation can choose an apprenticeship or vocational school. Most programs end with either a secondary school diploma (*matura*) and skilled worker certification combined, or students can continue their studies in the same school after gaining a secondary school diploma for one or two years, finally receiving vocational certification at a higher level (Figure 1).

Formerly, teacher trainees had four choices depending on the level of education they wanted to work at:

1. Kindergarten teachers trained for 4 years in a purpose-oriented college (BA)
2. Lower primary teachers trained in teachers' colleges for 4 years separately from upper-primary teachers, studying all lower primary subjects but foreign languages equally in-depth (BA)
3. Upper primary teachers trained in teachers' colleges for 4 years separately from lower-primary teachers, for 4 years, studying 2 subjects and pedagogy in-depth (BSc or BA)
4. Secondary school teachers trained at universities for 5 years, studying one or two subjects in great depth and pedagogy specific to the target population (MSc or MA).

With the introduction of the Bologna process, teacher education changed quite significantly in the last two cases: both future upper-primary and secondary school teachers are first to complete a BSc or BA with a major in one subject and a minor in another one to be taught, and subsequently an MSc or BSc in subject-specific Teacher Education. This new scheme only started in 2008 and the first graduates will finish their programs in 2010, which means that in 2009 both frameworks co-exist in parallel.

In Hungary, continuing teacher education has always remained in focus. Each school district has subject-specific advisors who can be approached for consultation and who coordinate in-service training in the region. At the nationwide level, each teacher is encouraged to complete in-service training courses on a regular basis. There is a system of accredited teacher development courses that are recommended to be taken by the teachers. Teachers are advised to complete courses worth 120 credits (accounting for about 120 study hours) every 7 years and their remuneration is also linked to this achievement. Most of the courses offered are either subject-specific or focusing on improvement of skills of the teachers or a certain method. Since the late 1990s, the most popular

Figure 1. Education System in Hungary

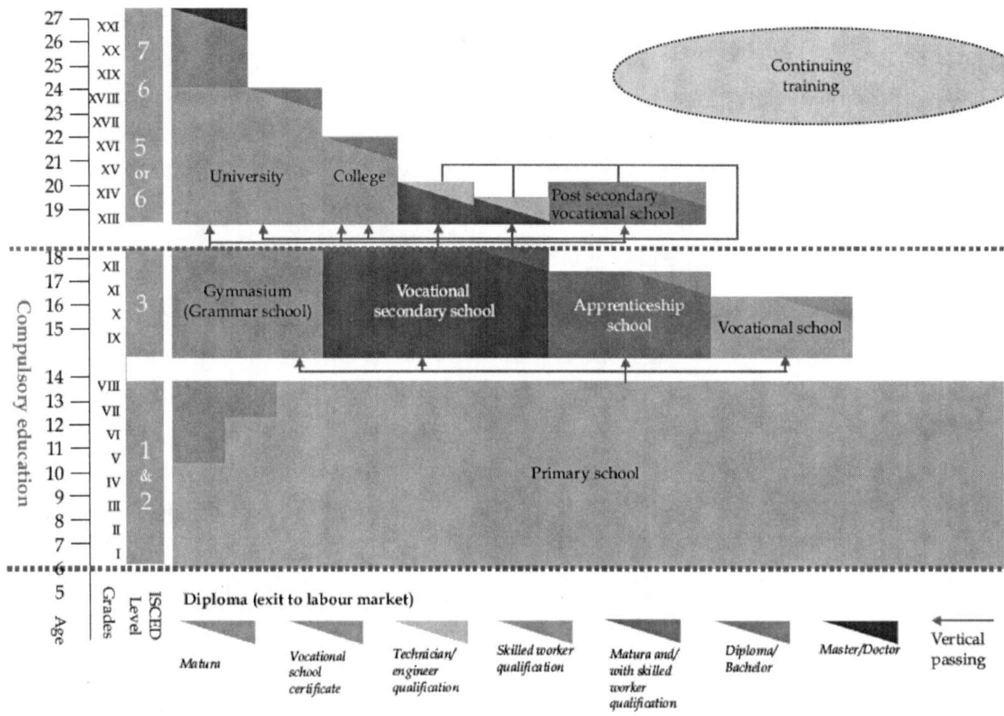

courses have been those integrating the Internet and education technologies in the curriculum.

As for teachers' ICT training, those trained after the mid-1990 received compulsory basic ICT training in upper-elementary and secondary schools, as well as at least one year's general ICT training in tertiary education. Certain teacher training institutions offer subject-specific ICT courses, where not only the technical aspect of using computers and electronic resources are discussed, but also the tools and their purpose-development and the pedagogical aspect of applications are also elicited.

Due to government initiatives, alternative delivery methods are encouraged to be used at all the levels of education, starting from kindergarten. This means there is a need for the provision and update of hardware and software on a competitive basis for teachers, the opportunity for bidding for tenders, professional development for staff in both the technical and methodological sense, as well as regular content development across the curriculum. A nationwide program called *Sulinet* (Schoolnet), sponsored and coordinated by the Hungarian Ministry of Education started in 1997, and has been underway ever since.

The integration of the uses of technology into the traditional education system typically happens through two types of schemes.

1. Top-Down Approach through Government Initiatives

The initiatives of the Hungarian Educational Information Strategy (1996-2006),

- delivery methods supported by ICT at all levels of education (Schoolnet Program);
- digitalization of learning content (LMS), providing access (Schoolnet Digital

Knowledge Base);

- institutional and individual IT infrastructure development (*Schoolnet Express*);
- a unified educational identification, infrastructure and IT applications for educational and administrative processes; and
- monitoring and analysis;

continued within the general framework of the *New Hungary Development Plan* (2007-2013) currently underway, aiming at regenerating Hungarian society and industries, including teachers and education, primarily by raising the level of employment and establishing conditions underpinning permanent growth.

Meanwhile, the 21st Century School Flagship Program (CSFP) was launched intending to prepare today's students for life long learning, and within this framework, the Intelligent School of the 21st Century Program was started. The goals of the program are:

- Equally accessible ICT infrastructure throughout the educational institution system to support the acquirement of ICT skills;
- Supporting the competence based educational methodology;
- Supporting social and community services providing ICT infrastructure which can help to develop appropriate skills;
- Creating the infrastructure for digital measurement or assessment;
- Creating the electronic information system of the public educational administration;
- Supporting teachers' pedagogical work; and
- Supporting community building, content provisioning infrastructure (Kárpáti and Horváth 2008, p. 7).

At a more specific level, it must be noted that the *Schoolnet* program, started in 1996, was launched by the Hungarian Ministry of Education in order to equip schools with computers having broadband access, but it also went beyond mere technical equipment and support: there have been teacher development courses offered within the scheme, subject-specific content development was provided by the Ministry but was and encouraged from the teachers' side, and the 2000s saw the development of the *Digital Knowledge Base*, which is not only a collection of teaching materials in an electronic format, but also an integrated learning management system with built-in tools that develop study skills beyond offering subject-specific knowledge. The scheme also comprised of a supplementary element in the early 2000s: *Schoolnet Express* allowed students and teachers alike to purchase IT equipment for educational use at a significant tax rebate.

Parallel with top-down initiatives from the Government side, professional organizations and NGOs started to pursue their own agenda as well to come up to the challenges created by technological changes.

2. Bottom-up Approach through Teachers' Initiatives

- peer-consultation sessions within various teaching communities;
- student-teacher working groups; and
- life-long learning for teachers and students.

Based on experiences with a former OECD teacher development project, Andrea Kárpáti, the manager of the project in question, claims:

We should not think that pedagogues are ready and able to acquire methods necessary for using technology for teaching and become innovators overnight. It takes a lot of methodological and technical support to ensure that the role of ICT is appropriate and it in fact facilitates the education process. Basic IT skills in themselves are not sufficient. The most successful element of this Hungarian OECD project was that all 100 teachers participating in the six-subject methodological experiment already possessed basic ICT skills and they could rely on that for their innovative projects. In addition, during the entire course of the innovative project, in parallel with their fieldwork, they also needed subject-specific methodological development and continuous consultancy. With this preparation, while getting to know subject-specific ICT tools, methods and up-to-date pedagogical approaches, they became able to create lesson plans, syllabi integrating 'digital' elements (Kárpáti 2003, p. 48).

Supposing that a practicing teacher wants to develop his or her professional expertise and wants to come up to keep pace with the challenges, let us examine what kind of possibilities there are today for organized training in the area of Education Technology in Hungary (See Table 1).

Teachers can either choose a course from the catalogue of accredited courses run in Hungary, travel abroad and take a course offered through the in-service scheme of the European Council, which are also accredited for Hungary, or take other contact or online courses at their own discretion, if they want to develop their digital literacy or methodology. From the above diverse range of options, let us examine a complex one, originating from an international organization, but adapted to the local circumstances.

ORGANIZATION BACKGROUND

EPICT - The European Pedagogical ICT License is a comprehensive, flexible and efficient in-service training course introducing a European quality standard for the continued professional development of teachers in the pedagogical integration of information, media and communication technologies (ICT) in education.

EPICT comprises content, method, technology and processes, all of which are controlled internationally by the EPICT Group and nationally by the EPICT country, enabling the national environment to obtain both recognition and accreditation for its professional development (www.epict.org).

Originating from Denmark, EPICT is now used in Australia, Austria, Cameroon, Ghana, Greece, Hungary, Iceland, Ireland, Italy, Norway, Sri Lanka, Uganda and the UK. Each country developed its own teaching material adapted to local circumstances, teaching and learning styles.

EPICT is one of the very few – if not the only – trans-national approach to PD in the pedagogical application of ICT in teaching and learning. EPICT is not just about learning ICT skills; it is how to pedagogically apply those skills for student training.A European programme that is well-documented, tested, evaluated and in operation in seven European countries is without parallel in the area of in-service teachers' professional development in pedagogical ICT integration (www.epict.org).

The scheme was discovered by the head of the Education Technology Institute of Eötvös Loránd University (ELTE), who recognized its merits and the feasibility of its introduction to the Hungarian context. The Institute together with its UNESCO Chair for ICT in Education (MULTIPED) assists faculty and staff with technology-enhanced learning solutions, undertakes research activities as well as develops software and tools. Although the institute is not a degree-granting institution by itself, it offers courses that are accredited by various departments across the entire university at bachelor's, master's and PhD levels.

Founded in 1635, ELTE is one of the oldest and largest universities in Hungary. The university is internationally recognized and all of its programs are accredited by the Hungarian Accreditation Board and its course credits are transferable in the countries of the European Union. Over the last hundred years, Eötvös University has educated

Table 1. ICT for Education teacher courses 2007-2008. Source: Csoma, 2008 pp. 139-144

Title	Organizer	ICT level	Content 1	Content 2	Content 3	Content 4	Length (h)	Training format	Cost	Accreditation
Current methodologies, professional development in the areas of multimedia, testing and evaluation skills for teaching English for specific purposes	Borsod-Abaúj-Zemplén County Pedagogical and Vocational Advising Institute	B		✓	✓		60	C	€300	✓
Multimedia in the English lesson	IATEFL-HU	B+	✓	✓	✓	✓	30	C	€180	✓
The Web in ELT 1	RELO	B					30	O	€100	✓
The Web in ELT 2	RELO	A					30	O	€100	✓
Internet in Language Teaching	Hungarian Teacher Education Centre.	B	✓	✓	✓	✓	120	B	€300	✓
EPICT elementary	IT Teachers' Association	B	✓	✓	✓	✓	60	B	€200	✓
EPICT advanced	ISZE	B	✓	✓	✓	✓	60	B	€200	✓
Summer Teacher Training Course	Microsoft	A	✓	✓	✓	✓	30	C	×	✓
E-learning in Teaching German: Teaching materials, research, presentation and publication	Council of Europe Socrates Comenius 2.2 training course	A	✓	✓	✓	✓	30	B	€850*	✓
Web-based learning management systems for language teaching	Council of Europe Socrates Comenius 2.2 training course	A	✓		✓	✓	30	C	€890*	✓
Internet for international school projects	Council of Europe Socrates Comenius 2.2 training course	B		✓	✓	✓	30	C	€750*	✓
European Science and IT Comenius projects management	Council of Europe Socrates Comenius 2.2 training course	B					30	C	€750*	✓
A Classics & ICT Resources course for Europe (CIRCE)	Council of Europe Socrates Comenius 2.2 training course	B	✓		✓	✓	30	C	€600*	✓
Start up and co-ordinate your European partnerships by using electronic learning- and communication systems	Council of Europe Socrates Comenius 2.2 training course	B	✓		✓	✓	30	C	€660*	✓
COMP@CTIVE II	Council of Europe Socrates Comenius 2.2 training course	B	✓	✓	✓	✓	30	C	€500*	✓
A teacher's handbook to developing eLearning programmes	Council of Europe Socrates Comenius 2.2 training course	B	✓	✓	✓	✓	24	C	€700*	✓

continued on following page

Table 1. continued

Title	Organizer	ICT level	Content				Length (h)	Training format	Cost	Accreditation
			1	2	3	4				
eTwinning workshops	European School-net	B+		✓		✓	15	C	×	×
German Multimedia-License Basic	Goethe Institut	A	✓	✓	✓	✓	60	O	€108	×
German Multimedia-Licence Advanced	Goethe Institut	A	✓			✓	30	O	€64	×
User Training	The British Council	B	✓		✓		2	C	×	×
Computers and Adult Education Learners	TESOL	B		✓	✓		1-2	O	×	×
Electronic Village Online courses	TESOL	B+	✓	✓	✓	✓	30	O	×	×
Principles and Practices of Online Teaching	TESOL	B	✓		✓	✓	30	O	$95	×
Teaching Speaking and Real-Time Communication Online	TESOL	A	✓	✓		✓	30	O	$95	×
Teaching Listening Online	TESOL	A	✓	✓			30	O	$95	×
Teaching Reading and Writing Online	TESOL	A	✓	✓	✓	✓	30	O	$95	×
Teaching Vocabulary and Grammar Online	TESOL	A	✓	✓	✓		30	O	$95	×
Creating and Using Multimedia for Online Instruction	TESOL	A	✓				30	O	$95	×
Cyberculture and Cross-Cultural Issues	TESOL	B	✓		✓	✓	30	O	$95	×
Multiliteracies for Collaborative Learning Environments	TESOL	B	✓	✓	✓	✓	30	O	$95	×
Creating and Managing a Web-Based Course Management System	TESOL	A+	✓		✓	✓	30	O	$95	×
Designing Interactive Activities for the Web	TESOL	A	✓	✓			30	O	$95	×
Online Learning for Campus-based Teaching	TESOL	A	✓	✓	✓	✓	30	O	$95	×
ICT in the classroom	The Consultants-E	B			✓	✓	50	O	€475	×
E-moderation	The Consultants-E	A	✓			✓	30	O	€435	×
A training course to learn how to use *Moodle*	The Consultants-E	A	✓	✓		✓	40	O	€595	×
The Internet: collaborative tasks and project work	The Consultants-E	B			✓	✓	30	O	€305	×

Key:
*: possible to apply for funding
Content:
1. Education delivery tools
2. Tools facilitating the learning process
3. Tools to access information
4. Communication tools

Training format:
C: contact
B: blended
E: online

Table 2. Number of students at the host institution. Source: www.elte.hu

Number of students in 2006		
PhD, DLA	1.631	5,1%
Vocational training	2.900	9,1%
Bachelor level training	10.819	33,9%
Master level training	16.416	51,5%
Higher-level vocational training	116	0,4%
Total	**31.882**	**100%**

Table 3. Titles and degrees of academic staff at the host institution. Source: www.elte.hu

Titles and Degrees of the Academic staff in 2006	
Full member of the Hungarian Academy of Sciences	58
Corresponding member of the Academy of Sciences	19
Doctor of the Academy	139
PhD (CSc 339)	779
DLA	9
dr. univ.	86
Total	**1090**

and employed many world famous scientists and four Nobel Prize laureates. Currently, ELTE has 8 different faculties and more than 30,000 students and an academic staff of about 1,000 highly qualified teachers and researchers (See Table 2, Table 3).

The University is a state-run institution; however, besides government support, it also relies heavily on various European Union, public, corporate and private grants as well as sponsorship, tuition fees of students enrolled in self-financed programs, and it also takes advantage of Public Private Partnership projects. The university's main profile is pre-service education, thus an additional partner was involved that has extensive experience in teacher education in the area of ICT. This organization is the Hungarian Association of IT Teachers (ISZE).

ISZE was founded in 1991, and has a democratic structure. Besides the instruction of IT skills to other teachers, its other mandates are the professional development of their members and clients, research, the dissemination of digital literacy and culture, the facilitation of relevant information flow and liaising between the education and business sectors.

The activities of ISZE's involve professional events such as presentations, courses and discussions, with the preparation and publication of background and learning materials, curricula and syllabi, the development and distribution of instructional video and software. Besides production of the above materials, ISZE uses its professional expertise for providing consultancy and advice to educational institutions and governing bodies in order to enhance and direct the efficient and meaningful development of digital learning environments and culture. In addition, ISZE liaises with similar international organizations and regularly compares experiences with them in an international setting.

Given an academic institution with excellent research and development background and an organization with extensive hands-on experience and professional network at the grassroots level, in 2005 the cooperation started with the familiarization of the joint team with the EPICT training material and its consideration for adaptation for the Hungarian context.

THE EUROPEAN PEDAGOGICAL ICT LICENCE (EPICT)

Besides equipping teachers with useful computer literacy skills, EPICT provides a concept, a framework for teachers to work within. It draws on the pedagogical background of teachers, and through each activity, it makes teachers think critically of the tools they are planning to use and the environment they wish to use the tools in. The processing of the material is team-based, and involves process-oriented and problem-based learning rather than memorization or drills. In the course of course activities, teachers jointly develop materials and learning scenarios for use in their own daily practices.

The course is delivered in a blended format with continuous contact and monitoring by certified EPICT facilitators. Participants meet at the beginning and the end of the course, and process tasks online. All themes of the course have a pedagogical rationale and build on participants' ICT-skills. The course material offers ideas on how to teach about and with ICT and present further, learner context-specific inspiration. Participants work in teams of three or four, where the team is challenged pedagogically and ICT-wise through an online dialogue with their facilitator. The assumption of course developers is that "knowledge and competences do not arise through the transport of information from one person to another, but that learning is a result of collaborative learning through contributing, creating and acting" (www.epict.org).

Besides the initial induction meeting, team-members may meet during the course on a voluntary basis, as typically several teachers from the same school participate simultaneously. This may be the result of a strategic decision made at the administrative level, meaning that information technology and its role in teaching, learning, collaboration and communication is on the school's pedagogical agenda.

The concept and the scheme was originally devised and launched by the Danish Ministry of Education and UNI•C (The Danish IT Centre for Education and Research) in 1998, then adapted in various other Western European countries, training 85,000 teachers in 7 years. When the Hungarian partner selected EPICT in 2005 as its approach to teachers' professional development, the host institution got a well-documented and tested European and international concept that has proven its efficiency in a number of European countries, but also in Africa and a few other parts of the world. After the concept had been studied by the course adaptation team led by Professor Kárpáti and the business plan prepared, its 22 members were trained as facilitators by senior trainers and course developers from the Danish root institution. To ensure quality standards, the first group of facilitators is always trained by the original EPICT group. Similar to the course philosophy, facilitator training is also based on a hands-on approach, professional dialogue, debate and continuous feedback.

The local adaptation of the teachers' course was prepared in light of the fact that the course should substantially contribute to meeting the specific needs of local educators for ICT-pedagogical competencies; it should contribute to the improvement of the pedagogical practices of participants for the integration of ICT into their continued teaching practices; and that it should contribute to an increased use of digitally enhanced learning. Each of the 17 units of the adapted material was prepared by two or three teacher trainers, and reviewed by at least one other. Adaptation involved not only the mere translation of the text and localization of the tasks and examples, but also supplementation of the material with more detail or the omission of parts that proved unnecessary in the local context. After the pilot year, 3 additional modules were developed in Hungary that were completely new (Moving stories, Data collection and Digital Learning Repositories).

The course is realized through flexible learning using the Moodle learning management system. This means that it commences with an introductory day where teachers meet and get acquainted with each other, the course delivery tools and its content and have the opportunity to discuss the objectives of the course with each other and the facilitator, who also takes the opportunity to make sure all participants possess the ICT skills necessary for the use of the tools and the platform. The course usually covers about 30 weeks and participants are expected to jointly tackle eight assignments supported and evaluated by the facilitator. The submission of these tasks is flexible, but they

Figure 2. No fixed level of student competence. Source: www.epict.org

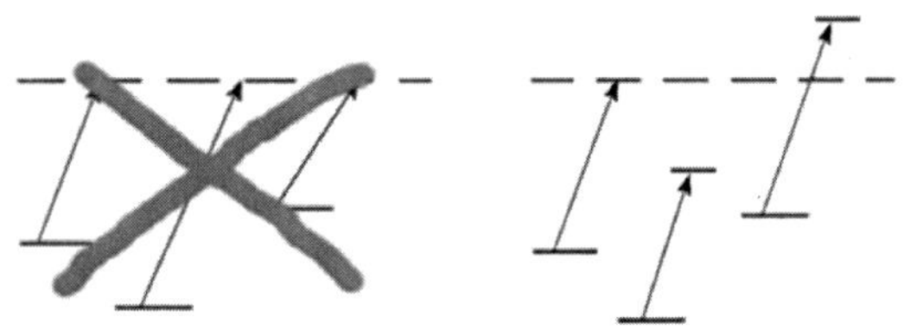

are to be done in a set order, with compulsory checkpoints in the process. If the facilitator judges the process as becoming unfeasible to finish, a reminder is given.

In the course of the learning process, participants get acquainted with various tools and methods using the same tools and methods that they are studying, in a meta-course manner. Teachers are put in the role of their students, testing the tools and the methods to be used with their classes after the training course. When facilitators recognize that a task is too easy or obvious for one team, they strive to provide more challenging tasks that follow up on the original one.

That is, there is no absolute level of task difficulty (Figure 2). Through the completion of tasks, professional dialogue and debate is encouraged not only by the tasks themselves but also by the facilitator, who participates in the discussion by commenting, reflecting on and constructively criticizing the developing product, providing continuous feedback.

Besides hands-on practice, participating teachers are also to discuss articles related to the unit they are studying and examples of good practice in their teams. At the same time, they are asked to describe a similar learning situation that they envisage in their own classes.

The core EPICT course consists of 8 modules, with three compulsory modules at the beginning of the program, followed by four elective ones, concluding in another compulsory one on school administration (See Figure 3).

A. Compulsory modules
- The Internet
- Texts and writing
- Communicating electronically

C. Optional modules (select 4)
- Using digital images
- Using spreadsheets
- Using presentations
- Producing educational websites
- A head start with databases
- Models and simulations

Figure 3. EPICT course structure. Source: www.epict.org

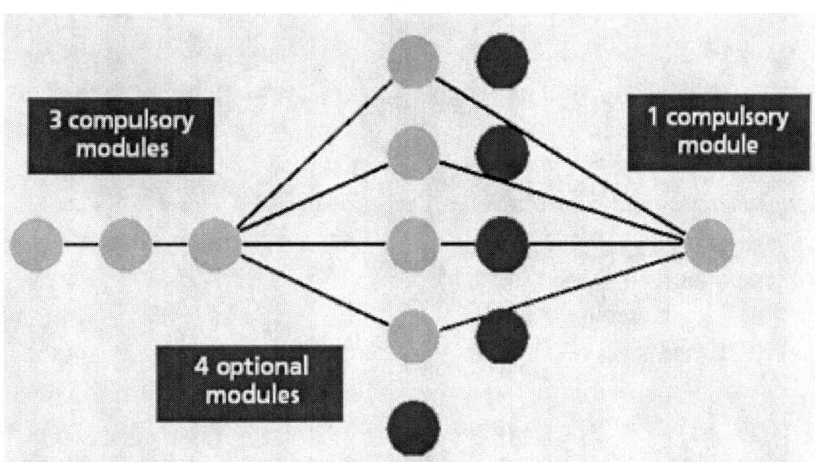

- Layout and DTP
- Educational software
- ICT, learning styles and classroom management
- ICT as a compensatory tool
- Games and learning
- Reading and ICT
- Data collection
- Moving stories (developed by the Hungarian team)
- Data collection (developed by the Hungarian team)
- Digital Learning Repositories (developed by the Hungarian team)

C. Compulsory

- School development and innovation

Upon completion of the 3+1 compulsory and 4 optional modules, teachers get a certificate that is internationally recognized on the one hand, and nationally accredited on the other, counting towards their compulsory in-service credits. At the end, participants are requested to evaluate the course. Besides research on student satisfaction, the questionnaire aims at the further enhancement of the tasks and materials to be revised regularly, as well as facilitator practices.

Surveying participant satisfaction is of course not the only quality assurance tool the host of the course employs. As discussed above, during the adaptation period prior to the launch of the scheme in Hungary, the localized version of each unit was prepared cooperatively by two or three authors and the product reviewed by an additional consultant. The appropriate distance learning environment was chosen based on usability studies comparing Moodle and CooSpace. The first year of the program (2005-2006) was spent on pilot studies with 120 participants. The participants could take the course for a nominal fee, while providing feedback for research, which employed action and skills research methods, ICT Attitudes and Use Questionnaires, as well as the California Personality Profile Test, aimed at discovering factors influencing the development of educational ICT skills using background variables such as age, discipline, professional rank, and personality traits. The second year saw the launch of regular, nationally accredited courses, after the careful selection of course providers by the Hungarian EPICT board. In the course of the sessions, facilitators carried out peer observation, a selection of submitted assignments was scrutinized, and at the end of each course, facilitators assessed modules and suggested revisions based on their own and their students' experiences.

The inference drawn from the past four years' experience is that there is continued demand for such a development course in Hungary and other countries as well. Experiences are discussed not only domestically but they are also comparable transnationally, and findings are shared on the central EPICT website (www.epict.org).

CURRENT CHALLENGES FACING THE ORGANIZATION

The main challenges of EPICT in the Hungarian context are:

1. Short time for course adaptation
2. Pioneering e-learning in teacher training
3. Competition of existing course providers
4. Sustainability (Kárpáti, 2007)

(1) Short time for course adaptation derives from the fact that the courses are offered one after the other and at the same time technology is advancing at a fairly rapid pace: new tools appear on a daily basis, electronic culture is changing and with the entrance of more and younger teachers the level of ICT expertise of the learning population changes as well. The applied solution is the employment of a large authors' and reviewers' team at the same time. It is important to enforce a continued assessment and evaluation of both content and delivery, as well as the feasibility of

the tasks to be tackled by course participants.

(2) In Hungary, e-learning is not a wide-spread phenomenon. In 2009, none of the universities offers a completely online degree, only certain courses can be completed online. The first accredited online teacher development course was launched jointly by the Regional English Language Office of the United States Embassy in Hungary (RELO) and the Hungarian branch of the International Association of Teachers of English as a Foreign Language (IATEFL Hungary) in 2003. However, this course was specific and limited to teachers of English as a Foreign Language, and employed only three tutors, whereas EPICT can take large amounts of teachers of any subject and has a great pool of facilitators.

(3) Since teachers must obtain 120 in-service training credits every 7 years, there is a great number of course providers that offer accredited programs. The EPICT board is constantly monitoring other players on the market and the variety of courses they offer. EPICT facilitators have experience with other ICT-based courses in various delivery formats (contact, blended and fully online), and the board is aware of their synchronous involvement in other training projects, which is an advantage as they can leverage this experience in their facilitator's practice within the EPICT course. At the same time, the range of approved EPICT course providers is expanding, thus enlarging the national EPICT network, and training facilitators for them.

(4) While there is constant demand for in-service training from both internal and external motivation, one recruitment challenge is potential participants' and their schools' financial situation, given the fact that a course costs about half of a state-paid teacher's monthly net salary. Fortunately, the Ministry of Education included EPICT in the European Union-funded National Development Plan, aiming for 40,000 pre-financed places.

SOLUTIONS AND RECOMMENDATIONS

From the past years' international experience, it is apparent that with initial support from the local authorities and the host institution, EPICT is economically feasible and sustainable. According to the model, participants pay a course fee to the regional course provider, while the course provider pays the facilitator's wages and royalties per participant to the national node, and finally, the national EPICT node pays royalties to the EPICT Group (Højsholt-Poulsen, 2007). The same relations characterize quality assurance reporting as well, thus contributing to the constant flow of information and relevant feedback.

The central provision of the concept, methodology and base material, and the national adaptation of the material in view of cultural and local educational peculiarities and the localization of the examples, case studies and tasks, as well as the customized approach of facilitators in view of the educational setting and the individual skills and abilities of participants, seem an ideal constellation. Ongoing consultations with local education authorities appear to be crucial in order to gain moral, professional and financial support and to ensure that the scheme can be seamlessly integrated with local policies.

Last but not least, after a careful study of personality traits of 120 participants in the pilot study, the Hungarian EPICT research team noted that besides realizing the importance of integrating ICT into their everyday schoolwork, even teachers with lower-level ICT skills enjoyed the team-building opportunities the course and the learning situation offered (Kárpáti, Török and Szirmai, 2007).

Stakeholders agree that staff development can certainly lead to school innovation, and on a larger scale, the change of the traditional teaching paradigm, which is desired by the rapidly changing environment our students live in both inside and outside the school.

REFERENCES

Csoma, K. (2008). Információs és kommunikációs technológiák a nyelvtanárképzésben. Budapest: Ad Librum.

Højsholt-Poulsen, L. (2007). EPICT *2007 presentation*. Retrieved June 20, 2009 from www.epict.org

Kárpáti. Andrea (2003). Az informatika hatása az iskola szervezetére, kommunikációs és oktatási-nevelési kultúrájára. Új Pedagógiai Szemle, 2(pp. 44-58).

Kárpáti, A. (2007). *Status 2007 Hungary presentation*. Retrieved June 20, 2009 from www.epict.org

Kárpáti, A., & Horváth, Á. (2008). National Policies and Practices on ICT In Education: Hungary. In T. Plomp, N. Law, R. Anderson & A. Quale, (Eds.), Cross-national ICT policy and practices in education. Charlotte, NC: Information Age Publishers

Kárpáti, A., Török, B., & Szirmai, A. L. (2007). *Bridges over Troubled Water -- The Effects of Personality Traits and ICT Skills on Changes in Teaching Style of Experienced Educators*. Paper presented at the EDEN Research Workshop, Poitiers.

New Hungary Development Plan. (n.d.). Retrieved March 10, 2009 from www.nfu.hu/doc/125

Prensky, M. (2001). On the Horizon. New York: NCB University Press.

Prensky, M. (2009). H. sapiens digital: From digital immigrants and digital natives to digital wisdom. *Innovate* 5 (3). Retrieved June 13, 2009 from www.innovateonline.info/index.php?view=article&id=705.

Robinson, R. (1953). Plato's Earlier Dialectic. Oxford, UK: Clarendon Press.

The European Pedagogical ICT Licence. (n.d.). Retrieved June 20, 2009 from www.epict.org

ADDITIONAL READING

Cort, P. (2003). Approaches to teacher training – transnational trends. Retrieved June 20, 2009 from www.cedefop.europa.eu/etv/upload/etvnews/news/2123-att1-1-s3_-_presentation_pia_cort.pdf

Csoma, K. (2008). *Információs és kommunikációs technológiák a nyelvtanárképzésben*. Budapest: Ad Librum. *EDEN: European Distance and E-Learning Network*. Retrieved June 20, 2009 from www.eden-online.org

Eurydice: The Information Network in Education in Europe. Retrieved June 20, 2009 from eacea.ec.europa.eu/portal/page/portal/Eurydice

Højsholt-Poulsen. Leo. EPICT *2007presentation*. Retrieved June 20, 2009 from www.epict.org.

Journal of Technology and Teacher Education (JTATE). Retrieved June 20, 2009 from www.aace.org/PUBS/JTATE

Kárpáti. Andrea (2003). Az informatika hatása az iskola szervezetére, kommunikációs és oktatási-nevelési kultúrájára. Új Pedagógiai Szemle, 2, pp. 44-58.

Kárpáti, A., & Horváth, Á. (2008). National Policies and Practices on ICT In Education: Hungary. in: Plomp, Tjeerd, Law, Nancy, Anderson, Ron and Quale, Andreas (Eds.): *Cross-national ICT policy and practices in education*. Charlotte, NC: Information Age Publishers: Kárpáti, Andrea. *Status 2007 Hungary presentation*. Retrieved June 20, 2009 from www.epict.org

Medgyes Péter and Angi Malderez (Ed.). (1996). *Changing Perspectives in Teacher Education*. Oxford: Macmillan Heinemann. New Hungary Development Plan. Retrieved March 10, 2009 from www.nfu.hu/doc/125

O'Reilly. Tim (2005). *What is Internet 2.0?* Retrieved June 20, 2009 from www.oreillynet.com/pub/a/oreilly/tim/news/2005/09/30/what-is-web-20.html?page=1

Papert, S. (1996). *The Connected Family*. Atlanta, Georgia: Longstreet Press. *PT3: Preparing teachers for tomorrow*. Retrieved June 20, 2009 from www.pt3.org/resources.php

TeacherTube. Retrieved June 20, 2009 from www.teachertube.com

The European Pedagogical ICT Licence. Retrieved June 20, 2009 from www.epict.org

The European School Project – Teacher training. Retrieved June 20, 2009 from www.europeanschoolsproject.org/teacher_training.htm

UNESCO Teacher Education. Retrieved June 20, 2009 from www.unesco.org/en/teacher-education

Venezky, R. és Kárpáti Andrea (szerk.). (2004). ICT and the Quality of Learning. *Results of the OECD Study. Special issue. Journal of Education. Communication Information, 2004*(1).

KEY TERMS AND DEFINITIONS

Bologna Process: The Bologna Process is an intergovernmental initiative which aims to create a European Higher Education Area (EHEA) by 2010 and to promote the European system of higher education worldwide.

Distance Education: Delivery of education via alternative modes rather than face-to-face, now typically in an electronic format, using online learning management or content management systems.

ICT: Information and communication technologies.

Matura: The two-level school-leaving exam for Hungarian secondary education, necessary for university entry.

Moodle (Modular Object-Oriented Dynamic Learning Environment): A content and leaning management system, used as an electronic learning environment.

Professional Development: The formal or informal education of teachers either offered by another party or self-directed.

Teacher Training: The education of teachers before they start the profession (pre-service) as well as their continuing education throughout their careers (in-service).

Transnational Projects: Initiatives involving participants from more than one country.

Chapter 9
Japanese Students' Digitally Enabled Futures Images:
A Synergistic Approach to Developing Academic Competencies

Michael Vallance
Future University Hakodate, Japan

David L. Wright
Future University Hakodate, Japan

ABSTRACT

This chapter illustrates how a Futures Studies approach encourages Japanese students to strategically analyze their futures by anticipating problems and stimulating collaborative solutions. Supported by creative digital media integration, students become active participants of a learning process that results in measurable outcomes of academic competencies. Two foresighting contexts are provided: local community and personal employment futures. Data from both are analyzed for the effectiveness of digitally enabled Futures Studies in promoting academic competencies of students in Japanese Higher Education. The article concludes with personal critiques from digitally enabled learning and Futures Studies perspectives.

SETTING THE STAGE

Introduction

Conventional Japanese education is designed for fact-based, exam-oriented learning using government approved textbooks to facilitate the one-way hierarchical flow of information from knower to non-knower (Mima, 2003). *"Confucian hierarchy runs deep...to the notion of teacher as knower of the right answer and the student a humble imitator of the master"* (Drydan, 1998, p.101). This traditional pedagogy is making reform a slow process in an education system which *"puts a lot of emphasis on acquiring knowledge through memorization and repetition"* (Fujitani, Bhattacharya, & Akahori, 2003, p.34) subsequently accentuating an increasing gap between the subjects taught at school and the activities of real life (Mima, 2003). To be blunt, the public education system in Japan is failing in its basic education (Whittaker, 2001; Craft, 2004).

DOI: 10.4018/978-1-61520-779-4.ch009

Although Japan's image may be a nation of high-technology and robotics, the actual implementation of Information Communication Technology (ICT) for basic technology training or more informed creative media utilization in education at schools and universities, *"remains comparatively low, and ICT does not appear as a priority in national education policy"* (UNESCO, 2007). Immersing ICT into mainstream education has been a major education policy of governments throughout the world and yet Japan lacks a clear vision for technology integration from schooling to higher education (Bachnik, 2003; Morris-Suzuki & Rimmer, 2003; Vallance, 2008a). Bachnik (2003), in her critique of Japan's attempts, states that, *"the technology revolution appears to be caught in a series of organizational 'short circuits' that sap the forward momentum of those trying to implement IT so that real forward movement is blocked"* (p.309).

One major consequence of this lack of educational leadership is that universities in Japan are not considered to be having much of an impact on developing the nation's human capital. Citing research as a key indicator of university impact on a nation's science and technology knowledge base, Whittaker (2001) reported that patent applications in Japan from its universities were a *"minuscule 0.3%"* in 1997. Vallance (2008) compares the clearly constructed educational policies for the 21st century of Singapore to the vague directives from the Ministry of Education, Culture, Sports, Science and Technology (MEXT) in Japan. It was argued that if Japanese educators were released from the stranglehold of national policies bereft of specific guidance, opportunities for stakeholders (teachers, students, parents, education managers) to embrace change in understandable, meaningful and relevant ways in classrooms throughout Japan will occur. He provides a framework with strategic actions built upon the firm constructs of thinking, learning, creativity and communication.

Fegan and Field (2009) argue for reform in Japanese Higher Education that places a greater emphasis on transnational education: *"The knowledge-based society demands an educated population, and as the need and possibility for that knowledge expands, so will the need to provide opportunities for an education across-borders"* (p. 17). The importance and relevance of transnational education in Higher Education is the recognition of diversity of ideas, knowledge, methods and thinking for *"constructively building knowledge and opportunities for both the domestic constituents and for the stakeholders in the international community"* (Fegan & Field, 2009, p.17).

It is therefore posited that the sooner the process of educating Japanese students for this Digital Age begins, the more flexible the nation will be to the economic, industrial, and social adjustments occurring throughout the world. This means that students need to be provided with meaningful and relevant opportunities to engage with problems that require the retrieval of prior knowledge, offer multiple perspectives of problems and solutions, and facilitate a challenging process which results in achievable, diverse outcomes. Learning should not occur in isolation but involve communication, cooperation and collaboration with fellow learners and experts. In this Vygotskian social constructivist learning, personal interpretation, decision making and community cooperation will foster long term understanding and transference of learned concepts (Vygotsky, 1986). In short, the construction of knowledge requires learners (of science or other subjects) to be actively involved in and contribute to the learning process (Kolb, 1984). Unfortunately, at present, this would be unconventional for many Japanese students and academics.

The argument though is that at all levels of educational leadership, change for a 21st century Knowledge-based Economy requires a modernization of human capital. This need for change has been acknowledged by governments (the macro level), researchers (the meso level) and practitioners (the micro level) (Vallance, Vallance & Matsui, 2009). On the one hand education may be considered in a constant state of flux, always trying to hit a moving target called equilibrium. By sensing its environment, organizational change occurs almost naturally (Wilson, 1992). In other words, education is a complex system metaphorically likened to a chaotic phenomenon. Morrison explains:

A complex system comprises independent elements which interact and which give rise to patterned behavior in the system as a whole. Order is not totally predetermined and fixed but the universe (however defined) is creative, emergent, evolutionary and changing, transformative and turbulent (Morrison, 1998, p.4).

On the other hand, change is an evolving process; organic and dynamic with evolutionary planning, problem coping, empowerment, initiative taking, staff development, restructuring and vision building (Fullan & Stiegelbauer, 1991). Whichever pole of the dichotomy is preferred, a premium is placed on organizations such as universities that can respond to change, uncertainty and openness. The assumption appears to suggest that those organizations which fail to respond will consequently perish (Vallance, 2006).

This chapter aims to illustrate that by using a Futures Studies approach supported by informed, strategic creative media integration, Japanese students can become active participants of a learning process that results in measurable outcomes. The projects exemplified are not expected to present fixed recipes of best practice but demonstrate that a Futures Studies approach in traditionally established pedagogical situations can contribute to the emerging behavior of systemic change in Japanese Higher Education.

CASE DESCRIPTION

Futures Studies

Futures Studies is a relatively *"new field of social enquiry whose purpose is the systematic study of the future and whose aims are to discover, invent, propose, examine and evaluate possible, probable and preferable futures"* (Bell, 1996, p.3). The purpose of the enquiry is to

challenge people's thinking by encouraging them to examine critically their current routines of behavior, to consider alternatives, to search for currently unrecognized alternatives, to analyze their goals and values, to become more conscious of the future and the control they may have over it, and to care about the freedom and well-being of future generations. (Bell, 1996, p. 23).

One central concept of contemporary Futures Studies is Polak's 'The Image of the Future', defined by Slaughter (1996) as, *"representations in words or pictures of possible future states of being. These can act as warnings of futures to avoid, or as 'magnets' which attract people to work for their realization"* (p. 325). The importance of creating such images of the future is neatly embodied by Elgin:

We cannot build a future we cannot imagine. A first requirement, then, is to create for ourselves a realistic, compelling, and engaging vision of the future that can be simply told. If our collective visualization of the future is weak and fragmented, then our capacity to create a future together will be commensurately diminished. Without a strong sense of the future and meaningful orientation for our lives, we can lose confidence in ourselves, our leaders, and our institutions.(Elgin, 1991, p.----)

Futures Studies encourages and advances informed images of the future in order to find out how they influence the way people act in the present and how these actions subsequently influences their own futures. Individuals can construct, carry and iteratively reconstruct mental images of futures events in their heads. However, informed images have to be created in a disciplined way in order to transcend the obstacles to imaging. These obstacles are found in our social institutions, including educational institutions (schools and universities) which *"discourage imaging because it can lead to imagined alternatives that can challenge existing social arrangements"* (Boulding & Boulding, 1995, p. 98). The future images thus represent an expectation but such images need to be created and communicated with the aid of a range of systematic and acknowledged futures-oriented methods, tools, and concepts. Active image-generation techniques can be deployed to reactivate and reengage those dormant yet poorly-refined imaging capacities of individuals. To implement a Futures Studies project a number of assumptions have to be made:

- Futures thinking is essential for human action. Images of the future (goals, objectives, intentions, hopes, fears and aspirations) are part of the causes of present action;
- Future outcomes can be influenced by individual and collective action;
- In making one's way in the world, the only really useful knowledge is knowledge of the future. People must speculate about the future in order to make their way through their daily lives intelligently and effectively;
- There are no empirical facts about the future. Although there are past facts, present options, and future possibilities, there are no past possibilities and no future facts (Bell, 1996, p.11).

The context of the application of the Futures Studies methodology within this chapter is a Communications course at a Japanese university. Ihsan, Inayatullah & Obijiofor (1995) have written that *"the purpose of communication is to begin to create a shared reality"* (p. 898) which is brought about in real world situations via the conduit of on-going negotiation and compromise; as will be highlighted in two case studies later in this chapter. Communication is therefore *"fundamental to the way we construct visions of alternative futures and share these visions with each other. The future eventually comes about by acting on our understandings and misunderstandings of such visions in interactions with the world"* (Stevenson & Simpson, 1993, p.319). Core communication theories have found application over a range of sub- and emerging disciplines such as science communication, business communication, and behavior change communication. Of particular usefulness to this study though is foresight communication. In 'Consciousness, culture and the communication of foresight', Ramos (2006) sets out an argument for a new genre of futures research with some proposed roles for the communicator of foresight and futures:

This short reflection is an attempt at mending, or of yoking together what has been dissociated: futures research with its natural depth with larger mainstream popular debates about human and planetary futures. While the corporate colonized media has showcases idiosyncratic and outdated techno-futures, more valuable futures oriented research is ready to emerge. But while such rigorous futures research incubates, or decays on library shelves, and with many projects under-resourced in their capacity to diffuse and communicate the results of their work, the corporate media runs rampant over the present. When one man has media access to three quarters of the planet, and uses this for propaganda purposes, what matters of rigorous and deep futures work? All the valuable insights in the world, the deepest understanding of the challenges we are facing in the 21st century are totally worthless if they cannot diffused more broadly, and remain cut off from effective avenues of expression and their capacity to influence change. Futures research must move beyond its academic enterprise into the domain of the media, through coordinated and intelligent communications strategies, through a hybridized foresight practice, epistemically reflexive while being aesthetically infusive (Ramos, 2006, pp. 1119-1124).

Foresight communication as a central concept was operationalized during the Communications coursework and introduced to students as one emerging sub-field with the broader family of applied Communication Studies. Starting with one example of a core communication concept (specifically Lasswell's (1948) 'Communication Formula') students were subsequently introduced to a variety of applied contexts within science communication, with the emphasis on strategically communicating their images of the future by way of the short film media. In foresight communication, students are also encouraged to be strategically analytical in their own viewing of films and other apparently futures-oriented images of the future in order to be able to create their own more meaningful and strategically deployable images of the future crafted to specific audiences with specific strategic outcomes in mind from the onset. The students are conceived not only as the mere passive consumers of inherited images of the future but are alternatively placed centre stage as active creators and communicators of self-produced futures images. It is therefore the instructors' intention that students are enabled to subvert the conventional view that the production and dissemination of futures images come under the domination of what Polak (1973) refers to as 'futures-making elites', a veritable aristocracy whose social positioning bestows preferential rights in determining other peoples futures. Though beyond the scope of our research, anecdotal evidence in working with Japanese students strongly indicates an especially domineering futures-making elite at work who effectively subsume all non-elite efforts at self-futurizing. Furthermore, a cursory analysis of Japan's mass media indicates Japan as being a culture in which the 'future' as an abstract concept is appropriated as a buzzword, and in which people are rarely afforded the opportunity to operationalize and systemize the concept of futures, let alone conduct analyses and create their own images.

It is acknowledged that the image of the future constitutes a staple communication artifact of many media related organizations with a global shift away from a reliance on printed media. School pupils and university students growing up in early twenty first century social contexts with ubiquitous mobile communication technologies, media-rich, and multi-media and/or multi-sensorial communication strategies are expected to broaden their footprint upon emerging media-hungry generations. This would seem to provide and even more opportune time for the image of the future to be strategically disseminated through such media for greater effect.

An important additional consideration in the implementation of a systematic Futures Studies project in an existing educational course is the need for students to consider the broader community outside the confines of their classroom spaces. Community Futures can be contextualized within a broader field of study known as Community Development - a commitment to *"improving the lot of ordinary people"* (Kenny, 1994, p.21) and is primarily concerned with *"ordinary people's lives, their experiences, their hopes and visions"* (*ibid*). The aims of Community Development are to *"transform unequal, coercive and oppressive structures in society"* (*ibid*). To fulfill these aims, Community Development *"challenges, provokes, presents unpalatable information, and even disturbs"* (*ibid*). More precisely focused to the objectives of our own research is the concept of Community Futures; an emerging field of inquiry with inter-disciplinary, transnational origins rooted in futures research, development, community studies and rural studies. The focus of community studies in recent times has converged on revitalization strategies for depressed communities given that the impact of economic hardship has multiple causes, many of which can be traced back to problems associated with restructuring, globalization, and centralization-decentralization discourses. It is this premise that further supports the need for students to be aware of both local and transnational community consequences of possible or preferable futures.

Methodology

The theories of learning supported by digitized multiple media that have the greatest impact upon research are Sweller's cognitive load theory, Mayer's cognitive theory of multiple media learning, Schnotz's integrative model (Mayer, 2005), Kress' theory of multi-modality (Kress, 2003,) and Knipe and Lee's cognitive outcomes theory (Knipe & Lee, 2002). In order to test a theory of multiple media enabled learning there needs to be theoretical and empirical plausibility, testability and applicability. Moreover, to implement research in multiple media enabled learning there needs to be informed processes and measurable outcomes. Processes, for instance, involve assumptions and application of learning within pre-conceived contexts of multiple-media appropriacy: for example, students locating, evaluating, organizing, and communicating information related to, say, a science topic or an innovative design, or new ideas for social development. Outcomes can be measured by pre and post experiment tests, control and experiment group tests, factorial design where participants undertake iterative assessments, and also surveys supported by digital capture of processes (Martin & Vallance, 2008).

The research literature is bereft though of consistent theories that can apply to the numerous variables involved in educational multiple-media technology implementation and integration. Researchers involved in science education, for instance, are focusing upon task design (Towndrow, 2007) as central to knowledge transfer and learning. At the core of task design and any use of technology in the education space (whether in robotics, artificial intelligence, web-bot development, semantic web, etc.) is communication. It is communication that is affected by, and also affects, all processes of scientific discovery between people, and sometimes between people and machines (an example is the interplay of Artificial Intelligence and web-bots for more effective, personalized searching of the deep Web). Researchers must indeed gauge the effectiveness of technologies in an education setting but, more importantly, need to appraise perceptions of learning and measurable acquisition. These, in turn, provide empirical data upon which to continue the development of a theory of learning involving multiple media.

An instrument used to evaluate students' perceptions of learning is a cognitive outcomes survey. The survey used in this study, for instance, was initially developed by Knipe and Lee (2002) and implemented by Martin and Vallance (2008) in their research to quantify academic competencies (declarative, generic and epistemic) of Higher Education students. Self report surveys of learning, or perceived learning, provide valid evidence for analysis. For instance, Pace (1990) found consistency in results over time and with different populations when utilizing self reporting by students and evidence of learning. Moreover, Corrallo (1994) found that self report surveys of cognitive outcomes or gain (perceived cognitive learning) were indicative of results obtained through more direct forms of assessment (Rovai, Wighting, Baker & Grooms, 2009). On the other hand, critics point to students' overestimation of their learning or simply equating their enjoyment of a course to increased learning (*ibid*). However, given the in-depth analysis of Knipe & Lee's cognitive outcomes survey's validity by Martin and

Vallance (2008), the self report survey was considered appropriate for this study. In addition, the statements of the survey were considered suitable for collecting data on self-reporting of learning as a development of generic, epistemic and declarative competencies (Knipe & Lee, 2002; Vallance, 2006a). Generic competencies represent 'transformative potential' (Goodyear, 2001) and includes a willingness to learn, consolidate prior knowledge, have fresh ideas, and being critical. Demonstrating understanding, responding to different points of view, and expressing explanations represent declarative conceptual knowledge and applying such knowledge in problem solving or arguments is referred to as 'academic competence' (*ibid*). Epistemic fluency, where learners are required to be flexible in their use of knowledge (Morrison & Collins, 1996), was represented in this study by the students' connections to their university environment and community. The survey for this research (*see Table 4)* was available in Japanese and English on the Learning Management System for one week at the end of the course.

The participants in this research were a purposive select group of Japanese students studying Complex Systems at Future University Hakodate (hereafter referred to as FUN) in Hakodate city, Japan. The research was conducted with one group of second year Complex Systems students (n=27) in 2007 and a similar second year group of Complex Systems students in 2008 (n=38). The Futures Studies component implementation was conducted during their Communications course. The students met twice a week for 90 minutes over a 15-week period (total of 45 hours per semester) for 2 semesters. The aim of the Communications course is to introduce and develop students' literacy skills in media architecture and science education. Students use multiple media to locate, evaluate, present and respond to information as well as communicate ideas, facts and opinions within a science context. Higher education students nowadays are expected to use ICT to communicate their ideas in multiple formats in order to advance digital literacy (Gilster, 1997; Warschauer, 2007) and academic competency (Goodyear, 2001). At FUN, literacy is defined as the development of academic skills required to source, analyze, evaluate, manage, understand and make sense of information in a variety of modes, and communicate outcomes in multiple formats. It was additionally reasoned that the use of Futures Studies would facilitate the development of literacy and competencies deemed essential for undergraduates in a modern, research-oriented science university.

Implementation

Hakodate is a small city in the northernmost Japanese island of Hokkaido with a population 300,000. Hokkaido residents are considered less wealthy than most in Japan with its graying population reflecting Japan's demographics. Population in regional areas such as Hakodate is also declining as a large proportion (44%) of the nation reside in Japan's three main metropolitan areas of Tokyo, Osaka and Nagoya (Statistical Handbook of Japan, 2007). The uniqueness of Hakodate though, in educational contexts, is FUN. This is a small university of approximately 1,000 students specializing in Media Architecture, Complex Systems and Artificial Intelligence within a blend of science, design and communications courses. The university opened in 2001 and, as it is a public funded university, links to the local community are considered a priority in the implementation of research and study. With this in mind, the Communications course adopts a Futures Studies approach to implement projects that would satisfy curriculum aims and produce artifacts that can be accessible by the Hakodate citizens and the international community. An example is the development of science communication through multiple-media and Web 2.0 technologies.

Web 2.0 envisages the World Wide Web as a strategic platform in which data is inserted by users leading to a collective intelligence (O'Reilly,

2005). To expand upon O'Reilly's definition, Web 2.0 can be considered as a knowledge-oriented environment where users cooperatively create malleable content with shared presence that is synchronously and asynchronously distributed in wired and wireless networks to fixed and portable technologies (Vallance, Vallance & Matsui, 2009). This statement best serves the purpose for the implementation of the Futures Studies projects where content and delivery are created and managed collectively by students in Japan using asynchronous and synchronous tools for communication with each other and the community. These are undertaken by negotiating projects where students are required to apply knowledge of current science concepts to transform futures. Teamwork and a carefully planned process lead to unique outcomes which were presented in written and video formats.

The two projects implemented were called 'Hakodate 2017' and 'Futures Employment 2028'. The 'Hakodate 2017' project resulted in fifteen short movies displayed online at Google Maps. The 'Futures Employment 2028' project resulted in fourteen short movies and posters depicting working life through the eyes of today's science undergraduates in Japan. The unique representation and development of these ICT-enabled artifacts not only exposes the good work of FUN students on the international arena but also supports the unique (in the Japanese education context) desires of this university to inculcate dynamic, independent, novel and forward-thinking graduates to develop a post-industrial, post-information, knowledge-aware Japanese society. The next section will detail the implementation of the two projects.

Developing a Futures Studies Tool-Box

During the Communications course students were introduced to a number of Futures Studies methodologies, tools and concepts in the form of a rudimentary tool-box with which students were empowered to proceed with a systematic approach to creating their respective images of the future. The tool-box included a definition of Futures Studies, followed by a Guided Visualization technique, the Futures Triangle Analysis (FTA), scenarios planning, and SWOT Analysis, all of which are crystallized in a Communication Futures model building upon Lasswell's (1948) pioneering 'Communication Formula'.

Initiations into Futures Studies: Defining the Field

The course started with a definition of the term 'Futures Studies'. Of the numerous definitions, Bell's (1996) which defines Futures Studies as, *"a new field of social inquiry whose purpose is the systematic study of the future and whose aims are to discover or invent, propose, examine and evaluate possible, probable and preferable futures"* (p. 3) was chosen. Students were invited to share in the fact that such a field does indeed exist, though largely unrecognized in Japan; a paradox in itself given Japan's cultural image as a futures-oriented society.

Guided Visualization

An effective way to break the conceptual ice and initiate students with this unfamiliar world of Futures Studies is a technique known as Guided Visualization (GV). GV seeks to guide the individual with the aid of a facilitator conversant with Futures Studies into an alternative future. Once arriving at a mentally constructed location such as a utopia-like island, or simply the 'other side of the fence', the visualizer is asked a series of questions dependant on the circumstances and the objectives of the exercise, in order to stretch his or her imaginative capacities with a view to concretizing images of possible future states residing in the subconscious. Typical clues from the GV facilitator might include: 'Ten years from now where do you most want to be?', or, 'What kind of world is this? What does it look like, smell like, feel like?' and so on. Through such a confronting and deeply personal experience, the visualizer is encouraged to imagine, concretize and become aware of ideal future states, most of which are typically locked in the conceptual closet.

Lasswell's Communication Formula

After experiencing the Guided Visualization, students are then introduced to more systematic and methodical tools and frameworks in order to create futures films. As one aspect to strategically build coherent and communicatively rich images of the future, Lasswell's (1948) 'Communication Formula', which analyses communication artifacts according to the model 'Who says what in which channel to whom with what effect?' was introduced. The five components (who, what, which, whom, and what) can create a dynamic, iterative for a creative and considered communication process. Students were instructed to strategically craft their futures images following the five main components of Lasswell's Communication Formula but with an emphasis on the futures possibilities and potential in each. At first, students seemed to find the model simplistic but when actually attempting to articulate the 'who', as in 'who are you as the creators of a message about the future of a community?' the complexities of this deceptive question became readily apparent.

Futures Triangle Analysis

The Futures Triangle Analysis (FTA) is an applied futures tool with useful applications for mapping out the dynamics that collectively constitute a futures issue (Inayatullah, 2003). The apex of the triangle represents the pulls of the future, including a matrix of images-of-the-future, from dominant images to periphery and alternative/radical images as competing futures discourses. The bottom left angle represents the push, the drivers of change, such as new technologies, globalization, value shifts, demographics, and the push of the creative minorities. The bottom right angle represents the weight, factors resistant to transformative change, such as the mentality of the age, human relations, communication structures, and even geographical factors. From this dynamic triad of push, pull and weight, plausible futures emerge. The purpose is to engage in the deconstruction of the overall dynamics in order to reconstruct preferable futures as rehearsal for their societal implementation. The FTA was intended as a macro-mapping technique for providing a useful backdrop for the students to methodically and systematically map out the dynamics that inform their various communicative strategies. Tensions arising from the multiple factors also render visible hidden complex interactions.

Scenarios

In contemporary Futures Studies, one of the most important and influential tools of the futurists' tool-box is scenario creation. Amara's (1981) division into preferred, possible and probable remains the classic map of futures studies, with Masini (1993) describing three basic kinds of scenarios: a trend scenario - the most possible, probable and plausible; a contrast scenario - extreme situation, opposite to trend scenario; a utopia scenario - the most desirable future. Scenarios differ from Guided Visualization in that the futures are informed by a sense of what 'ought' to be. A consequence is the illumination in values and beliefs which are not consistent among individuals nor static over time. FUN students were encouraged to use scenarios for shaping their respective images of the future into coherent stories based on the above analyses and methodologies. Creating coherent images for all these scenarios types would have been unmanageable and therefore students were encouraged to focus primarily on the transformative, idea, utopian scenario.

SWOT Analysis

Although SWOT (Strength, Weakness, Opportunity and Threat) analysis is not a generic Futures Studies tool, it has become a favorite of practicing futurists as a first step conceptual mapping technique for a futures issue. Clearly all four of the SWOT dimensions have a potentially strong futures-orientation which can be stretched even more so when futures specific issues are analyzed. In the strategic creation of an image of the future for a community or city, a preliminary mapping out of the perceived strengths, weaknesses, opportunities, and threats provides a rich tapestry of data, information and insights and makes visible usually hidden connections between the complex of factors, from which the image creator can then explore and expand upon key issues. As it turned out, SWOT Analyses became the analytical tool of choice for most of the teams who felt an affinity with its apparent simple structure.

Having developed and rehearsed this rudimentary Futures Studies tool-box, the students were equipped with a new futures oriented language and vocabulary to proceed strategically in creating their own digitally enabled futures images (See Table 1).

Table 1. Implementation 2007 - Hakodate City 2017(---)

Course	Communications
Level	Undergraduate year 2.
Major Course	Complex Systems
Duration	Twice weekly for 1.5 hours each lesson over 2 semesters.
Technology	Classroom with 12 computers with Internet access and multimedia software.
Aim	At the end of the course students should be able to use a variety of media to create, analyse, organise, communicate, and make sense of new information.
No. of students	27
Summary of procedure	Project title: Hakodate City 2017. A systematic development of ideas, alternatives and communication for the city's futures.
Assessment	Formative: Electronic quizzes during the course. Personal e-portfolio of course activities and periodic reflections. Summative: Group multimedia artefact graded via an assessment rubric.

The project was introduced by presenting some statistics about Hakodate: lower income than other cities in Japan, less capital investment, and graying population. The students had to interpret the data and then define specific problems facing the city. For example, one student team wrote; 'Hakodate needs to increase its financial income and attract more visitors. We want more young people to live in Hakodate.' Next, the students voluntarily formed small teams (three students per team) to conduct a SWOT analysis. It was decided that ten years was a plausible period to consider as it would be understandable by the local community and implementable if deemed worthy. Moreover, it was anticipated that the futures scenarios developed by the students would encourage a discussion of change within the Hakodate community so that citizens could have an impact, or at least an input, on the city's medium term planning. In addition, the students had to type a business report seeking funds from overseas to implement and complement their chosen scenario. This fitted well with the linguistic aims of the Communications course in developing writing and presentation skills (See Table 2).

Students brainstormed ideas, sketched imaginary scenes, and searched the Word Wide Web for information. The first goal was to draw and summarize three ideas. The instructor also provided a model report template to support the students' English writing. Once the three ideas took shape the students then developed a survey and collected feedback from a minimum of 20 respondents. The survey data allowed students to consider which idea was most liked and then further that idea.

In addition, a long-term futures perspective was encouraged. The chosen scenario was ana-

Table 2. Example of students' SWOT analysis (Takeuchi & Nishi)

Strengths	Weaknesses	Opportunities	Threats
Beautiful night view Famous sightseeing spots Convenient transportation	Not vibrant Less young people Less disposable expenditure Few places to study	Develop tourist infrastructure Airport link direct to Taiwan Gather young people from around Japan	Demographic aging Increased crime Small shops go bankrupt Increased land price

lyzed in terms of being either static, nostalgic or transformative. This further encouraged students to consider their scenario as a tangible outcome that could be presented to the local community. The long-term view allowed for a more creative scenario, not simply presented as a wild prediction but a scenario grounded in quantitative and qualitative data of the present.

In the latter half of the course the student teams created short movies (duration of 2 to 3 minutes) to explain and justify each futures scenario. To support the students a 3-hour workshop on Apple's iMovie was held. The movies were later uploaded to a class account in YouTube. However, this was considered incomplete as each scenario was viewed without a recognizable context. It was agreed that the local community needed to visualize where the futures scenarios were to be implemented within the city. To enable this, a Google Map account was created for the class and students added Placemarks within Hakodate for their scenario. Each Placemark was edited with HTML code so as to connect to the individual movies residing at YouTube. The result was a series of Placemarks on a Google Map which, when selected, played a movie. A total of fifteen scenarios were created.

Having thus far used a social-constructivist approach to teaching and facilitating learning, it was appropriate to continue the process in a presentation of the students' futures scenarios for 'Hakodate 2017'. The final presentations were thus given at a Community Centre in Hakodate one evening and the Google Map with Placemarks and accompanying movies made accessible to the public; *seeFigure 1* and also link to the Google Map at http://web.me.com/mvallance/DRVALLANCE/BLOG/Entries/2009/4/2_Futures_Map.html

The implementation of 'Futures Employment 2028' was conducted in three distinct stages: prediction, foresight, and reflection. Each stage will be explained so that practitioners can consider implementation in their own local and transnational circumstances (See Table 3).

The first stage involved students making predictions about their expected employment upon graduating from FUN. The students listed possible prospects as doctor, teacher, systems engineer, programmer, researcher, entrepreneur, and actor. A poster template was provided and the aforementioned jobs assigned to groups of students. They then listed the required skills, duties, benefits and salary for each assigned job.

The next stage involved students considering possible futures as far as the year 2028 by which time many students would be forty years old and may be forced, by economic or other circumstances, to change occupation. From all the aforementioned posters the students selected a range of desired skills, duties, benefits and salary that they believed would apply to them in a possible 2028 scenario of occupation retrenchment in Japan. From these desired traits the students next created a unique job that may be available in 2028. In other words, the skills, duties, benefits and salary were used as a context to stimulate thinking about possible futures occupations. The resulting occupations included nano tech doctor, space travel conductor, space engineer, video game creator, information seller, robot designer, and organ maker. In the spirit of sharing, students

Figure 1. Google Map placemark with a futures movie

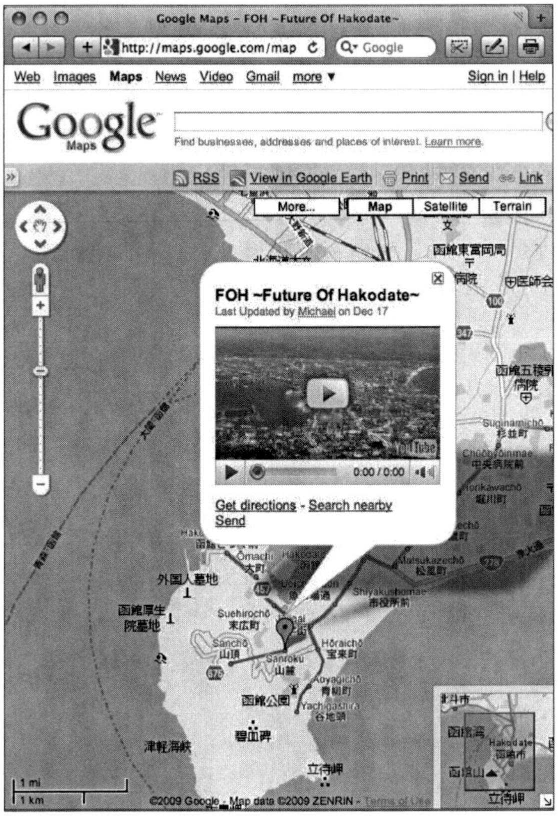

Table 3. Implementation 2008 – Futures Employment 2028(---)

Course	Communications
Level	Undergraduate year 2.
Major Course	Complex Systems
Duration	Twice weekly for 1.5 hours each lesson over 2 semesters.
Technology	Classroom with 12 computers with Internet access and multimedia software.
Aim	At the end of the course students should be able to use a variety of media to create, analyse, organise, communicate, and make sense of new information.
No. of students	38
Summary of procedure	Project title: Future employment 2028 A systematic development of ideas, alternatives and communication for personal employment futures.
Assessment	Formative: Electronic quizzes during the course. Personal e-portfolio of course activities and periodic reflections. Summative: Group multimedia artefact graded via an assessment rubric.

designed a suitable poster of a possible advertisement in 2028 for their particular occupation.

However, as with the 'Hakodate City 2017' implementation, students needed to consider how to present their ideas to a wider audience both locally and internationally. It was decided that a short movie portraying twenty four hours in the life of the occupation would be a suitable format of presentation. Moreover, the TV series, 24, was quite popular with the students so they wanted to see how they could use the media to depict a similar period of time. In this stage, tutor support was provided in the form of a text-based story of a day in the life of a fictitious virtual worlds architect. This allowed the tutor to present and contextualize language grammar, syntax, morphology and overall structure. The text was supported by online quizzes which tested students' grasp of the language and structure (*seeFigure 2*).

Additionally, movie storyboard and digital editing workshops were conducted as organization and technical support, respectively. Resources such as relevant YouTube movies, statistical data of future trends, and futures forecasts in magazines such as 'The Futurist' were provided. A rubric of the tutor's assessment criteria was also provided at this stage. The outcome was a variety of short (3-minute) movies entitled '24 - A day in the life of <occupation> 2028' prepared, filmed, edited and presented (in English) by teams of three students. All the short movies were uploaded to an online movie gallery for sharing and peer review (*seeFigure 3*).

In the final stage each individual student reflected upon their experience. Reflection is a reconstruction of experience which promotes in-

Figure 2. Online quiz

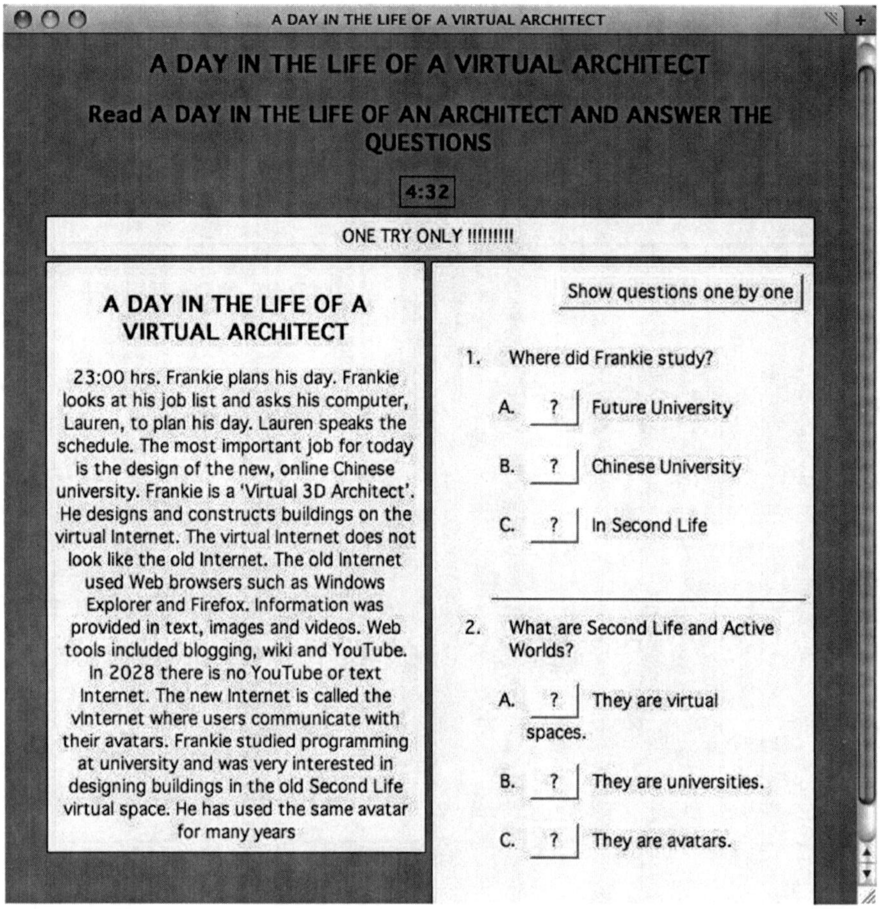

Figure 3. Web gallery of 'Futures Employment 2028' movies

dividual growth (Dewey, 1938). For the Japanese students (and many of their instructors) though, *"reflective practice would be considered unconventional"* (Vallance, 2008b, p.70). However, it was important for students to not only look ahead (the futures context of the communication) but to look back at their progress, successes and challenges in order to reconstruct their experience as communicators and learners. The students' reflections were typed into their individual online e-portfolio, with hyperlinks to their posters and movies. The e-portfolio was used by the instructor for a summative assessment of each student's work.

To conclude, the 'Futures Employment 2028' implementation facilitated the development of students' twenty first century literacy skills. To re-iterate, literacy has been defined as the development of academic skills required to source, analyze, evaluate, manage, understand and make sense of information in a variety of modes, and communicate outcomes in multiple formats. The 'Futures Employment 2028' project integrated text, images, audio and movies, and supported teamwork and individual reflection and responsibility. This, it was anticipated, would lead to learning that could, most importantly, be recognized by students, as well as measured by the instructor for assessment purposes. The next section will explain the efficacy of the implementation by focusing upon academic competencies and subsequent multiple media enabled learning .

Results

The cognitive outcomes survey by Knipe and Lee (2002) was conducted at the end of both projects. The degree to which the variables are related in surveys conducted in 2007 and 2008 was measured using a Pearson Product Moment correlation. A correlation of +1 means that there is a perfect positive linear relationship between variables. The value of Pearson's correlation in this study is 0.763; significant at $p=0.05$. This indicates that the strength of association between the variables is very high ($r = 0.763$), and that the correlation coefficient is significantly different from zero ($p < 0.05$). Therefore, it may be stated that the results of the two projects, even though involving different participating groups, are statistically worthy of comparison (See Figure 4, Table 4).

The results of the 2007 implementation (Hakodate 2017) indicate benefits of using futures scenarios in supporting students to develop as learners in a new educational environment that encourages creativity linked to academic competency. The results of Strongly Agree and Agree are combined. Although aggregating the choices of Strongly Agree and Agree provides a less comprehensive analysis, the combination does highlight the degree of success (or otherwise) in the development of academic competencies as an indication of learning. As mentioned above, academic competencies are categorized by Knipe and Lee (2002) as generic, declarative and epistemic.

Generic competencies were in evidence in the post course surveys and exemplified in the students' implementation. The survey data shows that the 'Futures employment 2028' project proved more beneficial in students' recognition of the components of generic competencies. The use of prior knowledge was far higher in the 'Futures Employment 2028'project (98%) compared to 'Hakodate 2017'project (67%). Similarly for new ideas (78%/ 63%) and analysis (86%/ 74%). This reveals that the utilization of futures scenarios had a greater impact on generic competencies. It should be acknowledged that the SWOT analysis within a Futures Studies approach produced high survey results and should not be rejected as a viable strategy in developing generic competencies.

The development of declarative competencies was also in favor of the 'Futures Employment 2028' project compared to the 'Hakodate 2017' project, although the percentages were much closer: viewpoints (86%/ 85%); explanation (84%/ 78%); decision making (93%/ 81%).

Figure 4. Post-course 2007 (n=27) and 2008 (n=38) survey results

	Strongly agree 強く同意する		Agree 同意する		Disagree 同意しない		Strongly disagree 全く同意しない	
	2007	2008	2007	2008	2007	2008	2007	2008
1.) I used some knowledge from **previous lessons**. 私は以前の授業で学んだ知識を利用した。)	22%	24%	63%	74%	15%	3%	0%	0%
2.) I had some **new ideas.** (私はいくつかの新しいアイデアを持っていた。)	11%	11%	52%	66%	37%	24%	0%	0%
3.) I **analysed** something so I could understand it. (私はある事柄を理解するために、それを分析した。)	11%	18%	63%	68%	26%	13%	0%	0%
4.) I learned about **different viewpoints** from other students IN MY CLASS. (私はMichael Vallance教授の授業で、他の学生から異なる視点について学んだ。)	37%	24%	48%	63%	15%	11%	0%	3%
5.) I **disagreed** with another student. (私は他の学生と意見が異なった。)	7%	13%	30%	55%	59%	29%	4%	3%
6.) I had to **explain** something to someone. (私はある事柄に関し、他の人に説明しなければならなかった。)	19%	18%	59%	66%	22%	16%	0%	0%
7.) I had to **solve a problem** (technical or other). (私は、ある問題 (技術的、またはその他の) を解決しなければならなかった。)	22%	26%	63%	58%	14%	16%	0%	0%
8.) I had to make a **decision.** (私はある決定をしなければならなかった。)	11%	11%	70%	82%	19%	8%	0%	0%
9) This project will help me **communicate** better in future. (このプロジェクトは将来、私によりよく情報交換することを助けてくれるだろう.)	48%	32%	41%	47%	11%	16%	0%	5%

An indication that the more challenging futures scenarios promoted negotiation is the result showing students with the 'Futures Employment 2028' project disagreeing more (68%/ 37%). The SWOT analysis can be considered too formulaic, providing lesser opportunities for negotiation and in-depth discussion.

The process involved in the Futures Studies projects facilitated action-oriented knowledge as students planned, justified, created and explained. This representation of epistemic fluency was also in evidence in the digital artifacts resulting from the implementation of the Futures Studies approach in both projects. For instance, through the application of the students' constructed knowledge, value was added to Google Maps in the form of creative, new ideas communicated in multimodal formats such as movies embedded within previously text-exclusive Placemarks. Students in both projects are thus communicating different ways of knowing subsequently realized in different expressions as multimodal, multiple media artifacts (movies, voice, text, posters, images, maps).

The next section will critique the implementation of digitally enabled Futures Studies. Michael Vallance will reflect upon the informed utilization of digital media supported by Futures Studies strategies to develop academic competencies of Japanese undergraduates. David L. Wright will critique the adoption of Futures Studies and the reported implementation process.

REFLECTION BY MICHAEL VALLANCE

As an educator implementing futures strategies to engage Japanese students in media communication, literacy enhancement, and academic competency development my own reflective practice is a *"process in which experience is recalled, considered and evaluated in relation to a broader purpose"* (Farrell, 1995, p.95). The purpose of adopting Futures Studies was to seek methods that could support Japanese undergraduate students in the development of much-needed but sorely lacking academic competencies. Collaborating with an expert colleague in Futures Studies and thinking subsequently inspired ideas for enhanced pedagogical practice, student engagement, task creativity and different modes of learning.

The context for the implementation was a Communication course which aims to develop a literacy that includes multiple modes of representation and presentation. Learning can be measured by tests of retention and transfer. However, the Communication course did not test students' retention as learning was measured by the students' ability to use taught or experienced information and skills to solve new problems. In our Futures Studies implementation the new problems were represented by futures scenarios 'Hakodate 2017' and 'Futures Employment 2028'. Subsequently, the assessment of students' learning was numerically graded using detailed and accessible rubrics. Additionally, the post-course surveys represented self-reporting of perceived learning by the students.

New media was utilized in the creative, multimodal representations of ideas using technologies such as Apple's iMovie editing software and Web 2.0 communication tools such as YouTube and Google Maps. The media artifacts designed by the students were considered a reflection of their understanding or meaning of the futures scenarios. Consequently, the final products convey a message to the viewer that represents the students' own interpretation of the scenarios which, in turn, illustrates a consideration of authorship, media format, audience, content and purpose in the development of media literacy.

Throughout the two implementations, language and multiple media communication were developed through sharing and discussing ideas in the process of media creativity. The role of social interaction is recognized as a major element of active learning (Sawyer, 2006). Meaning-making is thus derived from the interactions the learners have with the contexts they are working with so that their knowledge is enhanced and thus more meaning focused and more transferable. Hung, Jonassen and Liu (2008) state that, *"Knowledge constructed for solving problems results in epistemological (task-related procedural knowledge) and phenomenological (the world as we consciously experience it) knowledge types"* (p.488). These are richer, more meaningful and memorable representations.

The Japanese students used English in meaningful contexts. Although no target language was directly taught, the futures projects allowed students to utilize known language exponents and vocabulary within the context the students set for themselves. As the projects developed the students modified their own language output in multiple modes (text, voice and gestures) thus integrating new knowledge into existing knowledge. In short, the projects pushed learners to modify their comprehensible output (Swain & Lapkin, 1995). As stated by Plaas and Jones (2005): "

Table 4. Pearson correlation

Correlations			
		Total 2007	Total 2008
Total 2007	Pearson correlation	1	0.763(*)
	Sig. (2-tailed)		0.016662154
	N	9	9
Total 2008	Pearson correlation	0.763(*)	1
	Sig. (2-tailed)	0.016662154	
	N	9	1
	N	9	9
*** correlation is significant at the 0.05 level (2-tailed)**			

Meaningful interaction with output can enhance second-language acquisition just as much as input can" (p.476).

The projects also prompted students to reflect on their own thinking during the planning and critiquing discussions. These two actions in particular for reflective practice have been recognized in the learning sciences literature as key components of experts' engagement (Sawyer, 2006). It is not being proposed here that the students became experts simply due to being engaged in futures image construction but that the projects provided opportunities to promote reflective practice and thinking which in turn nurture students in their epistemic competency development. Furthermore, developing such academic competencies is a way of supporting students in seeking out how to understand. Krajcik and Blumenfeld (2006) state that: *"The development of understanding is a continuous process that requires students to construct and reconstruct what they know from new experiences and ideas, and prior knowledge and experiences"* (p.318).

On the other hand, the application of futures strategies may have been tainted with personal constraints of pedagogy (e.g. the need to broadcast some information), classroom practices (e.g. individual student work in undertaking online quizzes) and expected institutional outcomes (e.g. such as a numerical course grade). The limitations of the students' output and creativity may have been negatively influenced by these constraints. Adopting Futures Studies in its purist form may prove uncomfortable and quite intimidating for some educators and even some students. Having students present alternative futures though certainly broadens their thinking but care was taken here not to touch upon overly sensitive topics as the students' images were shared using communication technologies such as Google Maps and YouTube with the local and transnational community.

Nevertheless, the use of futures strategies resulted in remarkable media narratives of personalized futures with evidence of a development of much-needed academic competencies supported by, and supporting, multiple media enabled learning. Access to students' systematic ideas for futures scenarios using online tools such as YouTube and Google Maps furthers the link between university students, local citizens and transnational communities in helping one another shape a less uncertain future. It is thus posited that the adaption of Futures Studies actively prepares Japanese undergraduates with competencies that have been acquired by the shared, systematic development of creative new media for communication, meaning-making and understanding.

REFLECTION BY DAVID L. WRIGHT

In the following section I briefly critique and evaluate the students' short futures films from a Futures Studies perspective, followed by a macro self-critique of the overall project using a SWOT framework, thereby concluding with some recommendations for the implementation of a similar digitally enabled futures films project given the constraints of a non-Futures Studies course.

Critique of Student Future Films

Many Futures Studies researchers such as Hutchinson (1996) and Slaughter (2005) have pointed to an almost universal tendency across times and cultures to perceive the future in technological terms. Future-oriented solutions tended to cluster around superficial approaches, often dominated by the 'techno-fix' (Slaughter, 2005) rather than human-centric or 'social technology' solutions. FUN students too found it problematic to imagine, articulate or propose truly alternative images of the futures. Whether this is due to lack of guidance on the part of their instructors, a lack of imagination competencies, or a preference to 'play the future safe', is a question that remains for us to explore in our own on-going research into this line of inquiry. In depth reflective focus groups with students might reveal why the techno-fix featured so strongly.

To illustrate, one team suggested a future Hakodate City driven by an international Formula 1 (F1) racing car event as the strategy of choice to pull that city from its currently perceived socio-economic stagnation. Although F1 appears to be a future-oriented strategy at a superficial level, in that such an event does not currently exist in Hakodate, from a Futures Studies point of view, it is merely the past regurgitated in a different context using existing technologies and existing 'sporting as cultural event' strategies. A more creative and futures-oriented approach could have been applied to the same strategy. For example, an eco-friendly zero emissions racing car event, not necessarily F1, might be a more satisfying and futures-oriented proposal. In future projects, more thoughtful and thought provoking futures films might be produced if themes were limited to 'social technologies'.

Another problem area from a Futures Studies perspective questions the general analytic skills of the students. Japanese education tends to be weak in providing higher analytical skills during high school education leaving the would-be tertiary learner ill-prepared to deploy the kinds of analytical skills required for a true Futures Studies experience. Such a problem runs deep and cannot be superficially patched up with quick-fix solutions. Accordingly, prior to commencing a Futures Studies project, students such as those at FUN, would benefit greatly from a preliminary course in general research. This would include broader generalized components such as: what is a theory?; how to write a literature review; what is meant by an analysis?; how can we make sense of collected data?; etc.

Another concern is the degree of 'futureness' of the images created. It was the ultimate over-familiarity of the futures films that rendered them less 'of' and 'for' the future but as minimal extensions of familiar pasts and present societal structures, power relations and technologies. As Dator (1980) declared in a now famous futurist's axiom: Good futures work must at first seem ridiculous. Have our students erred on the side of caution within a comfortably numb future, or have they been over-zealous in trying to communicate messages about the future to satisfy what they think their instructors want to hear?

Nonetheless, it would be mean-spirited for a futurist to condemn such a project as without merits. Student themselves strove with vigor to express their ideas of how to create better futures for their communities and how such communities might look and be like to actually live in. Many teams had clearly struggled to use the various futures concepts as rigorously as they could given the constraints of time and their lack of experience with higher analytic skills. More generously we must imagine then what could be achieved with a more strategic approach from the course onset, with more time, more considered initiation into the novel world of futures thinking, and more personalized guidance with conceptually difficult and subversive futures ideas.

SWOT Analysis of the Overall Project

Strengths

An obvious strength for this project was the matrix of synergies emergent from our respective expert inputs: namely, the digitally enabled aspect, supplementing and complementing the futures component, and vice-versa. Stevenson (2008) and other futurists frequently point to the stagnant nature of present day Futures Studies and the need for futures to be taken to the streets, be created by those usually without a voice, and communicated across time and space with the most appropriate ICTs. According to Polak's (1973) theory of the image of the future, such images are conventionally under the domination of a 'futures-making elite'. If nothing else, this project represents, at least from a futures perspective, one small step towards undoing and subverting Japan's hierarchy of images producers and disseminators, providing young people with not only an appropriate futures tool-box and language but also the media technologies to support the creation and communication of their own personally created futures films.

Weaknesses

Firstly, in terms of Futures Studies, to make this kind of learning experience more effective for on-going projects, my personal post-facto reflection clearly indicates the need to deploy a more strategic approach to the project design. Of the various Futures Studies tools and methodologies initially introduced to the students, not all were effectively deployed for structuring their future films with meaningful and 'deep' images, ideas and concepts for the future. Further courses might be better served using fewer tools, at a deeper level. Perhaps the tools that were introduced were not necessarily the most appropriate, or, demanding enough to truly stretch students' imaginations and analytic skills into more creative futures spaces. To produce more robust futures-oriented films, one suggested methodology is Inayatullah's (2004) Causal Layered Analysis (CLA). CLA first explores the litany or the mass media produced superficial descriptions of a given futures issue. This is followed by an analysis of the social causes of the issue. At the third level is the worldview or paradigm, the epistemological base that supports the litany and causes. Finally at the deepest level are the social myths and metaphors whose authority are conventionally unquestioned, the taken-for-granted superstructure that underlies all else.

Opportunities

One opportunity from the education provider perspective suggests that any university offering a learning environment such as this digitally enabled Futures Studies project, is itself in a unique position. Though Futures Studies has become increasingly popular around the world over the last decade, Japan is still to offer a single course at any university. A Futures Studies course in combination with a digitally enabled component is even more rare and signals a new sphere of opportunity for educational futures (Shostak, 2004).

A second opportunity came vicariously from a fourth year FUN student who pointed out that once recruiting season comes around the Japanese student is often confronted for the first time with the need to deal with the concept of future-ness. This student reported that he wished that he understood the concept of future at a deeper level and had been taught such futures-oriented concepts, supported by futures methodologies and tools, from an early age in order to equip him and his peers with 'futures literacy' competencies. He felt that throughout his younger life he had been intentionally robbed of his innate futures thinking capabilities, until he was reduced to a being capable only of living in the 'creature present'; an ironic predicament for a young graduate-to-be from the Future University.

On this note, it has become popular for Japanese companies during recruiting season to ask of their prospective employees what their 'Dream Map' for the future is. A futures-literate would-be graduate could find him/herself advantageously positioned to impress a prospective employee if armed with a systematic and strategic approach to thinking about the future, and being aware of futures issues that could affect the organization. Such a competency must produce an attractive win-win situation for both employer-employee relations for the future. This is an opportunity that ought to be recognized by the educational institution, the teacher and the learner, to form a synergistic and strategic response to this recruiting trend.

What the above 'lesson' so vividly illustrates, is that once students are newly equipped with a new kind of language and tool-box fit for strategically and meaningfully engaging in issues and problems of and for the future, the future as a once invisible space, immediately becomes open to negotiation and engagement, in turn promoting the students capacities to positively articulate and construct alternative futures.

Threats

One threat to the very objectives of the program is a half-hearted approach to its delivery, especially in terms of the range, quality and depth of futures concepts introduced to the student. If too shallow the student may feel, with justification, that the future really is what it appears to be as expressed in the conventional mass media (technologies and more of the same) leaving the non-technological as mere impractical flights of fancy or something best left to corporate leaders and politicians.

It is not imaginable that management in Japanese universities could feel threatened by the field of Futures Studies whose explicit dissatisfactions with the present could lay the foundations for a subversive and radical element to emerge, developing into a disruptive force. At the extreme, educational management could conceivably conspire to forbid the teaching of Futures Studies.

As my co-author pointed out in the very first page of this chapter, *"Confucian hierarchy runs deep ... to the notion of teacher as knower of the right answer and the student a humble imitator of the master"* (Drydan, 1998, p.101), a cultural construct that could apply to educational management, as well as to academic colleagues similarly threatened by the notion of Futures Studies as an affront to teacher authority.

Another threat is that in times of economic depression, as was the case at the time of completing this paper, thinking about the future often appears to be a luxury. Parents concerned with their children securing jobs after graduating could perceive such a course project as ultimately futile in finding the 'right job'. Conversely, a Futures Studies perspective would posit the opposite point of view that during times of adversity a healthy dose of futures-oriented thinking and praxis are just the kinds of antidotes that provide positive perspective as well as ways out of the apparent adverse present. To not offer Futures Studies is the real threat.

CONCLUSION

This chapter has illustrated how informed implementations of Futures Studies in an existing higher education course have led to increased academic competencies. These are deemed essential for students in Higher Education but it has been argued that Japanese education does not actively promote the academic competencies of being critical, consolidating prior knowledge, having opportunities to express fresh ideas, willing to independently learn, and others mentioned above. Explicitly creating and communicating futures images based upon strategic and systematic methodologies supported by digital technologies, the Japanese students have thus negotiated unchartered intellectual territory which, as a result, produced measured outcomes. The result is a transformation of the student from a passive recipient of information to an active learner who can make sense of and communicate complex ideas for directing their own and society's futures. It would be prudent, therefore, of educational practitioners and policy makers to recognize that competencies which support systematic and strategic transformation create synergistic links between university students, local citizens and transnational communities thus giving shape to uncertain futures.

REFERENCES

Amara, R. (1981). The Futures Field. *The Futurist.* April/June.

Bachnik, J. M. (2003). Roadblocks on the information highway. Oxford, UK: Lexington Books.

Bell, W. (1996). An Overview of Futures Studies. []. Foundation Futures Study Centre, Qld: Australia]. *The Knowledge Base of Futures Studies, 1*, 29–58.

Boulding, K. E., & Boulding, E. (1995). The Future: Images and Processes. Thousand Oaks, CA: Sage Publications.

Corrallo, S. (1994). A preliminary study of the feasibility and utility for national policy of instructional good practice indicators in undergraduate education, (pp. 94-437). National Center for Higher Education Statistics.

Craft, L. (2004). *Remade in Japan.* ASSE Prism. Retrieved 26 August 2007 from http://www.prism-magazine.org

Dator, J. (1980). Emerging issues analysis in the Hawai'i judiciary. A report published by the Hawai'i judiciary, Honolulu, Hawai'i.

Dewey, J. (1938). Experience & education. New York: Touchstone.

Drydan, L. M. (1998). What Does Multiple Intelligence Theory Tell Us About CALL? In P. Lewis, (Ed.), Teachers, Learners and Computers: Exploring Relationships in CALL. JALT, Computer Assisted Language Learning National Special Interest Group, Japan.

Elgin, D. (1991). Awakening Earth. []. Queensland: Australia: Foundation Futures Study Centre.]. *The Knowledge Base of Futures Studies, 1*, 122.

Farrell, T. (1995). Reflective teaching. Principles and practice. *Forum, 4*(36). Retrieved November 6, 2007, from http://exchanges.state.gov/forum/vols/vol36/no4/p10.htm

Fegan, J., & Field, M. H. (Eds.). (2009). Education Across Borders: Politics, Policy and Legislative Action. Berlin: Springer.

Fujitani, S., Bhattacharya, M., & Akahori, K. (2003). ICT Implementation and online learning in Japan. *Educational Technology, 43*(3), 33–37.

Fullan, M. G., & Stiegelbauer, S. (1991). The New Meaning of Educational Change (2nd Ed.). New York: Teachers College Press.

Gilster, P. (1997). Digital Literacy. New York: John Wiley & Sons.

Goodyear, P. (2001). Psychological foundations for networked learning. In C. Steeples & C. Jones, (Eds.), Networked learning: perspectives and issues. London: Springer Verlag.

Hung, W., Jonassen, D. H., & Liu, R. (2008). Problem-based learning. In J.M Spector, M.D. Merrill, J. Van Merrienboer & M.P. Driscoll (Eds.), Handbook Of Research On Educational Communications And Technology (3rd ed.). New York: Lawrence Erlbaum Associates

Hutchinson, F. (1996). Educating Beyond Violent Futures. New York: Routledge.

Ihsan, S., Inayatullah, S., & Obijiofor, L. (1995). The futures of communication. *Futures*, *27*(8), 897–903. doi:10.1016/0016-3287(95)00053-Y

Inayatullah, S. (2003). Teaching Futures Studies: From Strategy to Transformative Change. *Journal of Futures Studies*, 35-40.

Inayatullah, S. (2004). Causal Layered Analysis: Theory, historical context, and case studies. In The Causal Layered Analysis Reader, (pp. 1-52). Tamkang University Press.

Kenny, S. (1994). Developing Communities for the Future. Melbourne, Australia: Nelson ITP.

Knipe, D., & Lee, M. (2002). The quality of teaching and learning via videoconferencing. *British Journal of Educational Technology*, *33*(3), 301–311. doi:10.1111/1467-8535.00265

Kolb, D. A. (1984). Experiential learning: experience as the source of learning and development. Englewood Cliffs, NJ: Prentice-Hall.

Krajcik, J. S., & Blumenfeld, P. C. (2006). Project-based learning. In K. Sawyer (Ed.). The Cambridge Handbook Of The Learning Sciences. Cambridge, UK: CUP

Kress, G. R. (2003). Literacy in the new media age. New York: Routledge.

Lasswell, H. D. (1948). The structure and function of communication in society. In L. Bryson (Ed.), The Communication of Ideas. New York: Harper & Row.

Martin, S., & Vallance, M. (2008). The impact of synchronous inter-networked teacher training in Information and Communication Technology integration. *Computers & Education*, *51*, 34–35. doi:10.1016/j.compedu.2007.04.001

Masini, E. B. (1993). Why Futures Studies? London: Grey Seal Books.

Mayer, R. E. (2005). Multimedia Learning. Cambridge, UK: CUP

Mima, N. (2003). Online technology is not enough: transforming the teacher-student learning process. In J. M. Bachnik (Ed.), Roadblocks on the information highway. Oxford, UK: Lexington Books.

Morris-Suzuki, T., & Rimmer, P. J. (2003). Cyberculture, society, and education in Japan. In J. M. Bachnik (Ed.), Roadblocks on the information highway. Oxford, UK: Lexington Books.

Morrison, D., & Collins, A. (1996). Epistemic fluency and constructivist learning environments. In B.G. Wilson (Ed.), Constructivist learning environments: Case studies in instructional design (pp. 107 - 119). Englewood Cliffs, NJ: Educational Technology Publications.

Morrison, K. (1998). Management Theories For Educational Change. Thousand Oaks, CA: Sage Publications.

O'Reilly, T. (2005). *What Is Web 2.0. Design Patterns and Business Models for the Next Generation of Software.* Retrieved Dec 30, 2007, from http://www.oreillynet.com/pub/a/oreilly/tim/news/2005/09/30/what-is-web-20.html

Pace, C. R. (1990). The undergraduates: a report of their activities and progress in college in the 1980's. Los Angeles: Center for the Study of Evaluation, University of California, Los Angeles.

Plaas, J. L., & Jones, L. C. (2005). Multimedia learning in second language acquisition. In R. E. Mayer, (Ed.), The Cambridge Handbook Of Multimedia Learning. Cambridge, UK: CUP.

Polak, F. (1973). The Image of the Future. New York: Elsevier Scientific Publishing.

Ramos, J. (2006). Consciousness, culture and the communication of foresight. *Futures*, *38*, 1119–1124. doi:10.1016/j.futures.2006.02.015

Rovai, A. P., Wighting, M. J., Baker, J. D., & Grooms, L. D. (2009). Development of an instrument to measure perceived cognitive, affective, and psychomotor learning in traditional and virtual classroom higher education settings. *The Internet and Higher Education*, *12*, 7–13. doi:10.1016/j.iheduc.2008.10.002

Sawyer, K. (2006). The Cambridge Handbook Of The Learning Sciences. Cambridge, UK: CUP

Shostak, A. B. (2004). High Schools for Futurism: Nurturing the next generation. *The Futurist*, (November-December): 23–27.

Slaughter, R. A. (1996). The Knowledge Base of Futures Studies. Victoria, Australia: DDM Media Group.

Slaughter, R. A. (2005). Futures Thinking for Social Foresight. Taiwan: Tamkang University Press.

Statistical Handbook of Japan. (2007). Retrieved 25 April 2009 from http://www.stat.go.jp/english/data/handbook/c02cont.htm

Stevenson, T. (2008). *The future's history: Let's reframe it.* Personal communication.

Stevenson, T., & Simpson, L. (1993). Creating Futures among uncommon cultures: A Methodology for Exploiting the Chaos to find new Coherence. In M. Mannermaa, S. Inayatullah & R. A. Slaughter (Eds.), *Coherence and chaos in our uncommon futures - Visions, means, actions, Selections from the XIII World Conference of the World Futures Studies Federation*, Turku, Finland, (pp. 319-328).

Swain, M., & Lapkin, S. (1995). Problems in output and the cognitive processes they generate: a step towards second language learning. *Applied Linguistics*, *16*, 371–391. doi:10.1093/applin/16.3.371

Towndrow, P. A. (2007). Task design, implementation and assessment: Integrating information and communication technology in English language teaching and learning. Singapore: McGraw-Hill.

UNESCO. (2007). *ICT in education: Japan.* Retrieved 25 August 2007 from http://www.unescobkk.org/index.php?id=1381

Vallance, M. (2006). Responsibility without power: reflections of an IT Coordinator in education. Perspectives: policy & practice in Higher Education, 10(4), October, 109-114.

Vallance, M. (2008a). Beyond policy: Strategic actions to support ICT integration in Japanese schools. *Australasian Journal of Educational Technology*, *24*(3), 275–293.

Vallance, M. (2008b). Using a database application to support reflective practice. Tech Trends: linking research and practice to improve learning, 52(6), Nov/Dec, 69-74

Vallance, M., Vallance, K., & Matsui, M. (2009). Criteria for the implementation of learning technologies. In M. Thomas (Ed.), Handbook of Research on Web 2.0 and Second Language Learning (pp. 1-19). Hershey, PA: IGI Global.

Vygotsky, L. (1986). Thought and language. Cambridge, MA: MIT Press.

Warschauer, M. (2007). Laptops & literacy, Learning in the wireless classroom. New York: Teachers College Press.

Whittaker, D. H. (2001). *Crisis and innovation in Japan: a new future through techno-entrepreneurship? MIT.* Japan Program Working Paper 01.02. Retrieved 21 December 2008 from http://dspace.mit.edu/bitstream/handle/1721.1/16566/JP-WP-01-02-52124684.pdf

Wilson, D. C. (1992). A Strategy For Change. New York: Routledge.

ADDITIONAL READING

Cuban, L. (2003). Why is it so hard to get good schools? New York: Teachers College Press.

Dewey, J. (1938). Experience & Education. New York Simon & Schuster.

Galtung, J., & Inayatullah, S. (1999). Macrohistory and macrohistorians: Perspectives on Individual, Social and Civilizational Change. USA: Praeger.

Hicks, D. (2002). Lessons for the Future: The Missing Dimension in Education. London: Routledge Falmer.

Inayatullah, S. (2005). Questioning the Future: Methods and Tools for Organizational and Societal Transformation (Second edition). Taiwan: Tamkang University Press.

Kress, G., & Van Leeuwen, T. (2001). Multimodal Discourse: The Modes and Media of Contemporary Communication. London: Arnold.

Masini, E. B. (1993). Why Futures Studies? London: Grey Seal Books.

Masini, E. B. (1996). Visions of Desirable Societies. New York: Pergamon Press.

Polak, F. (1973). The Image of the Future. New York: Elsevier Scientific Publishing.

Sardar, Z. (1999). Rescuing All Our Futures: The Future of Futures Studies. USA: Praeger.

Slaughter, R., & Bussey, M. (2006). Futures Thinking for Social Foresight. Taiwan: Tamkang University Press.

Thornburg, D. D. (1991). Edutrends 2010. Restructuring, technology, and the future of education. USA: Starsong.

Trochim, W. M. K. (2005). Research methods. The concise knowledge base. USA: Atomic Dog Publishing.

KEY TERMS AND DEFINITIONS

Futures Studies: The systematic research and analysis of images of the future (business as usual, collapse, nostalgic, and transformative) with the aim of creating, communicating, practicing and implementing preferred futures in the real world.

Image of the Future: A representation of a future object, society, system or world depicted in one or more media such as text, illustration, film, and so on.

Academic Competencies: Competencies expected of students in Higher Education that can be sub-categorized into generic, epistemic and declarative competencies.

Digital Enablement: To comfortably utilize technology for a wide range of tasks, in particular, communication.

Web 2.0: A knowledge-oriented environment where users cooperatively create malleable content with shared presence that is synchronously and asynchronously distributed in wired and wireless networks to fixed and portable technologies.

New Media: A technology experience of multimedia and hypermedia.

Hakodate 2017: A systematic development of ideas, alternatives and communication for the city's futures.

Futures Employment 2028: A systematic development of ideas, alternatives and communication for personal employment futures.

Guided Visualization: A creative technique for guiding an individual through a series of steps in order to 'arrive' at a future world which can then be articulated and used for on-going analyses and be built into an image of the future or futures scenario.

Futures Triangle Analysis: The Futures Triangle is a tool for mapping the dynamics that collectively produce plausible future outcomes consisting of three dimensions: pushes of the present, pulls of the future, and weights of history.

Scenario Creation: The activity of building a plausible and coherent story of a possible future world based on a series of systematic analyses typically consisting of continued growth scenarios, collapse scenarios, nostalgic/return to the past scenarios but, most importantly, transformative scenarios.

Chapter 10
Development of a Transnational Framework for E-Learning Technologies

Deryn Graham
University of Greenwich, UK

ABSTRACT

This case study looks at the creation of a Transnational Framework for e-Learning Technologies. It describes how the original study which aimed to "Develop a Framework for e-Learning" through a given exemplar in a United Kingdom institution, has gone through several iterations. From initially considering e-Tutoring/e-Moderating from a Human-Computer Interaction (HCI) point of view, to the adoption of Blended Learning as a solution to problems revealed by the Framework. Proceeding to evaluate e-Learning in terms of PESTE (Political, Economic, Social, Technical and Environmental) factors, restated here in the form of STEP (Social, Technological, Economical and Political) factors, which led to the realization of major external issues for e-Learning. Most recently, the study evolved to revisit e-Learning from an HCI and Computer-Supported Cooperative Work (CSCW) perspective, by applying a Cooperative Work Framework. The resulting final incarnation, a Transnational Framework for e-Learning, is thus presented.

ORGANISATION BACKGROUND

The University under reference is a large modern university in the UK with more than 25,000 students and 2,500 staff, offering approximately 1,000 different courses. It typically generates around £20 million in research, consultancy and enterprise activities annually. The School of Computing and Mathematical Sciences (CMS), within this University, has a range of interdisciplinary and multidisciplinary research consisting of some 80 plus cooperating researchers. It attracts considerable funding from the EU and UK government departments and agencies and is currently involved in many substantial industrial collaborations. It has won many awards for its work such as the Queen's Anniversary Prize for Higher and Further Education, the European

DOI: 10.4018/978-1-61520-779-4.ch010

IST prize, and has been a British Computer Society Gold Medal winner.

Students attending the University mirror the local populations and are therefore extremely diverse in terms of ethnicity and culture. This applies equally to the School which has a predominantly male contingent. Student ability varies but is reflective of most universities, with very strong and very weak students and an increasing absence of the middle of the Normal Distribution.

The development of the Transnational framework was initiated whilst at the School of Computing and Mathematical Sciences, of the university, and uses Teachmat, the School's in-house system, as a case study exemplar.

SETTING THE STAGE

The work began as an academic study initially considering e-Tutoring/e-Moderating from an HCI point of view, inspired by reports that the main reason for the failure of the United Kingdom eUniversity (UKeU) was attributable to the lack of research into potential customers' needs and a "supply-driven approach" (Sammuels, 2005). This was one of many examples of problems with the development and employment of e-Learning at that time. The investigation was further motivated by comments by Mason and others. Mason (2004) states that:

There is absolutely no evidence that learners are able or willing to do without teachers, no matter how well designed the materials, how extensive the resources or how 'just in time' the learning. The fundamental role of the teacher or tutor has not changed but the mode of operation has.

This view was supported by experiential data from students on Information Systems, Multimedia, and Computer Science programmes within the organization's (university's) School of Computing and Mathematical Sciences (Jones, 2004) insisting on no more than thirty percent of their courses in total (their management, content and delivery, etc) be "e".

A complete timeline (historical summary) for the case study follows. This summary also constitutes a generic template for a Transnational Framework for e-Learning Technologies, and the 9 stages involved:

1. Creation of a diary "synthesis of common interaction examples that constitute teaching and learning" (Figure 1) within the organization.
2. Generating from 1 above a list of "activities and skills required for Tutoring and e-Tutoring" (Figure 2).
3. Mapping the skills required for e-Tutoring against Salmon's (2004) stages in the "Framework for supporting e-Tutoring" (Figure 3), determining the "knowledge to be acquired" and the "action to be taken" for the organization, for e-Learning within the organization.
4. If necessary, revisiting activity 3 if blended learning is/becomes prevalent within the organization.
5. Evaluating e-Learning within the organization in terms of STEP or PESTE factors, which may be completely external to the organization, and yet have significant influence.
6. Take a Computer Supported Cooperative Work view of the organization's e-Learning technologies:
   (i) Instantiate "a time/space matrix" (Figure 4).
   (ii) Apply a "Cooperative Work Framework" (Figure 5), instantiating the roles of participants and artifacts, identifying where and in what form feedback, control and understanding occur.

7. From the above stages (1-6), determine critical factors and impediments to e-Learning within the organization.
8. Organizational review of the Framework findings.
9. Adopt suitable strategies for e-Learning.

The last point is where the goals of the organization's management (the STEP or PESTE factors) will decide the future shape of e-Learning within the organization. What is presented here is an academic framework based upon empirical evidence, which may be extremely distant from any individual organization's strategic management policy, for example, the adoption of e-Learning technologies may be mandatory and deemed to be imperative to the financial survival of the organization.

CASE DESCRIPTION

The following coverage includes a consideration of: Technological Concerns, Technological Components, and Management and Organizational Concerns. Some of these concerns and components are implicit, for example, the use of technologies and skills within the Framework (Figure 3). The original study in 2005 (Graham, 2005) looked at the skills and knowledge required for both traditional and e-Tutoring in an attempt to discover the reasons behind the apparent lack of success of current e-Learning systems. It tried to establish whether this lack of success was: an issue of requirements gathering and analysis; a tutoring problem; or simply a communications problem and an issue of Human-Computer Interaction (HCI). HCI is now more commonly referred to as Interaction Design. These endeavors led to the development of a Framework for e-Learning (Graham, 2005).

In order to identify typical tutoring activities, a representative week in the calendar of several university lecturers was elicited, resulting in a synthesis of common interaction examples that constitute teaching and tutoring (Figure 1). Highly noticeable was the significant amount of time spent dealing with e-mail. In Figure 2, the activities and tutoring skills required were identified from this diary synthesis. A third column was added which suggested the new skills required for e-Tutoring. The inference was that e-Tutoring requires all the same skills as traditional face-to-face (f2f) tutoring, plus some additional skills.

These additional skills were considered to be firstly, technological and secondly, skills which dealt with managing mostly remote and often asynchronous communication. Such skills relate directly to perceived problems with computer-mediated communication (CMC), and are equally inherent in Computer-Supported Cooperative Work (CSCW) and HCI. CSCW is about groups of users and designing systems to support their group work, understanding the effect of technology (products often called groupware) on group work patterns (Dix et al., 2003; Preece, Rogers, & Sharpe, 2002). Groupware can be classified as synchronous or asynchronous, co-located or remote, supporting computer-mediated communication and shared applications and artifacts, facilitating meeting and decision support systems. Interaction problems such as the lack of visual and audible cues, gestures, intonation, turn-taking, context, collaboration, group dynamics etc have long been recognized by HCI and CSCW practitioners (Maier & Warren, 2000). A further related area is Information Visualisation. Information Visualisation (Shneiderman & Plaisant, 2005) can be defined as "the use of interactive visual representations of *abstract* data to amplify cognition". Learning is arguably a social activity, and communication is widely accepted as being central to any successful teaching and learning strategy (Sutherland, 1992). A system will fail, even if it fulfils all its functional requirements, if it does not address the requirements of the user.

The mapping of the relationship between the skills identified and those given or suggested by

Figure 1. Synthesis of common interaction examples that constitute teaching and tutoring

DAY	TIME	INTERACTION	STUDENTS/SUBJECT	COMMENT
Mon	09:00-10:00	Checking e-mails. Collecting keys, handouts, etc for lecture.		Only ever get to make a start on the numerous e-mails!
	10:00-12:00	Lecture followed by tutorials/labs.	125 level 3 degree students, then two of the four tutor groups of around 30.	A lot of preparation simply because this is a constantly changing field and at level 3 it should be state of the art.
	12:00-13:00	Tutorial/Lab (Group A).	30+ students.	Mostly formative exercises which build upon the lectures. In the labs this week.
	13:00-14:00	Tutorial/Lab (Group B).	30+ students.	
	14:00-15:00	Office Hour.	Usually project students (level 3 and MSc).	Saw 3/3 of the UG students, gave academic feedback.
	15:00-16:00	Meeting with PhD student.	PhD student on FP5 EU project in DM.	New student. Discussed progress.
	16:00-18:00	Checking/ replying to e-mails.		Too many, too often!
Tue	13:00-14:00	Telephone conference, AE FP5 project.	One of the partners only.	Discussion on a matter resulting from the Partner Meeting last week.
	14:00-15:00	AE FP5 team meeting.	With RF and PhD student.	Progress meeting post Partner Meeting.
	15:00-16:00	Meeting with PhD student.	Meeting with student for AE FP5 project.	PhD progress meeting. Discussed a joint paper.
	16:00-18:00	Checking/ replying to e-mails.		
Wed	13:00-14:00	Open day duty.	80+ students. IS and CS programmes.	Teach on both programmes.
	14:00-16:00	Learning and Quality Meeting.	School Board.	
	16:00-18:00	Checking/replying to e-mails. Preparation for Personal and Level 1 academic Tutorial tomorrow.		
Thurs	09:00-10:00	Checking/ replying to e-mails.		
	10:00-12:00	Research Group Meeting.	Research Group.	
	12:00-13:00	Departmental Meeting.	Department.	Had to leave early to go and teach at 1pm.
	13:00-14:00	Personal Tutorial.	25 students, level 1.	
	14:00-15:00	Office Hour.	Usually project students (level 3 and MSc).	Saw 4/10 MSc students, gave feedback.
	15:00-16:00	Update materials for lecture course.		Post a reminder about next week's coursework deadline.
	16:00-17:00	Academic Tutorial.	30 students, level 1.	Personal tutees plus others from other Schools.
Fri	08:00-20:00	Checking e-mails. Writing papers and grant applications. Preparing lectures. Assessing work. Assessing courses as an external examiner. Work on FP5 projects.	Attended to some of the considerable work generated by the Partner Meeting for one FP5 project.	Currently working on two grant applications and three papers. Preparation for next week's External Examiners Meeting.

Figure 2. Activities and skills required for Tutoring and e-Tutoring

Tutoring Activities	Tutoring Skills	New (e)Tutor Skills required
Tutorials.	**Personal and academic.**	Technology.
Lecturing.	**Communication, enthusing.**	Coping with the lack of f2f contact, visual and audible cues.
Assessment.	**Feedback, plagiarism.**	Dealing regularly with asynchronous and remote communication.
Research supervision.	**Knowledge, support, enabling.**	Remote, asynchronous enthusing!
Preparing teaching materials.	**Presentation, authoring.**	e-Motivation.
Mentoring.	**Mentoring.**	Committed time management.
Queries.	**Communication via e-mail and telephone.**	Extending the application of traditional tutoring skills, such as authoring and the scheduling of activities.
Scheduling.	**Time management, organisational skills.**	Adding to repertoire of teaching methods through the media.
Updating skills.	**Learnability.**	Information Visualisation!
Industrial training visits.	**People skills, assessment skills.**	Adopting a more student centred approach?
External exam moderation.	**Subject knowledge, assessment regulations, etc.**	e-Socialising.
Administration and meetings.	**Academic judgement.**	Culture/attitude shift.
Taught project supervision (UG and PG).	**Knowledge, support.**	
EU project management.	**More of all the above!**	

Figure 3. A Framework for supporting e-Tutoring. Maintenance is deemed to be an issue for all stages of the model. STAGE refers to Salmon's (2004) 5 stage Model of e-Tutoring.

SALMON STAGES	SKILLS TO BE ACQUIRED	KNOWLEDGE TO BE ACQUIRED	*ACTION TO BE TAKEN*
STAGE 1: Access & Motivation	There is now an abundance of tools available, which may be W3C compliant (and SENDA compliant to some degree). These tools have much of what is required for all of the five stages, so what must be acquired are the skills and knowledge necessary for their use. It is the non technical aspects which are therefore the focus.	Vis. skills to be acquired. Tools are easier to adopt (and have often been adopted) for stages four and five, with forums etc available, to cater for stages two and three in particular.	Computer Science, Multimedia, and Information Systems students should be capable of attaining access! Motivation is the main problem which could be assisted by improvements to the course site Welcome? F2f meetings to be arranged prior to e-Tutoring?
STAGE 2: Online socialization			Use of tool's news and course forums to be adopted for conferencing etc. Regular checking of forums is very important.
STAGE 3: Information exchange			Ditto stage 2 above.
STAGE 4: Knowledge construction			Stage 4 is often fully implemented and operational. Further improvements to the presentation and compliance could be made.
STAGE 5: Development			Achieved in most cases, but could be further improved upon, e.g. the links to past papers and other resources.

Salmon's (2004) five stage model of e-Tutoring, was next explored. Salmon's model for e-Moderating gives more weight to the social aspects of e-Tutoring, adapting to the e-Learning environment and the group dynamics (three of the five stages). The last two stages are those concerned with the actual knowledge construction and development. From direct experience, this emphasis is probably correct and this is the main implication for practice. In the Framework proposed (Figure 3), the human factors associated with stage 1 of Salmon's model appeared to be paramount to the success or failure of a system. Referring here to human factors such as; the current learning situation, communication, cultural and social aspects, all of which are well known to other aforementioned disciplines and have much in common with the user requirements. Learning is achieved by providing appropriate scaffolding, whether for traditional tutoring or e-Tutoring. Instead of motivation there is e-Motivation, socializing becomes e-Socializing. Fundamentally, the nature of human interaction and the lack of visual and social cues etc provided by the technology is likely to be a major reason for Salmon's e-Tutoring stages 1 to 3 being more difficult in non f2f situations.

One possible solution implied by the "Action to be taken" above and often proposed to resolve the inadequacies of e-Learning identified, the human requirements; such as "Motivation" and the lack of "Online Socialisation" described by Salmon's early stages (2004), is the application of Blended Learning. A further study (Graham & Valsamidis, 2006) investigated whether the use of Blended Learning can fulfill or at least accommodate some of the human requirements presently neglected by current e-Learning systems. The study evaluated the in-house system Teachmat, the in-house system of the School of Computing and Mathematical Sciences (CMS)'s, used as a reference for the Framework (Figure 3) below, and discussed how the use of Blended Learning has become increasingly prevalent as a result of its enhancement and expansion, its relationship to human and pedagogical issues, and both the positive and negative implications of this reality. There is currently a movement towards Blended Learning, with in-house course management tools invoking a creeping change in teaching practice from traditional tutoring to e-Tutoring. Blended Learning (Teach-nology, 2006) has been defined as:

An educational formation that integrates elearning techniques including online delivery of materials through web pages, discussion boards and/or email with traditional teaching methods including lectures, in-person discussions, seminars, or tutorials.

In developing a Framework for e-Learning, it was apparent that many of the technological requirements necessary to enable e-Learning were provided by an in-house tool, namely; Teachmat (Graham, 2006). On reflection, it led also to the realization that many aspects of this Framework in relation to Salmon's 5 Stages had been attained for many courses; effectively these courses were using technology led Blended Learning. Teachmat and the CMS intranet are treated as synonymous, although strictly speaking Teachmat is part of the CMS intranet. Teachmat was originally developed primarily for course content management support, a pseudo Content Management System. It has been extended considerably, and indeed since the framework was suggested (for example, printed handouts are no longer given, and links to past papers and other resources now exist), from a mere repository for course materials to a comprehensive on-line intranet system. Teachmat now resembles more an in-house Virtual Learning Environment (VLE) for Computer Supported Collaborative Learning (CSCL), employing Web 2.0 technologies, wikis, blogs, video conferencing (optional) and attempts to incorporate social networking, i.e. Second Life (Second Life, 2008). It now handles everything from; learning material, assignment uploads, assessment and examinations management, forums, student advice, registration and attendance, curriculum and institutional policies management, lecturer and student handbooks, etc, etc. The result is that the Teachmat environment has changed the learning and teaching style from traditional to Blended. The level of Blended Learning employed is being individual to courses, with some courses employing multimedia course delivery, such as video. The facilities used for courses are presently a matter of choice; however, virtually all coursework is uploaded on-line and there is a growing pressure for on-line assessment. Submissions generate automatic electronic receipts and staff e-mail notifications in the case of final year projects, for instance. Electronic registers record both weekly attendance and uploads for each week linked to the files themselves. Forums are available to students and staff at course level. The level of electronic communication with students and other staff has exploded as a by-product. Fundamentally, more and more elements of the teaching and learning are now electronic. Face to face (co-located and synchronous) teaching is still the predominant method employed in the organization for local (co-located) students, but much of the related activities are now remote and asynchronous. Lecturers still give lectures, tutorials and workshops in person but via personal computers, stored on data sticks or directly linked to Teachmat. Teachmat is being further exploited for external institutions, where both teaching and supporting activities are being carried out remotely and asynchronously, using video for example. Here learning is moving from Blended to fully "e".

The pros of this situation, the deployment of Blended Learning, appear to be mostly managerial: For example, a reduction in the amount of printing and photocopying costs, and paper; moderated work is immediately available electronically, indeed almost everything is now available at the click of a mouse. All learning material for each course (schedules, coursework, room bookings, etc) is on the system so staff absence can be more easily accommodated. Staff absence is also recorded on the system and news bulletins provided on Teachmat inform students of the absence of staff; extenuating circumstances and coursework extensions are also dealt with on-line; everything is on Teachmat.

Teachmat, whilst having provided for many of the mostly technical requirements of Blended Learning or the Framework for e-Learning support, has yet to completely resolve the human issues: tutors are expected to be on-line 24/7; traditional tutoring is still superior in terms of flexibility and the accommodation of unforeseen circumstances; it is still much easier to flick through paper coursework submissions than electronic ones; a register only actually shows that a file has been uploaded for a course that week by the student; there are restrictions on the file size of uploads; any printing of uploaded coursework is restricted to black and white, which is a weakness for assessing HCI criteria in particular, adding further pressure for tutors to mark on-line; students and especially staff feel that are being dictated to by the system; there are issues associated with the ownership of teaching materials which are obviously more accessible in electronic form; Teachmat has furthered the vast increase in "e" administration, continuously monitoring forums, plus the propagation of electronic communication and documents being required to be completed for tasks; the management system is becoming unmanageable; anxiety and resentment within staff and students is being created by this "wandering into" Blended Learning; there are still health and safety, pedagogical, as well as social issues regarding e-Tutoring which have yet to be addressed. Finally, everything is on Teachmat.

Wannermacher (2006, p.72) identifies the following categories for incentives for increasing Faculty acceptance of e-teaching at German universities:

a) Financial Incentives
b) Infrastructural and Technical Incentives

c) Accounting and Reducing Workload
d) Distinctions Incentive
e) Competitive Advantage for Universities
f) Creating a Climate Conductive to E-teaching

Sociology uses PESTE factors (Political, Economic, Social, Technical, and Environmental). Reclassifying Wannermacher's incentives in terms of PESTE factors, it can be seen that for the normal interpretation of Environmental issues, these issues are not pertinent to e-Learning. However, a looser interpretation could classify incentive f) as Environmental (educationally environmental).

a) Financial Incentives (E)
b) Infrastructural and Technical Incentives (T)
c) Accounting and Reducing Workload (E)
d) Distinctions Incentive (S/E)
e) Competitive Advantage for Universities (E)
f) Creating a Climate Conductive to E-teaching (P)

Where: P: Political; E: Economic; S: Social; T: Technical; En: Environmental

Restating these as STEP (Social, Technical, Economic and Political) factors, leads to the same classification, identical to the PESTE classification as none of the incentives were deemed to be sufficiently environmental.

The major concern with the incentives identified by Wannermacher is that pedagogical motives are not evident. This significant absence is true of the evaluation of the application of Blended and e-Learning through in-house tools such as Teachmat (Graham & Valsamidis, 2006). The findings of Wannermacher (2006) and Graham (2006) indicate that e-Learning is management driven, the pros given above are mostly managerial and, as they originate from the higher echelons of the institution, are likely to be externally politically driven. Haydn (2006) suggests that the current e-Learning trend in the UK is highly political, but again it is the lack of the employment of e-Learning to improve pedagogy as the primary motivation that raises considerable unease.

The most recent study involved the application of a Cooperative Work Framework from CSCW to e-Learning groupware (Graham, 2008). Groupware can be classified in several ways, one of these is by where and when the participants are performing the cooperative work, as summarized in a time/space matrix as: synchronous or asynchronous, co-located or remote. Another classification is by the function of the system they primarily support: CMC supporting the direct communication between participants; meeting and decision support systems capturing common understanding; shared applications and artifacts supporting the participant's interaction with shared work objects (the artifacts of work). CMC includes: email and bulletin boards; structured message systems; text messaging (IM, SMS and MMS); video conferences and communication; Collaborative Virtual Environments, and; Meeting and Decision Support Systems. Some CMC systems are asynchronous, including traditional e-mail and structured messaging systems. Various forms of video communication support synchronous communication, such as video conferences, direct person-to-person video or social contact. Many systems such as those for e-Learning and CSCL may support more than one of these system functions, and this can be seen as a sign of good groupware. Furthermore, there can be some additional relationships between these functions.

Using a time/space matrix e-Learning would be classified as mainly asynchronous and remote groupware, as it is these features that are purported to be the strengths of e-Learning. Australia's "School of the Air" is categorized as being remote but synchronous. The time/space matrix has become a common language amongst the CSCW community. It can also be useful during design, as one of the earliest decisions is what sort of interaction is planned. The design space

Figure 4. Learning in a refined time/space matrix.

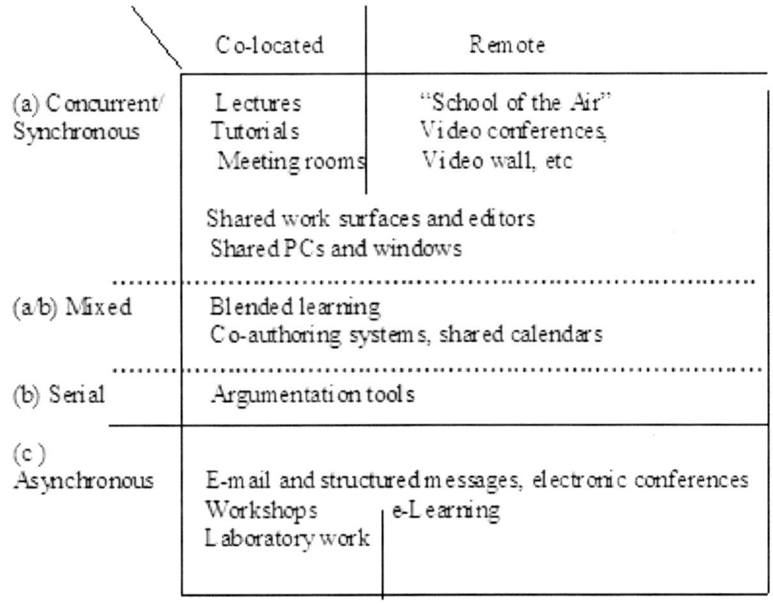

for synchronous interaction is entirely different from the asynchronous. A useful distinction is to look at the data stored and classify systems as synchronized when there is a real-time computer connection, or asynchronized when there is none. Laboratory work can be synchronous, but is usually asynchronous as in this case. Figure 4 places learning systems into this refined matrix.

The cooperative work framework can be applied to e-Learning (Figure 5). The groupware is the e-Learning system, often an in-house intranet or open-source based system. The artifacts of work are the assignments, tests, etc., those elements that are assessed formatively or summatively. The participants would be the students and the tutors, however, after the initial set-up the tutor may not be part or a full part (replaced by some sort of course administrator) of the framework. Direct communication is likely to be in the form of e-mail or forums, and may be supported by electronic conferences and video connections. Common understanding can be supported by argumentation tools, meeting rooms and shared work surfaces. Control and feedback from shared artifacts may be supported by shared PCs and windows, shared editors, co-authoring systems and shared diaries. The problem relates to explicating common understanding. Feedback from the artifacts to the participants would take the form of assessment, for instance. However, control from the participant to the artifact is likely to be distinct from the feedback due to its asynchronous nature. The major issue for the cooperative work framework for e-Learning is actually where understanding occurs. In the classroom setting with f2f communication, understanding is more achievable through the subtle cues and gestures exhibited by both students and tutors. Even in large classes, there is a common awareness for both parties – "deadly silence" or smiles of acknowledgement resulting from a tutor's question to the class. Many of these cues are still present in remote, but synchronous learning; Australia has many years of experience with distance learning. Large distances and low population density led naturally to the "School of the Air". This retained the teacher pupil verbal interaction and much of the strict time frame with few of the problems that

Figure 5. Cooperative work framework

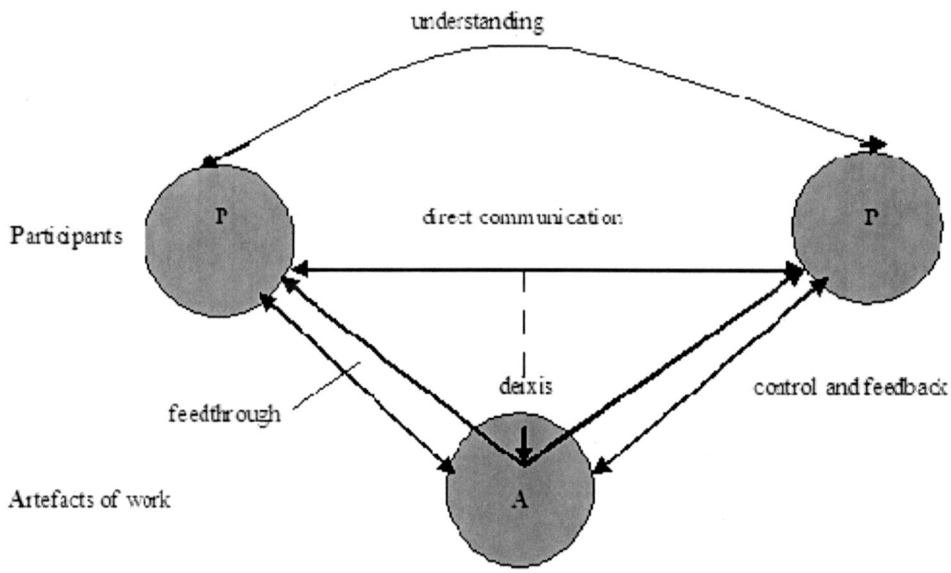

today's e-Learning environment faces (Howgate, 2007). e-Learning not only lacks these important visual and audio cues and synchronicity, but if the tutor is responsible for the initial setting-up of a system and then involved only via the artifacts of work, it is difficult to see where the common understanding so vital for any learning exists. Other considerations are with respect to shared information (Clark & Brennan, 1991; Clark & Schafer, 1989). e-Learning essentially necessitates communication through collaborative models. For asynchronous groupware (and even some synchronous systems) used in e-Learning, the major form of direct communication is text-based. Exceptions to this are other media that may be used in addition to text such as graphics, voice animation or video clips. Despite these, text is still the dominant medium. Text-based communication in groupware systems and CSCL is acting as a speech substitute, thus, there are some problems adapting between the two media. Text-based conversation, has reduced feedback for confirmation, less context to disambiguate utterances, slower pace of interaction, but is more easily reviewed.

CURRENT CHALLENGES FACING THE ORGANISATION

In developing the Framework, it had been suggested that the problems of e-Learning were not new and were as for other forms of interaction and their requirements. It was further suggested that e-Learning should heed the lessons learnt from other areas such as HCI and CSCW and that the problems of e-Learning and associated requirements were no longer fundamentally technological but human. It was concluded that it was these problems that needed to be addressed in any proposed framework if progress was to be made. This might be enabled by greater improvements in communications technology becoming sufficiently sophisticated as to convey subtle cues etc, but subsequent progress may ultimately necessitate a cultural and social shift in the attitudes of tutors and tutees towards teaching and learning per se. It was yet to be seen whether or not the Department for Education and Skills' latest e-Strategy "Harnessing Technology: Transforming Learning and Children's Services" (Dfse, 2005) would prove successful in addressing the issues raised.

It was also concluded that the use of Blended Learning has been an indirect consequence of the in-house technologies now employed. Tools like Teachmat are directing teaching and learning practices towards Blended Learning. The development of such in-house tools has caused a technology led proliferation in the employment of Blended Learning. This sea change was not a conscious decision by staff and students, who are highly unlikely to request e-Learning. This raised questions about the pedagogy behind systems developed. HCI and communications issues remain, as do some technical problems. The major concern is that although many (but not all) of the technical requirements have been catered for by tools like Teachmat (as demonstrated by the list of pros, in the main associated with Salmon's Stages 3-5), many important issues, namely those referred to as "human" have not been addressed (reflected by the list of cons, mostly associated with Salmon's Stages 1 and 2). There has not necessarily been any cultural or social shift in attitudes however, concluding that the successful embodiment of human factors; pedagogical, social, etc, is still key and requires most effort for fully "e" or Blended Learning. Blended Learning is presently not providing a solution; it has yet to accommodate the attainment of Salmon's motivational or social stages identified by the Framework and the constant focus on the technology is merely aggravating the situation.

After evaluating the application of e-Learning using PESTE factors from Sociology, it was proposed that e-Learning should adopt its own PESTE factors, where PESTE stands for Pedagogical, Educational, Social, Technical and (Educationally) Environmental (Graham, 2007). The order of these PESTE factors for e-Learning is highly significant. Pedagogy should be the main concern. Obviously this overlaps with Education, but Social factors should also be high on the agenda in accordance with the findings that human issues are paramount, as learning is inherently a social activity, most fundamentally founded on the instinct to survive. Equally in relation to the findings, Technology and the Environment should carry less weight. If e-Learning were to adopt its own STEP factors, they would stand for Social, Technical, Educational and Pedagogical, with the order reversed except for Social and Technical, i.e. PEST, which is rather an unfortunate acronym (so best to keep to PESTE even if the last "E" is a little contrived).

A deliberate, conscious decision was made to exclude Political and Economic factors which are credited as the present drivers for much of the expansion of e-Learning. In practice, economic incentives are likely to prove to be a myth as serious attempts to realize e-learning are experientially at least as expensive as f2f learning.

Applying a cooperative work framework resulted in the identification of further current challenges facing organizations (Graham, 2008). Human communication is very rich (Benyon, Turner & Turner, 2005), CMC is impoverished (but humans cope to a point). Despite the development of ubiquitous communications systems, distance still matters; however, the sheer richness is not merely verbal but is also reflected in the use of gesture, body posture and so on, all of which make up non-verbal communication. All this is highly relevant to e-Learning where the richness of f2f communication is replaced with impoverished CMC. Whilst humans cope with the inferiority of CMC there appear to be limits. The absence of one or two aspects e.g. co-located and use of gesture is manageable. However, e-Learning lacks non-verbal communication and social norms of behavior, web-cam images are renowned for their distortions. It can be argued that Salmon's (2004) Stages 1 and 2 (Access and Motivation, and On-line Socialization) are where grounding (constructing a shared understanding) occurs. It is these two stages that are repeatedly being affirmed as difficult and fundamentally key to e-Learning. It appears to be the compounding of factors in an e-Learning environment, which make understanding and therefore e-Learning difficult or impossible. Lack of visual cues, or lack of audio cues, or lack of synchronicity alone are not insurmountable, but combined may prove to be so. This is why Blended Learning is so attractive. The crux of the problem is that understanding is a human attribute and can only take place between people (participants) and is not possible by current technologies. If the tutor is absent or remote from the framework in the sense that communication is only via the artifact (the system and/or the assessment) then understanding, and therefore learning, cannot take place. The continuous understanding, feedback and control, natural to humans are not present, or indeed possible for computer systems. Feedback and control would be restricted to that implemented. These are weaknesses fundamental to the nature of e-Learning. Impediments to understanding, and factors key to collaboration and learning: grounding; synchronicity; feedback (back channels); control (breakdown and repair); visual cues; audible cues; technologies and architectures. Feedback and control are linked to cues and are obviously affected by synchronicity. As humans are adaptive, they can accommodate the absence of one or some limited combination of these factors. The problem for e-Learning is that often the lack of many or all of these factors is inherent. Blended Learning relieves some of the impediments, but does not solve them. The reality is that many current e-Learning systems and technologies, especially intranets, are essentially glorified web-enabled databases (content management systems), rather than knowledge-bases. Unlike the structured "How" and "Why" answers derived from the semantic and cognitive-based architectures of knowledge-based systems, web-enabled databases simply retrieve answers to such questions from their databases. Such information retrieval is not pedagogically sound and somewhat removed from human cognition.

The framework identifies challenges to organizations per se, and the framework is transnational in both its approach and findings. For the case study organization, the fact that Teachmat is in-house is a considerable advantage to the School, compared with other Schools and organizations, in terms of the control and management of technologies employed, but there are still overriding problems common to the deployment of e-Learning within all organizations as stated above.

SOLUTIONS AND RECOMMENDATIONS

In order to achieve some form of practical understanding within any e-Learning system, the impediments and factors listed need to be adequately addressed (Graham, 2009). Understanding has been determined as the critical factor for any learning system and the main reason for its propensity for failure. The political and economic undertones motivating a relentless push for such systems make the desire for their existence questionable. In general, humans still make the best teachers of other humans, because they are more capable of true human understanding in spite of the occasional misunderstanding or ambiguity (breakdown). The promotion of e-Learning would be more palatable if the primary motivation were pedagogical. In consideration of the application of a Cooperative Work Framework, the lack of understanding requires explicit and continuous mechanisms for feedback and control, as a substitute for those intrinsic and implicit in f2f communication (the all important cues and backchannels facilitating breakdown repairs amongst other things). Just employing more communication through the artifacts would lead to another set of problems, for example, greater pressure for online assessment which has already raised concerns: more assessment of "e" assignments; a move to more recognition rather than recall based on-line tests, which are easier to manage and require little expertise to assess once created. Electronic marking has recently been criticized by the Association of Teachers and Lecturers (Metro, 2007, p. 16): "Pupils are at risk of receiving the wrong grades in their exams under plans to extend electronic marking", due to fatigue. "Question papers could be 'dumbed down' to make the scripts easier to process and markers could make mistakes if they do not take regular screen breaks" which reinforces the need for attention to be given to health and safety issues in relation to CMC. Electronic marking "was introduced to speed up the process and cut the cost of posting scripts to assessors". There is also the responsibility of learners, when most learners are not the ideal "independent learner" aspired to for e-Learning. Skilled professionals may be employed for the initial content design of systems, with the long-term management designated to non-teaching professionals. The number of experts required at the front-line, thereby being substantially reduced, reducing costs. Salmon's (2004) Stages 1 and 2 also need to be overtly tackled for the necessary grounding. Blended Learning has been the approach often used. The manner of its application could be lessening its effectiveness (mixing the learning with the socializing in the first instance). A purely social (short) meeting of tutors and tutees prior to any teaching and learning has from previous anecdotal evidence improved student retention, and may be a way forward. Taking a more magnanimous viewpoint, e-Learning systems and the use of computers in general can, and should, be exploited for their inexhaustible patience, memory, asynchronous nature and remoteness, and other such attributes, where they would be most appropriate; teaching a new language, aiding those with learning difficulties, etc. using multi-modal approaches. The latter is now the basis of a new large multidisciplinary research project into multi-modal learning.

ACKNOWLEDGMENT

The support of the other participants of the Certificate of professional development in e-Learning, Teaching and Training (CeLTT) workshops, their contributions to the synthesis and to Figure 2 is gratefully acknowledged. Proof reading for this chapter was carried out by Dr. George Goodsell.

REFERENCES

Benyon, D., Turner, P., & Turner, S. (2005). Designing Interactive Systems: People, Activities, Contexts, Technologies (pp. 676-756). Reading, MA: Addison-Wesley.

Clark, H. H., & Brennan, S. E. (1991). Grounding in communication. In L. B. Resnick, J. Levine, & S. D. Behreno (Eds.), Socially Shared Cognition. Washington DC: American Psychological Association.

Clark, H. H., & Schaefer, E. F. (1989). Contributing to discourse. *Cognitive Science*, *13*, 259–294.

Dfse Web site (2005). *Dfse, Harnessing Technology: Transforming Learning and Children's Services*. Retrieved April 21, 2005, from http://www.dfes.gov.uk/publications/e-strategy/

Dix, A., Finlay, J., Abowd, G., & Beale, R. (2004). Human-Computer Interaction, (3rd Ed., pp. 476-508; 664-713). Harlow, UK: Prentice Hall.

Graham, D. (2005). Developing a Framework for e-Learning. In *Proceedings of the 6th Annual Conference of the Higher Education Academy*, University of York, 30th August – 1st September 2005, (pp. 111-114).

Graham, D. (2006). Developing a Framework for e-Learning 2006. Keynote Paper. In D. Graham (Ed.), *Proceedings of the Developing a Framework for e-Learning Workshop 2006, part of the 7th Annual Conference of the Subject Centre for Information and Computer Sciences, Higher Education Academy*, Trinity College, Dublin, 29th August 2006, (pp. 4-9).

Graham, D. (2007, June). PESTE Factors in Developing a Framework for e-Learning, *ELEA E-Learning journal, 4*(2), 194-201.

Graham, D. (2008, December). e-Learning in a Cooperative Work Framework. *ELEA E-Learning journal, 5*(4), 475-484.

Graham, D. (2009). Explicating Understanding. In A., Mendez-Vilas, A., Solano Martin, J., Mesa Gonzalez, & J. A., Mesa Gonzalez, (Eds.), *Research, Reflections and Innovations in Integrating ICT in Education (2009), Proceedings of the V International Conference on Multimedia and Information and Communication Technologies in Education (M-ICTE2009)*, New University of Lisbon, Lisbon, Portugal, 22-24 April 2009, (Vol. 2, pp. 739-743).

Graham, D., & Valsamidis, A. (2006). A Framework for e-Learning: A Blended Solution? In A. Mendez-Vilas, A. Solano Martin, J. Mesa Gonzalez, & J. A. Mesa Gonzalez, (Eds.), *Current Developments in Technology-Assisted Education (2006), Proceedings of the IV International Conference on Multimedia and Information and Communication Technologies in Education (M-ICTE2006)*, University of Seville, Seville, Spain, 22-25 November 2006, (Vol. 1, pp. 233-237).

Haydn, T. (2006). Multimedia, interactivity and learning: some lessons from the United Kingdom. In A. Mendez-Vilas, A. Solano Martin, J. Mesa Gonzalez, & J. A. Mesa Gonzalez, (Eds.), *Current Developments in Technology-Assisted Education (2006), Proceedings of the IV International Conference on Multimedia and Information and Communication Technologies in Education (M-ICTE2006)*, University of Seville, Seville, Spain, 22-25 November 2006, (Vol. 1, pp. 110-114).

Howgate, P. (2007). *Personal communication.*

Jones, R. (2004). *Personal communication.*

Maier, P., & Warren, A. (2000). Integr@ting [London: Kogan Page.]. *Technology (Elmsford, N.Y.)*, 103–106.

Mason, R. (2004). In M. Ryan, (2005), CeLTT teaching materials. School of Education and Training, University of Greenwich, London.

METRODigest. (2008, March 20). Electronic marking 'puts grades at risk.' *METRO*, (pp. 16).

Preece, J., Rogers, Y., & Sharp, H. (2002) Interaction Design Beyond Human-Computer Interaction, (pp. 105-137). Hoboken, NJ: Wiley.

Salmon, G. (2004). *All things in Moderation*. Upper Saddle River, NJ: Prentice Hall. Retrieved March 18, 2005, from http://www.e-tivities.com

Samuels, M. (2005, March 3). MPs identify where UKeU went wrong. In Computing, VNU Business Publications, (pp. 1, 4-5, 28).

Second Life Web site. (2008). Retrieved August 24, 2008, from http://secondlife.com/

Shneiderman, B., & Plaisant, C. (2005). Designing for the User Interface, (4th Ed., pp. 580- 601). Boston: Addison Wesley.

Sutherland, P. (1992). Vygotsky and Vygotskyans. In Cognitive development today: Piaget and his critics, (pp. 45-46). London: Paul Chapman.

Teach-nology Web site. (2006). Retrieved April 24, 2006, from www.teach-nology.com/glossary/terms/b/

Wannermacher, K. (2006). Functional Differentiation of Incentives for E-teaching at Universities. In A. Mendez-Vilas, A. Solano Martin, J. Mesa Gonzalez, & J. A. Mesa Gonzalez, (Eds.), *Current Developments in Technology-Assisted Education, Proceedings of the IV International Conference on Multimedia and Information and Communication Technologies in Education (M-ICTE2006)*, University of Seville, Seville, Spain, 22-25 November 2006, (Vol. 1, pp. 72-76).

KEY TERMS AND DEFINITIONS

e-Learning: Using Computer-Mediated Communication (CMC) tools to facilitate e-Tutoring/e-Moderation.

e-Tutoring/e-Moderating: Either term is usually treated as synonymous with e-Learning. Enabling tutoring or moderating by "e", electronic means. This communication is often asynchronous and remote, using technologies such as Web 2.0.

Cooperative Work Framework: A framework suggested for demonstrating cooperation between participants and artefacts for Computer-Supported Cooperative Work.

STEP Factors: Also PESTE factors from Sociology. In both cases, P stands for Political, E, Economic, S, Social and T, Technical. The last E for PESTE stands for Environmental.

Blended Learning: A combination of traditional face-to-face and e-Learning.

ADDITIONAL READING

Rather than prescribing specific journals and books, what is provided here is an anthology of topics which were extensively researched for this case study. Reading of these topics is recommended to truly appreciate e-Learning in a wider context, being more aware of its historical background, enabling a greater insight into its origins and raison d'etre. Topics include Artificial Intelligence (Expert/Knowledge-based Systems, Computer Aided Learning, e-Tutoring Systems), Human-Computer Interaction/Interaction Design, Computer-Supported Cooperative Work, Computer-Mediated Communication, Education (Theories: Piaget, Vygotsky, etc), Cognitive Psychology (Cognivitism, Behaviorism). A reflection of the times is the requirement to read-up on Educational Policies (Organizational, National and International), in addition to Sociology (PESTE or STEP factors). Finally, there's e-Learning of course!

Chapter 11

Second Life Brought to Life: A Case of Usability In-World

Kevin Yee
University of Central Florida, USA

Jace Hargis
University of the Pacific, USA

ABSTRACT

This case presents the challenges and successes encountered when a university attempts to offer a course in a new online virtual learning environment (VLE). Overcoming the resistance towards change requires many aspects—innovation, expertise, funds, culture, persistence, attitude, collaboration, willingness to take risk and possibly open to experiencing a failed event. Most importantly, there is a need for addressing the individual needs of student learning. Being able to develop networks and reach outside of those networks for expertise, input, and commitments are essential to moving forward and becoming successful at offering a unique and innovative VLE. Ultimately, the social, technological, economic, and political parameters involved in this process are all significant and requires workarounds in order to provide an innovative, individualized teaching and learning model.

ORGANIZATION BACKGROUND

The organization, from which this case is drawn, is among the top 100 liberal arts university for higher education in the United States of America. This private university provides a wide variety of programs throughout its eleven schools boasting an innovative approach to teaching and learning for over 150 years. The management structure follows a traditional academic hierarchy, which includes a board of regents, president, provost, associate/assistant provost, academic deans, department chairpersons and faculty members. The financial status is solid, even in recent times of market downturn, private institutions are typically well endowed and the enrollment has increased due to the limiting of new enrollment at state-operated higher education institutions. Enrollment at this institution is approximately 8,000 undergraduate, graduate and pre-professional students. The strategic planning in this University focuses on active pedagogy, innovation, the Scholarship of Teaching and Learning (SoTL),

DOI: 10.4018/978-1-61520-779-4.ch011

Figure 1. Second Life

leadership development, experiential learning, and diversity. The organizational culture encourages creativity, fosters non-linear solutions and awards progressive thinking.

SETTING THE STAGE

Typically educational institutions have struggled to advance as quickly as corporate businesses with identifying and implementing useful, application instructional technology, which is a commonplace amongst educational institutions. Institutional management of technology in this University is two-fold: the infrastructure is maintained centrally by an Instructional Technology (IT) department; and secondly, the support for classrooms and faculty with respect to technology are decentralized through each school. Therefore, everyone is a potential player in this process from the faculty to the department chair, dean, IT professional, etc. Like many, the institution adopted a course management system (CMS), which enables faculty to post their syllabus, hold discussion boards, collect and return assignments electronically, as well as provide online assessments and active learning modules. However, as common in the academic world, these electronic environments have not been uniformly utilized by all faculty members, so we were not surprised when initially exploring the possibility of enhancing our current CMS with a new VLE, that there would be a smaller pool of faculty members to engage, as well as there might be resistance to moving ahead with the technology when the current infrastructure had not been fully utilized.

The VLE which we reviewed, evaluated and recommended for our faculty members is called Second Life (See Figure 1). Second Life (SL) is a persistent online virtual world hosted on Internet servers run by Linden Lab; participants download and install free client software to view and enter the virtual world. Resembling a video game in appearance and range of motion, SL is unlike a game in that there is no proscribed series of actions, and no task that must be performed. The servers and virtual world persist even after individual clients log off, generating a unique amalgam of synchronous and asynchronous experiences for users. Most SL inhabitants "in-world" set up a virtual shop and attempt to make money (the currency, called lindens, can be exchanged for dollars and vice versa) by selling virtual goods useful to other characters. Players can customize their avatars, or use the software tools to create structures, furniture, or any other conceivable object. While membership is free, land on which to build a permanent presence in-world depends on renting land from Linden Lab.

The promise of SL in education revolves around community, and the connecting of individuals through a new, avatar-driven interface. Unlike the text- and picture-based network available courtesy of the World Wide Web (WWW), SL offers an immediacy of experience and companionship. It's hard to ignore the reality of another person behind the keyboard when their avatar runs toward "the camera" or flies overhead. The entire notion of interactivity, not to mention engagement, becomes such a visual and visceral experience that it hardly compares to text-based "interactions" of the WWW and traditional CMS platforms.

While SL has existed for some years, the early adopters envisioned a commercial space akin to a souped-up WWW, yet the hordes of paying customers have by and large failed to materialize. Niche markets catering to gambling and pornography established a foothold, and there remain adult-oriented sections of SL to this day. The slow adoption of SL by the masses is likely a by-product of the commercial nature of SL's early adapters. In the early WWW, hobbyists created content purely for the love of sharing (or the establishment of like-minded social communities) and thoughts about commercialization came later. By virtue of starting after the dot-com boom (and bust), SL burst onto the scene with users holding commercialization foremost in their minds, and as a result, fewer community-based projects entice newcomers to SL, and adoption has been slow. Owen Thomas, columnist for the influential blog Valleywag, conjectured in early 2009 that "the end is near" for SL, with commercial parties seemingly fleeing in droves and only education remaining. With a few tweaks, however, SL could become not just conducive, but indeed ideal for a distance education platform, and one might say that while the "the end is near" for commercial use, "the beginning is (potentially) near" for educational uses of SL as a dynamic, interactive learning environment.

There is a distinctly social component which is readily apparent in SL. Yet it would be a mistake to assume automatic acceptance by today's college students, members of the so-called Millennial or Y-generation (1982-2000) and often touted as "digital natives" as though they formed a homogeneous whole. Gen-Y folks are perceived as good at change, comfortable with technology, independent, financially savvy, not intimidated by authority, creative, group-oriented, diverse and in search of a balance in their lives. In fact, many young people (some of whom could also be called part of the "Homeland" generation that cannot recall life before terrorism on American soil) do not easily embrace virtual networks, and even digital applications are not a given. It's worth remembering that the average age of video game players is now 35. Nor should the viability of virtual worlds be automatically assumed. There are many different types of proprietary virtual worlds, with many of them browser-based (running on a WWW platform) such as virtual MTV, There.com, or Google's already-closed experiment in virtual worlds, Lively. Given the challenges, it's possible that SL may itself not survive, a notion that puts a further chill on institutions pondering a possible migration to the VLE.

Still, for the most part, the trend in American higher education has recently been to increase class size enrollments, often by migrating the content, as well as the instructional methods to an online venue. Usually, such classes are offered asynchronously, with the student free to log in and perform the required work at whichever point during the week matches his or her own availability (if not current mood). While today's students may not uniformly embrace video games or virtual worlds, there is little doubt that they embrace technology as the lens through which they view much of their social lives. One need merely to watch the exodus from a lecture hall to witness how quickly students flip open their mobile phones, impatient to chat with a friend about critical social events or peruse text messages missed during the lecture. Entire streams of students pass by each other oblivious, each glued only to their own mobile technology device, as if feeding an insatiable addiction. Second Life, by virtue of its avatar-based immediacy, hopes to capitalize on that level of technology-inflected sociality in a way that text-based CMS systems never have. It may be an unhealthy metaphor, but some hope that instead of providing the alcoholic with a drink (i.e. providing more technology to students who seem to be addicted to digital modes of communication), that we can align instructional material with how students behave.

Second Life has enjoyed growth since its introduction in 2003, and now counts 15 million members. While residency at any given moment is typically near 30,000 "residents," the number of unique visitors per month exceeds 700,000 (Linden Lab, 2009). The high volume of visitors provides an increasingly large base of pre-existing users for Second Life. Over 300 universities now have a presence in Second Life, with faculty experimenting in Second Life via modules, case studies, optional activities, and in a few isolated cases--mostly involving computer-science, communications, or design classes--entire courses taught online in the VLE (Sussman, 2007).

CASE DESCRIPTION

Technology Concerns

Because SL requires a client-side software installation and does not simply run in the Web browser, the program is able to generate greater range of movement and infinitely scalable graphics. The downside to such an approach, however, is a requirement for a graphics-capable computer. The minimum specifications to run SL are often not met by low-end desktop and notebook computers, even if brand new, and it becomes likely that some students will not have access to the necessary high-end computing equipment at home. Campus computing labs and library walk-up computers become the next logical resources to tap for needed IT support, yet installing the program would require an institutional will and local buy-in greater than is presently the case at most campuses.

Part of the hesitation by IT professionals may be the frequent, often weekly, updates to the program sent out by Linden Lab. One could further imagine instructor hesitancy to offer a course in SL if the program itself needed to update frequently. Unlike a Web-based CMS, which often allows for asynchronous completion of work, SL's interface argues for synchronous virtual meetings, yet those are the very types of arrangements most at risk if the system suffers from downtime and required installations.

More grave may be the lack of intuitiveness in using SL for educational purposes. On the one hand, there are bountiful resources explaining how to do things in SL: explanations on secondlife.com, YouTube video demonstrations, a SL wiki, book-length downloadable PDF guides, and indeed even books like Sarah Robbins' *Second Life For Dummies*. On the other hand, however, the need for such a variety of assistance points to a problem unto itself: it's not obvious to the first time (or even intermediate) user how to create items, how to customize one's avatar, or how to program objects to perform functions when clicked. An educator exploring SL for potential adoption would likely become frustrated not only at all of the above, but also by the lack of plug-and-play, turnkey solutions for education. There is no clear tool or method for uploading slide shows, videos, or images. Nor is there a simple to use dropbox or student survey/vote solution. There are work-arounds for all of the above, but some of them cost money and none of them are apparent simply from looking at the objects as they appear in the virtual world. At this point, little seems geared for the educational experience in SL.

The much-touted ability to create any item from scratch in SL typically requires countless hours of dedication that vanishingly few educators could actually afford to donate. Similarly, the native ability of SL to allow users to imbue objects with programming is lost on most teachers. The WWW and Photoshop similarly allow today's instructors to painstakingly craft custom images or write their own programming to deliver quizzes online via C+ and Javascript, but the vast majority of teachers would rather just use the existing tools of the CMS to handle programming functions. In order for SL to be more successful in an educational environment in a menu-driven set of tools that approximate for the VLE what CMS's, such as Blackboard, Angel, Moodle or Sakai do for the WWW: make it simple, programming-free, and painless to perform teaching tasks in the VLE. In the best of all possible worlds, an educational consortium could even make prefabricated objects available for free to teachers, possibly via a kind of warehouse shopping experience. Why bother creating a medieval table and chairs or a chemistry laboratory with beakers and flasks if someone else has done it already? The economics of SL, however, presently dictate that little is available for free; the hobbyist crafting a medieval table hopes to recoup some lindens for the trouble of assembling the table.

If the technology is daunting for the professor, it can be equally vexing for the undergraduate students. Even among today's youth, not everyone is technologically advanced, and if a class is to be avatar-based, this poses special problems. How can students, some of whom have difficulty navigating even a text-based CMS like Blackboard, hope to function in the more-free (but ultimately less proscriptive, and therefore more confusing) world of SL? Our eventual solution was to craft video tutorials, playable through the Web browser, courtesy of screen capture technology like Camtasia and Captivate (See Figure 2).

Even with optimally-prepared students, however, instructors in SL must prepare for connectivity issues. Network traffic, server reliability, and even Internet connections can all cause minor to major disruptions, and it is absolutely essential to have a secondary (perhaps even a tertiary) backup in place for a synchronous distance educational experience. Second Life offers audible voice communication, but this may be prone to network slowdowns, and a preferable mode of audio communication is to mute SL but simultaneously turn on free Internet telecommunications such as Skype for verbal interactions.

The notion of using multiple programs simultaneously to interact synchronously at a distance expands easily to other applications. While SL may lack a whiteboard; there are numerous free online whiteboards that offer a digital equivalent to lecturing in front of a class. Why stop there? PowerPoint presentations distributed by the CMS could be opened independently, and students can flip through them at their own pace while the class proceeds. Or the same could be done with image files, or document and PDF files. The end result could look like a mess of windows and programs simultaneously open on the operating system, with the main action occurring via avatar interaction in SL, but voice communication proceeding over Skype and the virtual whiteboard employed for the occasional sketch.

Over time, the technology workarounds listed above may not even be necessary. Presently, SL servers and the limitations of Internet bandwidth

Figure 2. An example of Second Life screen shot

cause performance degradations (ranging from mildly annoying all the way up to unbearable) when the number of users on an island increases. Over twenty users taxes the system, especially client computers with less-advanced graphics cards, and thirty users on a single island represents the limit for most participants at home. On the one hand, this would seem to indicate a cap on participants that argues against the typical larger class size. But if the past is any indication, technology marches faster than we usually anticipate. It was not that long ago, in the years before broadband, that video application on the WWW were widely questioned and seen as not viable.

The less-intuitive "next step" revolves not around hardware, but around the maximization of the software's potential. In brief, it's a problem of education for the teachers, who do not often intuitively grasp how to use the new interface creatively. The first, reflexive reaction is often one that attempts to extend or extrapolate familiar tools into the new interface. As a result, faculty members seeing SL for the first time ask about hosting lecture notes or PowerPoint slide presentations online, as if the avatar-based world were capable only of reproducing the same tools used in the physical, face-to-face classes.

The more prosaic uses of SL leap quickly to mind. It is possible to visit previously-established and built-out locations in SL, ones created and hosted by uninvolved third parties, that offer architectural reproductions of actual (or fictional) locations such as the Sistine Chapel, Amsterdam, Tombstone, Dante's Inferno, Shakespeare's Globe Theater, or ancient Rome and Greece, to name only a few examples. The benefits of interacting with live human participants on an international stage also appeal quickly to language teachers with little need of explanation. Indeed, it takes but the simplest search inside of SL to locate areas where a desired target language is spoken by actual users, and these are some of the more populous areas of SL.

Locating other people in real-time might be an aim of researchers, too, perhaps lured by the potential of a random sampling of human research participants that cuts across multiple demographics. Yet the reality of Institutional Review Board (IRB) approvals looms large in such projects, and SL consequently more often serves as an informal test bed than a more formal, rigorous test environment for social questions.

The authors of this case study—working on opposite coasts of the United States—recognized the myriad challenges facing faculty who were considering SL as a platform option, and attempted to address them via weekly online meetings and systematic exploration of SL. The weekly agenda included learning how to build simple objects, locating existing assessments of potential student work, and uncovering existing technology, architecture, and pre-programmed objects in SL that would prove useful to instructional faculty members.

While an uninitiated newcomer to SL might assume that orientation issues may take but a few hours to resolve, in practice a significant amount of time, energy, and effort must be expended to firmly orient a new faculty member to the realities and possibilities of SL. The exploration necessary must be systematic, and the interactions must be longitudinal in nature. Low-level interactions were possible with a minimum of investment, but deeper and more meaningful interactions required longer time commitments to understand or implement. In other words, it may not look hard to get started, but in doing anything meaningful required a longer commitment—a bit like comparing the learning of easy phrases in Spanish to being able to converse about metaphysical concepts in the target language.

The largest challenge remains an entire shift in thought processes, from thinking in physical terms to thinking in virtual terms, a paradigm shift on the order of magnitude in moving from two-dimension to three-dimensional thought processes. Indeed, the ease with which instructors can imagine third-dimension objects and processes invites entirely new methodologies in SL. "Thinking three-dimensionally" in the virtual world is quite a different process from the physical world, and faculty will need guidance.

For instance, in the physical world a classroom exists as a static concept, beholden to the laws of physics and that troublesome inability to create or delete matter. But in SL, a room can be switched off and all its furniture, settings, and current arrangement merely stored for future reincarnation, while a replacement room full of furnishings is commanded into view. Such a programmed room in SL is called a holodeck, borrowing the terminology from the Star Trek universe. One cannot help but notice the sublime irony of a holodeck existing within an already-virtual space; in essence, this is a virtual space within a virtual reality—a replacement for "what is real" by that which is twice faked. It's not a far jump to investigate the boundaries of reality in general.

The existence of three dimensions opens up the possibility for lending new appearances to older, established teaching tools. Terms that need to be highlighted can be created as three-dimensional, block objects in space. They can be picked up, placed in the air, or thrown around. They can be imbued with programming so that "touching" one yields a programmed response, either to the environment or the avatar itself doing the touching (this is how avatars are made to "dance," for instance). Graphic organizers, such as concept mapping, take on a whole new meaning when one works not with sticky notes on a flat surface, but with objects in 3D space that can be physically re-arranged, put on top of each other, or expanded in size to indicate relative importance.

In fact, the pedagogical tools are so radically different from ones in the traditional classroom that it may be worthwhile to return to first principles and examine the teaching practice from start to finish. Theories of teaching and learning encourage us to begin with learning objectives, and work backward from these "end goals" to determine what assessments to use, which (and how much) information to impart, and how to let students practice the learning. In the analog world, those initial learning objectives are often inflected through the Taxonomy of Educational Objectives (Bloom, 1956). Bloom's categories in the cognitive domain are particularly relevant: knowledge, comprehension, application, analysis, synthesis, and evaluation. At the risk of being over-reductive, these levels could be seen as asking students to perform in one of three "super-categories": internalize information, apply the learning, or analyze something.

Does the new VLE offer a way to think differently about those super-categories? Asking students to internalize information could take several forms: be exposed to it, memorize it, learn it on their own time, or practice it with others. All of those forms certainly could exist in SL. Exposing students to new information is perhaps the most difficult to imagine in a virtual world. It can be extremely time-consuming to construct physical objects (let alone program them), so one thinks first of existing tools to spread information. Yet the lack of well-integrated tools for PowerPoint presentations or MS-Word document files provides a chilling effect on any attempt to "inform" using the virtual environment. It would be orders of magnitude simpler to email information-level material separately, apart from the VLE, and reserve SL time for other activities toward internalizing information, such as memorization practice or group work. Time spent in-world is arguably even better spent on the other super-categories of applying the learning or analyzing objects.

These remaining concepts of application and analysis seem easier to map onto SL's unique tool set. In particular, it might be most fruitful to consider the problem statement from the reverse angle: rather than identify existing teaching tools (spreadsheets, slide show presentations, beakers and Bunsen burners, etc) and attempting to imagine a match inside SL, it would be advantageous to start with SL's strengths and unique abilities. These include flying, building objects, constructing (and changing) identity via the avatar, decorating, and teleporting to gather information from other people in-world, or from other virtual spaces. Each of the above abilities could work in service of application or analysis, particularly when combined with synchronous (simultaneous) conversation. If instructors utilize the VLE to perform the usual types of instruction (listen to the teacher, work independently, work with a partner, work with a group, report out to other groups, report out to the whole class), the virtual space approximate a face-to-face classroom quite a lot more than the typical "online course" experience of anonymous, asynchronous reading and task-performing (which usually takes the form of writing independently).

Management and Organizational Concerns

Organization concerns seemed to focus around the economics of this project, as one might expect. Funding is a difficult topic regardless of the situation, however, in education, funding is frequently the reason for rejecting many initiatives. However, in our case, we were fortunate to work at an institution whose forward thinking kept them in front of the virtual world concept, as they re-created a campus which closely resembled their physical campus in SL. The facade of their in-world campus mimicked the core of their campus quad, while the inside of the buildings were allowed to be open, modified and where active learning objects were encouraged to be housed. In SL, there are several items which are not free, such as land and buildings. However, the price of land, especially for educational purposes, is very reasonable and if an institution can use their faculty or students in the area of computer science, they can build their own buildings in SL. We, however, used an outside contractor to build our campus, mainly because we wanted to stay on the forefront and knew it would require time to secure faculty and possibly time to learn to write the code. Some may see this as high barriers to entry into SL and may not be able to secure these institutional costs, however, like everything on the net, these all will come down in short time. Two of the potential cost issues to consider are land and uploads.

There is a one-time cost for purchasing land, plus an ongoing small rental fee, although there is a significant educational discount. The larger issue is how large and detailed one wishes to create an online equivalent to the physical campus, since the more 'prims' (primitive objects, the basic building block of most everything in SL, excepting the ground and avatars) that are used goes against the island's 'limit' - the limit exists merely as a safeguard so that the graphics gain resolution ("res-in") well. So, ideally, each institution should have clear goals ahead of time as to their priorities - aesthetic or functional and to what degree, both requiring prims, so making this decision upfront allows the builder to place emphasis on one or the other. If the institution is paying to build an island, they may want to duplicate their original campus, or duplicate the exterior of the building with the inside being different, or to duplicate nothing. One philosophy is that taking a risk and building something unusual may bear unexpected yields, such as a quiz-booth suite as a use of space that would never happen in real life. Or considering the virtual environment for use in public relations, so that parents and prospective students can view the institution, the residence halls, dining areas and/or well-known landmarks of the university.

There is a certain level of expertise required to build a campus in world, although at this point of the history of virtual realities, there are many items which can be bought, or available in a similar shareware model as developed historically on the Internet. If the expectations are high for the environment, the institution would need expertise for programming objects in a specific way in which the university or faculty would want to use them. Examples could include classrooms or laboratories which allow students to manipulate virtual chemicals or medical/dental labs that require students to perform operations. There may be other creative ways to accomplish this, if the institution could develop a program where students from engineering and/or graphical art departments are asked to build virtual worlds as part of their class assignments, internships, coop programs, etc. One aspect to keep in mind is that Second Life Scripting (SLS) language is an Object-Oriented Programming (OOP) language, like C+ and others, so it is highly recommended that the institution partner with faculty members to discuss their needs first, identifying the specific needs and desired outcomes. One word of caution is not to underestimate the level of programming, because it could be a significant issue aligning what the professor actually wants with what the programmer can do. The most important factor is to keep in mind lead time, as it could take up to one year to fully develop. We need to keep in mind that some faculty may want areas of their island/classroom where there is limited flying or voice chat available, which needs to be programmed in, and there are similar questions as to whether to allow visitors or lurkers, and even prosaic questions like walls which the faculty member can see through (or not), as required by the teaching space.

There is a small fee to upload items, textures, pictures, sound, video, although the rates are low. We recommend that if institutions take this route, they might wish to apply a technology fee to the course which passes this cost directly to the student who benefits; or provide the faculty member or department with a small budget, in which they can purchase these during the creation of their course. A third alternative would be to discuss the idea and plan for the course and uploads with the company who owns SL, Linden Lab, and prepare a contract which would allow a certain amount of uploads as an institution.

While many items cost money, it is important to note that there are many free activities, such as simply visiting others sites/islands, talking to others avatars from around the world, and possibly partnering with institutions which have land for a bartering agreement. The bottom line is that it costs absolutely nothing for the students or faculty to enter and wander around SL; it is only when someone wants to build a permanent presence that funds become an issue.

CURRENT CHALLENGES FACING THE ORGANIZATION

Some of the major challenges in academia are the same as ones throughout the universe, and they involve the politics that go along with every decision and potential change. Ideally, there should be ample up-front discussions involving faculty and various stakeholders who will be high-end users of the virtual environment. These meetings should allow everyone to voice their concerns and even if the administration or a dedicated group of faculty wish to move forward without unanimous acceptance, then the community is more likely to embrace the change due to the perception of buy-in, which often time is the most significant challenge.

For this case, the story began two years ago, when after several preliminary discussions with faculty, the administration decided to dedicate some funds to build a campus in-world that resembled the physical campus. It took about a year to gather the information, identify a builder, build it, and deploy it. Once it was built, we had a grand opening, with in-world visitors and an auditorium of students observing that the university SL island was available. Over this past year, there have been limited activities in-world. Occasionally traditional classes would meet their students in world for a dedicated assignment. The course which is the backbone of this case will be offered this summer entirely in-world and taught by an instructor 3,000 miles away, in different a state of the United States.

Ultimately every new course or teaching environment has to be vetted through colleagues, departments, colleges, academic councils, curriculum committees and academic affairs. Through each of these steps, depending on the institution, each step is handled differently and with varying levels of difficulty. Our experiences are that the peer review and acceptance of the new approach as well as the experimental learning environment may be the one filled with the most landmines. In our case, the initial attempt was to identify a faculty member from one department, believing that SL could offer significant and readily realized power due to its ability to offer quick connections for the discipline. Although we were able to identify an eager and participatory faculty member, we were quickly met with resistance by their department, who ultimately did not approve the offering. Next we turned to another department proposing a somewhat different course, that we believed favored an online environment and one that was taught previously by the potential in-world instructor in an offline environment, would be attractive to the department. Unfortunately, even with the course already vetted through another university and a viable instructor, the department also rejected the proposal, favoring a philosophy of using an internal model of faculty delivering an online course using the institutional CMS. The next step was to approach the administration of the college in hopes that they would be interested in this innovative approach and be able to assist in identifying both an interested faculty member and a viable department, and then the college administration could approve the course and we would be on our way. However, it seemed that the college administration did not see the value in this novel learning environment. So, since it seemed that the standard route of gaining approval had been met with dead-ends, we tried to think of non-traditional routes in which we could achieve our goals. Through several weeks of pursuing our networks, we serendipitously found our path through our university Professional and Continuing Education School. They could offer the course as an academic extension course, offering units which the students could transfer in as a free elective and used for a degree-earning major. With this department, we were able to move efficiently through the approval process and have the course on the calendar for the second summer session. We advertised both internally and externally (nationwide), and will be offering the course this summer. We will collect data on its effectiveness using a Scholarship of Teaching and Learning (SoTL) approach, providing pre and post-assessments and detailing qualitative data to assess the aspects of the in-world environment which are conducive to active learning.

In addition to the internal politics of working through this process, there are always other institutional politics, which should be considered, such as who actually received the funds at an institution, for what purposes, and how are the funds for educational technology distributed and subsequently spent. There is no specific or consistent procedure on how to address this, as the politics and those in decision-making political realms differ from each institution. The only thing we can do it is to try to pursue initiatives such as teaching in-world for the right reasons, which is to attend to our students' learning styles and hope that most institutions can recognize that we have no other agenda other than addressing student needs.

One of the most severely lacking aspects of in-world teaching and learning is that at this point, there is very little assessment practices of any type; either ways for faculty to assess student learning, or just as importantly, assessment on how effective the mode of teaching in-world actually is for students. The problem with this scenario is that few people want to buy in as a first adopter, so we end up with a Catch-22 scenario. No one wants to be create an in-world class until they have seen it successfully done, but until someone jumps in, there is no way we can even determine if this environment has the potential to assist learning. This is one of our major goals: to systematically determine the value, or lack of value, in these environments - the only way to truly do this is jump in and collect plenty of data. However, we need to be cognizant of boosterism by early adopters, which may paradoxically be counter-productive, as some like technology for its own sake. Then again, this is a fairly common step for every emerging technology.

SOLUTIONS AND RECOMMENDATIONS

The solution which was produced was to identify an organization on campus that both had an innovative attitude AND was in a position to offer the academic courses. Fortunately, we found such an organization in our Professional Continuing Education School, which can both offer academic courses for credit and currently posses the mechanism for a varied pay schedule, collection of fees and a mechanism to involve the registrar and an open online environment, with associated appropriate clients/students. We are now able to offer a completely in-world learning experience and attract students from across the world, as well as secure an instructor from a different part of the country (or world). One literature instructor recruited for Second Life was a colleague at a previous institution. In the past, existing relationships in established networks, such as professional organizations or former employers, did not necessarily generate new collaborations, especially across great distances. With Second Life offering the possibility of teaching from remote locations, the primary limitations became relational (one still must find the instructor from other networks) rather than logistical. Recruiting students across the globe is similarly possible, though more work must be done to experiment with marketing avenues. The literature instructor mentioned above had attempted to advertise the Second Life course via Web-based blogs and forums, where he was a founding member of the site with over 50,000 readers, but this marketing did not result in any enrolled students. Two students from other countries (Australia and Denmark) did contact the instructor for additional information, but apparently chose not to follow through. Local marketing efforts at the University of the Pacific yielded better results, with several students signing up for the course.

Our recommendation for other institutions hoping to gain a presence in a unique VLE is to first identify a department or college who is secure enough in their teaching to take risks and student-centric enough to take calculated risks to assist them. Then find viable in-world faculty who are interested and assist them with developing dynamic, interactive learning objects, which they could embed in their VLE courses. Above all, we highly recommend developing an experimental design prior to the class offering to overtly collect qualitative and quantitative data on the experience, so upon completion each institution can reflect, assess, and determine exactly what works well and what to avoid when offering VLE's at their institution.

REFERENCES

Bloom, B. S. (1956). Taxonomy of Educational Objectives, Handbook I: The Cognitive Domain. New York: David McKay Co Inc.

Boyer, E. L. (1990). Scholarship reconsidered: Priorities of the professoriate. Princeton, NJ: Carnegie Foundation for the Advancement of Teaching.

Dillenbourg, P. Mendelsophn, P. & Jermann, P. (1999). Why spatial metaphors are relevant to virtual campuses. in Levonen, J. & Enkenberg, J. (Eds.), Learning and instruction in multiple contexts and settings. Bulletins of the Faculty of Education, 73. Joensuu, Finland: University of Joensuu, Finland, Faculty of Education.

Life, S. (2009). Accessed and downloaded at http://www.secondlife.com on March 27, 2009.

Linden Lab press release. (May 20, 2009). *Over 15 billion minutes of voice have been delivered in Second Life.* Accessed and downloaded from http://lindenlab.com/pressroom/releases/19_05_09 on July 2, 2009.

Sussman, B. (2007). *Teachers, college students lead a Second Life.* Accessed and downloaded from http://www.usatoday.com/news/education/2007-08-01-second-life_N.htm on June 13, 2009.

Ullman, C., & Rabinowitz, M. (2004, October). Course management systems and the reinvention of instruction. *THE Journal.* Retrieved from http://www.thejournal.com/articles/17014

University of Bridgeport. (2009). Accessed and downloaded from http://www.bridgeport.edu/pages/3530.asp on March 28, 2009.

Webopedia. (2009). Accessed and downloaded from http://www.webopedia.com/TERM/O/object_oriented_programming_OOP.html on March 29, 2009.

ADDITIONAL READING

Bugeja, M. J. Chronicle of Higher Education. "Second Thoughts About Second Life." [Online]. Available: http://chronicle.com/jobs/news/2007/09/2007091401c.htm

Campus Computing Project. (2000, October). *The 2000 National Survey of Information Technology in US Higher Education.* Available: http://www.campuscomputing.net/pdf/2000-CCP.pdf

CCarter. "Introducing Your RL Students to Second Life." [Online]. Available: http://www.cxknowledge.com/Intro_SL.html

College of Communication. Ohio University, The GRID Lab: The Game Research and Immersive Design Lab [Online.]. Available: http://gridlab.ohio.edu

Conklin, Megan. Elon University. "101 Uses for Second Life in the College Classroom." Pdf. [Online].

Fetscherin, M. Second Life Research Blog. [Online]. Available: http://secondliferesearch.blogspot.com/

Gartner. (2007, April 24). Gartner Says 80 Percent of Active Internet users will have a "Second Life" in the Virtual World by the End of 2011 [Online.]. Available: http://www.gartner.com/it/page.jsp?id=503861

Geoghegan, W. H. *Whatever happened to instructional technology.* Paper presented at the 22nd Annual Conference of the International Business Schools Computing Association, Baltimore, MD, 1994

Israel, S. Global Neighbourhoods. "Putting Second Life into Education." [Online]. Available: http://redcouch.typepad.com/weblog/2007/01/farrels_part2.html

Jarrett, K. The Story of my Second Life [Online]. Available: http://www.storyofmysecondlife.com/

Lagorio, C. (2007, January 7). Pepperdine in a treehouse. *New York Times*, Section 4A, p. 22.

Life, S. (2007, July 25). Second Life [Online]. Available: http://secondlife.com

Lim, K. Theory. IstheReason. "How NOT to Teach in Second Life." [Online]. Available: http://theory.isthereason.com/?p=1363

McGolerick. Elizabeth Weiss. "Online Degrees. Second Life University" [Online]. Available: http://encarta.degreesandtraining.com/index.jsp

New Media Consortium. (2006, August 1). About the NMC [Online]. Available: http://www.nmc.org/about

New Media Consortium. (2007, March 8). *2007 Horizon Report.* [Online].Available: http://www.nmc.org/pdf/2007_Horizon_Report.pdf

Oblinger, D. G., & Oblinger, J. L. (2005, June 23) Educating the Net Generation [Online]. Available: http://www.educause.edu/educatingthenetgen

Olsen, S. CNET News "Universities Register for Online Future." [Online]. Available: http://news.cnet.com/2100-1032_3-6157088.html?part=rss&tag=2547-1_3-0-20&subj=news

Read, B. (2006, August 29), Second Life keeps chugging along. *The Chronicle of Higher Education,* [Online.] Available: http://chronicle.com/wiredcampus/article/1529/second-life-keeps-chugging-along

Reuters, A. (2006, November 9), IBM accelerates push into 3D virtual worlds. *Reuters*, [Online.] Available: http://secondlife.reuters.com/stories/2006/11/09/ibm-accelerates-pushinto-3d-virtual-worlds

Reuters, A. (Adam Pasick). "Prof Gets Funding for Virtual Shakespeare World." [Online]. Available: http://secondlife.reuters.com/stories/2006/10/18/prof-gets-funding-for-virtual-shakespeare-world/

Robbins, S. Intellagirl's Second Life Education Research. Available: http://www.secondlife.intellagirl.com/

Schultz, N. My So-Called Second Life. Accessed October 2008 http://mysocalledsecondlife.com

Tebbutt, D. IT Week Online. "Is Second Life a Brave New World?" [Online]. Available: http://www.computing.co.uk/information-world-review/features/2184795/second-life-brave-worlds

Terdiman, D. WIRED online. "Second Life Teaches Life Lessons." [Online]. Available: http://www.wired.com/gaming/gamingreviews/news/2005/04/67142

Terry, A. Virtual Canuck. "An Educator Discovers his Second Life." [Online]. Available: http://terrya.edublogs.org/2006/07/17/an-educator-discovers-his-secondlife/

Tettegah, S. University of Illinois. "Teaching and Learning in a Virtual World." [Online]. Available: http://faculty.ed.uiuc.edu/stettega/virtualworlds/index.html

The Second Life Best Practices in Education: Teaching, Learning, and Research 2007 International Conference [Online.] Available: http://slbestpractices2007.wikispaces.com/

Wagner, J. A. Edutopia. "The School of Second Life." [Online]. Available: http://www.edutopia.org/school-second-life

Wong, G. CNN Online. "Educators Explore Second Life Online." [Online]. Available: http://www.cnn.com/2006/TECH/11/13/second.life.university/index.html

KEY TERMS AND DEFINITIONS

Second Life (SL): SL is a persistent online virtual world hosted on Internet servers run by Linden Lab; participants download and install free client software to view and enter the virtual world. Resembling a video game in appearance and range of motion, SL is unlike a game in that there is no proscribed series of actions, and no task that must be performed.

Virtual Learning Environment (VLE): VLE is a designed information space; a social space; is explicitly represented; where learners are not only active, but also actors; are not restricted to distance education; integrates multiple tools; overlaps with the physical environment; and can be a space for effective learning as well as innovation. (Dillenbourg, et. al., 1999).

Instructional Technology: Instructional technology applies research in learning theory, psychology, and emergent technologies to solve instructional and performance problems. The Presidential Commission on Instructional Technology highlighted four performance areas of Design of instruction; Production of instructional products and events; Management of instructional settings and resources and Evaluation of instructional programs. (University of Bridgeport, 2009)

Avatar: An avatar is a computer user's representation of himself/herself or alter ego, whether in the form of a three-dimensional model used in computer games, a two-dimensional icon used on Internet forums and other communities, or a text construct found on early systems. It is an "object" representing the embodiment of the user. The term "avatar" can also refer to the personality connected with the screen name, or handle, of an Internet user. (Second Life, 2009)

Prim: A Prim is a primitive object or building block. They are used to build objects in Second Life (everything in SL, except the ground terrain and avatar - if you can right click/edit, it is a prim). (Second Life, 2009) An Island in Second Life is simply the area or space upon which one may build, and interact. The 'islands' may be in the sky, on 'land', or as a 'island' surrounded by water.

Course or Learning Management System (CMS): A Course Management System is Internet-based software that manages student enrollment, tracks student performance, and creates and distributes course content. In this way, the CMS enables teachers to extend the classroom beyond its traditional boundaries of time and space. (Ullman and Rbinowitz, 2004)

Object-Oriented Programming (OOP) Language: OOP Language is a type of programming in which programmers define not only the data type of a data structure, but also the types of operations that can be applied to the structure. In this way, the data structure becomes an object that includes both data and functions. In addition, programmers can create relationships between one object and another. For example, objects can *inherit* characteristics from other objects. One of the principal advantages of object-oriented programming techniques over procedural programming techniques is that they enable programmers to create modules that do not need to be changed when a new type of object is added. A programmer can simply create a new object that inherits many of its features from existing objects. This makes object-oriented programs easier to modify. To perform object-oriented programming, one needs an *object-oriented programming language (OOPL)*. Java, C++ and Smalltalk are three of the more popular languages, and there are also object-oriented versions of Pascal. (Webopedia, 2009).

Scholarship of Teaching and Learning (SoTL): SoTL involves planning, assessing, and modifying one's teaching and applying to it the same exacting standards of evaluation that are used in research. According to Boyer (1990), "Excellence in the classroom is all too often undervalued".

Chapter 12
Perspectives on the Influences of Social Capital upon Internet Usage of Rural Guatemalan Teachers

Douglas Tedford
Fundación Rigoberta Menchú Tum, Guatemala

ABSTRACT

The Fundación Rigoberta Menchú Tum and the researcher collaborated to identify the influences of bonding, bridging and linking social capital upon teacher Internet usage in the rural Guatemalan town of San Lucas Toliman. The Participatory Rural Appraisal was employed to draw upon community perspectives for identifying the study problem, designing interview questions, and evaluating data, with the researcher in the role of facilitator. Of 34 teachers invited to participate in online coursework free of charge, only 5 completed it. Among them, 20 were interviewed by a native Spanish speaker, and 42 local community educators synthesized interview responses into recommendations for improving local engagement of teachers in online learning. Bonding and bridging social capital influences of family, friends, technology experts and school administrators were shown to levy significant positive and negative effects upon teacher decisions to use the Internet in a region challenged by inadequate buying power, and limited telecommunications infrastructure.

ORGANIZATION BACKGROUND

The Fundación Rigoberta Menchú Tum (FRMT), named after the recipient of the 1992 Nobel Peace Prize, was established for the purpose of promoting and sustaining the educational and social progress of the indigenous peoples of Guatemala, the Americas and the world (Cifuentes, 2007; Duque Arellano, 1999; FRMT, 2007b; Zapeta, et. al., 1998). It is a fully non-profit organization with a small paid staff and large cadre of volunteer professionals within Guatemala and worldwide, all dedicated to the development and progress of indigenous peoples as equal participants in education and industry, for which computer and Internet literacy is essential (Koss, 2001; Organization of American States, 2006; United Nations Educational, Scientific and Cultural Organization, 2008) and skills are required

DOI: 10.4018/978-1-61520-779-4.ch012

Figure 1. An English teacher of San Lucas Toliman, Guatemala receives guidance for using the Internet at a community technology center of the Fundación Rigoberta Menchú Tum, a non-profit educational and social services organization led by the 1992 recipient of the Nobel Peace Prize.

for speaking English and Spanish, as principal languages of commerce (Barshefsky, 2002; Douglas, 2006). The FRMT's secondary vocational school, the Centro Educativo Luciano Pavarotti, situated in San Lucas Toliman, Guatemala is also the site of a community technology center (CTC) which houses 22 Internet-ready computers donated by friends of Luciano Pavarotti, the municipality of Alcobendas, Spain, and the Quetzal Club of France, with technical support supplemented by the Republic of China (Taiwan) (Cifuentes, 2007; Galvez, 2007). Access to computers and the Internet is limited by a number of factors, but it was found that issues other than access affect engagement in online learning. The researcher, a volunteer educational consultant, facilitated the development of a study which explored the social influences upon decisions of rural Guatemalan teachers relative to participating in distance education via the Internet- a study called for in academia, and the first of its kind in research linking relationships between social capital, teacher education and online learning in the developing world (Creed & Joynes, 2005; Lorenzetti, 2004; Trucano, 2005).

SETTING THE STAGE

From 1960 to 1996, a civil war was waged in the mountain highlands and jungles of the Republic of Guatemala, in Central America (Central Intelligence Agency, 2006). Difficulties imposed by the war upon transportation and communication disrupted the development over time of Information and Communication Technology (ICT) infrastructures in remote areas of the nation, and of knowledge and practices for the use of ICT in education, constituting a digital divide between metropolitan and rural regions (Attewell, 2001; Caniz, 2006; Koss, 2001). The rhetoric of the 1996 Esquipulas Peace Accords (Conciliation Resources, 2007) and of subsequent agreements demonstrated a commitment of the Guatemalan government to support equal educational opportunities for its indigenous peoples. A few years thereafter, this commitment was enriched through the promise of enhancing educational opportunities by provision of equal Internet access throughout Guatemala (ITFORCEGT, 2006; Ordoñez, 2006; United Nations Educational, Scientific and Cultural Organization, 2008, p. 2).

This objective has been followed up most effectively in the nation's capital and least successfully in mountainous, rural regions such as San Lucas, Toliman, the site of the study (Menchu, 2007). Researchers have postulated that provision of Internet access does not guarantee usage (Crump & McIlroy, 2003; Foth, 2003), extending the polemic about the digital divide into questions of why the Internet is neglected when available (DiMaggio & Hargittai, 2001; Natriello, 2001). Although evidence of a digital divide has been noted between developed and developing nations (Leavey, 2003; Rogers, 2003), few research studies discuss disparities of ICT access or usage in third world online education. Creed and Joynes stated,

In general distance education is an under-researched area and the need for improvement in the quality and quantity of research and evaluation is widely acknowledged... What research exists tends to be strong on description but weak on evaluative data, both quantitative and qualitative, on which to make judgments about effectiveness and this is particularly so in developing countries. What are the reasons behind this? The usual suspects, common to research in any area, are there: poor dissemination, limited research skills and constrained resources which often push research and evaluation to the bottom of the agenda. But there are also other reasons specific to distance education itself. (2005, p. 6)

This lack of resources to support research on distance education in the developing world impedes the dissemination of knowledge within and between third world cultures about the common concerns which face them.

Such challenges to the spread of third world online education are addressed through the promotion by intergovernmental organizations, such as the International Bank for Reconstruction and Development, of applying social capital to improve the quality of Internet access and usage in the developing nations (International Bank for Reconstruction and Development, 2006, 2007a, 2008). Although journal articles and websites have advanced an agenda of interactivity between educators via the Internet, and have suggested the value of social capital for the diffusion of the Internet in the developing world, specific research studies which investigate the contribution or influence of social capital for online education of any sort were not found. In an interview, Kowch commented,

[S]o far the education sector has little to say about (the)... contribution (of)... social capital at... global levels. Little research is done to provide measures of social capital accretion and depreciation in the education sector... Are we measuring this macro policy phenomenon in distance learning? I have seen no evidence of it... While social capital concepts may seem abstract or disconnected from most educational technology leadership today... technology-enhanced education offers more social capital capacity for our nations than do most subfields in education... (Lorenzetti, 2004, p. 6)

What is known about the disparities of Internet access for rural sections of the developing world is tied to the mutually-dependent factors of infrastructure and buying power, both of which are scarce in rural, remote sectors. Rutherford, Gillespie and Richardson (2004) defined the Internet as a principally "urban technology" (p. 1) and shared,

The telecommunications infrastructures which support the Internet are predominantly deployed within and between major cities (and)....broadly speaking, core urban regions have significant

advantages over peripheral rural regions in terms of access to telecommunications... In large cities, the monetary and academic necessity of ICT skills, including facility with the Internet, is a given, driving achievement in higher education and business... Infrastructure, pricing and training function (work) in tandem to expand the use of services for profit and public benefit. (p. 1)

Goodman, Gottstein and Goodman (2001) commented that satellite technologies have made the Internet available in the most remote sectors, but that the question remains, "Who pays?" for these services (p. 21). Apart from financial resources, the principle challenges for fomenting Internet usage in rural, remote sectors are the lack of Internet sophistication among potential users and a dearth of ICT experts to guide them. Discussing the digital divide, they indicated,

There are a number of divides even if only the Internet is considered, with distinctions between populations based on.... income, education, language, occupation, and ethnicity. Multiple distinctions make for stark gaps. Thus, poor, semiliterate, ethnic minorities in small, isolated rural villages in the world's poorest countries are not as likely... to be frequent or sophisticated users as are people not characterized by any of these traits. (p. 21)

The ICT market has been identified as favoring best quality of services to be situated in and between large urban centers (Rutherford et al., 2004). The only way in which an online teacher development program could be successfully introduced in a rural sector of the developing world would be through the infusion of donated resources and a staff of experts in ICT and teacher training, funded by government social welfare resources, non-profit collaborations, private industry initiatives, or a combination of these sources, because wholly private, for-profit efforts would be considered as unwise (Romo-Rodriguez, 2005). San Lucas Toliman is representative of many remote, rural towns in Guatemala which could benefit from this type of cooperative effort. In San Lucas, the Fundación Rigoberta Menchú Tum operates a small school and CTC which is connected to the Internet.

The Centro Educativo Luciano Pavarotti, Programa Utzilal Tijonikel offers local secondary students a curriculum of academic and vocational courses in Spanish and supports the perpetuation of Guatemala's Mayan cultures (FRMT, 2007b). The school is funded through donations, and is fee-based with scholarships provided based on evidence of need. Weekly studies of all students at the Pavarotti include online student learning in a CTC with 22 Internet-connected computers donated by friends of Luciano Pavarotti, the municipality of Alcobendas, Spain, and the Quetzal Club of France, with technical support supplemented by the Republic of China (Taiwan) (Cifuentes, 2007; Galvez, 2007). The school's teachers were allowed access to the CTC according to availability. Schedules of the CTC have varied, but correlate with the school's day schedule of morning to mid-afternoon instruction, with interruptions to accommodate administrative meetings or occasional paid usage by groups scheduling the school's adjacent conference center for meetings or presentations.

Up until February of 2009, Internet access for the school's computers was contracted as a measured-usage service received by satellite dish, so usage hours were rationed in order to guarantee availability throughout each day of each service month. Internet-based features requiring higher data transmission, such as viewing of videos, were discouraged. Files such as these which were data heavy took a long time to download and were blamed for jamming Internet reception for all users. Earphones were not available in the CTC because this encouraged viewing of videos or music listening. Service interruptions were frequent due to rainy weather.

Before free Internet usage became available to the 34 teachers participating in a teacher training project with the researcher, free use of the foundation's CTC was limited to the school's students and teachers. The hours of operation for student use were flexible and subject to cancellation to make way for administrative meetings, donor usage and repairs. Students were notified of these changes by the school's teachers. Paid usage of the CTC by members of the community was allowed, at a rate equaling approximately $1.20 US per hour. The center was managed by an ICT-trained employee of the school. Guidance rendered to the paid participants was limited to assistance with turning the Internet on and off, and with printing of files. The CTC was viewed primarily as an advanced study tool for the school's students.

The education director oversaw all education initiatives of the FRMT from offices based in Guatemala City and traveled regularly to oversee progress of programs at the Pavarotti school, including utilization of the computer lab. An operations manager and headmaster locally governed the school and CTC. The researcher has functioned as a volunteer educational consultant to the FRMT since August of 2006. With the intention of playing a more active role in the educational development of rural teachers throughout Guatemala, the FRMT education director invited the researcher to conduct seminars for English teachers at the Pavarotti school. In tandem with data for enhancing teacher involvement and persistence in online education, recommendations and refinements for practices in the management of the CTC resulted from this project.

CASE DESCRIPTION

The ICT project described herein was initiated in July of 2007. At that time, and by invitation of the education director of the FRMT, 34 teachers who had participated in a teacher training program led by the researcher at the FRMT's school and led by the researcher, were offered free usage of the Internet to participate in follow-up training online with the researcher in a 26-week course. Of the 34, only 19 elected to try out free online access, and only 5 of them completed the course. This perplexed the FRMT education staff, local leadership of the Ministerio de Educación de Guatemala (MINEDUC), and the researcher (Cifuentes, 2007; Galvez, 2007). In reaction to a comment that perhaps the non-participating teachers lacked motivation, the FRMT agreed to support the researcher in the role of facilitating a study to shed light on challenges and potential resolutions to teacher rejection of the Internet.

In order for the results of such a study to foment lasting change in practices tied to teacher Internet usage in San Lucas Toliman, it would be necessary to select a research approach which validated the norms and values of Community-Driven Development (CDD), making the input of local leadership endemic to the research plan and its implementation (International Bank for Reconstruction & Development, 2007, ¶ 1). As suggested by multiple sources the study should deflect its focus from issues of improving Internet access to questions of how to improve Internet usage (Crump & McIlroy, 2003; Foth, 2003) and should integrate learning about the effect of social capital for enhancing teacher involvement with ICT (International Bank for Reconstruction and Development, 2007a; Lorenzetti, 2004). Compatibility of such an approach was found in the Participatory Rural Appraisal (PRA) (Chambers, 1990, 1992, 1994, 1998) which had been previously employed to study interactions between rural indigenous groups in developing nations, including Guatemala (Dudwick et. al., 2006; Ibañez, et. al., 2002). The PRA is known as "a growing family of participatory approaches and methods that emphasize local knowledge and enable local people to make their own appraisal, analysis, and plans... to enable (entities) to work together to plan context-appropriate programs" (International Bank for Reconstruction & Devel-

Figure 2. The researcher (the author) provided free teacher training at the Centro Educativo Luciano Pavarotti for three periods during 2007 and 2008, with continuing follow-up. Low responsiveness to the FMRT's offer of free Internet use brought about this study.

opment, 2007c, ¶ 2) Use of the PRA was found to eliminate distortions of data collection and findings (Chambers, 1998) which could result from cultural differences between developed and developing nations (Laungani, 2005), and to support culturally-meaningful styles of collecting and evaluating data. The PRA foments community-driven identification of problems and involves the community in devising methods, conducting data collection, interpreting data and developing solutions to be implemented locally (Gonsalves, 2005).

Coleman explained that definitions of social capital could be molded to match a variety of needs or functions (1988). Sabatini (2007) provided a website-linked gateway to diverse applications of social capital for research. Alsop, Chase and Owen (2003) considered social capital as norms and values transmitted through social networks. Lin described social capital as "resources embedded in social relations" (2001, p. xi). The term suggested a context for understanding needs for guidance to overcome barriers to the use of the Internet, as provision of the apparatus of Internet access were not found to guarantee usage (Crump & McIlroy, 2003; Foth, 2003). Woolcock (1998, 2002) favored viewing social capital as knowledge, norms and values originating from three types of networks, namely bonding, bridging, and linking. For this study, and in line with Woolcock's definitions, bonding social capital refers to close associations of equals, such as teachers. Bridging social capital connotes associations with locally-accessible experts, such as ICT technicians. Linking social capital describes individuals originating from outside the immediate social setting, such as the researcher and the education director of the Fundación Rigoberta Menchú Tum.

Through this perspective, social capital in networks was particularly significant because it had been identified as both a medium for long-distance sharing of ICT knowledge, norms and values and as a catalyst for local change in ICT skills and preferences (Van Bavel, Punie & Tuomi, 2007), empowering community-driven development of solutions to locally-identified problems.

Table 1. Characteristics of 34 teachers invited to enroll in a 26-week online course

Sub-Group Size	Course Completion	Description of Participation	Interview Sample
5	yes	consistent	5
6	no	consistent, then dropped out	5
8	no	logged on once or twice only	5
15	no	never logged on	5

The perspective of social capital was also seen as valuable for identifying the effectiveness of opinion leaders and change agents in encouraging online participation (Rogers, 1995, 2003). For the task of interviewing teachers during the summer of 2008, the researcher would take the role of non-invasive facilitator, and relegate duties involving direct contact with the teachers to a culturally-sensitive, native Spanish-speaking research assistant. Research questions addressed teacher concerns about using the Internet, teacher satisfaction with Internet resources, and social influences upon Internet usage. The native researcher reconstructed the interview questions into shorter units and conferred individually with 20 of the 34 teachers, who had been selected in a purposive sample, as in Table 1.

Led by the research assistant, digitally-recorded interviews were transcribed in Spanish at the end of each interview period. Representative statements were culled from the transcriptions and assigned response categories identical to the research questions. These representative statements were then copied in large print onto five sets of sentence strips for analysis after conclusion of the 20 interviews. Next, employing the principles of the Permanent-Group Interview (PGI) method within the PRA approach (Grenier, 1998), 42 community educators attended an open-invitation meeting and dinner to review, prioritize, interpret and discuss the representative statements, in order to present their suggestions for enhancing the involvement and persistence of local teachers in online education. The PGI was led by the FRMT education director, and the meeting was facilitated through support of the researcher and research assistant.

This meeting crystallized the community's understanding of specific teacher ICT concerns and temporal ICT challenges. The meeting brought to light how teacher decisions to use free Internet services for online professional development were influenced positively or negatively by bonding, bridging and linking social capital. This data supported the FRMT, the researcher and the community in its shared goals to enhance participation of rural Guatemalan teachers in online learning. Evidence for the forms of social capital and their influence is cited through translated excerpts from the interviews and through descriptions of the community's evaluation of findings in the PGI. Comments of both types are presented as an English-language translation of the original Spanish. The interview data and community findings provide an example of the challenges and promises of online education for remote, rural towns in Guatemala, and demonstrate how such a study design could be of value in other regions of the developing world.

Temporal Impediments to Internet Access

Although the emphasis and value of the study is to learn about the influences of social capital upon usage, it is essential to provide brief background data covering the physical and economic context within which teachers made the choice to accept or reject free Internet services and coursework in San Lucas Toliman and environs. Comments

Figure 3. Teachers learn English via their online course, with free Internet services subsidized by the FRMT. The course was of 26 weeks duration. Of 34 teachers, 19 initiated the course and 5 completed it. This study incorporated interviews of 20 of the teachers to learn their reactions to the Internet.

offered by teachers in the interviews mirrored notions presented by prior research about how buying power increases eligibility to pay for Internet services but also revealed new information about how the scarcity of services in a remote, rural location can be affected not only by the presence of satellite dish receivers but of electrical power and land-line telephone services. Getting access to an Internet-connected computer is a significant challenge for the majority of teachers residing within or near to the town of San Lucas Toliman. A variety of factors can contribute to a teacher's physical proximity to Internet services and to their freedom to use those services.

Lack of buying power and of electrical and telecommunications infrastructures in communities impeded the purchase or usefulness of a home computer and of Internet services. Some of the interviewed teachers lived outside of town in small settlements located on hillsides or in forested areas. Buying power limited access to higher-priced dwellings within the town limits or in larger nearby settlements, where the presence of electrical utility lines could make home computer use with Internet service a remote possibility, if teachers were able to purchase them. Barriers to Internet usage were further exacerbated by the limited availability of land-line telephones, requiring the purchase of satellite-based connections in place of lower-cost dial-up services. Teacher 1, a resident of a settlement outside of San Lucas Toliman, described what happened when he followed up on an advertisement for home Internet services:

Just a while back I asked... but it needs an antenna and a lot of other things. That made it very complicated to get-with the antenna and with a lot of things... but... there's not enough... recently when I asked about it, they were asking for 300 (quetzals) monthly [aprox. 40 U.S. dollars].

In a region where a teacher's starting salary is equivalent to 200 U.S. dollars monthly (or $1.40 hourly) (Galvez, 2007), these prices are fully out of range of their buying power. Teacher 6 shared:

I say to myself if I had the means necessary to have the Internet in my house, I'd get it. Because here it is very expensive.... with the equipment, I believe that with a down payment of one thousand quetzals for one-for the Internet-Hmm-because I was-I was studying and since I can't pay-If I had it, then I'd work more hours at night.

Other teachers were even less hopeful of obtaining home service, due to lack of electrical power in their communities. In almost all of the 20 interviews, pay scale played a significant role in limiting teacher choice or opportunity for getting home Internet service.

Added to buying power and electrical and telecommunications infrastructures, distance to a public Internet-connected location represented another level of challenge for teachers seeking to obtain online educational resources or participate in online coursework. Travel into town was essential for accessing any public Internet site, and the price per hour at Internet cafés was prohibitive for all but a few, making free access through the FRMT's CTC a very attractive option. To get to an Internet café or the CTC, the teachers relied on public transportation for mobility from homes as far as two hours from the center of town, while others walked. Transportation ranged from motorcycle taxis and small buses to flatbed trucks. Night travel was considered unwise due to the possibility of crime, requiring teachers to leave town in time to arrive home before dusk.

Teacher 1 divulged, "[T]he Internet is hard for me because of bus fare-bus fare and time. Eh, really I (am a) teacher in the mornings, and by midday I dedicate the afternoon to working in the field." Without time, proximity or financial resources on his side to support desires for professional development, Teacher 1 had committed all of his daylight hours to meet basic financial needs, and without personal transportation, was virtually locked out of the potential to utilize a free Internet resource during hours permitted by any form of public transportation, which in his case, was a flatbed truck. Teacher 3 revealed, "I don't have money to come every day. I had to go fifteen kilometers...and the only thing is there is-there is no money." Most teachers, lacking money for transportation, lacked opportunity for practicing or observing others to develop Internet skills. Although they acknowledged the relative advantage of the Internet for enhancing professional development, they could not take advantage of the offer of free usage.

Influences of Bonding Social Capital upon Internet Usage

Durston (2002) noted that bonding social capital was an essential resource for getting things done in rural Guatemalan communities. This correlated with Fazio (2007) who indicated that Guatemala's mountainous landforms provided the resources and infrastructure for building of an agricultural-based economy but also promoted close, bounded relationships which grew out of exclusion from the (metropolitan Spanish-speaking) host culture. Thereby, analysis and findings from the rural teachers of this study should manifest a bonding social capital effect of strong interdependence for using the Internet within the community of San Lucas Toliman and should reveal the presence of traditions or values which were distinct from larger city cultures. These were found to be present, and bonding social capital influences were found to both support and deter Internet usage of the interviewed teachers.

Many of the teachers indicated the need for others to accompany them while they worked on the Internet, either as co-learners, experts, or companions. Teacher 16 explained:

Well, I go to a bookstore [Internet café] in San Lucas Toliman, and the boy indeed operates the computer very well, and there I gain courage... I have to go with people because alone-alone I can't.

Some felt less willing to go to a public place to utilize the Internet in favor of working alongside siblings or friends in a home setting. Teacher 9 described:

For me it's a little uncomfortable to get over there [to the CTC]. I am going to be honest and sincere again. I have only gone onto the Internet from the capitol because I have three sisters there and one of my sisters-She installed the Internet...

Others described their thankfulness to family members or others for assisting them with childcare and words of encouragement. Teacher 6 indicated:

I get discouraged because my husband takes care of my oldest daughter, and my parents, my father-They are the ones who motivate me. They support me... because it takes time, and I don't want them to suffer because of my studies...So, I worked at twelve at night and in the early morning. I got up at three in the morning in order to finish an assignment.

Many teachers relied on these forms of mutual support while others expressed a higher level of self motivation in managing their time and activities, a value which was promoted in the permanent-group interview (PGI) meeting of community educators.

However, not all teachers enjoyed the support of family or friends to fulfill their aspirations for getting an education and particularly for taking the time off from family duties to study online. Teacher 16 shared: "Every day of the week, mornings and afternoons, I was occupied, since my brothers were studying, [and] I stayed there in charge of the house, so I couldn't go anywhere." The cultural expectation of women to jettison their own goals in favor of domestic work in support of the educational advancement of their male siblings was also reflected in Teacher 5's comment about interruptions to her timeline for getting an advanced degree

First and foremost, I dreamed as a child of becoming a teacher, but my father died when I was twelve. And, my mama said, "You are staying in the kitchen. Your brothers must be attended to." And, I had to obey my mama, but over time my brothers grew up and I said to my mama, "Mama, I didn't study, but my brothers indeed studied," because I wanted to work too. And I achieved it when finally the last one graduated.

This experience profoundly impacted Teacher 5, who lamented the taunting and ridicule she continued to receive from her brothers who said she was too old to be trying to study online. She nevertheless persisted in her commitment to utilize the Internet regularly.

Most teachers who were interviewed discussed their goals for studying English online as part of a service mission to the community, reflecting a strong commitment to social capital bonding and mutual support among the members of the community. Teacher 17 shared her appreciation of the Internet as a tool for teaching:

Well, besides a lot of information, related to a variety of subjects that can help one as a teacher, I always look for one or another ways of how to share with the children... After all, it is part of one's development and is knowledge that one can share with the children.

Teacher 3 looked upon online education as stepping stone to a higher degree and greater opportunities to serve the community:

I have desires (to pursue)... higher education... What I like is community development. It's my area-something I like, because I know what rural poverty is. And, thanks to Ajaw [God]-thanks to God, because not everyone has this habit (of Internet use).

Figure 4. Guatemalan teachers, school principals and community leaders met together at the Centro Educativo Luciano Pavarotti in the summer of 2008 to discuss and prioritize statements of 20 rural English teachers interviewed about their Internet usage

Teacher 16 considered learning English online as a facet of a personal mission to aid in alleviating the suffering experienced in a settlement of plantation workers residing outside of the town limits:

This community suffered a lot two years ago. Can you see over there from where we are? (points to a wooded mountainside) They were living there at the base of the volcano, and because of a storm due to the famous Hurricane Stan there was a mudslide. A lot of people died. Many of the women lost their husbands-ended up as widows. And, many of the children that we have here [in the school]-many are orphans. Whole houses were swept away. Because of that I want to each day prepare myself more, giving away the resources that are here, eh-and in that way supporting their education better, because I know that it's a small place here but many things can be done also.

The minimum requirement for teaching in the community is the completion of the ninth grade. Independent of their own attained grade levels, the majority of the teachers viewed the learning of English online only as a short-range objective associated with improving teaching quality, and not as part of a plan to obtain an online college degree.

These interview excerpts bear clear witness to the positive and negative influences which bonding social capital associations can levy upon teacher attitudes and goals about using the Internet. As in all cultures, studying online requires the displacement of other activities, rearranging of task commitments, and negotiation in family units about how available resources will be applied. The 42 community educators which met in the permanent group interview extolled teachers for managing their time to allow for online study, encouraged women to act independently, and recommended the exploration of methods for educating families about the importance of supporting all genders in a commitment to learn online. These injunctions represent the first stage of a plan for developing the social capital supports necessary to sustain online teacher professional development practices in the region.

Influences of Bridging Social Capital upon Internet Usage

Within this study, the concept of bridging social capital referred to seeking the involvement of expert resources to learn to use the Internet. Randolph and Krause (2002) emphasized, in addition to the need for effective ICT mentors, the important role students can plan in providing mutual aid in learning how to utilize technology. They cited a "lack of knowledge about and discomfort with computers" as a precedent to the formation of negative attitudes leading to avoidance of the Internet. Rowe-Whyte et al. (2002) commented upon the potential reactions of novice adopters, including the holding of "negative attitudes that can undermine persistence and achievement" (p. 2).

Some Mayan teachers, for whom Spanish is a second language, struggled with poor adaptation to the Internet as a technological innovation which integrated advanced instructions in Spanish or English. Teacher 1 explained his concerns about trying out the Internet:

The truth is, the only thing that I do is enter into the web page and struggle to reach an address. I really feel bad about it. The truth is that I lack a knowledge about what it is, how it is operated, how to write and in what form, and how to utilize it. The only thing that can be done now is-is this! Stick my address into the web page and go in there and that's as far as I can get. I feel like what I know about the Internet is miserable. I am lacking a lot. Really, a lot.

Teacher 16 expressed a similar level of anxiousness for guidance in specific functions of the Internet:

how to go in, how to call up (a web page)... I get very nervous that I am going to break the machine. I know I have to study a lot to know how to operate the Internet well... Since one doesn't go (online) regularly, one perceives it as (even) more difficult.

Teacher 11 explained the sense of futility she shared with other teachers in trying to understand and use the myriad of systems offered on computers:

Hmm. It has been quite difficult, because we [teachers] don't have a lot of knowledge about computers. We don't have much time on the computer. One has to know Word, [Power] Point, Excel and a lot of other things. He [the IT technician at the Pavarotti school CTC] taught us, but it was worthless for us because we don't know about the Internet. He did us the favor but we don't know how to do it, because we don't know about the Internet. He did us the favor but we don't know about it.

Most need in depth guidance and sensitive follow up. For some, it's their first encounter with computer technology of any sort. Teacher 1 recommends:

I'd like-What would it be? That they'd give us some training. Yes-I'd like to know everything about the Internet-everything, really. The truth indeed for me is that computers have-have been a pleasure for me. Computers have really helped me. But, slowly but surely, as we say in Guatemala. I have learned many things half way. Yes, and I have learned to operate it (but)... I have not-not-not ever seen English in print and I attempt and it never works out... As such, one advances little...

Most of the teachers of San Lucas Toliman and environs have little or no previous experience with the Internet, only a few of those interviewed speak Spanish as the primary language, and many find English language instructions online to be a significant challenge.

From within the bonding social capital groups that teachers form, some are esteemed for their skills in using the Internet and they serve a bridging social capital function. Teacher 4 comments that she "almost always ask[s] for a little help is of the (experienced) teachers who are here in the school and of the director who always is always watchful to guide everyone-always." Teacher 7 shared her concern about the apathy of some of the teachers:

other teachers... ha(ve) a different image of what it in reality could be... (if only) my teaching companions, apart from coming to the onsite workshop, would take the opportunity to go in(to the Internet) and see how it changes them.

When teachers attend the CTC, they hope for guidance from the ICT technician, another potential source of bridging social capital. Because these technicians possess specialized knowledge about computers and the Internet, and because they control access to the CTC, these individuals can levy considerable influence in the decision of a teacher to use the Internet for learning. Contrasting experiences were related in the interviews. Teacher 7 was happy to relate:

[His] classes are always very friendly, the machines always operate very well. [The IT teacher] tells us which machines we will use....or if (one) has a problem (he is) to whom I ask help. Eh, you should note that he is a very available person-always very available.... He is always a very service-oriented person,

Anxiousness about in depth guidance over time for using the Internet is also tied to the weak ICT background knowledge presented by the teachers. Many teachers made comments similar to Teacher 15, who stated:

I touched something and all that could be seen was a line of colors. Then the technician came and said to me, "You touched something", and then he told me, "Since you don't get it, you're going to cause problems (on this computer)".

The divergent comments make one question how to improve teacher confidence in trying out technological inventions such as the Internet, and how to enhance mutual receptivity between teachers as learners and the ICT supervisor as mentor to improve teacher Internet confidence.

Something which was noted in multiple teacher interviews was tied to the role of the operations manager and ICT supervisor, as symbols of bridging social capital, in setting and maintaining consistent, reliable hours of availability of the CTC's computers. Comments of Teachers 2, 15 and 10 included:

[First] they told us Monday or Friday, however [later] they told us Monday [only]... once they were in a meeting and another time they were in I don't know what activity... when she [the teacher] went, well [he] was busy and he couldn't [help] either... when one get's there, [and] asks... he says, 'There aren't any-any machines-they're busy. Come later.' One goes another day-It's the same-they're busy.

Additionally, expectations of learning Internet usage in trial and error online activities without guidance in person were reported by teachers to be unrealistic, consistent with assertions by a number of researchers that online learning is most effective when combined with face-to-face learning opportunities (Batane, 2004; Chang, 2004; Henning, 2003; Olugebenga Ojo & Kayode-Olakulehin, 2006).

Figure 5. The education director of the Fundación Rigoberta Menchú Tum led the proceedings of a meeting of 42 community educators. During this meeting, they developed findings from teacher interview data and shared ideas about how to enhance local engagement in online teacher professional development.

Another very positive source of bridging social capital for studying online was identified in teacher interview comments about guidance and encouragement they had received from local educational administrators to study online. As an example, Teacher 6 declared:

I am about to finish a bachelor's degree in education... so I'll have it done in approximately one year... [The principal] told me, "The best thing is that you continue studying"...because of which I made the commitment...because he told me that it was going to be beneficial to me-That, in the years to come, more education would be required of me.

Many teachers openly acknowledged the professional incentive for participating in online coursework in education. Particularly the learning of English was seen favorably by school administrators, and was particularly of value for continuation of teaching contracts in privately-operated schools.

The comments of a group of 42 community educators, assembled for the permanent group interview meeting, included requests for the FRMT to enhance Internet training opportunities for teachers with no previous computer experience, and encouraged teachers to manage their time and priorities in order to utilize the free Internet services at the school. Although the Internet could provide a gateway for easing the transition to acquisition of Internet practices through contact with entities distant from the receiver, this was not at all found to be the case in San Lucas Toliman, where the best way to support Internet usage was found to be a combination of bonding and bridging influences in social networks. This finding in the permanent group interview meeting was fully consistent with assertions of Kavanaugh, et. al.

(2005) who indicated that a combination of bridging and bonding social capital sources made for a dynamic environment for community change:

Communities with "bridging" social capital... as well as "bonding" social capital ... are the most effective in organizing for collective action... When people with bridging ties use... the Internet, they enhance their capability to educate community members and to organize, as needed, for collective action. (p. 119)

Within the context of this study, linking social capital resources, transmitted through the conduit of the Internet to remote communities (Van Bavel, et. al., 2007) would be useless without the support of ICT experts, as a form of bridging social capital, to guide teachers supported by their associates in bonding social capital groups, for development as online learners.

Influences of Linking Social Capital upon Internet Usage

Teacher interviews clearly demonstrated a general appreciation for the value of Internet resources originating from outside their community. Teacher 3 described the Internet as "a powerful tool for learning." Teacher 4 said she could "find any kind of… (information) looking on the Internet," and Teacher 9 indicated it "opens the doors to the world." In interviews teachers made reference to specific types of information which attracted them to the Internet, including instant access to facts, surfing for news and ideas for lessons, email services and sites which promoted English-language learning. While these resources were looked upon as valuable or even essential, the multiple barriers of buying power, infrastructure and distance were viewed as insurmountable by most teachers. Of the 34 teachers invited to take advantage of free Internet usage for coursework under the auspices of the FRMT, only 11 persisted for one half of the 26-week course, with 5 completing.

Although online resources are hosted by entities from outside the community, the significance of linking social capital in the context of the study is limited to individuals from outside of the immediate societal context which through direct human interaction could have influenced the Internet usage of the teachers. The researcher served as the chief source of linking social capital, as facilitator of the 26-week course in English teaching which spurred this study, joined by the FRMT education director who extended the offer of free Internet services for the teachers. Other linking social capital sources were academic and professional contacts via email, college online study colleagues, and online prayer partners. However, bearing out research by Woolcock and Narayan (2000), the paucity of references in teacher interviews to resources qualifying as linking social capital underscored the influence of bonding and bridging social capital as the key supports for using the Internet to learn online.

With so few teachers accepting the offer for free Internet usage and such a small percentage of enrolled teachers completing the coursework, it was essential that this quandary should be studied from the perspective of the community, and an open invitation was extended to all members of the educational community to participate in the permanent-group interview meeting, which followed PRA guidelines for group derivation of findings based on the interview data, and eliminated the potential for distortion of findings which could have resulted from cultural insensitivity of the researcher. This approach heightened the propensity of the study's findings to result in permanent systemic change driven by community decision making. The FRMT as provider of free Internet services, the FRMT education director as an agent of change and opinion leadership, and the researcher as an ongoing promoter of online teacher education worked in tandem to support the implementation of a research project designed to meet the community's specifications.

Figure 6. Community-Driven Development processes for enhancing teacher engagement in online learning are essential for promoting permanent systemic change. The Participatory Rural Appraisal relies upon local decision making to identify problems, form questions, conduct research, evaluate data and summarize findings.

CURRENT CHALLENGES FACING THE ORGANIZATION

The collaboration between the researcher, native-speaker research assistant, staff of the Fundación Rigoberta Menchú Tum, teachers receiving training services and community educational leadership resulted in the establishment of a new level of dialogue for developing a system of online professional development in rural, remote sections of Guatemala. After completion of just a few of the interviews, it became apparent that low responsiveness of teachers to the offer of free Internet usage was not due to a simple lack of motivation, as had been asserted. Specifically, the study advanced the cause of social justice for an underserved rural teacher population in a developing nation, by demonstrating (a) indicators for improving Internet availability per location and hours of access, (b) community recommendations about how to develop new skills, habits and priorities for online education, (c) levels of interest for creation of specialized online coursework matching the community's needs, and (d) needs to address a general scarcity of resources to overcome challenges of buying power, infrastructure and distance for gaining access to Internet hardware, connections, and training.

Approximately one month after the completion of the interviews and permanent-group interview meeting of community educators, a focus group was convened in San Lucas Toliman by FRMT leadership with the purpose of identifying a series of next steps to enroll teachers in a long-term program of professional development online. As an intermediary step, an agreement was made with the researcher to offer a 12-week short course, running September through November of 2008, as follow-up for teachers interested in continuing to sharpen their English-language teaching skills. The following January, a plan was agreed upon between the researcher and the FRMT to create an online link on the FRMT main page (www.frmt.org) to a teacher forum, or Campus Virtual, with an extensive library of English-language learning websites for exploration, and to also add forums for young adults and children with the same purposes. An offer was extended from a third-party organization for donated website design services, but this offer was not fulfilled.

Notably, in February of 2009, the FRMT also entered into an agreement with the Guatemalan government to cosponsor the development of the Universidad Maya (U-Maya), proposed as a Mayan multicultural, multilingual educational resource for vocational and professional training of rural and city populations, which would eventually include online study components. Development of this project is contingent upon the securement of sustainable funding sources and the commitment of educators and educational administrators to assist in the design and ongoing management of the U-Maya. This plan is fully integrated with objectives of multiple national and international organizations which promote educational progress for indigenous peoples, as exemplified by the Consejo Nacional de Educación Maya (2007) (National Council of Mayan Education).

SOLUTIONS AND RECOMMENDATIONS

The involvement of community educational leadership for analysis of the 20 teacher interviews resulted in a series of specific recommendations for ameliorating identified challenges. The first recommendation resulting from the permanent group interview related to the improvement of Internet availability per location and hours of access. The educators suggested that as teachers work at varying or multiple shifts and free Internet access is limited to the FMRT's community technology center, similar services should be offered at other private schools in the community with extended evening hours, and with at least a few work stations continuously open for use by community teachers.

The permanent group interview meeting also resulted in community recommendations about how to develop new skills, habits and priorities for online teacher education. The group emphasized that teachers are requesting introductory guidance for performing basic computer functions as a part of Internet training, hope for patience and ongoing support during a period of adjustment, and succeed when attending a computer lab in small groups to provide mutual encouragement. Community educational leaders requested the FRMT's consideration of regularly-scheduled Internet orientation sessions. The FRMT recommended the utilization of seasonal interns to assist in this process.

The community's educational leadership indicated high levels of interest for the creation of online coursework which melds governmental requirements with teacher capacity for using the Internet and their buying power. Many teachers reject notions of professional development due to difficulties in obtaining enrollment, paying for, and traveling for higher education and see free accredited online coursework as a positive option. Content knowledge, literacy and computer literacy levels present challenges which can be addressed by strategic online coursework design that is considered user-friendly.

The permanent-group interview brought out the need to address a general scarcity of material resources related to using the Internet and for training to utilize those resources. The group reminded that teachers who reside in and/or teach in remote settlements lack transportation, financial resources and ICT infrastructure necessary to guarantee regular access to the Internet. The group stated that wiring the town and environs of

San Lucas Toliman for universal Internet access would be beneficial to many teachers.

Family expectations upon women of domestic work for family members impeded online professional development activities outside the home. The community educational leaders indicated that they and the FRMT need to devise methods for diffusion of new values for socioeconomic development through online learning and assure that these values are permanently integrated into the community's traditions. They reminded that opinion leaders in the community, such as school administrators, respected older teachers and other individuals can influence the realignment of norms leading to support for online learning.

Members of the FRMT staff, led by the education director, the area representative of the MINEDUC, and five local teachers of San Lucas Toliman who completed the original 26-week online coursework are the few pioneers who, in collaboration with the researcher, are actively engaged in promoting the diffusion of the innovation of online learning for the community's teachers. This study has provided significant data about factors which can be enhanced to accelerate that phenomenon, through employment of methods which empowers the identification of resolutions through a Community-Driven Development process.

Local comments pointed up the essentiality of a cooperative agreement between private and public entities to coordinate pay scales, work schedules and proximity of Internet services, so that all teachers of the region might benefit from equal opportunities for professional advancement with the Internet as a prime tool in the process. The potential integration of efforts between these entities represents a fusion of local bonding and bridging social capital sources and external, linking social capital. Most importantly, this study has brought to fruition findings based on an analysis of social capital forces which directly affect teacher decisions to study online, dispelling baseless assertions about their unresponsiveness.

The ideal solution, requiring the greatest commitment of funding and manpower, would be to equip the town of San Lucas Toliman, and environs with universal Internet access free of charge, supply all teachers and students with low-cost, solar-powered wirelessly-connected laptop computers, and conduct Internet training for all recipients with regular follow-up training and individualized assistance to promote the development of a digitally-literate population. In line with the evidence supplied by this study, systemic change to close the digital divide in rural sectors of the developing world such as San Lucas Toliman will depend upon the close collaboration of industry, government and intergovernmental entities and the non-profit sector to support engagement and persistence in online teacher professional development.

REFERENCES

Alsop, R., Chase, R., & Owen, D. (2003). *Social capital, empowerment, and community driven development: Presentation notes. PSIA Sourcebook.* World Bank: Geneva. Retrieved at http://info.worldbank.org/etools/bspan/PresentationView.asp?PID= 936 &EID=482

Attewell, P. (2001). The first and second digital divides. *Sociology of Education*, *74*, 252–259. doi:10.2307/2673277

Barshefsky, C. (2002). Trade policy for a networked world. *Foreign Affairs (Council on Foreign Relations)*, (March/April): 134–147.

Batane, T. (2004). Inservice teacher training and technology: A case of Botswana. *Journal of Technology and Teacher Education*, *12*, 387–410.

Caniz, E. (2006). Evaluation of technological needs and resources at five middle schools in Totonicapán, Guatemala. *CLASPO Report: Summer 2006.* Austin, TX: Center for Latin American Social Policy at the University of Texas. Retrieved at www.utexas.edu/cola/insts/llilas/claspo/ research/ noformat/claspo/PDF/field reports/tzoc 06.pdf

Central Intelligence Agency. (2006). *The world factbook—Guatemala.* Retrieved at https:// www. cia.gov/library/publications/the-world-factbook/ geos/gt.html

Chambers, R. (1990). *Rapid but relaxed and participatory rural appraisal: Towards applications in health and nutrition.* Retrieved at www.unu. edu/unupress/food2 /UIN08E/ uin08e 0u.htm

Chambers, R. (1992). Rural Appraisal: Rapid, Relaxed, and Participatory. *Institute of Development Studies Discussion Paper 311.* Sussex, UK: HELP. Retrieved at www.worldbank. org/wbi/ sourcebook/sba 104.htm

Chambers, R. (1994). Participatory rural appraisal: Challenges, potential, paradigms. *World Development, 22*(10), 1437–1454. doi:10.1016/0305-750X(94)90030-2

Chambers, R. (1998). Beyond "Whose reality counts?" New methods we now need? *Studies in Cultures, Organizations and Societies, 4*, 279–301. doi:10.1080/10245289808523516

Chang, T. (2004). Transborder tourism, borderless classroom: Reflections on a Hawaii–Singapore experience. *Journal of Geography in Higher Education, 28*(2), 179–195. doi:10.1080/0309826042000242431

Cifuentes, W. (2007). *Online chat with the Assistant Education Director of the Fundación Rigoberta Menchú Tum by Douglas Tedford,* December 6, 2007.

Coleman, J. (1988). Social capital in the creation of human capital. *American Journal of Sociology, 94*(Supplement), S95–S120. doi:10.1086/228943

Conciliation Resources. *(2007).* Agreement on social and economic aspects and agrarian situation: 1996, Mexico City. *Conciliation Resources, website. Retrieved at*http://www.c-r.org/our-work/ accord/guatemala/socio-economic-accord.php

Consejo Nacional de Educación Maya (CNEM). (2007). Xka xmolomil li k'anjel chirix li tzolok Mayab', 4to congreso nacional de educación maya: consensos, planteamientos y demandas (Fourth national congress of Mayan education: consensus, considerations and demands). Cobán, Alta Verapaz, Guatemala.

Creed, C., & Joynes, C. (2005). Education for all global monitoring report: Improving the quality of primary school through distance education. Study undertaken by IRFOL: Distance Learning and Improving the Quality of Education Report. International Research Foundation for Open Learning for the EFA Monitoring Team. Paris: UNESCO.

Crump, B., & McIlroy, A. (2003). The digital divide: Why the don't-want-to's won't compute—Lessons from a New Zealand ICT project. *First Monday, Peer Reviewed Journal on the Internet 8*(12). Retrieved at http://www.firstMonday .org/ issues/issue8_12/crump/#c6

DiMaggio, P., & Hargittai, E. (2001). *From the 'digital divide' to 'digital inequality': Studying Internet use as penetration increases.* Sociology Department, Princeton University. Princeton, New Jersey. Retrieved at http://www.princeton.edu/~ arts pol/workpap/ WP15%20-%20 DiMaggio%2BHargittai.pdf

Direccion de calidad y desarrollo educativo (DICADE), (2006). *Curriculum nacional base: nivel primaria y preprimaria.* (Basic national program of study: primary and preprimary levels). Guatemala City: Ministerio de educacion, Guatemala.

Douglas, R. (2006). Interview with Professor Rogelio Douglas, Director of English Language Programs, Ministry of Education, Republic of Panama. August 30, 2006. Panama City, Panama.

Dudwick, N., Kuehnast, K., Nyhan Jones, V., & Woolcock, M. (2006). *Analyzing social capital in context: a guide to using qualitative methods and data.* Washington, DC: World Bank Institute. Retrieved at http://siteresources.worldbank.org/WBI/ Resources/Analyzing_ Social_Capital_in_ Context-FINAL.pdf

Duque Arellano, V. (1999). Forjando educación para un nuevo milenio: Desafíos educativos en países multiculturales (Forging an education for a new millennium: Educacional challenges in multicultural nations). Guatemala City: Fundación Rigoberta Menchú Tum, Instituto Indígena para la Educación FRMT, Países Bajos, UNESCO.

Durston, J. (2002). *El capital social campesino en la gestión del desarrollo rural: Diadas, equipos, puentes y escaleras.* Santiago de Chile: CEPAL: Comisión Económica para America Latina y el Caribe. Retrieved at http://www.eclac.org/ publicaciones/xml/0/ 11700/Capitulo_ III.pdf

Fazio, M. (2007). *Economic opportunities for indigenous peoples in Latin America: Guatemala, Conference Edition,* February 2007. Washington, DC: World Bank. Retrieved at http://web.worldbank.org/WBSITE/EXTERNAL/TOPICS/EXT EDUCATION/0,content MDK:21185632~menuPK: 282391~pagePK:64020865 ~piPK:51164185~theSitePK:2823 86,00.html

Foth, M. (2003). *Connectivity does not insure community: on social capital, networks, and communities of place.* The International Conference on Information Technology in Regional Areas, December 15-17, 2003. Caloundra, Queensland, Australia. Retrieved at http://www. mobilecommunity design. com/ research/Foth-Connectivity_does_not_ ensure_community-on_social_capital_networks_and_ communities_of_place.pdf

Fundación Rigoberta Menchú Tum (FRMT). (2007b). *Website of the Fundación Rigoberta Menchú Tum.* Guatemala City, Guatemala. Retrieved at http://www.frmt.org/

Galvez, O. (2007). Telephone interview, September 20, 2007, between Douglas Tedford and Osbaldo Galvez, chief administrator of the Centro Educativo Luciano Pavarotti. San Lucas Toliman, Guatemala.

Gonsalves, J. (2005). Participatory research and development for sustainable agriculture and natural resource management: A sourcebook. Ottawa, Canada: International Development Research Centre.

Goodman, S. E., Gottstein, J. B., & Goodman, D. S. (2001). International perspectives: wiring the wilderness in Alaska and the Yukon. *Communications of the ACM, 44*(6), 21–25. doi:10.1145/376134.376143

Grenier, L. (1998). Working with indigenous knowledge: a guide for researchers. Ottawa: International Development Research Centre.

Henning, E. (2003). 'I click, therefore I am (not)': is cognition 'distributed' or is it 'contained' in borderless e-learning programmes? [Retrieved at EBSCO Host database.]. *International Journal of Training and Development,* 7(4), 303–317. doi:10.1046/j.1360-3736.2003.00188.x

Ibañez, A., Linder, K., & Woolcock, M. (2002). Social capital in Guatemala: a mixed methods analysis. *Guatemala Poverty Assessment Program, Technical Paper No. 12.* Geneva: International Bank for Reconstruction and Development.

International Bank for Reconstruction and Development (IBRD/World Bank). (2006). *Social capital, empowerment, and community driven development, description.* Retrieved at http://info.worldbank.org/etools/vod/PresentationView.asp?PID =936&EID=482

International Bank for Reconstruction and Development (IBRD/World Bank). (2007a). *Social capital and information technology.* Retrieved at http://www1.worldbank. org/prem/ poverty/scapital/topic/info1.htm

International Bank for Reconstruction and Development (IBRD/World Bank), (2007b). *World Bank Participatory Sourcebook, Appendix 1: Methods and Tools.* Retrieved athttp://www. worldbank.org/wbi/sourcebook/sba104.htm

International Bank for Reconstruction and Development (IBRD/World Bank). (2008). *PovertyNet: Information and Communication Technology.* Retrieved at http://web.worldbank. org/WBSITE/EXTERNAL/TOPICS/EXTPOVERTY/EXTEMPOWERMENT/0,contentMDK:20265884~menuPK:543261~pagePK:148956~piPK:216618~theSitePK:486411,00.html

ITFORCEGT. (2006). *India – Guatemala IT Education Centre of Excellence.* Retrieved at http://www.itforcegt.org/

Kavanaugh, A., Reese, D., Carroll, J., & Rosson, M. (2005). Weak ties in networked communities. *The Information Society, 21*, 119–131. doi:10.1080/01972240590925320

Koss, F. (2001). Children falling into the digital divide. *Journal of International Affairs, 55*(1), 75–90.

Laungani, P. (2005). Building multicultural counseling bridges: The holy grail or a poisoned chalice? *Counselling Psychology Quarterly, 18*(4), 247–259. doi:10.1080/09515070500435476

Leavey, T. (2003). The Internet remains a mystery to most people. *UN Chronicle, 4*(34), 34–35.

Lin, N. (1999). Building a network theory of social capital. *Connections, 22*(1), 28–51.

Lorenzetti, J. (2004). Strategic planning and social capital in distance education: a conversation with Eugene Kowch. *Distance Education Report, 8*(18), 5–7.

Menchú, P. (2007). Letter re: Douglas Tedford, Fundación Rigoberta Menchú Tum

Menou, M., Day, P., & Schuler, D. (2007). *Liberating Voices! A Pattern Language for Communication Revolution: Telecenters, harnessing ICT in support of community development.* Retrieved at http://diac. cpsr.org/cgi-bin/diac02/pattern.cgi/public? pattern_id=867

Natriello, G. (2001). Bridging the second digital divide: What can sociologists of education contribute? *Sociology of Education, 74*, 260–265. doi:10.2307/2673278

Olugebenga Ojo, D., & Kayode Olakulehin, F. (2006). Attitudes and perceptions of students to open and distance learning in Nigeria. *International Review of Research in Open and Distance Learning, 7*(1), 1492–3831.

Ordoñez, A. (2006). *India abrira un centro de entratenimiento informatico (India will open an ICT training center).* El Periodico: Guatemala, September 30, 2006. Retrieved at http://www.itforcegt.org/ photos3.php

Organization of American States (OAS). (2006). Foreign ministers vow to strive so everyone in the Americas can benefit from the knowledge-based society. *Website, OAS General Assembly, 36th Regular Session, Santo Domingo, June 2006.* Retrieved November 12, 2007, at http://www.oas.org/36ag/english/

Randolph, K. A., & Krause, D. J. (2002). Mutual aid in the classroom: an instructional technology application. *Journal of Social Work Education, 38*(2), 259–272.

Rogers, E. (1995). Diffusion of Innovations, (4 ed.). New York: The Free Press.

Rogers, E. (2003). Diffusion of innovations, (5 ed.). New York: The Free Press.

Romo-Rodriguez, G. (2005). Information and communication technologies and non-governmental organizations: Lessons learnt from networking in Mexico. *The Electronic Journal of Information Systems in Developing Countries, 21*(3), 1–29.

Rowe-Whyte, A., O'Sullivan, P., & Hunt, S. (2002). Immediacy on the web: Narrowing the digital divide. Department of Communication, Illinois State University, Normal, Illinois. Retrieved from EBSCO Host Database.

Rutherford, J., Gillespie, A., & Richardson, R. (2004). The territoriality of pan-European telecommunications backbone networks. *Journal of Urban Technology*, 11(3): 1–34. doi:10.1080/10630730500064166

Sabatini, F. (2007). *Social capital gateway: resources for the study of social capital, website.* Retrieved at http://www.socialcapitalgateway.org/NV-eng-education.htm

Trucano, M. (2005). *Knowledge Maps: ICT in Education*. Washington, DC: *info*Dev/ World Bank. Retrieved at http://www.infodev.org/en/Publication.8.html

United Nations Educational, Scientific and Cultural Organization (UNESCO). (2008). *Latin American and Caribbean ministers approved new plan of action for the information society 11-03-2008 (San Salvador)*. Communication and Information Resources, website. Retrieved at http://portal.unesco.org/ci/en/ev.php-URL_ID=26186&URL_DO=DO_ TOPIC&URL_ SECTION=201.html

Van Bavel, R., Punie, E., & Tuomi, I. (2007). *IPTSICT-Enabled Changes in Social Capital, in The IPTS Report*. Institute for Prospective Technological Studies (IPTS) of the European Commission, Directorate General, Joint Research Centre. Retrieved at http://www. jrc.es/home/report/english/articles/vol85/ ICT4E856.htm

Woolcock, M. (1998). Social capital and economic development: toward a theoretical synthesis and policy framework. *Theory and Society, 27,* 151–208. doi:10.1023/A:1006884930135

Woolcock, M. (2002). *Social capital and development: concepts, evidence and applications.* Power point presentation, Workshop on understanding and building social capital in Croatia, Zagreb, Yugoslavia. Cambridge, MA: World Bank and Harvard University.

Zapeta-García, J., Vásquez-González, R., Pérez, F., & Alfonso, L. (1998). Diagnóstico de la realidad educativa de los pueblos indígenas y otros pueblos de Mesoamerica: informe - Guatemala. Guatemala City: Países Bajos/ Fundación Rigoberta Menchú Tum/ UNESCO.

ADDITIONAL READING

Agency for Educational Development (AED). (2007). *ICT@AED, website.* Retrieved at http://ict.aed.org/

Agency for International Development (AID). (2006). ICT for professional development in Uganda: impact and scalability assessment. *Center for Applied Technology, Academy for Educational Development.* Retrieved at http://www.dot-com-alliance.org/documents/ Uganda_Evaluation_Report_ Full1.pdf

Ajb'atz' Enlace Quiché. (2007). *Bienvenidos a Ajb'atz' Enlace Quiché, website.* Retrieved at http://www. enlacequiche.org.gt

Bennett, W. L. (2003). Communicating global activism: Strengths and vulnerabilities of networked politics. *Information Communication and Society*, *6*(2), 143–168. doi:10.1080/1369118032000093860

Bessette, G. (2004). Involving the Community: A Guide to Participatory Development Communication. Ottawa: International Development Research Centre.

Bordieu, P. (1983). *The forms of capital.* Website article translated from German by Nice, R. Retrieved at http://www.viet-studies.org/Bordieu_capital.htm

Cheung, D. (2002). Refining a stage model for studying teacher concerns about educational innovations *The Free Library*. (2002). Retrieved from http://www.the freelibrary.com/ Refining a stage model for studying teacher concerns about...-a096695274

Chronicle, U. N. (2000). Unwiring the Internet in Costa Rica. Zooming in on information technology. *UN Chronicle*, *2*, 32.

Coupal, L. (2004). Constructivist learning theory and human capital theory: Shifting political and educational frameworks for teachers' ICT professional development. *British Journal of Educational Technology*, *35*(5), 587–596. doi:10.1111/j.0007-1013.2004.00415.x

Dickson-Swift, V., James, E., Kippen, S., & Liamputtong, P. (2007). Doing sensitive research: What challenges do qualitative researchers face? *Qualitative Research*, *7*(3), 327–353. doi:10.1177/1468794107078515

Farr, J. (2003). Social capital: a conceptual history. *Political Theory*, *31*(X), 1–28.

Frank, K., Zhao, Y., & Berman, K. (2004). Social Capital and the Diffusion of Innovations within Organizations: Application to the Implementation of Computer Technology in Schools. *Sociology of Education*, *77*, 148–171. doi:10.1177/003804070407700203

Fukuyama, F. (1999). Social capital and civic society. Prepared for delivery at the IMF Conference on Second Generation Reforms. Washington, D.C.: International Monetary Fund.

Fundación Rigoberta Menchú Tum (FRMT). (2007a). *Biblioteca publica virtual Rigoberta Menchú Tum, website.* Retrieved at http://www. biblioteca rigoberta.org

Glaeser, E., Laibson, D., & Sacerdote, B. (2002). The economic approach to social capital. *HIER: Harvard Institute of Economic Research*, Harvard University: Cambridge, MA. Retrieved at http://64.233.179.104/scholar?hl=en&lr=&q=cache:4d0TSckJx2gJ:post.economics.harvard. edu/hier/2001papers/HIER1916.pdf+

GLOBE Program. (2007). GLOBE Program, Guatemala, website. Retrieved at http:www. globe. gov/fsl/INTL/main.pl?ctry=GT&lang=en&nav=1

Grootaert, C., Narayan, D., Nyhan Jones, V., & Woolcock, M. (2004) Measuring social capital: an integrated questionnaire. *World Bank Working Paper, No. 18.* Geneva: International Bank for Reconstruction and Development.

Gülseçen, S., & Kubat, A. (2006). Teaching ICT to teacher candidates using PBL: a qualitative and quantitative Evaluation. [Retrieved at EBSCO Host database.]. *Educational Technology & Society*, *9*(2), 96–106.

Herie, M., & Martin, G., (2002). Knowledge diffusion in social work: a new approach to bridging the gap. *Social Work, January 2002, 47*(1).

Hirschmann, D. (2003). Keeping 'the last' in mind: incorporating Chambers in consulting. *Development in Practice*, *13*(5), 487–502. doi:10.1080/0961452032000125866

Hung, C. L. (2003). Income, Education, Location and the Internet-The Digital Divide in China. *Conference Papers-International Communication Association, 2003 Annual Meeting, San Diego, CA,* 1-28. Retrieved at EBSCO Host database.

International Development Research Centre. (2007). *The International Development Research Centre, website.* Retrieved at http://www1.world bank.org/prem/ poverty/scapital/topic/ info1. htm

Jung, I. (2005). ICT-pedagogy integration in teacher training: Application cases worldwide. *Educational Technology & Society*, *8*(2), 94–101.

Kapoor, I. (2002). The devil's in the theory: a critical assessment of Robert Chambers's work on participatory development. *Third World Quarterly*, *23*(1), 101–117. doi:10.1080/01436590220108199

Laferrière, T., Lamon, M., & Chan, D. (2006). Emerging e-trends and models in teacher education and professional development. *Teaching Education*, *17*(1), 75–90. doi:10.1080/10476210500528087

Lin, N. (2001). Social capital: A theory of social structure and action. Cambridge, MA: Cambridge University Press.

Maksakovskii, V. P. (2006). What is hampering the development of our education? *Russian Education & Society*, *48*(3), 18–30. doi:10.2753/RES1060-9393480302

Mendler, J., Simon, D., & Broome, P. (2002). Virtual development and virtual geographies: using the Internet to teach interactive distance courses in the global South. *Journal of Geography in Higher Education*, *26*(3), 313–325. doi:10.1080/0309826022000019891

Paldam, M. (2000). *Social capital: one or many? Definition and measurement.* Department of Economics, University of Arbus, Denmark. Retrieved at http://www.business.aau. dk/oecon/undervisning/Skema%e6ndring/2003/ soka2.pdf

Patrinos, H., & Skoufias, E. (2007). *Economic opportunities for indigenous peoples in Latin America, Conference Edition,* February 2007. World Bank. Retrieved at http://web. worldbank.org/WBSITE/EXTERNAL/TOPICS/ EXTEDUCATION/ 0,contentMDK:21185632~menuPK:282391~pagePK:64020865~piPK:511641 85~theSitePK: 282386,00.htmlir

Proenza, F. (2002). A poverty reduction strategy for the information age: FAO Investment Centre. *TechKnowLogia,* July-September, 58. Retrieved at www.Tech KnowLogia.org

Proyecto Educacional de Latinoamerica y el Caribe (PRELAC). (2004). Management in Latin America and the Caribbean: Education-Are we on the right track? ECLAC-UNESCO High Level Seminar, June 30, 2004. San Juan, Puerto Rico: UNESCO.

Putnam, R. (1995). Tuning in, tuning out: The strange disappearance of social capital in America. PS: Political Science and Politics (December). 664-83.

Putnam, R. (2000). Bowling alone: The collapse and revival of American community. New York: Simon & Schuster.

Robinson, L. (2002). Participatory rural appraisal: a brief introduction. *Group Facilitation*, Spring 2002. Retrieved at http://findarticles.com/p/articles/mi_qa39 54/is_200204/ai_n 9029098?tag=content;col1

Rudra, N. (2005). Globalization and the strengthening of democracy in the developing world. *American Journal of Political Science*, *49*(4), 704–730. doi:10.1111/j.1540-5907.2005.00150.x

Selwyn, N. (2002). *Defining the 'digital divide': developing a theoretical understanding of inequalities in the information age.* Occasional Paper 49. Cardiff: Cardiff University. Retrieved at http://www.cf.ac.uk/socsi/ict/defining digitaldivide.pdf

Sobel, J. (2002). Can we trust social capital? *Journal of Economic Literature*, 40, 139–154. doi:10.1257/0022051027001

United Nations Educational, Scientific and Cultural Organization (UNESCO). (2001). *Symposium on indigenous identities: Oral, written expressions and new technologies.* UNESCO, May 15-18. Retrieved at http://www.unesco.org/culture/ indigenous/ html_eng/bookfair.shtml

United Nations Educational, Scientific and Cultural Organization (UNESCO). (2002). *Information and Communication Technologies in Teacher Education.* Paris: UNESCO. Retrieved at http://www.unescobkk.org/index.php? id=3565\

United Nations Educational, Scientific and Cultural Organization (UNESCO). (2003). *Communication and Information—Education—Literacy Portal—United Nations Literacy Decade (2003 – 2012).* Retrieved at http://portal.unesco.org/education/ en/ev.php-URL_ID=53811&URL_DO=DO_TOPIC& URL_SECTION=201.html

Woolcock, M., & Narayan, D. (2000). Social capital: implications for development theory, research, and policy. *The World Bank Research Observer*, *15*(2), 225–249.

KEY TERMS AND DEFINITIONS

Bonding Social Capital: Denotes "ties between people in similar situations, such as immediate family, close friends and neighbours" (Woolcock, 1998, p. 13).

Bridging Social Capital: "Encompasses more distant ties of like persons, such as loose friendships and workmates" (Woolcock, 1998, p. 14).

Community-Driven Development (CDD): "An approach to development that supports participatory decision making, local capacity building, and community control of resources" (International Bank for Reconstruction & Development, 2007, ¶ 1).

Community Technology Center (CTC): A place where the community may utilize ICT resources at no cost or at a fair cost to the public.

Digital Divide: "the gap that exists between individuals advantaged by the Internet and those individuals relatively disadvantaged by the Internet" (Rogers, 2003, p. 468).

Fundación Rigoberta Menchú Tum (FRMT): Foundation headed by 1992 Nobel Peace Prize Winner Rigoberta Menchú Tum, which has advocated for improvements in education and social services for indigenous peoples of Guatemala, and the Americas.

Indigenous: This term referred to a racial characteristic of individuals who are native to a developing nation, present before invasion or conquest.

Information and Communication Technology (ICT): "Facilitate(s) by electronic means the creation, storage, management and dissemination of information... (and) a means of communicating… from... networked computers and the Internet." (Romo-Rodriguez, 2005, p. 4).

Linking Social Capital: A type of social capital which implied reaching out "to unlike people in dissimilar situations, such as those who are entirely outside of the community, thus enabling members to leverage a far wider range of resources than are available in the community" (Woolcock, 1998, p. 14).

Ministerio de Educación de Guatemala (MINEDUC): Guatemalan Ministry of Education

Participatory Rural Appraisal (PRA): "A growing family of participatory approaches and methods that emphasize local knowledge and enable local people to make their own appraisal, analysis, and plans... to enable (entities) to work together to plan context-appropriate programs" (International Bank for Reconstruction & Development, 2007c, ¶ 2).

Social Capital: For purposes of this study, would be limited to its generally-accepted working description as norms within social networks (Alsop et al., 2003; Narayan & Woolcock, 2004).

Chapter 13
Interactive Hypermedia-Based Learning Environment:
Models of Making Sense of Dynamic Visualization

Billie Eilam
University of Haifa, Israel

Ofir Gurtler
University of Haifa, Israel

ABSTRACT

Seven students learning art in the 12th grade, experienced for the first time the processes involved in the interpretation of a dynamic performance art in a hypermedia-based learning environment, followed by learning a hypermedia-based curriculum unit concerning this complex skill, and concluding by transferring this acquired knowledge for interpreting a new, different artwork. Cognitive aspects of students' profiles of understanding and models of enactment are described. Interpretation of performance art is highly complex, but is important in current era of visual culture. Generally, this learning environment enabled most students to overcome some of the difficulties involved in this dynamic visualization, but presented them with other difficulties. A careful considerations of these issues as related to the design, by curriculum developers and teachers may yield a successful students' performance.

DOI: 10.4018/978-1-61520-779-4.ch013

PRO AND CONS OF TECHNOLOGY

The use of technology in current formal and informal learning environments is not a rare sight any more. Diverse technologies may constitute powerful cognitive tools for enhancing students' learning of various content domains in numerous ways; they afford students' access to updated local or international, static or dynamic information and data, frequently unavailable in textbooks or schools; enable students' interactions with the information and its active processing; present students with multiple representation-types of same phenomenon thus promoting students' awareness to different emphases or their development of multiple views and cognitive flexibility; it may extend the immediate learning environment beyond its physical borders by providing the means for establishing networks of communication and cooperation, and so forth. However, at the same time, students using technology in the course of learning were found to confront many related difficulties, pointing at the many flaws such use may have; the overwhelming available information may hinder students' ability to deal with it efficiently; the need to integrate diverse representation-types or understand a dynamic phenomenon in order to construct a coherent body of knowledge; the need for cultivating thinking through symbolic systems, and more. It seems that technology alone, although offering many advantages to learning, has to be applied with cautious, accounting for students' characteristics and abilities, the target task at hand or the domain to be studied. An advantage in one situation may become a hinder in another, and vice versa.

Being an important goal of learning visual arts, the purpose of the present chapter is to describe possible implications of our examination of the use of hypertext for promoting students' ability to make meaning and understand social criticism. As noted by Freedman (2003, p. xi):

"The process of learning to make and adequately respond to the complexities of the visual arts is unlikely to occur without guidance. Unless people are given instruction, they may never get beyond the surface of the images and designed objects they see every day. When students develop a deeper understanding of their visual experiences, they can look critically at surface appearances and begin to reflect on the importance of the visual arts in shaping culture, society, and even individual identity."

LEARNING WITH HYPERMEDIA TECHNOLOGY

Hypertext and Hypermedia: Definition as well as Advantages and Limitations

The term "Hypertext" was coined by Theodor H. Nelson in the 1960s, referring to a form of electronic multi-linear or multi-sequential series of text chunks connected by electronic links in an open-ended, reversible mode, having no beginning or end, offering readers different navigational pathways and access to information through several entrances, without any one of them surpassing the rest. The integration of various modalities - visual information, sound, animation and other forms of data - within the hypertext, created an expansion of the hypertext, named "Hypermedia", terms usually used interchangeably (Landaw, 1992).

Hypermedia Advantages

Hypermedia technology is widely use for its many advantages for learning in any domain. These environments allow learners non-linear, on demand access to deep and efficient exploration of large amounts of complex information and multiple-representation learning materials, in accordance with personal learning styles, personal preferences for navigational modes, pace, time, and interest (Barrett, 2000; Collier, 1987; Dillon & Gabbard, 1998; Dillon & Jobst, 2005; Landow, 1992; Nielsen, 1995). Materials composing hypermedia learning environments - diverse contents and relevant representations - may be designed and organized to reflect human knowledge organization, decreasing involved mental efforts. They may be linked according to any desired principles and are subjected to continuous updating by modification, elaboration, and reorganization of composites, constituting a high-potential tool for promoting acquisition of complex topics (Carpenter & Taylor, 2003; Delany & Gilbert, 1991; Jonassen & Reeves, 1996). Learning with hypermedia was found to promote independent study, problem solving (Bera & Liu, 2006; Tabatabai & Shore, 2005), meta-cognitive abilities (Moos & Azevedo, 2006), and learners' motivation (Wishart, 2000). Many of these studies are related to literacy and to science – examining the promotion of knowledge and skills as well as self regulation of learning (Koehler, 2002; Moos & Azevedo, 2006; Liu, 2005).

Hypermedia Constraints and Limitations

However, some researchers cautioned against the overarching use of hypertext, due to the lack of empirical evidences that demonstrate the educational benefits of learning with it and the multiple factors that may shape learning outcomes (Chen & Rada, 1996; Dillon, 1996; Dillon & Jobst, 2005; Landauer, 1995; McKnight, Dillon & Richardson, 1991, 1996). Some reviews of results and meta-analysis concerning studies reporting observations of learning with hypertext revealed large individual differences in users' responses to this technology and mix benefits (Chen & Rada, 1996; Nielsen, 1989). In their review of experimental findings concerning quantitative effects of hypertext/hypermedia on learning outcomes, Dillon and Gabbard (1998) found that the benefit gained were quite limited. They noted that advantages are seen when a rapid search through a large number of documents is required, that the increased control over access to information may be detrimental for low ability students, and particular interface designs have to be suited to certain learning styles to be effective. They concluded that learners' style of interaction with the hypermedia was crucial for understanding learning in this environment. They suggest that passive learners are more influenced by cuing of information, and that the combination of an active motivated search with learners' ability probably determines the outcomes of their use of this medium (Dillon & Gabbard, 1998).

Learning in hypermedia environments may be influenced by any number of factors, shown to affect learning processes in general; among them are: the characteristics of the knowledge domain involved (e.g., ill- or well-structured, complexity); nature of the materials to be studies and the extent of its overloading the working memory (e.g., organizational structure - possibly initiating a split attention effect and minimizing the contiguity effect; spatiality – increasing the complexity of perceptional processes and information processing while, for example attempting to link among detached information pieces; dynamics – requiring the perception of a large amount of information per time unit; multimodal and/or multimedia - burdening the visual channel with both text and images), all which may impose on learners a high cognitive load, which may result in a low level processing of the presented information (Chandler & Sweller, 1991, 1992; Mayer, 2005; Moreno & Mayer, 1999; Sweller, 1988); or individuals' relevant prior knowledge and beliefs, cognitive abilities, interests, learning styles or cognitive flexibility (Spiro et al., 1991). Small differences were found for gender, but not enough to produce gains (Dillon & Jobst, 2005).

Therefore, an examination of the cognitive benefits of the hypermedia medium for learning and instruction of certain ill-structured and complex materials like art and performance art in particular, is called for. The present chapter attempts to follow Dillon and Gabbards' (1998) conclusions and shed some more light on students' style of interaction with the hypermedia and relevant cognitive outcomes of their constructed knowledge and understanding of performance art.

LEARNING ART WITH HYPERMEDIA: THE CASE OF PERFORMANCE ART

Art: An Ill-Structured Domain

Contrary to Science domains, art is an ill-structure knowledge domain, characterized by continuous change of its concepts and their meanings as well as of its ideas - while being applied in diverse situations, and by its deficiency in strict rules to guide learners in their attempts to understand information and process it. To arrive at deep understanding, learners have to acquire and actively construct networks of concepts and principles concerning a phenomenon, which they may apply for its interpretation (Efland, 2002; Short, 1995). In spite of this complexity, high school students were shown to mostly respond to images on a level of recognition – rather than analysis, unless intentionally taught to analyze images and decode their intended meaning (Beach & Freedman, 1992; Freedman & Wood, 1999).

Artworks are created in diverse contexts regarding periods, political, religious or social variables. They are being influenced by these contexts as well as by their creators' biography, perspectives, and beliefs. Constructing artwork interpretations involves paying attention to all their specific interacting components, which therefore, may give rise to many different interpretations with no specific one being preferred or correct. Rather, art seeks 'credible' interpretations that account for as many as possible internal relations among artwork components and their meaning as well as external influencing components like, the artist biography and artwork contexts (Efland, 2002). Freedman (2003) defined the low-level interpretive skills as "discernment of a simple, intended message of a symbolic representation or personalizing a situation that one sees represented" (p. 87) to be distinguished from high-level interpretive skills, which includes individual's unpacking of underlying assumptions and representing the context, forming multiple associations – thus meanings, and performing a self-conscious, critical reflection, being aware of associative knowledge (Freedman, 2003).

Multiple interpretations of an artwork may also evolve from observers' (learners) interactions with it through processes of sensation and perception as well as possible effects of their prior knowledge, beliefs, abilities, and more. Such factors may lead learners to notice and focus their attention on certain aspects of an artwork but not others, hence constructing different interpretations. Great attention is currently placed in art education on the importance of makers-viewers relationships. Awareness of different interpretations, combining interpretations, comparing among them and challenging interpretations increase understanding of artworks and enriches culture – new insights granting new meanings to traditional artworks (Efland, 2002; Freedman, 2003).

Learning Art with Hypermedia

As described above, art education is inherently complex: an ill-structured domain, interdisciplinary in nature, involving many forms of representations and requiring many layers of analysis for constructing deep understanding. Such characteristics may favor the use of hypertext as a learning environment that may reduce some of these complexities and make learning art more feasible. Such learning requires high cognitive flexibility for the construction of networks of interrelated ideas that may grant meaning to various artworks (Spiro, Feltovich, Jacobson & Coulson, 1991). New information perceived, activates relevant knowledge stored in these networks in the long-term memory, enabling their retrieval for further processing and elaboration. Therefore individuals' repeated encounters with the same phenomenon but from different points of view, increase the formation of links that enable entrance points to these networks, and thereby the chance for the retrieval of relevant knowledge, it's processing and the making meaning of it. Spiro, et al., (1991) used the hypermedia as an environment that may promote such learner-materials encounters.

However, in spite of the belief that hypermedia enhances the focus and purpose of art education, few studies only investigated learning art in this environment, using mostly authoring software (Carpenter & Taylor, 2003; Taylor, 2000; Taylor & Carpenter, 2002). Mostly they examined the learning of static art, demonstrating the advantages of the hypermedia-based environment. Dynamic art, as any other dynamic visualization, imposes on students additional difficulties.

Performance Art: A Dynamic External Visualization

The term "performance art" (PA) is used to describe a live dynamic artistic event, performed by artists in front of an audience, at a certain place and point in time. Artists' voices are conveyed via a medium chosen by them, responding to political, social, economic, or other aspects of present reality, expressing their engagement in social examination and reconstruction as well as shaping self- and ethnic identities (Leigh-Green, 1999). PA messages emerge from weaving implicitly interrelated images – some of them symbolic - frequently perceived as detached, into new conceptual realities – requiring observers to make meaningful connections among these bits of messages (Goldberg, 1995). They may be international, touching upon universal, national or local issues (e.g., ecology, racism, feminism). Thus, PA as an ill-structured domain poses a great challenge for learners on the one hand but as a major, current form of art, common in museums, its instruction becomes imperative.

However, studies concerning the teaching of PA, its analysis and interpretation are scare. Basic pedagogies for the instruction of dynamic PA have therefore, to draw on theories concerning other types of artworks (Barrett, 2000, 2003; Efland, 2002; Freedman, 2003; Short, 1995; Stout, 1995). Artworks represent a variety of complex ideas, partly explicit and easily identified and partly implicit. Implicit ideas require the identification of relevant information that would enable the understanding of the artwork meaning. The processes involved in the construction of deep understanding of artworks were described in a model (Short, 1995). It suggests that artworks embody seven distinct levels of information, that may be identified and defined in accordance with the extent of learners' depth of understanding as it materialized while observing and analyzing the artwork, and constructing its 'credible' interpretation: (a) Identify structural elements (e.g., the medium: oil, video art) in relation to formative qualities of the PA (e.g., composition, harmony); (b) Describe the artwork's components/elements – namely, what is seen in it, their interrelations and the artwork as a whole; (c) Identify expressional characteristics and related symbols; (d) Revealing the meaning of the various artwork components/elements and symbols, as well as of the artwork as a whole, by identifying the artwork cultural/historical context of creation, artist's biography, and his/her additional artworks; (e) Construct comprehensive interpretations and arrive at a global understanding of the complete artwork; (f) Develop a sense of aesthetics based on awareness of beauty and artistic value; (g) Construct a critical appraisal of artwork qualities as compared to other artworks and based on its importance in the particular social and artistic context (Short, 1995).

Awareness of the first three levels (a to c) - the artwork internal structural elements - is expressed in the ability to describe the artwork, and constitutes the basis for making meaning of it (Barrett, 2000). Levels d to f relate to the utilization of relevant external information, including aesthetic considerations. Meaning is granted to this information based on the context of artwork as well as on the artist's ideas, beliefs, and messages as they - and the various components/elements they contain - are frequently expressed in his/her other artworks as well (Efland, 2002). This process leads to the construction of a global understanding of the artwork (Walker, 1996). The seventh and last level integrates the entire knowledge constructed in the prior six levels, into the ability to critically appraise the artwork. Such appraisal requires the observers' aesthetic awareness, which is developed by their exposure to a large variety of artworks, representing diverse contexts, cultures, and styles (Stout, 1995). The importance of social and cultural critique as a constructive force in arts communities is well established. It constitutes a form of artists responding to and expressing of positions and opinions concerning various social, political and economic phenomena occurring in the society or milieu (Freedman, 2003).

Hence, art instruction seeks to develop students' ability to construct valid and reliable, credible interpretations, which accounts for the seven information levels described above, rather than a single 'correct' interpretation. Due to the aforementioned characteristics of PA closely fitting hypermedia advantages, and due to hypermedia being a high-potential tool for promoting acquisition of complex topics (Jonassen & Reeves, 1996), we have selected this medium and constructed a hypermedia-based environment for the learning and instruction of PA, as is described next.

HYPERMEDIA-BASED CURRICULUM UNIT

Hypermedia-Based Unit Content and Structure

The PA selected for this curriculum unit is Joseph Beuys' PA, *"I like America and America likes me,"* presented in the Rene Block Gallery in New York (1974), being well known and typical example of PA. This PA is rich with cultural, political and social elements and symbols. The meaning of the artwork may be weaved in various ways from these many detached meanings and facts. Being a prototypical PA, well known and researched, large amount of easy to access information is available on the internet about the artist, his work, this PA and its context of creation. Since the main purpose of this chapter is a discussion of the hypertext as an environment for learning a dynamic, ill-structure knowledge domain rather than of the art itself, no description of the artwork is discussed here.

The hypermedia-based curriculum unit was specially designed for the instruction of PA interpretational skills. It contains information presented in diverse representations on the hypermedia different 24 pages (i.e., text, photographs and video clips). Links among various pages enabled an easy nonlinear access to information. Unit structure and function were designed in accordance with (a) the aforementioned research-based instructional pedagogies; (b) cognitive aspects of learning regarding skill acquisition and instruction, metacognition, and knowledge transfer (for example, Anderson, 1993; Eilam, 2004; Nickerson, 1987; Salomon & Globerson, 1987; Salomon & Perkins, 1989); and (c) promotion of cognitive and metacognitive processes in hypermedia-based environment (for example, Azevedo, 2005; Calcaterra, Antonietti & Underwood, 2005; Moos & Azevedo, 2006; Tabatabai & Shore, 2005).

The hypermedia-based unit structure matched the characteristics of the ill-structured PA and composed of four parts, paralleling the four main levels of artwork analysis: (a) artwork details - presented in English, including artist's and artwork names, artwork medium and location of its performance; (b) PA description – in 24 pages eliciting awareness to its various scenes. Each page contains a static picture of a typical PA scene view, a verbal description of the elements and activities presented in it, and navigation arrows that enable the returning to a previous scene or proceeding to the next one. The 24th page contains a link for proceeding to the third part of the curriculum; (c) artwork interpretation – focusing learners on relevant information regarding the artwork, on ways of identifying and granting meaning to its components and symbols as well as integrating it all into a meaningful creation. Pictures of the artwork components/elements are presented with links to multimedia information about each of them, the artists' biography, his other artworks, and the historical/cultural context in which this artwork was created. These representations support and complement each other, but also constrain learners' many possible interpretations of the artwork (Ainsworth, 1999). The presentation of components as distinct rather than as unnoticed parts of a dynamic continuous whole may decrease cognitive load (Chandler & Sweller, 1991). In addition, the contiguity between relevant presentations (Mayer & Moreno, 2002) frees mental efforts for carrying out processes involved in the artwork interpretation. In the upper part of each of the interpretation pages, two lines of navigation icons enable the moving to any other page; and (d) aesthetic and critical appraisal of the artwork - a page containing in addition to relevant contents also the lines of navigation icons, to enable the reexamination of any previous part.

Two modes of navigation among pages were designed. The first, performed through the interpretation page. This page contains pictures, each constituting a link to a specific information page, enabling users to return to the interpretation page from any other unit page and proceed from it to any other page by pressing a picture. The second, by using icons in a line located on the top of each unit page, which enable users to move to any other unit page at any desired order. Learners' exposure to this amount and type of information, presented nonlinearly, as well as to various possible interpretations constitutes cognitive scaffolding in the process of acquiring independent ability to analyze PA (Yelland & Masters, 2007).

HYPERMEDIA-BASED CURRICULUM UNIT EFFECTIVENESS

Our Case Study

Students were given the relevant PA video on a computer screen, and were asked to interpret independently this artwork, with no guidance or time limitation, using any web information source they desire as well as paper and pen, while thinking aloud. During the 2nd phase they were given in addition to the artwork also the hypertext-based learning unit, which taught them the processes of PA interpretation. In order to expose learners' detailed behaviors (e.g., strategies, thoughts, navigation) as they gradually unfold in the course of learning art and interacting with the hypermedia-based unit we focused on several individual learners only. These learners were seven 12th graders (age 17-18 years old), four girls and three boys majoring in art who were selected by their teachers for their high scores in art, ability to express thoughts clearly, to use the computer and the web, and for their knowledge of English. The analysis of learners' detailed behaviors yielded some core patterns underlying learners' learning modes.

A screen capturing software and camera as well as a web camera recording learners' faces revealed the advantages of learning art with hypermedia (e.g., navigation modes, screen manipulations) and enabled a fine grain analysis of learners activities and their captured 'think aloud' transcripts. Observational protocols of engagement with the unit and of task performance in addition to learners' written notes supplemented the data. Video-recorded interviews with each learner concerning his/her notions and product of each learning phase, were conducted and further clarified observed processes.

Outcome knowledge and understanding were examined by applying a fine grain analysis to the various data gathered during the three learning phases, each performed by students individually, with interviews conducted several days following each phase, and next phase being performed several days after each interview: (a) First phase – Beuys' PA interpretation, having no prior knowledge of PA; (b) Second phase - learning the hypermedia-based curriculum unit followed by same PA interpretation; and (c) Third phase - transfer of acquired knowledge for the interpretation of a new, entirely different PA - Carolee Schneemann's *"Up to and including her limits"* (1976). The comparison between the outcomes of phases (a) and (b) for each learner enabled the evaluation of the hypermedia-based unit contribution to learning, whereas phase (c) outcomes revealed the extent of learners' understanding and their acquisition of the skill of PA interpretation, using hypermedia environment.

Two profiles of learning processes emerged for each learner from two distinct microanalyses: (a) An *activity profile* – emerging from the application of criteria defined as "units of activity," describing the learning activities performed by students all through their PA interpretation (e.g., watching whole/parts of PA video, raising questions on observed video, entering sites, navigational mode, examining reading materials superficially/deeply). This detailed profile enabled learning characterization; and (b) *Level of understanding profile* - emerging from the application of eight criteria for understanding based on Short's model (1995) (see p. 5). This profile enabled the evaluation of learners' ability to interpret a PA, and as an outcome of their activity profile.

PA Interpretation Ability

Performance usually reflects the interactions between student and task characteristics. Students attended the task equipped with some general prior knowledge concerning the content of several PA elements (e.g., 2nd world war, native Americans, feminism), knowledge concerning art and the analysis of static art - but deficient in knowledge of and experiences with PA as a form of art and its interpretation (e.g., identify elements, awareness of artist biography, symbolization, medium characteristics), some knowledge concerning web information search, and hypermedia (e.g., navigation, sites search, Babylon search), and limited knowledge of English as a second language (required for most web searches). Students' knowledge in each of these areas was quantitatively and qualitatively different. In addition, students' interactions with the task may have been affected by factors like personal characteristics (e.g., motivation), and abilities (e.g., cognitive, perceptual), interest in various topics, and more.

The task involving interpretation of PA, as mentioned above, is far from being intuitive or easy, due to PA complexity; its many internal and external, concrete and abstract interacting elements, mostly having symbolic meanings; PA being a dynamic medium - presenting large amounts of spatial information per time unit; and PA being ill-structured – interpretation is constructed by gradually weaving distinct bits of knowledge about PA components into a coherent, founded, and credible interpretation, which may constitute one of several possible interpretations. It is a highly complex cognitive operation, involving the application of diverse declarative and procedural knowledge. Experiencing the interactive hypermedia-based curriculum, is expected to increase students' awareness of this complexity and to demonstrate possible modes of orchestrating the application of various operations in the aim of weaving interpretation/s. In addition, since none of the participants ever studied about PA, saw PA or knew anything about it, they had to transfer their knowledge of static art interpretation to perform this new, much more complex task.

General Characteristics of Students' Performance

Generally, as reported for most learning situations, students' understanding profiles and PA interpretations were found to be directly related to their interest in the presented content (e.g., dominating cultures, feminism) and their motivation to go on searching and deepening their knowledge, even after feeling their interpretation is ready. Awareness of, and the ability to evaluate one's own quality of interpretation involve the application of metacognitive knowledge throughout the interpretation process, while monitoring and evaluating the information found on the web, the extent to which it explains various PA components and their interrelations, grant them meaning, or how much additional information is required for weaving the comprehensive final interpretation. All these cognitive and metacognitive operations require students' investment of mental efforts, resulting in large differences among their final interpretation products. The mental model they construct in the course of the interpretation process is expected to guide future interpretations. The more experiences involving the application of metacognition, the better students are able to refine and tune the accuracy of this constructed mental model.

Few students were characterized by low interest and motivation and low metacognitive ability regarding the present task. In addition, they seemed to ignore the dynamics and complexity characterizing the PA as a form of art and tried to interpret it as a static form of art; namely, being satisfied in all three phases with the identification of a small number of PA components while performing limited PA observations. Being satisfied with a small amount of superficial information found on the web about PA components and background, students' constructed relations among these few components was limited and their understanding of symbolic meaning highly deficient and concrete. In addition, their deficient monitoring throughout the interpretation process, yielded altogether a shallow, superficial and partial PA interpretation. Contrary to these students, some exhibited high motivation and interest in the presented PA, demonstrating thorough attempts to arrive at a comprehensive interpretation. Although they have employed similar basic activities to achieve their goal (i.e., observation, searches, note taking, and reporting the constructed interpretation), the large differences in outcome products emerged from the qualitative and quantitative characteristics of these activities and of their efficient metacognitive orchestration of these activities, as described next.

(a) Observations: Variations in PA observations were expressed in the number of observations performed, points in time along the interpretation process they were performed, and type of observations performed (i.e., continuous - from beginning to end; alternating – starting and stopping at different points along the PA video according to need; or going back and forth in selected limited video parts). The continuous observation-type allows for the construction of a general impression of the PA and an initial identification of elements and their interrelations, thus constituted a starting point for all students. The second observation-type enables note taking and web searches for clarification and information gathering, thus came latter on in the process. The third observation-type enables clarification of particular instances in the PA or examination of specific details, thus was applied when students had already some understanding of what was going on. The first, continuous observation-type was enacted by all students. The other two types appeared with accordance to students' individual motivation, knowledge and interest in the PA exploration, characterizing more successful students. Only those performing repeated observations were found to overcome to a certain extent, the difficulties inherent in the dynamic PA, by being able to identify a larger number of elements.

(b) Internet Searches: Searches were characterized by several criteria and reflected students' web searching skills, prior knowledge, metacognitive awareness, as well as their interest and motivation to continue deepening their understanding of the art. The selected criteria were: students' choice of a search engine (i.e.., Google), of a web dictionary (i.e., Babylon), of search values (e.g., artist name, artwork name, crossing of artist with artwork names, gallery of PA presentation), language of sites (e.g., English, Hebrew), type of sites, use of links, and mode of processing of located information (i.e., ignoring information, deep reading, superficial reading).

Mostly, all students used Google as a search engine and only few used the Babylon for clarifying unfamiliar words/terms by translating them from English into Hebrew (English being a second language). Some used the translation as is, without making sense of it in the wider context of the PA. Others attempted to clarify the meanings of unknown words as part of the PA holistic conceptual meaning. Frequently it meant perceiving words as symbolic expressions of various PA components, granting them meaning accordingly, advancing considerably students' ability to interpret the PA. This in contrary to a deficient understanding of core words/concepts/terms in the information found, due to not using the dictionary, ignoring them in spite of their being crucial for understanding the PA. Such behaviors hindered students' ability to construct the desired interpretation resulting usually in a superficial and partial one. In addition to web searching skills, it soon became clear that students' motivation and interest, was an important factor in determining how much time and efforts they were ready to invest in the searching for information and in making sense of the PA as a whole by integrating the information found, as directly expressed in students' products quality.

Search focus was greatly determined by the search values students applied. For example, searching according to the name of the artist resulted in a large amount of information about the artist, his life and his works including many links, whereas crossing the artist name with the particular artwork name enabled students to find focused information relevant to the PA interpretation. However, the former brought about students' comparisons among the artist works and ideas, transferring information from one to another, deepening their understanding of the particular PA and promoting their interpretation. In general, large amounts of information brought about students' shifts into a shallow reading, skip most of it, and lose their patience, resulting in a superficial interpretation due to their deficient understanding of many PA details, symbols in particular, and inability to relate among them.

When exposed to the learning hyper-based curriculum unit (in the second study phase) students mostly preferred its exploration by applying a sequential, linear mode of entering the unit pages, ignoring the advantages inherent to the non-linear hypermedia, which allow learners to explore information in accordance with their understanding and their gradual mode of knowledge construction/revision. Instead, the sequential linear entries seemed to ensure students' examination of all 24 unit pages. In any case, skipping many links in the unit meant that students did not collect the entire information relevant for the PA interpretation.

Generally, students entered pages presenting information about components only once, probably because the presented unit information was focused and directly relevant for initial understanding of the PA. They entered few times those pages presenting artist's biography and artwork cultural-historical context, probably since the processing of this information was more complex than the processing of distinct components. Processing information concerning artwork context and artist biography required more entries and time, especially following students' recognition of their potential important contribution to PA interpretations.

Learning the unit increased most students' awareness of the importance of information regarding all PA components and of the complexity involved in weaving these distinct information bits into a comprehensive coherent interpretation. Still, most students entered just a small number of the many links presented in the unit pages, claiming they are tired, lacking interest in the information, having enough information already, feeling they already know it all, preferring to focus merely on important information that would advance their interpretation or claiming they enter only those links that "attracted" them. Some of these explanations reflect a deficient metacognitive ability. In addition, names of links not necessarily reflect their importance and relevance to the PA or cannot be properly evaluated by students who, frequently at this stage, are still deficient in information for evaluating the link.

(c) Notes taking (in addition to writing their final interpretation report): The more information students found and had to integrate – the higher became their cognitive load, due to the limited capacity of working memory. In addition, the dynamics of the PA could have contributed to students' high cognitive load, requiring them to notice, identify, and remember many details that pass before their eyes in a short instance of time, for future processing. Surprisingly, as described above, students made little use of the ability to stop the video or to repeat observations of it's over loaded instances. Taking notes along observations and searches may indeed decrease some of the cognitive load of all students by providing them with an external support.

Notes reflected different levels of information processing during observations and search, therefore were directly related to final products. The most basic level of note taking was expressed in copying full sentences or even paragraphs of the information found on the web as is, hoping to make sense of it latter on. This type of note taking resulted in the accumulation of too much unrelated, distinct bits of written information, which then had to be processed jointly with the PA video information. Since integration of a large amount of unrelated information is not an easy task, mostly these students' interpretation was far from being coherent and holistic. Occasionally, students wrote a list of elements or other details, each with its meaning according to the internet – a more organized and useable form of notes.

Another type of note taking was characterized by students' making sense of the information read by linking it to their own existing knowledge and to details they have identified in the PA, summarizing their integrated ideas in short remarks written in their own words. One student, for example, constructed a table for comparing two artworks of the artist, whereas another drew a diagram representing a sequence of causes and effects linked by arrows. Since this type of notes taking, already involved some processing of information, notes were highly effective in advancing these students' understanding and thereby interpretation of the PA. Writing down single distinct words, concepts, processes or main points, constituted an additional type of note taking. Such notes served mainly as triggers for further activities like observations or searches.

All together, students used notes for various purposes; they were used to decrease cognitive load that was created due to students' attempts to identify and remember large amount of information; to indicate a particular order of events or relations among elements, as encountered by students along task performance; they promoted students' ability to organized and integrate the vast information collected from both the internet and the video; they triggered students' memory regarding the need to further search for a particular information, to process particular information, or the need to discuss the issue/element in the final report.

(d) The final Interpretation Report: As can be expected, interpretation was influenced by all the aforementioned factors and their interactions, yielding very different students' reports. For example, students of high motivation, who have found more information about the PA or its creator, as well as invested larger amounts of efforts in carrying out deep reading, in performing several observations, and in the processing of information into a coherent full interpretation – exhibited full comprehensive reports. This in contrary to students of lower motivation, who limited their observations and were satisfied with the identification of only few PA elements; who stopped searching after having a limited amount and quality of information, thereby exhibited a deficient and superficial interpretation of the PA message; who for the most parts ignored symbols, metaphors and other modes of expression, which constitute the core of PA messages. Another example is that of students that were experienced in web searching, hence arrived at a large amount of information, but had no motivation to pursue the task as far as they could, and were satisfied with a partial and superficial interpretation.

In addition to reflecting students' motivation to invest efforts in observations, searches, and processing of the dynamic PA information, interpretation reports reflected students' profiles of levels of understanding. These profiles showed each student's achievements regarding the seven levels constituting PA interpretation. None of the students offer any interpretation right after their observations (one or two) of the PA. They have begun suggesting some ideas only after reading information about it in the internet. This behavior may evolved from their low self confidence regarding the new dynamic art medium, very different from the static art they have interpreted until that day, or from their being overwhelmed by the vast information and lacking experiences concerning how to deal with it.

Performance Models: Students' Construction of PA Interpretation

Examining students' variations in enacting the described core activities, three types of prototypical performance models emerged. Some variations in the enacted models were found among the three phases of the study and among students. Generally, students' understanding profiles matched the prototype model they applied for achieving the goals of learning how to interpret a PA and transfer the acquired knowledge for the interpretation of a new, different PA. Three prototypical models were found: (a) the multi-stage interactive model, (b) the model of intermediate stages, and (c) the deficient stages model. These models are described next.

The Multi-stage Interactive Model

This model is characterized by cycles of alternating observations and searching, accompanied by notes taking: one to two consecutive observations, web search and reading, an additional observation followed by an additional search and reading, all through accompanied by note taking and completed by reporting the constructed interpretation. Variations among students and phases were expressed in the number of observation-search cycles performed, number of observations in each cycle, type of observation performed – continuous or focused – point in time notes were taken, mode of taking notes, etc. These, in turn were highly influenced by students' motivation and prior knowledge.

However, in spite of these differences, the principle guiding this model, including its variations, is the student-observations-searches-interactions. These interactions promoted the gradual expanding and deepening of students' bodies of knowledge regarding the PA; namely, identifying initial salient PA components, partially making sense of them based on observed video and prior knowledge, searching information about the their meaning and the PA, which in turn revealed more details in the PA, which students tried to identify in a second observation, which brought about the construction of an initial interpretation, which required some more clarification, which led to an additional information search, and raised interest in more general information, which may shed more light on the PA, its context of creation, its ideas and symbols, the artist biography, etc. until students are satisfied with their interpretational product and write the report. This model responds to the need to weave a network of distinct information bits into a coherent whole, by gradually discovering and revealing the meaning of increasing number of PA components and their interrelations.

As seen above, this model also enabled students to overcome the difficulties inherent in the dynamic PA they have just encountered (e.g. identifying as much elements, relations and symbols in it). A gradual increase in most students' interest was evidenced as they became more acquainted with its content and meaning. This brought about their search for details and for information through indirect sources, like the artist biography and artwork context – rather than being satisfied with information directly related to the identified components, yielding a more elaborated, comprehensive and frequently more than a single deep interpretation.

Unsurprisingly therefore, this model yielded profiles of highest understanding levels, including the highest number of identified elements and activities, of interpreted PA symbolic meanings and relations, of application of details from artist biography and context of creation in the construction of the PA interpretation, and a high integration of all the knowledge collected into the most comprehensive interpretation.

The Model of Intermediate Stages

The model is composed of double consecutive observations, search and reading, both accompanied by notes taking, and a final reporting of interpretation. Evidently, it lacks the cycles of interactivity evidenced in the multi-stages model, which seemed to promote the gradual construction of a rich body of knowledge. Instead, each activity type was enacted linearly after the other, resulting in the finding of a certain amount of components during the double observations, and a search, mostly limited to finding information that would explain these components and grant them some acceptable meanings, rather than enrich the second observation and in turn also the following search, etc. Usually, the initial double observations characterizing this model, promoted students' ability to partially overcome the difficulties involved in the PA being dynamic and enabled them to detect more components, have a better general feeling of the PA, a better knowledge of its content (not meanings) and what is seen in it. However, due to deficient information about all relevant elements (including artist biography or artwork context), students were not able to relate among the various identified components, yielding a deficient meaning of particular PA parts or a concrete perceptions of symbolic components. This resulted in a partial and superficial as well as mostly a single PA interpretation.

Another important aspect was that when a particular element in the PA drew students' attention during the observations, they perceived it as central to the PA and constructed their interpretation around it with little chance of changing this first impression. Contrary to this phenomenon, in the cyclic interactive model, the alternations between observation and searches was found to change students' focus and impressions drawing their attention to other, core PA elements, thereby changing the course of their interpretation.

Profiles of understanding of students applying this model reflected these limitations in all levels. Namely, a smaller number of components were identified, fewer relations were formed, symbolic meanings were seldom decoded as well as the small number of relevant details found about artist biography and artwork context having a limited contribution to the understanding of the PA. The artwork was treated as static, ignoring its complex dynamic nature.

The Deficient Stages Model

This model composed of a single observation, followed by a search and reading, sometimes accompanied by notes taking, followed by the writing of interpretation report while conducting a partial observation for the examination of particular selected PA instances. The dynamics and complexity involved in a PA as well as the increased cognitive load, hindered students' ability to identify many of the important PA components and interrelations, most of the components passing through without any notice. Hence, these initial findings constrained the search for information, leading to a deficient interpretation. Deficiency in this case was expressed in the interpretation essentially composing of few identified components – not necessarily core one but rather the salient ones. Mostly, these components were explained separately with no relations to others, to context of creation or to artist biography. Explanations and meanings were frequently concrete rather than abstract; namely, overall interpretation was dull and shallow, lacking comprehensiveness, holism, depth or symbolic meaning.

Observing parts of video during the writing of the report seemed to support recall more than to carry out any other function. The many details described in students' interpretations were mostly a description of what has been seen, rather than an integration of these details into a comprehensive whole with valid meaning. Thus, although each of the two latter models contained two observations, their order and way of enactment as related to the information searches, greatly influenced the outcome interpretation.

Initially, in all three models, students addressed only partially or even not at all, few PA structural elements that could affect the PA understanding and interpretation (i.e., its medium type and characteristics, name, and technical details), but are more salient in a PA than in static art. Since these elements are important for a full PA understanding, it is desired that they would be treated already in the first level. Latter on, after learning the PA unit, several students, mostly those of the multi-stages interactive model, learned to notice these elements and reveal their meaning – improving their interpretation.

The first multi-stage interactive model enabled students to construct the fullest and most efficient mental model of PA interpretation, model that may guide such task in the future. However, this was possible due to interactions with other factors like students' prior knowledge and in particular their metacognitive abilities, interest, and motivation. Students' exposure to the learning unit, frequently promoted their ability, each students according to his/her own characteristics, to construct such a mental model by increasing their awareness of direct relations between the making sense of as many as possible PA components and symbols and the holistic comprehensive outcome interpretation.

SUMMARY AND CONCLUSION

The present study examined the processes involved in students' performance art interpretation, while learning and interacting with information in a hypermedia-based environment. In spite of differences founds among students and differences relating to the dynamic complex task at hand, all students applied the same three basic operations for constructing an interpretation: observation, searching information, and notes taking. Differences among students evolved from the order of enactment of these operations, and from modes of enactment of each operation, including number of times or length of operation use, depth of searching for information, investment of effort in processing information, etc. Modes of operation are in part the outcome of students' interest in the PA, their existing declarative and procedural knowledge, and their motivation, factors usually related to each other.

An analysis of students' order of enactment of the aforementioned operations was found to yield three prototypical models of enactment: (a) the multi-stage interactive model, (b) the model of intermediate stages, and (c) the deficient stages model. As described above, the first model utilized the hypermedia advantages, whereas the third one constituted a linear model, and the second model being an intermediate one, with a partial utilization of the hypermedia environment. This was true for both using the web and learning the unit. The outcomes of a linear or non linear enactment of operations, information searches, and learning were very different, in spite of these models being composed of the same operations. The outcomes of students' enactment of the first multi-stage interactive model were the most valid, credible, comprehensive, and deep PA interpretations. Such interpretations were based on the identification of the larger number of PA components, their interrelations, symbols and events that was made possible and was promoted by the interactions between the products of observations and the information products of searches that explained the products of observations and revealed some new, initially unnoticed ones, and so forth. It seems that this mode of enactment makes the most of the hypermedia advantages, and is most efficient in overcoming the shortcomings inherent to the dynamic visualization, namely, the limitations of perception and the cognitive load evolving from the large amount of information that has to be perceived and processed in a short time, as well as prevail over the high PA complexity with its many layers of processing and understanding. This successful interpretation was contrary to other interpretations, and in particular those constructed by students that enacted the third deficient models, that lacked validity and coherency due to their being based on a limited number of identified PA components and related information found, yielding a partial and highly superficial PA interpretation.

Generally, the PA learning unit successfully introduced the topic and promoted art students' ability to interpret PA. This was evidenced in students' understanding profiles, being higher in most of its criteria in the second phase, after learning the unit, than in the first phase, when students' first encountered this form of art. As is usually the case, performance decreased marginally in the third phase that required students to transfer this acquired knowledge for interpreting a new, very different PA. Students' performance suggested some improvements in the learning unit, for emphasizing and demonstrating those parts and levels of interpretation that students ignored or accounted for unsatisfactorily.

It is most desirable that before using the hypermedia environment for learning and achieving specific targets, students would receive some explanations and training regarding its efficient use, and in particular when the target is dynamic in nature. Such training may increase students' focus and monitoring toward the target, thereby yielding better outcomes than with no training, leaving students to attempt achieving their goals by trial and error. Such mode of using the hypermedia may bring about the construction of an erroneous or deficient mental model that would hinder students' future performance.

This case constitutes an example of learning a dynamic, ill-structured knowledge domain - the performance art - in hypermedia environment. Its conclusions may shed some light on students' decoding of dynamic external visualization like advertizing and the danger of their being manipulated by such and other media messages due to poor decoding that focuses on denotations rather than on connotations. In present visual culture, the abilities examined in the present case may be crucial for future citizens.

REFERENCES

Ainsworth, S. E. (1999). A functional taxonomy of multiple representations. *Computers & Education, 33*(2/3), 131–152. doi:10.1016/S0360-1315(99)00029-9

Anderson, J. R. (1993). Rules of the mind. Hillsdale, NJ: Erlbaum.

Azevedo, R. (2005). Computer environments as metacognitive tools for enhancing learning. *Educational Psychologist, 40*, 193–197. doi:10.1207/s15326985ep4004_1

Barrett, T. (2000). Criticizing art: Understanding the contemporary. New York: McGraw-Hill.

Barrett, T. (2003). Interpreting art: Reflecting, wondering and responding. New York: McGraw-Hill.

Beach, R., & Freedman, K. (1992). Responding as a cultural act: Adolescents' responses to magazine ads and short stories. In J. Many, & C. Cox (Eds.), Reader stance and literary understanding: Exploring the theories, research, and practice, (pp. 162-188). Norwood, NJ: Ablex.

Bera, S., & Liu, M. (2006). Cognitive tools, individual differences, and group processing as mediating factors in a hypermedia environment. *Computers in Human Behavior, 22*, 295–319. doi:10.1016/j.chb.2004.05.001

Beuys, J. (1974). I like America and America likes me. Presented in the gallery Rene Block, New York.

Calcaterra, A., Antonietti, A., & Underwood, J. (2005). Cognitive style, hypermedia navigation and learning. *Computers & Education, 44*, 441–457. doi:10.1016/j.compedu.2004.04.007

Carpenter, B. S., & Taylor, P. G. (2003). Racing thoughts: Altering our ways of knowing and being through computer hypertext. *Studies in Art Education, 45*(1), 40–55.

Chandler, P., & Sweller, J. (1991). Cognitive load theory and the format of instruction. *Cognition and Instruction, 8*, 293–332. doi:10.1207/s1532690xci0804_2

Chandler, P., & Sweller, J. (1992). The split-attention effect as a factor in the design of instruction. *The British Journal of Educational Psychology, 62*, 233–246.

Chen, C., & Rada, R. (1996). Interacting with hypertext: A meta-analysis of experimental studies. *Human-Computer Interaction, 11*, 125–156. doi:10.1207/s15327051hci1102_2

Collier, G. (1987) Thoth-II: Hypertext with explicit semantics. In Proceedings of hypertext '87 (pp. 269-289). Chapel Hill, NC: University of North Carolina.

Delany, P., & Gilbert, S. (1991). Hypercard stacks for Fielding's Joseph Andrew: Issues of design and content. In P. Delany & G. Landow (Eds.), Hypermedia and literary studies (pp. 287-298). Cambridge, MA: MIT Press.

Dillon, A. (1996). Myths, misconceptions and alternative view of information usage and the electronic medium. In J. Rouét et al. (Eds.), Hypertext and cognition (pp. 25-42). Mahwah, NJ: Erlbaum.

Dillon, A., & Gabbard, R. (1998). Hypermedia as an educational technology: A review of the quantitative research literature on learner comprehension, control, and style. *Review of Educational Research, 68*(3), 322–349.

Dillon, A., & Jobst, J. (2005). Multimedia learning with hypermedia. In R. E. Mayer, (Ed.), The Cambridge handbook of multimedia learning, (pp. 569-588). New York: Cambridge University Press.

Efland, A. D. (2002). Art and cognition: Integrating the visual arts in the curriculum. New York: Teacher College Press.

Eilam, B. (2004). The instruction and acquisition of cognitive skills in Israel: Difficulties and accomplishments. In K. Mutua & C. Szymanski Sunal (Eds.), Research on Education in Africa, The Caribbean, and The Middle East (Vol. 1, Chap. 10, pp.183-202). Greenwich, CT: Information Age Publishing.

Freedman, K. (2003). Teaching visual culture. Curriculum, aesthetics, and the social life of art. New York and London: Teachers College, Columbia University and National Art Education Association.

Freedman, K., & Wood, J. (1999). Students' knowledge of visual culture: Images inside and outside of school. *Studies in Art Education, 40*(2), 128–142. doi:10.2307/1320337

Goldberg, R. (1995). Performance Art: From futurism to the present. London: Thames and Hudson.

Jonassen, D., & Reeves, T. (1996). Learning with technology: Using computers as cognitive tools. In D. Jonassen (Ed.), Handbook of research on communications and technology (pp. 694-719). New York: Mcmillan.

Koehler, M. J. (2002). Designing case-based hypermedia for developing understanding of children's mathematical reasoning. *Cognition and Instruction, 20*(2), 151–195. doi:10.1207/S1532690XCI2002_2

Landauer, T. (1995). The trouble with computers. Cambridge, MA: MIT Press.

Landow, G. P. (1992). Hypertext: The convergence of contemporary critical theory and technology. Baltimore, Maryland: John Hopkins University Press.

Leigh-Green, G. (1999). The return of the body: Performance Art and art education. *Art Education, 52*(1), 6–12. doi:10.2307/3193779

Liu, M. (2005). The effect of technology enhanced learning environment on middle school students' motivation, attitude, and science knowledge. *Computers in the Schools, 22*(3), 159–171. doi:10.1300/J025v22n03_13

Mayer, R. E. (Ed.). (2005). The Cambridge handbook of multimedia learning. New York, NY: Cambridge University Press.

McKnight, C., Dillon, A., & Richardson, J. (1991). Hypertext in context. Cambridge, England: Cambridge University Press.

McKnight, C., Dillon, A., & Richardson, J. (1996). User centered design of hypertext and hypermedia for education. In D. Jonassen (Ed.), Handbook of research on educational communications and technology (pp. 622-633). New York: Macmillan.

Moos, D. C., & Azevedo, R. (2006). The role of goal structure in undergraduates' use of self-regulatory variables in two hypermedia learning tasks. *Journal of Educational Multimedia and Hypermedia, 15*(1), 49–86.

Moreno, R., & Mayer, R. E. (1999). Cognitive principles of multimedia learning: The role of modality and contiguity. *Journal of Educational Psychology, 91*, 358–368. doi:10.1037/0022-0663.91.2.358

Nickerson, R. (1987). Why teach thinking? In J. B. Baron, and R. J. Sternberg (Eds.), Teaching thinking skills: Theory and Practice (pp. 27-37). New York: W. H. Freeman.

Nielsen, J. (1989). The matters that really matter for hypertext usability. Paper presented at the Hypertext '89' Second ACM Conference on Hypertext, Pittsburgh, PA.

Nielsen, J. (1995). Multimedia and hypertext: The internet and beyond. Cambridge, MA: Cambridge Academic Press.

Salomon, G., & Globerson, T. (1987). Skills may not be enough: The role of mindfulness in learning and teaching. *International Journal of Educational Research, 11*(6), 623–627. doi:10.1016/0883-0355(87)90006-1

Salomon, G., & Perkins, D. (1989). Rocky road to transfer: Rethinking mechanisms of a neglected phenomenon. *Educational Psychologist, 24*(2), 113–142. doi:10.1207/s15326985ep2402_1

Schneemann, C. (1976). *Up to and including her limits*.

Short, G. (1995). Understanding domain knowledge for teaching: Higher-order thinking in preservice art teacher specialist. *Studies in Art Education, 36*(3), 154–169. doi:10.2307/1320906

Spiro, R. J., Feltovitch, P. J., Jacobson, M. J., & Coulson, R. L. (1991). Cognitive flexibility, constructivism, and hypertext: Random access instruction for advanced knowledge acquisition in ill-structured domains. *Educational Technology, 31*(5), 24–33.

Stout, C. J. (1995). Critical conversation about art: A description of higher order thinking skills generated through the study of art criticism. *Studies in Art Education, 36*(3), 170–188. doi:10.2307/1320907

Sweller, J. (1988). Cognitive load during problem solving: Effects on learning. *Cognitive Science, 12*, 257–285.

Tabatabai, D., & Shore, B. M. (2005). How experts and novices search the web. *Library & Information Science Research, 27*, 222–248. doi:10.1016/j.lisr.2005.01.005

Taylor, P. G., & Carpenter, B. S. (2002). Inventively linking: Teaching and learning with computer hypertext. *Art Education, 55*(4), 6–12. doi:10.2307/3193962

Taylor, (2000). Madonna and hypertext: Liberatory learning in art education. *Studies in Art Education, 41*(4), 376-389.

Tisdall, C. (1979). Joseph Beuys. London: Thames and Hudson.

Tisdall, C. (1990). Beuys in America, or the energy plan for the western man. In C. Kuoni (Ed.), Energy plan for the western man/Joseph Beuys in America: Writings by and interviews with the artist (pp. 7-18). New York: Four Walls Eight Windows.

Walker, S. R. (1996). Thinking strategies for interpreting artworks. *Studies in Art Education, 37*(2), 80–91. doi:10.2307/1320509

Wishart, J. (2000). Students' and teachers' perceptions of motivation and learning through the use in schools of multimedia encyclopedias on CD-ROM. *Journal of Educational Multimedia and Hypermedia, 9*(4), 333–347.

Yelland, N., & Masters, J. (2007). Rethinking scaffolding in information age. *Computers & Education, 48*, 362–382. doi:10.1016/j.compedu.2005.01.010

ADDITIONAL READING

Ainsworth, S., & VanLabeke, N. (2004). Multiple forms of dynamic representation. *Learning and Instruction, 14*, 241–255. doi:10.1016/j.learninstruc.2004.06.002

Azevedo, R. (2002). Beyond intelligent tutoring systems: Using computers as METAcognitive tools to enhance learning? *Instructional Science, 30*, 31–45. doi:10.1023/A:1013592216234

Azevedo, R. (2005). Using hypermedia as a metacognitive tool for enhancing student learning? The role of self-regulated learning. *Educational Psychologist, 40*(4), 199–209. doi:10.1207/s15326985ep4004_2

Bennet, L. T., & Dwyer, F. M. (1994). The effect of varied visual interactive strategies in facilitating student achievement of different educational objectives. *International Journal of Instructional Media, 21*(1), 23–32.

Bodemer, D., Ploetzner, R., Feuerlein, I., & Spada, H. (2004). The active integration of information during learning with dynamic and interactive visualization. *Learning and Instruction, 14*, 325–341. doi:10.1016/j.learninstruc.2004.06.006

Carpenter, B. S., & Taylor, P. G. (2006). Making meaningful connections: Interactive computer hypertext in art education. *Computers in the Schools, 23*(1/2), 149–161. doi:10.1300/J025v23n01_13

Chandler, P. (2004). The crucial role of cognitive processes in the design of synamic visualizations. *Learning and Instruction, 14*, 353–357. doi:10.1016/j.learninstruc.2004.06.009

Efland, A. D. (1995). The spiral and the lattice: Changes in cognitive learning theory with implications for art education. *Studies in Art Education, 36*(3), 134–153. doi:10.2307/1320905

Emmison, M., & Smith, P. (2000). Researching the visual. London, Thousand Oaks, New Delhi: SAGE Publications.

Freedman, K. (2003). Teaching visual culture. Curriculum aesthetic and the social life of art. New York and London: Teachers College, Columbia University and National Art Education Association.

Freedman, K., & Hernandez, F. (Eds.). (1998). Curriculum, culture, and art education. Comparative perspectives. Albany, NY: State University of New York.

Goldstein, B. E. (2002). Sensation and perception (6th ed.). Pacific Grove, CA: Wadsworth- Thomson Learning. Goodman, N. (1069). Languages of art. An approach to a theory of symbols. London, UK: Oxford University Press.

Hebet, M., Ponce, J., Boult, T., & Gross, A. (Eds.). (1994). Object representation in computer vision. International NSF-ARPA Workshop, New York City, NY, USA, December 5-7, 1994 proceedings. Springer.

Hegarty, M. (2004). Dynamic visualizations and learning: Getting to the difficult questions. *Learning and Instruction, 14*, 343–351. doi:10.1016/j.learninstruc.2004.06.007

Lowe, R. (2004). Interrogation of a dynamic visualization during learning. *Learning and Instruction, 14*, 257–274. doi:10.1016/j.learninstruc.2004.06.003

Mare, E. R. (2001). Multimedia learning. New York, NY: Cambridge University Press.

McDonald, S., & Stevenson, R. J. (1998). Effects of text structure and prior knowledge of the learner on navigation in Hypertext. *Human Factors, 40*(1), 18–27. doi:10.1518/001872098779480541

Morrow, J. (1997). Dynamic visualization from middle school through college. In J. R. King, & D. Schattschneider, (Eds.), Geometry turned on! Dynamic software in learning, teaching and research. Washington, DC: Mathematical Association of America.

Puntambekar, S., & Stylisnou, A. (2005). Designing navigation support in hypertext systems based on navigation patterns. *Instructional Science, 33*, 451–481. doi:10.1007/s11251-005-1276-5

Rose, G. (2001). Visual methodologies. An introduction to the interpretation of visual materials. London, Thousand Oaks, New Delhi: SAGE Publications.

Schwan, S., & Riempp, R. (2004). The cognitive benefits of interactive videos: Learning to tie nautical knots. *Learning and Instruction, 14*, 293–305. doi:10.1016/j.learninstruc.2004.06.005

Taylor, P. G., & Carpenter, B. S. (2005). Computer hypertextual "uncovering" in art education. *Journal of Educational Multimedia and Hypermedia, 14*(1), 25–45.

van Leeuwen, T., & Jewitt, C. (Eds.). (2001). Handbook of visual analysis. London, Thousand Oaks, New Delhi: SAGE Publications.

Van Someren, M. W., Reimann, P., Boshuizen, H. P. A., & de Jong, T. (Eds.). (1998). Learning with multiple representations. Oxford, UK: Elsevier Science Ltd.

Zahn, C., Barquero, B., & Schwan, S. (2004). Learning with hyperlinked videos – design criteria and efficient strategies for using audiovisual hypermedia. *Learning and Instruction, 14*, 275–291. doi:10.1016/j.learninstruc.2004.06.004

KEY TERMS AND DEFINITIONS

Hypertext: This term was coined by Theodor H. Nelson and it refers to a form of electronic multilinear or multi-sequential series of text chunks connected by electronic links in an open-ended, reversible mode, having no beginning or end, offering readers different navigational pathways and access to information through several entrances, without any one of them surpassing the rest

Hypermedia: It is integration of various modalities - visual information, sound, animation and other forms of data - within the hypertext.

Performance Art: It is used to describe a live dynamic artistic event, performed by artists in front of an audience, at a certain place and point in time.

Artworks: These are created in diverse contexts regarding periods, political, religious or social variables. They are being influenced by these contexts as well as by their creators' biography, perspectives, and beliefs.

Chapter 14
Using Email as a Cultural Bridge in the Learning Process for Transnational Students

Sandra Wilson Smith
Rowan University and Union College, USA

ABSTRACT

Today many American composition and rhetoric courses are theme-based and have an embedded focus on social, political, and/or popular cultural issues. This kind of course can be especially challenging for transnational students who are less conversant with this cultural information than many of their native-born peers. In these classes, writing assignments that incorporate interviewing as a part of the information gathering process often allow transnational students to build a kind of cultural bridge between their native country and the U.S. Email can be used to help facilitate this process. What the author focuses on in this case is how email discussion can be incorporated organically into a learning/writing task, and how this discussion can be student-framed. The fact that the students initiate the email communication of their own volition taps into the positive qualities that computer-mediated communication (CMC) has. The students are empowered to act autonomously and construct their own learning activity.

ORGANIZATIONAL BACKGROUND

This case involves a satellite campus of a large public university in the northeastern part of the United States. The main campus serves approximately 10,000 students while the satellite campus serves about 500 students. The satellite campus is located in an economically disadvantaged urban community of roughly 80,000 residents. Although this community had once been a thriving city that offered secure employment for its residents with jobs at manufacturers such as RCA Victor and Campbell Soup, in the late 1960s it began to experience a significant decline in manufacturing, as did many urban centers in the United States. The city eventually experienced major urban decay and currently suffers from a high crime rate and a troubled public school system. Data from the United States Census Bureau indicates that in 2005 approximately 44% of the city's residents lived in

DOI: 10.4018/978-1-61520-779-4.ch014

poverty. The 2000 Census reports that the city has a very high minority population, with 53.3% of the residents identifying as African-American and 38.8% as Hispanic.

The satellite campus offers a variety of courses that meet the general education requirements for most majors, and it provides complete four-year programs for a limited number of majors, such as early childhood education, sociology and criminal justice. Most of the students eventually move on to the main campus to complete their degree requirements. A high percentage of the students at the satellite campus are enrolled in the university through the Educational Opportunity Fund Program, which is designed to support financially and educationally disadvantaged students. In addition, a high percentage of the students are English as Second Language (ESL) students, and many complete our ESL program before matriculating to the university.

SETTING THE STAGE

As the primary instructor of the required first-year composition and rhetoric courses at the satellite campus, I have had to seek out effective ways of enhancing the language learning experiences of the ESL students in my classes. Complicating matters, the ESL students themselves fall into several categories. The first group could be labeled "transnational students." On rare occasions these transnational students are international students, who come to the United States to complete their college degree and then return to their home country; more often, though, these are students who have recently immigrated to the United States, having lived here for one to six years. These students completed their high school education, or even some college, in their home country. They tend to still have significant ties to their country of origin and remain in close contact with family members and friends there. The second group of ESL students immigrated to the U.S. with their families when they were children or teens and attended some elementary and/or high school in this country, often in ESL or bi-lingual programs. The last group of ESL students immigrated to the U.S. as very young children or were born here, and thus, grew up speaking both English and their family's native language. These students generally speak the family's native language at home. While the students themselves tend to be quite Americanized and speak idiomatic English, their writing still demonstrates many of the grammatical errors that characterize the writing of ESL students, such as problems with verbs (tense and agreement), prepositions, and articles. I am primarily focused on the transnational population in this case.

As matriculated students at the university, all these ESL students are enrolled in the regular, required composition classes with native speakers. In recent years, my composition classes have had an enrollment of between 50 to 90% ESL students. In the last few years, the largest ESL populations have come from Vietnam, the Dominican Republic and Puerto Rico. Students at the satellite campus often begin their writing course work with a Basic Writing class, a non-credit pre-college level writing course, before moving on to the required College Composition I and II courses. In this case, I focus on a College Composition I class.

The transnational student population that I am examining in this case tends to be fairly technologically savvy. They often have their own email account as well as the one provided by the university. They frequently use cell phones, webcams, and instant messaging services like Yahoo! Messenger to stay connected with friends and family. They regularly use the Internet to find information.

However, the satellite campus does not provide much in the way of computer technology or training to support instruction. It does provide two computer labs for the students to use and good access to electronic databases through the library's web page, but no computer technology is available for classroom use. While Blackboard is available on-line for instructors to post class materials on, no training has been offered at the satellite campus on how to use this (or any other) technology.

CASE DESCRIPTION

Considering Transnational Students in American Composition Courses

We have come to understand that writing is a socio-cultural activity. For instance, Brian Street (1995) explains how "social and material conditions affect. .. a given form of communication" (p. 1). As an instructor of writing at a state university in an urban center in the United States, I have grappled with the socio-cultural nature of writing because many of my students were born and raised for a significant portion of their lives in another country, and now they are performing the act of writing in the U.S. These students not only contend with issues such as learning English grammar, syntax and vocabulary; they also have to learn the conventions of the American academic essay/research paper. In addition, the reading and writing required in composition courses often demand that students employ wide-ranging knowledge about national history, popular culture, contemporary political issues, and other cultural phenomena. In fact, today many composition courses are theme-based and have an embedded focus on social, political, and/or popular cultural issues. For example, an instructor might design a composition course around the topic of popular entertainment and focus on American music, television and movies in the reading and writing assignments. This kind of course can be especially challenging for students who have lived in the country for only a few years and are consequently less conversant with this cultural information than many of their native-born peers. College professors who have been used to working almost exclusively with native-born students may not at first recognize the complex network of cultural information that we expect our students to have at their fingertips; however, as the college-bound immigrant/ESL population continues to rise in the U.S., more professors will have to consciously consider how the construction of their courses has an impact on the learning of this population.

I, too, use a theme-based approach in my composition courses, employing a non-fiction book as a point of focus. In previous years my classes have concentrated on popular culture, and I have used Steven Johnson's book *Everything Bad Is Good For You: How Today's Popular Culture Is Actually Making Us Smarter* (2005), which examines popular media, such as video games, television shows, and the Internet. For the 2008-2009 academic year, I decided to use Jean M. Twenge's book *Generation Me* (2006), which provides analysis of generational differences between the Baby Boomers, born between 1946 and 1964, and today's young generation that Twenge labels "Generation Me." I chose this text because I thought that it would be effective in terms of allowing the students to develop a good understanding of research-based argumentative and analytical writing, and I also thought that the students would enjoy reading a book about their own generation. They would have a knowledge base with which to evaluate the argument Twenge makes. For the native-born students in my class, this was clearly the case; however, I also had a group of Vietnamese students in the class who had lived in the U.S. for only one to five years, and they had less of a knowledge base with which to evaluate the argument in the book, which focuses on differences between two generations of Americans.

However, two factors arose that made the use of this book a very effective learning experience for these transnational students. The first factor was that after reading the first couple of chapters, these Vietnamese students perceived that the generational differences Twenge provides analysis of regarding the behavior and attitudes of older and younger American generations holds true for the older and younger generations in Vietnam today. Although I had not considered it when selecting the book for my course, in recent years, Vietnam has experienced significant westernization as the government has moved away from a more closed Communist system to a more open free-market system. In the last ten years, significant foreign investment has come into the country and Vietnam's business climate has been internationalized. The traditionally agricultural country has increasing moved towards an economy based on manufacturing and information technology industries. These material changes in the economy have influenced people's behavior and value systems, and thus, my Vietnamese students saw that much of Twenge's commentary on American young people could describe themselves as well.

The second factor that allowed for more effective learning with this population was the use of interviewing as part of the first essay assignment. In the composition courses that I teach, I like to include interviewing as part of the process of gathering information for at least one of the essays written during the semester. The educational experiences that most of my students have had privilege written, published sources. During their school careers, the students have been asked to write research papers and reports that draw on articles and books for information. However, I also want my students to consider how oral and/or unpublished sources of information, such as interviews with knowledgeable people, can be valuable. Unforeseen by me, this interviewing process often opens up a window between the two cultural environments that my transnational students have experienced; it has allowed them to build a kind of cultural bridge between their native country and the U.S. Mary Louise Pratt (1991) describes this kind of writing activity as one of the "literate arts of the contact zone" in the "transnationalized metropolis of the United States" (p. 36), the contact zone being a location where elements of two cultures meet and grapple with each other, producing new kinds of texts and/or knowledge.

An examination of how I used *Generation Me* that first semester in my College Composition I course will help illustrate the concept of this contact zone and will also illustrate how email can come into play to help facilitate learning in this contact zone. The research methodology that I have used in this case is ethnographic in nature. I collected information in three ways: through first-hand observations of my students in the classroom and during individual conferences outside of class; through informal conversations with students; and through formal interviews conducted with the transnational students in the class. Before presenting my case, however, I will provide some background information on the use of CMC in connection with teaching composition.

Computer-Mediated Communication and Composition Courses

Both writing and learning are inevitably affected by new technologies. As the computer and the Internet made their way into the everyday lives of more people, instructors of writing began to consider how CMC could be effectively incorporated into their teaching and classrooms. Instructors of composition and rhetoric were often the first to incorporate CMC into their pedagogy and to theorize its effect on learning, but second and foreign language instructors quickly followed. Both synchronous electronic discussions, such as those offered in networked classrooms, and asynchronous communication, such as those offered by electronic discussion boards and email, have received significant scholarly attention in the last few years. Many scholars, especially as CMC technology was emerging, have focused on the positive effects of using this kind of communication as a part of writing instruction. People have argued that this kind of discussion, which does not take place face-to-face but rather inside the more level playing field of a virtual space, democratizes learning and empowers students, giving them a more equal voice in the knowledge-building process (Cononelos and Oliva, 1993; Warschauer, Turbee and Roberts, 1996, Yan, 2008). These scholars and others have suggested that this virtual space tends to empower groups of students who may be less likely to participate in classroom discussions—for instance, students who are shy or self-conscious about their foreign accent—and minimizes "cues related to gender, race, position in established organizational hierarchies, social status, and appearance" (Self and Meyer, 1991, p. 170).[1] Scholars have emphasized the collaborative nature of this kind of learning process and have theorized that the instructor takes on the role of a facilitator rather than as an authority figure, which makes the learning process more student-centered (Hawisher and Moran, 1993; Cononelos and Oliva, 1993; Faigley, 1999).

However, as instructors have gained more experience using CMC in their teaching, a number of them have acknowledged the complicated nature of this kind of communication and that it is not always productive or supportive for students. Lester Faigley (1992) comments that "equality of participation... does not necessarily lead to 'community building' as some teachers have theorized" and explains that electronic conversation can be "agonistic" (p.185). Reporting on exchanges between students in his networked classroom discussions, he comments that these kinds of discussions "are just as likely to move toward dissensus as consensus, toward name-calling rather than agreement" and can allow students to make "racist, sexist, and homophobic" comments without taking responsibility for the harm they are doing to others (p.189, 198). However, Faigley does not see this dissensus as uniformly negative because it is a result of the expression of a diversity of voices. Terry Craig, Leslie Harris, and Richard Smith (1998) describe their experiences using MOOs (text-based online discussion environments) in their classes and how the initial polite student discussion degenerated, some students even "resorting to swearing and virtual violence" when communicating with each other (p.138). While acknowledging that CMC does encourage critical thinking, they also warn that instructors must teach "students to respect those who hold opposing views, so that disagreement can lead to productive exchange, rather than to a destructive silencing" (p.143). Indeed, instructors have become wary of "flaming," a kind of virtual verbal attack. In a CMC environment, people do not have to encounter others face-to-face, and this seems to make people more susceptible to using vitriolic verbal attacks than they would if they had to look their victim in the eye.

The CMC learning activities that the scholars above describe are typically initiated and framed by the instructor, and while the instructor may be displaced to a certain degree as the students take control of the discussion on the electronic platform, generally speaking, the instructor maintains a virtual presence to monitor and/or influence communications. Under certain circumstances, perhaps especially with email activities, the instructor may play a more hands-off role. For instance, second/foreign language instructors often arrange for their students to communicate with native speakers as "pen pals" through email. Thus, the instructor would initiate the CMC activity but not necessarily monitor it. The fact remains, though, that these kinds of CMC activities are organized and directed by the instructor, suggesting that the instructor still holds a privileged position in facilitating the learning task. What I focus on in this case is how email discussion can be incorporated more organically into a learning/writing task, and how this discussion can be student-framed. The fact that the students initiate the email communication of their own volition taps into the positive qualities that CMC has. The students are empowered to act autonomously and construct their own learning activity.

Fall 2008 College Composition I

In the fall 2008 semester, I had selected a new non-fiction book, Twenge's *Generation Me*, to use in my College Composition I class. Typically for homework, I assign students to read about 20 pages of the text and to produce some kind of informal writing in connection with the reading. For instance, I might ask the students to identify the author's main argument in a chapter and to give examples of the evidence he provides to support his claims. In class we discuss the reading, commenting on issues such as the effectiveness of the argument, the various argumentative strategies the author uses, and whether we are convinced by the author's discussion. I also answer any questions the students have about the reading and clarify points that the students are having trouble understanding. In this course, I usually tie all the formal essay assignments to the book we are reading as a class. I have found this to be an effective approach because the students have already done a significant amount of reading, writing, and talking about the topic and consequently have already begun to think complexly about the topic. Thus, when they receive the essay assignment, they are not "starting from scratch." When working on the essay, they continue to build on the knowledge base that they have already been developing in the class. To produce complex writing, one must engage in complex thinking.

Because Twenge's discussion is a comparative one that focuses on generational differences, I thought that this would be the logical place to start for the students' first essay. The essay prompt began with the following paragraph:

In Generation Me, Jean M. Twenge argues that people in the younger generation are more focused on the self and care less about social conventions than people of previous generations. She gives a number of examples, including child-rearing practices, weddings/marriages, and the use of profanity, to support her claims. In an essay partially based on a series of interviews you will conduct, focus on one of these three social practices (child rearing, marriage, or profanity) and come to your own conclusions about generational differences/similarities.

(See Appendix A for the complete assignment sheet.)

As part of the assignment, the students were required to interview two to four Baby Boomers (or, if they were older students, members of Generation Me) so that they could more easily draw their own conclusions about generational differences. Also, the interview material would be used in the essay to provide support for the claims about generational differences that the students made. Because Twenge's argument about generational differences focused on Americans, I had envisioned that the students would also focus on Americans in their essays, even though I knew that at least half of my class would probably be ESL students. I had assumed that they could interview American Baby Boomers and use their observations of their young American peers to develop their essays. I had not carefully considered all the cultural information that these students would not necessarily have had access to that would be crucial to make this kind of argument.

Out of my class of fifteen students, thirteen were ESL or bi-lingual; however, only four of these could be labeled "transnational," as per my definition above. Three of these students were female and in their twenties, and one was male and in his mid-fifties. The most recent arrival had only lived in the U.S. for one and a half years, and the most "veteran" had lived in the country for about five years. They all came from Vietnam, and they all essentially had one foot in Vietnam and one in the U.S. They had family and friends still living in Vietnam with whom they communicated regularly, but they also had family and friends in the U.S. and were probably going to spend the rest of their lives in this country. It was this group of students who approached me after I had introduced the essay assignment and asked me if they could write their comparison/contrast of generations on the Vietnamese rather than Americans. They explained that it would be very difficult for them to come to conclusions about American generations because they did not have enough knowledge or experience to draw on. Later, when I interviewed these students, I asked them what had gone through their minds when they first received the essay assignment. One student stated, "That it's hard for me because I know nothing about the American culture, so I think it's impossible for me to write that essay." Another student said, "First, when I got the assignment, I was wondering how I was going to get information from Americans. If I could discuss my culture, then it would be easy for me. If I talk with my people, it is better for me."

I agreed to their focusing on generational differences in the Vietnamese population in their essays and urged them to position their observations about the older and younger Vietnamese generations with/against Twenge's observations about Americans. Then the students set out busily gathering interview information from their relatives, friends, former teachers and former colleagues. The students used two distinct interviewing processes, in-person and through technology. When interviewing other Vietnamese people who had recently immigrated to the U.S., they conducted face-to-face interviews. When interviewing friends, family, and acquaintances who still lived in Vietnam, they tended to use email. For instance, the male student interviewed a number of his former colleagues in Vietnam by email. One of the female students interviewed a former teacher who had been her tutor in Vietnam by email. Because the student had spent a significant amount of time in the teacher's house during tutoring sessions, the student knew that the teacher would be able to provide useful information on the topic of marriage. Another female student interviewed a close friend's mother who lived in Vietnam. This student reported that she had several back-and-forth exchanges through email with her friend's mother. In addition, several students used cell phones and instant messaging services to conduct some interviews. Clearly email is not the only technology system students can use for gathering interview information, although email may have some advantages over a phone call because responses are written down (and thus do not have to be recorded in a rush by the interviewer) and, often, are more detailed than verbal ones exchanged during a phone call. Text messages sent by cell phone, although written, tend to be abbreviated as well. Instant messaging has the advantage of a being written communication, but it is different from email in that the interviewee is responding immediately (as an interviewee would in a face-to-face interview) while with email the respondent has time to consider his/her answer. Again, sometimes this consideration leads to more developed responses.

The students' use of email (and other CMC) discussion as part of the learning process was not directed by the instructor. The students acted on their own and took on the position of power in this process. They were able to dip into their home culture, through the use of email and other technologies, and gain more control over their topic, to shape it the way that they wanted to. In their essays, they stitched their own experience and information that they had gathered from people still living in their native country onto their new knowledge about their adopted culture.

If we examine one student's essay (I will call the student Ngoc), we can clearly see this stitching together of information about both cultures. Ngoc presented her thesis in her introductory paragraph:

Although Twenge's arguments concern the young American generation, one can still apply them to young Vietnamese. As a Vietnamese Gen Me-er, I realize that my generation struggles with difficulties within their culture regarding living their own lives. One of their struggles is against the strict rules and traditions in marriage. Nowadays, young Vietnamese have more chances to pursue their happiness because of changing perspectives about choosing their partners and changing attitudes about divorce.

Twenge argues that the young American generation's attitude about marriage is much different from previous generations', and Ngoc uses Twenge's idea as a basis for her own thesis about the Vietnamese. One point that Twenge makes in her book is that young Americans are much more open to inter-racial and inter-religious marriage than their parents were. Ngoc takes Twenge's idea and sees how it applies to her own culture. In the essay, Ngoc explains how traditionally in Vietnam the religion of one's marriage partner has been an important issue. Catholics have tended to marry Catholics, and Buddhists Buddhists. If there were an inter-religious marriage, one partner would be required to convert, but often this would cause a rift in the family. To demonstrate how things have changed with the younger generation, Ngoc gives the example of her boyfriend and herself, who have different religions. They have agreed that after they marry, she will remain Catholic and he will remain Buddhist. They will not give in to her future mother-in-law's urgings that Ngoc convert. Ngoc states in her essay,

She [the boyfriend's mother] has argued with my boyfriend about this topic a few times, and she was very mad when my boyfriend said, "I am going to marry her, not you. Please, let me live my life." My boyfriend is a good person. He usually respects and obeys his mother, but in marriage issues, he wants to have, what Twenge terms, his "personal choice" (31). Not only my boyfriend, but Gen Me also expresses their desire to make their own choices about marriage. A difference in religion does not ruin their happiness.

Again Ngoc makes explicit connections between Twenge's argument about Americans and her home culture.

An example of how Ngoc's writing about her own culture helped to acculturate her to her new American environment can be found in her concluding paragraph. In this paragraph, she argues that the changes in attitudes towards marriage seen in the young Vietnamese population are unconditionally positive. She comments, "[W]e are free to choose and build a happy relationship with our partners without regards to their race or religion. Family and society are no longer big obstacles that affect our decisions in marriage anymore." She ties these ideas to a classic American movie, *West Side Story*. This movie, based on the musical, is about a young, cross-cultural couple who seek love together despite the disapproval of those around them, and it is a perfect allusion to use in her essay. She uses a quotation from the movie, "When love comes so strong there is no right or wrong. Your love is your love" to illustrate the young Vietnamese generation's attitude about marriage. She concludes her essay with the following assertions: "The important thing is my generation never gives up looking for happiness. As times change and traditions weaken we are able to liberate ourselves from the past. When family becomes a place of misery, we should free and give ourselves other chances to find happiness." The fact that Ngoc used a reference to an American cultural icon to help emphasize her point about Vietnamese generations suggests that her knowledge about American culture is developing. (See Appendix B for a complete copy of Ngoc's essay.)

Another student, who I will call Kim, makes a similar argument in her essay. Her thesis is "In doing research for this essay, I have figured out that Vietnamese young people have experienced similar changes to Americans when it comes to choosing marriage partners. While the older people found themselves stuck in traditional marriages, the younger generation has more freedom to run their own lives." In one of her body paragraphs, Kim focuses on differences in generational attitudes regarding interracial marriage. She quotes her teacher, who is 50 years old and lives in Vietnam, as saying that her father "did not allow her to have that kind of 'crazy thinking,'" i.e. about marrying outside of her race. Immediately, Kim follows up in her essay, "Similarly in *Generation Me*, Twenge asserts that in America people were considered strange if they got married with people from other races until quite recently (19)." She is making meaningful connections between the two cultures.

Two of the four transnational students in the class who chose to write about differences in Vietnamese generations felt that this first essay of the semester was their "best" one. (The students completed three other formal essays for a total of four during the semester.) One student commented that this first essay was her best because she had "experienced this" (generational conflicts regarding attitudes towards marriage). She also stated, "With the other essays, I didn't feel as connected with the topic. I had to do more research" (as opposed to drawing from personal resources and experiences). She didn't seem to perceive collecting information through personal and email interviews as burdensome research. Finally, she stated that when writing the first essay, "I [could] express my ideas clearly." The second student who thought that this first essay was his best one commented, "I had experience with the topic, and I knew a lot about the topic. I could interview a lot of people. I knew a lot about my country."

The topic itself (generational differences in their native country populations) and the students' ability to gather meaningful information about the topic (through email and other types of interviews) seem to have given these students a sense of control over their writing and to have made them feel as though they could produce writing that accurately communicated their ideas. Mark Warschauer (1996) has done research on how using computers for writing and communication in connection with teaching ESL and EFL (English foreign language) students affects students' motivation. While the computer-assisted writing activities that were a part of his study were generally more integrated into the classes than those in my class, his survey of 167 students in 12 university writing courses in Hong Kong, Taiwan, and the U.S. suggests that students respond positively to using the computer, and email specifically, as part of the writing and learning process. Students gave statistically significant positive responses to the following statements: "Computers help people overcome weakness and powerlessness." "Computers help people overcome isolation." "Using a computer gives me more control over my learning." "Writing to others by e-mail helps me develop my thoughts and ideas." "E-mail helps people learn from each other" (pp. 6-7). The students' positive responses to these statements suggest that CMC, and email in particular, contribute to students feeling more in control of their writing and learning. Their responses also indicate that they feel that the use of email helps them to articulate their ideas more effectively in writing. Warschauer concludes that, with CMC, students feel a sense of empowerment, independence, and control over their learning. This is what my transnational students seemed to experience.

Using Email and Community Building

Traditionally, the concept of community has been conceived of as local and place-based. The people in this kind of traditional community would go to meetings in the town hall together and would meet and greet at the local coffee shop, beauty salon, and barber shop. Their children would go to school together, and the adults would organize church fundraisers and attend Parent-Teacher Association meetings as a part of being good citizens of the community. These activities and the regular face-to-face connections that would result from them would often give people a sense of belonging. In recent decades, with urbanization and global relocation, this kind of community is on the wane. Sociologists have studied this trend and have provided new analysis of and new definitions of community. Barry Wellman and Scot Wortley (1990) describe what they call a "personal community network," which is "a person's set of active community ties" and "is usually socially diverse, [and] spatially dispersed" (p. 559). While Wellman and Wortley are still focused on community networks that are mainly based on face-to-face and phone contact, other scholars, especially those concerned with new media, have considered how CMC may come into play in building a sense of community. Douglas Schuler (1996) examines community networks, which are "community-oriented computer services" that local institutions such as libraries, schools, government agencies, and non-profit organizations tie into with the idea that civic and political interchanges will be enhanced (p.25). Schuler concludes that community networks "help anchor and ground 'new communities'" (p.412). While Schuler's conception of a computer-mediated community network is still locally place-based, other scholars have looked at cyberspace as a kind of new frontier for community. Charles Soukup (2006) discusses how many social critics have argued that CMC "contexts such as chatrooms, multi-user environments and bulletin board systems can function as one of Ray Oldenburg's 'third places' or 'Great Good Places,'" the kind of traditional community gathering places like the coffee shop that I describe above (p.422). While Soukup cautions that "virtual third places" are not a panacea for the loss of community connection we have experienced in recent decades, he does assert that they offer "possible remedies for. .. alienation and fragmentation" and may allow people to feel more "intrinsically connected to political and social life" within a community (pp. 437-438). Steven Jones (1995) goes even further when he asserts that CMC is a "socially produced space" and "allows us to customize our social contacts from fragmented communities" (pp. 16-17).

In regards to the case that I am presenting, David Holmes (2005) provides particularly useful analysis of community and communication structures. Holmes discusses how community has been "re-spatialized," going both micro and global (p. 175). He comments on how "physical and electronic urban architectures" have contributed to this reconfiguration of community and explains that the more integrated our lives become with electronic networks, the less we depend on physical and local community. He adds, "Conversely, the less individuals get to know their neighbors, the more important it is to" be connected to electronic networks (p. 68). He argues that it is not entirely accurate to claim that "the contemporary public sphere is breaking down and becoming fragmented" (p. 81); rather this public sphere "is sustained across increasingly more complex and dynamic and global kinds of communication environments" (p. 81). Holmes concludes that people need to be integrated into a community and that "media spaces" like the Internet offer people valuable "forms of connection" (p. 222).

A few researchers have discussed how interaction in online communities contributes to English-language learners' (ELLs) literacy development and enhances their sense of community. Youngjoo Yi (2008) describes a site, Welcome to Buckeye City, which was created, maintained, and used by Korean adolescent students who had immigrated to the U.S. The site was used in various ways, as a place to discuss their daily lives or problems and as a place to post and/or create stories, poems, and pictures. The majority of the postings were in Korean, emphasizing the students' shared ethnic identity. Yi focuses especially on the relay writing the students produced on the site; one student would begin a novel, and then multiple people would continue the storyline. Yi concludes that this kind of literacy practice that took place outside of the school setting allowed the students to develop a "'diasporic' network," to maintain important native language and cultural connections, and to reinforce literacy practices, such as composing (p.679). Also, Rebecca Black (2005) examines ELLs' participation in online fanfiction communities where people post their original fiction based on elements of popular television shows, movies, books, etc. This fiction is generally written in English, so ELLs who participate in this kind of creative endeavor are likely to enhance their English literacy skills. However, Black also focuses on how an ELL in this online community can develop an identity as an "expert." For instance, anime and manga are popular inspirations for the fiction on many fanfiction sites, so ELLs with Japanese or Chinese backgrounds are often perceived as experts because of their knowledge of the language, culture, and/or folklore that anime or manga involves. Black argues that this online participation allows ELLs "to construct identities as successful writers within the anime-based genre and thus increase their acceptance as English-language users within the community" (p. 122). Black concludes that socially based writing practices are enhanced by student participation on these sites.

While the scholars discussed above have a variety of CMC spaces—chat rooms, MOOs, MUDs (a multi-user, real-time virtual world), social networking sites, MMOGs (Massively Multiplayer Online Games)—in mind when they analyze the concept of virtual community, email allows for the development of a particular kind of virtual community. While people may develop email communities with people they have never met face-to-face—usually because of a mutual interest or shared professional expertise—the students involved here use email to maintain a connection with people they know personally but who are physically separated from them. The students are members of dual communities, their native one and an adopted one in the U.S., and they use email to maintain their connection with their native community. John Schilb (1996) points out that "postmodern theory evokes a self who may occupy multiple positions, form various allegiances, and teem with conflicting ideas" (p. 88), and this is what my students are experiencing in the postmodern world they inhabit. They are Vietnamese, and they are Americans. They refer to Vietnam as "my country," and they earn their U.S. citizenship. They integrate multiple identities, and email helps them to do this. This is similar to the process Homi Bhabha (1994) describes when he discusses how colonized people can resist authoritative culturalization. He describes "the possibilities of being, somehow, *in between*, of occupying an interstitial space. .. not fully governed by the recognizable traditions from which you came" (p.190). Bhabha identifies this position as a third space and suggests that this kind of "in between" space allows an individual to maintain a distinct identity and point of view. (This "third space" is very different from the "third place" associated with Ray Oldenburg that I mentioned above, the Oldenburg third place involving public spaces like the community coffee shop that allow for informal social interaction.) Bhabha suggests that when the subject occupies this space, he/she achieves a position of power. Interestingly, email can help to create this third space, the space between two cultures. Like the cities that create computerized community networks, which Schuler (1996) describes, the students are building their own community networks around their multi-valent selves. Warschauer's survey (1996) indicates that students do associate email with a sense of community. They strongly agreed with the statement "Using email and the Internet makes me feel part of a community" (p. 6). In fact, Holmes reports that the people who designed ARPANET, a network that has evolved into the Internet, were very surprised at how people ended up using email. The designers had expected people to use email to "communicate with computers," but people actually seized on email to "communicate with other people" (p. 47). Instructors of composition can tap into the positive qualities that email possesses by designing some of their writing assignments carefully. Approaches friendly to the use of email might be especially helpful when working with the transnational student population.

CURRENT CHALLENGES

The field of composition is a growing one in higher education. Most colleges and universities require students to take several composition courses, and more students need to take remedial (developmental) writing courses before they take the required college-level ones. The supply of Ph.D.s with a focus on composition and rhetoric does not come close to meeting this teaching demand. Thus, too often inexperienced instructors who lack appropriate expertise end up teaching freshman composition courses. This problematic situation is compounded when universities cut costs by using part-time instructors at a reduced pay rate. These instructors often find themselves teaching two courses at three or more institutions to try to cobble together a living wage. The use of part-time instructors is especially high in the area of composition. Thus, many of those who teach composition to first-year students do not have the time, energy, or expertise to do so well.

Universities often do not offer these instructors appropriate training in how to effectively teach ESL/transnational populations, a rapidly growing population in higher education. Frequently little professional development is offered on how to effectively incorporate technology in their writing classes or how to use technology in connection with the various kinds of student populations present at most universities today. Thus, it falls on the shoulders of individual instructors to develop expertise in these areas on their own, often through a process of trial and error. My own experience is representative of this situation.

All the challenges that I mention here are present at the university involved in this case, and I do not foresee any changes in these areas in the immediate future.

SOLUTIONS AND RECOMMENDATIONS

The solutions and recommendations can be categorized into two areas, first what individual composition instructors can do and second what steps can be initiated by colleges and universities in this context. The individual composition instructors can recognize that they may have a growing population of ESL/transnational students in their classes; they can consider these students when designing courses and assignments; when developing a theme-based class that focuses on American social, political, or popular cultural issues, they can consider ways students can use their knowledge about their native culture in connection with their writing about American cultural issues. For example, in the spring semester when I was teaching the same course I describe above, I simply added one sentence to my assignment sheet: "You could focus on generational differences/similarities with Americans or your home country populations." This one sentence reduced the panicked feeling my students were experiencing that first semester and allowed them to move forward immediately and productively with the writing assignment. Thirteen of the sixteen students in my spring semester College Composition I class chose to write about their non-American native populations. Finally, instructors can consider including writing assignments that are friendly to the use of email to gather information, as email and other kinds of CMC seem to be especially effective in empowering transnational student writers.

More research needs to be conducted regarding the use of technology in teaching writing to ESL/transnational students, especially in connection with the student population that is mainstreamed into regular (non-ESL) composition courses. Individual instructors or groups of instructors should pursue this research. While my case provides analysis based on ethnographic research involving a limited number of students, future research should also include quantitative studies with larger numbers. Additional research is also needed on how CMC can contribute to community building for the transnational student population.

Also, colleges and universities can provide more training for instructors regarding the teaching and learning of the ESL/transnational student population and provide more training for instructors about how to effectively incorporate CMC into their teaching.

REFERENCES

Bhabha, H. (1994). Between identities: Homi Bhabha interviewed by Paul Thompson. In R. Benmayor & A. Skotnes (Eds.), Migration and identity (pp.183-197). Oxford, UK: Oxford University Press.

Black, R. W. (2005). Access and affiliation: The literacy and composition practices of English-language learners in an online fanfiction community. *Journal of Adolescent & Adult Literacy*, *49*(2), 118–128. doi:10.1598/JAAL.49.2.4

Cononelos, T., & Oliva, M. (1993). Using computer networks to enhance foreign language/ culture education. *Foreign Language Annals*, *26*(4), 527–534. doi:10.1111/j.1944-9720.1993.tb01186.x

Craig, T., Harris, L., & Smith, R. (1998). Rhetoric of the "contact zone": Composition on the front lines. In T. Taylor & I. Ward (Eds.), Literacy theory in the age of the internet, (pp.122-145). New York: Columbia University Press.

Faigley, L. (1992). Fragments of rationality: Postmodernity and the subject of composition. Pittsburgh, PA: University of Pittsburgh Press.

Faigley, L. (1999). Beyond imagination: The internet and global digital literacy. In G.

Hawisher, G., & Moran, C. (1993). Electronic mail and the writing instructor. *College English*, *55*(6), 627–643. doi:10.2307/378699

Hawisher & C. Selfe (Ed.). Passions, pedagogies, and 21st century techologies (pp. 129-139). Logan, UT: Utah State University Press.

Holmes, D. (2005). Communication theory: Media, technology, society. London: Sage.

Johnson, S. (2005). Everything bad is good for you: How today's popular culture is actually making us smarter. New York: Riverhead Books.

Jones, S. G. (Ed.). (1995). Cybersociety: Computer-mediated communication and community. London: Sage.

Pratt, M. (1991). Arts of the Contact Zone. [New York: Modern Language Association.]. *Profession*, *91*, 33–40.

Schilb, J. (1996). Between the lines: Relating composition theory and literary theory. Portsmouth, NH: Boynton/Cook.

Schuler, D. (1996). New community networks: Wired for change. New York: ACM Press.

Selfe, C., & Meyer, P. (1991). Testing claims for online conferences. *Written Communication*, *8*(2), 163–192. doi:10.1177/0741088391008002002

Soukup, C. (2006). Computer-mediated communication as a virtual third place: Building Oldenburg's great good places on the world wide web. *New Media & Society*, *8*(3), 421–440. doi:10.1177/1461444806061953

Street, B. V. (1995). Social literacies: Critical approaches to literacy in development, ethnography and education. London: Longman.

Twenge, J. (2006). Generation me: Why today's young Americans are more confident, assertive, entitled—and more miserable than ever before. New York: Free Press.

U.S. Census Bureau. (2006). *Press release.* Retrieved May 18, 2009, from http://www.census.gov/Press-Release/www/releases/archives/income_wealth/007419.html

U.S. Census Bureau. (2009). State & county quickfacts, Camden (city), New Jersey. Retrieved May 18, 2009, from http://quickfacts.census.gov/qfd/states/34/3410000.html

Warschauer, M. (1996). Motivational aspects of using computers for writing and communication. In M. Warschauer (Ed.), *Telecollaboration in Foreign Language Learning: Proceedings of the Hawaii Symposium: Report #12* (pp. 29-46). Honolulu, HI: University of Hawaii, Second Language Teaching & Curriculum Center.

Warschauer, M., Turbee, L., & Robers, B. (1996). Computer learning networks and student empowerment. *System, 24*(1), 1–14. doi:10.1016/0346-251X(95)00049-P

Wellman, B., & Wortley, S. (1990). Different strokes from different folks: Community ties and social support. *American Journal of Sociology, 96*(3), 558–588. doi:10.1086/229572

Yan, J. (2008). Social technology as a new medium in the classroom. *New England Journal of Higher Education, 22*(4), 27–30.

Yi, Y. (2008). Relay writing in an adolescent online community. *Journal of Adolescent & Adult Literacy, 51*(8), 670–680. doi:10.1598/JAAL.51.8.6

ADDITIONAL READING

Bizzell, P. (1994). "Contact zones" and English studies. *College English, 56*(2), 163–170. doi:10.2307/378727

Bolter, J. D., & Grusin, R. (1999). Remediation: Understanding new media. Cambridge, MA: MIT Press.

Calhoun, C. (1998). Community without propinquity revisited: Communications technology and the transformation of the urban public sphere. *Sociological Inquiry, 68*(3), 373–397. doi:10.1111/j.1475-682X.1998.tb00474.x

Eldred, J. (1991). Pedagogy in the computer-networked classroom. *Computers and Composition, 8*(2), 47–61. doi:10.1016/8755-4615(91)80048-I

Finnegan, R. (2002). Communicating: The multiple modes of human communication. London: Routledge.

Frechette, J. (2002). Developing media literacy in cyberspace: Pedagogy and critical learning for the twenty-first-century classroom. Westport, CN: Praeger.

Graham, S. (2000). Splintering urbanism: Networked infrastructures, technological mobilities and the urban condition. London: Routledge.

Hawisher, G., & LeBlan, P. (Eds.). (1992). Reimagining computers and composition: Teaching and research in the virtual age. Portsmouth, NH: Boynton/Cook.

Hawisher, G., & Selfe, C. (Eds.). (2000). Global literacies and the world-wide web. London: Routledge.

Herman, A., & Swiss, T. (Eds.). (2000). The world wide web and contemporary cultural theory. London: Routledge.

Holmes, D. (Ed.). (1997). Virtual politics: Identity and community in cyberspace. London: Sage.

Johnson, S. (1997). Interface culture: How technology transforms the way we create and communicate. New York: HarperCollins.

Jones, S. (1998). Cybersociety 2.0: Revisiting computer-mediated communication and community. Thousand Oaks, CA: Sage Publications.

Kendall, L. (2002). Hanging out in the virtual pub. Berkeley, CA: University of California Press.

Kress, G. R. (2003). Literacy in the new media age. London: Routledge.

Liff, S., & Steward, F. (2001). Community e-gateways: Locating networks and learning for social inclusion. *Information Communication and Society*, *4*(3), 317–340.

Peters, M., & Lankshear, C. (1996). Critical literacy and digital texts. *Educational Theory*, *46*(1), 51–70. doi:10.1111/j.1741-5446.1996.00051.x

Porter, D. (Ed.). (1997). Internet culture. London: Routledge.

Rheingold, H. (1993). The virtual community: Homesteading on the electronic frontier. New York: HarperCollins.

Rheingold, H. (1994). The virtual community: Finding connection in a computerized world. London: Secker and Warburg.

Smith, M., & Kollock, P. (Eds.). (1999). Communities in cyberspace. London: Routledge.

Snyder, I. (Ed.). (1998). Page to screen: Taking literacy into the electronic era. London: Routledge.

Spears, R., & Lea, M. (1994). Panacea or Panopticon? The hidden power of computer-mediated communication. *Communication Research*, *21*(4), 427–459. doi:10.1177/009365094021004001

Taylor, T., & Ward, I. (Eds.). (1998). Literacy theory in the age of the internet. New York: Columbia University Press.

Turkle, S. (1995). Life on the screen: Identity in the age of the internet. New York: Simon and Schuster.

Van Dijk, J. (1999). The network society: Social aspects of new media. London: Sage.

Weigel, V. B. (2002). Deep learning for a digital age: technology's untapped potential to enrich higher education. San Francisco, CA: Jossey-Bass.

Wise, J. M. (1997). Exploring technology and social space. London: Sage.

KEY TERMS AND DEFINITIONS

CMC: Computer-mediated communication. This term refers to any kind of communication that is any way mediated by a computerized system, which would include email, Internet chat rooms, electronic discussion boards, text messaging, instant messaging, social networking sites, word processing, MUDs, etc.

Contact Zone: A location where elements of two cultures meet and grapple with each other, producing new kinds of texts and/or knowledge. It is associated with transnational encounters. An underlying idea of the contact zone is that communication often involves "dissensus," struggle, and protest, as well as consensus.

EFL: English as a Foreign Language. This term is associated with students who are learning English as a foreign language to use for travel, business, or personal purposes (as opposed to as a language they will use on a daily basis).

ESL: English as a Second Language. This term is associated with students who are learning English as their second language; i.e., they are aiming for native-speaking-level competency in the language.

Third Space: A term coined by sociologist Ray Oldenburg. It refers to public spaces, such as the local coffee shop or town square, that allow for informal social interaction, contributing to a feeling of shared community. It is a concept associated with a "traditional" community.

Third Place: A term used by Homi Bhabha, a theorist of Post-colonialism. It refers to the in-between space colonized people can use to resist authoritative culturalization. In this space, an individual can maintain a distinct identity and point of view. An individual can develop a hybrid identity, not completely governed by the colonizing culture or the traditional culture.

ENDNOTE

1 In this quotation, Selfe and Meyer are summarizing the findings of other researchers. Their own study conducted during an on-line conference involving instructor participants, which they discuss in this article, suggests that gender and status are factors in how people participate in CMC (the males and individuals with high professional status posting more comments and arguing their points more assertively).

APPENDIX A

Essay #1

In *Generation Me*, Jean M. Twenge argues that people in the younger generation are more focused on the self and care less about social conventions than people of previous generations. She gives a number of examples, including child-rearing practices, weddings/marriages, and the use of profanity, to support her claims. In an essay partially based on a series of interviews you will conduct, focus on one of these three social practices (child rearing, marriage, or profanity) and come to your own conclusions about generational differences/similarities.

Step 1: Interviewing

Interview two to four people who are 45 years old or older regarding your selected topic. (You might want to interview several young people as well.) You should have a list of 4 to 7 questions written down to ask during the interview, and you should record each person's answers. You should ask each interviewee the same questions. For instance, if you wanted to focus on the issue of child rearing practices, you might ask questions such as the following: What qualities did your parents try to instill in you when they were raising you? Were they concerned about nurturing your self-esteem? Explain. Describe the rules of your household and how you parents disciplined you if these rules were broken? Be careful to design your questions so that you receive developed responses rather than one-word, yes-or-no responses. Also, if your interviewee's answer calls for a follow-up question, feel free to ask question(s) not on your original list—just make sure you write them down shortly after the interview!

Step 2: Writing the Essay

Use the following as guidelines when developing your essay:

Early in the Essay

- **Give an overview of Twenge's argument about generational differences** in connection with focus on self and attitude towards social conventions. You may want to include background information on and/or define "Generation Me" and "Baby Boomers" as part of this discussion. You might want to summarize Twenge's discussion regarding child-rearing practices, marriage choices, or use of profanity (whichever one you are discussing in your essay) as well. The first time you mention Twenge's ideas, make sure you use the title of the book in a signal phrase. Also, if you use Twenge's exact language, use quotation marks and give the page number in parenthesis at the end of the sentence.
- **Provide a thesis**. Your thesis should communicate your conclusions about generational differences/similarities in connection with child rearing practices, marriage choices, or use of profanity. You may situate your views on the topic in connection with Twenge's views, i.e., do you agree (completely or partially) or disagree with her arguments.
- You could open your essay with an illustrating scenario, especially if you are discussing how the two generations are different, and move your background information/thesis to the second or third paragraph. This is simply an option.

Middle Section of the Essay

- **Provide support for your thesis**. This could come in the form of personal examples, observation, expert opinion, general discussion, etc. If you agree with Twenge, you could use information from *Generation Me* to help support your claims. Also, you should use relevant information that you have gathered through your interviews as evidence to support your thesis. When you use information from an interview, sometimes you may want to paraphrase what the person has said, and other times you may want to use a direct quotation. Make sure you attribute any information that you use from an interview. Remember, for any claim that you make, you must provide significant evidence. Thus, don't make claims that are too extreme, e.g., "Baby Boomers always…."

This is a comparison/contrast essay. Thus, you need to think carefully about how you should organize the information in your body paragraphs. Will you examine the Baby Boomer generation first and then Generation Me? (This would be a subject-by-subject—or block—organizational structure.) Or will you take a point-by-point approach?

Closing Section of the Essay

This is a very important section of the essay because this is where you provide your analysis of the topic. What conclusions can you draw from examining these two generations? Have things stayed the same? Why? Have things changed significantly? Are these changes positive or negative? Why? Why is this important information for the reader to think about?

Length

700-750 words, or about 3 pages, word-processed and double-spaced

Audience

Carefully consider your intended audience. Do you have a very broad audience in mind, like a newspaper's readership? Are you addressing older generations, trying to help them understand the behavior of the younger generation? Are you directing your argument towards a more academic audience—experts in psychology, sociology, child development? Keep your intended audience in mind when making choices about organization, vocabulary, evidence, etc.

APPENDIX B

Marriage and Its Story between Two Generations

Jean M. Twenge, who has a Ph.D. in psychology, researched and published a book entitled *Generation Me* to argue that Generation Me (Gen Me), those who are under thirty-five years old, tend to focus on individualism. In this book, she provides a lot of evidence to verify her thesis that there are changes in many aspects of Gen Me such as conduct, beliefs, etc., compared with the Baby Boomer generation. The young generation's motto, "do what makes you happy and don't worry about what other people think" (20), reflects these changes. Although Twenge's arguments concern the young American generation, one can still apply them to young Vietnamese. As a Vietnamese Gen Me-er, I realize that my generation struggles with difficulties within their culture regarding living their own lives. One of their struggles is against the strict rules and traditions in marriage. Nowadays, young Vietnamese have more chances to pursue their happiness because of changing perspectives about choosing their partners and changing attitudes about divorce.

Vietnamese people in the previous generations were more influenced in choosing partners by their parents than many of us today. In general, people had to marry someone who had the same race as them. My mother, who is of the older generation, said, "There was no such thing as interracial marriage in the 1950s. The only kinds of people who did that were prostitutes." For this reason, some true loves in interracial relationships were stamped out. About five years ago, I watched a Vietnamese movie called *La Thu (The Letter)*. It was about a love story in the 1960s between a Vietnamese girl and an American soldier. They were forced to break up because the girl's family did not accept this marriage. In that period, it was taboo for a girl to marry a foreign man, and it caused shame for the family. However, the soldier was still looking for his girlfriend because he did not understand the Vietnamese culture. Thus, the girl's family hid her away from the soldier. She cried a lot, and in the end she ran away from her home country to follow the American soldier. She came back to visit and received her parents' forgiveness after 30 years. Nevertheless, it just was a movie and a movie usually has a happy ending. My aunt, Hue, born in the 1950s, explains real life: "In my time, if a girl had fallen in love with a foreign man, she would be forced to marry a native one and end her true love." Now, everything has changed. People in my generation are very free to choose their partners. The development of the Vietnamese economy gives my generation many opportunities to work and be in contact with foreign people. Therefore, interracial relationships are increasing in my country. There are many of them that have a very happy wedding with wishes from their family, friends and neighbors. These weddings are becoming the norm in my country. My friend, Uyen, confided with me that," If I fall in love with a foreign man, I prefer to marry him rather than a Vietnamese man, even though I know we will have misunderstandings sometimes. I cannot live and be happy with a man whom I do not love for the rest of my life." My friend, who is 21 years old, said what my young generation thinks: follow your heart and do whatever makes you feel happy.

Similarly, the past generation tended to obey their parents and marry in the same religion. Traditionally, Vietnamese people have respected and believed in God. In some families that had the utmost belief in God, converting to another religion meant betraying their roots. Some families abandoned their child because he/she converted from his/her own religion, especially with Catholicism. My Mom had to convert from her own religion, which was Buddhism, to marry my Dad who is Catholic. Yet, not everyone had the agreement from their family like my Mom. Kim, my mother's friend, told me a touching story. Her aunt loved a Buddhist man. His family requested that Kim's aunt convert her own religion, Catholicism, to Buddhism, but her family did not accept it. Consequently, they broke up with each other in tears. Later, it was arranged that she marry her first husband, but they were not happy. Sometimes her husband was physically abusive towards her. When she could no longer handle her husband, she ran away from him, but not until her parents passed away. This story is similar to a situation I have faced today, but my solution is completely different from hers.

My boyfriend and I have decided to keep our own religions if we marry each other. However, his mother is not satisfied with this decision. She wants my boyfriend to convince me to follow her religion,

Buddhism. She has argued with my boyfriend about this topic a few times, and she was very mad when my boyfriend said, "I am going to marry her, not you. Please, let me live my life." My boyfriend is a good person. He usually respects and obeys his mother, but in marriage issues, he wants to have, what Twenge terms, his "personal choice" (31). Not only my boyfriend, but Gen Me also expresses their desire to make their own choices about marriage. A difference in religion does not ruin their happiness.

Another change in Vietnamese perspectives regards divorce. The past generation was used to enduring their marriage even if it was not successful. They could not make a decision to stop their suffering because it could involve their family's honor. Hue told me that "someone who divorced back then would be scorned by their neighbors and it would be shameful for her family." In fact, divorce never happened officially in Hue's generation because nobody accepted it. The only way a wife could end her marriage was by running away from it. When a couple got married, they were supposed to be with their partner for the rest of their lives. In contrast, my generation can divorce for abundant reasons, such as money, sex problems, gambling, domestic violence, etc. Like Twenge says, "We are told to follow our dreams, to pursue happiness above all else" (19). This generation was taught to love themselves more than anything. Therefore, if they do not find their own benefits and happiness, they can divorce their partner without being concerned about what other people think (Twenge, 25). A research study done in 2001 showed that "one in six marriages" came to an end in Ho Chi Minh City, a large city in Vietnam (http://www.highbeam.com/doc/1P2-13394654.html). That is a high rate for a country that has so many traditions in marriage. This rate also illustrates that there is now a rapid change in attitudes about marriage and divorce among my generation and the elder generation.

There have been a lot changes in Vietnamese attitudes toward marriage through two generations. The differences have brought advantages to my generation. Nowadays, we are free to choose and build a happy relationship with our partners without regards to their race or religion. Family and society are no longer big obstacles that affect our decisions in marriage anymore. This is like the line from *West Side Story*, "When love comes so strong there is no right or wrong. Your love is your love." The important thing is my generation never gives up looking for happiness. As times change and traditions weaken we are able to liberate ourselves from the past. When family becomes a place of misery, we should free and give ourselves other chances to find happiness.

Chapter 15
Integrated Cross-Cultural Virtual Classroom Exchange Program:
How Adaptable Public Schools are in Korea and the USA?

Eunhee Jung O'Neill
Center for International Virtual Schooling, USA

ABSTRACT

As information and communication technology (ICT) evolves, the scope of social interactions expands globally through the Web, and knowledge has become a key source for economic production. The capacity to understand diverse cultures and the ability to utilize ICT for knowledge acquisition and application have become critical to increasing and sustaining global solidarity, peace and development. Accordingly, society expects educational institutions to provide students with cultural learning opportunities and ICT skills. In an effort to address these issues, a cross-cultural virtual classroom exchange program using an online course management system was introduced to public schools in Korea and the USA. By investigating technological, pedagogical, and organizational factors, this paper analyzes the adaptability of public schools in Korea and the USA with respect to integrating cross-cultural virtual exchange activities within their respective curricula. Ultimately, this case recommends solutions for increasing adaptability, and invites international collaboration among education stakeholders to disseminate the cross-cultural virtual learning worldwide.

ORGANIZATION BACKGROUND: PUBLIC SCHOOLS AND ICT POLICY

The Republic of Korea (South Korea)'s public K-12 schools are composed of six-year elementary schools, three-year middle schools, and three-year high schools. The K–12 curriculum is centralized at the national level. Since 1954, the Korean Ministry of Education (currently renamed as Ministry of Education, Science and Technology: MEST) has developed and advanced the national curriculum every eight to ten years. The centralized national curriculum reflects the governments' political and economic stances. For example, the government

DOI: 10.4018/978-1-61520-779-4.ch015

put great emphasis on education as an engine of the nation's economic growth in the 1970's. Diverse research and reports have disclosed the power of Korea's education as related to its rapid economic development (Korea Education & Research Information Service, 2008; Morris, 1996; UNESCO, 1993). Accordingly, science, mathematics, and technical education have been core subjects. Since 1997, with an emphasis on globalization, the English language has been taught from the third grade and has become one of the biggest interests of Korean society.

By providing the vision for adapting education to the Information Age (Korea Education & Research Information Service, 2000), MEST has directed educators to participate in and follow school innovation using ICT. There is a very structured and linear connection between the central department of education, local office of education, and each level of public schools.

The policies for the informatization of education were introduced in two stages. In the First Comprehensive Plan (1997–2000), all elementary and middle schools were provided with ICT hardware, one PC with high-speed Internet connection, a large screen TV projector per every classroom, and one or two computer laboratories. The Second Stage Plan started in 2001 and focused on developing ICT software, such as digital online content materials. The Korean Education & Research Information Service (KERIS) led the development of ICT content material and its distribution. KERIS also supplied ICT resources for teachers and students including cyber learning services and the promotion of public education through the Internet (KERIS, 2004).

The central administration and its policy systematically planned and supported the provision of public schools' ICT equipment and contents materials. Since funding amounts were based on school size, i.e., the number of students, classrooms, and facilities, all public schools in Korea were set up equally with ICT infrastructures (KERIS, 2001). The plan for adapting ICT in elementary and secondary education has been continuously implemented. Emphasizing educational welfare and information culture, MEST has focused on "narrowing the education gap" since 2006. Also, MEST enacted Regulations for the Center of Safe On-line Learning, which requested schools to teach the ethics of information and communications, and to install software that blocks students from any harmful information (MEST & KERIS, 2007, p. 19).

The United States of America (USA) has a decentralized educational system. The U.S. Department of Education (DOE) is not responsible for the whole nation's education, instead, each state DOE is accountable for their state's education. Thus, the U.S. DOE makes overarching educational policy and provides an educational technology plan as suggestions and recommendations, and the state level departments set the concrete plans for implementation. This decentralized structure brings a dynamic quality of education according to a state's unique environment and policies. Typically, states follow either a 5-3-4 compulsory education system (five years of elementary school, three years of junior high school, and four years of high school), or a 6-3-3 system. Since the American school in this case study is located in Virginia, reviewing the respective educational ICT policy will be appropriate.

Under the No Child Left Behind Act of 2001 (White House, 2002) whereby public schools are required to administer a state-wide standardized test to all students every year to enhance academic achievement, the U.S. DOE announced a national technology plan to inform and guide policy makers to implement ICT in education (Culp, Honey & Mandinach, 2003). In addition, since the Enhancing Education Through Technology (EETT) Act of 2001 was passed by Congress, the Virginia Department of Education established the Educational Technology Plan for Virginia: 2003–2009 (State Board of Education, 2003). This plan addresses technology integration, professional development and support programs, connectivity, educational application, and accountability. It aims to ensure that "all students develop the technology skills and knowledge to realize their potential as leaders in a technology-supported information economy." The plan emphasizes "long-range, effective, statewide integration of educational technology into teaching, learning, and school management." (State Board of Education, 2003, p. v)

Unlike South Korea where the government established a nationwide ICT infrastructure equally, the Virginia plan diagnosed that "all public schools and school division offices in Virginia do not have the same level of connectivity to local and outside resources. Infrastructures vary widely from school division to school division and even among schools in the same division" (State Board of Education, 2003, p. 53). The Virginia State Board of Education suggests a standardization of schools' connectivity, thus allowing all classrooms to be networked through the high-speed Internet connections. Educational funding in the U.S. is based on regional tax rates, and each school applies to a district office of education for any additional project funding.

SETTING AND PARTICIPANTS

Three elementary schools in Seoul (Korea) and one elementary school in Virginia (USA) performed International Virtual Elementary Classroom Activities (IVECA) activities for a whole semester. As shown in Figure 1, participants of this case study include six classrooms of total 154 students, six classroom teachers (T), ten support teachers (ST), four school administrators (P) in four public elementary schools in both countries. In particular, in the one American school, there were two 5th grade Reading and Writing in English (RWE) classes (indicated with the codes, Class1 and Class2, respectively in Figure 1.), their teachers (T1 and T2), one 6th grade RWE class (Class3) and their teacher (T3), four technological and instructional support teachers (ST1– ST4) and a school administrator (P1). The data collection sources in the three Korean schools were three regular 6th grade classes (Class 1– Class 3), their teachers (T1–T3), two support teachers (ST1 and ST2) in each school, and three school principals (P1– P3). A cross-cultural virtual classroom exchange program, IVECA, consists of three virtual classrooms. Each virtual classroom was paired with one American classroom and one Korean classroom.

CASE DESCRIPTION

This case study aims to discuss the adaptability of public schools in Korea and USA in a cross-cultural virtual classroom exchange program for their students. The ultimate goal of this paper is to recommend international collaboration for the dissemination of cross-cultural virtual classroom exchanges in public schools worldwide. Thus, it is important to first understand the inclusive context of this educational effort. Introduction to an integrated cross-cultural classroom exchange program will demonstrate the value of analyzing the adaptability of public schools and will serve as a guide to problems in this case study. The subsequent three narrative sections will illustrate realistic situations of the public schools in Korea and the USA during their adaptation processes of the cross-cultural virtual exchange program.

Contextual Background

Rapid evolution of information and communication technologies (ICT) has globally networked diverse societies and economies. Economic trade and social interaction occur in virtual spaces without limitations of physical boundaries and distance between nations. Infinite information and knowledge introduced through ICT has become a key source of economic production (Asian Development Bank, 2003; Bloom, 2004). Due to the unprecedented scale of globalization, people

Figure 1. Setting and participants (T: Teacher, ST: Support Teacher, P: Principal)

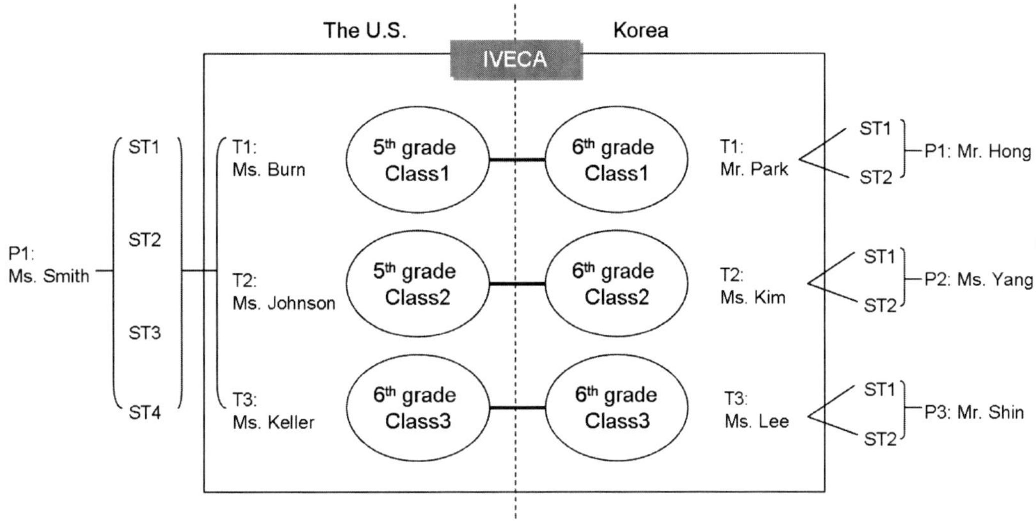

frequently encounter others from different cultures of distant regions or overseas. However, differences in culture, including language and religion, have often resulted in conflict due to intolerance, prejudice, and misunderstandings among peoples and nations (UNESCO, 2006a).

Intercultural competence is the ability to work appropriately and effectively in international and multicultural working environment with others who are linguistically and culturally different from oneself in collaboration (Fantini, 2006; Lasonen, 2006). Intercultural competence develops most effectively as people communicate and interact directly with others in environments of different cultures and diverse languages (Fantini, 2000). At this point, the means of fostering interculturally situated communication opportunities into school curriculum become an issue.

Fortunately, ICT has evolved enough to facilitate direct and regular intercultural interaction among students around the world through their respective school systems. Emphasizing the benefits of ICT for vitalizing societies, Burke addressed the uses of ICT for students' intercultural learning when featured at the 2003 Intercultural Education Summit as the keynote speaker:

> *... I see the dramatically-increasing availability of tools and resources other than that of the schoolroom (or even of the established information media).... in the way information and communication technology (ICT) is enhancing the abilities of even small communities to survive without having no submerge themselves in larger, more powerful cultures, ... it has also become urgent that we find ways to inform students about modes of thought other than that of their own locality. The world is already too interconnected for us to continue in the old isolationist paradigm. Nowhere is now too 'far away' to matter. It is no longer acceptable in a world of proximity, to ignore the views of other cultures. Fortunately, the same technology that has given rise to this complication also provides means to deal with it (Burke, 2003, pp. 2-3).*

International Virtual Elementary Classroom Activities (IVECA) was thus designed to provide cross-cultural learning opportunities by using ICT to effectively develop intercultural competence through public school curricula.

Integrated Cross-Cultural Classroom Exchange Program: IVECA

IVECA is an online classroom exchange program where K-12 school students in different countries share their thoughts and ideas through a web based, course management system (CMS). Its curriculum was developed by integrating local curricula with the framework of improving intercultural competence. With the school curricula integrated with the IVECA program, students in different countries perform individual and group projects in their classrooms according to the weekly activity topics provided in the IVECA program. The topics consist of activities such as personal introductions, comparison of school lives and cultures, discussions of cause and effect, and finding solutions regarding international issues. Completed projects are posted using the CMS communication and collaboration tools. Students from each country share their ideas, collaborate, and search and exchange information with each other every week. Depending on the needs and objectives of local schools, communication and collaboration platforms may include mainly discussion board and optionally blogs, wikis, and other images, not excluding podcasting and videocasting as well as synchronous audio and video interactions. The following vignette illustrates how IVECA is integrated in a public school classroom.

Monday afternoon after all students went back home, American English teacher Ms. Medlin visits her international virtual classroom on the web to see what activities are planned for this Thursday. The first page of the site shows an announcement describing this week's teaching and learning topic. The topic of this week is "what do you think about this issue?" The objective is to teach students how to search for events or news related to the U.S. and Korea, and logically write and talk about the cause and effect of the events. The goal of the discussion activities of this topic is to make students realize that there are different viewpoints in understanding an issue according to their cultural background and to cultivate open-mindedness and flexibility to these differences.

Since writing cause-effect sentences are the objectives in the English class, Ms. Medlin easily makes the connection between her English class objectives and the virtual classroom topic and starts designing lesson plans for this week. From her standard of learning objectives, she selects relevant local teaching materials to use as an introduction on how to find cause and effect in a story and how to use supporting ideas to write about the relationship. She feels that the first unit of this week would work with the materials. Thinking of the next English unit, she wants to prepare more interesting activities. "Let me see what is in the virtual classroom resource menu...," she says as she clicks on the course material menu on the virtual classroom website. She checks through all the relevant links and materials, and she finds that some very interesting events happened between the U.S. and Korea. She wants to use the material for this week's discussion with Korean students. Some creative ideas come to her mind. She thinks that it will be great to do some role-play with the story, to exchange the video clip, and then to share student ideas about the causes and effects of the events. Thinking that maybe the role-play itself might reveal different student perspectives and understanding of the events, she is getting excited about the activities.

However, wondering how the Korean teacher will design this activity and whether or not she will like her idea, Ms. Medlin opens her mail box and types a message to the virtual administrator about her idea. While waiting for a response, she keeps opening other resources that the virtual classroom website provided. "Wow.... um..... really?" Finding other news and events currently happening in Korea, she realizes how differently Korean society understands and solves certain problems.

When Ms. Medlin returns home, she finds an email response from the virtual administrator. The message says that the Korean teacher is also very excited about the idea and agrees to follow the suggested lesson plans of Ms. Medlin. In addition, the Korean teacher provides some additional stories in their textbook, which are relevant to the events that Ms. Medlin wants to use for the exchange activity. The additional materials will be helpful for both Korean and U.S. students, as well as for the teachers, in understanding the background of the events.

On Wednesday, she brings her students to the class library and reads the events she selected for the students. After studying some difficult words together, Ms. Medline lets them find and share the causes and effects of the events. Also, they share their supporting ideas about why they think the events caused the results and brought about those effects. When students return to their seats, they start writing cause and effect paragraphs in their notes. Also, she allows them to ask questions when they do not clearly understand the situation and bring ideas they want to share with the Korean students. Also they write about what they need to ask Korean students to have a better understanding of the events. Thereafter, the teacher gives students time to plan the role-play with the events.

On the exchange day, Thursday, Ms. Medlin distributes hand-outs including additional stories that the Korean teacher provided a few days ago. At first, each student reads the stories and shares his/her idea with a partner and jots down the reflection of his/her readers' response. In the classroom library, students volunteer to present their notes while others give feedback, including compliments and suggestions to the readers. Now Ms. Medlin takes out the school digital video camera and sets up the role-play stage in the open space at the back of the classroom. Students are very concentrated on the role-play preparation. While seeing her students work so hard and even enjoy what they are doing, Ms. Medline is very satisfied....

Multiple studies on IVECA in public elementary schools in Korea and the USA have proved its effectiveness in improving students' intercultural competence. Students attain knowledge about diverse cultures including their own, open their minds to accepting and adjusting to cultural differences, interact appropriately with people in different cultures and communicate effectively—share information, ideas and feelings—with others who have culturally and linguistically different backgrounds. In addition, IVECA has a positive influence on students' writing skills, it helps students broaden their worldviews by overcoming prejudice, misunderstandings, and racism, and it motivates students to learn (O'Neill, 2007; 2008). Below is the final voluntary posting of a Korean sixth grade student regarding her IVECA experience. It shows the potential impact of intercultural education in reducing world conflicts and contributing to peace and solidarity.

...I think IVECA activities are really great for students to develope [develop] their ways of thinking. It's hard to explain but, this is the way. If you continue to share stories with foreign countries, you students naturally get used to think widely. What I mean is that their thoughts and the basic structure and ways they think will become based on the whole world not only their own country. And if that happens, all students would care about overseas friends and further more, the danger and worries about war between each countries would decrease as well. The International Virtual Elementary Classroom Activities are the first start of all those great stuff. I fill [feel] proud and honorable for being the first class to experience it. I believe this activity would spread to more countries and help students all over the world develope [develop] themselves.

As the student envisioned, the impact of IVECA will be greater when it is diffused widely around the world and when it is implemented sustainably in public school systems. Now, the question is whether or not public schools worldwide can adapt to such transnational and intercultural learning environments facilitated by ICT. Seeking the answer to this question, this paper first investigates the adaptability of public schools in Korea and the USA. The following problems will guide finding the solution.

Problem Statement

How adaptable are public schools in Korea and the USA with respect to implementing IVECA, an integrated cross-cultural virtual classroom exchange program?

1. What technological concerns arise when the public schools in Korea and the USA implement IVECA?
2. How do teachers and students perform IVECA in their teaching and learning at school?
3. What are the organizational issues that influence IVECA integration in the public school systems of both nations?

Data Collection and Analysis

Data was collected during the previously conducted research on the implementation of IVECA. It included direct observation (recorded classroom video reviews for the Korean site), participant observation as a virtual administrator, student journals, interviews with students, teachers, support teachers and principals, informal talk with American teachers before, during, and after their IVECA class hours, instant messaging with Korean teachers, email exchanges, and archived postings of students in the Moodle discussion boards. Documents including each school's educational goals, curricula, American teacher pacing guides, Korean teacher guide books, class schedules, computer lab schedules, and school event calendar were also collected. American state standards of learning objectives and Korea's national curriculum were also obtained.

Miles and Huberman's (1994) analytic technique was used for the data analysis. Corpuses of data were reduced by coding and categorizing events and episodes into major themes. Patterns and relationships among the themes and role players (students, teachers, and administrators) were explored and analyzed by displaying the data through the forms of charts, graphs, matrices, and networks. Answers to the questions of this case study were concluded and verified throughout the continuous analytic comparison of data.

Technology Components and Implementation Procedure

While IVECA was integrated as a part of local classroom activities, its transnational exchange activities were performed through Moodle, an open source online content management system. With the guidance of the teachers, students searched information from the Internet and inserted relevant images into their postings. On special occasions, such as introducing themselves or conducting role-play through audio/video message, either students or teachers used multimedia production tools. Video/still cameras and multimedia editing software were utilized for the activities. Paint, iPhoto, Movie Maker, and iMovie, which were installed as default programs on PC and Mac computers, were used for the image and video editing. Also, microphones for audio recording were sometimes used. Especially for Korean teachers, a commercial web video conference system, WebEx, was used for the IVECA teacher training sessions at a distance. Teachers Room, a Moodle discussion board created for teachers, was used as the basic communication and discussion channel among the teachers in both countries; email was also used. Communication channels of the students were two

Moodle discussion boards—one was for formal weekly discussions and the other was for informal daily conversations. For the communication with the investigator (virtual administrator), both email and instant messaging were used in addition to Moodle's Teachers Room.

IVECA weekly topics/activities were introduced to the public school teachers and instructional coordinators. Once each of the schools revised and approved the IVECA curriculum based on their respective curricula's pace/schedule, a final syllabus was posted and distributed through the IVECA classrooms in Moodle. Teachers in both nations were trained through both face-to-face meetings and online training using Moodle. Before beginning IVECA weekly activities, teachers of each nation introduced IVECA to their students and trained them how to use the computer keyboard and Moodle system. IVECA was implemented for a whole school semester.

Three major issues—technological, pedagogical, and organizational factors—influenced adaptability of public schools in Korea and the USA in their integration of IVECA. The following sections relevant to each issue are presented in narrative form in order to illustrate realistic situations of adaptation of IVECA in the public schools. Each scene is based on observation field notes, interviews, informal talk, instant messaging, and journals. There was also a need to pay attention to the conflicts, ineffectiveness, and incoherency of the situations and perspectives of the key players in order to determine the specific problems in this case. Also, searching for positive potentials or alternatives should reveal solutions to the problems. In these narrative sections, the investigator speaks in the first person and appears as a virtual administrator providing instructional consultation, technological training and support.

Technological Issue: What were the Technological Concerns?

"Didn't we have Movie Maker on our school laptops?"

American school technology specialist, Ms. Thorne was talking on the phone with a city technology officer. While examining the programs and capacity of the school laptops in preparation for IVECA, Ms. Thorne and I could not find Movie Maker in the program menu. The city officer informed her that unnecessary programs had been blocked to prevent students from playing with the programs in their classes.

"Well, let's schedule to meet this week or next week. I will come by your school and unblock any programs your school needs," said the officer. Ms. Thorne typed all programs and multimedia tools that would be required for IVECA activities in the technology check-up request form and submitted it to the city technology officer by email.

"Is it very hard to unblock the path to the programs?"

Ms. Thorne answered my question, "I doubt it, but we are not allowed to change the setting by ourselves. You need to have a security password. The city office manages all computers distributed to the city schools. I guess, if a school messes up something while manipulating their computer settings, it makes harder to get it fixed later on. So, that's why I think the city office wants to have the control over the city school computers maintenance."

In the evenings, while setting up the American school computers with the city technology officer, I also communicated with Korean schools via email and instant messages to check their technology capacity and availability. Each school technology assistant provided information about their computer systems and multimedia production tools. Unlike the American school, where students and teachers used both Mac (at the computer lab) and

PC (laptops in this school), the Korean schools only used PC desktop computers. Teachers and students could access all programs on the school PCs—each school was managing their computers. The Korean schools had digital video and still camera for recording school events. However, they did not have multimedia production equipment for students use.

Ms. Kim, the Korean Class 2 teacher, said, "I am not worried. These days, many students have their own digital still or video cameras at home. You know, still camera also can take quite considerable amount of video. I am sure we will figure out how to make video with my students. My students know technology better than me."

As for Internet access, some schools in Korea have installed software to limit students' Internet searches if they use inappropriate keywords such as "sex" or "nude." Korean public schools teach students how to use the Internet appropriately and productively. Consequently, the school computers were basically open to any sites on the World Wide Web.

About a month later, with the help of Ms. Thorne and the American school media specialist, Ms. Laura, the teacher training session was set up at the school. Both Mac and PC computers, video/still cameras, mini DV tapes, microphones were prepared. I asked them,

"Were you able to find the Firewire cables with both 6-4 pins and 4-4 pins?"

A few weeks ago, Ms. Laura and I found that their PCs and Macs had different types of Firewire ports, and that the school did not have the two types of Firewire cables. Ms. Laura expressed her frustration while realizing that her school has multimedia tools, but they are neither compatible with each other, nor are they fully set up for a whole multimedia production process. However, Ms. Laura answered with a big smile,

"Yes, we got it through the city office media center. All our equipment will finally work together!"

Shortly after her excitement, in the middle of the training session, however, I began to hear,

"The page does not open!"

"You might need to wait for a while. The page might have a lot of images."

"No, no, I have been waiting forever. I don't think the site works."

Ms. Perkins, a city office instructional technology teacher, commented,

"Ah, you know what? The site might be blocked by the school network system. We are trying to protect our students from harmful video clips on the web, but it sometimes blocks things too much, you know."

I was introducing the teachers to a website to show some example video clips that will be helpful for their activities on video production of the day. I also planned to provide the teachers with an additional option using a secured web platform to upload students' videos and make them appear in the Moodle system. However, for the day, I emphasized that teachers should be careful in helping their students produce only short-length video clips, which can be handled in Moodle system. Ms. Perkins and I also decided to have another meeting to continue our discussion.

The same training course that the American school teachers took was provided for Korean teachers, but it was delivered only through the online video-conference system, WebEx. Since the teacher training module was designed and offered through the Moodle system as a distance learning course, Korean teachers were also able to follow all the course work with minimum guidance. The participating homeroom teacher in each school attended the session with their support teachers—either a school technology assistant or a technologically competent peer teacher. When asked her reflection on the training experience, Ms. Lee, the Korean Class 3 teacher, answered,

"I am not so proficient in using technologies like this. So I was afraid if I might not be able to follow these required activities, but I feel more confident now. I think I can perform my task. In addition, I have my peer teacher who I can ask a help if I forget how to do this again"

In fact, it was observed through the web conference system that she and her support teacher were laughing together as they worked on their joint video production. They also completed their tasks in the given time. However, Ms. Kim and her school technology assistant imported their video clips with Korean multimedia software. Due to codec incompatibility, the clips would not play properly through Windows Media Player on the American site. Thus, teachers were instructed to use only default multimedia tools as guided in the training module.

The training session was very intensely delivered in four hours instead of two weeks as was initially planned, since the teachers could not find *time* to attend the training together. Although the teachers were enthusiastic and clearly enjoyed experiencing IVECA activities, posting messages, creating video messages, and practicing Moodle functions, I was sorry that they could not have sufficient time to practice collaborating on an actual lesson plan. At the end of the session, Ms. Johnson, the America's Class 2 teacher walked to me and said,

"I really enjoyed today's activities and presentations… I am not still so confident about dealing with the technology and I'm a bit confused about how I should teach my kids and how my students' exchange will happen in Moodle. However, I think I am getting it gradually and I would like to learn more. Let me keep practicing it through the online materials and tutorials you provided, and I hope you would keep helping me to play my work right"

I did not realize at the time the significance of her comment until the end of the IVECA intervention when the program was over.

Pedagogical Application: Did Teachers and Students use IVECA Effectively?

I like IVECA but feel like I haven't really gotten to know anyone because no one's written back to me yet. (Journal)

At the early stage of IVECA implementation, an American Class 2 student, Sara, wrote in her journal that she felt disengaged since she actually had not exchanged messages with any specific counterpart student. I found that her postings were typically posted close to the last one in each discussion thread. Students tended to read messages from the top and reply to the messages as they read. Usually, the computer lab hour was not long enough for students to read and reply to all messages posted. In one of our conversations, Ms. Kim, the Korean Class 2 teacher asked,

"Should I tell my kids to reply to all messages? I am trying to guide my kids to reply as evenly as possible for all American kids' messages, but they usually read the first few postings from the top and it is hard for them to know who is replying to which messages."

While Ms. Kim was trying to find effective ways to engage more students in message exchanges, Ms. Johnson, her counterpart teacher, showed a lack of understanding in how to use Moodle for the exchange activities,

"Are we posting our message this time [at the follow-up's week] or replying to the Korean kids' messages?"

Ms. Keller, the American Class 3 teacher, was also having difficulty guiding her students where to post their messages for the follow-up week activities. Ms. Keller was with one of the students and was trying to guide him:

"Yes, they are gonna reply… If you guys reply in the What's Up board in week three, and they are gonna… is it right [looking at me, investigator]?"

What's Up board allowed students to exchange informal notes about their daily life at anytime. Somehow, she thought that the board was for follow-up activities, which gave additional time for students to edit and complete their unfinished messages, discuss similarities and differences between the two countries' information, and or reply to counterpart student messages. I later found that in the weekly discussion boards from her class, some students had replied to some of the Korean's postings while others had posted new messages in the What's Up board.

After half way through the implementation, Ms. Keller, however, began to integrate her RWE class time with computer lab hour. During her RWE class hours, she showed the IVECA topic announcement page to her students through a projector she checked out in advance. She helped her students have enough time to grasp the objectives and activities of the week's writing topic. She handed out worksheets that she redesigned, based on the IVECA weekly activity guides. Using the worksheet, her students brainstormed in groups what to prepare and to write for the week's postings. A few days later, on the day her class was assigned to use the computer lab, she brought her students to the lab. Students took out their worksheets including the information they had gathered over the week. Ms. Keller made multiple groups with the students and guided them as they discussed and completed their final postings as a group on the IVECA discussion board.

The following week, after the Korean students had posted their messages, Ms. Keller grouped her students again and assigned each group to a certain number of Korean postings. The group members read, discussed, and replied together to the assigned postings first and then freely read and replied to either Koreans' or their own classmates' postings. However, since she had not asked her students to list their names as a group on each posting, there was some misunderstanding among the Korean students:

IVECA activities are very good experience to learn USA's cultures and English. I satisfied with most things, but I was disappointed to a friend who writes a letter very careless [carelessly]. There are kind of cheater who write a letter same with their friends. Think of it, when you did a very good work with your best with very long time, but someone cheat your great ideas! When I'm victim, I will miss a fun to write my idea. Without that, IVECA was very good activity that I have ever done... (Journal)

Since the American students posted the paired group work individually, the same messages were being posted under different author names so that Korean students thought one of them had "cheated" by copying someone else's response. When I was recalling this incident with teachers at the end of the program, Ms. Johnson commented,

I mean it is an experience matter. If you experienced this beforehand, it would be easier. If I do this again, I will be definitely better. I think knowing ahead of time about how I could implement it will be great. (Interview)

While each class lessons were getting formulated over the implementation period, Ms. Keller was often observed reserving the computer lab for IVECA activities. However, it was also observed that she was spending quite a lot of time in checking whether any projectors were available and she would borrow projectors spontaneously. Also, she occasionally asked her students to bring laptops from other classrooms during the RWE class hour. Ms. Burn who participated in IVECA a second time commented on the differences between having a complete technology package set up in one place and having each piece in different locations.

Last year the laptop that we used had the projector on the cart with the computers. So, it was just easy to pull out the projector and put it on the screen. Now, the projector is in another room. It's like

when I was thinking about checking out, I just feel like.. Before, it was right there, I just could use it. Now, it's really pathetic excuses....But, I think at this point, it's kind of shame that every classroom doesn't have projector everyday to use. I mean for the kids to read Social Studies books, they can be reading off the Internet and teachers should be showing where to go. (Interview)

In the other site, Mr. Park, the Class 1 teacher in Korea, was showing weekly activities through the built-in projector in his classroom before bringing his students to the computer lab. He integrated many of his subject classes with IVECA activities whenever the topics were relevant to the subject matter.

I once had an objective in my Korean class; Students can identify the organization of the writing and can demonstrate their understanding in the writing through comparison and contrast. I've been emphasizing that we need to be aware of differences between their posting and ours on IVECA. And, it's good chance to apply what they learned about stanza in their Korean class and also good for interdisciplinary learning and application. They have been enjoying learning about other countries in their social studies class also. Well, I design my classes from interdisciplinary approach. For example, we have unit on Internet manner in our practical course subject. I've tried to integrate that unit in IVECA activities. I'm trying to integrate any other related subject matters rather than stick to certain one subject.... (Interview)

Ms. Lee also used the large screen TV in her classroom, which had been distributed to all public school classrooms under the Ministry of Education Information Age project. She used a computer lab for students' actual computing activities—searching for information and relevant images, and posting and replying to messages on IVECA discussion boards. During the week, she took advantage of the TV projector to view IVECA announcement pages at anytime, she guided students in brainstorming topics, and she assigned homework ahead of time.

For the preparative homework assignments, Ms. Kim utilized her class homepage and let her students gradually upload the information they found over the week to use it collaboratively for the IVECA weekly activities. When asked about her teaching strategies, Ms. Kim commented,

Korean students have learned how to use computer software like Microsoft Word, PowerPoint and Hangul and they know even better than teachers in using the Internet, playing with images, multimedia and so on. You know computer education is a required curriculum in public schools in Korea... But, of course, there are some kids who left behind than others. But they teach and learn with each other. I actually didn't do much with technology for IVECA. My students did follow the IVECA instruction. I just guided them to understand the value of this cultural learning, help them to grasp topics and find the appropriate contents for them to write effectively. As we used to use our homepage for the class homework submission, I guided them to use it for IVECA preparation, too. It is just like my Korean language education class. (Interview)

As Ms. Kim mentioned, the Korean students easily found relevant images and embedded them into most of their postings. The American students showed their excitement when they read the Korean's messages including images:

Bruce was concentrated on reading each message from the beginning of the class. As he saw pictures of dessert, "Wow~", he smiled with his friend, Walt. Bruce found another picture [in the Korean students' postings], "Look at this" John responded, "Oh, my god"... "Woah... hahaha"

Bruce and John are talking about images of vegetables. When they scrolled down and read another message, "Oh, they like steak... Wohoo!!!" They read every single message carefully and expressed their excitement and surprise. Tom was looking at John's screen. Carol was not even looking around as she read the Korean students' messages and replied to their messages (Field note)

Such images also helped the Korean students understand the American students' messages written in English. When Donsuk was asked about what he learned through the activities. He answered,

Culture. But I could not fully understand. I could guess the meanings by looking at pictures. [And then] friends who are good at English told me the [exact] meanings. (Interview)

Since students enjoyed using images, which were helpful for communications as well as increased students' interests, they were motivated to use images appropriate for their counterparts. The Korean teachers allowed their students to search image files on the Internet, and the students were able to attach them once their teacher guided them through the process. However, the American students had restricted Internet access. The school technology specialist, Ms. Thorne, usually found images and stored them on the school sever in advance and students could only use images from this pool in their postings.

As the implementation progressed, it was often observed that many American students were typing messages with only one finger or just one hand. They gradually showed improvement in typing and some of the students said that IVECA motivated them to practice typing faster. However, a few students who had poor typing skills and very low writing proficiency reported that throughout the entire program, typing made it difficult for them to perform writing tasks for IVECA.

I mean the only part I really didn't like was the typing part....But to actually talk to them and actually read what they have to say, because they do have like pretty cool stuff, I actually liked that part.... And like other people [his close friends who had the same problem in typing with poor writing skill] it's the same way and like I think it's just because of the typing because they don't really like to do it [typing] and it get's really boring. (Interview)

Knowing that America also emphasize technological literacy, I wondered why these kids had not yet been trained in typing, at school. I asked one of the American teachers about the possible reasons. One of the answers led me to further explore the school's policies and administrative functions.

Teachers and schools are very focused on students' academic achievement. We have State level tests. School's major interest is whether or not our students will pass the standard of learning. Keyboarding? It is not included in the test. Our students begin to learn typing from 6th grade. (Informal talk)

Organizational Influence: How were the Schools Managed?

"Oh, I am sorry. We could not post anything yesterday."

"No, no, you don't need to apologize. What happened?"

"All 6th grade students had to take SOL test prep at the time we normally use for IVECA, and I could not change my computer lab hour ahead of time"

When I encountered Ms. Keller in the cafeteria during her lunch time, she explained why her students could not post any messages to that week's IVECA board. I sat down next to her and asked about how she was doing with IVECA and whether she had any difficulties. She said,

"No, I am enjoying IVECA. Remember? At the beginning, my students were like, I-don't-know-what-to-write, why-do-we-write-this... kind of attitude. But now they write a couple of paragraphs much faster and their writings make sense better than before. I think they also try to get attention from Korean kids, and you know what? As a matter of fact, my kids were sort of open their mind because they could see Korean kids use two languages and some of the Korean kids' life styles are better than their lives, and foods and traditions are so rich and interesting to them. My kids are realizing that they have not known well even their own culture, the meaning of the flag and history and so on. I think IVECA is really good for them to learn not only different culture but also their own culture. They learn from the students overseas. So, how interesting it is! Ha-ha-ha..."

Ms. Keller kept going on and on about IVECA, but finally she began to talk about her concerns.

"These weeks, we had not enough time for IVECA preparation because of SOL preparation. My kids' level is low, so I had to pay attention to their SOL test score....It will be good if the principal let public to know this program will be good, this is pretty cool, and how we integrate teaching with our kids. I think it would be a good role as a principal."

She reminded me of a conversation with Ms. Burn in the computer lab. She said,

Ms. Johnson and I were talking about this the other day. You know kids are doing NCLB thing and take test. But this [IVECA] is much meaningful activity. They have reasons why they are writing and enjoy it. And they express something they could do by going there for the people [Korean kids]. Won't you need go and let principal know this? This is real experience and meaningful. They need to do this at RWE mainly! (informal talk)

When Ms. Keller had almost finished her lunch, I asked her if she had informed her Korean counterpart of when her students would be able to do the weekly activities. I was concerned since the Korean students could move to the next week activities based on American students' postings this week. Furthermore, I had seen some messages from some Korean kids, at the What's Up board, wondering why their American friends had not been posting. Ms. Keller said she hadn't and explained that it was because of her busyness at school due to the test preparation. I told her that I would check with Korean teacher about the pacing adjustment.

Later that evening, I left a message in the virtual Teacher Room to inform Ms. Keller's counterpart, Ms. Lee, about the situation in the American site and suggested an alternative pacing option. Although I did not receive a response from Ms. Lee, I saw that her students had moved on to the next week's activities. In the mean time, I received an email from Ms. Lee. She understood the American school situation and mentioned that her school would be very busy over the next a couple of weeks since they had a very important school function to attend to.. Much later, when the program ended, I found out how busy she really was those days. She explained,

My principal Mr. Shin does not know much about this activity. He is more interested in Art. He devoted his whole career to Art education. Since my school is a model school, I had to turn in activity reports of seven different topics with my 6th graders. To be honest, my formal vice-principal introduced me to IVECA, but (after he moved to another school) neither the principal nor new vice-principal were interested in IVECA....As my class is the only one for IVECA, I felt isolated from other classes. (Interview)

I responded to her email by asking if it would be hard to follow the IVECA pace during school hours. I suggested that she encourage her students to keep interacting with American kids freely through the What's Up board. I also suggested encouraging individual participation in weekly discussions before the whole class could come back to the topic. She agreed to my suggestions and left a message for Ms. Keller regarding her school situation and activity plan, in the Teacher Room.

I also observed that the number of students' postings in Korean Class 2 had been decreasing over the last two weeks and the consistency of postings was not as good as that of previous weeks. As a result, many of the American student postings did not have any replies. Since in the Teacher Room I could not find any messages written by Ms. Kim regarding a pacing problem, I proposed an on-line meeting with her. At the end of the school day, when she became available online, she began to type messages:

"I just came back to my classroom from school playfield. How are you?"

"Pretty good thanks. What's going on in your school?"

"It's autumn sports festival season. It's been so crazy these couple of weeks. Because all of our 6th grade students will be doing a Taekon-Dance performance in the festival next week, we have to rehearse during class time. It has been hard to find time for any activity including IVECA because of these practices."

"Ah… that's why I could not see your student postings as usual. You know kids are very sensitive about the replies. They might wonder if the Korean kids do not like to talk to them anymore"

"Oh, they might, I know. My kids are also eager to receive replies. I should've informed Ms. Johnson. I've been just so pre-occupied. But you know my kids love IVECA. Actually they have been asking when we are going to computer lab for the activities all the time. Next week, once the festival is over, I am sure my kids will be able to go back to normal pace."

So, I suggested that she do another follow-up activity the following week instead of working on next week's topic. I also conveyed the pacing adjustment to Ms. Johnson through the Teacher Room.

When I was about to log-off from the instant messaging application, Mr. Park sent me a text message saying his kids might not be able to do IVECA because they had a mid-term exam and would be going on a field trip after the exam. I told him that I wished he could have included some questions related to IVECA activities in the exam questionnaire. Along with a smile emoticon, he said that he thought it should be that way and that it would be possible if all 6th grader teachers participated in IVECA together. He further noted that in elementary schools in Korea, teachers develop their exam questionnaire based on the national curriculum objectives. I also asked him if IVECA had been too much work. He said,

Since IVECA bulletin board has clear instructions on it and is well managed, students can use it without calling out for help. Thus, it's not been a big burden to teachers. Honestly, I don't think I've done anything. Rather, it lightened the burden on the teacher-discretion class [Da-neem Jai-riang class that teacher can run the class curriculum as they want], which we need to utilize computer in my class. (Interview)

I asked him if his principal, Mr. Hong, had ever talked about IVECA with him. Mr. Park said that Principal Hong was very interested in IVECA, and in fact it was the principal introduced who had introduced him to IVECA. Whenever the principal saw Mr. Park, he would check to see how he was doing with IVECA and offer encouragement. Mr. Park commented that his principal's encouragement reaffirmed that he was doing the right thing for his students. After the project ended, I visited the principal and learned that the he was linking IVECA to English education and cultural learning integrated with other relevant subject matters:

[Through IVECA] we not only learn other language but also can pick up the culture and apply that in using that language. Since learning the language helps students learn about the culture automatically, it would help them in communicating with foreigners. We call it an interdisciplinary subject. It would be great to use the subject in which computers, English, or other subject matter are integrated. (Interview)

Mr. Hong additionally commented that IVECA fits perfectly with Korean society's interest in globalization, English education, and the missions of his school—producing global citizens, promoting English proficiency and cultural understanding, and utilizing ICT in education.

Near the end of the program, as suggested by American teachers during the project period, I also tried to convey the value of IVECA to the school administration. First, I met with the instructional coordinator, Ms. Spreen. She is a school leadership team member as well as one of the IVECA support teachers. I asked how she saw IVECA with respect to the Standards of Learning (SOL) and No Child Left Behind (NCLB) issues at school. She very confidently expressed her perspective on IVECA:

I think that, to me, the biggest piece of the IVECA is the exchange of cultures. But within exchange of culture then can you weigh up infuse what we are required by the State to teach. So, you know, when we are thinking about skills, that skills is going back into a piece of literature or an article and picking up some details or answering some questions, and then we could use the articles that they read or maybe they are summarizing and giving their opinions back to somebody else. Those are good skills and that something that our kids need to know.... And then we will be pointing out to the teachers how this is not a stand-alone, this is not something in addition to what you have to do. This could be in places something and maybe pointing out where our standards are really in there. (Interview)

She also added that it could be about whether or not teachers can make the link between the State requirement and IVECA activities. In fact, Ms. Spreen could not attend the initial training course due to schedule conflicts. Nor was she observed giving any instructional support for teachers over the program implementation period, which is why, she explained, most IVECA teachers had not come to her for help. Nevertheless, her perception about IVECA made me think that other IVECA teachers should have worked with her earlier. I wondered what the principal would want to say about IVECA.

"How are you? Ms. Smith. We are all done with IVECA this semester. Have you had a chance to hear about the program from anyone?"

"No, actually not, I think Ms. Spreen is the person who communicates with the teachers."

"Oh, then you might have talked with Ms. Spreen about IVECA."

"Well… no, we had not had a chance to talk about it specifically. This is my first semester as a principal. The leadership team has had to dealt with many things, haha. But I know which teachers were working on the project and what the program is about"

Ms. Smith commented on her perception of IVECA,

Everybody says these days... is global economy and world are spread everything, but I do think it is true. My students need to be able to understand other cultures and communicate with people of all different types. (Interview)

To the question about the goals and mission of her school, Ms. Smith clearly stressed that the mission of the school was to facilitate students' high achievement in SOL test scores, and to conform with the NCLB Act regulations. She also described how IVECA is related to the school goal and RWE curriculum.

I think the project like this fits in because there was a still teacher choice in how you deliver the curriculum so a project like this that has a strong writing component to it where the kids have written it fits perfectly in for our RWE class because we are doing concentration on reading and writing during the two hour block...I think that like anything needs to fit. Teachers need to see this as something well the children in learning communication skills, writing skills, thinking about how they want to formulate their idea to communicate fits into my RWE program. (Interview)

Consequently, I did not need to explain the benefit of IVECA to her, since Ms. Smith was of a like mind. However, I did need to tell the IVECA teachers what the principal thought.

In light of the issues set forth in the narrative sections above, what needs to be done?

CURRENT CHALLENGES FACING THE ORGANIZATION

As illustrated above, the study revealed that technological, pedagogical, and organizational issues affected the adaptability of public schools in both Korea and America in integrating cross-cultural virtual learning activities, IVECA. Additionally, schools faced challenging issues for further adoptions of IVECA.

Specific Problems Addressed

Technologically, the American school needed to set up all the different types of equipments to be compatible and access to the required programs needed to be unblocked. Both American and Korean schools had to make sure they used common multimedia software so that the created video files could be viewable in both countries. All participating teachers should be trained how to utilize online course management system (CMS) and how to produce diverse types of communication forms including text, audio, and video. This is also related to pedagogical issues.

To provide effective instruction and interculturally meaningful learning opportunities for students, teachers needed to be familiar with how IVECA exchange processes work and how IVECA is integrated with local curricula. Efficient and easy access to technologies helped teachers effectively adapt integration of IVECA with their class activities. While Korean classrooms were equipped with built-in projectors and large screen televisions, American schools needed to check out the equipment ahead of time. Technological competence of the students also influenced the implementation of IVECA. The Korean teachers let their students handle image files and allowed them to utilize the Internet for their activities. American students had a technology specialist assist them in the use of image files, and their Internet searches were relatively restricted. Some American students had difficulties in typing for IVECA activities. A school's organizational management based on state or national policy affected these differences.

Korea's public elementary schools are required to teach computer education from the first grade. While the Virginia emphasizes technology utilization in schools, at the local level, schools are more focused on SOL testing, which does not test computer skills. Official approval of IVECA integration by school principals was desired by participant teachers in both Korea and American schools in managing their time to adapt IVECA. The benefits of IVECA need to be connected to a principal's educational focus and a school's mission, state/national learning objectives, and national curriculum goals. However, communication and sharing perspectives between the teachers and administrators need to be established for adapting IVECA effectively under the support of school administration.

Challenges and Current Status

After the project was completed, participant teachers and administrators discussed with the investigator how they could continue to implement and integrate IVECA into their school activities.

American school teachers suggested that classrooms be set up in a way that teachers do not need to plan for and check out technology equipment in advance, bring it to classrooms and set it up in their classroom every time. The teachers agreed they should at least be able to view the IVECA website in any class hour for effective integration and efficient class time management. However, Principal Smith stated that her school does not have enough funds to install such equipment in every classroom nor set up an additional room with a full set of multimedia and computing equipment. Ms. Smith said that someone at school level should persuade the school board or city office. A principal may suggest the need for technology funding, but actual decision making for granting the funds comes out of the board. Alternatively, an investigator from a university and school members could write up grant proposal to obtain funding from an educational technology fund resource or state/federal level grant program. Ms. Smith said someone should be dedicated to such work.

All American participating teachers thought IVECA had high-quality activities and were willing to rejoin the project in the future. However, they were not sure if it would be possible to have all of the same-grade teachers join IVECA to make it fully adapted to their school. They said that since the pressure from SOL testing is heavy, most teachers tend to avoid implementing creative teaching. To meet the state and school requirements, they preferred to drill students in content and test-taking skills. Helping such teachers understand that IVECA is integrated with their curriculum and training them to be capable for IVECA utilization seemed challenging. Along with it, providing students with computer education from younger grade would become a challenge.

As for the matter of having all same-grade teachers participate in IVECA, Korean teachers were rather positive. Since Korean teachers already tend to work collaboratively with the same-grade teachers, they thought it would make their schools more adaptable to IVECA integration. If some teachers did not know how to use technology, they said other teachers would help them. However, one of the participant teachers expressed a concern that older teachers might be hesitant to join because of their limited English proficiency. The other two teachers pointed out that this issue would be also resolved by working together with the same-grade teachers.They also commented that students could be used for the communication. English could be a problem, but they agreed it would simply be a matter of how to provide training for those hesitant teachers to take advantage of IVECA and the collaborative work from peer teachers.

One of the growing problems in using the Internet was also pointed out. Korean students are very exposed to cyber games, such that child Interent addiction has become a significant social issue. In 2007, Korea Agency for Digital Opportunity and Promotion reported degree of elementary students' Intenet addition—1.2% (high risk) and 11.0% (potentially at-risk) (MEST & KERIS, 2007). During the IVECA impelementation, a student who thought he was addicted to Internet gaming reported that he did not pay attention during the program. He found out too late that there were, in fact, some very interesting activities. However, he said that he could not resist his desire to play games when sitting at the computer lab. Developing the instructional strategies to engage such children in IVECA and helping them overcome such addiction would be one of the next challenging tasks for Korean schools.

Currently, the American school installed a projector and an electronic white-board in every classroom and they are connnected to the teacher's computer. City office of education supported the installations so that the school's adaptability of

Figure 2. Adaptability factors in public school. Integration with cross-cultural classroom exchange programs

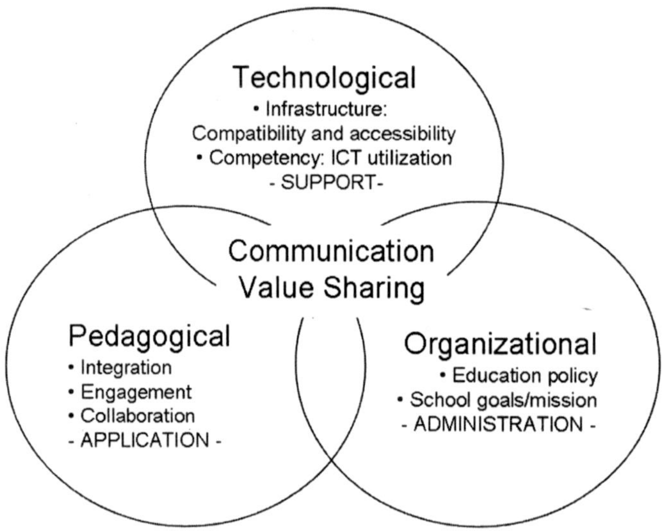

technology infrastructure has been improved dramatically over a year. This American school is planning to join IVECA and interact with several schools in Korea elementary schools soon.

SOLUTIONS AND RECOMMENDATIONS

As described above, investigating technological, educational, and organizational issues identifies specific problems determining public schools adaptability of cross-cultural classroom exchange activities (in this study, IVECA). The problems that schools can resolve internally are not an issue. However, the challenges come from problems that schools cannot find any alternatives to, or that they have difficulties adopting a solution. In an attempt to provide schools with a solution guide, this section first clarifies the factors that influence public school adaptability. Second, solutions to the challenges schools faced will be discussed in economic, social, cultural and political contexts. Ultimately, this paper will provide recommendations to diffuse further cross-cultural virtual classroom exchange programs integrated with pubic school systems.

Adaptability Factors as Solution Guides

Figure 2 presents the primary factors and its subordinate elements of public schools adaptability to IVECA.

The technological factor consists of two elements—technological infrastructure and competency of ICT users (key players: students, teachers, and resource teachers) in schools. Although schools have technologies for online activities and multimedia production, all equipments and computer systems need to be compatible in the system. In addition, the easier it is for users to access the technologies, the more adaptable schools are. Research has also addressed the positive relationship between easy access to technologies and technology integration in teaching (Williams, Coles, Richardson, Wilson, & Tuson, 2000; Dexter, 2002). Additionally, schools are more adaptable to IVECA when the teachers and students are competent in using ICT including online content management systems, typing, diverse media tools, and software. This factor is about how school infrastructure and key players are technologically supportive to the implementation process.

The pedagogical factor is related to how well teachers integrate IVECA with their classroom activities. Teachers in a decentralized curriculum system need to be proficient in grasping the relationship between IVECA topics/activities and state learning objectives. Teachers in a centralized curriculum system can link IVECA topics/activities to relevant subject unit objectives. They can also use their textbooks for IVECA activity content material. Appropriate engagement skills for intercultural exchange are critical to successful cross-cultural learning. Teacher intercultural sensitivity influences student intercultural understanding (Van Hook, 2005). Teachers need to have instructional strategies when applying student group projects, thereby enabling each member to contribute to achieving the goal of the group cooperatively. The more group projects promote collaboration with counterparts, the more successful the adaptation to IVECA will be. In addition, collaborative teaching with peer teachers increases the adaptability.

Since state and national education policy governs the goals, missions and curricula of local public schools, the organizational factor significantly affects a schools' adaptability. When school administrators find the connection between the benefit of IVECA and emphases of education policy, schools become more adaptable to IVECA. However, appropriate managerial strategies of school administrators are required in fostering the adaption processes of schools. For example, establishing clear communication channels among teachers, resource teachers, and leadership teams help them know that school authorizes IVECA. This facilitates the adoption of IVECA as part of school curricula. Such communication channels include meetings to enhance pedagogical and technological adaptation. Such meetings provide teachers with opportunities to collaborate and to share experiences and insights that could enhance adaptability. As Rogers (2003) also emphasizes, sharing the benefits of innovation (IVECA) among adopters (teachers) expedites its adaptation.

Additionally, to adopt IVECA as a formal school curriculum, public schools under a strictly centralized system need authorization from local offices of education in the context of education policy established by a Ministry of Education. Thus, the adaptability of such public schools has greater influence from higher level organizations and national education policy. However, once it is approved, the scope of IVECA dissemination becomes large and schools' adaptability can dramatically increase.

The factors clarified above will guide local schools in solving the specific problems identified in this case study. The following section discusses solutions for the current challenges that the schools faced in broader context. Recommendation of the solutions will be provided beyond local school level to the economical, cultural and political context.

Solutions and Recommendations

The challenges that the public schools met in further adapting IVECA include: 1) obtaining funds or support from State/National offices of Education to construct technological infrastructure 2) helping teachers avoid limiting their teaching due to the SOL test, 3) promoting teacher competency and collaboration, and 4) engaging students addicted to Internet gaming.

The first challenge involves technological policy matters in terms of distributing technologies to schools. The second challenge also is relevant to educational policy along with professional development issues. The third challenge pertains to pedagogical and organizational aspects of teacher preparation. The last challenge is related to pedagogical and technological issues. Overall, these challenges are related to educational technology policy, teacher preparation and professional development. Thus, the solutions lie in identifying the roles of key players, policy makers and higher education teacher educators.

- **Recommendation one:** Policy makers increase educational technology budgets to enhance technological infrastructure for public schools in order to promote adaptability of cross-cultural virtual exchange activities worldwide. Such support would foster social and economic potential as well as educational advancement.

The theme of this case study—public school adaptability in cross-cultural virtual classroom exchange program integration—implies a relationship with political, cultural, technological, and educational issues. Elucidation of these relationships should provide policy makers with sufficient reason to act on this recommendation. Society demands that education facilitate cultural understanding among people and nations. The use of information and communication technology (ICT) as means to that end is very promising. Furthermore, the utilization of ICT in education will contribute to society's economic growth due to the nature of our global knowledge-based economy.

Recently, international organizations have paid marked attention to promoting mutual understanding and respect for cultural differences among nations and culturally different groups of people. Established in 2005, United Nations Alliance of Civilizations (AoC) identified four main fields of action—*education, youth, migration, and media*—to resolve cultural conflicts around the world (United Nations, 2007; 2008). AoC addresses the significance of improving "mutual respect and understanding through the positive experiences resulting from increasingly direct encounters between people of diverse cultures" (Kerim, 2007). Since 2006, the United Nations Global Alliance for ICT and Development has been dedicated to enhancing world harmony and facilitating co-development through the use of ICT (UNGAID, 2009). Asia-Europe Meeting also emphasizes "promoting dialogue among cultures and civilizations and mutual understanding between people of Asia and Europe" (Xinhua News, 2008).

Such international organizations and academia agree that education plays a critical role in producing global citizens who are respectful of cultural differences and capable of interacting and cooperating with people from other countries and cultures. Reimers (2006) stresses that schools should cultivate students to possess global citizenship by teaching them how to communicate in peaceful and constructive ways across-cultural differences. He also posits that schools need to inculcate global values in their students through curriculum. At the UNESCO Expert Meeting on Intercultural Education, scholars underscored the need to implement intercultural education in all levels of education to help students become interculturally competent global citizens (UNESCO, 2006b).

Currently, due to the increased rates of international marriages, illegal immigrants, North Korean refugees, and international trainees, Korean society has become more multicultural. Educators and society in general are urged to develop best practices in multicultural education, and to that end, the use of an e-learning format is considered to be the most promising (Park & O'Neill, 2009).

In response to America's economic crisis, an emphasis has been placed on education as a fundamental resource for long-term and sustainable development of the nation. In the American Recovery and Reinvestment Act of 2009, investment for education technology was underscored by the motto of Education for the 21st Century. It was to ensure economic competitiveness of the next generation (House of Representatives, 2009). Exchange programs of "online learning for teachers and children around the world" were also specifically suggested as ways to promote development and preserve different cultural value through education (New York Times, 2009).

Cross-cultural virtual classroom exchange programs, such as IVECA, promote children's intercultural competence and provide them with opportunity to utilize and develop ICT skills (e.g. information searches, creating electronic projects, and utilizing information for international exchanges). By exchanging ideas, discussing issues, and sharing thoughts and feelings with classmates and international counterparts, students develop analytic and critical thinking, and communicative strategies. These skills are essential to being a competent human resource for 21st century global society. Most importantly, IVECA helps students broaden their worldview and grow as global citizens by providing them with ways and means to define their own cultural identity and overcome racism and prejudice through the acquisition of global knowledge and values in diverse cultures (O'Neill, 2007; 2008).

It is certain that cross-cultural virtual classroom exchange activities fulfill social, economic, cultural needs. Therefore, policy makers need to plan immediate actions to help public schools adapt to cross-cultural virtual exchange activities through their regular school curricula and provide financial support at the state and national levels. The wider such cross-cultural learning opportunities are diffused, the greater the impact on society and the economy will be.

- **Recommendation two:** Teacher educators in higher education need to internationalize teacher education programs and provide intercultural dialogues among pre-service teachers through the Web. Internationalized interdisciplinary teacher education programs integrated with educational technology and intercultural/multicultural education will produce quality teachers required for adapting cross-cultural virtual classroom exchanges in schools.

Studies have stressed the importance of the teacher's role in promoting intercultural learning in second/foreign language students (Byram, 2001). Genuine engagement strategies based on intercultural sensitivity and competence are known to positively influence minority student performance (Nel, 1992) and increase the effectiveness of intercultural virtual classroom exchange (O'Neill, 2008).

The effectiveness of teacher technology competence on students learning has been addressed. Albee (2003) focuses on increasing pre-service teachers' technology skill preparedness in stating teachers' technology competence increases the effectiveness of teaching. Experienced teachers also have recommended that pre-service teacher education programs include technology competence development (Fisher, 1997). Teachers who experienced IVECA also noted the importance of developing technological proficiency in online classroom activities and multimedia communication.

IVECA teachers testified they could better grasp how cross-cultural learning can be integrated with their curriculum after they experienced the activities over the course of a semester. Kearsley (1998) posits that teacher training should be planned in the form of long term, on-going and experience-based training. He also stresses that the training focus should be on instructional applications of the technologies and contents.

Therefore, pre-service teachers need realistic opportunities to develop their intercultural competence and their utilization of technology for cross-cultural virtual classroom exchange activities. By linking interdisciplinary teacher education programs overseas through the Internet, teacher education programs should facilitate pre-service teachers' real experience in cross-cultural virtual exchange activities. As a result, pre-service teachers will be able to enhance their intercultural understanding and will be trained how to utilize technologies for online cross-cultural learning. Developing student teaching programs in local schools will promote sustainable adaptability to cross-cultural exchange activities. At the same time, continued scholarly discourse and research through this exchange program would advance the quality of cross-cultural classroom exchange programs benefiting not only students and society in each nation but also global society.

Furthermore, state and national offices of education can collaborate with universities in providing professional development courses for cross-cultural virtual classroom exchanges. In addition, it will be more practical if policy makers establish a teacher education and employment policy that credits such pre- and in-service teachers, who took the training course or experienced cross-cultural virtual classroom exchange activities.

Naturally, these two recommendations will require systematic collaboration. The vision is that such collaborative efforts will increase the adaptability of local schools in cross-cultural classroom exchange activities, and ultimately produce an international virtual schooling system. As more students can join such schools, there will be greater reduction in cultural conflicts and a collaborative development of a world economy. Universities and nonprofit organizations in Korea and America have established and are seeking further international collaboration from academia, ministries, technology firms, and international organizations. The nature of such collaboration supports the long-standing efforts of the United Nations and UNESCO to create a better world.

The education of the young and exchanges of young people and of ideas in a spirit of peace, mutual respect and understanding between peoples can help to improve international relations and to strengthen peace and security (General Assembly resolution 2037 (XX) of 7 December 1965).

REFERENCES

Albee, J. (2003). A Study of Preservice Elementary Teachers Technology Skill Preparedness and Examples of How It Can Be Increased. *Journal of Technology and Teacher Education*, 11.

Asian Development Bank. (2003). *Key Indicators: Education for Global Participation*. Retrieved from http://www.adb.org/Documents/Books/Key_Indicators/2003/pdf/theme_paper.pdf

Bloom, D. E. (2004). Globalization and Education: An Economic Perspective, In M. Suarez-Orozco & D. Qin-Hillard, (Ed.), Globalization: Culture and Education in the New Millennium. (pp. 58-77). Ewing, NJ: University of California Press.

Burke, J. (2003). *Intercultural Education Summit Keynote*. Retrieved from http://people.ucsc.edu/~pmmckerc/IEA.html

Byram, M., Nichols, A., & Stevens, D. (Eds.). (2001). Developing Intercultural Competence in Practice: Languages for Intercultural Communication and Education. Multilingual Matters, Ltd.

Culp, K. M., Honey, M., & Mandinach, E. (2003). A Retrospective on Twenty Years of Education Technology Policy. Washington, DC: Center for Children and Technology Education Development Center, U.S. Department of Education, Office of Educational Technology.

Dexter, S. (2002). eTIPS-Educational Technology Integration Principles. Designing instruction for technology-enhanced learning. Hershey, PA: Idea Group Publishing.

Fantini, A. E. (2000). A CENTRAL Concern: Developing Intercultural Competence. In *SIT Occasional Papers Series,* (1). Brattleboro, VT: School for International Training.

Fantini, A. E. (2006). Final Report of a Research Project conducted by the Federation of The Experiment in International Living with funding support from the Center for Social Development at Washington University, St. Louis, Missouri (The Initial Phase of An Extended Project to Explore and Assess Intercultural Outcomes in Service Program Participants Worldwide). Brattleboro, VT: Federation EIL

Fisher, M. (1997). The Voice of Experience: Inservice Teacher Technology Competency Recommendations for Preservice Teacher Preparation. *Journal of Technology and Teacher Education*, *5*(2-3), 139–147.

Kearsley, G. (1998). Educational Technology: A Critique. *Educational Technology*, *38*(2), 47–51.

Kerim, S. (2007, September). S*tatement of the 62nd Session of the United Nations General Assembly at the Ministerial Meetings of Group of Friends of the Alliance of Civilizations*, New York. Retrieved from http://www.unaoc.org/images/articles/min_pga.pdf

Korea Education & Research Information Service. (2000-2004). *White Paper: Adapting Education to the Information Age.* Seoul: Korea, Retrieved from http://english.keris.or.kr/etc/whitepaper.jsp

Korean Culture and Information Service Ministry of Culture. (2008). Facts about Korea. Korean Government Publication.

Lasonen, J. (2006). *Expert Meeting on Intercultural Education: Intercultural Education in the Context of Internationalization, Localization and Globalization*. Paris: UNESCO Headquarters.

MEST & KERIS. (2007). 2007Adapting Education to the Information Age. Seoul, Korea: Ministry of Education, Science and Technology & Korea Education and Research Information Service. Retrieved from http://www.keris.or.kr/download/data/2007-WhitePap.pdf

Morris, P. (1996). Asia's Four Little Tigers: a comparison of the role of education in their development. *Comparative Education*, *32*(1), 95–109. doi:10.1080/03050069628948

Nel, J. (1992). The Empowerment of Minority Students: Implications of Cummins. *Action in Teacher Education*, *14*(3), 38–45.

New York Times. (2009, June 4). Obama's Speech in Cairo. *New York Times*. Retrieved June 4, 2009, from http://www.nytimes.com/2009/06/04/us/politics/04obama.text.html?pagewanted=7

O'Neill, E. J. (2007). Implementing International Virtual Elementary Classroom Activities for Public Schools Students in the U.S. and Korea. *Electronic Journal e-Learning, 5*(3), 207-218.

O'Neill, E. J. (2008). *Intercultural Competence Development: Implementing International Virtual Elementary Classroom Activities for Public Schools Students in the U.S. and Korea.* Doctoral dissertation, University of Virginia.

Park, N., & O'Neill, E. J. (2009). *Adapting to Cultural Diversity: Policy to Promote Intercultural Education Policy in Korea.* Paper presented at 2009 World Civic Forum, Seoul, Korea.

Reimers, F. (2006, September). Citizenship, Identity and Education: Examining the public purposes of schools in an age of globalization. *Prospects*, *36*(3).

Rogers, E. M. (2003). Diffusion of Innovations (5th ed.). New York: Simon and Schuster.

State Board of Education. (2003). Educational Technology Plan for Virginia: 2003-2009. Virginia Department of Education.

Tellis, W. (1997). Introduction to Case Study. *Qualitative Report*, *3*(2).

UNESCO. (1993). World Education Report, Paris: UNESCO Publishing.

UNESCO. (2006a). Guideline on International Education. Paris: UNESCO Headquarters.

UNESCO. (2006b). *Expert Meeting on Intercultural Education*. Paris: UNESCO Headquarters.

United National Global Alliance for ICT and Development. (2009). *Our Mission*. Retrieved June 3, 2009, from http://www.un-gaid.org/About/OurMission/tabid/893/language/en-US/Default.aspx

United Nations. (1965). *Declaration on the Promotion among Youth of the Ideals of Peace, Mutual Respect and Understanding between Peoples*. Retrieved April 22, 2007, from http://www.unhchr.ch/html/menu3/b/65.htm

United Nations. (2006, November). *Alliance of Civilizations Report of the High-level Group*. New York: U.S. from http://www.unaoc.org/repository/HLG_Report.pdf

United Nations. (2007, September). *UN High Representative for Alliance of Civilizations: Address to the AoC Group of Friends (Ministry Level)*. New York: U.S., ECOSOC Chamber, Retrieved from http://www.unaoc.org/images/articles/hr_final_remarks.pdf

United Nations. (2008, January). *The First Alliance of Civilization Forum, Madrid.* New York: U.S., Alliance of Civilization. Retrieved from http://www.unaoc.org/images/aoc%20forum%20report%20madrid%20complete.pdf

Van Hook, C. W. (2005). Preparing Teachers for the Diverse Classroom: A Developmental Model of Intercultural Sensitivity. *University of Illinois at Urbana-Champaign: Clearinghouse on Early Education and Parenting (CEEP), Early Childhood and Parenting (ECAP). Collaborative*, *22*(6), 67–72.

White House. (2002, September). Remarks on Implementation of the No Child Left Behind Act of 2001. *Weekly Compilation of Presidential Documents, 38*(36), 1482-1486. Washington, DC: US Government Printing Office, Retrieved from http://www.gpo.gov/fdsys/pkg/WCPD-2002-09-09/html/WCPD-2002-09-09-Pg1482.htm

Williams, D., Coles, L., Richardson, A., Wilson, K., & Tuson, J. (2000). Integrating Information and Communications Technology in Professional Practice: an Analysis of Teachers' Needs Based on a Survey of Primary and Secondary Teachers in Scottish Schools. *Technology, Pedagogy and Education*, *9*(2), 167–182. doi:10.1080/14759390000200089

Xinhua News. (2008, October 25). ASEM Resolves to Further Promote Interfaith Understanding and Exchanges. In *the news of 7th Asia-Europe Meeting*. Retrieved January 9, 2009 from http://news.xinhuanet.com/english/2008-10/26/content_10252340.htm

ADDITIONAL READING

Bennett, J. M., & Bennett, M. J. (2001). Developing Intercultural Sensitivity: An Integrative Approach to Global and Domestic Diversity. *Paper delivered to the Diversity Symposium, Diversity Collegiums, Bentley College, Waltham, MA.*

Davis, N., & Cho, M. O. (2005). Intercultural competence for future leaders of educational technology and its evaluation. *Interactive Educational Multimedia, 10*, 1–22.

Davis, N., & Niederhauser, D. S. (2007). Virtual Schooling. *Learning & Leading with Technology, 34*(7), 6.

Dawes, L. (2001). What stops teachers using new technology. Issues in teaching using ICT. New York: Routledge Falmer.

Earle, R. S. (2002). The integration of instructional technology into public education: Promises and challenges. *Educational Technology*, *42*(1), 5–13.

Elbaum, B., McIntyre, C., & Smith, A. (2002). Essential Elements: Prepare, Design, and Teach Your Online Course. Madison: Atwood Pub.

Fantini, A. E. (1995). Introduction-language, culture and world view: Exploring the nexus. *International Journal of Intercultural Relations*, *19*(2), 143–153. doi:10.1016/0147-1767(95)00025-7

Grant, A. C. (2006). The development of global awareness in elementary students through participation in an online cross-cultural project. Unpublished Ph.D., Louisiana State University and Agricultural & Mechanical College, United States -- Louisiana.

Guiherme, M. (2002). Critical citizens for an intercultural world: Foreign Language Education as Cultural Politics: LICE: Language for Intercultural Communication and Education

Hammer, M. R., Bennett, M. J., & Wiseman, R. (2003). Measuring intercultural sensitivity: The intercultural development inventory. *International Journal of Intercultural Relations*, *27*(4), 421–443. doi:10.1016/S0147-1767(03)00032-4

Hanvey, R. G. (1982). An Attainable Global Perspective. *Theory into Practice*, *21*(3), 162–167. doi:10.1080/00405848209543001

Harms, C. M., Niederhauser, D. S., Davis, N. E., Roblyer, M. D., & Gilbert, S. B. (2006). Educating Educators for Virtual Schooling: Communicating Roles and Responsibilities. *The Electronic Journal of Communication*, *16*(1-2).

Huang, Y., Rayner, C., & Zhuang, L. (2003). Does intercultural competence matter in intercultural business relationship development? *International Journal of Logistics*, *6*(4), 277–288. doi:10.1080/13675560310001626963

Kincaid, T., & Feldner, L. (2002). Leadership for Technology Integration: The Role of Principals and Mentors. *Educational Technology & Society*, *5*(1).

Korhonen, K. (2002). *Intercultural competence as part of professional qualifications: A training experiment with Bachelor of Engineering students*. Unpublished doctoral dissertation, Jyvaskylan Yliopisto, Finland.

Kozma, R. B. (Ed.). (2004). Technology, Innovation, and Educational Change, A Global Perspective, A Report of the Second Information Technology in Education Study (SITES) Module 2, A Project of the International Association for the Evaluation of Educational Achievement (IEA). Eugene: International Society for Technology in Education (ISTE).

Law, N., & Plomp, T. (2003). Curriculum and Staff Development for ICT in Education. Cross-national Information and Communication Technology Policies and Practices in Education.

Mahlstedt, A. (2003). Global Citizenship Education in Practice: An Exploration of Teachers in the United World Colleges. Monograph, International Comparative Education, School of Education, Stanford University.

O'Dowd, R. (2009). Online Intercultural Exchange--An Introduction for Foreign Language Teachers. *ELT Journal*, *63*(1), 81–84. doi:10.1093/elt/ccn065

Pieterse, J. N. (2009). Globalization and culture: Global mélange (2nd Ed). New York: Rowman & Littlefield Publishers.

Suarez-Orozco, M. M., & Qin-Hilliard, D. (2004). Globalization: Culture and education in the new millennium. Berkley and LA: University of California Press.

Tearle, P. (2004). Implementation of ICT in UK secondary schools. *Final Report: February 2004*. Devon: University of Exeter.

Thorne, S. L., & Payne, J. S. (2005). Evolutionary Trajectories, Internet-mediated Expression, and Language Education. *CALICO Journal*, *22*(3), 371–397.

Williams, T. R. (2005). Exploring the Impact of Study Abroad on Students' Intercultural Communication Skills: Adaptability and Sensitivity. *Journal of Studies in International Education*, *9*(4), 356. doi:10.1177/1028315305277681

KEY TERMS AND DEFINITIONS

Intercultural Competence: Ability to interact appropriately, communicate effectively, and work collaboratively in international and multicultural environments, with others who are linguistically and culturally different from oneself. Intercultural competence is composed of five dimensions: knowledge, skills, attitudes, awareness, and language proficiency.

Information and Communication Technology (ICT): All sorts of technologies that enable people to obtain, share, and utilize information and knowledge, and to communicate with each other. It includes technologies for communicating through text, audio, voice, images, or videos. In the field of education, ICT refers to digital and computing technologies that allow access to the Internet, facilitate the construction of knowledge, and manipulation of diverse digitized information through a wide range of networks. ICT also includes wireless mobile technologies such as cellular telephones or PDAs.

International Virtual Elementary/Secondary Classroom Activities (IVECA): Online intercultural classroom exchange programs providing elementary and or secondary school students with opportunities to learn cultural similarities and differences through direct communication with students in different countries via virtual learning spaces. The intercultural exchange activities are integrated with the curricula of local participating schools so that IVECA becomes a part of their school curricula—not as an add-on special project.

International Virtual Schooling: A form of intercultural schooling in which schools in multiple countries are connected through ICT and use cross-cultural classroom exchanges as a part of their curricula.

Course Management System (CMS): Web-based software platform allowing instructors to create online courses, manage course content, track student performance, and offer online collaboration and diverse means of communication.

Moodle: Free open-source course/content management system such as Sakai's Collaboration and Learning Environment, ILIAS, etc..

Global Knowledge-Based Economy: An economy wherein knowledge and information-based digital products are produced and traded through virtual market spaces that depend on ICT. In this economy, a firm's productivity relies on the quality of information and the promptness of obtaining and utilizing information for customer needs.

Chapter 16
Live Interactive Virtual Explorations via the High Performance Wireless Research and Education Network

Kimberly Mann Bruch
University of California at San Diego, USA

Hans-Werner Braun
University of California at San Diego, USA

Susan Teel
Southern California Research Learning Center, USA

ABSTRACT

Researchers affiliated with the National Science Foundation funded High Performance Wireless Research and Education Network (HPWREN), are conducting case studies and facilitating technology transfer activities that enable Live Interactive Virtual Explorations (LIVE) between hard-to-reach science sites and an array of education communities. This chapter discusses lessons learned – both technological and pedagogical – during a longitudinal study of HPWREN LIVE case studies and technology transfer activities.

BACKGROUND AND HISTORY OF LIVE INTERACTIVE VIRTUAL EXPLORATIONS

Though Live Interactive Virtual Explorations (LIVE) were not coined such until 2007, researchers with the National Science Foundation funded High Performance Wireless Research and Education Network (HPWREN) began experiments with real-time distance learning activities in 2001. The first activity occurred between the office of the HPWREN principal investigator and a computer laboratory at the Pala Native American Learning Center. Facilitated by the HPWREN team, this 2001 activity occurred during a semester-long community college class taught by an HPWREN researcher via collaboration with Palomar College. The Computer Science and Information Systems

DOI: 10.4018/978-1-61520-779-4.ch016

course introduced tribal members to computer and Internet fundamentals as well as multicast technology. While the course was primarily taught in a traditional classroom format, the real-time video/audio experiments occurred a few times during the semester and allowed researchers to better understand the current state of multicast across low-cost wireless access links. These early experiments included the use of vic, a multicast video tool, and rat, an audio tool. Meanwhile, Blackboard was the browser interface used for all class lecture presentations, assignments, and online discussions. The 2001 experiments did not continue into 2002, as both video and audio were consistently very choppy due to packet losses on the network infrastructure, which has subsequently been addressed with equipment upgrades.

A couple of years later, the researchers started experiments again with an IP-based conferencing product (Polycom) across the network. One such test occurred in March 2003 between a hard-to-reach site within Anza-Borrego Desert State Park and a conference in urban Irvine (California). Specifically, teachers attending the National Teacher Training Institute Conference participated in an underwater tour of Crystal Cove State Park and examined fossilized oyster beds in nearby Fish Creek – while sitting in a conference room about 100 miles away. The remote interactive presentations utilized Polycom software for both video and audio while the hardware setup at Fish Creek utilized a tripod-mounted four-foot antenna pointing to an HPWREN node atop a nearby mountaintop. This node connects to several additional mountaintop nodes ending up at the HPWREN originating node at the San Diego Supercomputer Center at the University of California – San Diego.

This March 2003 activity was evaluated with the use of informal Likert-scale pre- and post-surveys, which were distributed to participants. The respondents answered questions that measured compatibility, complexity, relative advantage, and adoption. The analysis of responses and quantification of variables is based upon prior research conducted by Rogers (1995), Valente (1996), Rice and Gattiker (2001), and Bruch (2002).

The survey respondents consisted of 13 elementary school teachers and two principals from southern California. Results from these surveys are as follows:

Compatibility Perceptions

Among pre-survey respondents, only 30 percent agree that the distance learning activity is compatible with their curricula while post-survey results increased to 85 percent. Likewise, 62 percent of pre-survey respondents agree that the activity meets their teaching needs while 85 percent of post-survey respondents agree.

Complexity Perceptions

Among both pre-survey and post-survey respondents, 39 percent agree that the activity requires too much technological knowledge. Similarly, before the activity, 46 percent agreed that technical assistance would be required to participate in a LIVE activity while 61 percent agreed after the activity.

Relative Advantage Perceptions

Among pre-survey respondents, 69 percent agree that the activities will improve teaching efforts while 100 percent of the post-survey respondents agree. Likewise, 92 percent agreed that the activities will allow for better information dissemination and 100 percent of the post-survey respondents agree.

Adoption

Among pre-survey respondents, 39 percent agree that they will use the technology in future classes; this number increased to 54 percent with the post-surveys. Before the activity, 85 percent agree that they will use it within the upcoming year and 92 post-survey respondents agree.

Survey Conclusion

Survey results imply that remote interactive exploration programs can be compatible with the most curricula and meet the teaching needs of most. However, the perceived complexity of the activities is rather high and perhaps one of the reasons why the adoption perception is not 100 percent.

In April 2003 a similar experiment was conducted between a conference being held in San Diego (the George Wright Society Cultural Resources 2003 Joint Conference) and the Fish Creek site. During this experiment, not only were conference participants able to interact in real-time with the on-site park ranger, but they were also able to view real-time data from environmental sensors and high-resolution cameras deployed at the site; this allowed participants to gain much more insight about the area. Participant feedback for this experiment was inconclusive as the number of survey respondents was less than ten. However, the majority of survey respondents had positive compatibility, relative advantage, and adoption perceptions regarding the activity.

Though several years have passed since these original studies, a large number of similar activities have transpired via the California State Park PORTS (Parks Online Resources for Teachers and Students) between an array of K-12 sites and the Fish Creek site. Specifically, the PORTS program continues to offer virtual fieldtrips of the Crystal Cove State Park by way of a videoconferencing software package that is run on the California High Speed Network, which provides Internet connectivity to thousands of California schools. The videoconferencing software offers the capability of multiple sites being connected at the same time, however, the PORTS staff discovered that point-to-point connections typically provide for the most life-like fieldtrips. Additional information about this technology transfer activity is in section "Technology Transfer" of this chapter.

After the Fish Creek experiments in 2003, the HPWREN researchers turned their attention to the implementation of an array of real-time sensors and high-resolution cameras throughout San Diego County science sites. This work, coupled with networking research, continued to be a focus of the group during 2004 and 2005. Then, in 2006, a series of experiments took place at the HPWREN-connected California Wolf Center, the Palomar Observatory, the Santa Margarita Ecological Reserve, and additional sites.

In early 2007, several LIVE activities were showcased within the National Science Foundation exhibition booth at the American Association for the Advancement of Science annual meeting in San Francisco. The experiments included multiple LIVE activities during the week-long conference; each real-time LIVE activity was displayed alongside applicable still images on a 15-screen display (Figure1).

Conference participants were able to interact with an array of field scientists such as those at the California Wolf Center and the Santa Margarita Ecological Reserve. Discussion took place in real-time between biologists at California Wolf Center wolf enclosures and conference participants while images and maps accompanied the real-time activity at the screen display. The ecological reserve portion of the experiment included real-time audio/video with two biologists while simultaneously viewing real-time graphs of river chemistry data being updated about once per minute, a three megapixal camera that updated every few seconds, and a 22+ megapixel three-camera 180-degree panorama that updated every few minutes. Another portion of the LIVE experiment at the AAAS annual meeting allowed conference participants to observe a LIVE activity taking place between a classroom at the California Science Center (Los Angeles) and the Palomar Observatory. While the California Wolf Center and the Santa Margarita Ecological Reserve events utilized Skype for the

Figure 1. LIVE Activity with still images in a 15-screen display

real-time activities, the Palomar Observatory portion used Polycom ViewStation FX equipment at the conference and Observatory with a Polycom v500 at the California Science Center. The Skype connections were all successful while the Polycom setup worked for testing, but the v500 failed during the actual scheduled activity.

The challenges with these early experiments primarily involve refining procedures associated with equipment and software. However, simple modifications, including assembly of a LIVE backpack system, completion of a LIVE manual, and experimentation with software solutions provided viable short-term solutions for the project team to continue with more LIVE experiments. These additional activities, as well as more details about each of the HPWREN-connected science sites, are described in the Case Studies and Technology Transfer sections of this chapter.

CASE STUDIES

Distance learning experiments conducted at HPWREN-connected science sites include the California Wolf Center, Cabrillo National Monument, the Palomar Observatory, and the Santa Margarita Ecological Reserve. The case studies at these four science sites provide both quantitative and qualitative data to better understand compatibility, relative advantage, complexity, and adoption perceptions of LIVE activities taking place across the network. Similar to the 2003 study described in the aforementioned Fish Creek experiment summary, Likert-scale surveys were administered throughout several case studies to measure these perceptions.

A. California Wolf Center

Situated just outside the rural town of Julian, California (San Diego County), the California Wolf Center is a non-profit wildlife education center committed to increasing public awareness and understanding of the importance of all wildlife

Figure 2. Camera with a built-in microphone and PDA

Figure 3. Use of backpack laptop and lightweight camera for the second test

by focusing on the history, biology, behavior, and ecology of the gray wolf (Canis lupus). This is accomplished by offering engaging educational presentations, participating in conservation programs, and hosting and funding research on both captive and free-ranging wolves. As one of the first HPWREN science sites to participate with the LIVE pilot project, the Wolf Center study took place in 2006 and included multiple experiments aimed at determining compatibility and adoption among the education and research staff at the facility.

The initial test consisted of a self-contained high-resolution network camera with an attached 12-volt battery and builtin wireless card (for the image stream). As shown in Figure 2, the camera was used alongside a PDA (with built-in-microphone) to support a bidirectional audio conversation using the free software package Skype. The setup was supported by a wireless access point with a directional antenna. Though remote participants (such as National Science Foundation staff in Washington, D.C.) found the experiment interesting, the video was choppy and the audio deteriorated with wind. On the science site end, the Wolf Center staff found the setup cumbersome, as the camera was heavy and difficult to hold steady while simultaneously carrying the PDA.

The second test replaced the PDA with a backpack holding a full-size laptop and connected to a digital video camera and headset. The laptop was equipped with Skype as well as Orangeware WebCamDV software for the video component. As shown in Figure 3, this backpack laptop and lightweight camera setup was much easier to carry; however, a tripod would have made it easier to take steadier video.

The primary improvement noted during this experiment was the superior audio quality; the headset eliminated the wind issues experienced when using the built-in PDA microphone. Also, the digital video camera allowed for auto-focus and zooming so that remote participants were able to see the wolves much clearer and better understand what they were experiencing during their real-time virtual exploration. Additionally, this video camera setup provided the wolf center presenter with the capability of seeing the video being presented to the remote participants; "I can see what I am actually showing" explained a wolf center educator.

Following these early experiments, the Wolf Center education staff developed a Powerpoint presentation to accompany the LIVE activity. Additionally, Center staff put together an array of wolf artifacts to supplement the experience at the audience end; these artifacts allow the remote participants to have hands-on activities during the remote real-time presentation between their site and the Wolf Center, as long as their site is in San Diego County.

The biggest challenge with the California Wolf Center case is insufficient staffing for LIVE activities at the Wolf Center end. Although Center

Figure 4. Real-time camera view of Palomar telescope with additional image of LIVE presenter

researchers and staff are very interested in making LIVE activities a component of their education program, there has not been an activity taking place between the wolf enclosures and an education site due to this lack of staffing. The Center staff hopes to conduct at least a few LIVE activities within the upcoming year. These presentations can be tailored to any age group/ grade level, and it is California state curriculum-based; the programming will consist of an educational presentation (including a hands-on artifacts presentation if the site is within San Diego county) and a live streamcast from the Center's wolf enclosures. The plan is for Center staff to work with students and teachers so that they are able to interact with the Wolf Center educator in real-time while biologists are observing and discussing the wolves' behavior. The Center also plans to have someone on site at the school end to answer questions and explore the artifacts with the students and teachers at any school in San Diego county.

B. Palomar Observatory

Perched atop the Palomar Mountain in San Diego County, the HPWREN-connected Palomar Observatory is home to some of the world's most powerful telescopes. The first LIVE activity with the observatory took place at an academic conference in February 2007 and is described on page --- of this chapter with the next case study occurring at the Pala Native American Reservation. The Native American activity included on-site curricula prepared by the reservation's learning center staff in addition to the Powerpoint presentation by the observatory's public information officer via LIVE (Figure 4). Following the hands-on activities and the Powerpoint presentation via LIVE, the public information officer showed off the powerful telescopes at Palomar to approximately 60 Pala tribal members and interested people from the community – discussing an array of concepts.

About a year later, in early 2008, the Reuben H. Fleet Science Center hosted a similar LIVE

Figure 5.Aerial view of Palomar Observatory telescope domes

event with the Observatory. This activity was held in conjunction with the Science Center's annual Astronomy Day and participants ranged in age from four-years-old to eighty-years-old. The real-time "tour" took place outside the 48-inch Samuel Oschin Telescope where the public information officer discussed its uses before moving to the outside of the 200-inch telescope. In addition to the LIVE activity itself, images taken by the observatory telescopes were also provided to participants as well as an HPWREN information booklet, the Palomar Observatory newsletter, and an aerial image of the observatory. This latter image (Figure 5) allows participants to easily realize how many telescopes there are at the observatory. While one participant asked "Is there a benefit to using a large telescope versus a small telescope?" another asked "Who built those telescopes?" During the discussion regarding this latter question, the child asking the question (along with details from her father) shared that her great-great grandfather was one of the people that worked on parts for the earliest telescopes at the observatory in the 1930s. These types of interactions are only possible via real-time interaction such as the bi-directional activities allowed by LIVE events.

Similar to the March 2003 Fish Creek study described in section I, the Palomar Observatory case studies were also evaluated via survey evaluation. The survey data was collected in April 2007 at the rural Pala Native American Learning Center and in April 2008 at the urban Reuben H. Fleet Science Center. Eighteen subjects (14 females and four males) participated in the data collection efforts. Of the 18 respondents, ten participated in a LIVE activity at the rural learning center while eight participated in a LIVE activity at the urban science education center. Of the 18 respondents, nine have a college degree, five have completed some college, and four have completed high school only. The ages of respondents range from 18 to 80.

Identical surveys were used to collect both the 2007 and 2008 data; specifically, compatibility, complexity, and adoption data was collected using the surveys described in section one of this chapter.

Because of the small sample, simple descriptive statistics were used to quantify participants' perceptions of compatibility, complexity, and adoption of the LIVE system. The quantitative data was then coupled with the collected qualitative data to compile the conclusion of the experiment.

Compatibility Perceptions

The majority (17 of 18) of participants reported that the video component of the LIVE system is compatible with their needs. However, 50 percent of participants reported that the audio component of the LIVE system is compatible with their needs and the other 50 percent reported that the audio is not compatible with their needs.

The wide range of comments regarding the audio helped to understand the inconsistency in the audio component of the compatibility measure:

"Too noisy from the wind."

"Everything was excellent."

"Noisy kids (unsupervised)."

"I enjoyed the kids asking questions."

"This was a great opportunity to tour the Observatory and learn more about it, and also visit with one another about other education opportunities for the young ones on the reservation."

"My children loved the pictures of the stars and they learned enough that it made them want to visit the telescope at the Observatory in person.

The latter two comments were specifically from parents of children attending the Little Feathers Preschool at the Pala Native American Reservation.

Complexity Perceptions

The majority (16 of 18) of participants reported that there were sufficient opportunities to interact with the presenter at the remote site. Thirteen of 19 participants reported that they felt the information was presented effectively by the LIVE presenters while five had "no opinion" about this measure.

There were only a few qualitative comments regarding the complexity measures:

"The best thing about the LIVE activity was the interactivity."

"The presenter had a good connection with kids and kept it entertaining."

"The information was a little above the age level here."

"The material content was a little too much...."

The latter two comments help explain the lack of opinion regarding the presented information while the first two comments explain why the majority of the participants felt that there were sufficient opportunities to interact with the presenter.

Adoption Perceptions

The majority (16 of 18) of the participants reported that they "learned a lot from the LIVE activity" and that they "would recommend LIVE to others".

Survey Conclusion

Based on the survey results, as well as conversations with staff from the Pala Native American Learning Center and the Reuben H. Fleet Science Center, these two experiments demonstrate that both urban and rural participants not only appreciate, but learn from LIVE activities with hard-to-reach science sites like the Palomar Observatory.

However, the audio issues need to be resolved prior to additional such activities taking place.

Because of this conclusion from the survey results, tests with an array of microphones and headsets were conducted. Once a suitable audio solution was in place (microphone improvement), the HPWREN researchers initiated another formal LIVE activity between the Observatory and the Reuben H. Fleet Science Center in early 2009. LIVE participants included a group of elementary school students participating in a week-long spring break science camp at the Science Center. Situated just in front of the 200-inch telescope, the observatory's public information officer discussed an array of astronomy concepts with the 45 students at the Science Center. While questions and answers flew back and forth between the Science Center students and the public information officer at the observatory, the real-time LIVE activity also included a Powerpoint slideshow of images taken by Palomar telescopes. The activity was such a success that HPWREN researchers decided to duplicate the activity for an additional student group on April 22, 2009; this time the students hailed from the Julian Charter School Astronomy Club, which meets weekly at a City of San Diego Library. The latter experiment was not as successful as the Science Center activity as the library's wireless network bandwidth was overloaded and did not allow for audio or video transmission via the Internet. In lieu of the local Internet connection, an alternate approach was tried via the AT&T 3G network, which provided choppy audio and no video transmission due to a low signal. The activity ended up consisting of a Powerpoint presentation regarding Palomar Observatory with audio via the 3G connection; the public information officer talked with the charter school students in real-time about the observatory as well as the growing light pollution issue atop Palomar Mountain. Though there was no video during the activity and the audio quality was not very good, the 30+ elementary school students agreed that the activity sparked their interest in visiting the observatory in person and the school is now looking into a fieldtrip before year's end.

Because the audio issues at the observatory have been solved, there are no major challenges for this site to conduct LIVE activities. The public information officer at the site is very engaging with LIVE participants and the researchers are hopeful to continue outreach activities with this important science site.

C. Santa Margarita Ecological Reserve

Located approximately 60 miles from central San Diego in Temecula, the HPWREN-connected Santa Margarita Ecological Reserve is home to the last free flowing river in southern California. To visit this pristine wildlife habitat is a privilege because the hard-to-reach, researched-focused reserve is only open to the public a few times per year. The first formal LIVE activity at the reserve occurred at an academic conference in February 2007 and is described in the first section of this chapter. Another similar activity took place in March 2007 at the San Diego Science Alliance High Technology Fair in Del Mar (San Diego County). Specifically, the California Mediterranean Research Learning Center and Cabrillo National Monument in partnership with HPWREN and San Diego State University Field Stations Program hosted a booth at the 2007 San Diego Science Alliance High Technology Fair. The partners collaborated to demonstrate how HPWREN LIVE activities enable the communication of real-time data and video from remote science sites directly to students, educators, and scientists through the Internet. The LIVE activities allowed for real-time video and audio communication between students at the High Tech Fair and scientists stationed at banks of the Santa Margarita River running through the ecological reserve. In addition to the real-time video and audio communication, a Remotely Operated Vehicle (ROV) was deployed in the river to show real-time underwater video to the technology fair participants. Real-time hydrologic sensor data was also available at the fair booth via the ecological reserve's website, which displays information collected by automated sensors every few minutes.

The LIVE activity utilized Skype with the video feed being displayed on one large screen at the fair booth. Another screen displayed the real-time underwater video from the ROV as well as another video feed that showed a shot of the overall river bank.

An Axis Server allowed booth staff to control live video from the ROV and river bank simultaneously or alternate between larger versions of the video feeds. The real-time water quality sensor data were displayed on a flat screen computer monitor in graphical format so that LIVE participants could better understand what is going on with an array of measures in the water shown on the other two screens.

Though a formal evaluation was not conducted for this activity, the fair participants were obviously excited about the variety of technology being used at the booth. They were especially engaged by the ecological reserve scientist talking with them in real-time about the water quality sensors at the river. The scientist talked with the students while manipulating hydrological parameters by inserting the hydro-sensor probe in several treatments such as: the river to establish ambient conditions, ice water to change water temperature, baking powder to influence dissolved oxygen, and vinegar to drop the pH level. The students at the fair were able to see, hear, and speak with the scientist via the LIVE system and simultaneously observe real-time graphical depictions of the hydrological parameter changes as the sensor probe was moved between various treatments. The data changes, river camera, and interactions with the reserve scientist kept the students asking questions during the entire event. By addressing the students by name, the scientist engaged the fair participants in discussions regarding the changes they were observing in the graphs depicting real-time hydrological parameters. This friendly, informal dialogue helped make the virtual event more like a field trip rather than a broadcast. As groups of students formed around the speakers and microphone to talk to the scientist, more students would crowd the table wanting to know what was going on. Several groups of students returned to interact a second time. By lunchtime, some of the students were telling staff booth that they had talked to the reserve scientist and wanted to try the system for themselves.

Another aspect of the activity that intrigued the fair students was their ability to see the researchers at the reserve controlling the ROV and working to unclog clumps of algae from the thrusters. When the scientist referenced the ROV as part of his discussion with the students, it brought an extra dimension to the presentation, though an underwater camera might have been just as useful. At one point, the scientist was talking to a student and simultaneously reached his hand into the water in front of the ROV and waved; the crowd roared comments like "Awesome!".

Perhaps most interesting for the students were times when the three video cameras, the video capable Skype camcorder, the river video, and the underwater ROV video camera all focused on the same area of action and the images overlapped. As a special on-site activity for fair participants, students donned a LIVE backpack system and explored the exhibit hall. The students roving around the hall interacted with their friends at the technology fair booth. This demonstration allowed the fair participants to gain first hand experience with the equipment being used at the reserve end of the experiment.

The biggest lesson learned during the technology fair LIVE activity was that pre-established questions for the students to ask the reserve scientist would have been useful. Another valuable lesson learned was that a Powerpoint presentation developed to lead students through a story board format did not hold the interest of students and was shelved early during the event. The Powerpoint presentation had been designed to inform participants how HPWREN connected all of the partners and enabled real-time communication, however, this information ended up being conveyed first hand by booth staff.

This 2007 technology fair study was very successful – largely due to the lessons learned during an earlier experiment that took place in 2006 between the Santa Margarita Ecological Reserve and the Pala Native American Reservation. Because of the positive response from the Pala Native American community regarding the Palomar Observatory case study described in section IIB of this chapter, the researchers chose this group as the first participants with the ecological reserve. Specifically, students from the Pala Native American Learning Center participated in the LIVE activity with a biologist at the ecological reserve. These LIVE activities were conducted in conjunction with the Tribal Digital Village Network, a high-speed wireless network that connects the 17 Native American Reservations in San Diego County. While the Pala students and their parents enjoyed the LIVE event, several lessons were learned by participating staff.

This Pala reservation activity took place via a T1 line and resulted in less than a half Megabits per second, which made the video and audio fairly choppy. One of the lessons learned from this technical glitch was that the students did not seem to mind the lag time on the video. Though formal evaluation surveys were not administered, informal data was collected and most students commented on the crayfish that was shown to them via the activity as the highlight of their LIVE experience. From the ecological reserve end, several lessons were learned, such as the need for additional staff at the science site end to assist with the camera. Additional lessons learned included the need for something more exciting than a mere discussion between the biologist and the LIVE participants as there was often a quietness between the education community and the science site due to a lack of conversation. This challenge was augmented with the use of the ROV and sensor experiments as described earlier in this section.

Another LIVE activity with this hard-to-reach site includes a study between the ecological reserve and the Reuben H. Fleet Science Center for their annual Green Day celebration. For this case, a group of college students were at the ecological reserve with scientists; this group communicated in real-time with Science Center visitors, who were also able to participate in a hands-on activity regarding water quality. This hands-on activity was similar to the activities taking place at the reserve with the students, who spoke with the Science Center participants in real-time about their experiments taking place in the Santa Margarita River.

D. Cabrillo National Monument

Beginning in late 2006, researchers started examining distance learning opportunities via the network at an intertidal area located at the National Park Service Cabrillo National Monument. The first formal test occurred in December 2006 between the intertidal area and the California Science Center in Los Angeles. The objective was a real-time interactive audio/video conference between a National Park Service interpreter at the tidepools and a group of third grade students at the Science Center School. The park ranger used a headset to provide interpretive interactive communication with the students and the connection was initiated using Skype software. At the California Science Center end, a single computer was equipped with external speakers and a microphone; the computer was connected to a projector that displayed the tidepool images on a large screen. The enthusiastic students took turns approaching the microphone to direct the park ranger to focus her handheld video camera on areas of interest. In addition, a submersible ROV was moving below the surface of the water in a large tidepool and open water, providing underwater video across the network. A digital network camera on a tripod was directed at the team while working to complete the final connections to the ROV video. This camera was then turned to capture activities of the team working in the tidepool area. The ROV and digital network cameras were also watched by the two Marine Magnet Schools in Florida.

Another LIVE study took place with the Cabrillo intertidal area and the Pala Learning Center. Specifically, approximately 15-20 Pala Learning Center children (grades K-5) participated in the early 2008 LIVE event. Prior to the tidepools "tour" led by a National Park Service interpretive park ranger, the students were given an explanation and able to ask questions about the geology of the area as well as the overall intertidal area at Cabrillo. This took place in a classroom at the learning center and was facilitated by NSF-funded Indigenous Earth Sciences Project geologist Norrie Robbins, who is known as "Doc" on the reservation as she works with San Diego reservation youth on a regular basis doing science activities. Though none of the children attending the event had been to an intertidal area, they were all familiar with the ocean in general and seemed to really enjoy both the pre-activities and the virtual real-time tour of Cabrillo tidepools.

The set-up on the Pala end of the LIVE activity consisted of a laptop equipped with an external microphone, web camera, speakers, and projector. Skype was utilized for the real-time communication between the Learning Center and the tidepools. This simple setup provided the students with an opportunity to not only explore the tidepools, but also better understand the technology behind the activity. Though surveys were not administered, all of the students seemed to learn a great deal from the activity and asked the facilitating HPWREN researcher to "please come back soon and show us more".

A number of additional LIVE activities have taken place at the Cabrillo National Monument since these two early studies. They are described in section IIIB of the Technology Transfer section.

TECHNOLOGY TRANSFER

A. California State Parks

As mentioned in first section (Background and History of LIVE), the HPWREN research team collaborated with the California State Parks on two distance learning activities in 2003. Since then, the Parks Online Resources for Teachers and Students (PORTS) project has provided thousands of California youth with opportunities to interact with real-time state park rangers via live interactive fieldtrips. In addition to the real-time Internet-based video/audio conferencing, the PORTS project provides teachers with applicable curriculum and supplementary activities to accompany the virtual fieldtrips to state parks throughout California. For instance, the Anza Borrego Desert State Park tour now includes paleontology curriculum that introduces student participants to geologic concepts prior to touring the Anza paleontology laboratory via PORTS. The interactive lesson at the paleontology lab then allows students to ask questions and receive feedback in real-time.

The greatest challenge faced by the PORTS project team is staffing needs at parks throughout the California State Parks system. While PORTS is successful at several state parks, there are other parks which the program could expand allowing for visits by people that otherwise would not have an opportunity to explore those sites. The Torrey Pines State Park in San Diego is one such example; Torrey Pines provides examples of vegetation and geology unique to the southern California area, however, PORTS activities are difficult to arrange at this site (and many others) due to staffing shortages.

B. National Park Service

Similar to the California State Parks' PORTS program, the National Park Service utilized the preliminary HPWREN LIVE studies at Cabrillo

National Monument to implement a collaborative Sea to Shining Sea (StSS) LIVE program, which expands the partnership between the National Park Service and HPWREN to include parks, schools, university on both coasts of the United States. Continued expansion of the StSS program now includes parks, school, and research learning centers throughout the country. The StSS program has completed more than ten case studies and two technology transfer workshops and researchers are currently working on additional StSS LIVE activities throughout the United States. Mammoth Cave National Park, Biscayne National Park, and Santa Monica National Recreational Area are examples of national parks that are modeling StSS programs after the Cabrillo National Monument study described in this chapter in D part of the second section (Case Studies).

The first phase of the StSS project involved the development of an instruction manual for the LIVE backpack system used at the science sites. The StSS LIVE manual provides step-by-step instructions on using the backpack system.

Phase two of the StSS project encompassed the development and maintenance of a web portal regarding the project's activities, real-time data, and contact information. The portal includes a homepage, a news page, a real-time data page, and a contact page. Additional portal components include an STSS LIVE reservations system, accompanying curriculum, and an array of accompanying resources.

The third phase of the StSS technology transfer project included 13 LIVE activities similar to those described in the case studies of this chapter. Many of these activities occurred between an array of education communities and Cabrillo National Monument. The education communities included a youth summer camp at the Reuben H. Fleet Science Center, a science class at a rural San Diego County middle school, and a couple of National Park Service conferences. Another StSS LIVE activity took place between Mammoth Cave National Park and a group of Native American youth (described in section IIIF) while additional activities involved Biscayne National Park, Loxachatchee National Park, and the Dry Tortugas.

Simultaneous with the LIVE activities, a technology transfer workshop was planned and conducted in November 2008. This two-day Technology Transfer Workshop and LIVE backpack system training for National Park Service staff and educators took place at the Cabrillo National Monument and was attended by participants from parks and schools from across the country including: Biscayne National Park (FL), Cabrillo National Monument (CA), Channel Islands National Park (CA), Cochise and Santa Cruz County Schools (AZ), Coronado National Memorial (AZ), Dade County Schools (FL), Death Valley National Park (CA), Fossil Butte National Monument (WY), Grand Canyon National Park (AZ), National Park Service Intermountain Regional Support Office (CO), Joshua Tree National Park (CA), Pinnacles National Monument (CA), South Broward Schools (FL), University of Arizona (AZ), Yellowstone National Park (MT), Yosemite National Park (CA), and Vista Unified School District (CA).

Participants learned the basics of how to plan and install a wireless system which supports LIVE distance education programs and environmental sensors. The goal of the workshop and training session was to cultivate expertise with wireless systems and LIVE distance education programs in the National Park Service. Workshop participants gained an understanding of wireless data systems sufficient to plan and implement a system at their parks. National Park Service staff practiced their skills with intentions to form regional teams to assist each other in planning and installing systems to meet the needs of their parks.

Four concurrent sessions were conducted, where participants rotated through four stations, while receiving hands-on experience and becoming familiar with wireless radios, access points, cameras, and environmental sensors. The HPWREN, National Park Service, and San Diego

State University Field Stations Program researchers introduced groups of five to six trainees to the equipment at the stations and led them through the basics of how to build, configure, operate, and explore opportunities with the equipment.

The first day of the workshop culminated at the Cabrillo National Monument lighthouse, where attendees assisted the instruction team in building a complete system at a remote location which included a point-to-point wireless link for Internet access, a local access point, environmental sensors, a camera, and a LIVE backpack. The second day of the workshop began with an informal review and question and answer session so that participants could discuss ideas for their parks. The LIVE backpack session also took place on the second day and allowed participants to set up and test the LIVE backpacks. Nine teams assembled and tested the backpacks, and used Skype to communicate with a science teacher located at a rural San Diego County school. In short time, the teams took the backpacks to the rocky intertidal area and initiated LIVE programs.

This technology transfer workshop was evaluated via informal Likert-scale surveys. The survey respondents consisted of 17 National Park Service employees ranging from interpretive park rangers to scientists. Results from these surveys are as follows:

Among survey respondents, 94 percent agreed that they learned a lot from the workshop, would recommend future workshops to others, and attained their primary goal in attending the workshop.

As for quality of the LIVE demonstration video quality and audio, 81 percent agreed that the video quality was good while 94 percent agreed that the audio quality was good.

When asked about workshop print materials, only 60 percent agreed that the handouts were helpful. In a separate section on the survey, respondents were able to list what they liked least about the workshop and handouts are definitely an area that needs improvement in future workshops. Specific comments in the section that asked "What did you like the least about the workshop?" are as follows:

"More handouts to refer to during class"

"No handouts or writing stuff handed out until end"

"Have handouts and simple diagrams on hand"

"Equipment lists might have been helpful"

"Information page on possible gear, prices, etc"

"Needed more positive examples"

To rectify this need for handouts, the project team put together print materials and uploaded them to a web server. The website information was then emailed to workshop participants, who responded that the materials were useful.

As for hands-on activities during the event, this was a strength during the workshop with 94 percent of survey respondents agreeing that there were sufficient hands-on opportunities. This was also illustrated in answers to the open-ended question "What did you like best about the workshop?":

"Hands-on demonstration"

"Hands-on"

"The availability of equipment for hands-on"

"Breakout sessions were good"

In addition to the multiple LIVE case studies and technology transfer workshop, LIVE off-shore communications tests have also been conducted. For example, the StSS team worked with HP-

WREN researchers on a LIVE experiment from a boat motoring near the kelp bed approximately two miles from the shoreline of Cabrillo National Monument. The test used an HPWREN connection to link the off-shore location and a central San Diego office using a cable modem connection. Real-time underwater video between an ROV equipped with a video camera allowed for the transmission of above and below water video as well as audio from the deck of the boat. Video and audio transmission utilized Skype and both were surprisingly excellent quality. An additional 12 mega pixel camera with an underwater housing was used to take pictures of the tidepools and this test was also very successful.

Several national parks, such as the Biscayne National Park and Dry Tortugas National Park, are now able to use the results of this test to implement a system which employs an ROV to explore the diversity and underwater beauty of coral reefs, sea grass meadows, and mangrove root systems in Florida. Further, the Submerged Resources Program, a national program within the National Park Service, is closely following the results of these experiments in anticipation that they can use similar equipment at multiple locations across the country. Some examples of park locations with underwater resources of interest include Lake Mead in Hawaii, Dry Tortugas in Florida, and the Channel Islands in California.

The biggest challenges for the National Park Service in utilizing the LIVE technology revolves around the Department of Interior (DOI) restrictions on video conferencing and streaming video. Because of this, participating parks are encouraged to form collaborative partnerships with universities, educational organizations, and schools similarly to the southern California NPS-HPWREN collaborative model that enables wireless connectivity and LIVE programming via an outside-DOI network.

Like the California State Parks challenge of short staffing. The typical national park has a chief of interpretation as well as a chief of science; these positions work closely together on a multitude of projects, however, unless one of these divisions (interpretation or science) makes the LIVE activities a priority, the LIVE events are unlikely to continue. While some parks appear to be embracing the technology, others are a bit hesitant. Like all types of technology adoption, this is not unusual and time will tell if the LIVE activities are embraced by educators and scientists within the community.

C. Reuben H. Fleet Science Center

In early 2008, the HPWREN researchers formed a collaboratory relationship with the Reuben H. Fleet Science Center in order to explore the effectiveness of LIVE activities among the Center's visitors. The first such case study occurred in May 2008 at the Science Center's annual Astronomy Day and took place between the Center's lecture hall and Palomar Observatory; evaluation results were correlated with a similar activity and are discussed in B part of the second section (i.e. Palomar Observatory in Case Studies) of this chapter. While the Astronomy Day activity participants ranged in age from young children to the elderly, middle school girls were the target audience for another experiment that took place at the Science Center in August 2008. Young girls attending summer camp participated in a LIVE program titled "Women in Science" and interacted in real-time with career scientists and science educators at the Cabrillo National Monument's intertidal area as shown in Figures 6 and 7. Formal evaluations of this activity were not collected, however, the informal comments were positive. The young girls not only enjoyed the activity, but the majority of them agreed that they learned a great deal from the LIVE event as well as the hands-on activities that were available to them in the lecture hall. Additionally, a National Science Foundation funded geologist was on site at the Science Center to share her experiences as a woman in science and to teach the girls a little about the geology they observed at the rocky intertidal area.

Four additional LIVE activities at the Science Center in Spring 2009 – ranging from a real-time interaction with an electron microscope facility (described in the next section of this chapter) to a spring break science camp between a group of elementary school students at the Science Center and a public information officer at the Palomar Observatory. Another LIVE experiment with the Science Center occurred in May 2009 in conjunction with Green Day; patrons were able to participate in a LIVE activity between the Science Center exhibition area and the Santa Margarita River at San Diego State University's Santa Margarita Ecological Reserve.

These activities equate a total of six LIVE events that have taken place over the past year between the Science Center and hard-to-reach science sites. While the education staff at the Center is enthusiastic about the use of the technology in their programs, a true technology transfer does not seem feasible without a great deal of additional effort. While the Science Center staff played a role in planning the activities, the discussed LIVE case studies at the Center have utilized HPWREN-owned equipment and there is no current plan of transferring the technology to the Science Center. The biggest challenge for the Science Center is the need for information technology support staff receptive to new concepts like the LIVE activities.

D. Nanoengineering Electron Microscope Facility

As aforementioned in C part of the third section (i.e. Reuben H Fleet Science Center in Technology Transfer) of this chapter, the Reuben H. Fleet Science Center visitors were able to participate in a LIVE activity between the Center's lecture hall and a scanning transmission electron microscope (STEM) at Nanoengineering Department of the University of California San Diego in April 2009. This activity occurred in conjunction with the Science Center's celebration of NanoDays, which is a national celebration of nanotechnology and organized by the NSF-funded Nanoscale Informal Science Education Network. Led by a university scientist, NanoWHAT LIVE participants were able to see first-hand how an electron microscope works via the LIVE activity with a materials scientist on hand at the Science Center end to answer questions before and after the activity.

Prior to the real-time demonstration, NanoWHAT participants had an opportunity to explore a number of hands-on activities such as a carbon nanotube balloon model, a liquid crystal sensor, and a nano noodle challenge. These hands-on activities, coupled with the materials scientist present during the LIVE activity, made the event seemingly successful. However, the audio for the activity was fairly choppy (though audible) while the video was good and allowed LIVE participants to experience an electron microscope that would otherwise be very difficult to access.

The technology transfer occurred between the general concept of real-time audio/video via the Internet and the Nanoengineering Core User Facility. That is, prior to the LIVE activity, training for the microscope was fairly cumbersome as the laboratory is situated in a different building from the scientist that teaches students and visiting researchers how to use the machine. The microscope trainer was often running back and forth between his office and the laboratory showing how to complete experiments with the microscope. Now, the use of Skype, a simple web camera and microphone allows the microscope user to "show" the microscope trainer questions via the Internet.

E. Birch Aquarium at Scripps Institution of Oceanography, UCSD

The Birch Aquarium is exploring ways to incorporate LIVE technology into their science education programs. To demonstrate the concept,

Figure 6.Park ranger shares science information via LIVE with young girl participants attending Women in Science" summer camp

Figure 7. Interaction of young girl participants with career scientists and science educators at the Cabrillo National Monument's intertidal area

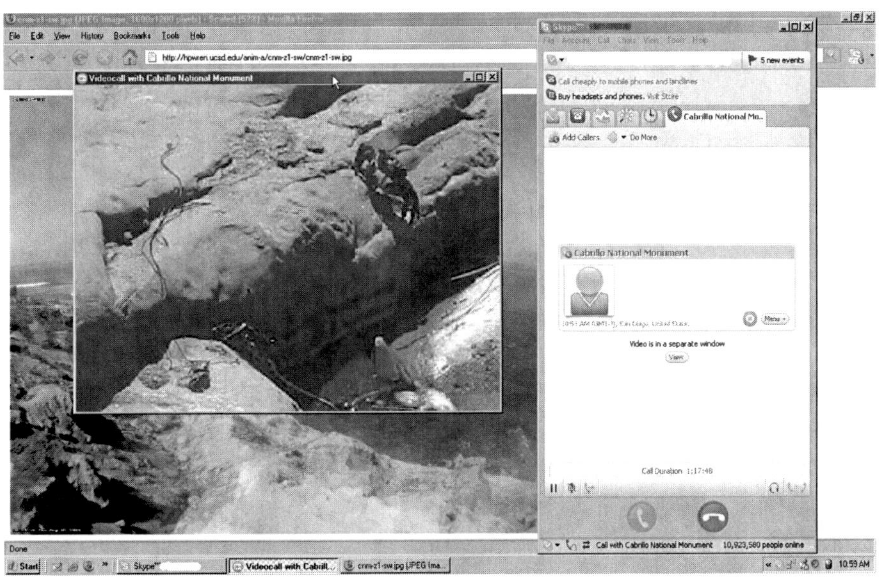

HPWREN researchers worked with Cabrillo National Monument staff to facilitate an activity between the intertidal area (Point Loma) and the Aquarium (La Jolla) in April 2009. During this brief test, a Cabrillo park ranger was able to speak with Aquarium visitors via LIVE. The audio was choppy due to high winds, however, researchers on the Aquarium end agreed that the study was a success and conducted a couple of their own tests within the same month. The Aquarium staff now aims to use the LIVE concept to share hard-to-access science sites with their visitors, ranging from oceanographic to seismologic field sites.

The biggest challenge with this technology transfer activity is the oceanographic component. Ideally, the LIVE activities would allow for the sharing of real-time off-shore audio and video as described in B part of the third section (i.e. National Park Service in Technology Transfer) section of this chapter. The complexity of this activity includes the use of boats, power generators, and likely additional support staff. Since the antenna would not be on firm ground, and given the anticipated distance between the wireless stations, it will require some experimentation with higher radio power and directional antennas, to achieve reliable high-speed network communication. On the other hand, it will also allow for new sources of interactive presentation materials, such as hand-held underwater cameras, perhaps even using a diver, remotely operated underwater vehicles, very high-resolution underwater cameras, as well as other real-time sensors in or above the water.

F. Southern California Tribal Chairmen's Association

The Southern California Tribal Chairmen's Association (SCTCA) is a consortium of 19 federally-recognized Indian tribes in southern California. The primary mission of SCTCA is to serve the health, welfare, safety, education, cultural, economic and employment needs of its tribal members and enrolled Indians in the San Diego County urban areas. The Association coordinates and administers numerous grant programs for its members and the southern California Indian community, including the Urban Adolescent Prevention Program (UAPP), which provides academic, cultural and prevention services to the North San Diego County Urban TANF (Temporary Assistance for Needy Families) participants under 18 years of age. Academic tutoring is provided at the UAPP site and students are also involved in Native youth conferences such as Dream the Impossible Conference, the I'm Going to College Conference, and the Juvenile Hall Open House Tour. Additionally, regularly-scheduled LIVE activities are now offered and share high-level science concepts with Native American youth.

The program coordinator downloaded and immediately starting experimenting with Skype in preparation for an activity between the Urban Adolescent Prevention Program and Mammoth Cave National Park, which took place in May 2009. The long-term plan for the association is to use the LIVE concept established at the Urban Adolescent Prevention Program as a model for additional programs within the tribal communities affiliated with the association. The program coordinator is using curricula developed by HPWREN to formulate a LIVE Passport Program for the Native American youth frequenting the association's site on a regular basis. This activity represents a successful technology transfer between the University researchers and the SCTCA.

The greatest challenges for this group's next steps is purely societal, as the participating youth come from impoverished residents that are unlikely to have a computer or afford high-speed Internet connectivity needed for online activities. Though the youth are able to use UAPP computers located at the program office and participate in LIVE activities, ideally they would be able to continue their inquiry regarding these science sites on their own time using Internet-connected computers at their home. Overcoming this challenge might be accomplished via a foundation grant focused on providing underserved communities with access to high-speed Internet.

ADDITIONAL STUDIES, CONCLUSION AND FUTURE RESEARCH

Another LIVE case study involved the October 2008 San Diego Supercomputer Center building dedication and featured audio/video transmissions between the new facility's dedication event and several HPWREN-connected science sites. The building dedication ceremony was followed by demonstrations of research housed at the center - including HPWREN LIVE research highlights. After a LIVE visit led by Cabrillo National Monument's Chief of Natural Resources Management and Science, Palomar Observatory public affairs officer discussed HPWREN-connected telescopes and recent discoveries made possible by the high-speed network. Next, a San Diego State University research technologist took the building dedication participants on a LIVE tour of the Santa Margarita Ecological Reserve – focusing on the river gorge and demonstrating the use of real-time remote sensors. This event allowed researchers to test and better understand the flow of ongoing LIVE activities between multiple remote science sites.

The HPWREN LIVE activities have generally been very successful – from both the audience and science site perspectives. However, it has to be understood that the implementation so far barely scratches the surface of what is possible in the future, based on new technologies and an increasing need for anywhere, any-time high performance data communication. The HPWREN LIVE activities are still in the research phase and have not been practically put into place at schools/universities at this time on a programmatic level. The researchers envision that being their next phase in the project.

The HPWREN LIVE concept attempts to be a system integration activity, utilizing common and inexpensive components, to make participation easy. New challenges include scaling in height and width, to allow for additional activities and audiences in general, as well as an anticipated need to reach multiple audiences simultaneously and in real-time. Another area of improvement is the need for higher video quality; ideally the current common Skype 320x240 video pixel (p) resolution could be scaled up to 640x480, and from there on to high-definition 720p and 1080p; it would also be useful to have the ability to achieve this higher video quality in a multi-point or multicast setting. While scaling up in video quality and its additional bandwidth needs, the system has to be designed so those with less bandwidth or less capable technology can still meaningfully participate with reduced video quality, without limiting high-performance sites. For interoperability reasons, future progress should also be driven by standards-based protocols, such as H.323. In addition, future LIVE enhancements will need to go beyond utilizing videoconferencing capabilities, and include other real-time data, such as various kinds of sensors, and supplementing the video feeds with very high resolution digital photos taken at the presenting site.

REFERENCES

Bruch, K. M. (2002). *Using a propositional diffusion model to examine the impact of broadband connectivity upon environmental monitoring.* Master's thesis. San Diego State University. Retrieved from http://kimbruch.com/thesis/

Rice, R. E., & Gattiker, V. E. (2001). New media and organizational structuring. In F. Jablin & L. Putman (Eds.), The new handbook of organizational communication: Advances in theory, research, and methods (pp. 544-581). Thousand Oaks, CA: Sage.

Rogers, E. M. (1995). Diffusion of innovations, (4th ed.). New York: Free Press.

Russell, C., Gregory, D., Care, W., & Hultin, D. (2007). Recognizing and avoiding intercultural miscommunication in distance education. *Journal of Professional Nursing*, *23*, 351–361. doi:10.1016/j.profnurs.2007.01.021

Valente, T. W. (1996). Social network thresholds in the diffusion of innovations. *Social Networks*, *18*, 69–89. doi:10.1016/0378-8733(95)00256-1

ADDITIONAL READING

Ahmed, H., Daim, T., & Basoglu, N. (2007). Information technology diffusion in higher education. *Technology in Society*, *29*, 469–482. doi:10.1016/j.techsoc.2007.08.011

Beck-Winchatz, B., & Riccobono, M. (2007). (in press). Advancing participation of blind students in science, technology, engineering, and math. *Advances in Space Research*.

Cardei, M., & Wu, J. (2006). Energy-efficient coverage problems in wireless ad-hoc sensor networks. *Computer Communications*, *29*, 413–420. doi:10.1016/j.comcom.2004.12.025

Chen, H.-M., Yu, C., & Chang, C.-S. (2007). E-Homebook system: A web-based interactive education interface. *Computers & Education*, *49*, 160–175. doi:10.1016/j.compedu.2005.05.003

Chetty, M., Blake, E., & McPhie, E. (2006). VoIP deregulation in South Africa: Implication for underserved areas. *Telecommunications Policy*, *30*, 332–344. doi:10.1016/j.telpol.2005.11.007

Dearing, J. W., Meyer, G., & Kazmierczak, J. (1994). Portraying the new: Communication between university innovators and potential users. *Science Communication*, *16*, 11–42. doi:10.1177/0164025994016001002

Dewiyanti, S., Brand-Gruwel, S., Jochems, W., & Broers, N. (2007). Students' experiences with collaborative learning in asynchronous computer-supported collaborative learning environments. *Computers in Human Behavior*, *23*, 496–514. doi:10.1016/j.chb.2004.10.021

Furlong, M., & Connor, J. (2007). The measurement of disability-related stress in wheelchair users. *Archives of Physical Medicine and Rehabilitation*, *88*, 1260–1267. doi:10.1016/j.apmr.2007.06.763

Gunasekaran, V., & Harmantzis. (2007). Emerging wireless technologies for developing countries. *Technology in Society*, *29*, 23–42. doi:10.1016/j.techsoc.2006.10.001

Hart, J., & Martinez, K. (2006). Environmental sensor networks: A revolution in the earth system science? *Earth-Science Reviews*, *78*, 177–191. doi:10.1016/j.earscirev.2006.05.001

Hawley, M., Cudd, P., & Cherry, A. (1994). Implementation of a PC-based integrated control system for children. *Medical Engineering & Physics*, *16*, 237–242. doi:10.1016/1350-4533(94)90043-4

Hewitt, J., & Brett, C. (2007). The relationship between class size and online activity patterns in asynchronous computer conferencing environments. *Computers & Education*, *49*, 1258–1271. doi:10.1016/j.compedu.2006.02.001

High Performance Wireless Research and Education Network News. Retrieved from <http://hpwren.ucsd.edu/>http://hpwren.ucsd.edu.

Howe, C., Tolmie, A., Thurston, A., Topping, K., Christie, D., & Livingston, K. (2007). Group work in elementary science: Towards organizational principles for supporting pupil learning. *Learning and Environments*, *17*, 549–563.

Jardine, P., Jerman, S., Seddon, N., & Rees, J. (1984). A communication aid for the physically handicapped. *Journal of Biomedical Engineering*, *6*, 230–236. doi:10.1016/0141-5425(84)90109-2

Kenward, M. (1971). An approach to the design of wheelchairs for young users. *Applied Ergonomics*, *2*, 221–225. doi:10.1016/0003-6870(71)90109-8

Kester, L., van Rosmalen, P., Sloep, P., Brouns, F., Kone, M., & Koper, R. (2007). Matchmaking in learning networks: Bringing learners together for knowledge sharing. *Interactive Learning Environments*, *15*, 117–126. doi:10.1080/10494820701332663

Mazzolini, M., & Maddison, S. (2007). When to jump in: The role of the instructor in online discussion forums. *Computers & Education*, *49*, 193–213. doi:10.1016/j.compedu.2005.06.011

Michinov, N., & Michinov, E. (in press). Face-to-face contact at the midpoint of an online collaboration: Its impact on the patterns of participation, interaction, affect, and behavior over time. *Computers & Education*.

Motiwalla, L. (2007). Mobile learning: A framework and evaluation. *Computers & Education*, *49*, 581–596. doi:10.1016/j.compedu.2005.10.011

Offir, B., Lev, Y., & Bezalel, R. (in press). Surface and deep learning processes in distance education: Synchronous versus asynchronous systems. *Computers & Education*.

Ozdemir, Z. D., & Abrevaya, J. (2007). Adoption of technology-mediated distance education: A longitudinal analysis. *Information & Management*, *44*, 467–479. doi:10.1016/j.im.2007.04.006

Richardson, S. (1971). Research report: Handicap, appearance, and stigma. *Social Science & Medicine*, *5*, 621–628. doi:10.1016/0037-7856(71)90011-4

Sandrasegaran, K., & Prag, K. (1999). Planning point-to-multipoint rural radio access networks using expert systems. *Expert Systems with Applications*, *17*, 145–166. doi:10.1016/S0957-4174(99)00031-7

Sea to Shining Sea News. Retrieved from <http://seatoshiningsea.org/>http://seatoshiningsea.org.

Sigelman, C. (1991). The effect of causal information on peer perceptions of children with physical problems. *Journal of Applied Developmental Psychology*, *12*, 237–253. doi:10.1016/0193-3973(91)90014-U

So, H.-J., & Brush, T. (in press). Student perceptions of collaborative learning, social presence and satisfaction in a blended learning environment: Relationships and critical factors. *Computers & Education*.

Sun, K.-T., Lin, Y.-C., & Yu, C.-J. (in press). A study on learning effect among different learning styles in a web-based lab of science for elementary school students. *Computers & Education*.

Tan, T.-H., Liu, T.-Y., & Chang, C.-C. (2007). Development and evaluation of an RFID-based ubiquitous learning environment for outdoor learning. *Interactive Learning Environments*, *15*, 253–269. doi:10.1080/10494820701281431

Tully, J., & Riekstins, A. (1999). License-free wireless internet access technologies. *Computer Networks*, *31*, 2205–2213. doi:10.1016/S1389-1286(99)00096-1

Valente, T. W., & Rogers, E. M. (1995). The origins and development of the diffusion of innovations paradigm as an example of scientific growth. *Science Communication*, *16*, 242–273. doi:10.1177/1075547095016003002

Wilson, S. (2008). Patterns of personal learning environments. *Interactive Learning Environments*, *16*, 17–34. doi:10.1080/10494820701772660

Young, A., & Lewis, C. (2007). (in press). Teacher education programmes delivered at a distance: An examination of distance student perceptions. *Teaching and Teacher Education*.

Zimmerman, C. (2007). The development of scientific thinking skills in elementary and middle school. *Developmental Review*, *27*, 172–223. doi:10.1016/j.dr.2006.12.001

KEY TERMS AND DEFINITIONS

HPWREN: High Performance Wireless Research and Education Network. The research project encompasses the creation, demonstration, and evaluation of a non-commercial, prototype, high-performance, wide-area, wireless network in southern California (USA).

LIVE: Live Interactive Virtual Explorations; distance learning activities that allow people to send and receive audio and video in real-time via an Internet connection.

PDA: Personal Digital Assistant; small portable hand-held computer.

Polycom: Software that allows people to send and receive both audio and video via an Internet connection.

ROV: Remotely Operated Vehicle; tethered underwater robot.

Skype: Free software that allows people to send and receive both audio and video via an Internet connection.

StSS: Sea to Shining Sea; distance learning project funded by the National Park Service (USA) that focuses on participants sending and receiving real-time audio and video via an Internet connection.

Chapter 17
Effectiveness of Problem Based Learning for Engineering Curriculum

J.I. Rojas
Universitat Politècnica de Catalunya (UPC), Spain

X. Prats
Universitat Politècnica de Catalunya (UPC), Spain

A. Montlaur
Universitat Politècnica de Catalunya (UPC), Spain

M. Valero
Universitat Politècnica de Catalunya (UPC), Spain

E. García-Berro
Universitat Politècnica de Catalunya (UPC), Spain

ABSTRACT

The main purpose of this case is to describe the process by which an initially limited-range practical experience, within the frame of a given course in an aerospace engineering degree, might be expanded to become the mother-course itself. Particularly, the practical experience is a Model Rocket Workshop (MRW), where students design, simulate, build, test and launch a small model rocket. The workshop is a Problem Based Learning (PBL) experience that covers a wide spectrum of educational aspects, ranging from theoretical disciplines, such as fluid dynamics and rocket dynamics, to topics more related to experimental work and hardware utilization like the certification of the rockets, as well as the rocket altitude measurements. Students get rapidly involved in the project, and acquire several practical and transversal abilities, while developing a solid knowledge of the physics underlying aerospace engineering. The case study shows some problems and improvements, academic results and lessons learned from the PBL approach. Finally, a series of new ideas related to MRW and to the course it belongs to are presented. The objective is to expand the MRW so that it embraces the totality of the activities that constitute this mother-course. As a consequence, the former would then become a new course entirely based on PBL. The strategy aims at enabling an optimum transition from conventional learning to PBL.

DOI: 10.4018/978-1-61520-779-4.ch017

ORGANIZATION BACKGROUND

The Universitat Politècnica de Catalunya (UPC) is a public higher education institution and one of the leading universities in Spain. The fields of research and education of the university are architecture, sciences and engineering. The schools and research centers are known, nationally and internationally, for educating and training technological professionals and for the high-quality research done in these areas. The university seeks excellence in teaching technical courses that are responsive to the training needs and requirements of traditional, evolving and newly-developing production sectors, including aerospace engineering, photonics, supercomputing, bioengineering, water resources and management and energy. All of them meet the criteria and requirements of the European Higher Education and Research Areas. Also, the substantial ability for technology transfer insures that the research generated by the technological and scientific teams has a real-world impact not only within Spain but also world-wide.

The University was officially founded in March 1971 and at present it offers 61 graduate and undergraduate official degrees, enrolling a total of about 29,500 graduate and undergraduate students. For some of these programs the university has international agreements with other technical universities to endorse double-degree diplomas, totaling 82 double-degree programs. Thus, the university has an international profile and it has about 2,300 students in international exchange programs. It is the Spanish university with the highest number of master's degree students from abroad. These programs have a natural continuation in 47 doctoral programs, enrolling 2,900 students.

The research activity of the university is undertaken by 40 departments, and it is funded by about 6,600 research projects, with a global research income of 72 million euros. It is the Spanish university with the highest research income from the European Union VI Framework Program. The overall scientific production during the last year was 1,600 papers, some of them in the most prestigious journals, like Science or Nature, to put some examples. It is the Spanish university with the highest citable output in the fields of Computer Science and Information Technologies; Mechanical and Aeronautical Engineering; Civil Engineering and Architecture; Electrical and Electronic Engineering and Automatic Control; and Electronic and Communications Technologies. The faculty and research staff amounts to 2,600 people, whereas the administrative staff amounts to about 1,500. The total budget of the UPC is 320 M€. Finally, the UPC is member of several international university networks (CLUSTER, CESAER and CINDA…).

The Escola Politècnica Superior de Castelldefels (EPSC) was founded in 1991 with the clear purpose of specializing in innovation in teaching methodologies. Since then, it has achieved a solid reputation among the Spanish universities in teaching excellence. It offers several bachelor degrees in engineering, including a bachelor degree in Aerospace Engineering. Special emphasis has been laid on using fully cooperative or Problem Based Learning (PBL) techniques. Student performance is evaluated using continuous assessment. Additionally, virtual campuses and interactive learning platforms have been developed from the very beginning and are intensively used in all courses (a couple of these tools are presented later on). Most of these techniques or tools have been subsequently used in other engineering schools or campuses of the different universities in Spain.

SETTING THE STAGE

Problem Based Learning (PBL)

Graduate coursework in aerospace engineering is intended in large part to prepare students for professional practice of engineering in companies and state or international agencies and, in some cases, for post-graduate research, either in public or private sector. Accordingly, the most complete and successful graduate programs in aerospace engineering are devised to provide a solid basis in physics and mathematics. Moreover, some topics – like, for instance, aerodynamics and flight dynamics or aeroelasticity, among others – involve an accurate knowledge of the underlying physics and a considerable load of relatively complex mathematical tools. Consequently, students quite frequently become overwhelmed by the intrinsic difficulties of these topics and, also quite usually, the success rate of regular courses is small. Furthermore, in most engineering schools and for most of the relevant topics, the assessment of student performance depends largely, or even entirely, on written exams. The traditional exams involve usually a variety of problems that are prepared to be completed in typically two hours of work in the classroom. A consequence of this way of assessing student performance is that the problems should be easy enough for the students to be able to solve them in a limited amount of time. However, in practice such simple problems do not occur in the professional exercise of aerospace engineering.

With the advent of physics and engineering education research as a research field, many initiatives are currently being developed. The generic goal of these initiatives is to improve the teaching of intrinsically complex topics using reform-based approaches. Consequently, there exists now an opportunity to move beyond the classical structure of engineering and physics courses to new experiences in which the students are the real and leading actors of their education. Many of these experiences involve the concept of PBL. In PBL experiences, students work in teams to explore real-world problems, learning whatever they need to learn in their way to the solution to the problem, under the conduct of their teachers. Additionally, in PBL, students identify problems of interest to them and experiment to find solutions. Moreover, they also design complex systems that integrate engineering fundamentals in a multidisciplinary approach. Compared with conventional learning, where the students work alone and learn from textbooks or class notes, this approach has several advantages. Among these advantages a few are worth mentioning. In particular, students develop a deeper knowledge of the subject, increase self-direction and motivation for the particular course, and, moreover, they reach improved research and problem-solving skills. In summary, PBL has now become a widespread teaching method in disciplines where students must learn to apply knowledge not just acquire it. More information on PBL can be found in literature (Doppelt 2005; Novack & Gowin 1988; Boud & Feletti 1997; Brodeur et al. 2002; Delisle 1997; Wilkerson & Gijselaers 1996).

However, PBL is not an easy thing to do, since it involves a deep transformation of the classical course organization. Students may feel disoriented and anxious as they have to decide how to proceed. On the other hand, teachers must devote time to follow the work of their students and give feedback, and may experience an increase in their teaching workload. And finally, teamwork, which is a central aspect of PBL, may be frustrating for both teachers and especially students.

Frequently, frustrating PBL experiences lack positive interdependence and/or individual accountability. When the PBL activity has positive interdependence, good performances of all team members are necessary for the project to succeed (e.g. everyone must complete his or her part). Moreover, when the activity has individual accountability, every team member is responsible for the whole task, and cannot concentrate in his or her part of the task, ignoring the tasks of the other teammates.

Group Puzzle Theory

One way to reinforce the positive interdependence and individual accountability in a PBL activity is to use the group puzzle technique (Freeman &

Jigsaw, 1994) to organize part of it. In a puzzle, the tasks to be done in a given phase of the project are split into several independent parts, so every member of the team ("core groups") is responsible for one of these parts. Then, it is said that every team member has a different role, or that each member is the expert in relation to a particular topic.

From time to time, members of different groups sharing the same role meet in groups of three or four (meetings of "expert groups") to clarify doubts about their roles or to complete together parts of the tasks they have been assigned. This in fact means the creation of a set of parallel groups, aside from the core groups. After these expert meetings and/or once the experts have finished their tasks and fulfilled their particular goals, they return to their core groups to share and to transfer the acquired knowledge to the rest of their teammates. Therefore, a significant part of the teaching process actually involves the students themselves.

Summarizing, each member must do his part of the task in order for the group to be successful in completing the activity (positive interdependence). Moreover, individual accountability is further reinforced if students must complete from time to time an individual exam about any of the roles of the activity. As a result, once the entire process is finished, each student should be able to understand the whole problem and develop a solution to solve it. Therefore, the success of a group means the success of all its members.

In the PBL, the puzzle technique is used as a key element to organize and distribute the tasks of the students.

CASE DESCRIPTION

Experimental Techniques in Aerospace Engineering (TEA) & Model Rocket Workshop (MRW)

The course called Experimental Techniques in Aerospace Engineering (*Tècniques Experimentals en Aerofísica*, TEA from now on) is a teaching unit of third-year course included in the Aeronautics Engineering degree at EPSC. This course addresses several experimental techniques and serves as a means to complement and intensify some of the theoretical aspects taught during the whole bachelor degree. For example, wind tunnel experiments are used to introduce experimental fluid dynamics to students, the functioning of an engine is taught in a practical way and some tests are proposed to study material properties. Further details are presented later on. The class involves weekly two hours of classes at the University, for which the attendance is mandatory, plus 4 to 6 hours of homework, but this latter number depends strongly on the activity.

Originally, the Model Rocket Workshop (MRW) was a PBL solution designed to conduct a limited-range aerospace educational activity and was proposed within the framework of TEA. In particular, this experience consists in the design, simulation, construction and launching of a model rocket. After the launch, the payload is recovered and the measured flight parameters are analyzed and compared to the numerical calculations. Above all, the activity is based on the utilization of cooperative learning and PBL techniques.

First Edition of the MRW

The first edition of the Model Rocket Workshop (MRW) took place during the academic year 2005-2006. Some changes and improvements have been made afterwards and will be presented later on.

Figure 1. Gantt Diagram showing the schedule of the MRW during the academic course 2008-2009. The diagram was elaborated with Gantt Project open access software (credit: this figure was obtained using Gantt Project[1]).

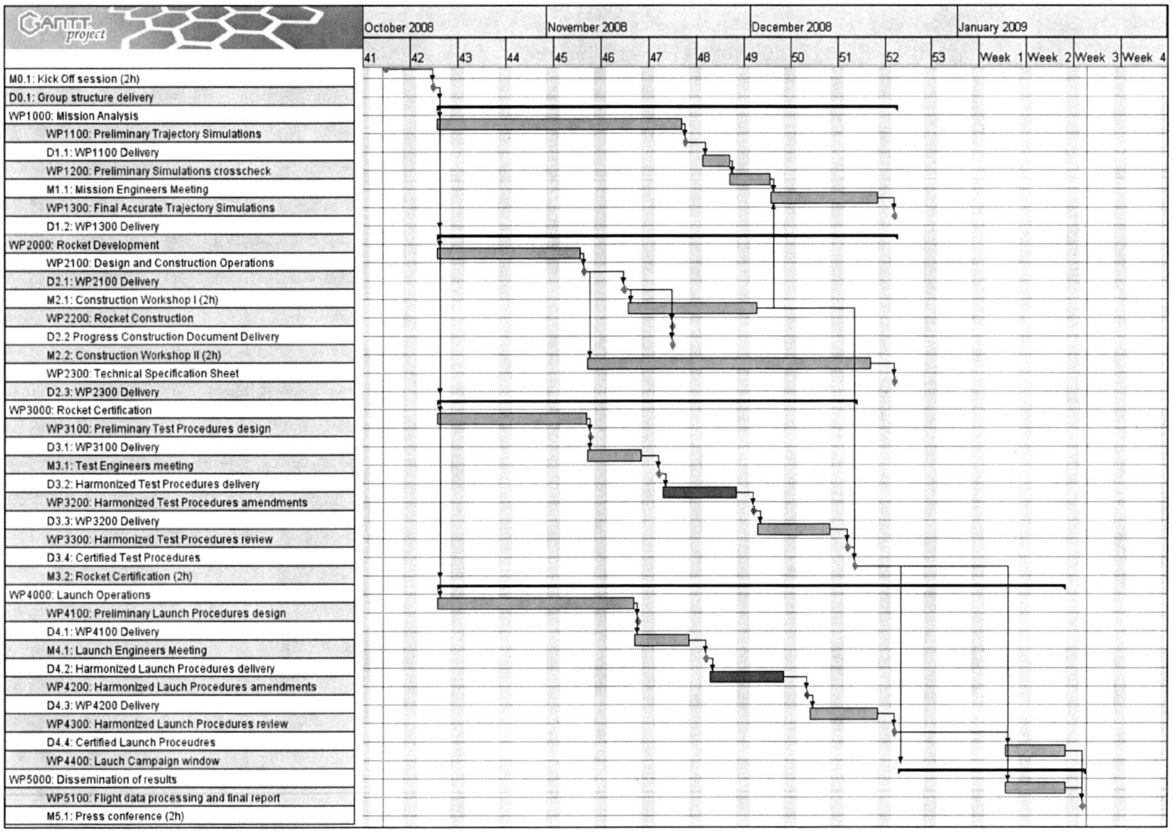

Organization of the Activity

In this section, the organization of the workshop as it was first completed is presented (Rojas et al. 2008). Regarding the schedule of the activity, the MRW lasts approximately twelve sessions. A Gantt Diagram of the schedule is shown in Figure 1.

The planning is strict and clearly sets up procedures and deadlines for every group. Several milestones are placed along the project, as well as deadlines to deliver partial reports and results.

During the first session, after the presentation of the workshop, the teaching staff assumes the role of a client company and gives the students information regarding the requirements to be fulfilled during the mission. Technical information is also provided such as, for example, the rocket engine thrust profile, given by the manufacturer of the rocket engines (see Figure 2). Also a list of available material is given to the students. Special emphasis has been made in using inexpensive and readily available material for all the equipment needed to complete the whole teaching unit. Most of the needed items, such as cutters, scissors, adhesive tapes, painting and so on, are inexpensive and readily available at regular stores, whereas others can be purchased either in specialized stores or directly from the manufacturers. In particular, rocket motors, fuselages and nose fairing are purchased to a specialized manufacturer.

As mentioned above, the learning methodology in the MRW is mainly inspired on the technique

Figure 2. Rocket engine thrust profile (in Newtons) versus time (in seconds) as provided by the manufacturer of the engine (credit: Noris-Raketen©).

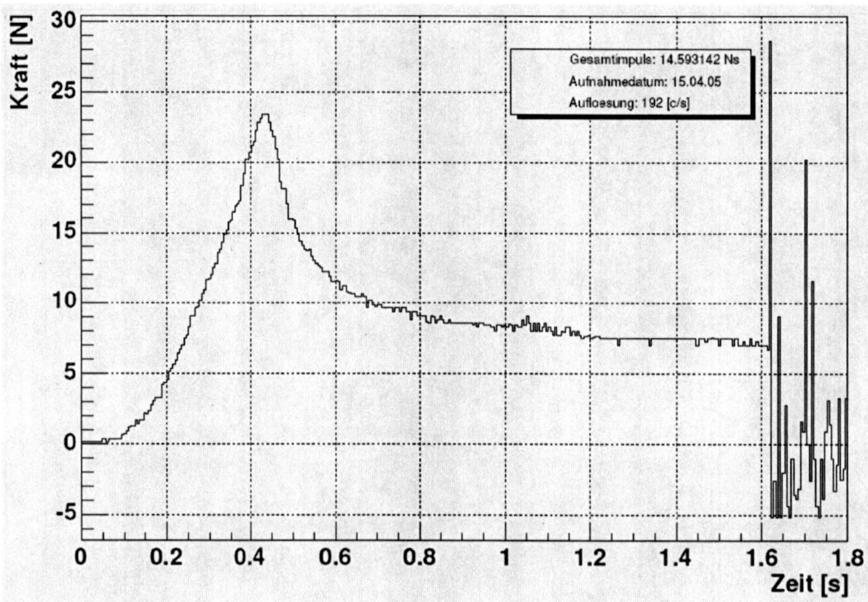

called group puzzle (Freeman & Jigsaw, 1994). Hence, in the class context, once the first session is over, the students are allowed to self-distribute and to organize themselves into the core teams. Shortly after this, each team decides how to assign the different roles to the several members within the group. These roles are explained later on in this section.

After its formation, each core group has to consider itself as a space agency, in charge of planning and accomplishing the design, construction and launching of the rocket, taking into account the mission requirements that the instructors have issued. All relevant tasks and duties are clearly indicated in Figure 1. The first task for the students consists in performing the mission analysis. It is followed by the development of the rocket. The rocket is then certificated and finally launched. Once the payload, the altimeter, is recovered, the flight parameters are analyzed and compared to the theoretical expectations. The software needed to download and to process the data acquired and stored by the altimeters during the flight is provided by the manufacturer of the altimeters.

Most of the data and information needed by the students is loaded and available in the dotProject web platform, which is explained in a further section. For instance, technical documents, such as rocket motor performances and features, safety code for rocket launching or list of materials, are available to students since the beginning of the activity.

All documentation of the project is in English and the whole teaching unit is also given in English, in order to create an environment with the highest degree of realism, that is, as similar as possible to the one found in international agencies or aerospace companies.

When designing the MRW, it was decided that the core groups were to be constituted of four members, although this number can be made larger if desired. Therefore, according to the Group Puzzle methodology, the project was divided into four main tasks. Again, in order to simulate the real environment of a space agency or an aerospace company, the task distribution inside every group is done as it occurs in real space agencies. To that end, four roles or types of Expert Engineers (EE) are identified, each one associated to clearly defined responsibilities and duties:

- Mission Engineer (ME):
  - Mission and team coordinator.
  - Leader for tasks related to mission analysis: rocket flight equation computation and simulation (assuming a two-dimensional, symmetric trajectory).
  - Team spokesman: presents the overall results during the final session of the workshop.
- Development Engineer (DE):
  - Leader for tasks related to rocket design.
  - Leader for tasks related to rocket construction.
- Test Engineer (TE):
  - Leader for tasks related to rocket certification tests design.
  - Referee for the certification tests of the rocket of another group during certification campaign.
- Launch Engineer (LAE):
  - Leader for tasks related to rocket launching procedures design.
  - Supervisor during rocket launching campaign to guarantee safety.
  - Ignites the rocket at the launching ramp.

The expert engineer acts as team leader and spokesman for the specific assigned tasks and work. It is important to remark that the expert engineer is in charge of leading these tasks, not of completing them all. Every member of the team should contribute and help the expert engineer in his specific responsibilities so that all team members participate in the learning process associated to that work. Note that the activity can be adapted to allow core groups of more than four members by extending the previous list with additional roles, according to the common practices in industry. A proposal for a new role will be explained later, in the description of the last edition of the MRW.

During the workshop, besides the individual work of each student, several meetings take place, bringing together either all members within a core group, or particular experts from every group. For example, the first session without instructors corresponds to a meeting where the roles of the experts have to be distributed within a group. Then experts from each team meet in order to identify their main tasks and responsibilities, the problems involved in designing and building the rocket and some other issues. Afterwards another meeting within a group is organized to share the acquired knowledge among experts and to transfer the results to all team members.

Both kinds of meetings are fundamental to guarantee the correct development of the tasks, which requires a high level of interaction between group members because of the existence of strong interdependency between data and results, inputs and outputs of every task. To make expert meetings more profitable and productive, experts are asked to deliver, before any meeting, brief and concise reports about the work they have previously done and about the matters to be commented in the corresponding meeting. This also gives the teaching staff relevant material in order to continuously evaluate the tasks of the students. Depending on the nature of the meeting, the minutes of the meeting may also be requested, stating the work done during the meeting and the achieved milestones. In total, the work completed by each core group consists in four partial reports and one final report, which must be delivered according to the deadlines given in the Gantt diagram shown in Figure 1. Details about these reports are given in the following section. If a group does not deliver a report within the deadline, the instructors can deny the launching permission for the model rocket of that group. The delivery of the reports is done through the dotProject platform, where the core group members can upload the files containing their respective reports.

The penultimate session of the workshop is the launch itself. In our case, the model rockets were launched from a site located in the vicinity of the University Campus, after having asked permission both to the City Council and to the owner of the launch site. In the present case, these two kinds of permits were the only ones needed to fly model rockets. Furthermore, according to Spanish regulations, no special permit from the Civil Aviation Authority is needed, since the site is outside any area controlled by the Air Traffic Management (ATM) and the maximum altitude reached by the rockets is below 1000 feet (the maximum allowable altitude above ground level for unmanned flying devices in Spain). The maximum flight altitude had been previously computed by integrating numerically the equation of motion and was confirmed by the experimental flight. An example of rocket velocity components versus time as obtained by numerical integration of the equations governing the rocket flight trajectory is shown in Figure 3. No license is neither necessary to use the rocket motors given that D-category motors were used and that a license is only compulsory when using H-category motors or above. Note that depending on the country where the workshop is realized, special permits may be required and local legislation concerning unmanned flying devices and motors should always be checked.

Finally, the final report is delivered during the last session. In addition, during the final session, each core group gives a formal presentation to present its work and results to the rest of students and teaching staff. Following the presentation, the team members are asked about technical, managerial and team performance issues. More details about this final session are given in the following section.

Calculation of the Rocket Trajectory

As they are important for further sections, we briefly present here some details related to the rocket motion equations integration. Particularly, we are requesting the students to make the following assumptions when performing the trajectory calculations (Heister & Messersmith, 1996):

- To consider a two-dimensional, symmetric (no slipping) trajectory.
- To assume that the rocket operates under a ballistic trajectory in which its angle of attack is zero (that is, the rocket longitudinal axis and its aerodynamic velocity are parallel).
- To assume there is neither lift nor lateral forces generation, which is valid provided we assume that the rocket's angle of attack is null.
- The engine thrust is aligned with the longitudinal axis.

According to these hypotheses, among the lift, drag and pitching moment coefficients, the drag coefficient is the only one that the students really need for their calculations.

Method of Evaluation

This section presents the main issues concerning the evaluation of the students in the first edition of the MRW, which took place during the academic year 2005-2006. On the one hand, the evaluation method was thought in accordance to the educational philosophy at EPSC, still valid nowadays, that is the method is to be based in continuous evaluation. On the other hand, it was decided for that edition that all the members of a same team would be assigned an identical mark. Thus, this section reports the criteria used to obtain a team's mark, not the mark of a particular member.

Generally, grading a PBL experience is a difficult matter, but it should be made as practical as

Figure 3. Plot of rocket velocity components (in meters per second) versus time (in seconds) obtained by numerical integration of the equations governing the rocket flight trajectory using Matlab© (credit: this figure was obtained using Matlab – MathWorks[2]).

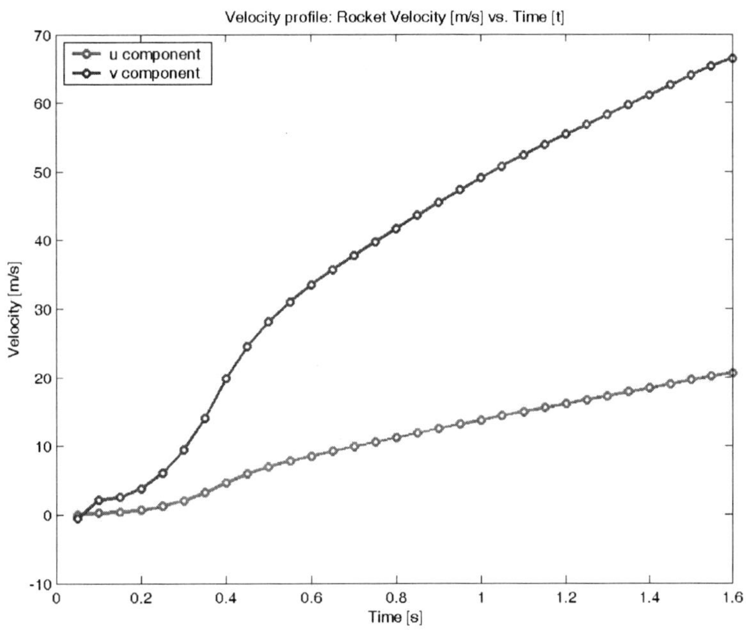

possible (Brügemann et al. 2005; Doppelt 2005). In accordance to this, we decided for the first edition that the final mark of a team would be based on the evaluation of the following concepts:

- The quality of a series of documents that the team has to deliver throughout the course. In this first edition, the delivery of these reports was made through the web tool named dotProject. In a later edition it was decided to migrate to Atenea (the Moodle-based institutional digital campus) due to several reasons, as explained further on. The documents to be delivered were the following ones, in chronological order of their due time (see also the Gantt diagram of Figure 1):
    - Report on rocket flight trajectory results obtained by numerical simulation of the rocket flight equations (see example plot in Figure 3).
    - Report on rocket test and certification procedures design.
    - Report on rocket launch procedures design.
    - Final report (see more information below).
- The degree to which the team had fulfilled the scheduled deadlines for the various deliveries. The students are properly informed about the deadlines at the beginning of the MRW, since they are clearly defined in the kick-off documentation relating to MRW planning provided by faculty members.
- The degree to which the team has achieved the objectives given by faculty members, as for instance, the accuracy in fulfilling the procedures published by faculty members in the kick-off documents. These

procedures refer to the management of reports, notification of the status and progress of tasks, etc.

- The quality of the presentation and final report. As previously mentioned, the presentation takes place during the last session of the course, which corresponds also to the deadline for the delivery of the final report. Both should be a concise summary of all the work done by the team throughout the workshop. Nevertheless, special attention should be paid to the following parts, which we consider the most relevant ones of the presentation and final report, since other matters have already been addressed in the previous reports:
  - The processing of the experimental results obtained from the readings of the altimeter on board the rocket (see example plot in Figure 4).
  - The comparison of these results with the theoretical results calculated by means of numerical simulations for previous deliveries.

Each team performs its presentation in front of an audience consisting of all other remaining MRW participants (faculty and students). A question time is allocated at the end of the presentation. Both the faculty and students may ask questions to each of the team members. This is especially valuable to ensure that all of them have properly assimilated the knowledge associated to each of the different roles, not only the knowledge associated to the member's particular role.

The authors would like to remark that up to four faculty members were used to conduct this activity and a minimum of two during the latter editions, and that all the deliveries represent a considerable amount of documentation to be evaluated by the educators. These facts are significant, since evaluation may require an important coordination effort or otherwise an important individual effort, depending on the number of participant faculty. For the first and following sessions, it was decided that all faculty members participating in the MRW would be responsible for assessing student performance in this activity.

RESULTS OF THE FIRST EDITION OF THE MRW

Marks of the Teams

The marks of most of the students in the first edition of the MRW were very high. The average mark was 8.71 over 10. Among the five participant teams, for three of them, constituted of five people, the marks were significantly high: two of these teams were rated 10.00 and the other one 9.00. The reason for this high marks is that these groups over-performed, that is, they worked even more than what were requested to do, and showed outstanding initiative. The average is lower due to problems occurred in another team. In this group, which was constituted of four members, we detected that a couple of students were not performing as requested. Exceptionally, they were rated with different, far lower marks respect to the other two members. This made us aware of the problems of the evaluation method, since maybe similar problems were taking place in other teams without us knowing.

Assessments & Comments from the Students

In the following section, some brief feedback is presented, as it was received from students or deduced from their comments after they conducted the first edition of the MRW:

- Students in general enjoyed the activities within the frame of MRW.
- Students liked to do hands-on activities that were based on a previous work they had done on paper (e.g. build physically

Figure 4. Plot of the altimeter readings of height (in feet) versus time (in seconds) presented in a typical window by PerfectFlite[3] Mini ALT altimeter software, after the data has been downloaded. The picture depicts some of the common features of these plots. Namely, for time 0 the height is higher than 0, since the altimeter stores data only starting from the moment it detects the launching has occurred, which happens after a given variation of height in time is exceeded (credit: this figure was obtained using PerfectFlite© Mini ALT altimeter software).

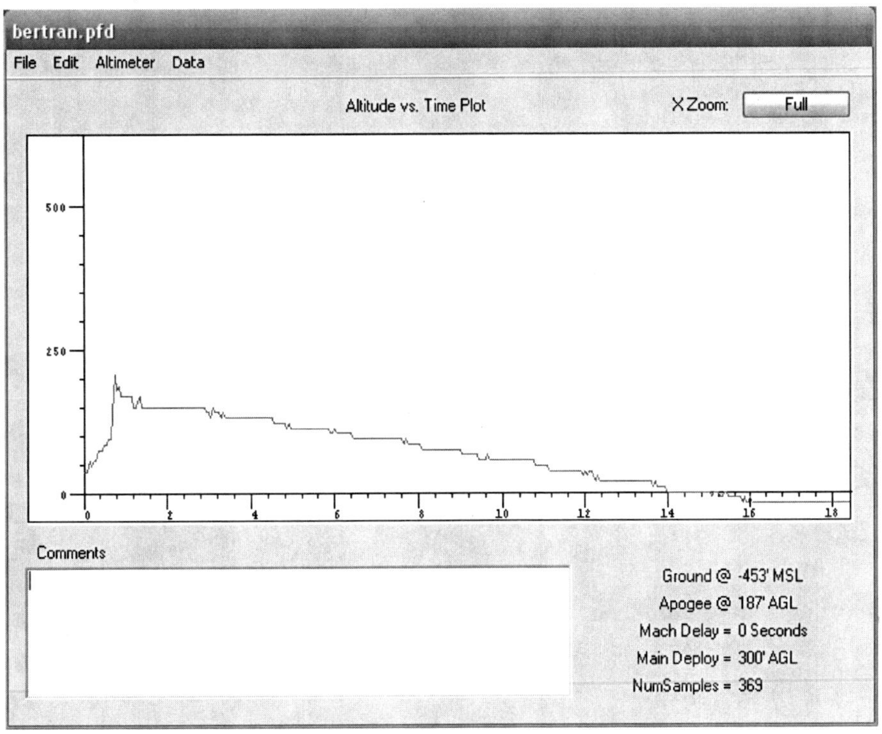

the model rockets or the recovery systems after they have designed them).

- Students appreciated the possibility of refining in parallel their former calculations and simulations as the hardware they used or built differed from their original designs.
- Students especially liked the MRW to be scheduled in 3rd grade, since at this point they have assimilated many theoretical concepts, but have not put most of then physically into practice yet.
- Students in general complained that in reality more allocated time was necessary than the one scheduled for some of the sessions or tasks, since they had to rush excessively in many cases and the quality of their work was affected.
- Students felt that the activities had been planned precisely in most of the cases, but they also commented that sometimes there was a lack of suited materials to properly perform some of the scheduled activities. For instance, students in this first edition of the MRW complained that the saws provided by the faculty were not suited for cutting the marquetry wood for building the fins (according to some students, the saws needed more teeth and harder, and also compatible handles). Other students complained that there were not enough

thermal blankets for every team to build parachutes, etc.

- Some students commented that the splitting of tasks and responsibilities among the expert engineers was not optimum. From their standpoint, during the MRW course each engineer was being sequentially overwhelmed by his particular tasks and deadlines during the corresponding period of the MRW. As a consequence, sometimes they felt they were not really doing any teamwork.

The last comment made us aware of an important problem, which is that some students had misunderstood what really was the role of the experts. This is addressed in the following section.

Problems Detected & Lessons Learned

First, some minor defects or problems that were detected during the first edition of the MRW are reported in the following list:

- It is important for the faculty staff to be aware of some deadlines too, not only relating to the deliveries of the teams but also related to the acquisition and renewal of some equipments and materials to be used by them. That is, it is important to accurately control and monitor the inventory and the schedule, and to remember to buy on time some missing items or materials, or to book on time some rooms, etc.
- It is critical to ensure that the students read, understand and use appropriately all the documentation that they have been provided with, since we noticed that some groups did not pay attention to certain documents (e.g. the altimeter user's guide).
- The upper load limit of the scales that the students use for the certification tests should be carefully taken into consideration, since the requirements of load to be applied to some parts of the rocket during the certification tests may exceed this upper limit.

Figure 5. Picture of an altimeter prior to its integration inside the nose fairing.

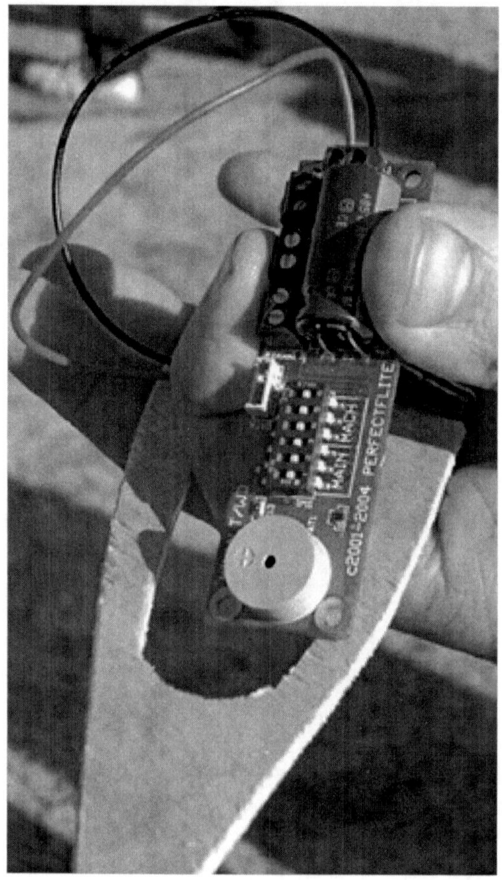

- Special attention should be paid to rockets having unnoticed excess weight or overweight, as compared with the maximum recommended take-off weight provided by the manufacturer.
- Some altimeters did not work adequately (see picture of an altimeter in Figure 5). A process of proof testing should be performed prior to the launch campaign.
- Some parachutes were not folded adequately by the students. Faculty should monitor

this process, for instance during the launch campaign.
- Some parachutes did not deploy adequately while the rockets were in flight.

Second, a more important problem is reported. Due to an excess of students, some groups were finally constituted of more than four people, which was not in accordance to what had been initially planned. As a consequence, there was an undesired redundancy of some roles in some teams. We decided to propose a new role, as explained later on, which in addition would help face a further increase in the number of students in subsequent editions, while preventing the number of teams and rockets to grow excessively.

Another aspect of the first edition that the authors did not consider satisfactory was the evaluation method, since in some cases the performance and commitment of different members of the same team had been significantly unbalanced. To better assess the performance and the achievements of every single member of a team, the authors opted in later editions for implementing a new evaluation method where the grading was individual. This method will be explained later on.

Finally, in many cases the students did not understand what the authors expected when designing the MRW, in relation to the role of the experts. For some reason, maybe due to a deficient communication or coordination, or to a misunderstanding, some teams did not realize that the experts were only the leaders or coordinators of some given tasks. Somehow these groups behaved and worked as if the experts were the ones to perform completely all their corresponding tasks. Instead, the students should have understood that the experts were the ones in charge of leading the team to fulfill the respective tasks. It is vital to ensure that the students understand this point. So this was an important problem that we had to deal with and to solve for future editions.

IMPROVEMENTS INTRODUCED

The last edition of the MRW so far, corresponding to the academic year 2008-2009, has been the fourth one. Next, some improvements introduced in the last editions of the MRW are reported. These modifications are related to the first version of the activity. In a particular manner, this section reflects the present day status of the MRW.

Modifications in the Rocket Certification Session

As reported above, among others, we detected the following problems:

- Some altimeters did work adequately.
- Some parachutes were not properly folded by the students.
- Some parachutes did not deploy adequately while the rockets were in flight.

To avoid these problems we decided to introduce some modifications in the MRW. Concretely, we specified new certification requirements for the rockets to obtain the launch authorization during the certification session:

- In order to assess the correct functioning of the altimeters, we included mandatory altimeter tests to be performed during the certification session.
- In order to guarantee the correct deployment of the parachutes during the launch campaign, we included mandatory tests to be performed on the recovery system during the certification session. Faculty should monitor the folding of the parachutes and should provide advice or guidance when necessary, either at the certification session or during the launch preparation.

A New Type of Expert Engineer is Proposed

As previously explained, each member of the team is assigned a different role, each of which has some specific responsibilities. The following expert engineers are those of the first edition of the MRW (Rojas et al. 2008), as this activity was initially designed for teams ideally constituted of four people:

- Mission Engineer (ME).
- Development Engineer (DE).
- Test Engineer (TE).
- Launch Engineer (LAE).

As mentioned before, the number of students for some teams exceeded four members in the first edition, which lead us to think about and create a new role for subsequent editions. This would prevent the number of teams and rockets to grow excessively over a given desired number, and would reduce the possibility of redundancy of roles. The proposed new role was:

- Logistics Engineer (LOE):
    - Leader for tasks related to rocket materials acquisition, storage and retrieval.
    - Leader for tasks related to laboratory equipment well-being maintenance, manipulation and storage.

Modifications in the Evaluation Method

Since the first edition in 2005-2006, there have been significant improvements in many facets, and particularly in the evaluation method. Nevertheless, it is worth saying that the present evaluation method is still coherent with the educational philosophy at EPSC, as was the initial one, i.e. it is based on continuous evaluation.

The main difference between the first and subsequent editions is that, in the latter, each member of the team is assigned a particular mark, so all members in a team may not have the same mark. This difference arose due to the following. We realized that credit had to be given effectively to the achievements of the team as a whole, but also the individual contributions to the team results had to be acknowledged. Consequently, the evaluation method had to allow each student to be graded individually.

The reason for this mark distinction within a group is also that on the one hand, pure team-based assessment might be a disadvantage to the stronger students and also be misused by weaker students. This should be prevented. On the other hand, the grade should reflect the evolution of each particular student during the workshop.

Thus, we still bear in mind the student evaluation criteria reported in a previous section for the first edition of the MRW. Nonetheless, there are some differences and innovations: 1) there have been some important changes in the first criterion, 2) we incorporated new criteria, and finally 3) as mentioned above, we use all these criteria to obtain a particular mark for every single MRW participant. These changes and new criteria are detailed in the following.

Regarding the first evaluation criterion in the last edition:

- Again, an important part of the mark of each participant depends on the quality of a series of documents that the team has to deliver throughout the course. As mentioned before, the delivery of these reports in this last edition was made through the web tool named Atenea, instead of dotProject. The reasons for the migration from dotProject to Atenea are presented in a later section. The documents to be delivered were the following ones, in chronological order:
    - Report on rocket design and construction operations.

- Preliminary report on rocket test and certification procedures design.
- Preliminary report on rocket launch procedures design.
- Progress report on rocket construction.
- Preliminary report on rocket flight trajectory results, obtained by numerical simulation of the rocket flight equations.
- Minutes of Test Engineers (TE) meeting.
- Harmonized rocket test and certification procedures.
- Minutes of Launch Engineers (LAE) meeting.
- Harmonized rocket launch procedures.
- Minutes of Mission Engineers (ME) meeting.
- Harmonized rocket test and certification procedures (after revision).
- Harmonized rocket launch procedures (after revision) (see for instance the ascending phase of a rocket in Figure 6).
- Rocket technical specification sheet.
- Final report on rocket flight trajectory results, obtained by numerical simulation of the rocket flight equations, using real updated data.
- MRW final report.
- Minutes related to some meetings of experts and meetings of core groups (these meetings have been previously scheduled when planning the MRW activity (see the Gantt diagram in Figure 1)).

In addition to the criteria previously reported for the first edition of the MRW, new evaluation criteria were considered in the last edition:

Figure 6. Rocket in the initial ascending flight phase, where the engine is still operative.

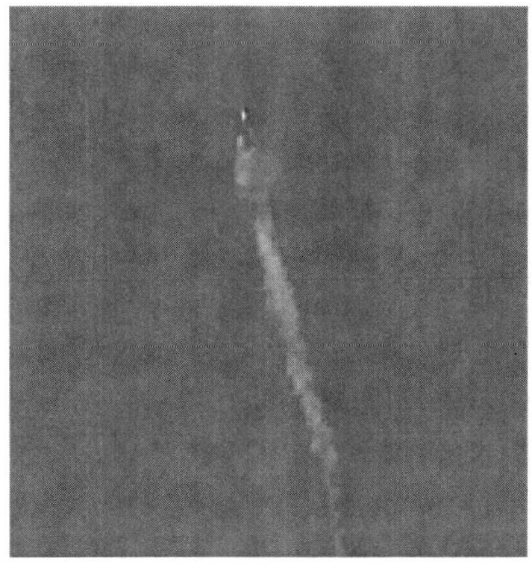

- To be able to define a particular mark for each student, we had to implement some innovations. First, the work done and knowledge acquired by each participant as the activity progressed had to be assessed on a continuous basis. We called this process "peer review". This evaluation was done through observation of:
    - Doubts raised by the student during and out of class-time.
    - Work done by the student during on-site sessions.
    - Answers to questions that faculty posed to the student after the delivery of some documents, during some meetings, etc.
    - The student performance at the final presentation.
- Second, all students must fill a self-evaluation form[4] the day of the presentation, taking place in the last session of the course. Through this form, the participants rate their team-mates and themselves and answer a series of concise questions confidentially. The list of questions includes, for instance, whether a given team member attended all team meetings, contributed to the activities, met deadlines by the team,

helped in keeping the team organized, cohesive, and progressing toward completion of the goals… and several others. The information provided is very valuable and may give clues to faculty about:
    - The attitude (degree of implication and participation), performance and functioning of each team member.
    - The member who has led the team.
    - Problems that arose during the course of the activity.
- We requested the teams to address new issues within the frame of their presentation and final report, e.g. suggestions, assessments, comments and opinions of students relating to the MRW, in order to improve the development of the workshop, etc.
- Frequently, the performance and initiative of one or more teams during an edition was outstanding, i.e. these teams have done much more work than requested. This has happened at least for one team for each MRW edition. We thought this should be especially taken into consideration.

The goal of the two first new criteria was to enable the monitoring and evaluation of the transfer of knowledge between group members with different roles, and the extent to which the work done and the reports delivered by the team are the result of teamwork, and not the result of the efforts of a single or a few individuals. Alternative or complementary options to allow grading of students individually were also considered. For instance, for the various reports delivered by the team during the teaching unit, each of the students is in charge of fixed duties and responsibilities. Accordingly, an individual grade can be assigned to each of them, although the reports are collective. The minutes of the meetings might also help in assessing student performances.

Finally, to obtain the global mark for a given student, we implemented a weighted mixture of team and individual assessment techniques, assigning 40% of the mark to teamwork, 30% to individual work and 30% to peer review.

Moving from dot Project to Atenea Web Tool

For the correct development of the MRW activity, a collaborative web platform is needed in order to manage the project, share documents, discuss some topics, etc. As mentioned before, the open access dotProject[5] platform was used in the first edition of the MRW activity. This web-based application is designed to provide project layouts and control functions, where a series of tasks can be structured, as well as the schedule associated with them. In addition, the platform provides a set of associated functions such as project planning, contract negotiation, risk management, cost management, task logging, forums for debate, file sharing, etc. Summing up, dotProject is a very user friendly platform to manage the day to day activities of a project progression and can be used by either project managers or down level project workers.

The initial idea was to use this web platform to achieve two main objectives. First, dotProject provides a standardized way of communication between the students (acting as industry) and the teaching staff (acting as the contracting company or customers). In this way, the description and scheduling of each task is presented at the kick-off session using the intrinsic functionalities that dotProject provides (automatic generation of Gantt diagrams, project organization, list of tasks, list of deliverables, file repository, etc). The second goal was to take advantage of the project management features of dotProject. In this context, the students were requested to enter task logs during the execution of the project, to update the tasks status and finally to use the forums to share experiences and doubts and to coordinate efforts, as it would be done in a real professional environment. However, this second goal was not achieved since the students only used the platform to share documentation (deliverables, input documents...) with the teaching staff.

In parallel, at University level, the web platform so-called Atenea was chosen to be the standard application to manage the different courses being taught at UPC. This platform is strongly based on Moodle, the most popular open source Learning Management System (LMS) nowadays. Atenea provides a wide range of tools aimed at a better management and promotion of learning. It is used at and among all the different schools that compose the UPC to conduct fully online courses, to promote blended learning and to establish a standardized and integrated way to exchange information between faculty and students.

For these reasons, and taking into account that the most significant features of dotProject were not being used by the students (partially because of the relatively small size of these projects and the teams involved), we decided to migrate from dotProject to the Atenea web application for the second and subsequent versions of the MRW.

RESULTS OF THE LAST EDITIONS OF THE MRW

Marks of the Students

The marks of the students in the last editions of the MRW have been 8.40 over 10 in average. Although we objectively think that the activity has been improved noticeably since the first edition, the average in the marks has diminished. The reasons for this fact might be the following:

- The level of complexity has aroused as we have been polishing the activity and enhancing the supplied documentation, etc. Thus, the MRW has become more demanding in relation to aspects such as quality, quantity and tightness-to-deadline of the various deliveries and reports, etc.
- Most of the students are still being rated with high marks. The average descent is due to very low marks that are assigned to students who do not show up, or significantly under-perform, etc. These cases are nowadays efficiently detected and assessed most of the times thanks to the modifications in the evaluation method.

Assessments & Comments from the Students

Next, some comments are listed. These come from feedback that was included by students in their final presentations in the last editions of the MRW (for these last editions, we requested them to do so, as previously explained):

- It would be very rewarding to make an important effort to minimize the total mass of the rocket. Namely, the battery (9V for which the mass is 40gr.) and some pieces of the fuselage are very heavy. Some solutions should be searched to reduce them in weight to the benefit of the rocket performance.
- The proper implementation of the recovery system is still problematic for the students (see example of descending phase in Figure 7). Maybe more guidance should be given to students on topics such as the gluing of parachute strings to the fuselage, the positioning of parachutes inside the body, how to correctly fold them, etc.
- Modify the engine bracket so the engine is completely fixed (it had about 5mm of free space).
- Students often complain about the altimeters, since in certain occasion they do not work well. In some editions a couple of altimeters obtained noticeably erroneous data. This issue should be studied in-depth, since the malfunction of the altimeters could be caused by an incorrect assembly

Figure 7. Descending phase in which nose fairing and fuselage glide and are recovered separately.

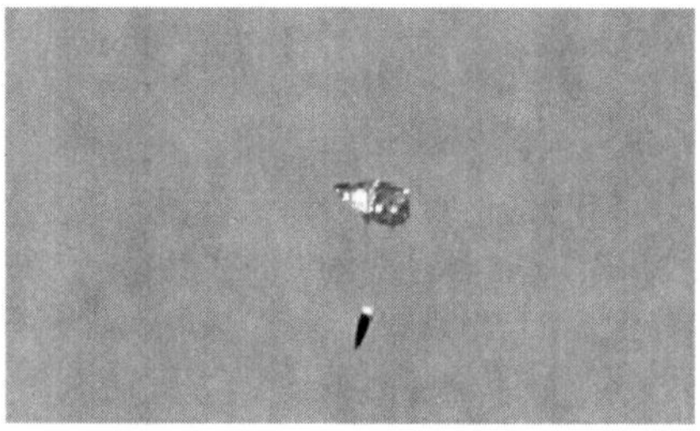

or disposal and not due to the altimeter itself.

- It might be interesting to keep track of the creative engineering solutions for the technological problems faced by the teams along the different editions. This way, we would detect which are the most common solutions, how students think and solve the problems, etc. This information sure would be important and helpful for the enhancement of the MRW and the formation of future students.

Problems Detected & Lessons Learned

A significant problem from our standpoint is that the launch campaigns often tend to evolve a bit anarchically. That is, even if there is an important work and organizational effort prior to the launch session (e.g. preparation of the harmonized rocket launch procedures), these sessions often turn into a small chaos. We should think of new ideas to guarantee that these sessions are conducted in a systematic and methodical way.

Some lessons were also learned from the past editions of the workshop:

- Some students and teams often perform complementary and/or un-requested work (e.g. CFD (Computational Fluid Dynamics) analysis of the rocket (see Figure 8), comparison of the trajectory simulation results with data obtained by other means like open access software (the Rocket Simulator[6]), etc.). This shows that they were really interested and motivated by the activity.
- Some teams elaborate excellent reports and complete a great work. This is a proof that the nature of the activity fosters the motivation of the students.
- Small groups of students perform better than big groups where two or more people assume the same engineer role. Thus, from our point of view it is highly recommended to stick to group sizes such that there is only one student per engineering role and exceptionally two people in the case of the Mission Engineer. In the last edition of the MRW it was preferred to form more groups (more rockets to be launched) rather than increasing the number of members per group. In our opinion, when a particular Engineering role is assigned to two or more students they do not commit with their responsibility as much as they would do if they were the only person assigned to that role. Regardless the fact that all the activity is strongly based on a team and that cooperative work is paramount, the fact that each student assumes an Engineering role implies that they assume as well a responsibility within the group and the quality of the cooperative work is improved.
- The continuous effort of the faculty members (improving the quantity and the quality of the documentation provided to students year by year) is also another key element for the incremental success of the activity. The unification of the documentation and an improved scheduling of activities and milestones have proved to be very important for a more correct and efficient evolution of the activity. The preparation of such detailed documentation involves a

Figure 8. Plot of path lines colored by velocity magnitude (in meters per second) obtained after a CFD (Computational Fluid Dynamics) analysis of a rocket (credit: this figure was obtained using Fluent© CFD[7]).

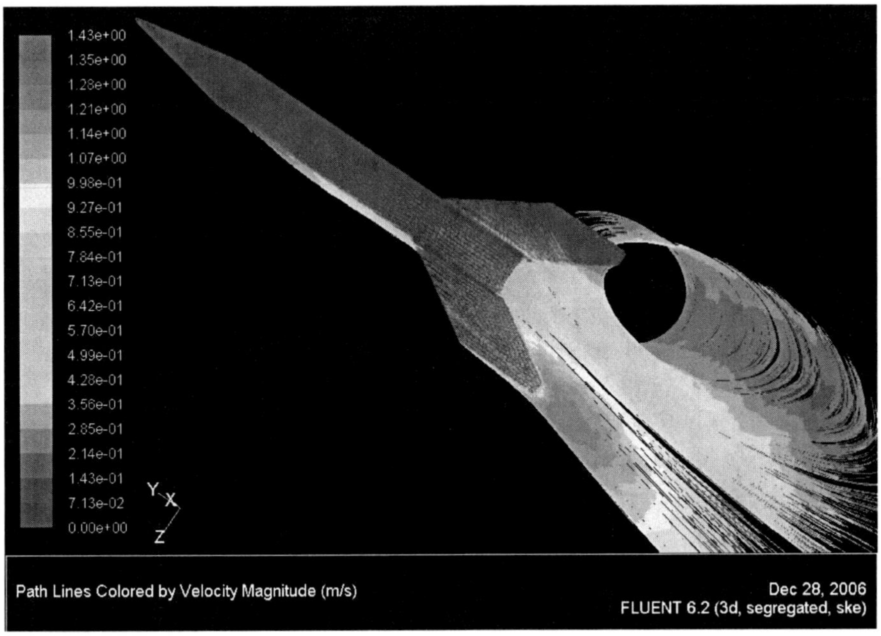

significant initial workload for the faculty. It is worth paying special attention when elaborating this documentation in order to eliminate the large amount of potential misunderstandings and to minimize the tedious job of solving them for each group.

ADAPTATION OF TEA TO PBL METHODOLOGY

This section contains a brief description of the activities within TEA, the course that MRW belongs to, and some ideas that the authors are considering in relation to them. As mentioned before, these ideas aim at expanding the MRW so it embraces the totality of the activities that constitute TEA at present day. As a consequence of the inclusion of these activities in the MRW, TEA would become a new course entirely under the umbrella of PBL.

Description of the Activities within TEA

Aside from the MRW, there is at present day a myriad of smaller independent activities included within the course called TEA. In principle, none of these activities is linked to the MRW in any way. Next we depict briefly all these activities:

- Fluid mechanics and aerodynamics workshops: to recall and enhance their knowledge on these subjects, the students perform an extensive series of hands-on activities. In the following, a list of these activities is presented:
  - Point measures in the fluid field: this activity consists in measuring physical and dynamical properties of a fluid. In particular, in the frame of this session the students perform the following tasks:

        - Analysis of experimental data of laminar and turbulent flows.
        - Direct pressure measurements.
        - Basis and utilization of a Pitot tube.
        - Pressure drop measurements.
        - Flow rate measurements.
    - Visualization of fluids: in this session several fluid visualization methods are described:
        - Particle image velocimetry.
        - Shadowgraphs.
    - Anemometry and velocimetry: this session consists of the following:
        - Description of hot wire anemometry and laser Doppler anemometry.
        - Measurements using hot wire anemometers in a wind tunnel (see picture of the wind tunnel in Figure 9).
        - Measurements of the average and turbulent velocity component in an airfoil wake.
    - Experimental measurement of aerodynamic performances of several models (e.g. NACA airfoils and a cylinder) in a wind tunnel.
- Hardness and tensile stress-strain tests: the students perform, in respective sessions, hardness and tensile stress-strain tests on samples made of several representative engineering materials (e.g. aluminum, copper, iron, steel and tin). Through the realization of these hands-on activities two goals are achieved:
    - The students learn the basis of the functioning and operation of a hardness tester and a Universal Testing Machine (UTM).
    - The students recall theoretical concepts and knowledge on materials' properties acquired in the frame of a previous course: Materials Science and Technology.
- Mechanics of gyroscopes: this is an introductory activity on mechanics of gyroscopes. It consists of a brief explanation on gyroscopes followed by a hands-on activity aiming at describing precession and nutation.
- Thermodynamic cycles: within this hands-on activity the students perform the following:
    - Review the Stirling cycle.
    - Record pressure and volume along the cycle.
    - Compute the mechanical work and the total power of an engine.
    - Compare the performances measured experimentally with the theoretical predictions.

Description of New Ideas & Future Work

The authors are considering the following ideas in relation to activities belonging to TEA:

- Fluid mechanics and aerodynamics workshops: as mentioned above, hands-on activities about fluid mechanics and aerodynamics are being performed nowadays as part of TEA, based on the use of a wind tunnel and other experimental equipment. These activities might be slightly redefined such that their particular contents become part of the MRW. The following possibilities are being considered in this sense, namely:
    - The student model rockets, once built, could be tested in the wind tunnel, instead of the models that are tested at present day in TEA, that is, instead of the NACA airfoils and the cylinder. The aim of these tests would be to characterize the aerodynamic

Figure 9. Picture of the wind tunnel for aerodynamic testing at the Aerospace Laboratory of the EPSC.

performances of the rockets, for instance the lift, drag and pitching moment coefficients. To perform the preliminary simulations of the trajectory, which take place before the rocket construction, students would use a drag coefficient provided by the faculty as initial data. Then, after the rocket construction and testing, they would use the drag coefficient and other data experimentally determined to refine their calculations and perform the final accurate simulations.

  - The students could use CFD software to characterize the aerodynamic performances of the rockets. Once the rocket has been designed and the coefficients have been calculated by this CFD analysis, they would use the data obtained by these simulations to compute the final accurate calculations of the trajectory.

These ideas can be implemented independently. Nevertheless, performing both experimental tests and CFD analyses to double-check the results would be a price-less educational asset to the benefit of the students.

- Hardness and tensile stress-strain tests: these tests might be easily included in the MRW by means of slight modifications only. There exists a variety of possibilities, for instance:
  - The tests may be performed by students on samples made of materials that they are using or will actually use to build their model rockets (e.g. marquetry wood, polymers).
  - The tests may be performed by students on samples made of other

materials (e.g. aluminum, composites, copper, iron, polymers, steel and tin) as if they were used in the model rockets, or as if they were from a real rocket launcher and actually had a structural application.

In any case, the students would proceed as if they were engineers from the Materials Department of their aerospace company. They would have to test the as-received materials to ascertain their mechanical properties and to verify that they fit to standards so that they will behave properly during their operational life.

- Mechanics of gyroscopes: again, this activity could be made part of the MRW by simply making a few changes. Namely, it could be reformatted such that, first, the fundamentals of rocket launchers' Attitude Control Systems (ACS) (e.g. space Inertial Navigation Systems (INS), Inertial Reference System (IRS)) would be explained in-depth to students. Second, this knowledge would be complemented when performing the practical experiences with the gyroscopes, which would be similar to the ones that students face at present day in TEA.
- Thermodynamic cycles: in this case, it might be more complex to adapt the actual hands-on activity such that it fits the contents and goals of the MRW. The reason is that the Stirling cycle and the Stirling engine have no relation to rocketry and launchers. Hence, a complete reformulation of the activity would be necessary. For instance, the session could be adapted in such a way that the fundamentals of rocket launchers' propulsion systems and space propulsion systems (e.g. solid, liquid and hybrid chemical propulsion) would be thoroughly explained to students. Afterwards, this knowledge would be put into practice by students by performing a set of hands-on activities.

Other important issues, ideas or modifications that should be addressed in the short-term are listed below:

- Modify and update the requirements relating to the rocket motion equations integration and simulation process. For instance, it would be interesting to assess the functionalities of the Rocket Simulator freeware. If feasible, it could be worth proposing the students to realize a comparison between the trajectories they compute numerically and the results obtained by using this open access software.
- It is necessary to redesign, rebuild and improve the present launch pad, since it is seriously degraded.
- Students often complain about the altimeters, since in some occasions they do not work properly. In some editions a couple of altimeters obtained noticeably erroneous data. This issue should be studied in detail, since the malfunction of the altimeters could be caused by an incorrect assembly or disposal and not because of an instrument error.
- Since the very beginning of the MRW, we consider that the batteries for the altimeters are too heavy (also students commented on that). Several ideas to counterbalance this problem are:
    - To increase the power of the rockets. So far, we have used rocket engines of category F, for which the maximum take-off weight is around 180 g. We could use category G engines, since still no license is needed for rocket engine operation in this case. Nonetheless, we should take into account that higher altitudes may be more dangerous depending on the

launching site and may require authorization from the civil aviation authorities.
- A circuit could be implemented such that smaller batteries could feed the altimeter.
- We could request the students or the University technical support team to design and build a cheaper, better altimeter.

Obviously, the implementation of all these new modifications represents a significant workload and would require an important coordination effort in order to schedule all activities in an optimum time. At present day, the activities that do not belong to MRW are almost scheduled randomly. Exception is made for the ones relating to fluid mechanics and aerodynamics.

CONCLUSION

The evolution of an initially limited-range practical experience within the frame of a given subject, in an aerospace engineering degree, is described in this paper. The original activity was the Model Rocket Workshop, which was successfully implemented within the Aerospace Engineering Program of the Escola Politècnica Superior de Castelldefels, belonging to the Universitat Politècnica de Catalunya. Within this practical experience, students design, simulate, build, test and launch a small model rocket. Also, students compare the theoretical results for the trajectory obtained by numerical integration with the experimental readings of altimeters on-board the rockets. The workshop is an experience based on cooperative learning and PBL, covering a wide spectrum of educational aspects, and that allows students to become familiar with the development and different phases of a space mission.

In addition to the description of the original workshop and its organization, the proposed case shows some problems that the designers have encountered while conducting the activity. Some modifications and improvements to solve these problems are also described, as well as several of the learned lessons. For instance, the authors review the evolution of the methods of evaluation, the educational results (student ratings) and some comments and assessments from the students, collected along the several editions. Finally, a series of new ideas related to the workshop and to the course it belongs to are presented. The objective is to expand the MRW so it embraces the totality of the activities that constitute its mother-course at present day.

As final conclusions we would like to emphasize that first, students are in most cases really interested and motivated by the activity. It fosters their creativity and initiative, while also improving their transversal skills. As a consequence, they often elaborate excellent reports and realize a great work. Second, a great sustained effort is necessary from the faculty members to ensure the success of the activity.

REFERENCES

Boud, D., & Feletti, G. I. (Eds.). (1997). The Challenge of Problem-Based Learning. London: Kogan Page.

Brodeur, D. R., Young, P. W., & Blair, K. B. (2002). *Problem-Based Learning in Aerospace Engineering*. Paper presented at the 2002 American Society for Engineering Education Annual Conference & Exposition, Montréal, Quebec, Canada.

Brügemann, V., Van Brummelen, H., Melkert, J., Kamp, A., Reith, B., Saunders-Smits, G., & Zandbergen, B. (2005, June). *An Example of Active Learning in Aerospace Engineering*. Paper presented at the Fifth International Workshop on Active Learning in Engineering Education, Delft, The Netherlands.

Delisle, R. (1997). How to Use Problem-Based Learning in the Classroom. Alexandria, VA: Association for Supervision and Curriculum Development (ASCD).

Doppelt, Y. (2005). Assessment of Project-Based Learning in a MECHATRONICS Context. *Journal of Technology Education*, *16*(2), 1–17.

Freeman, C., & Jigsaw, H. (1994). A Case Study Technique Where Students Become Experts. *Journal of College Science Teaching*.

Heister, S. D., & Messersmith, N. L. (1996). Launch Competition for Rocket Propulsion Education. *The International Journal of Engineering Education*, *12*(3), 229–238.

Novack, J. D., & Gowin, D. B. (1988). Learning how to learn. Cambridge, UK: Cambridge University Press.

Rojas, J. I., Prats, X., Montlaur, A., & Garcia-Berro, E. (2008). Model Rocket Workshop: a Problem-Based Learning experience for engineering students. *International Journal of Emerging Technologies in Learning*, *3*(4), 70–77.

Wilkerson, L., & Gijselaers, W. H. (Eds.). (1996). Bringing Problem-Based Learning to Higher Education: Theory and Practice, New Directions for Teaching and Learning, (No. 68). San Francisco: Jossey-Bass.

ADDITIONAL READING

Astorg, J. M., Bec, R., Bernard-Lepine, C., de Groote, K., & Amouroux, F. (2007). *PERSEUS: A Nanosatellite Launch System Project Focusing on Innovation and Education, IAC-07-E1.I.01*, Paper presented at the 58th International Astronautical Congress, Hyderabad, India.

Dupont, C., Bullock, M., Prevost, M., Maisonneuve, Y., Bec, R., Pillet, N., & Barenes, R. (2006). *The PERSEUS Student Launcher Project & Associated Hybrid Propulsion Activities, AIAA 2006-4317*. Paper presented at the 42nd AIAA/ASME/SAE/ASEE Joint Propulsion Conference & Exhibit, Sacramento, California, USA.

Felder, R. M., & Brent, R. (2001). Effective strategies for cooperative learning. [from http://www.ncsu.edu/felder-public/Papers/CLStrategies][JCCCT][.pdf]. *Journal of Cooperation and Collaboration in College Teaching*, *10*(2), 63–69. Retrieved July 13, 2009.

Felder, R. M., Woods, D. R., Stice, J. E., & Rugarcia, A. (2000). The future of engineering education. 2. Teaching methods that work. *Chemical Engineering Education, 34*(1), 26–39. Retrieved July 13, 2009, from http://www.ncsu.edu/felder-public/Papers/Quartet2.pdf

Fortescue, P. W., Stark, J., & Swinerd, G. (Eds.). (2003). Spacecraft Systems Engineering. John Wiley & Sons, 3rd ed.

Goddard, R. (2002). Rockets. Dover Publications. Mineola, NY, USA.

Hoerner, S. F. (Ed.). (1958). Fluid Dynamic Drag. Hoerner, S.F.

Johnson, L. W., & Riess, R. D. (1982). Numerical Analysis. Addison-Wesley.

Kolmos, A., & Graaff, E. (2003). Characteristics of Problem-based Learning. *International Journal of Engineering Education*, *19*(5), 657–662.

Larson, W. J., & Pranke, L. K. (Eds.). (2000). Human Space Flight – Mission & Analysis. McGraw-Hill Companies. New York, NY, USA.

McMaster University. (2009). Problem-Based Learning. Retrieved July 13, 2009, from http://www.chemeng.mcmaster.ca/pbl/pbl.htm

Oberth, H. (1923). *By Rocket into Planetary Space*.

Oberth, H. (1929). *Ways to Spaceflight*.

Ramsden, P. (1994). Learning to Teach in Higher Education. London, UK: Routledge.

Rugarcia, A., Felder, R. M., Woods, D. R., & Stice, J. E. (2000). The future of engineering education. 3. Developing critical skills. *Chemical Engineering Education*, *34*(2), 108–117.

Schneider, S. P., & Sullivan, J. P. (1992). *Aerodynamics Laboratory Education at Purdue University; Ground Testing Facilities, AIAA 92 4018*. Paper presented at the 17th AIAA Aerospace Ground Testing Conference, Nashville, Tennessee, USA.

Stine, G. H. (1983). Handbook of Model Rocketry. Arco.

Sutton, G. P. (1993). Rocket Propulsion Elements. John Wiley & Sons.

Tajmar, M. (2003). Advanced Space Propulsion Systems. Springer Cop., New York, NY, USA.

Thomas, J. (2003). Project Based Learning Handbook. A guide to standards-focused project based learning for middle and high school teachers. Buck Institute for Education, Novato, CA, USA.

Tsiolkovsky, K. E. (1935). On The Moon. USSR.

Turner, M. J. L. (Ed.). (2005). Rocket & Spacecraft Propulsion. Springer-Praxis, Chichester, UK.

Wertz, J. R., & Larson, W. J. (Eds.). (1999). Space Mission Analysis & Design. Kluwer Academic Cop., 3rd ed. Dordrecht, The Netherlands.

White, H. (1995). 'Creating problems' for PBL. Retrieved July 13, 2009, from http://www.udel.edu/pbl/cte/jan95-chem.html

KEY TERMS AND DEFINITONS

Altitude Control System (ACS): Spacecraft on-board system responsible to maintain its own correct orientation. These devices consist of a set of measurement devices, an active control system and one or several actuators that can induce movements to the spacecraft in order to point it towards the desired direction or orientation.

Computational Fluid Dynamics (CFD): Software package that uses numerical methods to solve problems involving fluid flows, like for example, the study of an airfoil.

Group Puzzle: Type of teaching activity where the tasks to be completed to achieve a specific goal are split into several independent parts, so every member of the team is responsible for one of these parts. Then, it is said that every team member has a different role, or that each member is the expert in relation to a particular topic. This kind of activity is usually found in Problem Based Learning courses.

Inertial Navigation Systems (INS): Navigation or positioning system that uses accelerometer sensors to continuously measure the acceleration that an aircraft or spacecraft is experiencing. From these measurements, the velocity, the orientation and the position of the aircraft/spacecraft can be drawn by the aid of some computational calculations.

Model Rocket Workshop (MRW): Activity that the authors propose in this work consisting into building a small model rocket as a central element in a Problem Based Learning teaching course.

Problem Based Learning (PBL): Learning strategy in which students solve one or some problems in a collaborative way. Students are separated in a few groups and the teaching staff gives them guidelines and a framework for the problem. Then, each group is responsible for organizing themselves and finding the way to solve the problem(s) with the support of the teaching staff.

Universal Testing Machine (UTM): Machine tool that allows testing the tensile and compressive properties of different materials. The applied force and the deformation on the material are measured and, in this way, the mechanical properties of the test sample can be drawn.

ENDNOTES

1 http://www.ganttproject.biz
2 http://www.mathworks.com
3 http://www.perfectflite.com
4 http://clte.asu.edu/active/team.htm
5 http://www.dotproject.net
6 http://www.rocket-simulator.com
7 http://www.fluent.com

APPENDIX

LIST OF ACRONYMS

ACS: Altitude Control System
CFD: Computational Fluid Dynamics
DE: Development Engineer
EE: Expert Engineer
EPSC: Escola Politècnica Superior de Castelldefels
INS: Inertial Navigation System
IRS: Inertial Reference System
LAE: Launch Engineer
LOE: Logistics Engineer
MRW: Model Rocket Workshop
ME: Mission Engineer
PBL: Problem Based Learning
TE: Test Engineer
TEA: Teaching unit dealing with experimental techniques in Aerospace Engineering, which is called *Tècniques Experimentals en Aerofísica*
UPC: Universitat Politècnica de Catalunya
UTM: Universal Testing Machine

Chapter 18
Using the How People Learn Framework for Online Course Design in Teacher Education

Sharon Dole
Western Carolina University, USA

Lisa Bloom
Western Carolina University, USA

ABSTRACT

The demand for online teacher education programs continues to grow in the United States. Two trends have fueled this dramatic growth for such programs: (1) The shortage of teachers in certain areas has prompted the spread of alternative routes to teacher preparation; (2) The nature of the higher education student in alternative programs has transformed from a traditional to a non-traditional profile. With the growth of online programs comes the need for effective courses. This case study uses the How People Learn (HPL) framework as the conceptual model to examine online courses in a teacher education program for evidence of high level learning outcomes. The case study involved data collection in the form of surveys, interviews and artifacts from four online classes using the HPL framework. Results of the study demonstrate that the HPL framework provides a powerful structure for creating and assessing environments conducive to the work of prospective professionals.

ORGANIZATION BACKGROUND

The organization is a mid-sized state university in the southeastern section of the United States with a strong tradition in teacher education. Founded in 1889 as a semi-private secondary school, it became a four-year teachers college in 1929. The teachers college served as a model for other regional colleges in the state. The college was designated a regional university in 1967 and in 1972 became a member of the state university system. In fall 2008 total enrollment at the university was 9,050 students.

DOI: 10.4018/978-1-61520-779-4.ch018

SETTING THE STAGE

In order to meet the critical shortage of special education teachers in the state, the special education program became an early adaptor of online teaching. The program received a small grant in 2002 to pay faculty to develop online courses. Currently three programs in special education are totally online: the Master of Teaching (MAT) program, an alternative teacher education program; the Master of Education (MAED) program for those who already have a teaching license; and the Academically and Intellectually Gifted (AIG) licensure program, an add-on license for teaching students in gifted programs. Enrollment in these three programs has grown substantially over the years and now stands at approximately 170 students.

Online technology methodologies are transforming the nature of both teaching and learning. Instructors are moving from deliverers of information to facilitators; likewise, students are becoming participants in a learning environment where the focus is on knowledge construction rather than knowledge reproduction. In addition, standards for learning are higher than they have ever been in the past for teachers. Many educational reformers advise putting teachers in a professional role as problems solvers and collaborators as well as both producers and consumers of research (Liston, Whitcomb, & Borko, 2007). Not only do teachers need the knowledge and skills of their craft, they need to be able to improve their teaching through reflection and evaluation (Darling-Hammond & Bransford, 2005).

CASE DESCRIPTION

Introduction

Collaboration, critical thinking, and problem solving are critical skills for teachers in the 21st century. While teaching in the past century tended to be more of an isolated activity, teachers today are expected to be active participants in decisions that affect the entire school and to work collaboratively in teams to address school and student issues. In addition to that of a collaborator, the role of the teacher has been described as one of an adaptive expert (Darling-Hammond, 2007; Darling Hammond & Bransford, 2005) who is able to solve problems, construct new knowledge and in turn, solve new problems as opposed to a worker who engages in routine tasks. Filling the role of an adaptive expert requires considerable reflection, critical thinking and evaluation. As an adaptive expert, teaching is viewed as the work of a professional as opposed to that of a technician. While technicians practice a set of known solutions to known problems, the work of professionals involves crafting new solutions to problems and predicaments that change on a daily basis.

Preparing teachers for their work as collaborators and problems solvers is a challenge facing teacher educators. Online courses are often criticized for focusing on the knowledge acquisition level rather than engaging students in complex problem-solving activities. Additionally, collaboration in online courses is often limited to superficial discussions on discussion boards. In this case, faculty used available technology and the How People Learn (HPL) framework as a conceptual model to design courses to maximize collaboration, reflection, and problem solving. The distance teacher preparation program provides evidence of high level learning outcomes that involve collaboration, reflection, mentoring, and problem solving

The Learners

This case study involved the examination of four online courses held over two years. The first year, one course was studied in depth. The following year, three additional online courses were included in the case study to follow up on themes and issues identified the first year. There were twenty-four students enrolled in the first online course in which the case study was conducted. The following year fifty additional students participated. The students taking the courses were non-traditional, with a wide range of experience and backgrounds. They were either lateral entry teachers seeking licensure in special education, teachers seeking the add-on Academically or Intellectually Gifted (AIG) license, or masters' students in the Master of Arts in Teaching (MAT) or the Master of Arts in Education (MAED) program. Some of the students were in their first year of teaching while others had considerable experience in teaching and were expanding their knowledge base. Online courses offered the students flexibility and convenience, as they were all teaching full time. Geographically, they were from both rural and urban areas across the state.

Course Design

The HPL framework stems from a project sponsored by the National Research Council that synthesizes what is known about learning and teaching (Bransford, Brown, & Cocking, 1999, 2000; Donovan, Bransford, & Pellegrino, 1999). The HPL framework focuses on the following four components of the learning environment:

- **Knowledge-centeredness**; what should be taught and how it is organized. Learners use their existing knowledge to construct new knowledge; what they know and who they are affects how they interpret new knowledge.
- **Learner-centeredness**; who learns, how and why. Concepts must be presented in ways that link students' existing knowledge to new understandings and build higher level thinking skills.
- **Community-centeredness;** the kinds of school and classroom environments that enhance learning. Instructors need to create psychologically safe environments in which communities of learners can thrive.
- **Assessment-centeredness;** the kinds of evidence that can be used to see if effective learning is occurring. Teachers need to have a toolbox of assessment strategies to guide students' learning and give them feedback to improve their achievement.

The Star Legacy or Legacy template (Brophy, 2000) was used in the design of the four online courses included in the case study. The template was developed at the Vanderbilt Learning Technology Center and is based on the principles of the HPL framework. The Legacy template is problem or inquiry-based and presented as a "learning cycle," with the learner progressing through a series of phases in exploring a multifaceted challenge.

Following the Legacy template, the course was divided into modules, with each module having a challenge based on an important concept of the course (See Figure 1). This modular design helps the instructional designer prioritize the concepts and skills of the course, set objectives for what the learners should understand by the end of the course, and arrange activities to help develop the students' understanding (Brophy, 2000). In each module, the learners progress through all phases of the learning cycle. The six phases of the learning cycle can be described as follows:

- *The Challenge*—presents a statement or scenario that poses a complex objective for the students. The challenge should be related to a major concept of the course that learners should come to understand in order to meet the objective.
- *Generate Ideas*—provides learners an outlet for showing what they know about the challenge. It can serve as a baseline or pre-assessment and the learners can go back at the end of the module to see what they have learned or how their thinking has changed.
- *Multiple Perspectives*—provide insights on the challenge. These statements or comments from experts do not provide a solution but should help the students see the many dimensions to the challenge.
- *Research and Revise*—engages students in learning activities linked to the challenge. These can be readings, homework problems, simulations, or other activities.

Figure 1. The Legacy template (Adapted from Brophy, 2000)

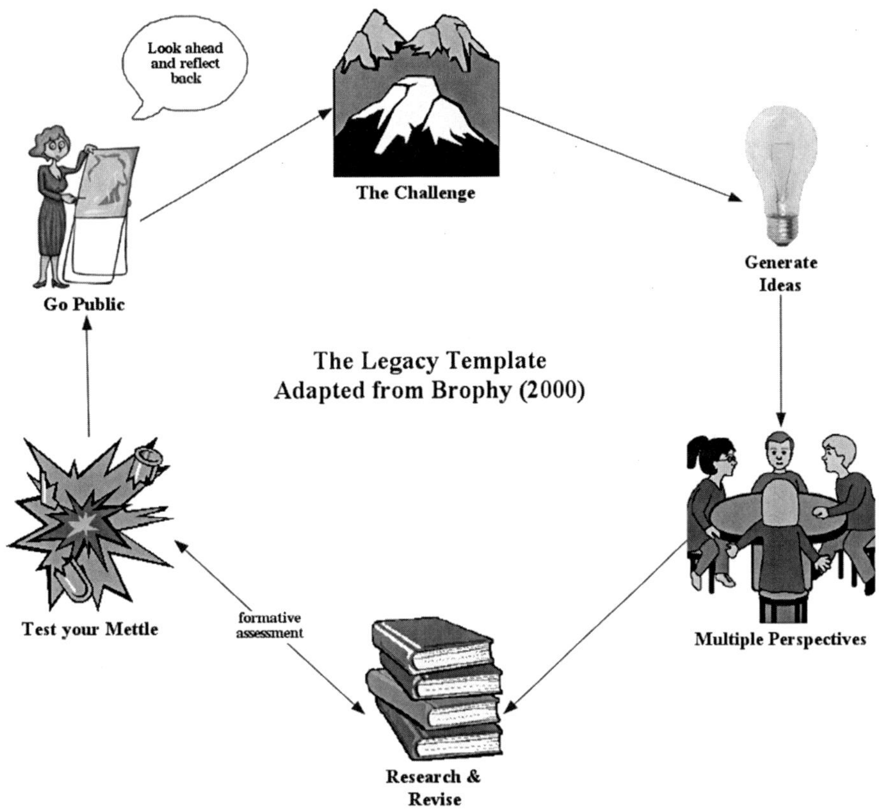

- *Test Your Mettle*—application of what students have learned and evaluation of what they need to know more about. This step helps students reflect on and synthesize what they know. Test your Mettle serves as a formative assessment measure as the learners may have to go back to the *Research and Revise* phase if they find that they need to do more research.
- *Go Public*—provides students an outlet to demonstrate what they know at the end of the module. This could be in the form of a test, a presentation, or other assignment.
- *Look Ahead & Reflect Back* serves to connect the learning goals of the previous module with those of the next module.

Method

A qualitative case study approach was used for the design of the study. Merriam (1998) defines a qualitative case study as "a thing, a single entity, a unit around which there are boundaries" (p. 27). Case studies are particularly relevant when the researcher is interested in process, as in this study. A qualitative case study should give the researcher and reader a feel for the context of the issue and the purpose of the inquiry. A case study approach was particularly well suited for this project, as we attempted to ascertain how the process represented by the HPL framework influenced student learning outcomes as well as collaboration, reflection and engagement within the courses.

Table 1. Courses & levels, data sources and corresponding enrollment

Course and Level	Description	Enrollment	Data Sources
SPED 401 Undergraduate	Concepts and theories of learning disabilities and educational characteristics of children with learning disabilities.	24	Discussion Board Posts
			Phone Interviews
			Student Products
			Course Evaluations
			Email Interviews
SPED 555 Graduate	Theoretical approaches and practices for creating positive classrooms.	18	Student products
			Survey
			Course Evaluations
			Discussion board posts
SPED 471 Undergraduate	Characteristics and unique needs of gifted students; screening and identification procedures.	17	Student Products
			Survey
			Course Evaluations
SPED 571 Graduate	Characteristics and unique needs of gifted students; screening and identification procedures.	15	Student Products
			Survey
			Course Evaluations

Data Collection

Data collection and analysis were ongoing, simultaneous (Merriam, 1988) and recursive (LeCompte & Schensul, 1993). Data were collected from four online courses, two undergraduate and two graduate (See Table 1). Initially, discussion board posts, student products, student course evaluations and phone interview data from one course were analyzed resulting in the several themes: professional growth, peer learning, teaching presence, and collaboration (Dole & Bloom, 2009). The following year, data from three other courses were collected and analyzed to triangulate data from the first year. Sources of data included the following:

- *Discussion board posts.* Asynchronous discussions are a part of each module of each course. Students post their reflections on course content and post substantial responses to their peers. Additionally, private discussion areas both synchronous and asynchronous are for collaborative projects. Archived postings from these discussion board areas from the initial course, Special Education (SPED) 401 were printed for data analysis. Discussion board posts from collaborative projects in one other course, SPED 555 were also printed and included in data analysis.
- *Student projects.* Student projects were collected from each class. Student projects included both collaborative projects and individual assignments. Collaborative projects included case studies, group annotated bibliographies, group brochures, group interviews and presentations. Individual assignments included lesson plans and action research projects.
- *Email Interviews.* Questions regarding online course design were sent via email to participants in the initial course, SPED 401. Students were asked two questions. In what ways did the design of SPED 401 facilitate your learning? In what ways did the design of the course promote collaboration? Eight students returned comments.

- *Interviews.* Phone interviews were conducted with six out of twenty-four students from SPED 401. Handwritten notes were collected from these interviews. Students were asked to describe their online course experience, discuss the HPL framework, their perceptions of their learning and their experience with collaboration in the course.
- *Course evaluations.* Course evaluations using the university course evaluation forms were collected for each class. Course evaluations include items ranked on a Likert scale and open-ended items.
- *Survey.* Students from three of the courses were sent a survey electronically. Thirty students out of fifty from three courses responded to the survey representing a return rate of sixty percent. This survey included Likert items and open-ended questions. Likert items were rated on a five point scale with one representing Strongly agree and five representing Strongly disagree. The items included the following:

The design of the course contributed to learning from my peers.

The design of the course contributed to higher level learning outcomes for me.

The design of the course contributed to collaboration among class members.

There were eight open-ended questions that asked students to comment on each aspect of the HPL framework. For example, students were asked, "To what extent did the multiple perspectives component of each module contribute to your learning?"

Data Analysis

From SPED 401 archived data from the discussion posts were triangulated with student products as well as personal, telephone, and email interviews with students who were enrolled in the course. A holistic approach was used to get an overall feel for the content before moving on to a more detailed analysis (Dey, 1993). Discussion posts were read and reread by both researchers in an attempt to find categories or themes. Using colored markers, each researcher separately identified emerging themes. The next step was to use worksheets to record the participant's words in one column and the researcher's interpretation in another column. The researchers then compared themes and identified patterns. Open ended comments from student course evaluations and the survey data from the second set of courses, SPED 471, 571 and 555 were analyzed with a similar process and corroborated our initial analysis. Student projects provided further evidence of the impact of the HPL framework on collaboration and student learning. We compared initial thoughts with final projects in each module for evidence of student growth and learning. Additionally, we analyzed student products to get a feel of the impact of the student work on their own classroom and the learning of their K-12 students. For example, action research projects that were assigned in two of the graduate classes require an assessment component in which our graduate students collect data from their own classrooms to answer questions about the impact of their practices on the learning and behavior of their students. Additionally, collaboration was included in all the rubrics for team projects. Including collaboration in the rubric allowed us to gauge the extent and quality of collaboration. Table 2 includes a rubric used in one of the courses.

Results

Data provided strong evidence that course design had a positive impact on student learning as far

Table 2. Rubric for interviews and team summary report

	Awesome	Admirable	Acceptable
Organization	Well organized Logical format Transitions from idea to idea were excellent, enhancing the project	Thoughtfully organized Easy to follow most of the time Transitions easy to follow, but at times ideas unclear	Somewhat organized Somewhat incoherent Transitions not always smooth
Cooperation	Worked extremely well with others Solicited, respected, and complemented each other's ideas Highly productive	Worked very well with others Worked to get everyone involved Productive team	Attempted to work well with others At times off task and not everyone was actively involved
Content	Excellent job of interviewing Utilized information effectively	Good job of interviewing Utilized information in an efficient manner	Acceptable job of interviewing Limited information
Presentation	Original, unique approach Engaging, provocative	Clever, at times unique Well done, interesting	Few original touches At times interesting

as complex problem solving, reflection and collaboration with peers. Analysis of the first set of data resulted in themes that coincide with the elements of the HPL framework. Themes that emerged included professional growth, peer learning, teaching presence, and collaboration. Each is described below. Subsequent analysis of data from the three additional courses corroborates the initial themes and resulted in an additional theme, transformational student learning. Each of the themes is discussed below.

Professional Growth Professional teacher growth was the first theme identified. This theme refers to the acquisition and practice of the knowledge, skills and craft of the profession and the connection of class content with professional practice. We found evidence of this theme in course evaluations, interviews, and discussion posts. The theme of professional growth relates both to the component of learner-centered environment and the component of knowledge-centered environment of the HPL framework. With regard to learner-centered environment, students made mention of opportunities to apply what they were learning to their own classroom practices as well as an appreciation of the opportunity to engage in problem solving. Students made several comments such as "Helped a great deal in dealing with problem behaviors within the classroom." And "The assignments were thought provoking and I could apply the situations to my school so I could see ways that might help and changes I could make personally." While all the components of the HPL framework seemed to contribute to professional growth, the course and module "Challenges" and the "Test your Mettle" phases specifically gave students a chance to apply their learning to opportunities and predicaments they faced in their own classroom and professional practice. As one learner commented, "I found the Challenge to be consistently rigorous. It allowed me to think analytically and then synthesize obtained information." Another learner wrote that

The greatest part of all was the class challenge. I did not realize how much I had learned until it was time to write my final definition of LD [learning disabilities]. This was when I truly realized that I had developed enough background to create something of my own thoughts and wouldn't be copying somebody else's article!

With regard to knowledge-centered environment, students commented on the opportunity to acquire new information relevant to their work. One new teacher remarked,

Wish this assignment had been covered before I started teaching last fall." A more experienced teacher stated, "I have a greater understanding of how LDs [learning disabilities] affect students across the spectrum of their academic experience and their lives in general. This will surely impact how I view and work with LD students in the future."

As stated previously, the "Multiple Perspectives" phase of the learning cycle exposes students to the many dimensions of the learning challenge. This phase appeared to motivate the students to continue learning. As one student commented,

I really enjoyed the way you had us dip into the research in so many directions, just getting a taste of all the many facets of LD [learning disabilities] and Special Ed. Issues. It whetted my appetite to learn more more more...

Another student remarked, "I found this online course to be stimulating and challenging intellectually and also personally. Every module was interesting and prompted me to search further on the WWW [World Wide Web] for more information...."

A third student stated, '"The modules offered awesome readings, ones that I have printed and will keep for future use...." Many students recognized the value of the "Multiple Perspectives" phase in helping them grow professionally. "This was extremely important because it changed beliefs that I had held and caused some to change."

Peer Learning

One of the most obvious themes that appeared over and over again was the learning that took place among peers. Evidence of peer learning was found in interviews, discussion posts, and student products. We define peer learning as the learning that occurs or is facilitated by peer interactions and peer feedback. Peer learning correlates with the HPL components of learner-centered environment as well as community-centered environment.

Many students commented on the value of peer feedback with comments such as the following: "Reading other's thoughts in an online class is essential to making the classroom feel whole. I learned a lot from their posts and have gotten good feedback about mine. It's gooood."

Posting my Classroom Mgmt [Management] Project has been helpful because I have learned so much from reading other papers. I worry that mine is not good enough and would have no idea how to do it without being allowed to look at my classmates' projects. I have received many helpful comments from classmates but being able to read their projects as they continue to develop them has been invaluable. The same holds true for other papers we published to the class; reading the thoughts of my classmates has really helped me...

Being able to share your thoughts and ideas with classmates enables you to openly communicate and see the differences in the way people react and think about specific issues. It gave you an opportunity to share your opinions and suggestions about things related to teaching and managing a classroom. I have learned a lot from reading my classmates notes or comments.

Appreciation for peer learning was especially evident in student comments about "Going Public." Students posted their assignments on the discussion board and were encouraged to be creative in their presentations. This led to a wide variety of presentations, appealing to every learning style. Examples of responses to assignments included the following:

I loved the diagram and printed a copy for future reference. You were very creative to use this representation to contrast the differences and compare the similarities. Great for a visual learner, you have added a lot to the class.

Teaching Presence

The theme of teaching presence came out in course evaluations, surveys and interviews with students. Teaching presence can be correlated with the HPL component of assessment, especially formative assessment. There is research to show that teaching presence is highly connected to student satisfaction (Palloff & Pratt, 2003). A student commented, "Her remarks are outstanding for all assignments. She finds points to tell us good and bad about assignments...." Timely feedback is important to students' perceptions. One student replied, "It says a lot when the instructor gives you almost immediate feedback. Many of us were first timers at this and if this course is used as a comparison or a model to the rest I would say you would have many informed and satisfied students." Another student said, "I really appreciated how organized you are and your prompt replies to all my ponderings and questions." " I always looked forward to the instructor's 'take' on my journal entry."

Collaboration

Evidence of the value of collaboration to student learning permeates all data sources. Collaboration correlates with the HPL component of community-centered environment. We define the theme of collaboration as students working together to achieve a common goal. At the beginning of each course and after the students posted their personal profiles, students were assigned to support groups of three to four members. In each course, the collaborative teams worked on one long-term assignment such as an annotated bibliography of online resources for teachers, parents, and/or students with learning disabilities. They also collaborated on shorter assignments such as PowerPoint presentations to present at a teacher in-service, case studies and so forth. Each team was assigned a chat room and an area on the discussion board. Archived chats and discussion board posts related to collaborative projects showed evidence of the influence collaboration had on student learning. Frequent questions and comments such as "What do you think the author means by..." and "oh, I never thought of it that way" and "Now I understand," "What do you think of addressing the case this way?" and so forth indicated that students were doing more than dividing assignment into tasks for each team member to work on independently.

Data analysis indicated that shorter group projects enabled the students to share leadership roles and learn group dynamics. One student commented

Well it was a little frustrating at first, and as the class unfolded, I began to better understand that this was group collaboration and an opportunity to participate in group sessions. I appreciated being able to convey my thoughts and classroom experiences with others and have the proper feedback. The design turned out to be great after all.

However, the group process worked better with some groups than others. One student, even though he/she was in a well functioning group, remarked that self-selection of group members may be preferable:

The group I was assigned was great to work with. They were very responsible, ready to get the work done, understanding of other responsibilities, and insightful, dedicated students! However, knowing a few folks in the class roster, several related dissatisfaction with their group members in terms of responsiveness, waiting to the last minute, etc. (always a biggie with group work). I would prefer to be able to CHOOSE my group members in the future.

On the other hand, another student had the opposite response about group selection,

My chat group was great!! Everyone participated well and worked to make our presentations a group effort. That was very gratifying to me. Others have suggested that we should be able to set up our own chat groups. In response to that I would like to say that in the class in which we were responsible for setting up our own groups, I found that extremely frustrating and problematic. Not knowing many of the folks in that class made it hard to find people to work with. I also felt that cliques of people who worked together elsewhere were formed. I was much happier with the group you put together, but as I said earlier, I had a great group!!

The above quotations are representative of the mixed reactions to the group work. Although the group process was sometimes frustrating as well as rewarding, the students realized its value in building community online. One student said, "I really enjoyed the groups we were placed in. At the first of the semester I was questioning it, however it allowed us to work together throughout the semester."

Transformational Student Learning

The theme of transformational student learning emerged as a theme when data from all four courses in the case study were taken together. We defined transformational learning as learning that affected a transformation of students' perceptions, knowledge and practice. The "Generating Ideas" phase and the later phases in the learning cycle provided our students as well as us with evidence of transformational learning.

This step reminded me of what I call jump starting your brain to think about the topic. I enjoyed communicating in an informal manner and comparing what I thought I knew was fact to what actually was fact. The initial thoughts made you think about your current ideas of the topic being presented. Once you were able to read the material presented, you could make a decision about whether or not your initial thoughts had changed.

The learner products provided numerous examples of learner application of course content in their own classrooms and the resulting progress of their K-12 charges. For example, one learner successfully used the HPL framework to design her own courses for middle school students in her own classroom. As a result of discussions regarding social and emotional needs of gifted students, several students in both SPED 471 and SPED 571 successfully arranged counseling services for gifted children in their own schools. Another student had transformed his classroom based on application of course content. Prior to the course, he had been criticized by other teachers and his principal for his inability to manage his classroom. Throughout the course, he had numerous discussions with his peers and the instructor about transforming his room. By the end of the school year, his principal was sending other teachers to his classroom to learn classroom management from him. Learners in the two gifted education courses became advocates for underrepresented groups of students in gifted programs such as culturally and linguistically diverse and twice exceptional students (students who both gifted and have disabilities). These learners were able to affect change in their home school systems' screening and identification process for gifted programs.

Discussion

This case study provides evidence of the contribution of course design to student learning. The application of the science of learning in the HPL framework to online course design can improve students' ability to become active learners. These learners understand complex subject matter and thus are more prepared to apply what they have learned to new problems in different settings (Bransford, Brown, & Cocking, 1999).

From the results of this study, it appears that the HPL framework is particularly relevant for courses preparing learners for professional roles such as that of a teacher. Using The HPL framework and technology available in online courses, students are engaged in course challenges that represent authentic problems encountered by professionals and afforded opportunity for reflection and collaboration. This experience closely resembles the type of work encountered by professionals on a daily basis. As the learners in this case study demonstrated, course design that engages students in authentic tasks, reflection and collaboration, can lead to high level learning outcomes such as changes in knowledge, perceptions and professional practices.

Merrill (2001, 2002a, 2002b; 2006, 2007) has examined instruction models for evidence of what he calls "first principles of instruction" and identifies the Star Legacy as a good representation of those principles because of its explicitness. The following five key principles of instructional design resulted from Merrill's meta-analysis of major instructional theories and models:

- *Learning is facilitated when learners are engaged in solving real-world problems (task-centered phase).*
- *Learning is facilitated when existing knowledge is activated as a foundation for new knowledge (activation phase).*
- *Learning is facilitated when new knowledge is demonstrated to the learner (demonstration phase).*
- *Learning is facilitated when new knowledge is applied by the learner (application phase)*
- *Learning is facilitated when new knowledge is integrated into the learner's world (integration phase).*

The synthesis of Merrill can provide a set of criteria for which to evaluate quality design and instruction in online courses.

Because enrollment in online programs in higher education continues to grow at a substantial rate, attention to course design is becoming even more critical. The most recent Sloan Consortium update (Allen & Seaman, 2008) reported a 12.9% increase over the previous year in students in higher education taking online courses. This represents a significant increase over the 1.2% growth of the overall student population in higher education. The current economic downturn resulting in rising unemployment and higher fuel costs will accentuate the demand for online courses (Allen & Seaman, 2008). As enrollment in online programs continues to grow, institutions of higher education must ensure quality of online courses. Case studies and surveys of students provide valuable information on quality of course design. There is research to show that students prefer consistent course design across courses (Swan et al., 2000; Young & Norgard, 2006). Additionally, with regard to student satisfaction, research on course design corroborates the findings of our study regarding the importance of community, peer learning, and teacher presence (Menchaka & Bekele 2008; Vesely, Bloom, & Sherlock, 2008). However, research that examines the effect of course design on student learning is just beginning to emerge (see for example Swan, 2001; Dunlap, Furth, &Tucker, 2009).

Course design that encourages high levels of student engagement, authentic learning tasks and collaboration involves a considerable investment of time for faculty, both in developing and in teaching the course (Boerema, Stanley, & Westhorp, 2007; Shea, 2007). Fink (2003) notes "faculty knowledge about course design is the most significant bottleneck to better teaching and learning in higher education" (pp. 23–24). As educators strive to provide high quality online courses there is a need to balance their workload with the realities of online teaching and provide support and training for course design.

CURRENT CHALLENGES FACING THE ORGANIZATION

Online course design requires extensive education and training. Not only do course designers need to become knowledgeable about the technological tools and techniques involved, they also need to gain experience in developing the practical and artistic skills and abilities required to design effective courses (Steen, 2008). Course design that moves beyond required readings and exams to one that focuses on interactive learning and challenging real-life problems requires a considerable investment of time on the part of faculty. It requires increased time in designing and also time to acquire new technological skills. Workload is a critical issue for courses that incorporate relevant professional activities, collaboration, and formative assessment. Likewise, effective facilitation of such a course makes it necessary for faculty to be accessible at all times to give prompt and constructive feedback and respond to students' questions individually. It is generally agreed that designing and teaching online courses is labor intensive and requires more time (Keeton, 2004; Shea, 2007) and smaller class size than face-to-face classes (F2F) (Collins & Gaylon-Keramidas, 2006). The university provides a centralized entity to assist all faculty members with the development of distance education courses through a faculty center for teaching and learning. However, the support deals more with practical and technology applications rather than theories of teaching and learning. Although faculty members are compensated monetarily with a small stipend for course design and revision, they do this on their own time. Course load is a major issue as online courses are treated the same as F2F courses with respect to course load. It is much more time consuming to teach three to four online courses a semester than to teach three to four F2F courses. A frequent faculty complaint is that teaching online classes is so demanding that there is little time available for research needed for promotion and tenure.

The current state of the economy in the United States and the subsequent budget crises facing institutions of higher education have further exacerbated the problem of time. Higher course enrollment is one of the steps taken by the university as a cost-saving measure. Online courses that were previously capped at twenty students per course are now capped at twenty-five students. Quality of instruction decreases with the increase in class size. Furthermore, it is yet unknown how the budget crisis will affect the technology infrastructure for maintaining distance programs and providing faculty support in designing and revising online courses.

SOLUTIONS AND RECOMMENDATIONS

The trend in online teacher education programs, particularly at the master's level, is not going to disappear; in fact, it has increased dramatically. Some institutions of higher learning have responded to this trend while others have appeared to ignore the demand for online programs. As distance education programs grow, quality control is a major issue. A successful online program requires extensive coordination among faculty and administration. The focus of administration should not be narrowly based on economics nor should academic departments be non-accountable. Based on the professional literature on online education (Ludlow, Collins, & Menlove, 2006) and on their own experience, the authors recommend that sufficient time be allocated for the design and delivery of online courses. In addition, faculty need to be given time and training to become familiar with the technology and course management system used for course delivery. As more online courses in education are offered and entire programs go online, institutions may consider an administrator for distance education in colleges of education (Maddux, 2006). This person would liaison with staff in other distance education units as well as be responsible for planning and scheduling. In addition, an assessment system should be in place specifically for online courses to monitor quality and modify the program as needed.

The knowledge that students learn in teacher education programs needs to be connected both at the course design level and at the program level (Darling-Hammond & Bransford, 2005). Basing course design on the HPL framework would not only lend coherence to a teacher education program but also model practices of good pedagogy.

The optimal number of students in an online course depends on many factors, including the nature of the course and the use of clinical faculty and/or graduate teaching assistants. The professional literature recommends between ten and twenty-five students in a class. The authors have found that twenty students in a class are optimal. In addition, the extra time required for developing and teaching online courses should be considered in course load. Incentives such as release time and stipends for developing online courses should be provided. Likewise, discussion should take place on how online course development and teaching is considered in the tenure and promotion process.

REFERENCES

Allen, I. E., & Seaman, J. (2008). Staying the course: Online education in the United States, 2008. Needham, MA: Sloan Consortium.

Boerema, C., Stanley, M., & Westhorp, P. (2007). Educators' perspective of online course design and deliver. *Medical Teacher*, *29*, 758–765. doi:10.1080/01421590701477332

Bourne, J., & Moore, J. (Eds.). (2002). Elements of quality online education: Practice and direction. Needham, MA: The Sloan Consortium.

Bransford, J., Brown, A., & Cocking. (Eds.). (2000). *How people learn: Brain, mind, experience, and school,* (Expanded Edition). Washington, DC: National Academy Press.

Bransford, J., Brown, A., & Cocking. (Eds.). (1999). *How people learn: Brain, mind, experience, and school.* Retrieved December 19, 2005, from http://www.nap.edu/html/howpeople1/

Brophy, S. (2000). *Guidelines for modular design*. Retrieved December 19, 2005, from http://www.vanth.org/white_papers.html

Brown, K. L. (2003). From teacher-centered to learner-centered curriculum: Improving learning in diverse classrooms. *Education*, *124*(1), 49–54.

Clark, R. W., Hong, L. K., & Schoeppach, M. R. (1996). Teacher empowerment and site based management. In J. Sikula, T. J., Buttery, & E. Guyton, (Eds.), Handbook of research on teacher education (pp. 595-616). New York: Macmillan.

Cochran-Smith, M., & Fries, M. K. (2001). Sticks, stones and ideology: The discourse of reform in teacher education. *Educational Researcher*, *30*(8), 3–15. doi:10.3102/0013189X030008003

Collins, B. C., & Gaylon-Keramidas, C. (2006). Planning and delivering online instruction. In B. L. Ludlow, B. C. Collins, & R. Menlove (Eds.), Online instruction for distance education delivery: Preparing special educators in and for rural areas, (pp. 43-75). Victoria, BC: Trafford Publishing.

Darling-Hammond, L., & Bransford, J. (Eds.). (2005). Preparing teachers for a changing World: What teachers should learn and be able to do. San Francisco: Jossey-Bass.

Dey, I. (1993). Qualitative data analysis: A user-friendly guide for social scientists. London: Routledge.

Dole, S., & Bloom, L. (2009). Online course design: A case study. *International Journal for the Scholarship of Teaching and Learning, 3*(1). Retrieved 5/11/09 from http://academics.georgiasouthern.edu/ijsotl/v3n1.html

Donovan, M. S., & Bransford, J. D. Pellegrino, (Eds.). (2003). How people learn: Bridging research and practice. Washington, DC: National Academy Press.

Dunlop, J., C., Furtak, T. E., & Tucker, S. A. (2009). Designing for enhanced understanding in an online physics course. *Tech Trends: Linking Research and Practice to Improve Learning, 53*(1), 67–73.

Fink, L. D. (2003). Creating significant learning experiences: An integrated approach to designing college courses. San Francisco: Jossey-Bass.

LeCompte, M. D., & Schensul, J. J. (1999). Designing and conducting ethnographic research. London: Alta Mira Press.

Liston, D., Whitcomb, J., & Borko, H. (2007). NCLB and scientifically-based research. *Journal of Teacher Education, 58*(2), 99–107. doi:10.1177/0022487107299980

Ludlow, B. L., Collins, B. C., & Menlove, R. R. (Eds.). (2006). Online instruction for distance education delivery: Preparing special educators in and for rural areas. Victoria, Canada: Trafford Publishing.

Maddux, C. D. (2006). Distance education: Some concluding thoughts. In B. L. Ludlow, B. C. Collins, & R. Menlove (Eds.), Online instruction for distance education delivery: Preparing special educators in and for rural areas, (pp. 249 261). Victoria, Canada: Trafford Publishing.

Marra, R. M. (2002). The ideal online learning environment for supporting epistemic development. *Quarterly Review of Distance Education, 3*(1), 27–44.

Menchaca, M. P., & Bekele, T. A. (2008). Learner and instructor identified success factors in distance education. *Distance Education, 29*(3), 231–252. doi:10.1080/01587910802395771

Merrill, D. (2002). First principles of instruction. *Educational Technology Research and Development, 50*(3), 43–59. doi:10.1007/BF02505024

Merrill, D. D. (2001). First principles of instruction. *Journal of Instructional Learning & Intelligent Systems, 14*(4), 459–466.

Merrill, M. D. (2006). Levels of instructional strategy. *Educational Technology, 46*(4), 5–10.

Merrill, M. D. (2007). First principles of instruction: A synthesis. In R. A. Reiser & J. V. Dempsey (Eds.), Trends and issues in instructional design and technology, (2nd ed., pp. 62–71). Upper Saddle River, NJ: Merrill/Prentice Hall.

Merriman, S. (1998). Qualitative research and case study applications in education. San Francisco: Jossey-Bass.

Northrup, P. T. (2002). Online learners' preferences for interaction. *The Quarterly Review of Distance Education, 3*(2), 219–226.

Palloff, R. M., & Pratt, K. (2003). The Virtual student: A profile and guide to working with online learners. San Francisco, CA: Jossey-Bass.

Shea, P. (2007). Bridges and barriers to teaching online college courses: A study of experienced faculty in thirty-six colleges. *Sloan-Consortium, 11*(2), 73–128.

Steen, H. L. (2008). Effective elearning design. *Journal of Online Learning and Teaching, 4*(4), 526–532.

Swan, K. (2001). Virtual interaction: Design factors affecting student satisfaction and perceived learning in asynchronous online courses. *Distance Education*, *22*(2), 306–331. doi:10.1080/0158791010220208

Vesely, P., Bloom, L., & Sherlock, J. (2007). Key elements of building online community: Comparing faculty and student perceptions. *Journal of Online Learning and Teaching*, *3*, 234–246.

Yang, Y., & Cornelius, L. F. (2004). Students' perceptions towards the quality of online education: A qualitative approach. *Association for Educational Communications and Technology*, *27*, 861–877.

Young, A., & Norgard, C. (2006). Assessing the quality of online courses from the students' perspective. *The Internet and Higher Education*, 107–115. doi:10.1016/j.iheduc.2006.03.001

ADDITIONAL READING

Allen, E.I., & Seaman, J. (2006). *Making the grade: Online education in the United States 2006.* Needham: Sloan Center for Online Education.

Barkley, K. Cross, P. & Major, C. H. (2005). Collaborative learning techniques: A handbook for college faculty. San Francisco: Jossey-Bass.

Bender, T. (2003). Discussion-based online teaching to enhance student learning. Sterling, VA: Stylus.

Bransford, J., Brown, A., & Cocking. (Eds.). (1999). *How people learn: Brain, mind, experience, and school.* Retrieved December 19, 2005, from http://www.nap.edu/html/howpeople1

Brown, D. G. (Ed.). (2003). Developing faculty to use technology: Programs and strategies to enhance teaching. Hoboken, NJ: Anker Publishing.

Brown, R. E. (2001). The process of community building in distance learning classes. *Journal of Asynchronous Learning Networks*, *5*(2), 18–35.

Carr, S. (2000). As distance education comes of age, the challenge is keeping the students. *The Chronicle of Higher Education*, *46*(23), A39–A41.

Caverly, D. C., & MacDonald, L. (2002). Online learning communities. *Journal of Developmental Education*, *25*(3), 36–37.

Collins, M., & Berge, Z. (1996). Facilitating interaction in computer mediated online courses. Retrieved on May 24, 2007 from: http://www.emoderators.com/moderators/flcc.html

Darling-Hammond, L., & Bransford, J. (Eds.). (2005). Preparing teachers for a changing world: What teachers should learn and be able to do. San Francisco: Jossey-Bass.

Hargis, J. (2005). Collaboration, community and project-based learning--does it still work online? *International Journal of Instructional Media*, *32*(2), 157–162.

Heuer, B. P., & King, K. P. (2004). Leading the band: The role of the instructor in online learning for educators. *The Journal of Interactive Online Learning*, *3*(1), 1–11.

LaRose, R., & Whitten, P. (2000). Re-thinking instructional immediacy for web courses: A social cognitive exploration. *Communication Education*, *49*, 320–338. doi:10.1080/03634520009379221

Lebaron, J., & Miller, D. (2005). The potential of jigsaw role playing to promote the social construction of knowledge in an online graduate education course. *Teachers College Record*, *107*(8), 1652–1674. doi:10.1111/j.1467-9620.2005.00537.x

Lou, Y. (2004). Learning to solve complex problems through between-group collaboration in project-based online courses. *Distance Education*, *25*(1), 49–66. doi:10.1080/0158791042000212459

Mandermach, B. J., Gonzales, R. M., & Garrett, A. L. (2006). An examination of online instructor presence via threaded discussion participation. *Journal of Online Learning and Teaching*, *2*(4), 248–260.

Palloff, R. M., & Pratt, K. (2003). The virtual student: A profile and guide to working with online learners. San Francisco: John Wiley & Sons.

Palloff, R. M., & Pratt, K. (2005). Collaborating online: Learning together in community. San Francisco: John Wiley & Sons.

Picciano, A. G. (2002). Beyond student perceptions: Issues of interaction, presence, and performance in an online course. *Journal of Asynchronous Learning Networks*, *6*(1), 21–40.

Salmon, G. (2005). E-tivities: The key to active online learning. London: RoutledgeFalmer.

Shea, P., & Bidjerano, T. (2009). Community of inquiry as a theoretical framework to foster "epistemic engagement" and "coginitive presence" in online education. *Computers & Education*, *52*(3), 543–553. doi:10.1016/j.compedu.2008.10.007

Shea, P., Sau Li, C., & Pickett, A. (2006). A study of teaching presence and student sense of learning community in fully online and web-enhanced college courses. *The Internet and Higher Education*, *9*(3), 175–190. doi:10.1016/j.iheduc.2006.06.005

Swan, K., Shea, P., Fredericksen, E., Pickett, A., Pelz, W., & Maher, G. (2000). Building knowledge building communities: Consistency, contact and communication in the virtual classroom. *Journal of Educational Computing Research*, *234*, 359–383.

Thompson, M. M. (2003). Instructor satisfaction in the online teaching-learning environment. In J. Mourne & J. Moore (Eds.) Elements of quality online education: Practice and direction. Needham, MA: Sloan Center for Online Education (pp. 189-212).

Whipp, J. L., & Lorentz, R. A. (2009). Cognitive and social help giving in online teaching: An exploratory study. *Educational Technology Research and Development*, *57*, 169–192. doi:10.1007/s11423-008-9104-7

Woods, R., & Ebersole, S. (2003) Social networking in the online classroom: Foundations of effective online learning. EJournal, 12-13 (1). Available at: http://www.ucalgary.ca/ejournal/archive/v12-13/v12-13n1Woods-browse.html

Yuen, A. H. (2003). Fostering learning communities in classrooms: A survey research of Hong Kong schools. *Educational Media International*, *40*, 153–162. doi:10.1080/0952398032000092198

KEY TERMS AND DEFINITIONS

Course Design: Refers to a systematic plan used to create a new class or revise an existing one to effectively attain instructional goals.

How People Learn (HPL) Framework: Is founded on recent research in cognitive science that puts emphasis on the learning environment and the extent that it is learner- centered, knowledge-centered, assessment -centered, and community-centered.

Star Legacy Template: Consists of six phases of the learning cycle based on the HPL framework: the challenge, initial thoughts, multiple perspectives, research and revise, test your mettle, and go public.

Teacher Education: Refers to higher education that leads to a degree and teaching license in a K-12 subject area.

Inquiry Based Learning: Refers to a student-centered, active learning approach focusing on questioning, critical thinking, and problem-solving.

Transformational Learning: Occurs as the result of a struggle or struggles that provide greater insight into one's thinking and/or practice.

Peer Learning: Involves student-student interaction that presents opportunities for students to formulate their own questions, discuss issues, and explain their viewpoints.

Collaboration: Refers to cooperative groups that provide social interaction that often deepens learning and gives the interpersonal support and synergy necessary for creatively solving complex problems.

Teaching Presence: Is the facilitation and direction of cognitive and social processes in order to achieve worthwhile learning outcomes among students.

Compilation of References

ACA*GIS. (2009). *Austria-Central Asia Centre for GI-Science*. Retrieved from http://www.aca-giscience.org/

ACCC. (2006). *Snapshop of Broadband Deployment as at 31 March 2006* [Report]. Australian Competition and Consumer Commission; Canberra, ACT. Retrieved December 12, 2008, from the World Wide Web: http://www.accc.gov.au/content/index.phtml/itemId/693170

Access Economics Pty Limited. (2009) *The Australian education sector and the economic contribution of international students.* Report for Australian Council for Private Education and Training. Retrieved from http://globalhighered.files.wordpress.com/2009/04/theaustralianeducationsectorandtheeconomiccontributionofinternationalstudents-2461.pdf

Adler, P. S., & Kwon, S.-W. (2002). Social Capital: Prospects for a New Concept. *Academy of Management Review*, *27*(1), 17–40. doi:10.2307/4134367

Aguti, J. N. (2006, October/November). *Education for national development: The Makerere University dual mode experience*. Paper presented at the Fourth Pan-Commonwealth Forum on Open Learning, Ocho Rios, Jamaica.

Ahamer, G. (2001). A Structured Basket of Models for Global Change. In C. Rautenstrauch & S. Patig (Eds.), Environmental Information Systems in Industry and Public Administration, (pp.101-136). Hershey, PA: Idea Group Publishing.

Ahamer, G. (2004). Negotiate your Future: Web Based Role Play. *Campus-Wide Information Systems, 21*(1), 35–58. doi:10.1108/10650740410512329

Ahamer, G. (2005). *Structural change in global energy economics*. University course materials. Retrieved from http://www.uni-graz.at/globalstudies/deposit/USW_VisionWirtschaftsEnergiekapitel.pdf

Ahamer, G. (2005). 'Surfing Global Change': How didactic visions can be implemented. *Campus-Wide Information Systems, 22*(5), 298-319. Retrieved from http://www.emeraldinsight.com/1065-0741.htm

Ahamer, G., & Jekel, T. (2010). Make a Change by Exchanging Views. In S. Mukerji & P. Tripathi, (Eds.) Cases on Transnational Learning and Technologically Enabled Environments, pp x-x.

Ahamer, G., & Schrei, C. (2006). Exercise 'Technology Assessment' through a gaming procedure. *Journal of Desert Research*, *5*(2), 224–252. doi:10.1504/JDR.2006.011364

Ahamer, G., Car, A., Marschallinger, R., Wallentin, G., & Zobl, F. (2009). *How to map perspectives: Moving GISc to IISc. 4th International Conference on Information Technology ICIT'09*, Al-Zaytoonah University of Jordan, Amman, June 3rd – 5th, 2009. Retrieved from http://www.alzaytoonah.edu.jo/ICIT/pages/index.aspx

Ainsworth, S. E. (1999). A functional taxonomy of multiple representations. *Computers & Education*, *33*(2/3), 131–152. doi:10.1016/S0360-1315(99)00029-9

Albee, J. (2003). A Study of Preservice Elementary Teachers Technology Skill Preparedness and Examples of How It Can Be Increased. *Journal of Technology and Teacher Education*, 11.

Alfred, M. V. (2003). Sociocultural contexts and learning: Anglophone Caribbean immigrant women in U. S. postsecondary education. *Adult Education Quarterly*, *53*, 242–260. doi:10.1177/0741713603254028

Allen, I. E., & Seaman, J. (2008). Staying the course: Online education in the United States, 2008. Needham, MA: Sloan Consortium.

Alsop, R., Chase, R., & Owen, D. (2003). *Social capital, empowerment, and community driven development: Presentation notes. PSIA Sourcebook.* World Bank: Geneva. Retrieved at http://info.worldbank.org/etools/bspan/PresentationView.asp?PID= 936 &EID=482

Amara, R. (1981). The Futures Field. *The Futurist.* April/June.

Anderson, J. R. (1993). Rules of the mind. Hillsdale, NJ: Erlbaum.

ASC. (2009). American Society for Cybernetics. Retrieved from http://www.asc-cybernetics.org/

Asian Development Bank. (2003). *Key Indicators: Education for Global Participation.* Retrieved from http://www.adb.org/Documents/Books/Key_Indicators/2003/pdf/theme_paper.pdf

Attewell, P. (2001). The first and second digital divides. *Sociology of Education*, *74*, 252–259. doi:10.2307/2673277

AusAID. (2009). *Where We Work.* Retrieved from http://www.ausaid.gov.au/about/ausaidmap.cfm

Azevedo, R. (2005). Computer environments as metacognitive tools for enhancing learning. *Educational Psychologist*, *40*, 193–197. doi:10.1207/s15326985ep4004_1

Bachnik, J. M. (2003). Roadblocks on the information highway. Oxford, UK: Lexington Books.

Banks, J. A., & Banks, C. A. (1997). Multicultural education: Issues and perspective (3rd ed.). Boston: Allyn & Bacon.

Barker, S. (2004). *Using Online Facilities to Support Face-to-Face Teaching.* Paper presented at the Online Learning and Teaching Conference: exploring integrated learning environments: a national forum for sharing information on engaging, designing, assessing and collaborating in online learning and teaching, Brisbane, Australia.

Barrett, T. (2000). Criticizing art: Understanding the contemporary. New York: McGraw-Hill.

Barrett, T. (2003). Interpreting art: Reflecting, wondering and responding. New York: McGraw-Hill.

Barrie, S. C., & P., G. (2007). The Linking of Institutional Performance Indicators to Improvements in Teaching in Classrooms. *Quality in Higher Education*, *13*(3), 275–286. doi:10.1080/13538320701800175

Barro, R. J. (1991). Economic growth in a cross section of countries. *The Quarterly Journal of Economics*, *106*(2), 407–443. doi:10.2307/2937943

Barro, R. J. (2001). Human Capital and Growth. *The American Economic Review*, *91*(2), 12–17.

Barshefsky, C. (2002). Trade policy for a networked world. *Foreign Affairs (Council on Foreign Relations)*, (March/April): 134–147.

Batane, T. (2004). Inservice teacher training and technology: A case of Botswana. *Journal of Technology and Teacher Education*, *12*, 387–410.

Bates, A. W. (1995). *The Future of Learning.* Paper first presented at the Minister's Forum on Adult Learning, Edmonton, Alberta, November 30 – December 1st, 1995. Retrieved April 12, 2007, from HTTP://bates.cstudies.ubc.ca/papers/side.html

Bates, A. W. (2005). Technology, E-Learning and Distance Education, (2nd Ed.). London: Routledge Falmer.

Bates, A. W., & Poole, G. (2003). Effective Teaching with Technology in Higher Education: Foundations for Success. San Francisco, CA: Jossey-Bass.

Bauer, C., Chin, K. L., & Chang, V. (2000). *Web-based learning: Aspects of cultural differences.* Paper presented at the 8th European Conference on Information Systems, Trends in Information and Communication Systems for the 21st Century. Austria. Retrieved July 1, 2007, from http://csrc.lse.ac.uk/asp/aspecis/20000068.pdf

Beach, R., & Freedman, K. (1992). Responding as a cultural act: Adolescents' responses to magazine ads and short stories. In J. Many, & C. Cox (Eds.), Reader stance and literary understanding: Exploring the theories, research, and practice, (pp. 162-188). Norwood, NJ: Ablex.

Becker, G. S., Murphy, K. M., & Tamura, R. (1990). Human capital, fertility, and economic growth. *The Journal of Political Economy, 98*(S5), 12–38. doi:10.1086/261723

Beckmann, E. A., & Kilby, P. (2008). On-line, Off-campus and in the Flow: learning from peers in development studies. *Australasian Journal of Peer Learning, 1*(1), 61–69.

Bell, W. (1996). An Overview of Futures Studies. []. Foundation Futures Study Centre, Qld: Australia]. *The Knowledge Base of Futures Studies, 1*, 29–58.

Benyon, D., Turner, P., & Turner, S. (2005). Designing Interactive Systems: People, Activities, Contexts, Technologies (pp. 676-756). Reading, MA: Addison-Wesley.

Bera, S., & Liu, M. (2006). Cognitive tools, individual differences, and group processing as mediating factors in a hypermedia environment. *Computers in Human Behavior, 22*, 295–319. doi:10.1016/j.chb.2004.05.001

Berding, J. W. A. (2000). John Dewey's participatory philosophy of education – Education, experience and curriculum. The history of education and childhood, Nijmegen University, http://www.socsci.kun.nl/ped/whp/histeduc/misc/dewey01.html.

Beuys, J. (1974). I like America and America likes me. Presented in the gallery Rene Block, New York.

Bickerstaff, K., & Walker, G. (2003). The place(s) of matter: matter out of place – public understandings of air pollution. *Progress in Human Geography, 27*(1), 45–67. doi:10.1191/0309132503ph412oa

Biggs, J. (2003). Teaching for Quality at University: What the Student Does (2nd ed.). Buckingham, UK: Society for Research into Higher Education and Open University Press.

Black, R. W. (2005). Access and affiliation: The literacy and composition practices of English-language learners in an online community. *Journal of Adolescent & Adult Literacy, 49*(2), 118–128. doi:10.1598/JAAL.49.2.4

Bloom, B. S. (1956). Taxonomy of Educational Objectives, Handbook I: The Cognitive Domain. New York: David McKay Co Inc.

Bloom, B. S., & Krathwohl, D. R. (Eds.). (1956). Taxonomy of Educational Objectives: The Classification of Educational Goals. New York: Longman, Green.

Bloom, D. E. (2004). Globalization and Education: An Economic Perspective, In M. Suarez-Orozco & D. Qin-Hillard, (Ed.), Globalization: Culture and Education in the New Millennium. (pp. 58-77). Ewing, NJ: University of California Press.

Boerema, C., Stanley, M., & Westhorp, P. (2007). Educators' perspective of online course design and deliver. *Medical Teacher, 29*, 758–765. doi:10.1080/01421590701477332

Boud, D., & Feletti, G. I. (Eds.). (1997). The Challenge of Problem-Based Learning. London: Kogan Page.

Boud, D., Cohen, R., & Sampson, J. (1999). Peer learning and assessment. *Assessment & Evaluation in Higher Education, 24*(4), 413–426. doi:10.1080/0260293990240405

Boulding, K. E., & Boulding, E. (1995). The Future: Images and Processes. Thousand Oaks, CA: Sage Publications.

Bourne, J., & Moore, J. (Eds.). (2002). Elements of quality online education: Practice and direction. Needham, MA: The Sloan Consortium.

Boyer, E. L. (1990). Scholarship reconsidered: Priorities of the professoriate. Princeton, NJ: Carnegie Foundation for the Advancement of Teaching.

Boyinbode, O. K., & Akinyede, R. O. (2008). Mobile Learning: An Application of Mobile and Wireless Technologies in Nigerian Learning System. *International Journal of Computer Science and Network Security, 8*(11), 386–392.

Brabazon, T. (2002). Digital Hemlock: Internet Education and the Poisioning of Teaching. Sydney, Australia: Report on e-learning for Department of Education and Training, University of New South Wales.

Bransford, J., Brown, A., & Cocking. (Eds.). (2000). *How people learn: Brain, mind, experience, and school,* (Expanded Edition). Washington, DC: National Academy Press.

Brodeur, D. R., Young, P. W., & Blair, K. B. (2002). *Problem-Based Learning in Aerospace Engineering.* Paper presented at the 2002 American Society for Engineering Education Annual Conference & Exposition, Montréal, Quebec, Canada.

Brophy, S. (2000). *Guidelines for modular design.* Retrieved December 19, 2005, from http://www.vanth.org/white_papers.html

Brown, K. L. (2003). From teacher-centered to learner-centered curriculum: Improving learning in diverse classrooms. *Education, 124*(1), 49–54.

Brown, T. H. (2005). Toward a model of m-Learning for Africa. *International Journal on E-Learning, 4*(3), 299–315.

Bruch, K. M. (2002). *Using a propositional diffusion model to examine the impact of broadband connectivity upon environmental monitoring.* Master's thesis. San Diego State University. Retrieved from http://kimbruch.com/thesis/

Brügemann, V., Van Brummelen, H., Melkert, J., Kamp, A., Reith, B., Saunders-Smits, G., & Zandbergen, B. (2005, June). *An Example of Active Learning in Aerospace Engineering.* Paper presented at the Fifth International Workshop on Active Learning in Engineering Education, Delft, The Netherlands.

Burke, J. (2003). *Intercultural Education Summit Keynote.* Retrieved from http://people.ucsc.edu/~pmmckerc/IEA.html

Burt, R. S. (2000). The network structure of social capital. *Research in Organizational Behavior, 22,* 345–423. doi:10.1016/S0191-3085(00)22009-1

Butcher, N., & Roberts, N. (2004). Costs, effectiveness, efficiency: A guide for sound investment. In H. Perraton & H. Lentell (Eds.), Policy for Open and Distance Learning. World review of distance education and open learning (Vol. 4, pp. 224 – 245). London: Routledge Falmer.

Byram, M., Nichols, A., & Stevens, D. (Eds.). (2001). Developing Intercultural Competence in Practice: Languages for Intercultural Communication and Education. Multilingual Matters, Ltd.

Caladine, R. (1997). Molta: A Model of Learning and Teaching Activities. *ultiBASE, 10*(1), 1-10.

Calcaterra, A., Antonietti, A., & Underwood, J. (2005). Cognitive style, hypermedia navigation and learning. *Computers & Education, 44,* 441–457. doi:10.1016/j.compedu.2004.04.007

Calvert, J. (1992). Deakin University. In I. Mugridge (Ed.), *Perspectives on Distance Education –Distance Education in Single and Dual Mode Universities.* Papers presented to a Symposium on Reforms in Higher Education in New Delhi, India. Vancouver: The Commonwealth of Learning.

Canete, A. (2004). Book Report on: The Production of Space by H. Lefebvre. *Thinking Culture.* Retrieved from http://thinkingculture.blogspot.com/2004/12/production-of-space-by-h-lefebvre-aloy.html

Caniz, E. (2006). Evaluation of technological needs and resources at five middle schools in Totonicapán, Guatemala. *CLASPO Report: Summer 2006.* Austin, TX: Center for Latin American Social Policy at the University of Texas. Retrieved at www.utexas.edu/cola/insts/llilas/claspo/ research/noformat/claspo/PDF/field reports/tzoc 06.pdf

Car, A. (2008). Towards a Quality Assurance Concept for Postgraduate Distance Learning Programmes for Professionals. In T. Jekel, A. Koller, J. Strobl (Eds.), Lernen mit Geoinformation II, (pp. 172-178). Heidelberg, Germany: Wichmann.

Car, A. (2009). *Time and Space*. GIScience, Austrian Academy of Sciences. Retrieved from http://www.oeaw-giscience.org/index.php?option=com_content&task=blogcategory&id=27&Itemid=38

Carpenter, B. S., & Taylor, P. G. (2003). Racing thoughts: Altering our ways of knowing and being through computer hypertext. *Studies in Art Education, 45*(1), 40–55.

Castells, M. (2001). *Identity and Change in the Network Society*. Institute of International Studies, UC Berkeley. Retrieved from http://globetrotter.berkeley.edu/people/Castells/castells-con0.html

Castells, M., & Arsenault, A. (2006). Conquering the Minds, Conquering Iraq. *Information, Communication & Society, 9*(3), 284–307. Retrieved from http://annenberg.usc.edu/Home/Faculty/Communication/~/media/Faculty/Facpdfs/Castells%20Iraq%20misinformation%20pdf.ashx

Center for World-Class Universities, Shanghai Jiao Tong University. (2008). *Academic Ranking of World Universities 2008*. Retrieved http://www.arwu.org/rank2008/EN2008.htm

Central Intelligence Agency. (2006). *The world factbook—Guatemala.* Retrieved at https:// www.cia.gov/library/publications/the-world-factbook/geos/gt.html

Central Intelligence Agency. (2009). *The World Factbook: China*. Retrieved March 1, 2009, from https://www.cia.gov/library/publications/the-world-factbook/geos/ch.html

Central Intelligence Agency. (2009). *The World Factbook: Malaysia*. Retrieved March 1, 2009, from https://www.cia.gov/library/publications/the-world-factbook/geos/my.html

Challis, D. (2006). Eroding distinctiveness: blurring the boundaries between on- and off-campus students by the adoption of learning management systems. In M. Tulloch, S. Relf, & P. Uys, (Eds.), *Selected papers from the 17th. Biennial Conference of the Open and Distance Learning Association of Australia: Breaking down boundaries: International experience in open, distance and flexible learning*, Adelaide, Australia: November 9-11, 2005, (pp. 87-96). Charles Sturt University: Open and Distance Learning Association of Australia.

Chambers, R. (1990). *Rapid but relaxed and participatory rural appraisal: Towards applications in health and nutrition.* Retrieved at www.unu.edu/unupress/food2 / UIN08E/ uin08e 0u.htm

Chambers, R. (1992). Rural Appraisal: Rapid, Relaxed, and Participatory. *Institute of Development Studies Discussion Paper 311*. Sussex, UK: HELP. Retrieved at www.worldbank. org/wbi/sourcebook/sba 104.htm

Chambers, R. (1994). Participatory rural appraisal: Challenges, potential, paradigms. *World Development, 22*(10), 1437–1454. doi:10.1016/0305-750X(94)90030-2

Chambers, R. (1998). Beyond "Whose reality counts?" New methods we now need? *Studies in Cultures, Organizations and Societies, 4*, 279–301. doi:10.1080/10245289808523516

Chandler, P., & Sweller, J. (1991). Cognitive load theory and the format of instruction. *Cognition and Instruction, 8*, 293–332. doi:10.1207/s1532690xci0804_2

Chandler, P., & Sweller, J. (1992). The split-attention effect as a factor in the design of instruction. *The British Journal of Educational Psychology, 62*, 233–246.

Chang, T. (2004). Transborder tourism, borderless classroom: Reflections on a Hawaii–Singapore experience. *Journal of Geography in Higher Education, 28*(2), 179–195. doi:10.1080/0309826042000242431

Chankova, S., Kombe, G., Muchiri, S., Decker, C., Kimani, G., & Pielemeier, N. (2006). *Rising to the challenges of human resources for health in Kenya: Developing empirical evidence for policy making.* Partners for Health Reformplus Project: Bethesda, MD. Retrieved May 30, 2009 from www.phrplus.org/pubs/Tech101_fin.pdf

Chen, C., & Rada, R. (1996). Interacting with hypertext: A meta-analysis of experimental studies. *Human-Computer Interaction, 11*, 125–156. doi:10.1207/s15327051hci1102_2

Chen, G., & Chiu, M. M. (2008). Online discussion processes: Effects of earlier messages' evaluations, knowledge content, social cues and personal information on later messages. *Computers & Education, 50*(3), 678–692. doi:10.1016/j.compedu.2006.07.007

Cifuentes, W. (2007). *Online chat with the Assistant Education Director of the Fundación Rigoberta Menchú Tum by Douglas Tedford,* December 6, 2007.

Clark, H. H., & Brennan, S. E. (1991). Grounding in communication. In L. B. Resnick, J. Levine, & S. D. Behreno (Eds.), Socially Shared Cognition. Washington DC: American Psychological Association.

Clark, H. H., & Schaefer, E. F. (1989). Contributing to discourse. *Cognitive Science, 13*, 259–294.

Clark, R. E. (1994). Media will never influence learning. *Educational Technology Research and Development, 42*(2), 21–29. doi:10.1007/BF02299088

Clark, R. W., Hong, L. K., & Schoeppach, M. R. (1996). Teacher empowerment and site based management. In J. Sikula, T. J., Buttery, & E. Guyton, (Eds.), Handbook of research on teacher education (pp. 595-616). New York: Macmillan.

Cloke, P. (2002). Deliver us from evil? Prospects for living ethically and acting politically in human geography. *Progress in Human Geography, 26*(5), 587–604. doi:10.1191/0309132502ph391oa

Coats, A. W. (1985). The American Economic Association and the Economics Profession. *Journal of Economic Literature, 23*(4), 1697–1727.

Cochran-Smith, M., & Fries, M. K. (2001). Sticks, stones and ideology: The discourse of reform in teacher education. *Educational Researcher, 30*(8), 3–15. doi:10.3102/0013189X030008003

Coffield, F. J., Moseley, D. V., Hall, E., & Ecclestone, K. (2004). Learning Styles and Pedagogy in Post-16 Learning: A Systematic and Critical Review. London: Learning and Skills Research Centre (University of Newcastle upon Tyne).

Coleman, J. (1988). Social capital in the creation of human capital. *American Journal of Sociology, 94*(Supplement), S95–S120. doi:10.1086/228943

Collier, G. (1987) Thoth-II: Hypertext with explicit semantics. In Proceedings of hypertext '87 (pp. 269-289). Chapel Hill, NC: University of North Carolina.

Collins, B. C., & Gaylon-Keramidas, C. (2006). Planning and delivering online instruction. In B. L. Ludlow, B. C. Collins, & R. Menlove (Eds.), Online instruction for distance education delivery: Preparing special educators in and for rural areas, (pp. 43-75). Victoria, BC: Trafford Publishing.

Conciliation Resources. *(2007).* Agreement on social and economic aspects and agrarian situation: 1996, Mexico City. *Conciliation Resources, website. Retrieved at*http://www.c-r.org/our-work/accord/guatemala/socio-economic-accord.php

Conner, M. (2000). *Global implications of e-learning.* Retrieved July 1, 2007 from http://www.linezine.com/2.1/features/mcgie.htm

Cononelos, T., & Oliva, M. (1993). Using computer networks to enhance foreign language/culture education. *Foreign Language Annals, 26*(4), 527–534. doi:10.1111/j.1944-9720.1993.tb01186.x

Consejo Nacional de Educación Maya (CNEM). (2007). Xka xmolomil li k'anjel chirix li tzolok Mayab', 4to congreso nacional de educación maya: consensos, planteamientos y demandas (Fourth national congress of Mayan education: consensus, considerations and demands). Cobán, Alta Verapaz, Guatemala.

Cookson, P. (2002). Online postgraduate education: some reflections. *International Review of Research in Open and Distance Learning, 3*(2), 1492–3831.

Corrallo, S. (1994). A preliminary study of the feasibility and utility for national policy of instructional good practice indicators in undergraduate education, (pp. 94-437). National Center for Higher Education Statistics.

Craft, L. (2004). *Remade in Japan.* ASSE Prism. Retrieved 26 August 2007 from http://www.prism-magazine.org

Craig, T., Harris, L., & Smith, R. (1998). Rhetoric of the "contact zone": Composition on the front lines. In T. Taylor & I. Ward (Eds.), Literacy theory in the age of the internet, (pp.122-145). New York: Columbia University Press.

Creed, C., & Joynes, C. (2005). Education for all global monitoring report: Improving the quality of primary school through distance education. Study undertaken by IRFOL: Distance Learning and Improving the Quality of Education Report. International Research Foundation for Open Learning for the EFA Monitoring Team. Paris: UNESCO.

Creese, E. L. (2003). Group Dynamics and Learning in an Organisation Behaviour Virtual Learning Community: The Case of Six Virtual Peer-Learning Teams. *ultiBASE, 3*(11), 1-11.

Creswell, J. W. (2003). Research Design: Qualitative, Quantitative, and Mixed Methods Approaches (2nd ed.). New York: Sage.

Croft, M. (1992). Single or Dual Mode: Challenges and Choices for the Future of Education. In I. Mugridge (Ed.). *Perspectives on Distance Education – Distance Education in Single and Dual Mode Universities.* Papers presented to a Symposium on Reforms in Higher Education in New Delhi, India, (pp. 49-78). Vancouver: The Commonwealth of Learning.

Crump, B., & McIlroy, A. (2003). The digital divide: Why the don't-want-to's won't compute—Lessons from a New Zealand ICT project. *First Monday, Peer Reviewed Journal on the Internet 8*(12). Retrieved at http://www.firstMonday .org/issues/issue8_12/crump/#c6

Csoma, K. (2008). Információs és kommunikációs technológiák a nyelvtanárképzésben. Budapest: Ad Librum.

Culp, K. M., Honey, M., & Mandinach, E. (2003). A Retrospective on Twenty Years of Education Technology Policy. Washington, DC: Center for Children and Technology Education Development Center, U.S. Department of Education, Office of Educational Technology.

Cunningham, D. J. (1992). Assessing constructions and constructing assessments. In T.M. Duffy, & D.H. Jonassen, (Eds.), Constructivism and the technology of instruction: a conversation, (pp. 35-44). Mahwah, NJ: Lawrence Erlbaum Associates.

Cutchin, M. P. (2002). Ethics and geography: continuity and emerging syntheses. *Progress in Human Geography, 26*(5), 656–664. doi:10.1191/0309132502ph393pr

Cybinski, P., & Selvanathan, S. (2005). Learning Experience and Learning Effectiveness in Undergraduate Statistics: Modeling Performance in Traditional and Flexible Learning Environments. *Decision Sciences Journal of Innovative Education, 3*(2), 251–271. doi:10.1111/j.1540-4609.2005.00069.x

Daniel, J. (2006). Foreword. In A. Hope & P. Guiton (Eds.), Strategies for Sustainable Open and Distance Learning. World review of distance education and open learning, Volume 6, p. xiv-xviii. London: Routledge.

Daniel, J. with Naidoo, V. (2005). Open and Distance Education for Africans and by Africans. Speech made at the African Council of Distance Education on Mobilization of African Leadership, at Tshwane, South Africa. In Commonwealth of Learning (Ed.). Speeches by Sir John Daniel and Colleagues, (pp. 5 – 9). Vancouver, Canada: Editor.

Darling-Hammond, L., & Bransford, J. (Eds.). (2005). Preparing teachers for a changing World: What teachers should learn and be able to do. San Francisco: Jossey-Bass.

Dator, J. (1980). Emerging issues analysis in the Hawai'i judiciary. A report published by the Hawai'i judiciary, Honolulu, Hawai'i.

Davis, D., O'Brien, M. A., Freemantle, N., Wolf, F. M., Mazmanian, P., & Taylor-Vaisey, A. (1999). Impact of formal continuing medical education: Do conferences, workshops, rounds, and other traditional continuing education activities change physician behavior or health care outcomes? *Journal of the American Medical Association, 282*, 867–874. doi:10.1001/jama.282.9.867

Delany, P., & Gilbert, S. (1991). Hypercard stacks for Fielding's Joseph Andrew: Issues of design and content. In P. Delany & G. Landow (Eds.), Hypermedia and literary studies (pp. 287-298). Cambridge, MA: MIT Press.

Delisle, R. (1997). How to Use Problem-Based Learning in the Classroom. Alexandria, VA: Association for Supervision and Curriculum Development (ASCD).

Demeritt, D. (2002). What is the 'social construction of nature'? A typology and sympathetic critique. *Progress in Human Geography, 26*(6), 767–790. doi:10.1191/0309132502ph402oa

Dennis, L. (1970). Dewey's Brief for the Fine Arts. *Studies in Art Education, 11*(3), 3-8. Retrieved from http://www.jstor.org/stable/1319771

DEST. (2009). *Australian Qualification Framework*. Commonwealth Department of Education, Science and Training (Sydney, NSW). Retrieved, from the World Wide Web http://www.dest.gov.au

Devereux, S., & Knowles, C. (2006). Introduction: challenging orthodoxies, influencing debates. The *IDS Bulletin* at 40. *IDS Bulletin, 37*(4), 1-5. Funaro, G. M., & Montell, F. (1999). Pedagogical roles and implementation guidelines for online communication tools. *Asynchronous Learning Network Magazine, 3*(2) 1-8. Retrieved from http://www.sloanc.org/publications/magazine/v3n2/funaro.asp

Dewey, J. (1938). Experience & education. New York: Touchstone.

Dexter, S. (2002). eTIPS-Educational Technology Integration Principles. Designing instruction for technology-enhanced learning. Hershey, PA: Idea Group Publishing.

Dey, I. (1993). Qualitative data analysis: A user-friendly guide for social scientists. London: Routledge.

Dfse Web site (2005). *Dfse, Harnessing Technology: Transforming Learning and Children's Services.* Retrieved April 21, 2005, from http://www.dfes.gov.uk/publications/e-strategy/

Dhanarajan, G. (1992). Dual Mode Institutions: The Off-Campus Centre of Universiti Sains Malaysia. In I. Mugridge (Ed.), *Perspectives on Distance Education – Distance Education in Single and Dual Mode Universities.* Papers presented to a Symposium on Reforms in Higher Education in New Delhi, India, (pp. 79 - 92). Vancouver: The Commonwealth of Learning.

Dick, W., Carey, L., & Carey, J. O. (2001). The Systematic Design of Instruction (5th ed.). New York: Addison-Wesley Longman.

Digital Dividend Replace Digital Divide? In Commonwealth of Learning (Ed.), *Speeches by Sir John Daniel and Colleagues,* (pp. 29 – 34). Vancouver, Canada: Editor.

Dillenbourg, P. Mendelsophn, P. & Jermann, P. (1999). Why spatial metaphors are relevant to virtual campuses. in Levonen, J. & Enkenberg, J. (Eds.), Learning and instruction in multiple contexts and settings. Bulletins of the Faculty of Education, 73. Joensuu, Finland: University of Joensuu, Finland, Faculty of Education.

Dillon, A. (1996). Myths, misconceptions and alternative view of information usage and the electronic medium. In J. Rouét et al. (Eds.), Hypertext and cognition (pp. 25-42). Mahwah, NJ: Erlbaum.

Dillon, A., & Gabbard, R. (1998). Hypermedia as an educational technology: A review of the quantitative research literature on learner comprehension, control, and style. *Review of Educational Research, 68*(3), 322–349.

Dillon, A., & Jobst, J. (2005). Multimedia learning with hypermedia. In R. E. Mayer, (Ed.), The Cambridge handbook of multimedia learning, (pp. 569-588). New York: Cambridge University Press.

DiMaggio, P., & Hargittai, E. (2001). *From the 'digital divide' to 'digital inequality': Studying Internet use as penetration increases.* Sociology Department, Princeton University. Princeton, New Jersey. Retrieved at http://www.princeton.edu/~arts pol/workpap/ WP15%20-%20 DiMaggio%2BHargittai.pdf

Direccion de calidad y desarrollo educativo (DICADE), (2006). *Curriculum nacional base: nivel primaria y preprimaria.* (Basic national program of study: primary and preprimary levels). Guatemala City: Ministerio de educacion, Guatemala.

Dix, A., Finlay, J., Abowd, G., & Beale, R. (2004). Human-Computer Interaction, (3rd Ed., pp. 476-508; 664-713). Harlow, UK: Prentice Hall.

Dixon, K., & Dixon, R. (2008). Capacity of an Electronic Portfolio to Promote Professionalism, Collaboration and Accountability in Educational Leadership. In J. Salmons & L. Wilson (Eds.), Handbook of Research on Electronic Collaboration and Organizational Synergy (pp. 472-493). Hershey, PA: IGI Global.

Dole, S., & Bloom, L. (2009). Online course design: A case study. *International Journal for the Scholarship of Teaching and Learning, 3*(1). Retrieved 5/11/09 from http://academics.georgiasouthern.edu/ijsotl/v3n1.html

Donovan, M. S., & Bransford, J. D. Pellegrino, (Eds.). (2003). How people learn: Bridging research and practice. Washington, DC: National Academy Press.

Doppelt, Y. (2005). Assessment of Project-Based Learning in a MECHATRONICS Context. *Journal of Technology Education, 16*(2), 1–17.

Dorst, K., & Cross, N. (2001). Creativity in the design process: co-evolution of problem-solution. *Design Studies, 22*(5), 425–437. doi:10.1016/S0142-694X(01)00009-6

Douglas, R. (2006). Interview with Professor Rogelio Douglas, Director of English Language Programs, Ministry of Education, Republic of Panama. August 30, 2006. Panama City, Panama.

Drent, M., & Meelissen, M. (2008). Which Factors Obstruct or Stimulate Teacher Educators to Use Ict Innovatively? *Computers & Education, 11*(1), 53–68.

Drydan, L. M. (1998). What Does Multiple Intelligence Theory Tell Us About CALL? In P. Lewis, (Ed.), Teachers, Learners and Computers: Exploring Relationships in CALL. JALT, Computer Assisted Language Learning National Special Interest Group, Japan.

Dudwick, N., Kuehnast, K., Nyhan Jones, V., & Woolcock, M. (2006). *Analyzing social capital in context: a guide to using qualitative methods and data.* Washington, DC: World Bank Institute. Retrieved at http://siteresources.worldbank.org/WBI/ Resources/Analyzing_ Social_Capital_in_Context-FINAL.pdf

Dunlop, J., C., Furtak, T. E., & Tucker, S. A. (2009). Designing for enhanced understanding in an online physics course. *Tech Trends: Linking Research and Practice to Improve Learning, 53*(1), 67–73.

Duque Arellano, V. (1999). Forjando educación para un nuevo milenio: Desafíos educativos en países multiculturales (Forging an education for a new millennium: Educacional challenges in multicultural nations). Guatemala City: Fundación Rigoberta Menchú Tum, Instituto Indígena para la Educación FRMT, Países Bajos, UNESCO.

Durston, J. (2002). *El capital social campesino en la gestión del desarrollo rural: Diadas, equipos, puentes y escaleras.* Santiago de Chile: CEPAL: Comisión Económica para America Latina y el Caribe. Retrieved at http://www.eclac.org/ publicaciones/xml/0/ 11700/ Capitulo_ III.pdf

Dzvimbo, K. P. (2005, September). The *African Researcher, the AVU Experiences and the Limits and Possibilities of Open, Distance and Electronic Learning in Africa.* Paper presented at the 11th Cambridge International Conference on Open and Distance Learning.

Efland, A. D. (2002). Art and cognition: Integrating the visual arts in the curriculum. New York: Teacher College Press.

Eilam, B. (2004). The instruction and acquisition of cognitive skills in Israel: Difficulties and accomplishments. In K. Mutua & C. Szymanski Sunal (Eds.), Research on Education in Africa, The Caribbean, and The Middle East (Vol. 1, Chap. 10, pp.183-202). Greenwich, CT: Information Age Publishing.

Eklund, J. (2005). Driving the Future of E-Learning. Taskforce Report, University of Sydney. Canberra, ACT: Industry Taskforce on Higher Education - Ministry for Employment, Education and Training, Australian Federal Government.

Eklund, J., & May, M. (2003). Evaluation of the Usage of National Flexible Learning Tookboxes (Series 3). Canberra, ACT: Australian National Training Authority.

Elgin, D. (1991). Awakening Earth. [). Queensland: Australia: Foundation Futures Study Centre.]. *The Knowledge Base of Futures Studies, 1*, 122.

ENP. (2009). *European Neighbourhood Policy*. Retrieved from http://ec.europa.eu/world/enp/

ESD. (2009). European Association for the Promotion of Sustainable Development, Vienna. Retrieved from http://www.esd-eu.org/

EU. (2009). *Boosting Co-operation through Twinning*. European Commission, EuropeAid. Retrieved from http://ec.europa.eu/europeaid/where/neighbourhood/overview/twinning_en.htm

Fantini, A. E. (2000). A CENTRAL Concern: Developing Intercultural Competence. In *SIT Occasional Papers Series*, (1). Brattleboro, VT: School for International Training.

Fantini, A. E. (2006). Final Report of a Research Project conducted by the Federation of The Experiment in International Living with funding support from the Center for Social Development at Washington University, St. Louis, Missouri (The Initial Phase of An Extended Project to Explore and Assess Intercultural Outcomes in Service Program Participants Worldwide). Brattleboro, VT: Federation EIL

Farrell, T. (1995). Reflective teaching. Principles and practice. *Forum, 4*(36). Retrieved November 6, 2007, from http://exchanges.state.gov/forum/vols/vol36/no4/p10.htm

Fazio, M. (2007). *Economic opportunities for indigenous peoples in Latin America: Guatemala, Conference Edition,* February 2007. Washington, DC: World Bank. Retrieved at http://web.worldbank.org/WBSITE/EXTERNAL /TOPICS/EXT EDUCATION/0,contentMDK:21185632~ menuPK: 282391~pagePK:64020865~piPK:51164185~theSitePK:2823 86,00.html

Fegan, J., & Field, M. H. (Eds.). (2009). Education Across Borders: Politics, Policy and Legislative Action. Berlin: Springer.

Fink, L. D. (2003). Creating significant learning experiences: An integrated approach to designing college courses. San Francisco: Jossey-Bass.

Fisher, M. (1997). The Voice of Experience: Inservice Teacher Technology Competency Recommendations for Preservice Teacher Preparation. *Journal of Technology and Teacher Education, 5*(2-3), 139–147.

Fontela, E. Guzmán, J., Pérez, M., Santos, F.J. (2006). The art of entrepreneurial foresight. *Foresight, 8*(6), 3-13. Retrieved from http://www.emeraldinsight.com/

Foth, M. (2003). *Connectivity does not insure community: on social capital, networks, and communities of place.* The International Conference on Information Technology in Regional Areas, December 15-17, 2003. Caloundra, Queensland, Australia. Retrieved at http://www. mobilecommunity design. com/ research/Foth-Connectivity_does_not_ensure_community-on_social_capital_networks_and_ communities_of_place.pdf

Freedman, K. (2003). Teaching visual culture. Curriculum, aesthetics, and the social life of art. New York and London: Teachers College, Columbia University and National Art Education Association.

Freedman, K., & Wood, J. (1999). Students' knowledge of visual culture: Images inside and outside of school. *Studies in Art Education, 40*(2), 128–142. doi:10.2307/1320337

Freeman, C., & Jigsaw, H. (1994). A Case Study Technique Where Students Become Experts. *Journal of College Science Teaching.*

Fresen, J. W., & Boyd, L. G. (2005). Caught in the Web of Quality. *International Journal of Educational Development*, *25*(3), 317–331. doi:10.1016/j.ijedudev.2004.12.002

Fresner, J., Angerbauer, C., Möller, M., Wolf, P., Dielacher, T., Schnitzer, H., et al. (2007). *ZERMEG III – Decision guidance for the visualisation of the achievements of sustainable corporate strategies.* Final report by STENUM, Austrian Federal Ministry of Traffic, Infrastructure and Technology, Vienna. Retrieved from http://www.fabrikderzukunft.at/results.html/id4132

Fujitani, S., Bhattacharya, M., & Akahori, K. (2003). ICT Implementation and online learning in Japan. *Educational Technology*, *43*(3), 33–37.

Fullan, M. G., & Stiegelbauer, S. (1991). The New Meaning of Educational Change (2nd Ed.). New York: Teachers College Press.

Galvez, O. (2007). Telephone interview, September 20, 2007, between Douglas Tedford and Osbaldo Galvez, chief administrator of the Centro Educativo Luciano Pavarotti. San Lucas Toliman, Guatemala.

Gao, T., & Lehman, J. D. (2003). The Effects of Different Levels of Interaction on the Achievement and Motivational Perceptions of College Students in a Web-Based Learning Environment. *Journal of Interactive Learning Research*, *14*(4), 367–386.

Gatliff, B., & Wendel, F. C. (1998). Inter-institutional collaboration and team teaching. *American Journal of Distance Education*, *12*(1). doi:10.1080/08923649809526981

Gilbert, P. K., & Dabbagh, N. (2005). How to structure online discussions for meaningful discourse: a case study. *British Journal of Educational Technology*, *36*(1), 5–18. doi:10.1111/j.1467-8535.2005.00434.x

Gilding, A., & Martino, J. (2001). *Learning About Online Learning in a Dual Sector University: Reflections, Issues and Challenges.* Paper presented at the Meeting at the crossroads: proceedings of the 18th Annual Conference of the Australasian Society for Computers in Learning in Tertiary Education (ASCILITE), Melbourne, Australia.

Gilster, P. (1997). Digital Literacy. New York: John Wiley & Sons.

Ginns, P., & Ellis, R. (2007). Quality in Blended Learning: Exploring the Relations between on-Line and Face-to-Face Teaching and Learning. *The Internet and Higher Education*, *10*, 53–64. doi:10.1016/j.iheduc.2006.10.003

Ginns, P., Prosser, M., & Barrie, S. C. (2007). Students' Perceptions of Teaching Quality in Higher Education: The Perspective of Currently Enrolled Students. *Studies in Higher Education*, *32*(5). doi:10.1080/03075070701573773

Global Studies. (2009). *Bundle of Electives and New Master Curriculum on "Global Studies" at Graz University.* Retrieved from http://www.uni-graz.at/globalstudies/

Goldberg, R. (1995). Performance Art: From futurism to the present. London: Thames and Hudson.

Gonsalves, J. (2005). Participatory research and development for sustainable agriculture and natural resource management: A sourcebook. Ottawa, Canada: International Development Research Centre.

Goodman, S. E., Gottstein, J. B., & Goodman, D. S. (2001). International perspectives: wiring the wilderness in Alaska and the Yukon. *Communications of the ACM*, *44*(6), 21–25. doi:10.1145/376134.376143

Goodyear, P. (2001). Psychological foundations for networked learning. In C. Steeples & C. Jones, (Eds.), Networked learning: perspectives and issues. London: Springer Verlag.

Graham, D. (2005). Developing a Framework for e-Learning. In *Proceedings of the 6th Annual Conference of the Higher Education Academy*, University of York, 30th August – 1st September 2005, (pp. 111-114).

Graham, D. (2006). Developing a Framework for e-Learning 2006. Keynote Paper. In D. Graham (Ed.), *Proceedings of the Developing a Framework for e-Learning Workshop 2006, part of the 7th Annual Conference of the Subject Centre for Information and Computer Sciences, Higher Education Academy*, Trinity College, Dublin, 29th August 2006, (pp. 4-9).

Graham, D. (2007, June). PESTE Factors in Developing a Framework for e-Learning, *ELEA E-Learning journal, 4*(2), 194-201.

Graham, D. (2008, December). e-Learning in a Cooperative Work Framework. *ELEA E-Learning journal, 5*(4), 475-484.

Graham, D. (2009). Explicating Understanding. In A., Mendez-Vilas, A., Solano Martin, J., Mesa Gonzalez, & J. A., Mesa Gonzalez, (Eds.), *Research, Reflections and Innovations in Integrating ICT in Education (2009), Proceedings of the V International Conference on Multimedia and Information and Communication Technologies in Education (M-ICTE2009)*, New University of Lisbon, Lisbon, Portugal, 22-24 April 2009, (Vol. 2, pp. 739-743).

Graham, D., & Valsamidis, A. (2006). A Framework for e-Learning: A Blended Solution? In A. Mendez-Vilas, A. Solano Martin, J. Mesa Gonzalez, & J. A. Mesa Gonzalez, (Eds.), *Current Developments in Technology-Assisted Education (2006), Proceedings of the IV International Conference on Multimedia and Information and Communication Technologies in Education (M-ICTE2006)*, University of Seville, Seville, Spain, 22-25 November 2006, (Vol. 1, pp. 233-237).

Grant, M. M. (2004). Learning to Teach with the Web: Factors Influencing Teacher Education Faculty. *The Internet and Higher Education Journal, 7*(4), 329–341. doi:10.1016/j.iheduc.2004.09.005

Grenier, L. (1998). Working with indigenous knowledge: a guide for researchers. Ottawa: International Development Research Centre.

Grippe, E. J. (2002). Pragmatism, Perspectivism and Education: A Critique of Habitual Social Constructivism. *Insights, 34*(3), 2–14.

Grushka, K., McLeod, J. H., & Reynolds, R. (2005). Reflecting Upon Reflection: Theory and Practice in One Australian University Teacher Education Program. *Reflective Practice, 6*(2), 239–246. doi:10.1080/14623940500106187

Haack, S. (2004). Pragmatism, Old and New. *Contemporary Pragmatism, 1*(1), 3–41.

Hager, M., Russell, S., & Fletcher, S. W. (Eds.). (2008). Continuing education in the health professions: improving healthcare through lifelong learning. Bermuda, NY: Josiah Macy, Jr. Foundation.

Hannum, W. H. (2007). When computers teach: A review of the instructional effectiveness of computers. *Educational Technology, 47*(2), 5–13.

Harasim, L. (2000). Shift happens: online education as a new paradigm in learning. *The Internet and Higher Education, 3*(1-2), 41–61. doi:10.1016/S1096-7516(00)00032-4

Harper, B., & Hedberg, J. (1997). Creating Motivating Interactive Learning Environments: A Constructivist View. In R. Kevill & R. Oliver & R. Phillips (Eds.), *What Works and Why: Proceedings of the 14th Annual Conference of Ascilite*. Perth, Australia: Curtin University of Technology.

Hawisher & C. Selfe (Ed.). Passions, pedagogies, and 21st century techologies (pp. 129-139). Logan, UT: Utah State University Press.

Hawisher, G., & Moran, C. (1993). Electronic mail and the writing instructor. *College English, 55*(6), 627–643. doi:10.2307/378699

Haydn, T. (2006). Multimedia, interactivity and learning: some lessons from the United Kingdom. In A. Mendez-Vilas, A. Solano Martin, J. Mesa Gonzalez, & J. A. Mesa Gonzalez, (Eds.), *Current Developments in Technology-Assisted Education (2006), Proceedings of the IV International Conference on Multimedia and Information and Communication Technologies in Education (M-ICTE2006)*, University of Seville, Seville, Spain, 22-25 November 2006, (Vol. 1, pp. 110-114).

Heidegger, M. (1977). Sein und Zeit. Tübingen, Germany.

Heister, S. D., & Messersmith, N. L. (1996). Launch Competition for Rocket Propulsion Education. *The International Journal of Engineering Education*, *12*(3), 229–238.

Henning, E. (2003). 'I click, therefore I am (not)': is cognition 'distributed' or is it 'contained' in borderless e-learning programmes? [Retrieved at EBSCO Host database.]. *International Journal of Training and Development*, *7*(4), 303–317. doi:10.1046/j.1360-3736.2003.00188.x

Højsholt-Poulsen, L. (2007). EPICT *2007 presentation*. Retrieved June 20, 2009 from www.epict.org

Holmes, D. (2005). Communication theory: Media, technology, society. London: Sage.

Hope, A. (2006). *Factors for Success in Dual Mode Institutions*. Retrieved April, 12, 2007 from HTTP://www.col.org/colweb/site/pid/3975

Hope, A., & Guiton, P. (Eds.). (2006). Strategies for Sustainable Open and Distance Learning. World review of distance education and open learning, (Vol. 6). London: Routledge.

Horx, M. (2007). *How We Will Live*. Vienna: Signum. Retrieved from http://www.zukunftsinstitut.de/verlag/medien_detail.php?nr=9

Howgate, P. (2007). *Personal communication*.

Huijser, H. (2006). Refocusing Multiliteracies for the Net Generation. *International Journal of Pedagogies and Learning*, *2*(1), 21–33.

Hung, W., Jonassen, D. H., & Liu, R. (2008). Problem-based learning. In J.M Spector, M.D. Merrill, J. Van Merrienboer & M.P. Driscoll (Eds.), Handbook Of Research On Educational Communications And Technology (3rd ed.). New York: Lawrence Erlbaum Associates

Hutchinson, F. (1996). Educating Beyond Violent Futures. New York: Routledge.

Ibañez, A., Linder, K., & Woolcock, M. (2002). Social capital in Guatemala: a mixed methods analysis. *Guatemala Poverty Assessment Program, Technical Paper No. 12*. Geneva: International Bank for Reconstruction and Development.

IEEE. (2006). *Instructional Management System (Ims) Content Packaging Best Practice and Implementation Guide*. IEEE Learning Technology Standards Committee (LTSC). Retrieved 30 June 2006, from the World Wide Web http://ltsc.ieee.org/

Ihsan, S., Inayatullah, S., & Obijiofor, L. (1995). The futures of communication. *Futures*, *27*(8), 897–903. doi:10.1016/0016-3287(95)00053-Y

Inayatullah, S. (2003). Teaching Futures Studies: From Strategy to Transformative Change. *Journal of Futures Studies*, 35-40.

Inayatullah, S. (2004). Causal Layered Analysis: Theory, historical context, and case studies. In The Causal Layered Analysis Reader, (pp. 1-52). Tamkang University Press.

International Bank for Reconstruction and Development (IBRD/World Bank). (2006). *Social capital, empowerment, and community driven development, description*. Retrieved at http://info.worldbank.org/etools/vod/PresentationView.asp?PID =936&EID=482

International Bank for Reconstruction and Development (IBRD/World Bank). (2007). *Social capital and information technology*. Retrieved at http://www1.worldbank.org/prem/ poverty/ scapital/topic/info1.htm

International Bank for Reconstruction and Development (IBRD/World Bank), (2007). *World Bank Participatory Sourcebook, Appendix 1: Methods and Tools.* Retrieved athttp://www. worldbank.org/wbi/sourcebook/sba104.htm

International Bank for Reconstruction and Development (IBRD/World Bank). (2008). *PovertyNet: Information and Communication Technology.* Retrieved at http://web.worldbank. org/WBSITE/EXTERNAL/TOPICS/EXTPOVERTY/EXTEMPOWERMENT/0,contentMDK:20265884~menuPK:543261~pagePK:148956~piPK:216618~theSitePK:486411,00.html

ITFORCEGT. (2006). *India – Guatemala IT Education Centre of Excellence.* Retrieved at http://www.itforcegt.org/

Jegede, O. (2000). Evolving a National Policy on Distance Education. *Education Today, 8*(2), 109–128.

Johnson, S. (2005). Everything bad is good for you: How today's popular culture is actually making us smarter. New York: Riverhead Books.

Jonas, H. (1984). The Imperative of Responsibility. *Search of Ethics for the Technological Age*, [transl. of "Das Prinzip Verantwortung"], University of Chicago Press; see also http://www.hans-jonas-zentrum.de/

Jonassen, D., & Reeves, T. (1996). Learning with technology: Using computers as cognitive tools. In D. Jonassen (Ed.), Handbook of research on communications and technology (pp. 694-719). New York: Mcmillan.

Jones, S. G. (Ed.). (1995). Cybersociety: Computer-mediated communication and community. London: Sage.

Joy, E. H., & Garcia, F. E. (2000). Measuring Learning Effectiveness: A New Look at No-Significant-Difference Findings. *Journal of Asynchronous Learning Networks, 4*(1), 33–39.

Kanouse, D. E., & Jacoby, I. (1988). When does information change practitioners' behavior? *International Journal of Technology Assessment in Health Care, 4*(1), 27–33. doi:10.1017/S0266462300003214

Kaplan, R. S., & Norton, D. P. (2001). The Strategy-Focused Organization: How Balanced Scorecard Companies Thrive in the New Business Environment. Boston: Harvard Business School Press.

Karemera, D., Reuben, L. J., & Sillah, M. R. (2003). The Effects of Academic Environment and Background Characteristics on Student Satisfaction and Performance: The Case of South Carolina State University's School of Business. *College Student Journal, 37*(2), 298.

Kárpáti, A. (2007). *Status 2007 Hungary presentation.* Retrieved June 20, 2009 from www.epict.org

Kárpáti, A., & Horváth, Á. (2008). National Policies and Practices on ICT In Education: Hungary. In T. Plomp, N. Law, R. Anderson & A. Quale, (Eds.), Cross-national ICT policy and practices in education. Charlotte, NC: Information Age Publishers

Kárpáti, A., Török, B., & Szirmai, A. L. (2007). *Bridges over Troubled Water -- The Effects of Personality Traits and ICT Skills on Changes in Teaching Style of Experienced Educators.* Paper presented at the EDEN Research Workshop, Poitiers.

Kárpáti. Andrea (2003). Az informatika hatása az iskola szervezetére, kommunikációs és oktatási-nevelési kultúrájára. Új Pedagógiai Szemle, 2(pp. 44-58).

Kavanaugh, A., Reese, D., Carroll, J., & Rosson, M. (2005). Weak ties in networked communities. *The Information Society, 21*, 119–131. doi:10.1080/01972240590925320

Kearsley, G. (1998). Educational Technology: A Critique. *Educational Technology, 38*(2), 47–51.

Keegan, D. (2000). Distance Training – Taking Stock at a Time of Change. London: Routledge Falmer.

Kennedy, G. E., Judd, T. S., Churchward, A., Gray, K., & Krause, K. (2008). First Year Students' Experiences with Technology: Are They Really Digital Natives? *Australasian Journal of Educational Technology, 24*(1), 108–122.

Kenny, J. (2003). *Student Perceptions of the Use of Online Learning Technology in Their Courses.* Retrieved May, 2004, from the World Wide Web http://ultibase.rmit.edu.au/Articles/march03/kenny2.pdf

Kenny, S. (1994). Developing Communities for the Future. Melbourne, Australia: Nelson ITP.

Kerim, S. (2007, September). S*tatement of the 62nd Session of the United Nations General Assembly at the Ministerial Meetings of Group of Friends of the Alliance of Civilizations*, New York. Retrieved from http://www.unaoc.org/images/articles/min_pga.pdf

Ketchell, M. (2003, February 28). Rmit to Scrap $47m Software System. [Fairfax Digital]. *Age*, 2–3.

Kilby, P., & Beckmann, E. A. (2008). So, what happened in Kabul today? Flexible learning in conflict and social justice programs at the Australian National University. In *Proceedings from Fifth Pan-Commonwealth Forum on Open Learning: Access to Learning for Development*, 13-17 July 2008, London. Retrieved from http://www.wikieducator.org/images/b/bc/PID_359.pdf

Kim, K. J., & Bonk, C. J. (2002). Cross-cultural comparisons of online collaboration. *Journal of Computer-Mediated Communication*, *8*(1).

Kimball, L. (2001). Managing distance learning: new challenges for faculty. In R. Hazemi, S. Hailes, & S. Wilbur (Eds.), The digital university: building a learning community (pp. 27-40). London: Springer.

Knipe, D., & Lee, M. (2002). The quality of teaching and learning via videoconferencing. *British Journal of Educational Technology*, *33*(3), 301–311. doi:10.1111/1467-8535.00265

Kobas, J. E., & Renzie, S. (Eds.). (2005). Innovation in Web-Enhanced Learning at University. Hershey, PA: IGI Global.

Koehler, M. J. (2002). Designing case-based hypermedia for developing understanding of children's mathematical reasoning. *Cognition and Instruction*, *20*(2), 151–195. doi:10.1207/S1532690XCI2002_2

Kolb, D. A. (1984). Experiential learning: experience as the source of learning and development. Englewood Cliffs, NJ: Prentice-Hall.

Korean Culture and Information Service Ministry of Culture. (2008). Facts about Korea. Korean Government Publication.

Koss, F. (2001). Children falling into the digital divide. *Journal of International Affairs*, *55*(1), 75–90.

Krajcik, J. S., & Blumenfeld, P. C. (2006). Project-based learning. In K. Sawyer (Ed.). The Cambridge Handbook Of The Learning Sciences. Cambridge, UK: CUP

Krathwohl, D. R., Bloom, B. S., & Masia, B. B. (1964). Taxonomy of Educational Objectives: The Classification of Educational Goals. Handbook Ii: Affective Domain. New York: David McKay Co., Inc.

Kress, G. R. (2003). Literacy in the new media age. New York: Routledge.

Landauer, T. (1995). The trouble with computers. Cambridge, MA: MIT Press.

Landes, D. S. (2000). The Wealth and Poverty of Nations: Why Some Are So Rich and Some So Poor. New York: W.W. Norton.

Landow, G. P. (1992). Hypertext: The convergence of contemporary critical theory and technology. Baltimore, Maryland: John Hopkins University Press.

Lasonen, J. (2006). *Expert Meeting on Intercultural Education: Intercultural Education in the Context of Internationalization, Localization and Globalization.* Paris: UNESCO Headquarters.

Lasswell, H. D. (1948). The structure and function of communication in society. In L. Bryson (Ed.), The Communication of Ideas. New York: Harper & Row.

Laungani, P. (2005). Building multicultural counseling bridges: The holy grail or a poisoned chalice? *Counselling Psychology Quarterly*, *18*(4), 247–259. doi:10.1080/09515070500435476

Laurillard, D. (1993). Rethinking University Teaching: A Framework for the Effective Use of Educational Technolgy. London: Routledge.

Laurillard, D. (2002). Rethinking University Teaching: A Framework for the Effective Use of Educational Technolgy (2nd ed.). London: Routledge.

Laurillard, D. (2007). Modelling Benefits-Oriented Costs for Technology Enhanced Learnign. *Higher Education*, *54*(1), 21–39. doi:10.1007/s10734-006-9044-2

Lawery, V. (2003). Quantifying quality – an examination of the factors which define 'quality' in a professional development program. In G. Davies & E. Stacey (Eds.), Quality Education @ A Distance (pp. 189 – 197). Boston: Kluwer Academic Publishers.

Lawless, D. V., & Roth, W.-M. (2001). The Spiel on "Spielraum and Teaching". *Curriculum Inquiry*, *31*(2), 229–235. doi:10.1111/0362-6784.00194

Leach, D. C., & Fletcher, S. W. (2008). Perspectives on continuing education in the health professions: improving health care through lifelong learning. *Chest*, *134*(6), 1299–1303. doi:10.1378/chest.08-1022

Leask, B. (2004). Internationalisation Outcomes for All Students Using Information and Communication Technologies (Icts). *Journal of Studies in International Education*, *8*(4), 336–351. doi:10.1177/1028315303261778

Leavey, T. (2003). The Internet remains a mystery to most people. *UN Chronicle*, *4*(34), 34–35.

LeCompte, M. D., & Schensul, J. J. (1999). Designing and conducting ethnographic research. London: Alta Mira Press.

Lefebvre, H. (1991). The Production of Space. Oxford, UK: Blackwell.

Leigh-Green, G. (1999). The return of the body: Performance Art and art education. *Art Education*, *52*(1), 6–12. doi:10.2307/3193779

Lentell, H. (2004). Framing policy for open and distance learning. In H. Perraton & H. Lentell (Eds.). Policy for Open and Distance Learning. World review of distance education and open learning (Vol. 4, 249 – 259). London: Routledge Falmer.

Lenz, W. (2005). Bildung im Wandel. Wien, Germany: LIT Verlag.

Life, S. (2009). Accessed and downloaded at http://www.secondlife.com on March 27, 2009.

Lin, N. (1999). Building a network theory of social capital. *Connections*, *22*(1), 28–51.

Liston, D., Whitcomb, J., & Borko, H. (2007). NCLB and scientifically-based research. *Journal of Teacher Education*, *58*(2), 99–107. doi:10.1177/0022487107299980

Liu, M. (2005). The effect of technology enhanced learning environment on middle school students' motivation, attitude, and science knowledge. *Computers in the Schools*, *22*(3), 159–171. doi:10.1300/J025v22n03_13

Lock, J. V., & Redmond, P. (2008). Working Collaboratively on the Digital Global Frontier. In J. Salmons & L. Wilson (Eds.), Handbook of Research on Electronic Collaboration and Organizational Synergy (pp. 262-277). Hershey, PA: IGI Global.

Logan, J. (2004). *Using an Online Database Searching Tutorial to Encourage Reflection on the Research Process by Undergraduate Students.* Paper presented at the Online Learning and Teaching Conference: exploring integrated learning environments: a national forum for sharing information on engaging, designing, assessing and collaborating in online learning and teaching, Brisbane, Australia.

Lorenzetti, J. (2004). Strategic planning and social capital in distance education: a conversation with Eugene Kowch. *Distance Education Report*, *8*(18), 5–7.

Ludlow, B. L., Collins, B. C., & Menlove, R. R. (Eds.). (2006). Online instruction for distance education delivery: Preparing special educators in and for rural areas. Victoria, Canada: Trafford Publishing.

MAAPD. (2009). *Alumni testimonials*. Retrieved from http://rspas.anu.edu.au/maapd/testimonials.php

Maddux, C. D. (2006). Distance education: Some concluding thoughts. In B. L. Ludlow, B. C. Collins, & R. Menlove (Eds.), Online instruction for distance education delivery: Preparing special educators in and for rural areas, (pp. 249 261). Victoria, Canada: Trafford Publishing.

Magagula, C. M. & Ngwenya, A. P. (2004). A Comparative Analysis of the Academic Performance of Distance and On-Campus Learners. *Turkish Online Journal of Distance Education (TOJDE)*, *5*(4).

Maher, M. L., & Tang, H.-H. (2003). Co-evolution as a computational and cognitive model of design. *Research in Engineering Design*, *14*(1), 47–63.

Maier, P., & Warren, A. (2000). Integr@ting [London: Kogan Page.]. *Technology (Elmsford, N.Y.)*, 103–106.

Mak, S. (1995). *Developing a Self-Access and Self-Paced Learning Aid for Teaching Statistics*. Paper presented at the Australian WorldWideWeb Conference 1995, Great Coral Reef Resort, Gold Coast, Australia.

Manathunga, C. (2002). Designing Online Learning Modules: An Australian Example in Teacher Education. *International Journal of Instructional Media*, *29*(2), 185.

Mankiw, N. G., Romer, D., & Weil, D. N. (1992). A contribution to the empirics of economic growth. *The Quarterly Journal of Economics*, *107*(2), 407–438. doi:10.2307/2118477

Marginson, S. (2004). Don't leave me hanging on the Anglophone: the potential for online distance higher education in the Asia-Pacific Region. *Higher Education Quarterly*, *58*(2/3), 74–113. doi:10.1111/j.1468-2273.2004.00263.x

Marra, R. M. (2002). The ideal online learning environment for supporting epistemic development. *Quarterly Review of Distance Education*, *3*(1), 27–44.

Martin, S., & Vallance, M. (2008). The impact of synchronous inter-networked teacher training in Information and Communication Technology integration. *Computers & Education*, *51*, 34–35. doi:10.1016/j.compedu.2007.04.001

Marton, F., & Säljö, R. (1976). On qualitative differences in learning 1: outcome and process. *The British Journal of Educational Psychology*, *46*, 4–11.

Masini, E. B. (1993). Why Futures Studies? London: Grey Seal Books.

Mason, R. (2004). In M. Ryan, (2005), CeLTT teaching materials. School of Education and Training, University of Greenwich, London.

Mayer, R. E. (2005). Multimedia Learning. Cambridge, UK: CUP

Mayer, R. E. (Ed.). (2005). The Cambridge handbook of multimedia learning. New York, NY: Cambridge University Press.

McClellan, R., & Dominguez, R. (2006). The uneven march toward social justice: diversity, conflict, and complexity in educational administration programs. *Journal of Educational Administration*, *44*(3), 225–238. doi:10.1108/09578230610664823

McCurdy, S., & Schroeder, R. (2005a). *Achieving diversity through online inter-institutional collaborations*. Paper presented at ED-Media World Conference on Educational Multimedia, Hypermedia and Telecommunications, Association for the Advancement of Computing in Education, Montreal, Quebec, Canada.

McCurdy, S., & Schroeder, R. (2005b). *Inter-institutional online class-sharing to promote diversity*. Paper presented at the Syllabus Conference, Los Angeles, CA.

McCurdy, S., & Schroeder, R. (2005c). *Inter-institutional collaboration in the delivery of online learning*. Paper presented at the annual Distance Teaching and Learning Conference, Madison, WI.

MCEETYA. (2009). *National Protocols for Higher Education Approval Processes.* Ministerial Council on Education, Employment, Training and Youth Affairs (Canberra, ACT). Retrieved, from the World Wide Web: http://www.mceetya.edu.au/

McFarlane, C. (2006). Knowledge, learning and development: a post-rationalist approach. *Progress in Development Studies, 6*, 287–305. doi:10.1191/1464993406ps144oa

McKnight, C., Dillon, A., & Richardson, J. (1991). Hypertext in context. Cambridge, England: Cambridge University Press.

McKnight, C., Dillon, A., & Richardson, J. (1996). User centered design of hypertext and hypermedia for education. In D. Jonassen (Ed.), Handbook of research on educational communications and technology (pp. 622-633). New York: Macmillan.

McLeod, S., Dawson, S., & Berg, L. (2002). Using online chat to enhance peer learning while on fieldwork placements. *CAL-laborate, 8.* Retrieved from http://science.uniserve.edu.au/pubs/callab/vol8/mcleod.html

Melton, R. F. (2002). Planning and Developing Open and Distance Learning – A Quality Assurance Approach. London: Routledge Falmer.

Menchaca, M. P., & Bekele, T. A. (2008). Learner and instructor identified success factors in distance education. *Distance Education, 29*(3), 231–252. doi:10.1080/01587910802395771

Menchú, P. (2007). Letter re: Douglas Tedford, Fundación Rigoberta Menchú Tum

Menou, M., Day, P., & Schuler, D. (2007). *Liberating Voices! A Pattern Language for Communication Revolution: Telecenters, harnessing ICT in support of community development.* Retrieved at http://diac. cpsr.org/cgi-bin/diac02/pattern.cgi/public? pattern_id=867

Mensch, G. (1975). Das technologische Patt: Innovationen überwinden die Depression. Frankfurt/Main: Umschau.

Menzel, U. (1996). *Lange Wellen und Hegemonie.* Inst. for Social Science. TU Brunswick, http://www-public.tu-bs.de:8080/~umenzel/inhalt/forschungsberichte/BlaueReihe13.PDF

Meriam, S., & Muhammad, M. (2000). How cultural values shapes learning in older adulthood: The case of Malaysia. *Adult Education Quarterly, 51*, 45–63.

Merrill, D. (2002). First principles of instruction. *Educational Technology Research and Development, 50*(3), 43–59. doi:10.1007/BF02505024

Merrill, D. D. (2001). First principles of instruction. *Journal of Instructional Learning & Intelligent Systems, 14*(4), 459–466.

Merrill, M. D. (2006). Levels of instructional strategy. *Educational Technology, 46*(4), 5–10.

Merrill, M. D. (2007). First principles of instruction: A synthesis. In R. A. Reiser & J. V. Dempsey (Eds.), Trends and issues in instructional design and technology, (2nd ed., pp. 62–71). Upper Saddle River, NJ: Merrill/Prentice Hall.

Merriman, S. (1998). Qualitative research and case study applications in education. San Francisco: Jossey-Bass.

METRODigest. (2008, March 20). Electronic marking 'puts grades at risk.' *METRO*, (pp. 16).

Meyer, K. A. (2003). Face-to-face versus threaded discussions: the role of time and higher-order thinking. *Journal of Asynchronous Learning Networks, 7* (3), 55-65. Retrieved from http://www.sloanc.org/publications/jaln/v7n3/pdf/v7n3_meyer.pdf

Mima, N. (2003). Online technology is not enough: transforming the teacher-student learning process. In J. M. Bachnik (Ed.), Roadblocks on the information highway. Oxford, UK: Lexington Books.

Mishra, S. (2002). A design framework for online learning environments. *International Journal of Educational Management, 33*(4), 493–496.

Mohan, G., & Mohan, J. (2002). Placing social capital. *Progress in Human Geography*, *26*(2), 191–210. doi:10.1191/0309132502ph364ra

Mokyr, J. (1990). The lever of riches. Technological creativity and economic progress. New York: Oxford University Press.

Moon, B. (2005, August). *Designing school-based training programmes for teachers through distance education*. Paper presented at the DETA Conference 2005, held at the University of Pretoria, South Africa.

Moore, D. (2001). Perspectives on quality assurance and distance education. In N. Baijnath, S. Maimela & P. Singh (Eds.), Quality Assurance in Open and Distance Learning. Roodeport, South Africa. A Joint publication between UNISA and Technikon SA. (pp. 55 – 63).

Moore, M. G. (1989). Three types of interaction. *American Journal of Distance Education*, *3*(2), 1–7. doi:10.1080/08923648909526659

Moos, D. C., & Azevedo, R. (2006). The role of goal structure in undergraduates' use of self-regulatory variables in two hypermedia learning tasks. *Journal of Educational Multimedia and Hypermedia*, *15*(1), 49–86.

Moreno, R., & Mayer, R. E. (1999). Cognitive principles of multimedia learning: The role of modality and contiguity. *Journal of Educational Psychology*, *91*, 358–368. doi:10.1037/0022-0663.91.2.358

Morris, P. (1996). Asia's Four Little Tigers: a comparison of the role of education in their development. *Comparative Education*, *32*(1), 95–109. doi:10.1080/03050069628948

Morrison, D., & Collins, A. (1996). Epistemic fluency and constructivist learning environments. In B.G. Wilson (Ed.), Constructivist learning environments: Case studies in instructional design (pp. 107 - 119). Englewood Cliffs, NJ: Educational Technology Publications.

Morrison, K. (1998). Management Theories For Educational Change. Thousand Oaks, CA: Sage Publications.

Morris-Suzuki, T., & Rimmer, P. J. (2003). Cyberculture, society, and education in Japan. In J. M. Bachnik (Ed.), Roadblocks on the information highway. Oxford, UK: Lexington Books.

Mukerji, S., & Tripathi, P. (2004). Academic Program Life Cycle: A Redefined Approach to Understanding Market Demands. *Journal of Distance Education, 19*(2), 14-27. Retrieved from http://www.jofde.ca/index.php/jde/article/view/97/76

Mukerji, S., & Tripathi, P. (2005). Quality of life of labour: a collaborative ODL approach towards humanising the society. In *ICDE International Conference*, November 19-23, New Delhi.

Mukerji, S., & Tripathi, P. (2009). *Editorial: Cases on Technological Adaptability and Transnational Learning: Issues & Challenges*, Riyadh. Retrieved from http://www.igi-global.com/requests/details.asp?ID=588

Munro-Smith, N. (2002). *A tale of two cities: Computer mediated teaching and learning in Melbourne and Singapore*. Paper presented at the 19th ASCILITE Conference, Auckland, New Zealand. Retrieved July 1, 2007 from http://www.ascilite.org.au/conferences/auckland02/proceedings/papers/105.pdf

Murphy, D., Walker, R., & Webb, G. (2001). Online learning and teaching with technology: Case studies, experience and practice. London: Kogan Page.

Natriello, G. (2001). Bridging the second digital divide: What can sociologists of education contribute? *Sociology of Education*, *74*, 260–265. doi:10.2307/2673278

NBEET. (2003). Australian Graduate Studies and Higher Degrees. (Report). Canberra: National Board of Employment, Education and Training - Higher Education Council.

Nduba, S., & Kinyu, M. (2003). *Consultative Meeting on Continuing Medical Education and the role of Information and Communication Technologies in Kenya*, AMREF International Training Centre. Retrieved May 30, 2009 from http://www.healthcomms.org/pdf/CME-ICTs-Kenya--report.pdf

Negroponte, N. (1995). Being Digital. Rydalmere, Australia: Hodder & Stoughton.

Nekongo-Nielsen, H. (2006, October/November). *The contributions of open and distance learning to national development in Namibia*. Paper Presented at the Fourth Pan-Commonwealth Forum on Open Learning held at Ocho Rios, Jamaica.

Nel, J. (1992). The Empowerment of Minority Students: Implications of Cummins. *Action in Teacher Education, 14*(3), 38–45.

Netto, A. (2009). *IT Literacy High on Government Priority List in Malaysia*. Retrieved March 1, 2009. from http://www.unesco.org/education/efa/know_sharing/grassroots_stories/malaysia.shtml

New Century Learning Consortium (NCLC). (2009). Retrieved May 4, 2009 from http://nclc-online.ning.com

New Hungary Development Plan. (n.d.). Retrieved March 10, 2009 from www.nfu.hu/doc/125

New York Times. (2009, June 4). Obama's Speech in Cairo. *New York Times*. Retrieved June 4, 2009, from http://www.nytimes.com/2009/06/04/us/politics/04obama.text.html?pagewanted=7

Newton, D., & Ellis, A. (2005). Effective Implementation of E-Learning: A Case Study of the Australian Army. *Journal of Workplace Learning, 17*(5/6), 385–397. doi:10.1108/13665620510606797

Nickerson, R. (1987). Why teach thinking? In J. B. Baron, and R. J. Sternberg (Eds.), Teaching thinking skills: Theory and Practice (pp. 27-37). New York: W. H. Freeman.

Nielsen, J. (1989). The matters that really matter for hypertext usability. Paper presented at the Hypertext '89' Second ACM Conference on Hypertext, Pittsburgh, PA.

Nielsen, J. (1995). Multimedia and hypertext: The internet and beyond. Cambridge, MA: Cambridge Academic Press.

Nonneman, W., & Vanhoudt, P. (1996). A further augmentation of the Solow model and the empirics of economic growth for OECD countries. *The Quarterly Journal of Economics, 111*(3), 943–953. doi:10.2307/2946677

Northcote, M. (2008). Sense of place in online learning environments. In *Hello! Where are you in the landscape of educational technology? Proceedings ascilite Melbourne 2008*. Retrieved from http://www.ascilite.org.au/conferences/melbourne08/procs/northcote.pdf

Northrup, P. T. (2002). Online learners' preferences for interaction. *The Quarterly Review of Distance Education, 3*(2), 219–226.

Novack, J. D., & Gowin, D. B. (1988). Learning how to learn. Cambridge, UK: Cambridge University Press.

Ntiro, S., & Mrema, J. (2003). *Information and Communication Technologies and Continuing Medical Education in East and Southern Africa*. Report of a Conference held in Moshi, Tanzania 8-10 April 2003.

O'Neill, E. J. (2007). Implementing International Virtual Elementary Classroom Activities for Public Schools Students in the U.S. and Korea. *Electronic Journal e-Learning, 5*(3), 207-218.

O'Neill, E. J. (2008). *Intercultural Competence Development: Implementing International Virtual Elementary Classroom Activities for Public Schools Students in the U.S. and Korea*. Doctoral dissertation, University of Virginia.

O'Reilly, T. (2005). *What Is Web 2.0. Design Patterns and Business Models for the Next Generation of Software*. Retrieved Dec 30, 2007, from http://www.oreillynet.com/pub/a/oreilly/tim/news/2005/09/30/what-is-web-20.html

Oakley, B. (2004). The value of online learning: Perspectives from the University of Illinois at Springfield. In J. C. Moore (Ed.), Elements of quality online education: Into the mainstream. Needham, MA: Sloan Consortium.

Oliver, R., & McLoughlin, C. (1997). Interactions in audio-graphics and learning environments. *American Journal of Distance Education, 11*(1), 34–54. doi:10.1080/08923649709526950

Olson, T. M., & Wisher, R. A. (2002). The Effectiveness of Web-Based Instruction: An Initial Inquiry. *International Review of Research in Open and Distance Learning, 3*(3).

Olugebenga Ojo, D., & Kayode Olakulehin, F. (2006). Attitudes and perceptions of students to open and distance learning in Nigeria. *International Review of Research in Open and Distance Learning, 7*(1), 1492–3831.

Ordoñez, A. (2006). *India abrira un centro de entratenimiento informatico (India will open an ICT training center).* El Periodico: Guatemala, September 30, 2006. Retrieved at http://www.itforcegt.org/ photos3.php

Organization of American States (OAS). (2006). Foreign ministers vow to strive so everyone in the Americas can benefit from the knowledge-based society. *Website, OAS General Assembly, 36th Regular Session, Santo Domingo, June 2006.* Retrieved November 12, 2007, at http://www.oas.org/36ag/english/

Ossimitz, G. (2009). *System Dynamics.* Retrieved from http://wwwu.uni-klu.ac.at/gossimit/pap.php?uk=6

Oxenham, J. (1980). Teaching development at graduate level in Britain. *IDS Bulletin, 11*(3).

Pace, C. R. (1990). The undergraduates: a report of their activities and progress in college in the 1980's. Los Angeles: Center for the Study of Evaluation, University of California, Los Angeles.

Palloff, R. M., & Pratt, K. (2002). Beyond the Looking Glass: What Faculty and Students Need to Be Successful Online. In K. E. Rudestam & J. Schoenholtz-Read (Eds.), Handbook of Online Learning: Innovations in Higher Education and Corporate Training (pp. 171-184). Thousand Oaks, CA: Sage.

Palloff, R. M., & Pratt, K. (2003). The Virtual student: A profile and guide to working with online learners. San Francisco, CA: Jossey-Bass.

Papenhausen, C. (2009). A cyclical model of institutional change. *Foresight, 11*(3), 4–13. doi:10.1108/14636680910963909

Park, N., & O'Neill, E. J. (2009). *Adapting to Cultural Diversity: Policy to Promote Intercultural Education Policy in Korea.* Paper presented at 2009 World Civic Forum, Seoul, Korea.

Pauli, D. (2007). Upskill on the Go [Macquarie University]. *Computerworld, 29*, 32–34.

Perraton, H. (2004 (a)). Aims and Purpose. In H. Perraton & H. Lentell (Eds.). Policy for Open and Distance Learning. World review of distance education and open learning (Vol. 4, pp. 9 – 41). London: Routledge Falmer.

Perraton, H. (2004 (b)). Choosing Technologies for Education. In H. Perraton & H. Lentell (Eds.), Policy for Open and Distance Learning. World review of distance education and open learning (Vol. 4, pp. 142 – 150). London: Routledge Falmer.

Peters, O. (2001). Learning and teaching in distance education: Pedagogical Analyses and Interpretations in an International Perspective. Open and Distance Learning Series. London: Kogan page.

Piaget, J. (1955). The Child's Construction of Reality. London: Routledge and Kegan Paul.

Picciano, A. G. (2006). Blended Learning: Implications for Growth and Access. *Journal of Asynchronous Learning Networks, 10*(3), 1–14.

Piña, A. A., & Scheinbuks, J. (2007). *Creating a culture of technology through inter-institutional online teaching partnerships.* Paper presented at the Association for Educational Communications & Technology, Anaheim, CA.

Piña, A. A., & Scheinbuks, J. (2008). *An e-learning partnership between racially and culturally different institutions.* Paper presented at the Technology in Education (TechEd) Conference, Ontario, CA.

Piña, A. A., & Scheinbuks, J. (2008). *Case studies of e-learning partnerships between racially & culturally diverse universities.* Paper presented at the Association for Educational Communications & Technology, Orlando, FL.

Piña, A. A., McCurdy, S., & Scheinbuks, J. (2007). *Building virtual bridges: Implementation of a collaborative online teaching partnership.* Paper presented at the Technology in Education (TechEd) Conference, Ontario, CA.

Piña, A. A., Sadowski, K. P., Scheidenhelm, C. L., & Heydenburg, P. R. (2008). SLATE: A community of practice for supporting learning and technology in education. *International Journal of Instructional Technology and Distance Learning, 5*(7).

Pivec, M., Koubek, A., & Dondi, C. (2004). Guidelines for Game-Based Learning. Lengerich, Germany: Pabst Science Publishers.

Plaas, J. L., & Jones, L. C. (2005). Multimedia learning in second language acquisition. In R. E. Mayer, (Ed.), The Cambridge Handbook Of Multimedia Learning. Cambridge, UK: CUP.

Polak, F. (1973). The Image of the Future. New York: Elsevier Scientific Publishing.

Popke, E. J. (2003). Poststructuralist ethics: subjectivity, responsibility and the space of community. *Progress in Human Geography, 27*(3), 298–316. doi:10.1191/0309132503ph429oa

Posnett, N. W., & Baulkwill, W. J. (1982). Working with Non-Conventional Literature. *Journal of Information Science, 5*(4), 121–130. doi:10.1177/016555158200500402

Pratt, D. D. (1992). Chinese conceptions of learning and teaching: A Westerner's attempt at understanding. *International Journal of Lifelong Education, 11*, 301–319. doi:10.1080/0260137920110404

Pratt, M. (1991). Arts of the Contact Zone. [New York: Modern Language Association.]. *Profession, 91*, 33–40.

Preece, J., Rogers, Y., & Sharp, H. (2002) Interaction Design Beyond Human-Computer Interaction, (pp. 105-137). Hoboken, NJ: Wiley.

Prensky, M. (2001). Digital Game-Based Learning. New York: McGraw-Hill.

Prosser, M., & Barrie, S. C. (Eds.). (2003). Using a Student-Focused Learning Perspective to Strategically Align Academic Development with Institutional Quality Assurance. Buckingham, UK: Open University Press.

Rainie, L., & Keeter, S. (2006). How Americans use their cell phones, Washington, DC: The Pew Research Center.

Rainie, L., & Madden, M. (2005). Podcasting catches on. Washington, DC: Pew Research Center.

Ramos, J. (2006). Consciousness, culture and the communication of foresight. *Futures, 38*, 1119–1124. doi:10.1016/j.futures.2006.02.015

Ramsden, P. (1991). A Performance Indicator of Teaching Quality in Higher Education: The Course Experience Questionnaire. *Studies in Higher Education, 16*, 129–150. doi:10.1080/03075079112331382944

Ramsden, P. (2003). Learning to Teach in Higher Education. London: Routledge.

Randolph, K. A., & Krause, D. J. (2002). Mutual aid in the classroom: an instructional technology application. *Journal of Social Work Education, 38*(2), 259–272.

Raskin, P., Banuri, T., Gallopín, G., Gutman, P., Hammond, A., Kates, R., & Swart, R. (2002). *The Great Transition. The Promise and Lure of the Times Ahead.* Stockholm Environmental Institute, Global Scenario Group. See http://www.tellus.org/seib/publications/Great_Transitions.pdf or http://www.sei.se

Rauch, H., & Strigl, A. (2005). *Die Wende der Titanic. Wiener Deklaration für eine zukunftsfähige Weltordnung.* [The Turn of the Titanic. Vienna Declaration of a Sustainable World Order.], Munich, Germany: oekom verlag. Retrieved from http://www.oekom.de/buecher/buchprogramm/

Reddy, V., & Manjulika, S. (1995). The Practice of Distance Education in Single and Dual Mode Institutions in India: Issues of Convergence and Integration. In Asian Association of Open Universities (Ed.), *Proceedings of the Asian Association of Open Universities IXth. Annual Conference. Globalized and Cooperative Distance Learning:* The National Open University, Taiwan, R.O.C.

Reding, V. (2003). *Student Approaches to Learning and Studying in Australia.* Paper presented at the Proceedings of the Learning Forum, Karlsruha.

Reimers, F. (2006, September). Citizenship, Identity and Education: Examining the public purposes of schools in an age of globalization. *Prospects, 36*(3).

Renard, G. (2003). The Disappearance of the Universe. Fearless Books.

Renwick, W. (992). Distance Education in Dual Mode Universities. In I. Mugridge (Ed.), *Perspectives on Distance Education – Distance Education in Single and Dual Mode Universities.* Papers presented to a Symposium on Reforms in Higher Education in New Delhi, India, (pp. 141 - 152). Vancouver: The Commonwealth of Learning.

Rice, R. E., & Gattiker, V. E. (2001). New media and organizational structuring. In F. Jablin & L. Putman (Eds.), The new handbook of organizational communication: Advances in theory, research, and methods (pp. 544-581). Thousand Oaks, CA: Sage.

Robbins, D. (2007). Sociology as reflective science - On Bourdieu's Project. *Theory, Culture & Society, 24*(5), 77–98. doi:10.1177/0263276407081284

Robinson, B. (2004). Governance, accreditation and quality assurance in open and distance education. In H. Perraton & H. Lentell (Eds.), Policy for Open and Distance Learning. World review of distance education and open learning (Vol. 4, pp. 181 – 206). London: Routledge Falmer.

Robinson, G., Dobson, M. & Sewell, J. (1999). Using C&IT for Continuing Medical Education in Africa - a pilot project in Zimbabwe. *Journal of Medical Internet Research,* Jul–Sep; 1(suppl1): e67.

Robinson, R. (1953). Plato's Earlier Dialectic. Oxford, UK: Clarendon Press.

Robson, J. (2002). Evaluating on-Line Teaching. *Open Learning, 15*(2).

Rogers, E. (2003). Diffusion of innovations, (5 ed.). New York: The Free Press.

Rojas, J. I., Prats, X., Montlaur, A., & Garcia-Berro, E. (2008). Model Rocket Workshop: a Problem-Based Learning experience for engineering students. *International Journal of Emerging Technologies in Learning, 3*(4), 70–77.

Romo-Rodriguez, G. (2005). Information and communication technologies and non-governmental organizations: Lessons learnt from networking in Mexico. *The Electronic Journal of Information Systems in Developing Countries, 21*(3), 1–29.

Roper, L., & Pettit, J. (2002). Development and the learning organisation: an introduction. *Development in Practice, 12*(3/4), 258–271. doi:10.1080/0961450220149654

Rosenberg, M. J. (2001). E-Learning - Strategies for Delivering Knowledge in the Digital Age. New York: McGraw-Hill.

Rosenzweig, M. R. (1990). Population growth and human capital investments: Theory and evidence. *The Journal of Political Economy, 98*(S5), 38–71. doi:10.1086/261724

Ross, C. J., & Klug, M. (1999). Attitudes of business college faculty and administrators toward distance education: A national survey. *Distance Education, 20*(1), 109–128. doi:10.1080/0158791990200109

Roth, W.-M., Lawless, D. V., & Masciotra, D. (2001). Spielraum and Teaching. *Curriculum Inquiry, 31*(2), 183–207. doi:10.1111/0362-6784.00191

Rovai, A. P., Wighting, M. J., Baker, J. D., & Grooms, L. D. (2009). Development of an instrument to measure perceived cognitive, affective, and psychomotor learning in traditional and virtual classroom higher education settings. *The Internet and Higher Education, 12*, 7–13. doi:10.1016/j.iheduc.2008.10.002

Rowe-Whyte, A., O'Sullivan, P., & Hunt, S. (2002). Immediacy on the web: Narrowing the digital divide. Department of Communication, Illinois State University, Normal, Illinois. Retrieved from EBSCO Host Database.

Rumble, G., & Latchem, C. (2004). Organisational models for open and distance learning. In H. Perraton & H. Lentell (Eds.), Policy for Open and Distance Learning. World review of distance education and open learning, (Vol. 4, pp. 117 – 140). London: Routledge Falmer.

Russell, C., Gregory, D., Care, W., & Hultin, D. (2007). Recognizing and avoiding intercultural miscommunication in distance education. *Journal of Professional Nursing, 23*, 351–361. doi:10.1016/j.profnurs.2007.01.021

Russell, T. L. (2002). The No Significant Difference Phenomenon as Reported in 355 Research Reports, Summaries and Papers: A Comparative Research Annotated Bibliography on Technology for Distance Education [Updated from 1999]. NC, USA: North Carolina State University: Office of Instructional Telecommunications.

Rutherford, J., Gillespie, A., & Richardson, R. (2004). The territoriality of pan-European telecommunications backbone networks. *Journal of Urban Technology*, 11(3): 1–34. doi:10.1080/10630730500064166

Sabatini, F. (2007). *Social capital gateway: resources for the study of social capital, website.* Retrieved at http://www.socialcapitalgateway.org/NV-eng-education.htm

Sahu, C. (2008). An evaluation of selected pedagogical attributes of online discussion boards. In *Hello! Where are you in the landscape of educational technology? Proceedings ascilite Melbourne 2008.* Retrieved from http://www.ascilite.org.au/conferences/melbourne08/procs/sahu.pdf

Salawu, O. & Ogunsola – Bandele, M. (2005). *Reminiscences on the Practice of Open and Distance Learning in Nigeria: Lessons for the Future.* Supplementary Paper Presented at the 11th. Cambridge International Conference on Open and Distance Learning, 22 – 23 September, 2005.

Salmon, G. (2004). *All things in Moderation.* Upper Saddle River, NJ: Prentice Hall. Retrieved March 18, 2005, from http://www.e-tivities.com

Salomon, G., & Globerson, T. (1987). Skills may not be enough: The role of mindfulness in learning and teaching. *International Journal of Educational Research, 11*(6), 623–627. doi:10.1016/0883-0355(87)90006-1

Salomon, G., & Perkins, D. (1989). Rocky road to transfer: Rethinking mechanisms of a neglected phenomenon. *Educational Psychologist, 24*(2), 113–142. doi:10.1207/s15326985ep2402_1

Samuels, M. (2005, March 3). MPs identify where UKeU went wrong. In Computing, VNU Business Publications, (pp. 1, 4-5, 28).

Sander, U., & Vollbrecht, R. (2000). Jugend im 20. Jahrhundert. München, Germany: Reinhardt.

Saviotti, P. P. (2007). *Diversity, efficiency and economic development & Variety, structural change and economic development.* Two lectures at the Graz Schumpeter School. Retrieved from http://www.uni-graz.at/schumpeter.centre/summerschool.php

Sawyer, K. (2006). The Cambridge Handbook Of The Learning Sciences. Cambridge, UK: CUP

Scheinbuks, J., & Piña, A. A. (2009). *An e-learning instructional partnership between culturally diverse minority institutions.* Paper presented at the Technology in Education (TechEd) Conference, Ontario, CA.

Scheinbuks, J., Schroeder, R., McCurdy, S., & Piña, A. A. (2006). *Online teaching partnerships.* Paper presented at the Supporting Learning and Technology in Education (SLATE) Conference. Chicago, IL.

Schilb, J. (1996). Between the lines: Relating composition theory and literary theory. Portsmouth, NH: Boynton/Cook.

Schneemann, C. (1976). *Up to and including her limits.*

Schön, D. A. (1983). The Reflective Practitioner - How Professionals Think in Action. Aldershot, UK: BasiAshgate ARENA.

Schön, D. A. (1986). Leadership as Reflection-in-Action. In T.J. Sergiovanni, J.E. Corbally. Leadership and Organizational Culture: New Perspectives on Administrative Theory and Practice, (pp. 59). Chicago: University of Illinois Press.

Schroeder, R., & McCurdy, S. (2005). *Inter-institutional class collaborations online*. Paper presented at the Midwest EDUCAUSE Conference, Chicago, IL.

Schuler, D. (1996). New community networks: Wired for change. New York: ACM Press.

Schumpeter, J. A. (1949). The theory of economic development. Cambridge, MA: Harvard Univ. Press.

Schunk, D. H. (2004). Learning Theories: An Educational Perspective. Upper Saddle River, NJ: Pearson Prentice Hall.

Second Life Web site. (2008). Retrieved August 24, 2008, from http://secondlife.com/

Selfe, C., & Meyer, P. (1991). Testing claims for online conferences. *Written Communication, 8*(2), 163–192. doi:10.1177/0741088391008002002

Shea, P. (2007). Bridges and barriers to teaching online college courses: A study of experienced faculty in thirty-six colleges. *Sloan-Consortium, 11*(2), 73–128.

Shneiderman, B., & Plaisant, C. (2005). Designing for the User Interface, (4th Ed., pp. 580- 601). Boston: Addison Wesley.

Short, G. (1995). Understanding domain knowledge for teaching: Higher-order thinking in pre-service art teacher specialist. *Studies in Art Education, 36*(3), 154–169. doi:10.2307/1320906

Shostak, A. B. (2004). High Schools for Futurism: Nurturing the next generation. *The Futurist*, (November-December): 23–27.

Siaciwena, R. (2006, October/November). *Challenges of a dual mode institution: The case of the University of Zambia (UNZA).* Paper Presented at the Fourth Pan-Commonwealth Forum on Open Learning held at Ocho Rios, Jamaica.

Sife, A.S.; Lwoga, E.T. & Sanga, C. (2007). New technologies for teaching and learning: Challenges for higher learning institutions in developing countries. *International Journal of Education and Development using ICT, 3*(2).

Simonson, M., Smaldino, S., Albright, M., & Zvacek, S. (2000). Teaching and Learning at a Distance – Foundations of Distance Education. Upper Saddle River, NJ: Prentice Hall, Inc.

Sinclair, R. (2003). Components of quality distance education – Distance education guidelines from different countries. In G. Davies & E. Stacey (Eds.), Quality Education @ A Distance, (pp. 257–264). Boston: Kluwer Academic Publishers.

Slaughter, R. A. (1996). The Knowledge Base of Futures Studies. Victoria, Australia: DDM Media Group.

Slaughter, R. A. (2005). Futures Thinking for Social Foresight. Taiwan: Tamkang University Press.

Sloan Consortium. (2009). *2007 Sloan-C excellence in online teaching and learning awards*. Retrieved May 12, 2009 from http://www.sloan-c.org/aboutus/awards.asp

Smith, R. G. (2003). World city topologies. *Progress in Human Geography, 27*(5), 561–582. doi:10.1191/0309132503ph447oa

Songini, M. L. (2000, November 1). Halloween Less Haunting for Hershey This Year. *Computer World.*

Soukup, C. (2006). Computer-mediated communication as a virtual third place: Building Oldenburg's great good places on the world wide web. *New Media & Society, 8*(3), 421–440. doi:10.1177/1461444806061953

Spiro, R. J., Feltovitch, P. J., Jacobson, M. J., & Coulson, R. L. (1991). Cognitive flexibility, constructivism, and hypertext: Random access instruction for advanced knowledge acquisition in ill-structured domains. *Educational Technology, 31*(5), 24–33.

Srisa-An, W. (2006). Making Distance Education Borderless. In S. Garg, A. R. Khan, A. K. Aggarwal, U. Kanjilal & S. Panda (Eds.), Open and Flexible Learning – Issues and Challenges – Prof. G. Ram Reddy Memorial Lecturers, (pp. 15 – 28). New Delhi: Viva Books Private Limited.

St Hill, R. (2000). *Modal Preference in a Teaching Strategy.* Paper presented at the Paper presented at the Effective Teaching and Learning at University Conference, Brisbane, QLD.

Stacey, E., & Rice, M. (2002). Evaluating an Online Learning Environment. *Australian Journal of Educational Technology, 18*, 323–340.

Stähli, F. (1998). Ingenieurethik an Fachhochschulen [Ethics for Engineers at Universities of Applied Science]. Fortis FH, Verlag Sauerländer AG, Aarau.

Stähli, F. (2005). *Warum muss Technik ein Gegenstand der Ethik sein?* [Why must technology be an object of ethics?]. Aarau. Retrieved from http://web.fhnw.ch/personenseiten/fridolin.staehli/_html/publ.html

Stalder, F. (2000). The Network Paradigm: Social Formations in the Age of Information. *The Information Society, 14*(1). Retrieved from http://www.indiana.edu:80/~tisj/readers/full-text/14-4%20Stalder.html

State Board of Education. (2003). Educational Technology Plan for Virginia: 2003-2009. Virginia Department of Education.

Statistical Handbook of Japan. (2007). Retrieved 25 April 2009 from http://www.stat.go.jp/english/data/handbook/c02cont.htm

Steen, H. L. (2008). Effective elearning design. *Journal of Online Learning and Teaching, 4*(4), 526–532.

Sterman, J. D. (2000). Business Dynamics. System Thinking and Modeling for a Complex World. Boston: McGraw-Hill.

Stevens-Long, J., & Crowell, C. (2002). The Design and Delivery of Interactive Online Graduate Education. In K. E. Rudestam & J. Schoenholtz-Read (Eds.), Handbook of Online Learning: Innovations in Higher Education and Corporate Training (pp. 151-169). Thousand Oaks, CA: Sage.

Stevenson, T., & Simpson, L. (1993). Creating Futures among uncommon cultures: A Methodology for Exploiting the Chaos to find new Coherence. In M. Mannermaa, S. Inayatullah & R. A. Slaughter (Eds.), *Coherence and chaos in our uncommon futures - Visions, means, actions, Selections from the XIII World Conference of the World Futures Studies Federation*, Turku, Finland, (pp. 319-328).

Stewart, B. L., Norwood, M., Ezell, S., & Waight, C. (2006). Case Study: Collaborative Creation of an on-Line Degree Program. *Innovations in Education and Teaching International, 43*(3), 197–211. doi:10.1080/14703290600618399

Stoekel, A., & Quirke, D. (1992). Services: Setting the Agenda for Reform. Canberra, Australia: Department of Industry, Technology and Commerce, Australian Government Publishing Service.

Stokey, N. L. (1991). Human capital, product quality, and growth. *The Quarterly Journal of Economics, 106*(2), 587–616. doi:10.2307/2937948

Stout, C. J. (1995). Critical conversation about art: A description of higher order thinking skills generated through the study of art criticism. *Studies in Art Education, 36*(3), 170–188. doi:10.2307/1320907

Strang, K. D. (2007, 14-16 February). *Building Quality and Interaction into Elearning: Applying Andragogy Theory to Synchronous and Asynchronous Online Course Design.* Paper presented at the Innovation, Education, Technology, and You: Online Conference for Teaching & Learning, Chicago.

Strang, K. D. (2008). Quantitative Online Student Profiling to Forecast Academic Outcome from Learning Styles Using Dendrogram Decision. *Multicultural Education & Technology Journal*, *2*(4), 215–244. doi:10.1108/17504970810911043

Strang, K. D. (2009). Using Recursive Regression to Explore Nonlinear Relationships and Interactions: A Tutorial Applied to a Multicultural Education Study. *Practical Assessment. Research Evaluation*, *14*(3), 1–13.

Street, B. V. (1995). Social literacies: Critical approaches to literacy in development, ethnography and education. London: Longman.

Strobl, J. (2001). *Information Spaces – Individualized Information in Context.* GIS and Remote Sensing Conference in Sopron, Hungary, 6-8 September 2001, http://www.geo.info.hu/sat/presentations/InfoSpaces_Sopron_elemei/frame.htm

Strobl, J. (2004). GIScience Education for Professionals – the UNIGIS Distance Learning Model. *Geospatial Today, 6*/2004.

Strobl, J. (2006). Regional Energy Potentials: Spatial Optimization of Renewable Resources. In *26th Annual ESRI User Conference, Track Ecology and Conservation.* Retrieved from http://proceedings.esri.com/library/userconf/proc06/papers/abstracts/a1818.html

Strobl, J. (2007). Geographic Learning. *Geoconnexion*, *6*(5-6), 42–43.

Strobl, J. (2007). Geographic Learning in Social Web Environments. In S. Catling & L. Taylor (eds.), Changing Geographies: Innovative Curricula, (pp. 327-332). Oxford, UK: IGU Commission for Geographical Education and Oxford Brookes University.

Strobl, J. (2008). Digital Earth Brainware. A Framework for Education and Qualification Requirements. In J. Schiewe, U. Michel, (Eds.), Geoinformatics paves the Highway to Digital Earth, (pp. 134-138). Osnabrück, Germany: Universität Osnabrück.

Strobl, J., & Car, A. (2009). Continuing Professional Education via Distance Learning: Success Factors and Challenges. In *FIG International Workshop on Professional Education 2009*, Vienna, 26-28 February 2009. Retrieved from http://www.fig.net/commission2/vienna_2009_proc/ppt/02_car_et_al_ppt.pdf

Strobl, J., & Lindner-Fally, M. (2007). *Global Learning - Pedagogical Concepts involving Virtual Globes.* Presentation at the conference "Geography for Society: Putting Bologna into Action", http://www.herodot.net/conferences/stockholm/esri/Lindner-Fally_Strobl(paper).pdf

Sukati, C. W. S., & Chandraiah, E. (2004). Effectiveness of Face-To-Face Sessions for Course Delivery at IDE, UNISWA. *Staff and Educational Development International*, *8*(2 & 3), 129–141.

Sukati, C. W. S., Chandraiah, E., Simelane, H. S., Sithole, M. M., & Magagula, C. M. (2008). Comparative Analysis of the Academic Achievement of a Cohort of B.A. (Hums) Students Studying Full-Time and Those Studying by Distance Learning Mode. Unpublished Final Report Prepared for the UNISWA Research Centre.

Sussman, B. (2007). *Teachers, college students lead a Second Life.* Accessed and downloaded from http://www.usatoday.com/news/education/2007-08-01-second-life_N.htm on June 13, 2009.

Sutherland, P. (1992). Vygotsky and Vygotskyans. In Cognitive development today: Piaget and his critics, (pp. 45-46). London: Paul Chapman.

Sveiby, K. E. (2001). A Knowledge-Based Theory of the Firm to Guide in Strategy Formulation. *Journal of Intellectual Capital*, *2*(4), 344–358. doi:10.1108/14691930110409651

Swain, M., & Lapkin, S. (1995). Problems in output and the cognitive processes they generate: a step towards second language learning. *Applied Linguistics*, *16*, 371–391. doi:10.1093/applin/16.3.371

Swan, K. (2001). Virtual interaction: Design factors affecting student satisfaction and perceived learning in asynchronous online courses. *Distance Education*, *22*(2), 306–331. doi:10.1080/0158791010220208

Sweller, J. (1988). Cognitive load during problem solving: Effects on learning. *Cognitive Science, 12*, 257–285.

Tabatabai, D., & Shore, B. M. (2005). How experts and novices search the web. *Library & Information Science Research, 27*, 222–248. doi:10.1016/j.lisr.2005.01.005

Tait, A., & Mills, R. (1999). The Convergence of Distance and Conventional Education. In A. Tait & R. Mills (Eds.), The Convergence of Distance and Conventional Education: Patterns of flexibility for the individual learner, (pp. 1 – 4). London: Routledge.

Tau, O. (2006, October/November). *Structure and Process in Dual-Mode Institution: Implications for Development.* Paper Presented at the Fourth Pan-Commonwealth Forum on Open Learning held at Ocho Rios, Jamaica.

Taylor, (2000). Madonna and hypertext: Liberatory learning in art education. *Studies in Art Education, 41*(4), 376-389.

Taylor, P. (2007). Space and sustainability: an exploratory essay on the production of social spaces through city-work. *The Geographical Journal, 173*(3), 197–206. doi:10.1111/j.1475-4959.2007.00241.x

Taylor, P. G., & Carpenter, B. S. (2002). Inventively linking: Teaching and learning with computer hypertext. *Art Education, 55*(4), 6–12. doi:10.2307/3193962

Teach-nology Web site. (2006). Retrieved April 24, 2006, from www.teach-nology.com/glossary/terms/b/

Tellis, W. (1997). Introduction to Case Study. *Qualitative Report, 3*(2).

The European Pedagogical ICT Licence. (n.d.). Retrieved June 20, 2009 from www.epict.org

Tisdall, C. (1979). Joseph Beuys. London: Thames and Hudson.

Tisdall, C. (1990). Beuys in America, or the energy plan for the western man. In C. Kuoni (Ed.), Energy plan for the western man/Joseph Beuys in America: Writings by and interviews with the artist (pp. 7-18). New York: Four Walls Eight Windows.

Towndrow, P. A. (2007). Task design, implementation and assessment: Integrating information and communication technology in English language teaching and learning. Singapore: McGraw-Hill.

Traxler, J. (2007). Defining, Discussing, and Evaluating Mobile Learning: The moving finger writes and having writ... *International Review of Research in Open and Distance Learning, 8*(2), Traxler, J., & Leach, J. (2006). Innovative and Sustainable Mobile Learning in Africa. Paper presented at the Fourth IEEE International Workshop on Wireless, Mobile and Ubiquitous Technology in Education (ICHIT'06).

Tripathi, P., & Mukerji, S. (2008). *Access and Equity to Education in India through Synergy of Conventional and ODL Systems: A Step towards Democratization of Education.* IGNOU. Retrieved from http://www.distanceetdroitaleducation.org/contents/OP2008-IGNOU.pdf

Tröhler, M. (2007). Leeway for wits and sense [Spielraum für Sinne und Sinn]. *Du: Zeitschrift Der Kultur, 778*, 45-61. Retrieved from http://www.du-magazin.com/

Trucano, M. (2005). *Knowledge Maps: ICT in Education.* Washington, DC: *info*Dev/ World Bank. Retrieved at http://www.infodev.org/en/ Publication.8.html

Tylee, J. (2001). *Cultural issues and the online environment.* Retrieved July 1, 2007, from http://www.csu.edu.au/division/landt/resources/documents/cultural_issues.pdf

U.S. News & World Report. (2005). Choosing a school: Campus diversity. *America's Best Colleges.* New Hudson, MI: U.S. News & World Report.

Ullman, C., & Rabinowitz, M. (2004, October). Course management systems and the reinvention of instruction. *THE Journal.* Retrieved from http://www.thejournal.com/articles/17014

Umpleby, S. (2007). Management Cybernetics: Tutorial on 5 DVDs. *The 11th World Multi-Conference on Systemics, Cybernetics and Informatics, July 8-11, Orlando, Florida*, organized by the International Institute of Informatics and Systemics (IIIS).

UNESCO. (1993). World Education Report, Paris: UNESCO Publishing.

UNESCO. (2002). Open and Distance Learning: Trends, Policy and Strategy Considerations. Paris: UNESCO

UNESCO. (2004). Global [*Comparing Education Statistics Across the World*. Montreal: UNESCO Institute of Statistics.]. *Education Digest*, 2004.

UNESCO. (2006). Guideline on International Education. Paris: UNESCO Headquarters.

UNESCO. (2006). *Expert Meeting on Intercultural Education*. Paris: UNESCO Headquarters.

UNESCO. (2007). *ICT in education: Japan*. Retrieved 25 August 2007 from http://www.unescobkk.org/index.php?id=1381

UniGIS. (2009). UNIGIS International Association. *Curricula*, Retrieved from http://www.unigis.net/

UniNet. (2009). *Eurasia-Pacific UNINET*. Retrieved from http://www.eurasiapacific.net/

United National Global Alliance for ICT and Development. (2009). *Our Mission*. Retrieved June 3, 2009, from http://www.un-gaid.org/About/OurMission/tabid/893/language/en-US/Default.aspx

United Nations Educational, Scientific and Cultural Organization (UNESCO). (2002). *Open and distance learning: Trends, policy and strategy considerations*. Retrieved March 1, 2009, from http://unesdoc.unesco.org/images/0012/001284/128463e.pdf

United Nations Educational, Scientific and Cultural Organization (UNESCO). (2008). *Latin American and Caribbean ministers approved new plan of action for the information society 11-03-2008 (San Salvador)*. Communication and Information Resources, website. Retrieved at http://portal.unesco.org/ci/en/ev.php-URL_ID= 26186&URL_DO=DO_ TOPIC&URL_SECTION=201.html

United Nations. (1965). *Declaration on the Promotion among Youth of the Ideals of Peace, Mutual Respect and Understanding between Peoples*. Retrieved April 22, 2007, from http://www.unhchr.ch/html/menu3/b/65.htm

United Nations. (2006, November). *Alliance of Civilizations Report of the High-level Group*. New York: U.S. from http://www.unaoc.org/repository/HLG_Report.pdf

United Nations. (2007, September). *UN High Representative for Alliance of Civilizations: Address to the AoC Group of Friends (Ministry Level)*. New York: U.S., ECOSOC Chamber, Retrieved from http://www.unaoc.org/images/articles/hr_final_remarks.pdf

United Nations. (2008, January). *The First Alliance of Civilization Forum, Madrid*. New York: U.S., Alliance of Civilization. Retrieved from http://www.unaoc.org/images/aoc%20forum%20report%20madrid%20complete.pdf

University of Bridgeport. (2009). Accessed and downloaded from http://www.bridgeport.edu/pages/3530.asp on March 28, 2009.

Useem, J., & Useem, R. (1963). Men in the middle of the third culture: The roles of American and non-Western people in cross-cultural administration. *Human Organization*, *22*, 169–179.

Valente, T. W. (1996). Social network thresholds in the diffusion of innovations. *Social Networks*, *18*, 69–89. doi:10.1016/0378-8733(95)00256-1

Vallance, M. (2006). Responsibility without power: reflections of an IT Coordinator in education. Perspectives: policy & practice in Higher Education, 10(4), October, 109-114.

Vallance, M. (2008). Beyond policy: Strategic actions to support ICT integration in Japanese schools. *Australasian Journal of Educational Technology*, *24*(3), 275–293.

Vallance, M. (2008). Using a database application to support reflective practice. Tech Trends: linking research and practice to improve learning, 52(6), Nov/Dec, 69-74

Vallance, M., Vallance, K., & Matsui, M. (2009). Criteria for the implementation of learning technologies. In M. Thomas (Ed.), Handbook of Research on Web 2.0 and Second Language Learning (pp. 1-19). Hershey, PA: IGI Global.

Van Bavel, R., Punie, E., & Tuomi, I. (2007). *IPTSICT-Enabled Changes in Social Capital, in The IPTS Report.* Institute for Prospective Technological Studies (IPTS) of the European Commission, Directorate General, Joint Research Centre. Retrieved at http://www. jrc.es/home/report/english/articles/vol85/ ICT4E856.htm

Van Hook, C. W. (2005). Preparing Teachers for the Diverse Classroom: A Developmental Model of Intercultural Sensitivity. *University of Illinois at Urbana-Champaign: Clearinghouse on Early Education and Parenting (CEEP), Early Childhood and Parenting (ECAP). Collaborative, 22*(6), 67–72.

Vesely, P., Bloom, L., & Sherlock, J. (2007). Key elements of building online community: Comparing faculty and student perceptions. *Journal of Online Learning and Teaching, 3*, 234–246.

Volery, T., & Lord, D. (2000). Critical Success Factors in Online Education. *International Journal of Educational Management, 14*(5), 216–223. doi:10.1108/09513540010344731

Vygotsky, L. (1986). Thought and language. Cambridge, MA: MIT Press.

Wagner-Döbler, R. (1998). Innovationsebben und Innovationsfluten: xxx. In S. Greif, H. Laitko, H. Parthey (eds.), Wissenschaftsforschung: Yearbook 96/97. Marburg, Germany: BdWi-Verlag.

Walker, S. R. (1996). Thinking strategies for interpreting artworks. *Studies in Art Education, 37*(2), 80–91. doi:10.2307/1320509

Wannermacher, K. (2006). Functional Differentiation of Incentives for E-teaching at Universities. In A. Mendez-Vilas, A. Solano Martin, J. Mesa Gonzalez, & J. A. Mesa Gonzalez, (Eds.), *Current Developments in Technology-Assisted Education, Proceedings of the IV International Conference on Multimedia and Information and Communication Technologies in Education (M-ICTE2006)*, University of Seville, Seville, Spain, 22-25 November 2006, (Vol. 1, pp. 72-76).

Warschauer, M. (1996). Motivational aspects of using computers for writing and communication. In M. Warschauer (Ed.), *Telecollaboration in Foreign Language Learning: Proceedings of the Hawaii Symposium: Report #12* (pp. 29-46). Honolulu, HI: University of Hawaii, Second Language Teaching & Curriculum Center.

Warschauer, M. (2007). Laptops & literacy, Learning in the wireless classroom. New York: Teachers College Press.

Warschauer, M., Turbee, L., & Robers, B. (1996). Computer learning networks and student empowerment. *System, 24*(1), 1–14. doi:10.1016/0346-251X(95)00049-P

Webopedia. (2009). Accessed and downloaded from http://www.webopedia.com/TERM/O/object_oriented_programming_OOP.html on March 29, 2009.

Weller, M. (2007). Virtual Learning Environments. New York: Routledge.

Wellman, B., & Wortley, S. (1990). Different strokes from different folks: Community ties and social support. *American Journal of Sociology, 96*(3), 558–588. doi:10.1086/229572

Werner, M. H. (2003). Hans Jonas' Prinzip Verantwortung [H. Jonas' principle of responsibility]. In M. Düwell, K. Steigleder (Eds.), *Bioethik: Eine Einführung* (pp. 41-56). Frankfurt, Germany: Suhrkamp. Retrieved from http://www.micha-h-werner.de/jonas.pdf

White House. (2002, September). Remarks on Implementation of the No Child Left Behind Act of 2001. *Weekly Compilation of Presidential Documents, 38*(36), 1482-1486. Washington, DC: US Government Printing Office, Retrieved from http://www.gpo.gov/fdsys/pkg/WCPD-2002-09-09/html/WCPD-2002-09-09-Pg1482.htm

Whittaker, D. H. (2001). *Crisis and innovation in Japan: a new future through techno-entrepreneurship? MIT.* Japan Program Working Paper 01.02. Retrieved 21 December 2008 from http://dspace.mit.edu/bitstream/handle/1721.1/16566/JP-WP-01-02-52124684.pdf

Wikibook. (2009). *Communication Theory / Network Society.* Retrieved from http://en.wikibooks.org/wiki/Communication_Theory/Network_Society

Wikipedia. (2009). *Education in the People's Republic of China.* Retrieved March 1, 2009 from http://en.wikipedia.org/wiki/Education_in_the_People's_Republic_of_China

Wikipedia. (2009). *Education in Malaysia.* Retrieved March 1, 2009, from http://en.wikipedia.org/wiki/Education_in_Malaysia

Wilkerson, L., & Gijselaers, W. H. (Eds.). (1996). Bringing Problem-Based Learning to Higher Education: Theory and Practice, New Directions for Teaching and Learning, (No. 68). San Francisco: Jossey-Bass.

Williams, D., Coles, L., Richardson, A., Wilson, K., & Tuson, J. (2000). Integrating Information and Communications Technology in Professional Practice: an Analysis of Teachers' Needs Based on a Survey of Primary and Secondary Teachers in Scottish Schools. *Technology, Pedagogy and Education, 9*(2), 167–182. doi:10.1080/14759390000200089

Wilson, B. G., Jonassen, D. H., & Cole, P. (1993). Cognitive approaches to instructional design. In G. M. Piskurich (Ed.), The ASTD Handbook of Instructional Technology (pp. 21.1-21.22). New York: McGraw-Hill.

Wilson, D. C. (1992). A Strategy For Change. New York: Routledge.

Wishart, J. (2000). Students' and teachers' perceptions of motivation and learning through the use in schools of multimedia encyclopedias on CD-ROM. *Journal of Educational Multimedia and Hypermedia, 9*(4), 333–347.

Woolcock, M. (1998). Social capital and economic development: toward a theoretical synthesis and policy framework. *Theory and Society, 27,* 151–208. doi:10.1023/A:1006884930135

Woolcock, M. (2002). *Social capital and development: concepts, evidence and applications.* Power point presentation, Workshop on understanding and building social capital in Croatia, Zagreb, Yugoslavia. Cambridge, MA: World Bank and Harvard University.

Xinhua News. (2008, October 25). ASEM Resolves to Further Promote Interfaith Understanding and Exchanges. In *the news of 7th Asia-Europe Meeting.* Retrieved January 9, 2009 from http://news.xinhuanet.com/english/2008-10/26/content_10252340.htm

Yan, J. (2008). Social technology as a new medium in the classroom. *New England Journal of Higher Education, 22*(4), 27–30.

Yang, Y. C., Newby, T., & Bill, R. (2008). Facilitating interactions through structured web-based bulletin boards: A quasi-experimental study on promoting learners' critical thinking skills. *Computers & Education, 50*(4), 1572–1585. doi:10.1016/j.compedu.2007.04.006

Yang, Y., & Cornelius, L. F. (2004). Students' perceptions towards the quality of online education: A qualitative approach. *Association for Educational Communications and Technology, 27,* 861–877.

Yelland, N., & Masters, J. (2007). Rethinking scaffolding in information age. *Computers & Education, 48,* 362–382. doi:10.1016/j.compedu.2005.01.010

Yi, Y. (2008). Relay writing in an adolescent online community. *Journal of Adolescent & Adult Literacy, 51*(8), 670–680. doi:10.1598/JAAL.51.8.6

Yin, R. K. (2003). Case Study Research: Design and Methods (3rd ed.). London: Sage.

Young, A., & Norgard, C. (2006). Assessing the quality of online courses from the students' perspective. *The Internet and Higher Education*, 107–115. doi:10.1016/j.iheduc.2006.03.001

Zapeta-García, J., Vásquez-González, R., Pérez, F., & Alfonso, L. (1998). Diagnóstico de la realidad educativa de los pueblos indígenas y otros pueblos de Mesoamerica: informe - Guatemala. Guatemala City: Países Bajos/ Fundación Rigoberta Menchú Tum/ UNESCO.

Zhang, D., Zhao, J. L., Zhou, L., & Nunamaker, J. F. (2004). Can E-Learning Replace Classroom Learning? *Communications of the ACM*, *47*(5), 75–79. doi:10.1145/986213.986216

Zimmer, T., Billaud, M., & Geoffroy, D. (2006). A Remote Laboratory for Electrical Engineering Education. *International Journal of Online Engineering*, *2*(3), 1–4.

About the Contributors

Siran Mukerji is Jawahar Lal Nehru scholar for her doctorate in HRD and also has Masters in Distance Education and Public Administration. She has been International Research Fellow of Open University Business School (2009), Open University, UK. She was associated with Arab Open University Saudi Arabia Branch for three years as a faculty member in Business Administration and co edited teaching case books and contributed articles in standard national and international journals and also presented papers in national and international conferences. Her current research interests are Performance management and HRM in open and distance learning institutions. She is a member of review committees of a number of international conferences / journals. In her parent institution IGNOU, India, she is Assistant Director.

Purnendu Tripathi, an International Research Fellow of Open University Business School (2009), Open University, UK, is Ph.D. in Management, with Masters in Distance Education also. He was associated with Arab Open University Saudi Arabia Branch for three years as a faculty member in Business Administration. In his parent institution IGNOU, India, he is Assistant Director. He has co edited teaching case books and contributed articles in standard national and international journals and presented papers in national and international conferences. He is a member of review committees of a number of international conferences and journals. His current research interest is Academic Program Life Cycle (APLC) and Educational Marketing.

* * *

Gilbert Ahamer was born as a physicist (i.e. developer of original world views), later on G. Ahamer has collaborated with several institutions and on various projects in order to see as many sides of as many medals as possible: assessing environmental radioactivity in his home county after the Chernobyl disaster, evaluating the global biomass energy potential of his home planet, computing the air emissions for his city, developing climate protection measures his country's administration, supporting ex-communist countries of Europe to accede to the European Union by better mastering their environmental legislation, promoting a developmental curriculum at his university and e-teaching Technology Assessment to his flock, namely to future engineers who are subjectively convinced to act for a better future. Consequently, *creating suitable sustainable structures* that *enable dialogic learning* and *discursive consensus finding* became the final aim of his mixed experiences.

Elizabeth Beckmann is a Lecturer in the Centre for Educational Development and Academic Methods at the Australian National University. She has an MA from the University of Cambridge, UK, a postgraduate Diploma of Natural Resources and PhD from the University of New England, Australia, and a Graduate Certificate of Higher Education from the Australian National University, where she is working towards a Master of Higher Education. A highly experienced educator, communicator and consultant, Elizabeth has worked in fields as diverse as environmental management, museums studies and public communication, including international education, and is very interested in the opportunities to transcend borders offered by online learning environments.

Wu Bing has been a lecturer with Shanghai TV University for numerous years – serving as the course coordinator and teacher for courses such as management information systems, operating systems, electronic commerce and network security. He also holds an administrative position as the Director of Database Center of Teaching Affairs Department and has been involving in various government and university-funded projects in the area of learning management systems, data mining systems and student enrolment systems. He possessed a Bachelor degree and a Master degree in Computer Application Technologies. At present, he is pursuing a PhD degree at College of Management, The University of Shanghai for Science and Technology. His research interests include information systems, data mining and multi-agent technology.

Lisa Bloom is a professor of education in the Department of Human Services at Western Carolina University. She has been teaching online classes approximately 10 years. Her research interests include constructivist approaches to teaching and learning, classroom management, and creativity. She recently published a textbook, *Classroom Management: Creating Positive Outcomes for All Learners*. She earned her Ed.D from West Virginia University and has been a member of the faculty of Western Carolina University for 20 years.

Hans-Werner Braun is a Research Scientist with the University of California San Diego at the San Diego Supercomputing Center. He is currently Principal Investigator for the High Performance Wireless Research and Education (HPWREN) project (http://hpwren.ucsd.edu/). Earlier Principal Investigator involvements included the National Laboratory for Applied Network Research (NLANR) and, while at the University of Michigan, the NSFNET project. These three activities are or were all based on National Science Foundation funding. Prior work included network engineering responsibilities for the regional computer network of the University of Cologne in Germany.

Kimberly Mann Bruch has been working with HPWREN and multiple collaborators since 2000 and most recently helped launch the HPWREN LIVE pilot project. She is principal investigator at UCSD for the National Park Service Sea to Shining Sea project, which is building on lessons learned from the HPWREN LIVE activities. CV is available at http://kimbruch.com.

Katalin Csoma: after completing her master's studies in Mathematics and English Linguistics and Literature at the University of Szeged in Hungary in 1995, Dr. Katalin Csoma studied Educational Policy and Management at the University of Oregon co-funded by the Soros Foundation and the University of Szeged. Consequently, she started her career as a teacher and teacher educator, instructing and developing courses in English Language Teaching Methodology, Technology-Aided Language Teaching,

Academic Writing and Study Skills. Subsequently, she worked for a Business College as head of the Foreign Languages Institute. With the help of a Fulbright Research Grant to the University of Washington, she was awarded a PhD in Education Technology in 2008, with her dissertation on Information and Communication Technologies in Language Teacher Education. Dr. Csoma is currently Academic, Cultural and Public Affairs Officer at the Embassy of Canada in Budapest.

Sharon Dole is an associate professor of education in the Department of Human Services at Western Carolina University. She has been designing and teaching online courses for several years. Her research interests include online teaching and learning, creativity, gifted education, and twice exceptional students. In 2008 she received the university's J. M. Robinson e-Teaching award. She earned her Ph.D. from the University of Georgia and has been a member of the faculty of Western Carolina University for 10 years.

Billie Eilam is the head of the graduate curriculum track, a director of the laboratory for research in cognitive processes of learning, and a staff member of the faculty of Education, University of Haifa, Haifa 31905, Israel. Tel. 972-4-8288379. E-mail: beilam@construct.haifa.ac.il. Her research interests are in the study of external visual representations as related to learning, instruction, curriculum and teacher education, with a focus on cognitive skills and learning processes. Her studies examine the application of curriculum and learning theories in authentic learning situations, and have been published in various journals like Learning and Instruction, Journal of Teaching and Teacher Education, The Learning Sciences, and more. She is currently writing a book about visual representations in teacher education (co-author Ben-Peretz, M.) to be published by Cambridge University Press. Eilam served on several national committees in education and has won several grants for developing curriculum materials and for conducting research on learning.

Miguel Garcia earned his PhD in Informatics from the Facultat de Informàtica de Barcelona (FIB), from the Universitat Politècnica de Catalunya (UPC), Barcelona, Spain, in 1989. He is Professor at the Department of Architecture of Computers at the Universitat Politècnica de Catalunya (UPC), Barcelona, Spain, since 2003. His research has been always focused on systematic design of diverse types of parallel algorithms. He has been Vice-Director of Studies at the Facultad de Informática de Barcelona (FIB-UPC), between 1993 and 1996, Vice-Director of the Institut de Ciències de l'Educació (ICE-UPC), between 1998 and 2003, and Director of the Escola Politècnica Superior de Castelldefels (EPSC-UPC), from 2003 until 2008 (email: miguel.valero@upc.edu).

Ofir Gortler received his B.A. degree in history of art and education in 2003 in the University Of Haifa, Israel. In 2005 he continued to study for M.A. degree in education in the University of Haifa, majoring in educational technology and the history of art studies. In his thesis he examined how senior students learning about a performance art piece while using a Hypertext based curricular unit. Ofir Gortler is currently working as an instructional designer in é-Learning knowledge solutions, a firm that provides knowledge solutions, as well as traditional and web-based training to educational and training departments in institutions and organizations.

Deryn Graham FHEA, C. Eng, FBCS, CITP, PhD, MSc, MA is an Associate Professor at Unitec, New Zealand and a Visiting Fellow at the University of Greenwich. Background is in Computer Science,

PhD from Brunel University in Artificial Intelligence. As a Lecturer at Brunel, began funded research projects into Education, and "Knowledge-Based Image Processing Systems", leading to a book. Visiting Professorship at Mid Sweden University then employed as a Senior Lecturer at Greenwich, successfully completing an EU FP5 project. Organiser/chair/editor of an annual workshop on e-Learning. A member/referee of programme committees/conferences, reviewed numerous papers, books and bulletins for several publishers. Well over 40 publications, has given keynote papers and been an invited speaker. Teaching and research interests, publications and grants are in diverse areas; Modelling, Networks, Information Visualisation, e-Learning, and HCI. Member of the HCI Disciplinary Commons in 2008. Institutional Nominee for the ILTHE National Fellowship Scheme in 2004.

Jose I. Rojas received his Masters degree in Aerospace Engineering from Universidad Politécnica de Madrid (ETSIA-UPM), Spain, in 2004, and the Advanced Studies Diploma within the Doctoral Program in Aerospace Science and Technology from the Universitat Politècnica de Catalunya (UPC), Barcelona, Spain, in 2006. He is currently pursuing his PhD at the Escola Politècnica Superior de Castelldefels (EPSC-UPC) in the field of viscoelastic properties of aerospace materials. As part of his PhD he made a research stage at the University of British Columbia (UBC), Vancouver, Canada, in 2008. He has participated in research and development projects in the field of aerodynamics (for instance, he has actively collaborated in the design of a panoramic vertical wind tunnel at EPSC-UPC for leisure and skydiving training purposes) and in applications of space- and ground-based technologies for the improvement of earthquake disaster management, during a stage at Beihang University, in Beijing, China, in 2007. Finally, he was working at the United Nations Headquarters (Air Transport Section), New York, USA, and working in a project related to heliport certification for Peace Keeping Missions in Africa. He is Assistant Professor at EPSC-UPC since the year 2005 (e-mail: rojass@fa.upc.edu).

Wallace Hannum is a faculty member in the educational psychology program at the University of North Carolina and Associate Director for Technology of the National Research Center on Rural Education Support. Dr. Hannum teaches graduate level courses on learning theories, instructional design, and the use of technology in education. Dr. Hannum's research focuses on instructional uses of technology, especially distance education. Dr. Hannum has consulted on instructional uses of technology with many organizations, both public and private. He has participated in the design and implementation of numerous technology-based programs and projects. He has worked extensively on education projects in Africa, Asia and Latin America. Dr. Hannum is author of five books and numerous articles on topics related to technology and instructional design.

Jace Hargis is an Assistant Provost at the University of the Pacific in Stockton, California and an Associate Professor of Education. He is the author of several books as well as over forty academic articles on professional development and over one hundred national and international presentations. He completed undergraduate and graduate degrees in the chemical sciences and earned a Ph.D. from the University of Florida in Science Education, specializing in the area of informal learning settings, which is the focus of my research agenda. Currently, he explores the connection between informal learning settings and virtual environments, such as Second Life.

Eunhee Jung (O'Neill) is the founder of the Center for International Virtual Schooling (C4IVS), Dr. Jung (O'Neill) is dedicated to formalizing an International Virtual Schooling (IVS) system by diffusing an intercultural program, International Virtual Elementary/Secondary Classroom Activities (IVECA), to public schools around the world in collaboration with universities, technology firms, NGOs, and international organizations. Her research on IVECA won the 21st Century Best Practice for Excellence in Distance Learning Award 2009 from the United States Distance Learning Association. Her expertise and research interests are in intercultural competence development, cross-cultural online classroom exchange for global knowledge-based societies, the use of ICT in education for intercultural understanding and capacity building, and the internationalization of teacher education and professional development of teachers. Dr. Jung (O'Neill) obtained her Ph.D. and M.Ed. in instructional technology from the Curry School of Education at the University of Virginia where she is currently a visiting scholar. She earned her B.A. in Elementary Education with concentration in Science Education from Seoul National University of Education in Korea.

Patrick Kilby has a BSc. (Agriculture) and Master of Agricultural Economics from the University of Sydney, and a PhD from the Australian National University (ANU). He coordinates and lectures in the ANU's Masters of Applied Anthropology and Participatory Development Program (MAAPD). This graduate program is aimed at people working in aid and development, with many of the students studying while working on challenging development situations in developing countries. Dr. Kilby has created and presented blended online and on-campus courses in Migration, Development Practice, and Program Management. He also supervises PhD students in participatory development and gender studies. Dr Kilby has evaluated both policy and programs for government and non-government organisations (NGO) in community development, humanitarian emergencies, and education, and is an adviser to the Australian Government on NGO Accreditation.

Xavier Prats earned his degree in Telecommunications Engineering from the Universitat Politècnica de Catalunya (UPC), Barcelona, Spain. He also has a master degree in Civil Aviation engineering from the French National School for Civil Aviation (ENAC), in Toulouse, France. He is currently pursuing a PhD within the Doctoral Program in Aerospace Science and Technology from the Universitat Politècnica de Catalunya (UPC), in the field of aircraft departure and approach routes optimization. He works as Assistant Professor at Escola Politècnica Superior de Castelldefels (EPSC-UPC) since 2002. His research interests also focus in air traffic management as well as the study of new Unmanned Air Vehicles (UAVs) technologies in order to use them in civil non-segregated airspace (e-mail: xavier.prats@upc.edu).

Ye Chun Ming holds a PhD and is currently a Professor, Deputy Dean and supervisor of doctoral students in School of Management, The University of Shanghai for Science and Technology. He is also the Secretary-General of the Shanghai Institute of Industrial Engineering. His research areas include industrial engineering, production and operations management, enterprise resource planning, supply chain management and enterprise information systems. He has been involving in numerous long-term research projects in production planning and scheduling. He has successfully completed a number of government-funded projects, published more than 80 papers in reputable local and international journals, and serves as reviewer to several journals.

Enrique Montilla earned his PhD in Astrophysics from the University of Barcelona in 1987. He has been Postdoctoral Research Associate at the University of Illinois at Urbana-Champaign. He is Professor at the Department of Applied Physics of the Universitat Politècnica de Catalunya (UPC), Barcelona,

Spain, since 1991. He is also Research Associate of the Institute for Space Studies of Catalonia (IEEC) since 1996. His research interests have a broad scope ranging from theoretical astrophysics to the design and implementation of scientific payloads for astronomical satellites. He has published more than 80 papers in refereed journals. He was Director of the Department of Applied Physics from 1997 to 2001. He is currently Vice-Rector of Academic Personnel of the UPC (e-mail: garcia@fa.upc.edu).

Adeline de Montlaur earned her degree in Aerospace Engineering from the École Nationale Supérieure d'Ingénieurs de Constructions Aéronautiques (ENSICA), in Toulouse (France) in 2002. She also has a Master degree in Mechanical Engineering from the State University of New York at Buffalo (2003). She is pursuing a Ph.D. in Aerospace Engineering at the UPC in the field of Computational Fluid Dynamics, and has also actively collaborated in the design of the vertical wind tunnel of the UPC at the premises of the Escola Politècnica Superior de Castelldefels (EPSC-UPC). She is Assistant Professor at EPSC-UPC since 2004 (e-mail: adeline.de.montlaur@upc.edu).

Anthony Piña is Dean of Online Studies for the Sullivan University System. He has both academic and industry experience and has been a professional consultant to Fortune 500 corporations, small businesses, government agencies, university consortia and the U.S. Military. Tony is a member of the board of directors of a charter school, the advisory board of two higher education institutions, the editorial board of two refereed journals. He has taught at the secondary, community college and university levels and has received eight national awards in the area of instructional technology. Tony is the author of the book "Distance Learning and the Institution" and has published several peer-reviewed journal articles and book chapters on instructional technology and distance learning. He has delivered over 100 invited presentations at professional conferences. Tony is a Past President of the Division of Distance Learning of the Association for Educational Communications & Technology (AECT).

Teoh Ai Ping is currently attached to the School of Business and Administration, Wawasan Open University, Malaysia, as a Senior Lecturer and Programme Leader in Accounting. She has industrial experience involving in various consultancy and implementation projects in the area of enterprise resource planning systems, quality management systems, accounting information systems and learning management systems. She obtained a Bachelor in Accountancy (Honors), a Master in Information Technology and a Doctorate degree in Business Administration specialized in enterprise risk management and internal auditing. Her research interests include web-based learning management systems, internal auditing and control, enterprise risk management and quality management systems.

Julian Scheinbuks was appointed Director of the Office of Distance Learning after working to initiate Distance Learning at Chicago State University. He was part of the initial group of 10 faculty members at Chicago State University who began teaching Biology online with both synchronous and asynchronous online technologies using an assortment of pedagogies. Julian Scheinbuks is a recipient of two 3 year State of Illinois Innovation Grant (HECA Grant) to study minority student accessibility to higher education using online instructional techniques and had initiated collaborations between three institutions within the state of Illinois each possessing unique and diverse enrollments. He has initiated the development of workshops to promote the use of instructional technologies that may be used to bridge the distances between courses offered at other institutions of Higher learning in the state of Illinois and has presented papers at various conferences that describe the approach to developing collaborations between courses at different institutions.

Sandra Wilson Smith recently received her Ph.D. in English from the Graduate Center of the City University of New York. She has had essays published in *E-Learning* and the *Southern Literary Journal*. She has been teaching first-year writing courses at various universities in Pennsylvania and New Jersey for the last nine years and has a particular interest in developmental writing and English as Second Language students. She has recently accepted a position as an Assistant Professor of English at Union College in Kentucky.

Kenneth D. Strang has a Doctorate in Project Management (high distinction, professional learning concentration), an MBA (honors), a BS (honors) and a Business Technology diploma (honors). He is a certified Project Management Professional® and is a Fellow of the Life Management Institute (distinction, specialized in actuary statistics and pension systems). His research interests include: leadership, multicultural e-learning, knowledge management, and e-business project management. He designs and teaches multi-disciplinary subjects in business, informatics and educational plus he supervises doctorate students.

Josef Strobl is an educator and researcher at the Centre for Geoinformatics, University of Salzburg, Austria. He holds degrees in Geography from Vienna University and has been teaching GIScience and related subjects at universities worldwide. He is current president of the Austrian Umbrella Organisation for Geographic Information (AGEO). As director of the Centre for Geoinformatics and the Austrian Academy of Sciences' GIScience Institute, Josef Strobl leads a group with an excellent record in distance education, spatial analysis and remote sensing, distributed architectures for SDI as well as real time and mobile services and applications ranging from planning for sustainability, regional energy systems and emergency preparedness to resource management. Prof. Strobl has been instrumental in developing and implementing the worldwide UNIGIS postgraduate distance learning programme, heads the annual AGIT and GI_Forum symposia in Salzburg and is working with a global network of partner institutions in education, basic and applied research in Geographic Information Science.

C. W. S. Sukati is a Senior Lecturer and currently the director of the Institute of Distance Education at the University of Swaziland. Dr. Sukati studied at the University of Botswana, Lesotho and Swaziland for his B.Sc. and B.Ed. degrees and at the University of Northern Colorado for his M.Sc. degree in Educational Research and Statistical Methodology. He further studied at the University of South Africa for the D.Ed. in Comparative Education and at Harvard University for the Ed.M. and Ed.D. degrees in Planning and Social Policy. His teaching and research interests are in educational planning and policy, comparative education, education and development, economics and politics of education, and in open and distance learning. He has published a book, a chapter in a book and several articles in refereed journals in the above areas.

Douglas Tedford is an educational consultant for the Fundación Rigoberta Menchú Tum with whom he is collaborating for the development of online rural education systems for learning English. He is an ELT Author, Editor and Teacher Trainer, based in Mexico City, and holds a Doctor of Education degree from Walden University and a Master of Science of Education degree from the University of Southern California. The study described herein was motivated by service experiences in rural Guatemala and by involvement, since 1988, in Spanish-bilingual classroom teaching, teacher training, online mentoring, adult literacy, and educational product development, with supervision in Mexico, Central America, and

South America. Dr. Tedford has taught workshops on English-language development in the United States and internationally, including at conferences of Teachers of English to Speakers of Other Languages (TESOL), MexTESOL, California TESOL, and the National Council of Teachers of English (NCTE).

Susan Teel directs the Southern California Research Learning Center, a program within the National Park Service, which recruits scientific, educational, and community partners to conduct research and education activities in national parks. While completing a dual M.S. in marine biology and coastal zone management, she launched a degree program at Miami-Dade College which linked local high schools, the college, and universities in a 2 plus 2 plus 2 program. She served as lead biologist on Comprehensive Everglades Restoration projects for both the Environmental Protection Agency and the Fish and Wildlife Service. Her most rewarding work has been teaching at Miami-Dade College, Florida International University, Florida Atlantic University, and Santa Monica College.

Michael Vallance is a Professor at Future University Hakodate (FUN), Japan. He has a Doctorate in Education from Durham University, UK and a Masters Degree in Computer Assisted Learning from Stirling University, UK. He is the co-author of Using IT in the Language Classroom (ISBN 0-13-127536-4) and is widely published in educational technology journals. He is involved in a number of ICT research projects such as Task Design for Web 2.0, Podmaps for iPods, and Virtual Collaborative Spaces. The research focuses upon the innovative utilization of ICT to support effective pedagogy, informed learning and measurable academic competencies. He has also been awarded funding from the UK Prime Minister's Initiative (PMI2) for his research of collaborative tasks and robot programming in Second Life. His Website is at http://web.mac.com/mvallance/

David L. Wright is currently Associate Professor at the Future University Hakodate (FUN), Japan. He completed his Masters of Business Communication within the Business Faculty, and his Doctorate with the Creative Industries Faculty from Queensland University of Technology in Brisbane, Australia. His principal research focus is in Futures Studies and Thinking, in which he integrates aspects from Communication Studies, the Creative Industries, and Complex Systems. Under the name TEST-TUBE STUDIOS he is currently developing new genres of future-oriented film making and media production including a multi-discipline collaboration producing Complexity related short films: Project Futurium – a proof of concept design for a synthetic environment for co-creative futures simulations; and JAPAN'S CREATIVE INDUSTRIES: An Evolutionary Anomaly of the C.I. Species. The above media productions are currently available for viewing on the FUN intranet.

Kevin Yee is the Assistant Director at the Faculty Center for Teaching and Learning in the University of Central Florida. He has previously taught at the University of California-Irvine, Pomona College, the University of Iowa, and Duke University. He completed a Ph.D. in German Literature from UC-Irvine in 1997. His disciplinary research includes German Romanticism, Goethe, fairy tales, and 19th-century German novellas. As a faculty developer, Kevin supports the UCF faculty in all respects intersecting with teaching. He is particularly interested in new technology tools for teaching, such as classroom clickers, wikis, blogs, podcasts, online pedagogy, and persistent online worlds. He has been teaching in Second Life since 2009.

Index

Symbols

6Ss quality assurance system 127
6Ss quality assurance system, concept system 127
6Ss quality assurance system, criterion system 127
6Ss quality assurance system, evaluation & feedback system 127
6Ss quality assurance system, implementation systems 127
6Ss quality assurance system, organization system 127
21st Century School Flagship Program (CSFP) 151

A

academically or intellectually gifted (AIG) license 361, 362
academic competencies 162, 185
academic enrollments 69, 71, 72, 73, 74, 76
access 69, 86
active learning 148
active participants 162, 164
aerospace engineering program 333, 334, 335, 355
Afghanistan 105, 113, 114
Africa 71, 75, 81, 82, 85, 86
Air Emissions Modeling Program (ALOHA) 34
Alliance collaboration environment 106, 110
altitude control system (ACS) 354, 357, 359
analysis-design-development-implementation-evaluation (ADDIE) 46, 54, 67, 68
andragogy 67, 68
anime 274
Anza-Borrego Desert State Park 312
art education 244, 247, 248, 249, 250, 251, 252, 253, 255, 257, 258, 259, 260, 261, 262, 263
artworks 244, 247, 248, 263
Asia 123, 124, 125, 128, 129, 130, 139, 140, 142
Association for Educational Communications and Technology (AECT) 31
Association for the Advancement of Computing in Education (AACE) 31
asynchronous communication 189, 193, 194, 195, 196, 199, 201, 205, 206, 210
asynchronous instruction 41
asynchronous online discussion forums 106
Australia 42, 43, 44, 45, 46, 47, 48, 49, 50, 51, 52, 54, 56, 57, 59, 60, 61, 62, 63, 64, 65, 66, 67, 68, 103, 105, 109, 111, 119, 152, 194
Australia Global Development Learning Network 104
Australian indigenous communities 105
Australian National University (ANU) 103, 104, 105, 106, 107, 109, 110, 113, 114, 116, 118
Australian universities 43, 46, 47, 48, 49, 51, 56, 57, 61, 67
Australia University Quality Agency (AUQA) 46, 47, 48, 50, 55, 56, 57, 59, 62, 67, 68
Austria 152
autopoiesis 25
avatars 205, 206, 207, 208, 209, 210, 211, 216

B

balanced learning assessment 42, 61, 68
balanced measure 43
balanced scorecards 68
Bangladesh 105
Bhabha, Homi 274, 276, 279
Blackboard 29, 30, 32, 33, 35, 36, 38, 41, 46, 47, 49, 52, 60, 207, 266
blended learning 187, 192, 193, 197, 198, 199, 201
blended teaching model 43
blurring boundaries 86
Bologna process 147, 149, 161

C

Cabrillo National Monument 314, 319, 321, 322, 323, 324, 325, 327, 328, 329
California 311, 312, 313, 314, 315, 316, 319, 321, 322, 325, 326, 328, 332
Cambodia 105, 108, 112, 113, 114, 119
Camden, New Jersey 264, 268, 272, 273, 274, 276, 277, 278, 279
Cameroon 152
Center for Off-campus Studies (Universiti Sains Malaysia) 124
Center for Teaching and Learning (CTL) (NEIU) 28, 29, 31
Central Queensland University 46
Centro Educativo Luciano Pavarotti 219, 221, 223, 228, 237
Chicago, Illinois 27, 28, 31, 33, 34, 35, 39, 41
Chicago State University (CSU) 28, 29, 31, 32, 33, 34, 35, 36, 37, 38
China 123, 124, 125, 126, 128, 139, 142, 143
Chinese Cultural Revolution 126
Chinese ethnic group 124, 125, 126, 128, 130, 139, 143
civilisational evolution 1, 4, 5, 9, 25
classroom overcrowding 79
cognitive learning 167
cognitive learning, perceived 167
cognitive load theory 167
cognitive outcomes surveys 167, 175
cognitive outcomes theory 167
cognitive theory of multiple media learning 167
cognitive tools 245, 260
collaboration 361, 368, 374, 376
College of Distance Education 70
co-located communication 189, 193, 194, 197
Colombia 105
community development 166
community-driven development (CDD) 218, 222, 242
community futures 166
community technology center (CTC) 219, 221, 222, 226, 227, 229, 230, 242
complex systems studies 168, 171, 173
composition and rhetoric courses 264, 265
computational fluid dynamics (CFD) 350, 351, 353, 357, 359
computer-mediated communication (CMC) 264, 267, 268, 270, 272, 273, 274, 275, 276, 278, 279
computer-mediated communication (CMC) tools 189, 194, 197, 199, 201
computer-supported cooperative work (CSCW) 187, 189, 194, 196, 201, 202
Confucian philosophy 124, 140, 162, 181
constructivism 2, 93, 361
contact zone 264, 278
continuing education 43
continuing medical education 90, 91, 92
conventional face-to-face (CF2F) university 70, 71, 72, 74, 75, 77, 78, 79, 80
cooperative work framework 187, 188, 189, 194, 198, 200, 201, 202
course design 360, 370, 371, 375
course management systems (CMS) 204, 205, 206, 207, 212, 216, 288, 300, 310
course objectives 29
Crawford, Sir John 104
cross-cultural virtual classroom exchange program 284, 286, 290, 304
cross-cultural virtual exchange activities 284, 304, 305
cross-cultural virtual learning 284, 300
Crystal Cove State Park 312, 313
cultural bridge 264, 267
cultural diversity 188

culture, differences in 287
curriculum unit 244, 249, 251, 253
curriculum unit, hypermedia-based 244, 249, 251

D

deontologic ethics 2
Department of Education (DOE) (USA) 285
Department of Immigration & Multicultural & Indigenous Affairs (DIMIA) (Australia) 47
developing world 219, 220, 221, 224, 235, 242
development engineers (DE) 339, 346, 359
development practitioner peers 103
development professionals 104
development studies 103, 122
development workers 103, 105, 113, 118, 122
Dewey, John 2, 20
dialogue 19, 25
digital divide 241, 242
digital enablement 185
digital era 148
digital immigrants 147, 148, 160
digital media integration 162
digital natives 147, 160, 205
digital wisdom 148, 160
discussion boards 361
distance education 123, 124, 125, 126, 127, 128, 143, 144, 161
Distance Education Association of Southern Africa (DEASA) 71
distance education (DE) 69, 70, 71, 72, 73, 74, 75, 76, 77, 78, 79, 80, 81, 82, 83, 84, 85, 86
distance learning 45, 106, 122
Distance Teaching & Learning (DTL) 31
diverse cultures 284, 289, 304, 305
Dominican Republic 265
dual-mode, challenges of 86
DVD players, portable 87, 89, 94, 95, 99

E

East Timor 105, 108, 110, 111, 113, 114
Educational Technology Plan for Virginia 285, 307
Education Technology Institute of Eötvös Loránd University (ELTE) 152, 155
EDUCAUSE 31, 39
e-learning 42, 43, 44, 45, 46, 47, 48, 49, 50, 51, 52, 53, 54, 56, 60, 61, 62, 63, 68, 92, 94, 100, 187, 188, 189, 192, 193, 194, 195, 196, 197, 198, 199, 200, 201, 202
e-learning, transnational framework for 187, 188
Elluminate 29, 30, 31, 32, 33, 34, 35, 36, 37, 38, 41
ElluminateLive 46, 52
Elon College 360
e-mail 264, 265, 267, 268, 270, 272, 274, 275, 278
e-moderation 187, 188, 192, 201
e-motivation 192
English as a foreign language (EFL) instruction 272, 278
English as a second language (ESL) 285
english as a second language (ESL) instruction 43, 47, 265, 266, 269, 272, 275, 276, 278, 279
English language learners (ELL) 273, 274
Enhancing Education Through Technology (EETT) Act 285
Escola Politècnica Superior de Castelldefels (EPSC) 334, 336, 340, 346, 353, 359
e-socializing 192
ethnic diversity 188
e-tutoring 187, 188, 189, 191, 192, 193, 201, 202
European Higher Education Area (EHEA) 161
European Pedagogical ICT License (EPICT) program 147, 152, 153, 155, 156, 157, 158, 159, 160
European Union (EU) 147, 149, 152, 155, 159
evolutionist learning approach 1, 2, 19
exchanges, categories of 123, 145
expert engineers (EE) 339, 359

F

face-to-face interaction 123, 189, 201
face-to-face tutoring 43
Faigley, Lester 268, 276
family planning (FP) 98, 99, 102

fanfiction 274, 276
fanfiction communities 274
feedback 89, 92, 93, 96, 97, 98
First Comprehensive Plan (Korea) 285
flexible learning 42, 68
fluid dynamics 333, 336
foresight communication 166
formal learning environments 245
Fourth Pan-Commonwealth Forum on Open Learning 70, 81, 83, 84
Fundación Rigoberta Menchú Tum (FRMT) 218, 219, 221, 222, 223, 224, 225, 226, 231, 232, 233, 234, 235, 236, 237, 238, 239, 240, 242
future, image of the 164, 184, 185
Futures Employment 2028 169, 172, 173, 174, 175, 176, 177, 186
futures studies 162, 164, 165, 166, 168, 169, 170, 171, 175, 176, 177, 178, 179, 180, 181, 182, 183, 184, 185
Futures Studies, digitally enabled 162, 177, 180
futures triangle analysis 169, 170, 186
Future University Hakodate (FUN) 168, 169, 170, 172, 179, 180

G

Generation D 148
George Wright Society Cultural Resources 2003 Joint Conference 313
Ghana 152
globalization 285, 286, 299, 307
global solidarity 284
Google Maps 169, 176, 177, 178
Greece 152
Green Technology Center 34
group discussions, asynchronous 43
group puzzle 335, 338, 357
groupware 189, 194
GSM (global system for mobile communication) 46
Guatemala 218, 219, 220, 221, 222, 224, 226, 228, 229, 233, 234, 236, 237, 238, 239, 240, 242, 243
guided visualization 162, 169, 170, 186

H

Hakodate 2017 162, 169, 172, 175, 177, 185
Hakodate, Japan 162, 168, 169, 171, 172, 173, 175, 177, 179, 185
Han ethnic group 124
health care services 91
health care workers 88, 89, 90, 91, 92, 93, 94
high crime rate 264
Higher Education Cooperation Act (HECA) 28, 30, 31, 36, 41
High Performance Wireless Research and Education Network (HPWREN) 311, 312, 313, 314, 315, 316, 317, 319, 321, 322, 323, 324, 325, 326, 328, 329, 332
High Performance Wireless Research and Education Network (HPWREN) project 311, 312, 313, 314, 315, 316, 317, 319, 321, 322, 323, 324, 325, 326, 328, 329, 332
HIV/AIDS 88, 89, 92, 98, 99, 102
Hofstede, Geert 125, 126, 130, 142, 143, 144, 146
Hofstede's dimensions of culture 125
Homeland generation 205
host communities 103
how people learn (HPL) framework 360, 361, 362, 363, 365, 366, 367, 368, 369, 370, 372, 375
human capital 163
human capital development 124, 163
human-computer interaction (HCI) perspective 187, 188, 189, 193, 196, 197
Hungarian Association of IT Teachers (ISZE) 153, 155
Hungary 147, 148, 149, 150, 151, 152, 153, 155, 156, 158, 159, 160, 161
hypermedia 244, 245, 246, 247, 249, 259, 260, 261, 263
hypermedia environments 246
hypertext 244, 245, 246, 247, 249, 250, 259, 260, 261, 262, 263

I

Iceland 152
Illinois Board of Higher Education (IBHE) 28, 38, 40, 41

Indian ethnic group 124
indigenous populations 218, 219, 222, 234, 237, 241, 242
individualism/collectivism 125, 145, 146
individual learning 1
Indonesia 105, 108, 109, 112, 114, 118
inertial navigation systems (INS) 354, 357, 359
inertial reference system (IRS) 354, 359
informal learning environments 245
information age 285, 295, 307
inquiry based learning 360, 376
Institute of Distance Education (IDE) (UNISWA) 69, 70, 71, 72, 73, 74, 75, 76, 77, 78, 79, 80, 84, 86
institutional change 1, 22
institution building 1, 4, 14, 16, 26
instructional technologies 203, 204, 216
integrative model 167
Intelligent School of the 21st Century Program 151
interaction 131, 136, 137, 144, 145
interaction, dimensions of 123, 145
interactive simulations 87, 88, 89, 96, 98, 99
intercultural competence 284, 287, 306, 307, 308, 309, 310
intercultural learning 25
international virtual elementary/Secondary classroom activities (IVECA) 284, 286, 287, 288, 289, 290, 291, 293, 294, 295, 296, 297, 298, 299, 300, 301, 302, 303, 305, 310
international virtual schooling 284, 310
Internet, instructor usage 218, 222
IP-based conferencing products 312
Ireland 152
Irvine, California 312
Italy 152

J

Japan 162, 163, 164, 165, 166, 168, 169, 171, 172, 175, 177, 178, 179, 180, 181, 182, 183, 184, 185
Japanese education 162, 169, 179, 181
Japanese education, conventional 162
Japanese higher education 162, 163, 164
Japanese public education system 162
Japanese students 162, 163, 164, 166, 168, 175, 177, 182

K

Kenya 87, 88, 89, 90, 91, 92, 93, 94, 95, 96, 99, 100
Kenya Medical Teaching College 88
Kenyan Ministry of Health (MOH) 87
Kenyan nurses 87, 88
knowledge acquisition level 361
knowledge-based economy, global 310
knowledge domain 246, 247, 249, 258
knowledge domain, ill-structure 247, 249
knowledge economy 125
Korea 284, 285, 286, 288, 289, 290, 291, 292, 295, 298, 300, 301, 302, 306, 307
Korean Education & Research Information Service (KERIS) 285, 301, 307

L

launch engineers (LAE) 339, 346, 347, 359
leap-frogging 25
learner interaction in the online asynchronous discussion forums 145
learner interactions 123, 135
learner interaction with online content 123, 145
learning achievements 123
learning activities 106, 115
learning, digitally enabled 162
learning environment 244, 245, 247, 260, 361, 362, 373, 375
learning environment, hypermedia-based 244
learning environments 103, 110, 115
learning experiences 87, 99
learning management system (LMS) 29, 30, 41, 46, 106, 107, 108, 109, 110, 123, 130, 131, 145, 203, 216
learning management systems (LMS) in Asia 123
learning materials 245
learning outcomes, high-level 360, 361, 370
learning patterns 123, 130
learning process 162, 163, 164, 183
learning settings 1, 10
Legacy template 360, 362, 363, 375

lifelong learning 125
Likert-scale surveys 312, 314, 324
Linden Labs 204, 205, 206, 211, 214, 216
lindens 205, 207
live interactive virtual explorations (LIVE) 311, 312, 313, 314, 315, 316, 317, 318, 319, 320, 321, 322, 323, 324, 325, 326, 327, 328, 329, 332
logical-positivistic philosophy 44, 45
logistics engineer (LOE) 346, 359

M

Madagascar 105, 112, 114
Malay ethnic group 124
Malaysia 123, 124, 125, 127, 139, 142, 143, 144
Mandarin language 124
manga 274
masculinity/femininity 125, 146
Master of Applied Anthropology and Participatory Development (MAAPD) 103, 104, 105, 106, 107, 109, 110, 111, 113, 114, 115, 118, 119
master of arts in education (MAED) program 361, 362
master of arts in teaching (MAT) program 361, 362
Matura exam 161
mental structural change 2, 10
mentees 28, 30
mentor-mentee relationships 28
mentors 28, 30, 32
Migration Law and Practice program 104
Millennial generation 205
Ministerio de Educación de Guatemala (MINEDUC) 222, 235, 243
Ministry of Education (China) 124
Ministry of Education, Culture, Sports, Science and Technology (MEXT) (Japan) 163
Ministry of Education, Science and Technology (MEST) (Korea) 284, 285, 301, 307
mission engineers (ME) 339, 346, 347, 359
model rockets 333, 336, 339, 355, 357
model rocket workshops (MRW) 333, 336, 337, 338, 339, 340, 341, 342, 343, 344, 345, 346, 347, 348, 349, 350, 351, 352, 353, 354, 355, 357, 359
Moodle 46, 52, 106, 107, 110, 207, 290, 291, 292, 293, 310
Moodle (modular object-oriented dynamic learning environment) 154, 156, 158, 161
multicasting 312, 329
multicultural students 44, 47, 49
Multimedia Super Corridor (Malaysia) 124
multi-modality, theory of 167
multi-user dungeons (MUD) 274, 278

N

National Centre for Development Studies (Australia) 104
national culture 123, 125, 130, 139, 141, 146
national culture, influence of 123, 139
National Park Service (USA) 321, 322, 323, 324, 325, 328, 332
National Science Foundation (USA) 311, 313, 315, 325
National Teacher Training Institute Conference 312
native-born students 264, 266
needs assessments 88, 90, 91, 92, 95
Nelson, Theodor H. 245, 263
Nepal 105, 118
network society 1, 10, 11, 14
new media 185
No Child Left Behind Act (USA) 285, 308
non-governmental organization (NGO) 87, 88, 89, 102
non-government organization (NGO) 112
Northeastern Illinois University (NEIU) 28, 29, 31, 32, 33, 34, 35, 37, 38, 41
Norway 152
nurses 87, 88, 89, 90, 91, 92, 93, 94, 95, 96, 97, 98, 99
Nursing Council of Kenya 88

O

object-oriented programming (OOP) language 211, 214, 216
off-campus study 103, 122
Office of Distance Learning (ODL) (CSU) 28, 29, 31, 38

Office of Technology-Enhanced Learning (OTEL) (UIS) 28, 29, 31, 36, 38
Oldenburg, Ray 273, 274, 276, 278
online content 135, 146
online courses 92, 210, 212
online discussion 103, 111, 122
online forum discussions 123, 130
online learners 123
online learners, behavior of 123
online learning 79, 86, 123, 129, 136, 141, 143
online learning activities 123, 141
online teaching 360, 371, 374, 375
Online Teaching Partnership (OTP) 27, 28, 29, 30, 31, 36, 37, 38
online teaching partnerships 27, 41
ontological approach 25
ontological learning approach 1, 2, 9, 19
open distance education (ODE) 125, 128, 130
open distance learning (ODL) 127, 128, 129, 130, 139, 141
open universities 126, 127
Open University Malaysia 124
Orangeware WebCamDV software 315
out-of-context teaching 104

P

Pala Native American Learning Center 311, 317, 318, 321
Palomar College 311
Palomar Observatory 313, 314, 316, 317, 318, 319, 321, 325, 326, 329
Panama 105
Parks Online Resources for Teachers and Students (PORTS) program 313, 322
participatory development 103, 122
participatory rural appraisal (PRA) 218, 222, 223, 224, 232, 233, 243
pedagogy 46, 63
peer learning 367, 376
performance art (PA) 247, 248, 249, 250, 251, 252, 253, 254, 255, 256, 257, 258, 260, 263
performance art (PA), dynamic 244
permanent-group interview (PGI) method 224, 227
personal digital assistants (PDA) 315, 332
personal learning styles 246
planning 69, 82, 86
political, economic, social, technical, & environmental (PESTE) factors 187, 188, 189, 194, 197, 200, 201, 202
Polycom software 312, 314, 332
postabortion care (PAC) 98, 102
postgraduate education 103, 104, 106, 114, 118
postgraduate study 122
power distance 125, 126, 139, 140, 146
practical abilities 333, 336, 340, 354, 355
practical experiences, limited-range 333, 355
Prensky, Marc 147, 148, 160
prim (primitive object) 203, 216
problem based learning (PBL) 46, 333, 334, 335, 336, 340, 351, 355, 357, 359
problem-solving activities 361
problem space 2
professional development 161
psychological learning approach 1, 2, 17, 19
Puerto Rico 265

Q

Qik 46
quality assurance 123, 125, 127, 128, 140, 141, 145

R

reflection-in-action 2, 3
remote communication 189, 193, 194, 195, 198, 201
remotely operated vehicle (ROV) 319, 320, 321, 322, 325, 332
rocket dynamics 333

S

Sakai 207
San Diego, California 311, 312, 313, 314, 315, 316, 319, 321, 322, 323, 324, 325, 326, 328, 329
San Francisco, California 313
San Lucas Toliman, Guatamala 218, 219, 221, 222, 224, 225, 226, 230, 231, 233, 235, 237

Santa Margarita Ecological Reserve 313, 314, 319, 321, 326, 329
scaffolding 93, 192
scenario creation 186
scholarship of teaching and learning (SoTL) 203, 213, 217
Schoolnet Digital Knowledge Base 150, 151
Schoolnet Express 151
School of Computing and Mathematical Sciences (CMS) 187, 188, 192
School of the Air (Australia) 194, 195
Sea to Shining Sea (StSS) distance learning project 323, 324, 332
secondary education 43
Second Life (SL) 46, 203, 204, 205, 206, 207, 208, 209, 210, 211, 212, 213, 214, 215, 216
Second Stage Plan (Korea) 285
Seoul, South Korea 286, 307
Seventh Malaysian Plan 124
sexual transmitted infection (STI) 102
Shanghai, China 123, 126, 127, 138, 145
Shanghai TV University (STVU) 126, 127, 128, 129, 130, 131, 133, 134, 136, 137, 138, 139, 140
Singapore 163, 184
Skype software 313, 314, 315, 320, 321, 322, 324, 325, 326, 328, 329, 332
social capital 218, 219, 220, 222, 223, 224, 226, 227, 228, 229, 230, 231, 232, 235, 237, 238, 239, 240, 241, 242, 243
social capital, bonding 218, 223, 224, 226, 227, 228, 230, 231, 232, 235, 242
social capital, bridging 218, 223, 224, 229, 230, 231, 232, 235, 241, 242
social capital, linking 218, 219, 223, 224, 232, 235, 242
social criticism 245
social impact 104
social interactions 284
social interactions, scope of 284
social mapping 104
social spaces 1, 10, 13, 16, 23, 25
social, technical, economic and political (STEP) factors 187, 188, 189, 194, 197, 201, 202
social, technological, economic and political (STEP) environmental factors 69, 71, 72, 75, 79, 80
societal learning 1, 3, 4, 7, 18, 25, 26
socio-cultural activities 266
Socrates 148, 153
Socratic method 148
solution space 2
spaces of understanding 25
Spain vi, xi, 333, 334, 340
spatial citizens 25
spatial planning 26
special education program 360
special education (SPED) 364, 365, 369
special education teachers 360
SPED 401 364, 365
SPED 555 364
Spielraum 2, 3, 21, 22, 24
Sri Lanka 152
Star Legacy 360, 362, 370, 375
star legacy template 360, 375
structural evolution 1, 5
structure building 26
student learning 203, 213
student learning needs 203
Sulinet (Schoolnet) program (Hungary) 150, 151, 154
Supporting Learning and Technology in Education (SLATE) 31, 38, 39
Swaziland 69, 70, 71, 72, 74, 78, 80, 81, 84, 85, 86
synchronous communication 189, 193, 194, 195, 196, 205, 206, 207, 210
synchronous instruction 41
synchronous interactions 43, 45, 47, 48, 49, 52, 53, 54, 62

T

Taiwan 219, 221
taxonomy of learning 42, 52, 68
teacher development programs 147
teacher development programs, transnational 147
teacher education 149, 153, 160, 161, 375
teacher education programs 360, 361, 372
teacher shortage 360

teacher training 161
teaching materials 151
teaching presence 368, 376
Teachmat system 188, 192, 193, 194, 197, 198
TechEd Events 31
technology 69, 75, 81, 84, 85, 86
technology-based learning 87
Tècniques Experimentals en Aerofísica (TEA) 336, 351, 352, 354, 359
teleologic ethics 2
test engineers (TE) 339, 346, 347, 359
Thailand 105, 108
third place 274, 276, 279
third space 274, 278
training delivery 91, 94
transformational learning 376
transnational education 163
transnational learning 103
transnational projects 161
transnational students 264, 265, 266, 267, 272, 275, 276
transnational study 122
transversal abilities 333
Twenge, Jean M. 266, 267, 269, 270, 271, 272, 277, 280, 281, 282, 283
twinning 14, 15, 17, 18, 19, 24, 26
Twitter 46

U

Uganda 105, 152
UK (United Kingdom) 43, 45, 46, 50, 63, 66, 152, 160, 187, 188, 194, 199, 200
uncertainty avoidance 125, 146
undergraduate education 103, 116
underserved populations 28
United Kingdom eUniversity (UKeU) 188, 200
universal testing machine (UTM) 352, 358, 359
Universitat Politècnica de Catalunya (UPC) 333, 334, 349, 359
Universiti' Sains Malaysia 73, 124
Universiti Tun Abdul Razak 124
university education 86
University of Botswana, Lesotho and Swaziland (UBLS) 69
University of Illinois 28, 31, 39, 41
University of Illinois at Springfield (UIS) 28, 29, 31, 32, 34, 35, 36, 37, 38
University of Swaziland (UNISWA) 69, 70, 71, 72, 73, 74, 75, 76, 77, 78, 79, 80, 81, 84, 86
University of Technology Sydney (UTS) 46
university system 187, 188, 199, 200
urban decay 264
USA (United States of America) 43, 45, 46, 50, 51, 55, 66, 67, 203, 205, 264, 265, 266, 267, 269, 270, 271, 272, 273, 274, 275, 277, 282, 284, 285, 286, 289, 290, 291, 294, 311, 332, 360, 371, 372, 374
Uzbekistan 105, 108, 111, 112, 115, 118

V

Vanuatu 105, 106, 108, 112
video simulations 87, 94, 99
video tutorials 207
Vietnam 105, 111, 114, 115, 265, 266, 267, 269, 270, 271, 272, 274, 282, 283
Virginia 285, 286, 300, 307
Virginia Department of Education 285, 307
virtual classrooms 123
virtual environments 28
virtual goods 205
virtual learning environments (VLE) 43, 46, 203, 204, 205, 206, 207, 210, 214, 216
virtual networks 205
virtual shops 205
virtual third places 273
virtual worlds 204, 205, 206, 207, 209, 210, 211, 215, 216
virtual worlds, persistent online 204, 216
visual arts 245, 259
visual culture 244, 258, 260, 262
voluntary counseling and testing (VCT) 98, 102

W

Wattle LMS 106
Wawasan Open University 124, 145
Wawasan (Vision) Open University (WOU) 127, 128, 129, 130, 131, 132, 133, 134, 136, 137, 138, 139, 140

Web 2.0 168, 169, 177, 183, 184, 185, 192, 201
web-based content 123, 141
web-based education 123
web-based environments 123, 137
WebCT 46, 47
whiteboards 207
Wimba 46, 52, 60
writing assignments 264, 266, 275

Y

Y-generation 205